Children Of The Presidents

George Washington to Donald Trump:

Includes legitimate, illegitimate, alleged,

and secret children of our 45 presidents

Cheryl Pryor

Arlington & Amelia

Copyright © 2017 Cheryl Pryor

Arlington & Amelia Publishers

ArlingtonAmeliaPub@cfl.rr.com

All rights reserved. No portion of this book may be reproduced or transmitted by any form or by any means, electronic or mechanical, including photocopy, recording, or any information storage and retrieval system without permission in writing from the author.

Photos from front cover: from left to right

Susan Ford   photo by White House photographer David Hume Kennerly, Courtesy of Gerald R. Ford Presidential Library.

Amy Carter – Courtesy of Jimmy Carter Presidential Library

Grandchildren & President Benjamin Harrison - Courtesy of Library of Congress

Julie Nixon & husband David Eisenhower, grandson of President Eisenhower - Courtesy of Library of Congress

Robert Lincoln - Courtesy of Library of Congress

Quentin Roosevelt, Courtesy of Library of Congress

First Lady Jackie Kennedy with children Caroline & John – White House photographer Cecil Stoughton, Courtesy John F. Kennedy Presidential Library

Barbara & Jenna Bush – Courtesy of George W Bush Presidential Library

First Printing

ISBN-10: 1-886541-15-9
ISBN-13: 978-1-886541-15-3

FOR PERRY

TABLE OF CONTENTS

	Introduction	i
1	George Washington	1
2	John Adams	9
3	Thomas Jefferson	23
4	James Madison	37
5	James Monroe	41
6	John Quincy Adams	47
7	Andrew Jackson	55
8	Martin Van Buren	61
9	William Henry Harrison	67
10	John Tyler	73
11	James Polk	93
12	Zachary Taylor	95
13	Millard Fillmore	101
14	Franklin Pierce	105
15	James Buchanan	109
16	Abraham Lincoln	113
17	Andrew Johnson	135
18	Ulysses S. Grant	141
19	Rutherford B. Hayes	157

20	James Garfield	169
21	Chester Arthur	181
22	Grover Cleveland	185
23	Benjamin Harrison	189
24	Grover Cleveland	199
25	William McKinley	207
26	Theodore Roosevelt	211
27	William Taft	239
28	Woodrow Wilson	249
29	Warren Harding	261
30	Calvin Coolidge	269
31	Herbert Hoover	277
32	Franklin D. Roosevelt	285
33	Harry Truman	309
34	Dwight D. Eisenhower	321
35	John F. Kennedy	331
36	Lyndon B. Johnson	361
37	Richard Nixon	375
38	Gerald Ford	387
39	Jimmy Carter	401
40	Ronald Reagan	413

41	George H.W. Bush	439
42	Bill Clinton	461
43	George W. Bush	481
44	Barack Obama	499
45	Donald Trump	515
	Bibliography	543

Introduction

We elected our first president well over 200 years ago and have been caught up in the lives and antics of not only the presidents but also in their families ever since. At the time this book was published we as a nation have just witnessed our 45th president sworn into office and to date have had just under two hundred children of presidents. Not all of them have been children during their White House days; some have been adults when their fathers became president – all the same; they are children of the presidents.

There have been alleged slave children by three different presidents, illegitimate children, and a "secret" child kidnapped from his mother and given up for adoption by another president. All the president's children and their stories are included - *the good and the bad.* Their good character traits and not so good will be revealed; after all this is what makes them interesting and gives a true look at who they are.

Not only are the just under two hundred children included but also some of the grandchildren that spent a good bit of time at the White House with their presidential grandfather and their grandmother the first lady.

In the years they live in the White House we watch the president's children with fascination and with as much interest as if they were movie stars or royalty. They live their lives in the spotlight with every move they make watched, every fashionable outfit they wear copied, and their romances leave us hoping there will be yet another White House fairy tale wedding. All their actions are scrutinized and judged by the press and the people, fairly or not. Then four years, and in some cases eight years later, they leave the White House and the spotlight fades; and we wonder what ever happened to them.

Some of the children of the presidents have had hard times trying to live in the shadow of their famous fathers while others have gone on to 'do their own thing,' whether that is in politics or another path of their own choosing, and done quite well. Some became alcoholics, committed suicide, or had gambling addictions - lives that soap operas mimic. One thing many of them had in common was to write books about their famous families.

Needless to say, they led fascinating lives living in the most famous house in America. They were given access to people and places they never would have had otherwise; just because of their famous family name and their father's title. Some used that to their advantage while others chose to make it on their own.

Some of our nations historical events that occurred while they were the First Family are included. Our nation has gone through many changes: The War of 1812 when the White House was burned, Prohibition, the Civil War, the Great Depression, the Wright Brothers first flight, along with many other 'firsts' as our nation aged and progressed. These presidential children were there to witness and experience these times in our nation.

The president's children are just as fascinating as their fathers, many times even more so. Here's a few things you will read about in 'Children of the Presidents':

- A presidential daughter and her immediate family are worth $500 million.

- One presidential son had his mother committed to an insane asylum.

- A president's son's body was stolen by grave robbers and discovered by his own son.

- Before they moved into the White House when her father was still the vice-president, his daughter was threatened to be kidnapped by the Symbionese Liberation Army (SLA), the fanatical, terrorist group that did kidnap Patty Hearst, granddaughter of William Randolph Hearst.

- A president's son was an adopted Creek Indian orphan who would have been killed by the other Indians of his tribe if the president hadn't saved him.

- A son of a president was on the scene of the Boxer Rebellion, the China Relief Expedition, and the Russo-Japanese War. He was part of the relief force that rescued the trapped Westerners in Peking, including the future president and first lady the Hoovers.

- A president's son was caught swimming nude in the South Lawn fountain of the White House with the prince of Siam.

- One president had a goat that he attached to a cart to pull his young grandson around. One day the goat took off across the White House lawn and escaped down Pennsylvania Avenue with the president running down the street after them.

- One president's youngest son rode his favorite horse up the White House elevator into the family quarters to surprise his brother who had been sick.

- A presidential son got the experience of a lifetime when he witnessed a Wright Brothers flying machine land on the South Lawn in 1911.

- A president's son, who was as unsociable as his parents, had a butler replaced merely because he didn't like the way he walked.

Whether you agree with their father's politics or not, we are fascinated by the president's children and often wonder what happened to them once they left the White House.

Ron, the youngest son of President Ronald Reagan said, "Once a President's kid, always a President's kid." It's a title you never shake off.

Regardless of any accomplishments they achieve or antics they pull once they leave the White House, they will always be remembered as the son or daughter of the president. It's a label they will carry with them for a lifetime.

I

GEORGE WASHINGTON

Children of Martha from her first marriage, stepchildren of George Washington:

John Parke "Jacky" Custis – Born: November 27, 1754   Died: November 5, 1781

Martha Parke "Patsy" Custis – Born: 1756   Died: June 19, 1773

Grandchildren that lived with and were raised by the Washingtons: Children of Jacky:

Eleanor "Nelly" Parke Custis – Born: March 31, 1779   Died: July 15, 1852

George Washington "Wash" Parks Custis – Born: April 30, 1781   Died: October 10, 1857

Great-granddaughter of Martha and George Washington was the wife of

General Robert E. Lee of the Civil War.

George Washington had no biological children, however; when he married the widow Martha Custis he became stepfather to her two surviving children. She had four children during her first marriage, two of which had passed away before Martha and George's marriage. Jacky and Patsy Custis were four and three years old at the time of George and Martha's marriage.

George would have been the only father they remembered. He loved the children and treated them very well.

When the children were old enough to be taught music lessons a harpsichord was purchased for Patsy while her brother received a violin and flute. The children had a music teacher who came several days a month to Mount Vernon.

A tutor came to live at Mount Vernon to teach seven year old Jacky and five year old Patsy. The tutor remained at Mount Vernon for seven years teaching the children until Patsy's health declined and Jacky was sent away to school.

Along with their studies and music lessons Jacky and Patsy also enjoyed dancing lessons. Music and dancing were an important part of life for children of the Washington's social standing. A few days each month children would visit neighbor's homes to participate in the lessons.

As Jacky grew older George Washington began worrying about his stepson. Schoolwork was not a priority in the teenager's life. While George was concerned about it, Jacky was not.

Washington reminded Jacky's teachers the importance of his studies. Jacky would one day be heir to a large fortune and Washington wanted him to be prepared and able to handle the responsibility. He wanted the lad to have a good character, be honest, hard working, and be knowledgeable in ways that would serve him well in his future. Jacky never did live up to those expectations.

Besides caring for the plantation and his family, George was hearing rumors about King George III that were disturbing. The debt of the French and Indian War was a burden on the British, and the king was trying to relieve that debt by taxing the colonists on goods they purchased and imported from England. Colonial leaders were adamantly opposed to this new taxation plan. George was kept informed and would soon become involved and in doing so secured his name in history.

At the age of twelve Patsy began experiencing violent epileptic seizures. There was no known cure or treatment for epilepsy at this time. George and Martha consulted with many different doctors desperately searching for a cure or for some relief for their daughter from this debilitating disorder. They tried everything the doctors thought might help, but nothing they tried made a difference.

Patsy over time became too ill to continue with her studies. Patsy's seizures increased over time in both frequency and severity.

During his teen years Jacky was sent to a school outside Annapolis, Maryland in hopes his studies would improve while studying with other young boys of his age. The school which was located close to Mount Vernon allowed him to visit and spend time with the family. While at school he studied very little and spent the majority of his time socializing and playing. Everything to Jacky was fun and games.

Jacky's lack of seriousness was a worry to his parents. He would one day be inheriting a large fortune from his father and perhaps he looked upon himself as a person of leisure; knowing he would never *really* have to work. His stepfather knew he would need to be educated enough to run a household of his own and not to be cheated financially. He would have not only a fortune but the burden of maintaining his inheritance.

One of the other students Jacky had become friends with was Charles Calvert. Charles was from the Calvert family who were descendants of Lord Baltimore. They were a prestigious family.

Jacky began spending more time at Mount Airy, home of the Calverts, than at Mount Vernon. Although he was only eighteen he had fallen in love with Nelly one of the Calverts' daughters and they became secretly engaged.

Nelly was sixteen while being courted by Jacky. She was young but of good character, pretty, and kind-hearted.

Jacky arrived at Mount Vernon with plans to inform his parents of his engagement. When he arrived home his parents thought it was for a visit but soon learned of their son's plan to get married. As far as continuing his education, that wasn't part of Jacky's plan.

Martha and Patsy were in favor of the marriage and were anxious to meet the girl who had captured Jacky's heart. George felt the boy needed to finish his education first. His desire was for Jacky to mature and make something of himself before contemplating marriage and taking on the responsibility of a family.

Nelly was invited to come stay at Mount Vernon so the family would have a chance to get to know her. After spending time with her the family approved of the marriage. She was liked by all who met her. It was felt she would be a good influence on Jacky, and she and

Patsy were about the same age and got along well. She was good company for Jacky's sister during her confinement.

One evening Patsy was seized with one of her epileptic fits. Nelly ran to her friend's aid but was helpless as what to do to help her. Patsy was lying on the floor in the midst of a violent seizure. Nelly shouted to Patsy's parents who rushed in to tend to their daughter.

George knelt beside the stepdaughter he had raised since she was a toddler with tears streaming down his face, sobbing and praying for the recovery of this precious young girl who he loved as his own. Only a few minutes passed and she was dead. Washington grief stricken bowed his head in despair. Martha too grieved terribly for her precious young daughter.

Following the death of his sister, Jacky became the sole heir of the Custis estate which was substantial. He was now a very wealthy young man.

Jacky was eighteen when he and Nelly married. His inheritance was enough to live on and he had no ambition to do anything other than enjoy life. For the first year of their marriage the young Custises divided their time between Mount Airy the bride's family home and Mount Vernon.

Relations with England and the colonies had disintegrated. Fellow patriots were urging Washington to take a role of leadership. While attending the Continental Congress John Adams put Washington's name forward to be the commander in chief. While initially the colonists were fighting for their rights, eventually it would change to fighting for their independence as a nation.

Martha along with Jacky and Nelly traveled to Philadelphia to be near George. Jacky and Nelly stayed with Martha until it was close to the time for the birth of their first child. The Washington's first grandchild Elizabeth "Betsy" Parke Custis arrived. Not long after Betsy's birth a second granddaughter followed, Martha "Patty" Parke Custis.

Jacky bought a home for his family, though it would be awhile before they moved in. Their estate called Abingdon included over one-thousand acres of land. Abingdon was located between Mount Vernon and Mount Airy. Washington felt Jacky had been cheated on the purchase, which had been one of his major concerns with Jacky's poor business judgment due to his lack of seriousness when it came to his education.

Nelly gave birth to yet another daughter their third, Eleanor "Nelly" Parke Custis. Jacky was a proud father and he loved his girls, but he longed for a son to add to his family.

During the summer Jacky and Nelly came to stay with Martha. Mount Vernon was filled with the voices of young children; music to Martha's ears.

The grandchildren were from five years old to an infant. They had come one after another, too close for Nelly to have time to recover and regain her strength. She had her hands full and was in fragile health after several births in such a short period of time. Martha often cared for the two youngest, two year old Nelly and the new baby George Washington "Wash" Parke Custis.

Jacky and Nelly would have seven children in all but only four would survive past infancy.

During the Revolutionary War when even Martha would spend harsh winters at Valley Forge tending to the soldiers and helping her husband in any way she could, Jacky continued with his life of privilege and leisure; never giving a moment's thought to joining the fight for the country's independence.

As the war was nearing the end, George was finally able to visit Mount Vernon for a few days. It was the first time he was able to set foot in Mount Vernon in over six years and it was his first opportunity to see his four grandchildren. After years of being at war it was wonderful to hear the voices of the children and hear laughter again. He was a proud grandfather.

Washington was devoted to Jacky Custis in his youth and did everything in his power to steer him in the right direction. Now his stepfather found it hard to respect a young man of privilege who chose to sit out the war and let others risk their lives while Jacky indulged himself. How could he ask others to put their lives on hold giving up so much when his own stepson wasn't willing to do the same?

When the General was ready to rejoin his troops after his short visit to Mount Vernon everyone was surprised when Jacky decided to join him. The Revolutionary War was coming to an end. Jacky Custis had shown no interest in the past in taking part in the war and fighting for this new nation. Martha was proud of her son for finally stepping up to fight alongside her husband while George was skeptical of his motives and wondered just how much of an asset he would actually be.

Jacky was assigned to his stepfather's personal staff and served as a civilian aide-de-camp to Washington during the Siege of Yorktown. He had only served a short time when he came down with camp fever, a form of dysentery soldiers in camps were all too familiar with.

Jacky was sent from the battlefield to a home nearby of a relative where he could recuperate. He never did regain his health.

When Washington received news of the critical condition of his stepson he left immediately to be with Jacky. Martha and Jacky's wife also rushed to be by his side. Within the hour of their arrival at the age of twenty-seven Jacky was dead.

Jacky hadn't achieved much in his life and wouldn't go down in history as a great man like his stepfather. The only thing about his life that would make others remember him at all was that he was the stepson of George Washington. Though not a hero, few of us are; Jacky had been a loving son, husband, and father. His family loved him regardless of his shortcomings and grieved for him deeply. Even though Washington was often exasperated by Jacky's behavior and lack of ambition, he loved his stepson dearly.

After eight and a half years of fighting George Washington was finally able to return home. All he longed for was to become a farmer and enjoy his life at Mount Vernon.

After a few years Jacky's wife would remarry and take her two oldest children with her. The two youngest, Nelly and Wash, stayed at Mount Vernon with George and Martha to live which was a common practice during these times.

Years after the end of the war George would go on to be elected the first President of the United States. The inauguration took place April 30, 1789 in New York. Martha and the grandchildren joined him in New York arriving about a month after his inauguration.

On their travels to the new home of the president, Wash was excited as they traveled and were met by parades and people coming out to wish them well along the way.

Nelly at age ten and Wash at age eight became the first kids or the first president's grandchildren in history. They became the *first* First Family.

Washington ran his presidency first from New York and later from Philadelphia with the family spending their summers at Mount Vernon.

Nelly loved school and was a good student. Wash however, didn't like to study. He was like his father in this respect. For the first few months Wash worked with a private tutor, and then it was decided to send Wash to a small school where he could study with other boys in hopes that it would have a better influence on him than it had on his father.

Nelly was tutored at home. She studied French and Italian in addition to her regular studies. She also studied music and painting, both subjects she loved.

On weekends George and the family spent time in the city taking in the sights. There was always something to see and do to entertain the children. They visited exhibits similar to what you see in museums today, zoos, and the theater. They once visited a wax museum that had a wax figure of George Washington in his military uniform which thrilled the children.

The eight years of Washington's presidency ended and it was time for the family to return to Mount Vernon. George had refused a third term as president setting a precedent for the future. George gave his Farewell Address and returned to Mount Vernon to retire.

By the time they returned to Mount Vernon Nelly was eighteen. She helped entertain their many visitors from all over the world of which there was a constant flow.

Wash was sent to St. John's College but he had no interest in studying and wanted to come home. He wrote to his grandparents asking if he could come home to stay. Washington wrote back that he would stay until he had finished his education.

Washington invited one of his nephews, Lawrence Lewis, to move to Mount Vernon and help with entertaining and running the plantation. George was getting up in years and he was at the point where he needed help. His nephew Lawrence came to live at Mount Vernon to help relieve some of the burden from the elderly Washingtons.

Lawrence, a childless widower, was twelve years Nelly's senior. She and Lawrence were soon spending a lot of time together and surprised no one when they decided to marry. They were married on George's sixty-seventh birthday.

Their first child was born only a few days before Washington's death. After Martha died

Nelly gave birth to seven more children. Four of the children died before reaching the age of two.

Nelly died at the age of seventy-three. She was buried alongside her grandparents at Mount Vernon.

At the age of twenty-three Wash married Mary Lee Fitzhugh. They had four children but only one daughter survived.

In later years Wash did mature and became a successful man who was respected. He completed his education at St. John's College and then went on to Princeton. Wash served in the military as an officer. His name became well-known not only as the grandson of the first president but as a successful playwright and orator. Wash dedicated much of his life in honoring his grandfather.

Wash built Arlington House that he built on land he had inherited from his father. The estate was located on a scenic hill overlooking the Potomac River across from the capital city of Washington, D.C.

At Arlington Wash received many visitors with whom he would reminisce about his grandfather who he had loved and revered. President Andrew Jackson was just one of his visitors at Arlington; many other of his visitors were also of the Washington elite. Wash displayed his collection of items from Mount Vernon and loved showing them to visitors, telling the story behind each and every piece in his collection. They were treasures and memories he cherished.

Wash's daughter Mary and her husband were married at and came to live at Arlington with Wash. Her husband was Robert E. Lee who would become a general and command the Confederate Army during the Civil War. Wash was a prominent figure in the lives of his seven grandchildren.

Wash's beloved Arlington would be confiscated by the United States government during the Civil War. The grounds on the estate were turned into Arlington Cemetery.

Before his death Wash wrote *'Recollection and Private Memoirs of Washington,'* an invaluable book about his famous grandfather.

2

JOHN ADAMS

Children of John and Abigail Adams:

Abigail "Nabby" Adams – Born: July 14, 1765   Died: August 15, 1813

John Quincy Adams – Born: July 11, 1767   Died: February 23, 1848

Grace Susanna "Suky" Adams – Born: Dec. 28, 1768   Died: Feb. 4, 1770

Charles Adams – Born: May 29, 1770   Died: November 30, 1800

Thomas Boylston Adams – Born: September 15, 1772   Died: March 13, 1832

Elizabeth Adams – Born: 1777   Died: 1777 Stillborn

Nabby Adams was the first child born of a president and her brother John Quincy Adams was the first presidential son to also become president.

Less than a year after the marriage of John and Abigail Adams their first child was born. Abigail Adams, or Nabby, was born in July of 1765. Nabby never had to do a thing except be born to become a footnote in history, as she would be the first child born of a President of the United States. At the time of her birth there was no such thing as a president; not only had there never been a president, there wasn't even a United States. At the time of her birth this nation was a British colony ruled by King George III.

John Quincy, Nabby's brother, was born just days before her second birthday. Not only would his sister make history, but so would her brother. Nabby would become the daughter of one president and the sister of another; while her brother would become the first presidential son to also become president.

John and Abigail Adams children came quickly one after the other. Not even a year and a half after John Quincy's birth Susanna Adams was born in December of 1768. Susanna was a frail child from the beginning and would live just a little over a year. At the time of Susanna's death Abigail was already pregnant with Charles who was born in May of 1770.

The Boston Massacre took place just months before Charles was born. John Adams was an attorney who believed everyone deserved a fair trial. He defended the British soldiers who were accused of the shooting at the Boston Massacre regardless of popular opinion against him taking the case.

John and Abigail's fifth child, Thomas Boylston Adams was born in September of 1772. When he was a year old in December of 1773 the Boston Tea Party took place.

While it would have been exciting in the eyes of a child for grown men to be dressed up as Indians and throwing chests of tea into the Boston Harbor, it must also have been a frightening time with the threat of war looming over their heads.

Their father had to travel to Philadelphia about three hundred miles from their home, which was quite a distance to travel in those times. He would be away from the family for quite some time participating in the Continental Congress.

While their father was in Philadelphia, it would be up to Abigail and the children to tend to the farm and take care of things at home. While away their father wrote letters in regards to the children's education. John's wishes were for his daughter to study along with her brothers. Education was of the utmost importance to both their father and their mother.

Patriots began collecting and stockpiling gunpowder thinking it inevitable that it would be needed in the days to come. The Continental Congress had sent King George III an Olive Branch Petition which the king rejected.

While out working the farm the Adams children stopped their work to watch as the militiamen of Braintree moved a store of munitions past their home. The militiamen were moving their stores to another location in fear the British would try to confiscate the gunpowder from them. Things were heating up between the colonials and the British.

The men had been wise in moving their stores. British troops marched to Concord with the intent to capture and seize the patriot's stockpiles of munitions. They spotted the militiamen on the town green. The militia weren't there to attack the troops as the British assumed, but to observe and report on their actions. Tensions were high. Both sides were on edge not knowing what the other side would do. No one knows for sure who fired the first shot, but regardless of who it was the Revolutionary War had begun.

Seven year old John Quincy woke in the middle of the night to sounds of cannons being fired in the near distance. At daybreak his mother and John Quincy made their way through the countryside and climbed to the top of Penn's Hill to see what was happening. The air was filled with smoke from all the cannon fire. You could smell the acrid smoke even from the distance of ten miles. They watched the flash as the cannons were being fired. What they were witnessing would become known as the Battle of Bunker Hill.

The family were now living in the midst of what had become battle grounds. Between the knowledge they gleaned from their father's letters written while away in the Continental Congress and what they were witnessing, the children were receiving more of an education than they ever could from their books alone. Unbeknownst to them they were watching history in the making; the beginning of the birth of our nation.

Battle weary soldiers found their way to the farm and Abigail opened her home to them in the days after the battle. Not only were soldiers welcomed but also families who were on the road leaving their homes fleeing to safety. Food was limited and space was so tight you had to step over people to move around, but no one was turned away.

Abigail and her children were kept busy tending to the soldiers whether in need of medical care or feeding them, tending to the farm, the animals, and crops; in addition to keeping up with their studies. Their tutor, a cousin of their mothers who had worked as a law clerk for their father lived with them and tutored the children.

The children were proud when they learned through one of their father's letters that he had been the one who had put George Washington's name forward to command the newly formed Continental Army. He kept them informed of what was happening in Philadelphia. They eagerly waited for their father's letters to arrive and would sit around their mother giving her their complete attention as she read the letters aloud.

In the summer of 1776 there was a major outbreak of smallpox. Abigail in order to protect the family was determined that they would be inoculated, which would ensure that if they came down with the disease it would be a lighter case. The inoculation only worked if the person actually came down with the virus. John Quincy and Nabby came down with the smallpox and recovered in a matter of weeks, but Charles and Thomas had to be reinoculated. Charles eventually came down with the smallpox, not from the inoculation but from exposure to someone who had the pox. He became very sick but recovered over time.

The Declaration of Independence completed, it was now read outside the Massachusetts State House. The crowd gathered close in order not to miss a word during the reading. At the conclusion of the reading loud cheers erupted.

John Quincy knew his father had a part in the writing of the Declaration of Independence. He knew that his father along with the other members of the Second Continental Congress were risking their lives. If they were captured by the British they could be put to death. Signing the document would be considered by the British a treasonous act.

For a time their father was able to return to Braintree. During his visit Abigail became pregnant yet again. The day John Quincy turned ten his mother gave birth to a baby girl. Baby Elizabeth was stillborn.

Congress chose John Adams to join Benjamin Franklin in France to convince the French to help finance the war and help the colonists fight. John planned to take his oldest son John Quincy with him. He felt he needed time with his father and it would be an educational experience for him.

Father and son sailed on a warship called the *Boston* leaving Massachusetts in February of 1778. There was a chance of being captured by the British on the voyage. It would have been a real coup for the British to capture John Adams one of the Founding Fathers. When British ships were seen their ship sailed in another direction out of their path. Once out to sea they had run into perilous weather. The waves rocked the ship convincing the passengers the ship would surely break apart. The passengers, both Adams included, suffered from seasickness. When they were in calmer waters John Quincy met a passenger on board who taught him the French language. John Quincy spent as much time as he could studying the language preparing for his time in France.

They arrived in France in April two months after they left from home. Once they left the ship to reach their final destination they still had to take a coach to Paris. This was a new world to John Quincy. He experienced new foods, customs, way of dress, lifestyle, and language which he had mastered while on board the ship. It was all thrilling to a young boy.

The senior Adams was in a country where he didn't understand the language. He was thankful he had brought his son along. John Quincy with his language skills was an asset to his father.

John Quincy was enrolled in a boarding school. Along with the typical subjects he had to study he was thrilled to learn the sport of fencing, music, and dancing. Fencing was used as a military training. Two competitors fighting with swords was something new to him and he enjoyed it immensely.

Weekends were spent with his father going out to dinner and trying new, exotic French food. They enjoyed the theater and getting out and meeting people. The people they met were impressed with the maturity and knowledge of young John Quincy. His father not easily impressed was proud of his son.

After a little over a year John Quincy and his father returned home. John Quincy had enjoyed his time in France but he was ready to go home and see his family.

They had only been home for a few months when his father was asked by Congress to return to Europe to help negotiate an end to the Revolutionary War and make peace with England. He would need to remain in France until England agreed to their terms. John Quincy wasn't excited about making a return trip so soon and would have preferred to stay home. His mother convinced him that since his younger brother nine year old Charles would be coming this time, it would help Charles to have John Quincy for a companion.

Charles was only four years old when his father left for the Continental Congress. He was six after the signing of the Declaration of Independence when his father returned home. His father after only being home for a few months left again to go overseas with John Quincy. Charles had been separated from his father for the majority of his life and he was practically a stranger. He knew him more through the letters he had written to the family than from spending time with him.

Again the seas were rough on the voyage. The ship had a leak and had to sail into a port in southern Spain instead of their destination of France. They would have to complete their journey of nearly one thousand miles on unfamiliar land crossing the treacherous Pyrenees Mountains on the backs of donkeys in the dead of winter. It was a difficult feat for the hardiest of men, but in the worst weather imaginable and for two young boys and their father it took all their strength to complete the journey. They crossed the mountains which separates Spain from France. Their clothes were constantly drenched from the rain and snow and at times the fog was so thick it made travel life-threatening. This part of the journey took them almost another two months arriving in France with both boys sick.

John Quincy and Charles were enrolled in the same school John Quincy had previously attended. They would only have time with their father on occasional weekends. He took them to visit museums and the theater when they were together to enrich their cultural education. Unlike his brother, Charles didn't speak or understand French and had a hard time making friends and adjusting. While John Quincy had thoroughly enjoyed the adventure of a new culture and customs and saw everything as a challenge, the younger Charles was lonely and missed home.

After a year in France John and his sons left for Holland where John was hoping to gain Dutch support for the American cause of independence. Charles and John Quincy were enrolled in school which had been unlike anything they had ever experienced. Their father described the Dutch schoolmasters in a letter to their mother as "mean-spirited wretches who punch and kick the students." The boys were withdrawn from the school posthaste and a tutor was hired to teach them at home. In addition to their tutoring Charles and John Quincy were allowed to attend lectures at the University of Leyden which benefited their education immensely. John Quincy would become a scholar of the university. He was an eager student and was excited to study under the masters on the arts and sciences. His brother Charles not so much so.

Charles was homesick and ready to return home. John wrote to Abigail that he was sending Charles home by himself. Abigail wrote back begging him not to send Charles, just eleven years old, on a voyage across the Atlantic alone.

A passenger on the ship, a major in the Continental Army, agreed to escort Charles. It turned out to be a traumatic journey for the young boy which he never recovered from. The ship ran into problems once on the seas and instead of heading to America as planned had to dock in Spain for repairs. Once in Spain his chaperone accompanied him to shore where they waited for passage home. After a time the chaperone could no longer wait and left Charles on his own. He was an eleven year old boy on his own in a country where he didn't speak the language, and had no idea how he was ever going to get home.

Normally it took about three weeks to a month to sail across the Atlantic. The seas were dangerous to cross with British ships threatening attack or imprisonment. They were also concerned about privateers. The seas were a treacherous place to be. Finally, months after he had initially boarded ship to sail home he was finally on his way again.

It had been five months since Charles left his father. The family was worried sick and after months of waiting for his arrival they feared he was lost at sea and presumed dead. He arrived home traumatized by his experience, refusing ever to speak of his trip.

Only a few days after he arrived home he and his younger brother Thomas were shipped off to school. He had been at the school for only a short time when he learned his mother and sister would be sailing for London. His father was to be the first United States representative to England and they would be joining him. It would be seven years before the two youngest boys ever saw either of their parents again.

John Quincy still in Holland had turned fourteen. His traveling days were not over. He would be traveling to Russia to serve as secretary to the American Minister of the Russian Empress Catherine the Great. His knowledge of the French language would be invaluable; as the Russian court spoke French.

The journey John Quincy took by coach through Germany and Poland would cover two thousand miles to reach St. Petersburg, Russia. The trip was quite an experience for John Quincy that would benefit him in years to come. It enabled him to see parts of the world few others in his time ever witnessed.

Similar to when he learned French John Quincy now studied and learned the German language. He eventually became fluent in six languages.

After a little over a year John Quincy returned to serve as his father's secretary. On his return trip he traveled through Sweden, Norway, Denmark, and northern Germany. John Quincy would be in France with his father who along with a few other men, including Benjamin Franklin and Thomas Jefferson, had negotiated a treaty with Britain ending the Revolutionary War. As his father's secretary John Quincy was there for that historical event and witnessed the signing of the Treaty of Paris.

As much as they would have liked to return to the United States at this time to see how the new country was flourishing, John's work was not yet finished. He had written home asking his wife Abigail and his daughter Nabby to join him.

Nabby, however; now a young woman of eighteen was in love and didn't want to leave. She had met and fallen in love with a lawyer named Royall Tyler. Her mother approved of him until she heard rumors that he had fathered an illegitimate child in his younger days. Abigail wrote John asking for advice on whether to allow her daughter to keep seeing him. John even though across the Atlantic had Royall looked into. The report came back which satisfied him but he thought his daughter too young and asked her to give the romance some time, then if she still wanted to marry Royall he would give his consent. His work for now was in London and he wanted his wife and daughter to join him. He had been deprived of their company for far too long.

Nabby reluctantly agreed that she would do as her father requested and give the relationship time. Abigail and Nabby boarded the ship *Active* and set sail. Her father in the meantime had a change of heart and had written to both Abigail and to Royall telling them he gave his consent to the marriage. The letters were still in transit as they set sail and Nabby's life history was altered.

Both women were terribly seasick on the voyage and at times had to be tied to chairs to keep them from being violently tossed to the deck of the ship. When land was finally sighted it would be an additional week before they were able to get up the Thames River due to the winds and rough waves.

Once they had their feet firmly planted on land again they had to take a carriage to London; an additional trip of seventy miles. It was here they met John Quincy and John. It had been so long since Abigail had seen her son she didn't even recognize him. From London they had to get in another carriage for another journey of hundreds of miles before arriving in Paris their final destination.

When John Quincy turned eighteen his parents thought it was time for him to return home and finish his education at Harvard. He would graduate in just over a year's time ranking second highest in his class. After graduation he began working as an apprentice to become a lawyer.

After a time in France John Adams was sent to England. John, Abigail, and Nabby moved again, which was fine with Nabby as she didn't care for the French people. While in England they were presented to King George III, the very king they had fought for their independence. The Adams were also invited to another event at the palace to celebrate the queen's birthday. At the birthday celebration Nabby and the princess, who Nabby had met and befriended, watched in amusement as the Prince of Wales the future King George IV made a fool of himself while dancing a minuet and fell down.

While in London Nabby met Colonel William Stephens Smith. Smith had served with George Washington in the Continental army. Having given up on her previous engagement with Royall after receiving no correspondence from him she accepted Smith's proposal of marriage. She would later learn Royall had been writing, but for some reason she never received the letters. If she had, it is doubtful she would have married Smith.

Nabby and Smith married in June of 1786, one month before Nabby would turn twenty-one. They had four children, three sons and a daughter; but it would not be a happy marriage. Nabby's husband was an alcoholic and was involved more than once in get rich schemes which were never successful.

A year after John Quincy's graduation from Harvard his parents returned home to the United States.

Charles who had been traumatized during his return trip home from France and then left behind as his parents were living overseas was happy to see his family return. As a young boy he had little time being nurtured by his parents. He had grown into a good looking young man and was attending Harvard, but he had never matured. He had been in trouble at Harvard on more than one occasion.

His parents felt Charles, even though now eighteen, needed to be watched over and guided on the right path. All the years he had been left by his parents his father now felt it his duty as a father to lambaste his son and compare him to his older brother John Quincy. His father expected a lot from his son and he let him know it in no uncertain terms. If he thought this would inspire his son to do better, he was wrong. Feeling he could never measure up to his father's expectations it had the opposite effect.

In 1789 George Washington was elected the nation's first president and John Adams became the first vice president.

As vice president John Adams lived in New York. Charles also moved there with his parents. His father made arrangements so Charles could study law under Alexander Hamilton. While in New York Charles pursued his law career which he failed at.

Nabby had also moved to New York with her family. Nabby at this time had three children one after the other – all boys. Some time later they would also have a daughter. The capital was moved to Philadelphia. John and Abigail had to move to Philadelphia leaving Charles and Nabby behind. Two weeks after her parents had moved, Nabby's husband announced he was leaving for England. He was involved in one bad deal after another often leaving his wife and children behind to fend for themselves.

Charles fell in love with Sally Smith the sister of Nabby's husband Colonel Smith. Regardless of how the family felt about Nabby's husband Sally was of a different personality and character than her brother and was well-liked. Charles and Sally were married in 1795. The family had hopes this would settle Charles down.

President Washington appointed John Quincy as minister to Holland. This time it was Thomas, the younger brother, who crossed the Atlantic with his brother to serve as his secretary. He served as John Quincy's secretary from 1794 - 1798 while in the Netherlands and Prussia.

Thomas had graduated from Harvard where he too had studied law. When his father was elected president he returned to the United States and lived with his parents in Philadelphia.

Thomas married Ann Harold and began practicing law. They had seven children. One of their daughters, Francis at only seven months came down with whopping cough and died.

Thomas was elected to the Massachusetts Legislature but resigned a year later. He was struggling with alcoholism.

Thomas would go on to become a state court judge. It was difficult for Thomas living up to the name his father and brother had made for themselves, and he never felt like he could measure up to their achievements. He got lost in the shadows of his brother and father. His father who could be cold, indifferent, and demanding, but not compassionate disowned his son for failure.

Charles struggled throughout his life. He had two children, a loving wife, and a law practice that was unsuccessful. He had become involved in a financial scandal. What made it even worse was he had lost money his brother John Quincy had entrusted him with.

He felt everyone around him in his family was highly successful. His father had been a patriot, Founding Father, and was now the vice-president of the United States. His older brother excelled at everything he did and was a diplomat. Even an uncle, Sam Adams, had been a Founding Father. His father relentlessly sent him letters telling him how disappointed in him he was. Charles felt like a failure and suffered from depression and became an alcoholic.

Things only got worse when John Adams paid a surprise visit to Nabby in New York. He was shocked to find that Charles' wife and two children were living there. He only now became aware of his son's drinking and financial problems. John Adams wrote to his wife Abigail: *"I renounce him!"*

For Abigail it wasn't quite that easy to give up on her son. She came to visit Charles and found him dying of cirrhosis of the liver. If it hadn't been for a caring friend who had taken him in, her son would have been dying alone and homeless. As a mother it broke her heart. When she left she walked out the door knowing there was a good chance she would never see him alive again. Leaving him behind had been one of the hardest things she ever had to do. She had barely arrived home before the news arrived that he had died.

John Adams became the nation's 2nd president.

In the time that John Quincy was serving as minister to Holland he met his future wife Louisa while traveling in London. His parents were opposed to the marriage as his mother thought it would hinder his political life being married to a foreigner. At the age of thirty John Quincy married his twenty-two year old English bride.

John Quincy was still working overseas when he learned his father had become the second president. His father assigned him the job of serving as our nation's first representative to Prussia.

John Quincy's first child was born while he and Louisa were living in Berlin. He was named George Washington Adams.

Thomas Jefferson won the next presidential election. John Adams having served as president for only one term was bitter at not being reelected. John Quincy and his family came home to Massachusetts to live. Unbeknownst to John Quincy his time in Europe was not over and when James Madison became president he would return overseas.

Arriving back in Massachusetts John Quincy wasn't sure what he would do. He and his family moved into his parent's home. Abigail Adams never did make Louisa feel welcome and while they didn't get along, John Adams was very kind to her.

After returning to law for a time John Quincy became a state senator. John Quincy and Louisa moved to Washington, D.C. while the Senate was in session and returned to Braintree, Massachusetts between Senate sessions.

John Quincy and Louisa had two more sons John Adams II and Charles Francis.

John Quincy resigned from the Senate knowing his votes, sometimes against his own party, were not always popular making his chances of reelection unlikely. This wasn't necessarily a bad thing, as there was now a new president. James Madison asked John Quincy to become a United States diplomat in Russia.

When John Quincy and Louisa left for Russia Louise begged her husband to bring all their children with them, but he would permit only their two year old son Charles Francis to accompany them. George and John would be left behind with relatives. Nabby's oldest son William asked if he could go with them. John Quincy agreed and William became his secretary. It would take them eighty days to cross the Atlantic and the Baltic before they arrived in Russia.

During their time in Russia Louisa gave birth to a baby girl they named Louisa Catherine. At a very young age she became very ill with a high fever and began having convulsions. She died a short time after her first birthday.

Back home Nabby confided in her mother of a lump she had discovered in her breast. She was examined by physicians and was informed that it was malignant. Months later the tumor was causing Nabby pain and she traveled to the home of her parents with two of her children to be seen by experts for advice. Nabby and her family were advised that her only hope for survival was to have a mastectomy.

The surgery took place at her parent's home with only a dose of opium or laudanum. After her recovery she returned to her home and after some time again began having pains yet again. They discovered the cancer had returned. As her days came to an end knowing she had little time left on this earth, Nabby desired to be with her parents when she died. Her mother Abigail sick herself was unable to travel. Nabby decided she would make the trip to her parent's home. Nabby with two of her children made the three hundred mile trip in a coach. Each bump in the road left her in excruciating pain, but she was determined to be with her family in her final days. She died at the home of her parents at the age of forty-eight.

John Quincy was in Russia when he heard about the War of 1812. President Madison had asked him along with two others to work out a peace treaty with England. John Quincy again was a witness to history in the making of the treaty as he was there to witness the signing of the Treaty of Ghent. President Madison made him United States minister to Great Britain.

When Monroe became president he asked John Quincy to serve as secretary of state. John Quincy became known as 'the nation's greatest secretary of state.' While in this position he was successful at negotiating with England for the Oregon Territory, he was responsible for the United States acquiring Florida from Spain, and he drafted the Monroe Doctrine.

John Quincy Adams would become our nation's 6th president. He went down in history as the first son of a president to also become president. The first of only two to be able to claim that honor. But his accomplishments didn't end there.

John Quincy spent the remaining years of his life serving as a member of the House of Representatives until in 1848 he collapsed on the floor of the House of Representatives suffering from a stroke and passed away two days later.

Similar to his father John Quincy wasn't a popular man. He would rather spend his time alone than with others, including his wife who he was harsh and demanding with and his children, who he also like his father made demands on them they never felt they could live up to. But unlikeable as he may have been, he is respected for his works. He gave his life to public service from the time he was in his teens until his death.

Many barely remember him as a president. The first thing many recall about him is that he went skinny dipping each morning in the Potomac River while president and he was the first son of a president to become president; but he accomplished much for this country in his lifetime.

3

Thomas Jefferson

Children with wife Martha:

Martha Washington Jefferson "Patsy" - Born: September 27, 1772   Died: October 10, 1836

Jane Randolph Jefferson – Born: April 3, 1774   Died: September, 1775

Peter Jefferson – Born: May 28, 1777   Died: June 14, 1777

Mary Jefferson "Polly" or "Maria" - Born: Aug. 1, 1778   Died: April 17, 1804

Lucy Elizabeth Jefferson #1 – Born: Nov. 3, 1780   Died: April 15, 1781

Lucy Elizabeth Jefferson #2 - Born: May 8, 1782, Died Oct. 13, 1784

Alleged Children with slave Sally Hemings:

The Thomas Jefferson Memorial Foundation, the foundation which owns and operates Monticello, announced that according to its extensive research Thomas Jefferson probably fathered one if not all of Sally Hemings's children.

Thomas Jefferson Hemings "Tom" - Birth: 1790   Died: Unknown, infancy

Harriet Hemings #1 - Born: October 5, 1795   Died: December 7, 1797

Edy Hemings – Born: 1799   Died: 1800

William Beverly Hemings – Born: April 1, 1798   Died: Unknown, sometime after 1873

Thenia Hemings – Born: 1799   Died: Unknown, died in infancy

Harriet Hemings #2 – Born: May 22, 1801   Died: Sometime after 1863

James Madison Hemings - Born: January 19, 1805   Died: November 28, 1877

Eston Hemings- Born: May 21, 1808   Died: January 3, 1856

The first baby born in the White House was during Thomas Jefferson's administration when his daughter gave birth to a baby boy.

Martha Jefferson had been married previous to her marriage to Thomas Jefferson. She had been married in her first marriage for less than two years when her husband died leaving her a wealthy young widow. In the time of her short first marriage she gave birth to a son named John who died at the age of three; just six months before her marriage to Thomas Jefferson.

Thomas and Martha were married for ten years in which most of that time Martha was not well. She gave birth to seven children, six of those children during her marriage to Thomas in which only two daughters would live to become adults. The Jeffersons lost four of their six children before the age of two and a half.

Just under nine months from the time of their marriage Martha gave birth to Martha Washington Jefferson who her father nicknamed Patsy. She was a little redhead like her father.

About a year and a half after the birth of Patsy, Jane Randolph Jefferson was born in April of 1774 who lived only for seventeen weeks. It was in March of 1775 when Thomas Jefferson was elected to Congress. He and Martha were often separated as he served in the First and Second Continental Congress. It was between the death of Jane and the birth of his son that Thomas Jefferson wrote the Declaration of Independence. The only son of Jefferson was born May 28, 1777 who lived only a few short weeks. Some historians list his name as Peter while others claim he remained unnamed.

Mary Jefferson was born August 1, 1778. Mary went by both Polly and later as Maria. She along with Patsy are the only two Jefferson children who would live to become adults.

Jefferson was the governor of Virginia when Lucy Elizabeth Jefferson arrived on November 3, 1780. She was born in Richmond, Virginia where the government had moved due to the Revolutionary War. The British invasion of Virginia in 1781 led to the decision of Thomas sending his wife and children to escape from the approaching British troops. They left Monticello and seeking safety made their way to their home Poplar Forest in Bedford County near Lynchburg. The family fled the approaching troops into the winter weather in snow and freezing temperatures which brought on the infant's illness from which she never recovered. Her death came just a few short weeks later. She lived for only a little over five months.

After Lucy's death Jefferson resigned as governor promising his wife that would be the end of any political assignments. He kept his promise throughout her lifetime.

Weakened from giving birth six times in less than fourteen years her health was already in a weakened state when she became pregnant yet again and died only four months after giving birth to the second daughter named Lucy (referred to as Lucy 2) in 1782. In the last months of her life Jefferson never left his wife's side. Martha Jefferson was only thirty-three years old at the time of her death.

Thomas Jefferson had promised his wife on her death bed he wouldn't marry again, and so it was Patsy at the age of ten who took over the position of running the household after the death of her mother. It was a position she held for the rest of her life, even during her own marriage.

President George Washington selected Jefferson to be a representative of the new government. It was 1784 when Jefferson was sent to France to join Benjamin Franklin and John Adams. Patsy would accompany her father to Paris while the two younger daughters Polly and Lucy would be left behind in the care of his wife's sister. Jefferson believed the younger girls would be safer left behind in the United States by avoiding the dangers of traveling across the Atlantic and in hopes of avoiding health problems they may have been exposed to in France.

France was an exciting place for young Patsy. Her father deeply enthralled at the culture in France must have shared experiences and tales of the things he admired in Paris. He was captivated by their architecture, music, and arts. Patsy met many of the elite of

France including the wife of Lafayette who had joined in the fight alongside George Washington in the Revolutionary War.

The wife of Lafayette sponsored Patsy into a school for girls in Paris, the Pentemont Abbey. Once Jefferson had been reassured she would not have to partake in religion classes he permitted his daughter to attend school at the Abbey.

Among the elite attending classes alongside Patsy were three princesses; even so life at the Pentemont Abbey did not cater to the whims of the rich and elite. Water would have to freeze before fires were built. Silence was to be observed unless called on in class or during recreation. There was no pampering regardless of your family name and status.

January of 1785 Lafayette returned to Paris and brought with him a letter for Jefferson from home. The letter informed him that Lucy Elizabeth (#2) his youngest daughter had died of whopping cough. Jefferson blamed himself for not having brought her with him to Paris. Yet another of his beloved children died at such a young age.

Patsy grieving after losing another sibling convinced her father to have her seven year old sister Polly brought to France to join them. Jefferson agreed, but Polly was happy where she was and didn't want to leave. She was young and barely remembered her family. Upon hearing that his daughter barely remembered them, Jefferson was even more convinced not to waste any more time in having his daughter brought to France to join him and Patsy.

In the summer of 1787 Jefferson made arrangements for the ship that was to transport his daughter and her escort to dock on the river near the plantation of the Eppes family where young Polly was staying with her aunt and family. Once the ship was docked the children were allowed to play aboard the *Arundel,* the ship they would be sailing on. The children had been playing on the ship one day and Polly had fallen asleep. After the other children left, the ship set sail with Polly and her escort. By the time the young girl woke up they were out to sea and the only family she remembered were left behind.

The ship sailed to London where her father had made arrangements with Abigail Adams who along with her husband and daughter were living in London to care for his daughter until he could arrange to pick her up and bring her to Paris. Polly who had just turned six, was taken from the only family she remembered to be brought to be with her father and sister who were strangers to her in a strange land. She was accompanied by her escort a young slave girl named Sally Hemings from the Jefferson plantation. Now Polly was being left in London for a time with even more strangers. After a time she grew close to Abigail and was content to stay with the Adams in London but would be uprooted yet again. Jefferson too involved with his work to make the trip sent a French servant who barely spoke English to pick his daughter up in London and bring her on a stagecoach to Paris.

At the time her father and sister had sailed to Paris Polly was so young that she had no memories of them. She would have to adjust yet again to living with her family in a strange country where the people spoke a different language from her own. She would join her sister at the Catholic school, the Pentemont Abbey. While in Paris she became known as Maria, a name she went by the rest of her life.

When Jefferson received a letter from his older daughter asking permission to become a nun and make the convent her home Jefferson showed up at the school bringing his daughters home. Patsy tutored her younger sister and became mistress of her father's house never to mention becoming a nun again.

It was the year the French Revolution erupted where people of wealth were being murdered and the guillotine was chopping off the heads of the French royals. Jefferson feared for his family's safety and after their home had been robbed three times he finally received word from Washington he could return home. It was autumn of 1789 when the Jeffersons sailed for home.

The year after their return to the United States Tom Randolph who had known Patsy as a child began courting her. He was well-educated and was studying and working towards a career in politics. Thomas Jefferson approved of the match and after an engagement of only three months, eighteen year old Patsy married Thomas Mann Randolph, Jr. As an adult Patsy reverted back to her given name of Martha.

Unfortunately, in such a short engagement period Tom hid a dark side that would only later reveal itself and cause Martha much heartbreak. She would eventually separate from her husband who suffered from alcoholism and mental breakdowns.

Martha and Tom's honeymoon came to an abrupt end when her father was named the nation's first secretary of state under Washington's administration. The newlyweds returned home early so Martha could run Monticello. Martha's husband, Tom Randolph, had idolized his father-in-law at one time, but after their marriage his attitude changed as he repeatedly had to compete for his wife's attention and always finding himself coming in second. He felt regardless of what he did he could never seem as worthy in the eyes of his wife. In time he would come to deeply resent his father-in-law.

Martha and her husband would have twelve children, losing only one of her children in their early childhood while the other eleven lived to become adults.

By 1797 when her father became vice president during John Adams' administration she had already had four children with another child arriving before her father became the nation's third president, and more soon following.

In 1797 Maria, Jefferson's youngest daughter, married her cousin from her mother's side John Wayles Eppes with whom she had grown up with as a young girl before moving to France. While Maria's husband admired his wife's father he never used him or his famous name for advancement, instead relying on his own intelligence and hard work to gain his accomplishments. He would become a member of the House of Representatives and the Senate.

A year after Maria was married she gave birth to a baby boy who died just three days later. A little over a year and a half later in September of 1801 she gave birth to another boy, Francis Eppes who was the only child of Maria to survive.

During his days in the White House Jefferson wanted his daughters to join him. There were times his daughters were unable to come due to pregnancies, births, and sick children. Martha gave birth to two more children during this time. Martha did join him during the social season and served as his hostess or acting first lady. When she wasn't available to fill the role Dolley Madison stepped in to serve as hostess.

Both Martha and Maria were married to congressmen in the early years of their father's presidency and Martha was able to serve as hostess at the White House while her husband served in Congress. During Tom's time in Congress he made many enemies due to his temper and his unstable mental condition.

During the time he was living in the White House with Martha and their children Jefferson believed his son-in-law's mental state to be psychosomatic and thought it to be a disease he could recover from if only he was willing. Tom looked at his brother-in-law

Jack Eppes, husband of Maria, as competition for his father-in-law's attention causing a nervous breakdown.

Maria didn't visit the White House as often as her sister Martha. She felt she was under her older sister's shadow stating people only commented on her beauty as she had nothing else of significance to offer, whereas her sister had much others admired about her. Her father loved them both dearly.

Both daughters would bring their children with them and lived part time in the White House filling the halls with sounds of laughter and little children running through the halls. Jefferson was enthralled with having his grandchildren with him and read to them, played with them, and spent as much time as possible with the youngsters.

During a White House visit a friend of Jeffersons looked on as the president played with his daughter's children. To them he was grandpa, not the president. Jefferson was enjoying himself with the grandchildren, a smile on his face and not a care in the world surrounded by a brood of little ones, with one standing behind him with his arms wrapped around his grandfather's neck and two of them climbing on his lap all vying for his attention - and getting it.

The grandchildren of Jefferson experienced many things other children were never able to. Jefferson's grandchildren were the first American children to eat ice cream. Zebulon Pike brought two grizzly bear cubs to the White House as gifts. Treasures collected from the travels of the Lewis and Clark Expedition were displayed in the White House for all to see such as antlers, stuffed animals, snake skins, pelts, collections of botanical specimens, and Indian costumes which mesmerized the grandchildren.

It is unknown if the grandchildren were in residence when the Indians came to visit the White House, but if not, no doubt they heard stories and vivid descriptions of their visit. Twenty one Indians from different tribes came to visit the president putting on a performance of their traditional dances on the North Lawn where they wore their traditional Indian clothing and paint. The Indians not only received gifts from the president but gave him gifts in return of tomahawks, blankets, and jewelry. The White House was a fascinating place to be for young children in the days of their grandfather's administration.

February 15, 1804 Maria gave birth to a little girl she named Maria Jefferson Eppes.

Word was sent to the president that his youngest daughter wasn't expected to live. The president was unable to leave Washington until Congress adjourned in March. He sent Maria's husband Jack, a congressman, to leave early to be with his wife. Jack had to struggle through icy weather often having to walk and lead his horse over routes that were frozen over and treacherous to pass through. When he arrived home he found his wife was in critical condition with her sister Martha caring for her.

The moment Congress adjourned Jefferson rushed to his daughter's home hoping and praying to reach his daughter in time. Devastated to see how frail she had become he had her moved on a litter to Monticello to be tended to in hopes she would recover. Maria died a short time later at the age of twenty-five on April 17, 1804 of complications from childbirth. The baby girl would also die a short two years later.

Jefferson was deeply grief stricken by the death of his daughter. He had lost so many loved ones in his lifetime. Only one daughter remained.

Martha, his surviving daughter, back at the White House gave birth to a son in 1806. The son, James Madison Randolph, would go down in history as the first child to be born in the White House. The boy was named by Jefferson who insisted on choosing all his grandchildren's names. He named the boy after his friend who was the secretary of state and would become the next president.

Martha would have another boy during her father's presidency and three more children after his retirement. Due to her duties of being a mother of a large brood and tending to Monticello, she was only at the White House part time. Martha educated her children at home with the aid of private tutors.

Once Thomas Jefferson retired he returned to Monticello. His home was filled with twelve grandchildren including Maria's son Francis Eppes who was a frequent visitor. Monticello's numerous visitors were always amazed to find a Founding Father and former president crawling around on his hands and knees playing with his young grandchildren. Those times with his grandchildren gave the former president great joy.

Once Thomas Jefferson retired his daughter lived with him at Monticello and devoted the rest of her life to caring for him. Jefferson had fallen seriously in debt to the point where he had to sell his extensive book collection that meant so much to him which would become the beginning of the Library of Congress. Jefferson, much to Martha's surprise, had also been paying the debts of her husband which put him further in debt; a debt he could ill afford to take on. His kindness and compassion brought on much of his debt between his continuous visitors coming and staying at Monticello that needed to be fed, loans to friends, giving to the University of Virginia, his generosity to others, all added to his debt; but he had a heart that couldn't turn others in need away.

During the War of 1812, Tom decided he would become a soldier and go off to fight the British. He wrote his will and made his wife Martha promise if anything happened to him she would never remarry. Whether his unsound reasoning was to die a hero and make a name for himself is unknown, but he returned from battle with his mind in a constant battle of retaining his sanity.

Thomas Jefferson died July 4, 1826, the 50th anniversary of the adoption of the Declaration of Independence. Five hours later, his friend and fellow patriot John Adams also lost his life on this historical day.

At the death of her father Martha not only inherited Monticello, but inherited her father's debts as well. Her troubles mounted two years later when her husband died also leaving a mountain of debt. Her son, Thomas Jefferson or Jeff, became executor of the estate. Jeff who was a man of honor was determined that whatever it took he would pay off all the creditors; both those of his father and of his grandfather.

After her father's death Martha took her son George Wythe and daughter Septemia to live with her daughter Ellen Coolidge in Boston. For the remainder of her life Martha would live with one or another of her children as she herself was now destitute.

Martha was the only one of Jefferson's *legitimate* children to survive past the age of twenty-five. Martha died at the age of sixty-four from what is believed to have been a stroke on Oct. 10, 1836. She was buried at Monticello next to her beloved father.

Did he or didn't he? That's the 225+ year old question that doesn't raise any less passion on the topic today than it did in Jefferson's day. The controversy of a relationship and children between Thomas Jefferson and his slave Sally Hemings brings out as much heated arguments as do opinions on which candidate, Republican or Democrat, is the better choice in an election year. Did Jefferson father the children of his slave Sally Hemings? If he did, does it make his place in history any less relevant?

Some argue that he as a slave owner sexually assaulted her, but there certainly isn't any evidence of that. Slavery was illegal in France where she had gone to escort Jefferson's youngest daughter. She could have stayed in France and been free and her unborn child would have been free at birth, not having to wait until he was 21 years of age as promised by Jefferson if she returned to Monticello. She chose of her own free will to return to America with Jefferson. Even years after his death she walked several miles in her elderly years over rough terrain several times a week to visit and care for his grave site. Doesn't sound like the actions of a bitter woman who was forced into a relationship. Is it possible to put emotions and preconceived ideas aside and consider there could have been a relationship of some sort?

People look at this through eyes of the 21st century rather than taking into account the era Sally and Jefferson lived in. It was a different world then and that must be taken into consideration before judgment is passed.

I am including Sally's children and will leave it up to you to decide what you believe on the issue. DNA has spoken on at least one of her children; but even that doesn't conclusively reveal if Jefferson is indeed the father or not, but it certainly points that way. The Thomas Jefferson Foundation Research Committee stated "a high probability that Thomas Jefferson was the father of Eston Hemings, and that Thomas Jefferson was likely the father of all six of Sally Hemings's children."

The Foundation didn't come to this decision lightly, but only after reviewing the facts with an open mind through documentary, scientific, statistical, and oral history evidence did they make their determination that he was most likely the father of her children.

Facts don't change because you want it to be one way or the other. The purpose of this isn't to try to convince you of anything, but to include the stories of what could very possibly be the children of a president; in which case they have as much right to have their story told as other children of presidents.

If you wish to read more about the findings from 'The Thomas Jefferson Foundation' and on the DNA testing go to monticello.org

Sally Hemings was the daughter of a slave and of slave owner John Wayles who was the father of Thomas Jefferson's wife Martha. Sally was the half-sister of Thomas Jefferson's wife. At the death of Jefferson's father-in-law, John Wayles, Thomas Jefferson inherited Sally as part of his wife's inheritance.

Jefferson was in France working for the new American government when he sent for his youngest daughter to be brought to France to join him. Polly, his daughter, was escorted from America to Paris by the Jefferson's fourteen-year-old slave Sally around 1787.

It was during the time in Paris that the alleged relationship between Jefferson and Sally began. This relationship was acknowledged by Sally's son Madison. By the time she returned to Monticello she was pregnant. The child, Thomas Jefferson Hemings "Tom," would live only a short time. Sally was approximately sixteen or seventeen at the time she returned to Monticello.

While in Paris Sally was trained as a lady's maid. Unlike in America slavery was illegal in France, so she was free during her time in Paris. She could have chosen to stay in France and she would have been free as would any children she had. She made the choice to return with Jefferson after he promised her she would be treated well and any of her children would be freed from slavery at the age of twenty-one. This was a promise he kept.

Sally had seven children in all. There are no photographs of the young slave girl, but she was described as pretty and practically white resembling her half-sister Martha.

The memoirs of Madison Hemings, son of Sally, in an article titled "Life Among the Lowly, No. 1," *Pike County, Ohio Republican* March 13, 1873 that was later published in *Frontline* of PBS, Madison said that his mother became Jefferson's concubine during their time in France. He also spoke of a baby boy she gave birth to after returning from France that lived only for a short time.

Thomas Woodson claimed to be Sally's first child. The information on Woodson is his name was originally Thomas Jefferson Hemings, but he changed his name after being sent from Monticello to live on a plantation of an owner by the name of Woodson. The story goes that after a visitor at Monticello commented on his similar looks to Jefferson to this slave, he had been shipped off to another plantation. Sally had several children that closely resembled Jefferson, but there is no record of any of her children having been sold or sent to live elsewhere. Woodson's birth date is given as the same year Sally gave birth to a Thomas, but according to Sally's own son Madison the baby named Tom died soon after birth. According to Woodson's descendants their oral history states him as being the offspring of Sally and Thomas Jefferson, but no record has been found to substantiate this claim. Slave records are sparse.

The first Harriet Hemings was born in 1798 and passed away just two years later. Sally's next child Edy was born in 1799 and died the next year. William Beverly Hemings, known as Beverly, was born in 1798 and died sometime after 1873, but no definite date other than he was alive in 1873 is known. Thenia was born the year after Beverly and died in infancy. The next child named Harriet Hemings was born in 1801 and lived to be sixty-two years of age. James Madison Hemings was born in 1805 and lived to be seventy-two. Eston Hemings was born in 1808 and lived to the age of forty-eight.

Beverly gained his freedom during Jefferson's lifetime and was given clothing and a few essentials that would help him get a start in his new life. He was given a ride from Monticello heading into a world completely foreign to him. Beverly was light enough to pass for white and he eventually did marry a white woman and had a child. His wife and child never knew he was black or the son of a slave. In order to pass into the white world he had to cut all ties with his family permanently.

Harriet was the next one to gain her freedom. She was given some money and clothing appropriate for a young white woman accepted into society and left Monticello at the age of twenty-one. She also was given her freedom during Thomas Jefferson's lifetime.

Harriet also passed into the white world marrying a white man in Washington, D.C. and raising a family. No one suspected she came from slavery or was of African American descent. She too had to cut all family ties for the rest of her life and after a time the family lost any trace of what happened to her. They kept her new name and identity as a white woman a closely guarded secret for her protection. Her new family was unaware of her heritage.

Jefferson wanting Madison and Eston to be prepared to entering the world as free men had them learn a trade so they would be in a position to support themselves once they left Monticello. They both served as an apprentice for a year with an uncle of theirs who was a carpenter. They were both freed in Jefferson's will after his death in 1826.

The *only* slaves Jefferson ever freed were his children with Sally and Sally's brother who had served as his chef while in France. Sally remained with Jefferson until his death. She would later be freed by Jefferson's daughter.

All of the other slaves of Monticello were sold after his death to pay off Jefferson's debts.

It's difficult to imagine how Beverly and Harriet were able to become absorbed into the white world directly from slavery when a life of slavery was all they had ever known. It was a completely different world, but they succeeded and did very well for themselves. Their secret was never discovered, and to the best of anyone's knowledge to this day their descendents have no idea of their background.

Madison and Eston would marry African American women. Madison's wife was born free but was the daughter of a slave. Eston who looked white married a woman of mixed ancestry similar to his own background of mixed races. They both did very well for themselves.

Initially Madison and Eston made their home in Charlottesville where their mother Sally lived with them once she was freed until the time of her death. For the last decade of her life, a few times a week she would walk over six miles to Monticello to care for Jefferson's grave. Sally and Jefferson had a relationship that lasted almost four decades.

After their mother's death both Madison and Eston moved to Ohio. Madison set up his home in Pike County. His name was listed on an 1870 census where the census taker had written next to his name, "This man is the son of Thomas Jefferson." Madison worked as a farmer and in the trade Jefferson had him apprentice for as a carpenter.

Eston also worked as a carpenter as he, like his brother Madison, had apprenticed to learn the trade before becoming free. He also made a living as a musician playing the violin. As a young boy he had shown interest in a violin Jefferson had and afterward he had arranged for the boy to have music lessons along with his brother Madison. They were both accomplished musicians.

Eston was a handsome man who was tall with straight hair and freckles resembling his father. He lived in Ohio until 1852 when he moved to Madison, Wisconsin. Once he made the move to Wisconsin he made a new life for himself. He had his name changed from Eston Hemings to Eston Hemings Jefferson and not only changed his name but his race. Eston's family from this time forward would pass as whites. Eston died just a few years after moving to Wisconsin leaving behind his wife and three children.

Madison was described as a man of intelligence, tall and thin, light gray eyes, and a complexion that was of a pale tan color. His friends and neighbors never questioned his relationship to Jefferson as the resemblance was great. Many of Sally and Thomas' children resembled their father. Madison and his wife had nine children.

Madison and Eston both passed down oral histories to their children and grandchildren telling them of their Jefferson lineage and how they were related to the third president of the United States. They told of their life histories and how they had grown up as slaves but were now free men. The oral history of descendants of Sally and Thomas Jefferson continues today and is still passed from one generation to the next.

4

James Madison

Children: son of Dolley Madison and stepson of James Madison

John Payne Todd- Born: February 29, 1792   Died: January 16, 1852

The title of 'the worst of presidential children' goes to Payne Madison the president's stepson who caused his own mother to live out her life in poverty.

The presidential son to hold the title of *'the worst of presidential children'* goes to Payne Todd, Dolley Madison's son from her first marriage and stepson of President James Madison. What made him so deserving of this title was not only his alcoholism, gambling, and womanizing as there were plenty of other presidential sons who could match him on that score; but also the fact that he was responsible for his mother living in poverty in her later years by not only covering his debts but from cheating his mother until Congress finally had to step in.

After the death of her first husband Dolley Todd moved in to her mother's boarding house in Philadelphia. She was a widow at the age of twenty-five after her husband and three month old son perished during a yellow fever epidemic which killed over five-thousand people in a period of four months. Her baby and husband died from the epidemic on the same day leaving her with a two-year old son John Payne Todd known as Payne.

James Madison, a forty-three year old bachelor, requested of his friend Aaron Burr to introduce him to Dolley. Madison would come to visit the young widow bringing toys for young Payne which endeared Dolley to him. It was only a matter of a few months before Dolley accepted Madison's marriage proposal. She was twenty-six years old when she became the bride of the forty-three year old Founding Father, delegate to the Continental Congress, and future president.

Dolley and Madison had no children of their own, but Madison treated and considered Payne as his own son. Madison would be the only father the young boy would remember.

Dolley spoiled her young son and gave in to all his demands. This would not change throughout his life as she continued to pamper and enable him. As time passed and Dolley realized there would be no more children she became even more indulgent. Madison was also lenient to Payne in his youth, but by the time he realized they had overindulged him to the point that he had become spoiled and lazy it was too late to undo the damage that had already been done.

Payne was a poor student and always preferred to play rather than study. James Madison, a brilliant man who achieved much in his life, hired tutors for Payne and even tutored Payne himself for a time. Payne never put any effort into his studies and did not improve as a student.

Madison eventually sent Payne to St. Mary's Seminary and University which was a Catholic boarding school in Baltimore, Maryland. He was enrolled at the boarding school from 1805 – 1812 studying French and Spanish among his other studies. He also learned to play the piano, but he never improved scholastically. For Madison this must have been frustrating to see the lack of discipline in his stepson.

Payne was seventeen years old when his stepfather became president. The press labeled him with the title of *'The American Prince,'* and he acted every bit the part of a pampered prince.

With his parents in the White House and Payne enrolled at St. Mary's he began going out into society with a friend of his mothers, the estranged wife of Prince Bonaparte, who was not a good influence on Payne. Madison seeing signs of trouble ahead knew he would have to do something before his stepson landed in trouble.

Madison sent the twenty year old Payne as a non-official with a delegation to a press conference to St. Petersburg, Russia in an attempt to end the War of 1812. Payne would serve as secretary for Madison during the war, though not a very good one. This attempt to kill two birds with one stone; to settle the War of 1812 and to get his stepson away from bad influences failed on both attempts.

Payne remained abroad between 1813 – 1815. During his time in Russia the nobility in Tsarist Russia treated the president's son as an American Prince. His every whim was not only given in to but encouraged, giving him a taste of living beyond his means. His drinking and gambling were becoming a major problem.

He had been sent overseas as a non-official so he was not being paid, though his stepfather had provided him with some funds in addition to his inheritance. Payne was going through his inheritance from his late father and still writing home for more money.

While overseas he fell 'in love' with a Russian princess who disappeared from sight and claims were made that she had been abducted and was never seen again. Whether the Russians were trying to protect one of their own or what the story is remains a mystery.

While abroad Madison began receiving gambling debts his son had incurred. Payne would later be sent to debtor's prison more than once for his debts.

Payne returned to the U.S. in 1815 but only after having spent $8,000; and remember this was in the early 1800's. Not only was the stepson of the president vain, irresponsible, and debt-ridden; but he was well on his way to becoming an alcoholic.

Payne out for a good time took one of his young cousins to a tavern slipping the innocent cousin alcohol who experienced being drunk for the first time. Payne was not a good influence. It wasn't uncommon for him to disappear on drinking and gambling sprees for long periods of time. It was only when his pockets were empty when his mother would discover where he was and that he was alive and in need of more money.

The actions of her only son was hard for Dolley to bear and also for the stepfather who loved him since he was an infant. Payne took advantage of them and their good hearts and refused to accept responsibility for his actions.

Madison loved Dolley, and many times to protect her from the heartbreak he would pay Payne's debts without letting her know. Madison got Payne out of debtor's prison by covering his debts. Dolley had no idea until after Madison's death when she received a sealed file of the amount of her son's debts Madison had paid off. The debt he had paid off unbeknownst to Dolley was approximately $20,000; and that was in addition to another $20,000 that she did know about. Madison had mortgaged his beloved plantation Montpelier and sold off acreage of land in order to pay his stepson's debts. Maybe if Payne had learned his lesson and stopped drinking and gambling it would have been a worthy cause, but his lifestyle of indulgence continued.

Dolley throughout her life would make excuses for her son even when she was hurting terribly from his actions. She would tell others, "His heart is good and he means no harm."

With all Payne's vices he had a likeable personality and could be a charmer. He was described as tall standing about 5'11" with blue eyes, black curly hair, and a dark complexion with a personality that captivated others. As an adult Payne never had a career. His mother thought he would settle down and find happiness if he could find himself a wife. He remained a bachelor for the rest of his life.

After Madison's death, Dolley getting up in years found Montpelier too much for her to keep up and sought her son's help in selling the plantation and the late president's papers. Payne cheated his mother of funds when selling the late president's personal papers. Congress agreed to purchase Madison's papers for the Library of Congress but they made arrangements to pay for them in installments; more for Dolley's protection from her son than for any other reason. Payne furious at being duped in his eyes attempted to sue the congressional trustees.

His mother who loved him dearly and hoped until her death that her son would change admitted she had spoiled her son and was partly responsible for his behavior. Due to paying his never ending debts was in large part why Dolley in her later years was impoverished. When her son threatened to sue the congressional trustees the outraged Dolley wrote him a letter begging him to take back his threats. She died the next year never hearing from her son again.

The last years of Dolley's life her niece, Anna Payne Cutts, took her in and cared for her. While initially Dolley's will had bequeathed everything to her only son Payne, three days before her death she changed her will dividing the funds for the sale of Madison's papers and half of her estate between her son and her niece. When Payne discovered she had changed her will he was furious and devious enough to have a fraudulent will written up showing him as the sole heir. Payne threatened to sue Dolley's niece, the woman who had been kind enough to care for his aging mother until her death.

Payne died two and a half years after his mother's death when he was not quite sixty years of age from typhoid fever. He left behind an unscrupulous reputation as an alcoholic, gambler, and thief. Perhaps the only worthy accomplishment he did in his life was to leave behind journals which provide an invaluable insight into the daily life of the son of a president.

5

James Monroe

Children of James and Elizabeth Monroe:

Elizabeth Kortright Monroe – Born: December, 1786   Died: January 27, 1840

James Spence Monroe – Born: 1799   Died: September 28, 1801

Maria Hester Monroe – Born: 1802   Died: June 20, 1850

Maria Hester Monroe, Monroe's youngest daughter, would go down in history as the first presidential daughter to have her wedding in the White House.

James Monroe was appointed U.S. minister to France in 1794 by President George Washington. His appointment in France lasted for two years. He and his wife and daughter Eliza, who was seven years old when the family moved to France and an only child at that time, were living in France during the French Revolution during a time known as the Reign of Terror.

Eliza the oldest daughter of James Monroe and his wife Elizabeth was born in December of 1786. Her name would one day become well-known throughout Washington. She would step into her mother's role as acting first lady following in the footsteps of Dolley Madison, the most beloved first lady – *and beloved Eliza was not.*

James the only son of James and Elizabeth was born in May of 1799. He was only a little over two years old, still a toddler when he died on September 28, 1801. He had been a sickly child throughout his young life. Whether his name was James Spence named after family as was a common practice at that time is mere speculation. His grave only identifies him as 'J.S. Monroe.'

Sometime after the birth of their son, Elizabeth began suffering with seizures which is assumed today to have been epilepsy. She would suffer these seizures the rest of her life.

Monroe and family would return to France in 1803 under President Jefferson to assist Robert Livingston in negotiating the Louisiana Purchase. They also lived in London for a time when Monroe was the U.S. ambassador to the Court of St. James.

There appears to be a good bit of conflicting information on birth dates on the Monroe's youngest daughter Maria Hester Monroe. She was born sometime in 1804 according to her grave marker. Some sources list her birth as 1802 and some as 1803; but the date most widely accepted seems to be 1802 which is more in line with her age when she moved into the White House and of when her marriage took place.

Eliza while living in France attended Madame Campan's prestigious school. Madame Campan was the lady-in-waiting for Maria Antoinette who was beheaded during the French Revolution along with her husband King Louis XVI.

Eliza returned to the school when her father was sent to France a second time by President Jefferson. It was during these days that she made a friend of Hortense Beauharnais who was the daughter of Josephine Bonaparte and stepdaughter to the Emperor Napoleon. Hortense would one day become the Queen of Holland and was the mother of yet another French Emperor, Napoleon III.

Eliza and Hortense remained friends throughout their lives. Her friendship with Hortense made a large impact on Eliza's life.

Eliza spent much of her younger years in Paris and London. During these formative years she had been greatly influenced by European ways which would one day be a bone of contention between Eliza, the press, and the people of Washington.

Eliza married George Hay in 1808. Hay was a prominent attorney in Virginia who was best known for serving as prosecutor in the trial of Aaron Burr for treason. He would also run his father-in-law's campaign in Virginia and after the completion of Monroe's administration he was appointed as a federal judge by President John Quincy Adams.

Hortense, Eliza's daughter, was named after her mother's friend The Queen of Holland Hortense de Beauharnais stepdaughter of Napoleon. Eliza's daughter came to live at the White House when she was seven years old.

Monroe was elected president in 1816. James Monroe, the nation's fifth president, was the last of the Founding Fathers to become president and the last president to wear a powdered wig and knee breeches. His administration ran from 1817 – 1825.

Eliza was a thirty year old married woman when her father was elected president. While living in the White House as the president's daughter Eliza and her mother brought some of the European elitist lifestyle with them in which the public and press didn't approve.

Maria was fifteen years old when she moved into the White House. She went down in the White House historical books twice; once for being the first presidential child under the age of nineteen to live in the White House and for being the first presidential daughter to be a bride and have her wedding take place at the White House.

Eliza spent her time in the White House years serving as her father's hostess standing in for her mother who declined assuming the role of hostess or First Lady stating it was due to her ill health. Eliza was more than willing to take over the role as she was a perfectionist and was well-qualified from her training at Madame Campan's school and from her days immersed in the European elitist class.

Eliza and her mother had already earned a name and reputation in the years they had been living in Washington and had rarely entertained others or followed the norm of Washington's social ways. She became renowned as haughty and pompous alienating the majority of Washington's social and political world when declining to follow the customs adhered to in Washington by refusing to call on the political wives.

When the Monroes moved into the White House First Lady Elizabeth Monroe and her eldest daughter Eliza decided to set their own rules of how things would be done. They tossed aside the old established ways of calling on society and decided to do things the European way. The fact that they were coming in and taking charge after Dolley Madison probably made it even more difficult; as Dolley was loved by all and holds even today the title of the best hostess of the White House. Dolley had lots of practice from the days of Jefferson when his daughter wasn't around to fill the role and then again throughout her husband's administration.

The women of Washington society decided to boycott dinners and receptions held by Eliza, leaving their husbands to make excuses for their absence. The Monroe women would get their revenge.

Seventeen year old Marie became engaged about a year after moving into the White House. The groom, twenty-one year old Samuel Lawrence Gouverneur, was her first cousin and one of her father's secretaries. The couple were making plans for their wedding when Eliza stepped in and took over. The young couple was given the excuse that affairs of state gave precedence to any ideas they may have had about their own wedding. Eliza ended up excluding everyone with the exception of family and a very few close friends. This would be a way for the first lady and Eliza to insert a little revenge to Washington society – at the expense of Maria and her groom.

The joy of planning her own wedding was taken out of Maria's hands. The groom was terribly upset demanding that the bride be able to plan her own wedding and make her own guest list. The first lady and Eliza won the battle.

The groom was furious and resented them taking over what should have been a joyous time in the planning of their own wedding, but even the president was powerless to stop them. The groom speaking his mind about his soon-to-be sister-in-law meddling into their affairs caused dissension between the sisters. Even so, it wasn't enough for Eliza to back down. It was her chance to show a little payback to the Washington socialites.

Not only were the bride and groom upset, but Washington society was outraged at being excluded to the first wedding of a presidential daughter to take place in the White House. Not only Washington society had been stricken from the guest list, but also Congress. Everyone had something to say and it wasn't pleasant.

Louisa Adams, who would be the next first lady, wrote in her diary about Eliza: *"No reputation is safe in her hands and I never from the first moment of my acquaintance with her have heard her speak well of any human being."* I imagine there were many tongues wagging in Washington with Eliza being the main topic.

The wedding took place on March 9, 1820 with forty-two guests who witnessed a candlelight ceremony with the bride and groom exchanging vows. The wedding is believed to have taken place in the Blue Room. After vows were exchanged the guests enjoyed a wedding feast in the State Dining Room.

Maria and Samuel had three children, two boys and a girl. Their first child, James Monroe Gouverneur, was a deaf mute. They had a daughter named Elizabeth Kortright Gouverneur, and their youngest child Samuel Lawrence Gouverneur, Jr. became the first U.S. Consul in Fuzhou, China.

Maria and Samuel moved to New York City where Samuel became postmaster, invested in racehorses, and in the Bowery Theater along with the son of Alexander Hamilton.

Eliza had made a name for herself amongst Washington society as being cold and heartless. However, it wasn't a heartless woman who tended to the victims of the fever epidemic during her father's administration. Eliza showed true compassion spending many a night caring for the sick and dying. Whether this changed people's attitude about this presidential daughter or not, she ministered to many victims spending sleepless nights by their side.

The invalid First Lady Elizabeth Monroe lived for another five years after they left the White House. President Monroe suffered from financial problems and moved to New York with his daughter Eliza accompanying him who was then a widow. Father and daughter moved in to the home of Maria and Samuel. President Monroe lived his final years with his daughters and son-in-law.

After the death of her father Eliza returned to her beloved France. While in Europe she visited her friend Hortense. With her friend she took a trip to Rome and in a private ceremony with Pope Gregory XVI she converted to Catholicism. She lived out her life in a convent in France and died on January 27, 1840; just a little over three years after her father's death. Her sister Maria survived her by ten years passing away in 1850.

6

John Quincy Adams

Children of John Quincy & Louisa Catherine Adams:

George Washington Adams – Born: April 12, 1801   Died: April 30, 1829

John Adams II – Born: July 4, 1803   Died: Oct. 23, 1834

Charles Francis Adams – Born: Aug. 18, 1807   Died: Nov 21, 1886

Louisa Catherine Adams – Born: August 12, 1811   Died: September 15, 1812

John II is the only presidential son to have married at the White House.

John Quincy Adams, the first presidential son to also become a president followed in his father's footsteps not only to the White House but also in expecting more from his children than they could possibly live up to. Sometimes a child in knowing they can never please their demanding parent turn to vices and a life of ruin. Two of John Quincy's sons died young at ages twenty-eight and thirty-one; both alcoholics and one most likely a suicide.

John Quincy Adams was serving as a diplomatic representative of the U.S. in the days of his own father's presidency when his wife Louisa gave birth to their first child George Washington Adams. George was born April 12, 1801 in Berlin; at that time the capital of Prussia. Just one month after his birth his grandfather, John Adams the nation's second president, left office having lost the election to Thomas Jefferson. Baby George's father was recalled to the U.S.

Just an infant when the family returned to the U.S. his father returned to law practice and soon after became a senator. In the days he was senator, John Quincy or JQA, was away in Washington and saw very little of his son.

John Adams II was born July 4, 1803. He was named after his grandfather, who twenty-seven years earlier had a hand in making that date infamous in America by being a part of the committee to draft the Declaration of Independence. His grandfather would also die on July 4th, 1826; the 50th anniversary of the adoption of the Declaration of Independence.

John's father was away from home so much that there was a time when John called everyone papa confused as to who his father was. His father had been out of his life more than a part of it and he didn't remember him. If that wasn't hard enough on a young lad, in November of 1805 his mother left for Washington to join their father leaving John and his brother George with family members.

There is no definitive family record left behind of a child named Carolina Adams that can be verified. Her name is mentioned in some ancestry sites, but otherwise the only notice that appears to even make note of her birth or death is from the record of a coffin that was ordered for her. The record came from the shop of a cabinetmaker who also made coffins. The listing in his record book is as follows "ADAMS John Q's child 6/23/1806."

I did not include Carolina in the list of children above as there just wasn't enough to prove or disprove that she was indeed a child of John Quincy and Louisa. Louisa did have a history of suffering several miscarriages and pregnancy issues throughout their marriage so it is very possible that this child was stillborn.

A third son, Charles Francis, arrived August 18, 1807. He would be the son to become the achiever of the family.

In 1809 George and John after having already been separated from their parents for the majority of their lives, an even bigger separation was soon to occur. Their father had been appointed by President Madison as the first ambassador to the Russian court of Czar Alexander I. John Quincy never known to be considerate of his wife's feelings accepted the post without even consulting her. In addition, John Quincy and his mother who considered her daughter-in-law a frail little thing, had made plans for the two older boys without her knowledge or consent.

George and John II were to stay behind in Massachusetts with their grandparents while the baby would travel with his parents to Russia. When Louisa learned of this plan she pleaded and begged her husband to allow her to take all their children, but to no avail. It had been decided. Louisa would not see her two sons again for eight years. In their most formative years they would be deprived of their parents attention, guidance, and even more important their love.

In their parents absence George Washington Adams and John II received letters from their father on what he expected from them. George especially received letters telling of his father's dissatisfaction of his son's studies and not living up to his expectations. George initially had shown signs of being an outstanding student but was never able to gain his father's respect or encouragement; never quite living up to the goals his father had laid out for his son.

During John Quincy's and Louisa's time in Russia they had another child, a little girl named Louisa Catherine born in 1811. Their little girl would die after just reaching her first birthday. Their daughter is believed to have died from the effects of the extreme Russian winter suffering from severe dysentery. She was born in St. Petersburg, the first American citizen born in Russia, and she also perished there. Both parents were devastated at the loss of their only daughter.

After the death of his daughter, John Quincy at the request of his wife pressed to return home to the United States so their family could be reunited. The U.S. was in the midst of the War of 1812 and President Madison instead of bringing John Quincy home sent him to Belgium to help negotiate a peace treaty to bring an end to the war. Instead of reuniting the family as hoped for his wife would now be left in Russia with only her son Charles.

Alone in Russia, Louisa was still expected to entertain as a diplomatic wife. She did a great job of it, even without her husband. After a time she received notice to meet him in Paris which began a journey few women in that time would be willing to face. To say it would be a dangerous journey would be putting it mildly.

Traveling with her young son Charles and Louisa's sister who had joined them in Russia they made what would be a six-week journey through war torn Russia, Poland, and Germany towards their ultimate goal of France. They would be making this journey during the middle of a harsh winter traveling by carriage which ran on a sleigh bottom to enable them to get through the snow and ice.

On the journey she was warned of the dangers she would be facing ahead, but still she was determined and kept on while passing fields with bodies of dead soldiers scattered along the way. There were times when their lives were endangered as they traveled over iced rivers with the threat of plunging into the freezing waters if the ice cracked. But they had yet to come to the larger danger they would yet face.

As they neared their ultimate goal of Paris their carriage was surrounded by hostile troops who demanded Louisa's death assuming she was of Russian descent. Louisa encouraged her servants to inform the troops that she was the sister of Napoleon and was traveling incognito. She stepped from the carriage in a regal manner standing tall and speaking in perfect French. She brought the troops to attention with salutes and cheers to Napoleon.

Her mother-in-law would never again refer to her as a frail little thing. When she learned of the travails of the journey of her daughter-in-law, she had a new-found respect for what she had experienced and how she faced her trials and tribulations.

John Quincy and Louisa went on to London where John Quincy served as U.S. minister in the land of his wife's birth. While in London he called for their two sons George and John to join them. After eight long years the family would be reunited.

President James Monroe gave John Quincy Adams the appointment as secretary of state in 1817 and the family would return to America. The following year Louisa's sister's three children who had been orphaned became a part of the Adams household.

George with assistance from his father gained admittance to Harvard. John Quincy wrote to his son telling him how to spend every moment of his day. Even once a college student at Harvard George received instructions on how to live his life - when to work and when to play; reminding him always that he was an Adams and to act accordingly and live up to the name.

George graduated from Harvard in 1821 and went on to study law under Daniel Webster. He would practice law in Boston and was elected to the Massachusetts State Legislature. He never did reach his father's expectations of him and continued to receive letters from him, caustic letters at that, letting his son know of his disappointment in him.

Living the majority of his life separated from his parents with only letters received, not loving letters; but letters of instruction and those that let him know how much he had let them down by not honoring his name and heritage did nothing to uplift him. By the time his father became president his father treated him as a persona non grata. He would earn the reputation of an underachieving son of an American president. To say it was difficult to try to live up to his father's and grandfather's reputations would be an understatement.

John unlike his moody brother George was active and excelled at sports while away at school. He had been educated at the best of schools but suffered from a short temper. He was an obnoxious prankster and some of his embarrassing behavior and antics led to his expulsion at Harvard during his senior year.

Charles graduated from Harvard in 1825 the same year his father became president. Charles did grow up to be the most promising of the siblings though he was not an innocent; he confessed to using prostitutes at times during his time at Harvard. After his graduation he, like his brother, also studied under Daniel Webster and practiced law in Boston. He wrote numerous reviews of works about both American and British history.

John Quincy Adams became the 6th president in 1825. The Adams wards, Louisa's dead sister's children, moved with them to the White House. Not only did they have to be concerned for their own children who were being quite worrisome but the additional responsibility of caring for these three were an additional burden.

Out of the three children who John Quincy and Louisa had become guardians to one boy became involved with a maid while the rest of the family was away from the White House and ended up marrying her, one of the sons was dismissed from Harvard due to lack of moral restraints and became an alcoholic, a recurrent theme in the Adams household, dying of alcoholism at the age of twenty-four, and the daughter ended up causing a major rift between the Adams own sons marrying one son and causing irreparable damage between the three brothers. In addition to these three wards there were two nephews and two nieces, children of Thomas Adams who often came to stay trying to escape their father's alcoholic stupors.

Mary Catherine the daughter of Louisa's dead sister was a scheming beauty. She would come to cause problems between the three Adams' sons. Flirtatious, she had each of the brothers fall in love with her going from one brother to the next. Charles was the first to fall under her spell, but she quickly moved on to George. She became engaged to George who would postpone the wedding in order to finish his education. That would be the end of their relationship. Once John arrived at the White House she began working her charms on him, the last brother to be conquered.

John II came to live in the White House after being expelled from college. After his expulsion he moved to the White House to work as his father's secretary.

George the oldest son remained a bachelor throughout his life. He had problems with depression and had a reputation for being a womanizer and an alcoholic. Feeling a despondency about the inadequacies his father was quick to point out, he found comfort from his grandfather John Adams and was at his side when his grandfather passed away.

From his grandfather John had found a father figure that accepted him for who he was. He had become close to his grandfather and after his death he became despondent and indifferent to life. He neglected his law practice and was voted off the Massachusetts State Legislature. The battle of alcohol had him beat.

John and his first cousin Mary, the orphaned niece the Adams had taken into their home, married February 25, 1828. John is the only presidential son to have married in the White House. Their wedding was similar to that of Maria Monroe's experience as far as the guest list goes. By marrying a girl that both brothers had previously fallen for had made enemies of his brothers who refused to attend the wedding. With problems within the family the guest list was kept to a minimum. The marriage took place in the Blue Room.

John and Mary gave birth to a baby girl on December 2, 1828 at the White House. Her name was Mary Louisa and she was the first baby girl to be born in the White House. Maybe as a reminder of his own daughter he had lost or for whatever reason, President John Quincy loved this little girl in a way that was uncommon for him. He showed her a love that he had neglected to show to his own children or even to his wife. He doted on the little girl he nicknamed Looly. John and Mary would also have another daughter named Georgiana Frances in September of 1830.

George Washington Adams the eldest son had fathered an illegitimate child in December of 1828 with Eliza Dolph, a chamber maid of the Adams doctor in Boston, Dr. Welch. She had been moved so George would be able to visit her and the child without anyone's knowledge or worry about the affair becoming public knowledge. If this had become public knowledge it would have been a black mark on the Adams' family name.

After George's brother John's White House wedding to a woman George had previously been engaged to, his alcoholism was out of control and his depression increased. He would die just a little over a year later.

After his father had lost his reelection he now had time to add pressure to his son's life who was already at the lowest point in his life. He demanded for George to come to Washington for a face-to-face to lecture his son on his scandalous lifestyle.

George responded to his father's summons and boarded the steamship The *Benjamin Franklin.* It was said while on board he began hallucinating and hearing voices. He had last been seen around 2:00 A.M. He either jumped or fell overboard. His hat and coat were found lying in a heap on the deck leaving the impression that he had jumped.

He disappeared on April 30, 1829. It was early May six weeks later before his body was washed ashore. He was twenty-eight years old at the time of his death. A coroner's inquest determined death by drowning. George had left notes behind insinuating that he intended to commit suicide. His death is considered by not only historians but from news accounts of his time that the death was suicide by drowning.

George's father and mother learned of their son's suicide from the newspapers.

After George's death it was discovered by personal papers that he had fathered an illegitimate child. He had been threatened by a blackmailer to pay him money to keep his silence about the affair or he would have the information published tarnishing the family name. After George's death his brother Charles refused to pay the blackmailer and the story was published.

At the end of his father's presidency John II managed a family business operating a flour mill in Washington that his father owned. The business began to lose money and between his failure at running the business and his despair over his brother's suicide he began drinking heavily to escape the pressures of life that he was ill equipped to handle. John II also became an alcoholic and died October 23, 1834 at the age of thirty-one.

Mary, John II's widow, lived with the former president and first lady for the remainder of their lives running their household and caring for them. Abigail's two granddaughters brought joy to Louisa's life which helped her cope with the death of her two sons. Mary outlived both of her daughters and returned to the White House to witness two other White House weddings before her death in 1870.

Charles, the only surviving child of Louisa and John Quincy Adams, may very well have become the first child to become the third generation to become a president following in his father's and grandfather's footsteps. Most likely the only thing that kept him from attaining the office of the presidency was his supporting causes that most of the public were not ready for. He was an advocate for abolition of slavery.

He married Abigail Brown Brooks at the age of twenty-two. They would have seven children.

Charles was an accomplished man who was respected by those who knew him. He was fluent in several languages, had graduated from Harvard at seventeen, and was a member of the Massachusetts State Legislature. He was elected to the Massachusetts House of Representatives in the year 1841. He served in the State Senate in 1844 and 1845.

As his father and grandfather before him he served as U.S. minister of Great Britain, the Court of St. James, under President Abraham Lincoln during the Civil War. When arriving in England he learned the king was about to step in using military power to support the Confederacy. Through his persistent negotiations he was able to keep England out of the war - perhaps changing history. Historian John S. Cooper stated that his work was "arguably the greatest contribution to Union victory made by any individual in the war."

Twice he was nominated for the presidency. By that time he had inherited his father-in-law's large estate which enabled him to pursue his dreams without financial pressures making his decisions one way or the other. Charles became a politician, diplomat, and historical editor becoming one of the best historical editors of his time.

Charles died of a stroke on November 21, 1886.

7

ANDREW JACKSON

Children of Andrew & Rachel Jackson

No biological children: Two adopted children

Andrew Jackson, Jr. - Born: Dec 4, 1808   Died: Apr. 17, 1865   Adopted at birth

Lyncoya Jackson – Born: circa 1811   Died: June 1, 1828   Adopted Creek Indian orphan

A president who was known as one of America's notable Indian fighters adopted an Indian orphan.

Andrew Jackson lost his wife Rachel just a month after the presidential election and a few months before he assumed the position of president. The gown she had bought to wear to the inauguration instead was used as her burial gown.

Andrew and Rachel had no biological children of their own but they were very loving and good Christians who had a reputation for taking in children. They took in at least ten children who came to become full time members of the family. They adopted children and took in nieces and nephews that they raised as their own. They never turned a child away that needed a home.

Jackson was guardian for several children. In the early part of the nineteenth century at the death of a child's father the courts would appoint a guardian for the child. This was done even if the child's mother was still alive and they were living with their mother.

Some of the children the Jacksons were guardians of were the children of General Edward Butler. The Butler children: Caroline, Eliza, Edward, and Anthony did live with the Jacksons occasionally at the Hermitage. In addition to the Butler children Jackson was also guardian to Rachel's brothers children: John, Samuel, Andrew Jackson, and Daniel who lived part time with the Jacksons.

Andrew Jackson, Jr. was born on December 4, 1808. Some records list his birth as the year 1809, but this is most likely due to the fact that he was adopted a few days into 1809. The Jacksons received the baby three days after his birth, adopting him a few weeks later and naming him after his adoptive father. No legal proof has been found showing the legality of his adoption.

Andrew Jr. was a twin. The twins were nephews of Andrew Jackson and his wife Rachel, sons of Rachel's brother Severn Donelson. It is unclear why the Jacksons adopted him or why the twins were separated with the birth parents keeping custody of the other boy. The twins Andrew Jr. and Thomas Jefferson Donelson were close throughout their lives.

Rachel and Andrew also adopted a young Creek Indian orphan named Lyncoya. That may seem like an odd turn of events for some who remember Andrew Jackson as being one of America's notable Indian fighters. So, how did a man with the reputation of fighting Indians come to adopt an Indian orphan?

In the year 1813 the young Indian child lost his entire family at the Battle of Tallushatchee during the War of 1812. Few of the Creek Indians survived the battle including women and children. One of the soldiers while looking for survivors found a young child by his dead mother. The ten-month old baby boy was brought from the battlefield to the fort. The boy was left with the other survivors who were taken as prisoners. It was here that General Jackson noticed the child. His heart went out to the little boy when the Creek women prisoners refused to care for him. Jackson went so far as to offer a reward to the women if one of them would nurse the child and care for him. The women refused; instead of caring for him they wanted to kill the child because his whole family had perished.

Andrew Jackson who had come out of the Revolutionary War as an orphan himself was moved by the predicament of the child. Andrew was a compassionate man, especially when it came to children. He searched the army for provisions to nourish the child. All that could be found to feed him was brown sugar and crumbs from biscuits which he mixed with water to feed him to make sure the child had some nourishment.

Lyncoya was close to the same age as his young son back home, Andrew Jr. General Jackson being able to relate to the child's circumstances stated, "He is a Savage but one that fortune has thrown into my hands."

General Jackson asked Colonel Pope's daughter Maria to care for the Indian child until he could send him home to the Hermitage. Maria Pope cared for the young child until the end of the Creek War when the General took him home to become a part of his own family. While under the care of Maria she had named the boy Lyncoya.

Lyncoya was raised as Jackson's son and later adopted into the Jackson family. Andrew Jackson loved the boy as his own. Initially the child was feeble and sickly but over time grew stronger.

When Lyncoya was only five years of age he astonished his family when he made a bow similar of that used by the Indians. The family was quite surprised by this as he had left the life of an Indian before the age of one. The only other Indians he had been around were on the few occasions when Indian chiefs came to the Hermitage, but they paid little attention to the boy. Lyncoya would pick up feathers found outside and placed them in his hair while playing with his bow.

He was sent to school when he became of school age along with the other children of the Jackson family. After attending school for an entire year he still didn't know the alphabet and showed little interest in learning. As he aged he did progress in his studies and then learned quite rapidly showing signs of genius.

General Jackson wanted the boy to attend West Point and pursue a life in the army but politics put an end to this desire of Jacksons. Lyncoya decided he would like to become a saddler and worked as an apprentice to a saddler in Nashville, Tennessee in 1827.

During the winter Lyncoya caught cold which he was never able to recover from. It settled in his lungs and he returned home to the Hermitage where he received tender care from his mother Rachel Jackson. He never did reclaim his health and declined rapidly. Lyncoya wouldn't live to see his adoptive father become president. He died most likely of tuberculosis on June 1, 1828 at sixteen years of age. His death came just a few months before Jackson won the presidency. His adoptive mother died just seven months later.

Lyncoya wouldn't be the only Creek Indian child at the Hermitage. There are unsubstantiated rumors that there were two other young Creek Indian boys to make the Hermitage their home for a short time. Theodore whose birth date is unknown died around 1813 is said to have been captured when soldiers invaded the Creek Indian town of Littafuchee. He died soon after arriving at the Hermitage. The other Creek child who was called Charley was given to Jackson by Jim Fife a Creek interpreter. There is little to be found on either of these two boys and it is thought that neither one of them lived long being in poor health by they time they arrived at the Jacksons' home.

It was just a matter of a few years after the death of Lyncoya, his adopted Creek son, when Jackson was in large part responsible for the Trail of Tears where the Cherokee Indians were forced off their homelands.

Hutchings another child the Jacksons took in was the grandson of Rachel's sister. His parents were both dead by the time the child turned five. He came to live at the Hermitage in 1817 attending school with Andrew Jr. and Lyncoya.

Andrew Jackson became president in 1829. Ten thousand people attended the inauguration. The White House had been opened to anyone who wished to come for a reception. It seemed as though every American citizen wanted to be there to join in the celebration.

After the inauguration the White House was so full of people, both Washington society and regular citizens, who wanted to congratulate the president that his staff had to sneak him out one of the windows and put him in a coach so he could return to Gadsby's Tavern where he had been staying in order to get a good night's sleep.

It would be another week before he could return to the White House. The crowd was a rambunctious lot who had left behind a bit of a mess with furniture and china broken. Jackson didn't seem bothered by the incident telling others he wanted to redecorate anyway.

Jackson's wife's twenty-one year old niece, Emily Donelson, moved in to the White House to serve as First Lady. Her husband was Andrew Jackson Donelson who was Jackson's nephew and had been a ward of Rachel and Andrew. He served as Jackson's secretary. They brought one child with them and would have three more who were born in the White House.

Emily even though only twenty-one did an excellent job as hostess for the president. She had been born and raised on a plantation and her duties as hostess and the size of the White House and staff didn't seem to be any trouble for the young lady. She even managed to convince Congress to give her money towards decorating and repairing the White House. Between being a mother and giving birth to three more children during her time in Washington she managed also to make social calls to the ladies and wives of Washington society, manage the White House staff, and was hostess for dinners and special events.

President Jackson not only brought Emily and his nephew with him to Washington, he also brought grandchildren with him to live in the White House. At the time he was president he had half a dozen grandchildren living with him who were all under the age of ten.

Children of all ages ran the halls of the White House. People would arrive at the White House for a meeting or to visit and find the president with a baby asleep in his arms. He loved having his house, whether at the Hermitage or the White House, filled with children. His nieces and nephews were also welcomed with open arms.

His young granddaughter Rachel was allowed to interrupt Cabinet meetings whenever she wanted. Grandpa never turned her away. He may have been known as Old Hickory, but he was a soft touch when it came to the grandchildren.

In December of 1835 President Jackson hosted the first White House party just for children. They had a "snowball" fight in the East Room; of course, the snowballs were made of cotton puffs, but the children had a wonderful time.

Family was everything to Andrew Jackson. He raised them with love but also taught them to give to others in need. The children in the White House would accompany Jackson to an orphanage to pass out gifts. He wanted to pass on the wonderful message to the children in teaching them about the gift of giving to those less fortunate.

More than once President Jackson could be found during the night walking the halls with a little one who was sick with a fever, measles, or the croup, soothing them until they fell asleep. He was a grandfather who was content to rock a child to sleep, soothe a crying child, or play with them.

All of the children of his household weren't young children. Some of the children living in the White House were ones he had taken in during their youth; his adopted son, nieces or nephews. Hutchings, an orphaned grandnephew of Rachel who Jackson had taken in when his parents died was attending college. He passed away just a few years after Jackson's administration ended.

For a time President Jackson had his hands full more with the older "children" of the White House than with the younger ones. Andrew Jr. and his cousin Hutchings were running around town chasing the young ladies. That all ended when Andrew Jr. met and fell for a beautiful young Quaker named Sarah.

Andrew Jr. married Sarah Yorke in 1831. They lived at the Hermitage managing the plantation until a fire broke out destroying most of the house in the year 1834. After the fire they moved to the White House with their two children. One of their children was the three year old Rachel who was never turned away when interrupting her grandfather's meetings and her little brother Andrew Jackson III who was eighteen months. Andrew III as an adult would graduate from West Point and fight in the Civil War in the Confederate army.

Sarah, in addition to Emily, served as hostess of the White House the last years of Jackson's presidency. It was the only time in history when there were two women acting as White House hostess simultaneously. Once Emily became ill Sarah took over the duties of acting first lady and did so until the end of Jackson's presidency in 1837. Emily died in 1836 of tuberculosis.

Andrew Jr. had a reputation from early on of collecting debts and mismanaging his affairs. That had not changed over time. After his father died in 1845 the state bought the Hermitage from him and allowed him and his family to live there rent free for the remainder of their lives. Andrew Jr. died from an accidental hunting accident in 1865. He had been climbing over a fence when his gun accidentally went off shooting himself in the hand. It appeared to be only a minor injury, but within a week he would be dead from lockjaw.

8

Martin Van Buren

Children of Hannah and Martin Van Buren

Unnamed daughter – Stillborn; date unknown

Abraham Van Buren – Born: Nov 27, 1807   Died: March 15, 1873

John Van Buren – Born: Feb 18, 1810   Died: Oct. 13, 1866

Martin Van Buren, Jr.- Born: Dec. 20, 1812   Died: March 19, 1855

Winfield Scott Van Buren – Born: 1814   Died: 1814

Smith Thompson Van Buren- Born: Jan. 16, 1817   Died: 1876

It was the first time in history the presidential children would be in attendance for their father's inauguration.

Martin Van Buren was a widower when he was president, one of the few presidents who were unmarried throughout their entire time in office. His wife Hannah died in 1819 eighteen years before he became president.

Hannah Van Buren had given birth to six children within a ten year period, only four of the children survived childhood. When Hannah died of tuberculosis at the age of thirty-five her husband Martin was crushed at the loss of his childhood sweetheart. He rarely again spoke of her even to his children and he never once mentioned her name throughout his entire 800 page autobiography.

After his wife's death Martin was distraught and left his four sons in the care of friends and family. Two years later when he won a Senate seat his oldest son was away at West Point, his thirteen year old son John was still living in the home of a political friend Rufus King, and the two youngest sons Martin and Smith were living with an aunt and family friends. Not only had they been deprived of their parents but were separated from each other as well.

Martin Van Buren went from the Senate to governor of New York which he resigned after just a few months to become President Jackson's secretary of state. President Jackson went on to make Van Buren his vice president in 1832 and would support Van Buren to succeed him as president in 1836. Van Buren was the first president to have been born a citizen of the United States.

Once Martin had become the vice president he asked his sons Abraham and Martin Jr. to come live with him in Washington. John was studying for the bar exam at the time and once Martin was convinced that the move wouldn't affect the outcome of his son passing the bar he was asked to join his father and brothers. The youngest son Smith, came to visit but not to live at this time. It's unclear why he didn't join the family in Washington other than to visit, but he did join them at a later date.

Abraham was the eldest of the Van Buren sons. He had been appointed to West Point when he was fifteen years old graduating in 1827. After his graduation Abraham served two years on the American frontier and another seven years as aide-de-camp to the Commanding General of the U.S. army. The year before his father became president he had been promoted to captain of the First Regiment of Dragoons.

John the second son and the favorite of President Van Buren was full of personality. At some point in his childhood days he had become critically ill where his father feared he could possibly lose his son. His father remained by his son's bed for hours watching over John who was on the verge of death. Whether it was from during this time when he came so close to losing him or due to his personality that just made it impossible not to be drawn to him, he had been his father's favorite from early on. Not only blessed with good looks and personality, John was incredibly smart as well.

John graduated from Yale and had passed the New York bar by the age of twenty. When his father was appointed U.S. minister to Britain, his son accompanied him as secretary. During John's time in London he picked up the bad habits of drinking and gambling. Both father and son returned to the U.S. in 1832. John returned to law opening a practice in Albany. He was a brilliant lawyer.

Martin Van Buren became president in 1837. It would be the first time in history the presidential children, all four of the Van Buren sons, would be in attendance for their father's inauguration and to celebrate his victory with him at the inaugural balls. Even though by now they were all adults, at one time or another they all made their residence at the White House.

The day before his father's inauguration Abraham resigned his commission to become his father's private secretary. Martin Jr. and Smith would also serve as personal secretaries and work with their father throughout his administration.

The first two years of Van Buren's administration were deprived of a first lady since he was a widow and there were no female members of the household to step in and take over the role.

Dolley Madison with the idea of a match in mind invited her niece Angelica Singleton who was a twenty-two year old Southern belle from South Carolina to attend a White House dinner with her. Angelica had come to Washington with her sister for the 1837 – 1838 social season. It was a private dinner that Dolley Madison had been invited to at the White House. She and her niece were to dine with the president and his three sons who were then living at the White House.

Abraham, the oldest son of the president, fell for Angelica and it appears his feelings were reciprocated as after they had known each other for just a short time he asked her to marry him and she agreed.

Abraham and Angelica were married eight months after they met in South Carolina and then returned to Washington to live in the White House with Abraham working for his father as secretary and Angelica assuming the role of hostess. Dolley Madison a former first lady gave the young woman tips and guided her into her new role. Angelica would serve as first lady for more than half of the Van Buren presidency.

The following spring in 1839 Abraham and Angelica took an extended visit to Europe. Angela still young and easily influenced returned home impersonating the royal traditions she had observed once back at the White House. Imitating their ways she presumed she was bringing a form of class into the White House that those of social standing would admire.

Instead of standing in a receiving line shaking hands beside the president as was customary, Angelica followed the lead of Queen Victoria and the royals of France and posed on a platform. This may have been the custom in Europe and accepted there, but here in America we had fought for our free and independent ways and the acting first lady's "royal ways" were met with utter disdain. She quickly received the message that she had conducted a faux pas and returned to shaking hands beside the president.

Abraham and Angelica would have one daughter and four sons. Their daughter Rebecca was born in the White House in 1840 but survived only for a few days. After they left the White House they would go on to have four sons: Singleton an unnamed son who was either stillborn or didn't live long, Martin III, and Travis Cole. The three sons that survived never married.

John Van Buren the second son is one of the most colorful and notorious of presidential children; though he would have a lot of competition with that title in the following years. Similar to Payne, the son of Dolley Madison, he had a drinking and gambling problem and was a womanizer. He had the promise of a great future ahead of him but chose his vices over a promising career.

His father sent him letters stating emphatically that he had the reputation of the Van Buren name to uphold. The letters didn't seem to have much impact on his son as the next letters would continue on the same theme with his father writing, *"What you may regard as innocent and harmless indulgence will take you years to overcome in the public estimation."* President or not, his words appeared to be going in one ear and out the other as another letter stated, *"Washington is full of reports...that you had twice been carried drunk from the race course."* Many presidential sons, and in later generations presidential daughters, seemed to take issue with the fact that it was their father who chose to be in public office - not them.

John however he chose to live his life, was brilliant and his father trusted him enough to send him to Europe on diplomatic errands. He was sent to England as a representative of the U.S. for the coronation of Queen Victoria. He would also attend other events and even danced with the Queen.

While abroad John rubbed elbows with the notable people of the United Kingdom including of course the Queen of England, the King of France, the King of Belgium, and the King of the Netherlands. In America he had been given the nickname 'Prince John' as he eased into being accepted as one of their own of the European elites and royals. He had personality, good looks, and charm that opened many doors for him.

Martin Jr., the third son and his father's namesake, spent most of his life working for his father. He lived at the White House serving as a personal assistant. He never married and devoted his life to his father's work. In the days after his father's administration he remained at the White House in order to copy and catalog all of his father's correspondence. He made it his life's work to organize all of the Van Buren Presidential papers for posterity.

Smith, the youngest son, also worked for his father during his presidency. He was one of his private secretaries and was his father's speechwriter and main spokesperson. He like his brother Martin devoted the majority of his life to his father and his work.

Martin Van Buren left the office of the presidency in 1841.

When Abraham's work at the White House was over he returned to the military. He would reach the rank of lieutenant colonel. His father who had been opposed to the Mexican War didn't stop his son from returning to active duty and accepting the position of paymaster. During the war he would become an aide to General Zachary Taylor who would one day himself become president. Abraham retired from the army in 1854.

Abraham worked with his brothers spending years of his life editing and publishing his father's presidential papers. Along with his brothers he worked on promoting the legacy of their father.

In June of 1841, John married his childhood sweetheart Elizabeth Vanderpoel. His marriage only slowed him down for a short period of time before he returned to his earlier vices. They had one daughter Anna who was born the year after their marriage.

John, a brilliant man who never lived up to his potential, served as New York state attorney general of New York. Unfortunately, his alcoholism left him in bad shape and left him an invalid. His health was in decline and he along with his daughter and a niece left for the spas of Europe. They traveled throughout England, Sweden, Norway, and Russia. He died on his return voyage of kidney failure while crossing the Atlantic Ocean in October of 1866 at the age of fifty-six.

At the end of his father's presidency Martin Jr. left with his father when he retired working at editing and copying his father's letters and working alongside his brothers in preparing their father's presidential papers for posterity.

Not a well man Martin Jr's health was deteriorating. He had contracted tuberculosis the same disease that had killed his mother. He left for Europe in the company of his father to seek in regaining his health with the restorative waters in France.

With his father remaining by his side Martin Jr would die in Paris at the age of forty-two on March 19, 1855. He would be the first presidential son to die in a foreign country. (The first presidential daughter to die in a foreign country was the young daughter of John Quincy and Louisa Adams in Russia.)

Not much has been revealed about Smith over the years. He had learned much about politics and political ways but never ran for office. He worked for just two years as a lawyer but never had much drive seeking to find success on his own; instead always being in the shadow of his father. He spent the rest of his adult live defending his father's reputation unconcerned about his own.

Smith married Ellen King James a wealthy woman who he had four children with. After the death of his wife he remarried Henrietta Irving, the niece of Washington Irving, who he had three more children with. He was the last survivor of the Van Buren family passing away in 1876.

9

WILLIAM HENRY HARRISON

Children of Anna and William Henry Harrison:

Elizabeth Bassett Harrison "Betsy" - Born: Sept. 29, 1796   Died: Sept. 26, 1846

John Cleves Symmes Harrison – Born: Oct 28, 1798   Died: Oct. 30, 1830

Lucy Singleton Harrison – Born: Sept. 5, 1800   Died: April 7, 1826

William Henry Harrison, Jr. - Born: Sept 3, 1802   Died: Feb 6, 1838

John Scott Harrison – Born: Oct. 4, 1804   Died: May 25, 1878

Benjamin Harrison – Born: May 5, 1806   Died: June 9, 1840

Mary Symmes Harrison – Born: Jan 22, 1809   Died: Nov 16, 1842

Carter Bassett Harrison – Born: Oct. 26, 1811   Died: Aug. 12, 1839

Anna Tuthill Harrison – Born: Oct 28, 1813   Died: July 5, 1845

James Findlay Harrison – Born: May 15, 1814   Died: April 6, 1817

Alleged children with Dilsia, a slave and William Henry Harrison:
Dilsia was his slave who he allegedly had 6 children with.

John Scott Harrison, son of one president and father of another president,

had his body stolen by grave robbers

Our 9th president William Henry Harrison wasn't the first in the family to be involved in politics, nor would he be the last. His father was a delegate to the Continental Congress who was one of the signers of the Declaration of Independence and his grandson Benjamin Harrison would become the nation's 23rd president. William Henry Harrison at the time he took office in 1840 was the oldest president and would hold that title until Ronald Reagan was elected in 1980. W.H. Harrison was the last president born a British subject.

It was a cold day in Washington on March 4, 1841 when Harrison took the oath of office. With neither a hat or coat on he gave the longest inaugural address in American history lasting one hour and forty-five minutes. Within a short period of time after the inauguration Harrison became ill with a cold that turned into pneumonia. His presidency lasted all of thirty-one days, the shortest tenure in history. He was the first president to die in office.

Anna Harrison, the first lady who never made it to the White House, would be the first presidential widow to be granted a pension by Congress. She received $25,000 in one lump sum.

The president and first lady had ten children. While growing up the family was vulnerable to the attacks of Native American Indian raids who were fighting against the government taking away their land. Their father, governor at the time, was involved with negotiations and treaty signings.

The governor and his wife Anna at times entertained Shawnee Chief Tecumseh in their home without fear. But Chief Tecumseh's brother Tenskwatawa was a different story, as he believed in the necessity of widespread war and slaughter against the white settlers. The Native American Indians were a fascinating sight for the young children.

The Harrison's first child was Elizabeth "Betsy" Bassett Harrison born in 1796. During her childhood her father was away from the home a good part of the time fighting Indians during the Northwest Indian War. She married her cousin John Cleves Short. Only two out of the ten Harrison children lived past the age of thirty-five, Betsy was one of the two. She died five years after her father's death.

John Cleves Symmes Harrison, the second child and first son, of the Harrisons lived in the Indiana Territory his entire life. He went by Symmes and was popular and well-liked.

His wife Clarissa Pike was the daughter of General Zebulon Pike who had discovered Pike's Peak. They had six children.

Symmes with the help of his father worked in the government land office in Indiana. Symmes was an honest man with strong ethics so when embezzlement charges were brought up against him he was shocked and devastated by the scandal.

Political enemies of his father were his accusers. There was an honest explanation which revealed the innocence of Symmes, but with desire to damage the reputation of W.H. Harrison his enemies covered the facts that would have exonerated Symmes.

Fired and living in shame he died at the age of thirty-four in the midst of the crisis. He died of typhoid fever with his father at his bedside leaving behind six children and a grieving widow. He did not live to see his father become president.

The third offspring of the Harrisons was Lucy Singleton Harrison who married a judge of Ohio's Superior Court. She had four children. She was dead just one week after giving birth at the age of twenty-six. She would not live to see her father become president.

William Henry Harrison, Jr., his father's namesake did not achieve much in his short life. He struggled through college and had an undistinguished law career. He married the daughter of a congressman who was a friend of the family. He like too many other presidential sons felt as though they could not live up to expectations made of them. He lived in poverty and died an alcoholic at the age of thirty-five. He also did not live to see his father become president. His widow Jane Findlay would become the acting first lady for his father's short time in office of the presidency.

The Harrison's fifth child John Scott Harrison would go down in history as the only son of a president who was also the father of a president. Ten years after his death his son Benjamin Harrison would be the nation's 23rd president. He did not live to see his son become president; nor did his father live to see John become a member of Congress serving two terms as a congressman.

John would marry twice having three children with his first wife and ten children with his second wife. He spent a large part of his life running his farm in Ohio where his mother eventually came to live until her own death.

Out of the ten Harrison children only two would live past the age of thirty-five; John and the oldest daughter Betsy. Within five years of his father's death nine out of ten of his children would also be dead leaving John Scott as the only surviving offspring of President Harrison.

On the day of John Scott Harrison's funeral the family discovered the body in an adjoining grave had been stolen. As strange as that may sound it was common for graves to be robbed in this era. The recently buried bodies would be sold to medical colleges and used to teach medical students.

Benjamin Harrison, a son of John's went to the Ohio Medical College in search of the missing body. To his astonishment he found not the body he was looking for, but the body of his own father which the family wasn't even aware was missing. The school wasn't aware they had the body of the son of a president until his own son, a future president, came upon his father's body accidentally. The naked body of his father was found dangling by his neck at the end of a rope hidden in a dumbwaiter.

Benjamin Harrison, not to confuse with the son of John but the son of President Harrison, became a physician. During the Texas War of Independence he was kidnapped and taken prisoner as the Mexican army was in need of doctors. He was married twice and had three children with his first wife and two with his second wife. He died at the age of thirty-three only a matter of months before his father became president.

Mary Symmes Harrison married a doctor and had six children. She died at the age of thirty-three just a year after the death of her father.

Carter Bassett Harrison, the eighth child of the Harrisons, attended Miami University at the age of fifteen. His father had been appointed as U.S. minister to Colombia and Carter left the university before graduation in order to go to South America with his father to serve as his private secretary. They were recalled by President Andrew Jackson and they returned to the U.S. in 1830.

After Carter returned to the U.S. he returned to Miami University. After he completed his studies he served as a clerk in a law office. Once he completed his bar exams he assisted his father in his business affairs. Carter was married in a double ceremony along with his sister Anna Tuthill Harrison. Carter married Mary Anne Sutherland who he had a daughter with. He died at the age of twenty-seven, a little over a year before his father was elected president.

Anna Tuthill Harrison was the youngest daughter of the Harrison children. She married her cousin William Henry Harrison Taylor named after her father. She died less than two years after her own father's death when she was thirty-one years of age.

James Findlay Harrison was the last of the Harrison children. He was born in 1814 and died in 1817. He was the last to be born and the first to die.

Three of the Harrison children passed away just a short time before their father's election: William Henry Harrison, Jr. at age thirty-five died in 1838; the following year Carter Basset Harrison died at age twenty-seven in 1839; and the year after that in 1840 Benjamin Harrison died at age thirty-four.

The First Lady Anna Harrison did not attend her husband's inauguration due to illness. The illness may very well have been caused by a depression from mourning the three sons she had lost in a short period of time before his election. She did go on to live another twenty-two years after her husband; outliving all but one of her ten children. She had been packing her bags ready to join her husband when she received word that he had died of pneumonia. She was a first lady who never did go to Washington.

By the time of the president's death he and his wife had lost six of their children that preceded them in death. They were: James Findlay in 1817, Lucy in 1826, Symmes in 1830, William Henry, Jr. in 1838, Carter in 1839, and Benjamin in 1840. The remainder of the girls were soon to follow: Mary Symmes in 1842, Anna Tuthill in 1845, and Elizabeth or Betsy as she was known in 1846. Of all the girls Betsy was the only one to live past the age of thirty-five. The only surviving offspring was John Scott Harrison.

In a period of eight years time the first lady had lost not only her husband but six of her children. Throughout her life she would go on to lose all but one of her sons and even some of her grandchildren. It was a lot for a woman to bear. She received comfort from the Bible, her favorite verse she often turned to was, *"Be still, and know that I am God"* from the book of Psalms.

The first lady had fixed up one of the rooms in her twenty-two room house as a museum of her husband's political items including campaign objects and his Presidential library of books to show to visitors. All was lost in a fire which completely destroyed the home in 1858. The fire was believed to have been set by a former disgruntled maid who was charged for setting the fire, but acquitted. The first lady survived with only the clothes on her back and from then until her death lived with her one remaining son John Scott Harrison.

The story of William Henry Harrison's children would not be complete without mentioning the fact that it is alleged that in addition to his ten children with his wife, he is claimed to have had six children with one of his slaves named Dilsia. As of the year 2016, the belief that he had children with a slave has not been verified one way or the other and no DNA tests have been done on surviving ancestors of Dilsia.

Rumor has it that when he was running for president he didn't want illegitimate slave children of his around and he gave four of the children to his brother who sold them down the river to a Georgia plantation. If true, he is the first president known to have sold his own children off.

It was revealed through historian Kenneth Robert Janken in a biography of Walter Francis White, an African American civil rights leader who was also president of the NAACP that Walter White's mother Madeline Harrison while working on the genealogy of her family traced some of her mixed white race ancestry back to William Henry Harrison. It isn't stated how that information was discovered or if it is accurate.

The family claims that Dilisa, a female slave that belonged to Harrison, had six of his children that were born slaves. Walter White would be a black great grandson of the former president if the claim is true. White inherited the looks and features of a white man; yet never denied being black or tried "passing" as white.

10

John Tyler

Children of first wife Letitia and John Tyler:

Mary Tyler – Born: April 15, 1815   Died: June 17, 1848

Robert Tyler – Born: Sept. 9, 1816   Died: Dec. 3, 1877

John Tyler V – Born: Born April 27, 1819   Died: Jan. 26, 1896

Letitia Tyler "Letty" - Born: May 11, 1821   Died: Dec. 28, 1907

Elizabeth Tyler "Lizzie" - Born: July 11, 1823   Died: June 1, 1850

Anne Contesse Tyler – Born: April 1825   Died: July 1825

Alice Tyler – Born: March 23, 1827   Died: June 8, 1854

Tazewell Tyler – Born: Dec. 6, 1830   Died: January 8, 1874

Children of second wife Julia and John Tyler:

David Gardiner Tyler "Gardie" - Born: July 12, 1846   Died: Sept. 5, 1927

John Alexander Tyler "Alex" - Born: April 7, 1848   Died: Sept. 1, 1883

Julia Gardiner Tyler – Born: Dec. 25, 1849   Died: May 8, 1871

Lachian Tyler – Born: Dec. 2, 1851   Died :Jan. 26, 1902

Lyon Gardiner Tyler – Born: August 24, 1853   Died: Feb. 12, 1935

Robert Fitzwalter Tyler – Born: March 12, 1856   Died: Dec. 30, 1927

Pearl Tyler – Born: June 20, 1860   Died: June 30, 1947

Gardie Tyler was one of two presidential sons who was at the Appomattox Court House during the surrender of Robert E. Lee

John Tyler the nation's 10th president had fifteen children; eight with his first wife Letitia and seven with his second wife Julia. John Tyler goes down in history as the president who fathered the most children.

While president all seven of his children with his first wife Letitia lived at the White House at one time or another. His second set of children were born in the days after he left the White House.

He was the first president to get married while in office. His first wife Letitia died in 1842 the year after he became president. He married his second wife Julia Gardiner in 1844. Julia was thirty years younger than the president, and his oldest child with first wife Letitia was five years older than her new stepmother.

Mary Tyler was the president's first child with his first wife Letitia. Mary married Henry Lightfoot Jones in 1835. Her father was a senator at the time she married. Her husband was a successful planter who owned land. By the time her father became president she had a son. Her mother was seriously ill so her father asked Mary to move in the White House. She gave birth to her second son while living in the presidential mansion. She had three sons two of which remained unmarried.

Robert Tyler was the second child and the first son of John and Letitia Tyler. He would become a lawyer and politician as his father before him.

His father encouraged his son to attend his alma mater the College of William and Mary. Robert was a good student making his father proud. Robert also wrote poetry and published a book of his poems.

In his twenties Robert married the actress Priscilla Cooper who he met when she performed in a play in Richmond, Virginia. As he watched her perform he fell head over heels for her and at the end of the performance he went backstage to meet the actress.

Priscilla grew up in a home her father, a drinker and gambler, won in a card game. Her mother died at a young age leaving Priscilla to be raised by her father. Priscilla joined her father on stage working as a father-daughter acting team. Neither one of them were exceptionally good actors and spent their acting career living in boardinghouses and performing in second-rate theaters.

Robert and Priscilla married in 1839 just a few months after having met. Robert's father served as his best man at his wedding. His mother had recently suffered a stroke and was unable to attend her son's wedding. The newly married couple came to live with the Tylers. Priscilla, a lovely girl, was loved by both her in-laws.

In the year 1841 John Tyler became vice president during the William Henry Harrison administration. That administration was short-lived with President Harrison dying just one month after his inauguration. It would be the first time in history a vice president succeeded to the presidency after the death of his predecessor. Due to the circumstances of how Tyler became president, he became known as "His Accidency." John Tyler, fifty-one years of age was at this time the youngest man to become president.

Tyler requested Priscilla to be the official White House hostess. His wife an invalid was unable to fill the role herself. The couple moved to the White House with Priscilla serving as acting first lady and Robert as his father's secretary.

Priscilla served as White House hostess for the first three years of Tyler's presidency. She was in President Tyler's words, "the presiding genius of the White House." Priscilla was quite a charmer, witty, and intelligent.

Priscilla already had one infant and was pregnant with her second child when she moved to the White House to assume the role of first lady. During her first formal dinner given for cabinet members she had been caring for a sick four month old infant all day, pregnant, dealing with the stress of the move to Washington, and learning to fulfill the role of first lady, and without all the help a first lady is blessed with today. In the middle of the dinner she fainted. Daniel Webster Secretary of State without hesitation scooped her up in his arms to remove her from the table to somewhere more comfortable when her astonished husband tossed a pitcher of cold water on not only his wife but the secretary of state.

Robert assumed the role as White House secretary at the age of twenty-five. After three years of serving as his father's secretary he moved his wife and children to Philadelphia to open a law practice. Politics had been a part of his life and it was in his blood. In addition to becoming a lawyer he became chairman of the Democratic party's central committee.

During this time he practiced law, served as sheriff's solicitor, and was chief clerk of the state Supreme Court. His law practice while successful was never prosperous. Even so, Robert refused many opportunities to use his father's name or his title of presidential son to gain favors for which he was respected and gained himself the reputation of a man of integrity. He was not a rich man by any means, but he certainly had people's respect.

When the Civil War broke out Robert Tyler was a well-known Southern name living in the north. A mob with anti-southern sentiments attacked his home forcing him and his family to leave Pennsylvania. He left for Virginia leaving behind all his worldly goods. At forty-four years of age he was too old to fight in the war, but was offered an appointment by President Jefferson Davis to serve as Register of the Treasury of the Confederacy. Due to his position his signature appeared on many Confederate dollars.

At the conclusion of the Civil War Robert returned to practicing law. He was off to a rough start and the former President Buchanan hearing of his dilemma sent him a personal check to help the young man he highly respected. As much as Robert needed the money he returned the check with appreciation of the thoughtfulness of the gift.

Eventually things turned around for him, and while not well off he was content with life and living comfortably. Now living in the South he became the Alabama Democratic state chairman and editor of the *Montgomery Advisor*.

He died in 1877 of a stroke and was remembered by those who knew him with respect as a man who was very giving while expecting nothing in return.

John Tyler's third child and second son was the president's namesake John, Jr. Like his older brother his father had desired for him to go to the College of William and Mary and to follow in his footsteps in studying law. His father's dream was for both his sons to join him and have a family law practice.

John, Jr. married Martha "Mattie" Rochelle in 1838. After being married for only a matter of months John, Jr. tried to get a divorce.

Like his father and his brother, John, Jr. did become a lawyer but had a hard time living up to the reputation of his father and older brother.

When his father became president John, Jr. served as one of his father's private secretaries. His wife Mattie tired of his drinking refused to move to Washington to join him while he lived in the White House. By this time the couple was apart more than they were together even though they were still married. They had three children together, two of which would remain unmarried.

John, Jr. was a talented writer and while in the White House he served as his brother's assistant with the press. He became famous when he defended his father in a very public duel with a newspaper editor. An editor had insulted his father and John, Jr. challenged the man to a duel. The editor full of hot air and bluster ranted about John, Jr. being a coward and proclaimed he wouldn't have the courage to show up for the duel. The editor was the one who ended up being absent at the time and place of the duel, and John, Jr. heard no more from him and gained the public's approval for standing up for his father.

John, Jr. drank heavily and his father was forced to fire him. He had done everything he could to encourage and stand by his namesake, but his drinking was causing bad behavior and embarrassment to the family and to the office of the presidency. John, Jr. was yet another presidential son who couldn't live up to the expectations expected of him as a presidential son and became an alcoholic.

After his days in the White House he had no interests. His marriage was still valid but the couple were mostly estranged. He appeared to be a lost soul who was his own worst enemy.

In Washington while drunk he and a friend were involved in a fight where they beat up a man. The *New York Herald* ran the story about the incident which humiliated the Tyler family.

Eventually he did settle down and joined his brother Robert in practicing law together in Philadelphia.

He became captain of the Virginia infantry during the Mexican War, a short-lived war. He later served as a colonel in the Civil War fighting for the Confederate cause and was assistant secretary of war. He was in his mid-forties by the end of the war when he again took up law. He secured a position in the IRS in Florida under President Grant.

His marriage was over, he was living in poverty, and never could measure up to his father or brother and gain the respect he desired. He lived the remainder of his life in the South.

Letitia, who was known to all as "Letty," was a beautiful young girl. In 1839 at the age of eighteen she married James Allen Semple. The marriage would not be a happy one. He suffered mental problems which from the early years of her marriage became evident. Alcohol would bring on rages which would terrify Letty. Over the years the unhappiness of her marriage left her an embittered young woman.

Letty's mother suffered a debilitating stroke and then not only did she have an unstable husband to worry about but Letty had to take over for her mother in caring for her younger siblings.

Two years after his wife's stroke John Tyler was elected vice president and just thirty days after that he assumed the presidency after the death of President Harrison. Robert's wife Priscilla became the hostess or acting first lady. Overtime Letty was called in to give a hand in the role. Letty, most likely relieved for an excuse to leave her husband for a valid reason became indispensable.

The president had Letty's husband Semple assigned as a purser in the navy. He would be out to sea for three years giving his wife some respite.

Letty having fit in and doing a good job as hostess after taking over for Priscilla allowed Robert and Priscilla to leave the White House and move to Philadelphia so Robert could pursue a long delayed law practice. The twenty-three year old Letty took over the daunting tasks of White House hostess on her own once Priscilla left. Suffering from a marriage that was strained and a husband who was a burden, her role as first lady likely gave Letty a great deal of pleasure and self-worth.

Elizabeth "Lizzie" Tyler was eighteen when her help was requested from her sister and sister-in-law to help with the workload as White House hostess. Letty had taken on the role of hostess for the president's mansion, caring for their mother, and caring for the younger children, and the work had become overwhelming. She was hoping for some relief with Lizzie's help.

Lizzie proved to be of little help as hostess. It would have been good experience for the young girl who was about to become a bride and would need to run her own household and care for a family, but she was more interested in planning her wedding than in helping out with the workload.

William Waller a staff member at the White House who was a young lawyer and neighbor from when they lived in Virginia was about to marry the eighteen-year old Lizzie.

John Tyler had become president when President Harrison died. It was the first time in history a vice president would assume the position of the presidency due to death and many of his political foes didn't consider his ascendency to the presidency valid due to how he claimed the title of the presidency. It was an unfriendly Congress he had to contend with. Congress was determined to make it as unpleasant as possible for Tyler, so with a White House wedding on the horizon and the condition of the White House declining, Congress allowed no funds for improvements on the president's mansion. It was a rundown setting for a wedding of a president's daughter.

Regardless of the condition of the White House on January 31, 1842 the wedding took place. It would be the one and only time First Lady Letitia Tyler would leave the family quarters and be involved in any White House event. That would be the last time the first lady was seen by the public. She died eight months later.

As the family of the bride witnessed this special event, little did they realize they would soon lose their mother and in a matter of years would lose their sister the bride too.

Lizzie and William moved to Lynchburg, Virginia and had five children. Eight years after their White House wedding twenty-six year old Lizzie died suffering complications after giving birth.

Anne Contesse the sixth child of Letitia and John Tyler born in April of 1825 died at birth.

Alice, the president's youngest daughter with his first wife, was described as tall and fat by the harsh, judgmental press. Alice was only fourteen when her father became president. She would still be a teenager when her mother died. It was a difficult time for the young girl.

With a father with his days occupied as president, a mother who was an invalid and then dealing with her death, family members marrying and moving away, and with others who were busy as secretaries to their father or hostess of the presidential mansion; it would have been a lonely time regardless of how many people were living under one roof for a girl her age.

Tazewell was the eighth and the last of the children of Letitia and John Tyler. He was ten years old when his father became president and not yet a teenager when his mother died the year after they moved into the White House.

It was only three months after the death of the first lady Letitia Tyler when word spread of a beautiful young lady who had arrived in Washington. The young, twenty-two year old beauty was Julia Gardiner of New York. The Gardiner family was invited to the White House for dinner. Not only did she spur the interest of two of the Tyler sons, but also that of the president.

While attending a White House social event the president led the young beauty away from the others giving her a tour of the presidential home. Only five months after the death of his wife he asked Julia to marry him. In response she said she would have to think about it and soon afterward returned with her family to New York. When Julia did agree to his marriage proposal the president kept the engagement a secret – even from his own children.

Letty's role as White House hostess came to an unexpected, brusque end when just two years after the death of her mother her father eloped with Julia Gardner. It was a complete surprise and a shock to his family.

Her father at fifty-four years of age had married a twenty-four year old socialite. The wedding was completely unexpected by the family and a surprise to all of Washington. While her brothers had no issues with their father marrying again, the girls were shocked and not happy about the marriage so quickly after the death of their mother and to such a young woman.

Mary, the oldest daughter, was five years older than her stepmother. Initially, Lizzie was upset about her father's marriage to a woman who was only three years older than she was, but over time she got past that and was on friendly terms with her stepmother. Eventually the other sisters accepted their new stepmother, but there would be a lifelong unrelenting contention between Letty and Julia.

Taz was fourteen when his father brought home a new wife to the surprise of the entire family. Taz young enough to appreciate having a mother in his life got along very well with his new stepmother. The feelings were reciprocated as Julia loved Taz as if he were her own. With so much opposition to her coming into the family by her husband's daughters, it was a respite with young Taz accepting her so wholeheartedly. Their relationship did not change as she added her own children to the family. Julia and Taz got along very well.

Julia Tyler is the only woman married to a sitting president whose children were all born after leaving the White House. John and Julia Tyler, his second wife, had seven children together.

Tyler's father's presidential administration was at an end and the family was moving to their home Sherwood Forest in Charles City County, Virginia. Sherwood Forest is the only private residence that has been owned by two presidents that weren't related: President William Henry Harrison who never actually lived there and John Tyler who retired from the presidency in 1845 and lived there with his second wife Julia and some of the children. Sherwood Forest has been owned by the Tyler family since 1842 and is currently owned as of the year 2017 by Harrison Ruffin Tyler, grandson of the president and son of Lyon Gardiner Tyler.

After the days of the presidency the battle between Letty and Julia continued. Julia was having her own family adding to the number of Tyler offspring and was quite tired of Letty and her relentless dispute.

James Semple, Letty's husband, resigned from his commission in the navy and had moved back with his wife for a time taking a position in the Confederate States Navy. The Tyler family were all staunch supporters of the Confederacy during the Civil War. Already suffering from mental problems, the south losing the war exasperated Semple's condition. He couldn't seem to grasp the war had come to an end and would go about in disguise to spy thinking he was working for the southern cause.

Letitia left her husband and opened a private girl's school, the Electic Institute in Baltimore. The couple never did divorce, they just simply lived apart for the rest of their years.

Letty, not one to let go of a grudge sued Julia for some family keepsakes and mementos she had in her possession. Letitia would outlive her stepmother, but her resentment of the woman her father loved never diminished.

Letty in her old age had become blind and was living in an impoverished state. She eventually moved to Washington, D.C. to live at the Louise Home a shelter for poor women. She lived to the age of eighty-six.

Alice a typical teenager was getting out of hand. At the age of eighteen she was stubborn and disrespectful to her stepmother and didn't take kindly to her stepmothers attempt at discipline. The life at Sherwood Forest was a bore to the young Alice who no longer was the "fat" young girl the press described in her days at the White House but had become quite a beauty.

Young adults at times can be moody and disrespectful and Alice made her stepmother suffer with her treatment of her. Julia decided it would be easier on both of them to send Alice away to boarding school. Alice did not like that idea at all, but her father heeded to his new wife's wishes.

While Alice was a romanticist who fell in and out of love quite often, she dug her heels in when it was suggested perhaps it was time for twenty-one year old Alice to be married. Alice responded with that suggestion by saying that she "felt she had not been a young lady long enough yet." She refused to be rushed into marriage.

She continued to exasperate her stepmother when she refused several marriage proposals, until she met the Reverend Henry Mandeville Denison. Denison was the new Episcopal rector who had caught all the young ladies eyes and stole many a heart; as the young girls one after another fell for the tall, handsome twenty-eight year old newcomer.

Alice fell for the handsome new reverend just like the rest of the girls. Alice was ready to give up the idea of enjoying her days as a young lady and set her sights on marrying Denison. And that's exactly what she did.

It is unknown what attracted her to Denison when she had refused so many other marriage proposals? It wasn't for his money as he had none to speak of, nor did he hold any place of distinction in society. It appears it truly was love as it never seemed to give her a moment's pause that he wasn't rich or had made a name for himself.

Alice and Denison married and had two children. Their first baby was premature and lived for only a week. She later had a daughter Bessy.

Alice's life was to be a short one dying at the age of twenty-seven of bilious colic. The former president was heartbroken at the loss of his daughter. Alice was the third daughter within the last seven years he had buried: Mary his oldest in 1847, Elizabeth or "Lizzie" in 1850, and now Alice in 1854.

Nearing the end of his teen years Taz got gold rush fever as did millions of people worldwide. He was anxious to join others as they were preparing to traipse across America to head to California and pan for gold. His father put an end to those dreams instead guiding his son to study medicine with his uncle who was a doctor.

Finances were extremely tight in the Tyler household, yet his father was more than willing to help his son so he could have a medical education and become a doctor. Taz respected his father's wishes and studied medicine and became a physician.

Taz married Nannie Bridges in 1857. They had two children, one a toddler and the other only an infant at the time he entered the Civil War.

Taz served in the Confederate States Army (CSA) as a surgeon. Perhaps due to the butchery he had seen firsthand in the war he succumbed to alcohol until it became a problem in his life. It is very possible he suffered from what today is known as PTSD, or post traumatic stress disorder, an unknown term in those days; but experienced by soldiers who had seen too much death and despair in any war. As a surgeon he had seen more than his share.

When he returned from the war he was angry with his stepmother who he had been so close to for what he considered deserting the family home Sherwood Forest. She had moved north to be with family during the Civil War. Angry at the outcome of the war he was determined not to live under Yankee occupation in his state of Virginia and headed to California.

Taz left his wife and two young children behind. His wife divorced him and he died an alcoholic at the age of forty-three. He lived only a year after his divorce.

The first child of former President Tyler and his second wife Julia was David Gardiner known as Gardie to all those who knew him. Gardie was the first of the seven children of John and Julia Tyler.

The fact that the former president was already father to seven living children with his first wife didn't dampen his enthusiasm for his next arrival of children with his second wife. He loved all of his children dearly and took great pride in them.

Gardie went to a private school in Charles City County, Virginia and at the age of sixteen entered Washington College which presently is the Washington and Lee University.

Abraham Lincoln was elected president the year previous to Gardie becoming a university student. When the Civil War broke out Gardie was fifteen. He dropped out of college a year later at the age of sixteen and enlisted in the Confederate Army serving in the infantry and also the artillery units.

Gardie found himself guarding prisoners at Libby Prison and was disgruntled that he wasn't out shooting Yankees. After a time he joined an artillery unit and at eighteen years of age he fought under Robert E. Lee in the Army of Northern Virginia.

The war was over as of April 9, 1865. Gardie was in attendance at the surrender of Robert E. Lee at Appomattox Court House. There was another presidential son also in attendance for this historic event, only this presidential son fought for the Union - Robert Lincoln, the oldest son of Abraham Lincoln.

Gardie's father, the former president, died in 1862 the year after the Civil War started and the year Gardie had left to be a university student.

At the advice of his mother Gardie returned to Washington College at the end of the war, while his brother Alex who had also fought returned to Sherwood Forest to work on repairs to the family home from the damage that occurred during the war.

Gardie struggled with living with the southern loss in the war and living under Union successors. He had a hard time accepting the 'united' part in the United States. It was decided it would be best for both Gardie and Alex to go to Germany to attend college. Gardie, Alex, and a cousin sailed aboard the *SS Hansa* headed to Germany.

The boys attended college in Karlsrube, Germany. Gardie struggled with the German language having a hard time sitting through classes where he understood little of what was being said. Gardie adjusted better once he and his brother Alex started an American baseball club with fellow students. Baseball was new to Germans and this was the first baseball club or baseball teams in Germany.

The boys enjoyed sports and outdoor activities. They joined a shooting club and helped put together a cricket club. The boys also became involved in boxing and gymnastics. Gardie became consumed with Germany's fervor for gymnastics to the point of writing home and prompting his mother to put up parallel bars for his brothers at home.

Gardie had been in Germany for two years when he decided to return home and finish his education. His brother Alex remained in Germany. He would complete his studies at the university he had previously attended, the law school of Washington and Lee. He graduated and became a lawyer passing the bar in 1870 and settled in Charles City County, Virginia.

During the period following the Civil War, known as Reconstruction, Gardie was an influential aid in Virginia's triumphant struggle against the influence of Carpetbaggers.

Politics was in his blood even though his father was no longer president by the time he was born. He entered politics on the Democratic party ticket.

He served on the Board of Visitors of the College of William and Mary where his father had attended.

For a time he was director of the state lunatic asylum in Williamsburg, Virginia and then served in the Virginia State Senate, was elected to the U.S. House of Representatives, and when defeated returned to his law practice. He served as a state circuit court judge until his death.

He married Mary Morris Jones. They had five children together. He died at Sherwood Forest Plantation, the Tyler family home, at the age of eighty-one.

John Alexander Tyler, or Alex as he was known, was the second child and second son to John Tyler and his second wife Julia. He was a healthy twelve pound baby that was born at the family home Sherwood Forest in Virginia.

The Sherwood Forest Plantation where Alex grew up was located on the James River in Charles City County, Virginia. The Tyler family moved to Sherwood Forest in 1842 once Tyler's presidential administration had come to an end. Tyler was a slave owner and there were approximately seventy slaves living at Sherwood Forest Plantation. John Tyler was a caring slave owner and saw to it that none of his slaves were ever whipped or their families split up. He had reservations about owning slaves, but nevertheless he did own slaves to help run his plantation.

Alex's younger days at Sherwood Forest of playing and fishing were his fondest memories. He had an endless supply of brothers and sisters to play with at the plantation along with the slave children.

In the early days of the Civil War Alex's mother encouraged him to enlist in the Junior Guard. He was thirteen at the time and served as second lieutenant in the Charles City Junior Guard.

Alex's father died when he was fourteen. After his father passed away Alex ran away from home to enlist in the Confederate States Army. He was turned down and sent home. He was too young at the age of fourteen.

By the time Alex had turned sixteen his brother Gardie had joined the army and he was determined he would join too. He begged his mother relentlessly to let him join. She didn't want to send another son to fight in the war but after a time she agreed on one condition. She said she would agree if he would join the Confederate navy, not the army. Her reasoning for this was the army suffered more casualties and she felt he would be safer in the navy.

Alex was assigned to a ship in the navy that was quarantined due to yellow fever. He spent most of his navy life aboard a ship isolated from others and away from the battles of the war. This was not what Alex had in mind when he joined up to fight so he left the navy and joined Gardie where he was serving as a prison guard.

Near the end of the war Alex joined the First Virginia Battalion of Artillery under General Robert E. Lee. Alex eager to fight for the cause came to the war at an early age but late in the war. The war was about to end. Two days after his seventeenth birthday General Robert E. Lee surrendered to General Ulysses S. Grant. The south had lost the war and this was a bitter pill for Alex to swallow.

For a time Alex returned home only to find the home had been damaged from the war and from the Union soldiers. The thought of Yankees in his childhood home left him even more morose.

Alex's mother sent his older brother Gardie and him to Germany to finish their education at college abroad. Alex was a good student with an aptitude for math and science. He studied to become a mining engineer.

Alex learned the German language well. He and his brother became involved in starting a baseball club, the first ever in Germany. The brothers also became involved in other sports such as boxing and gymnastics. He spent some time hunting, something he had enjoyed back home in Virginia.

His brother eventually returned to the United States to finish his education while Alex remained. He was still in Germany at the start of the Franco-Prussian War and joined the Saxon army. He joined the First Uhlan regiment under King John of Saxony and took part in the occupation of France. He served with distinction and was decorated by the Prussian government.

Alex returned home to the United States in 1873 poor but happy. He was able to speak fluent German and French. He had been trained as an engineer and was looking forward to finding work in this field.

Alex found work mining near Salt Lake City. The Panic of 1873 brought about by post-Civil War inflation, investments in railroads, and economic losses brought about a depression which put an end to his work in mining. He eventually found work at the Southside Railroad Company but it paid very little and cost of living was more than he was making.

Alex married Sarah Griswold Gardiner in 1875. The bride was his third cousin and wealthy. There would be times when they would see little of each other when he was working as an engineer and surveyor out west. Their first child was born Christmas of 1876. The boy was either stillborn or died soon after his birth. They would have three more children. Sarah outlived her husband and all her children.

Alex had been out of work for years and the former first lady reached out to friends and those in a position who might be able to help her son. She was able to help in securing from Congress an appropriation to survey Indian lands in the Dakota territory. President Rutherford B. Hayes appointed him as a surveyor for the United States Department of the Interior.

Alex while surveying land in the Dakota territory in Indian land the summer of 1883 appeared at the governor's palace in New Mexico. While out surveying he had run out of water in the desert and suffering from thirst and dehydration he drank alkaline water which gave him dysentery and died at the governor's palace from drinking the contaminated water at the age of thirty-five.

The third child and first daughter by former president and second wife Julia was Julia Gardiner Tyler known as Julie. She was born at Sherwood Forest the family plantation.

During the Civil War when Julie was twelve years old the family left the plantation and moved to New York. She had just turned thirteen at the time of her father's death.

Julie was tutored at home until about the age of sixteen. The young, sociable girl needed some direction and guidance and her mother decided to send her to the Convent of the Sacred Heart a convent school in Nova Scotia. She was homesick so far from home and away from family.

Julie was married at the age of nineteen to William Spencer. Spencer was a farmer from New York who has having financial difficulties whose future looked bleak. He had an astounding amount of debt. He went to work in the Colorado silver mines and then on to California citrus groves and eventually disappeared from the family after borrowing money to pay off his debts. He was never heard from again.

Julie died from childbirth complications after giving birth to a daughter at the age of twenty-one. The baby, a little girl named Julia, was raised by her mother the former first lady.

When Lachian Tyler was born in 1851 his father was sixty-one years of age.

Lachian studied medicine at the New York College of Physicians and Surgeons. After becoming a doctor he practiced in the north. Even though he was a doctor he lived in poverty for years.

Lachian married Georgia Webb Powell. Lachian and his wife never had any children.

He had moved to Washington and with a new wife to support and a private practice with few patients he appealed to his mother to use her influence as a former first lady to help him. There really wasn't anything she could do to help her son. For years he had tried to rely on his name as the son of a president to aid him in opening doors with no success.

In addition to his private practice he eventually found work on his own distinction not having to resort to relying on the family name. He worked in the U.S. Navy's medical division. He passed the exams and became a surgeon in the navy.

His private practice in time was lucrative. He practiced medicine in Washington and in 1887 he moved to Elkhorn, West Virginia where he practiced medicine until his death. He died at the age of fifty.

The fifth child of Julia and the sixty-three year old former president was Lyon Gardiner Tyler born in August of 1853. He was born at Sherwood Forest Plantation.

Lyon graduated from college with a master's degree in 1875 from the University of Virginia. He then went on to study law.

In 1878 Lyon married Annie Baker and had three children with her: John Tyler, Elizabeth Gilmour Tyler, and Julia Gardiner Tyler Wilson.

Lyon was elected to the state legislature where he used his influence to reopen the University of Williams and Mary College. He served as president of the College of William and Mary for thirty-one years from the years 1888 to 1919. He is given credit for restoring W&M's financial situation after the Civil War. (Presidents Thomas Jefferson, James Monroe, and John Tyler had all attended W&M.) During his time as serving as president of the university he also was an author, public speaker, and respected historian. He was awarded the title of Professor Emeritus.

In addition to his work at W&M he was the founder of a small college and taught for some time at a high school.

After the death of his first wife Lyon married Sue Ruffin and had another three children: Lyon Gardiner Tyler born in 1924, Harrison Ruffin Tyler born in 1928, and Henry Tyler who died as an infant. Lyon was seventy-one years old when his son and namesake Lyon Gardiner Tyler was born and he was seventy-five years old when his son Harrison Ruffin Tyler was born. His own father had been sixty-three at the time of his birth.

Lyon committed himself to historical research and was an expert in the fields of early Virginia history and genealogy. He like some of his brothers found themselves fighting his father's battles long after he was gone from this earth; defending and justifying his political career. He was a staunch supporter of his father's moral and political stance. He wrote 'The Letters and Times of the Tylers,' a detailed defense of his father's political career.

Our 10th president, born in the eighteenth century while George Washington was president, has two grandsons that are alive today. Grandsons, not great-great grandsons; but grandsons of our tenth president are alive in a year when our 45th president just took office. One of those grandsons, son of Lyon Gardiner Tyler, is living at Sherwood Forest Plantation today; the home of our 10th president. That makes former President John Tyler, a pre-Civil War president, the earliest former President of the United States with living grandchildren. Now think about that; their grandfather was born during the administration of George Washington our 1st president.

Robert Fitzwalter Tyler was born when the former president was in his late sixties. He was the fifth and last son of the former president and his second wife.

His father died before he was six years of age and would barely remember his father. He attended Georgetown College until due to financial difficulties he had to leave college and return home. Without a college degree to rely on or training of any kind he chose farming over a career in the business or legal world. He was successful at farming. He was a farmer in Hanover County, Virginia on leased land.

He had three children with his wife Fannie Glenn Tyler. While he may not have made achievements that were noteworthy enough to be put in history books or to be remembered by many, he lived a contented life and was significant in the lives of his family.

Pearl Tyler was the last of the Tyler children. Pearl was born on June 20, 1860. By the time the last of Julia and John Tyler's children Pearl was born their first child Gardie was fourteen years old. All of the former president's daughters from his first wife, with the exception of Letty, were dead by the time Pearl was born.

Pearl's father was seventy years old at the time of her birth. She was about a year and a half when her father died so she never had a chance to know him. He was a caring father who treasured his children. He had been waiting in Richmond at the time of his death to be sworn in as a member of the Confederate House of Representatives.

Pearl was born before the Civil War began and lived to the end of World War II. There were a lot of changes that took place in the world she lived in.

Pearl attended Georgetown Academy and after converting to Roman Catholicism at the age of twelve with her mother she changed schools and attended the Sacred Heart located in Washington.

Pearl married Major William Mumford Ellis. Her husband had been a member of the Virginia House of Delegates. She lived the remainder of her life near Roanoke, Virginia. They had eight children and had a good marriage. They were married for over fifty years.

I would be remiss to neglect to mention the allegations that President Tyler had fathered slave children. It isn't known exactly when these allegations were made by the ancestors of the slave family, even whether it was in the president's lifetime or came out much later; but there has never been any proof to substantiate the claims.

John William Dunjee who was an 'alleged' child of President John Tyler with a slave woman who was born in 1833 and died in 1903. John William Dungy was born a slave in New Kent County / Charles City County, Virginia. His family (no mention is made of what generation of the family made this claim) claimed that President John Tyler was his father and Dungy's mother was a slave. He was born slave to an owner on another plantation, not of the Tyler family. There has been no information found to base the legitimacy of this claim on and as of 2017 is unsubstantiated.

In the year 1841, abolitionist publisher Joashua Leavitt alleged that Tyler had fathered several children with his slaves and later sold his offspring. There has only been found one record to date of the president selling any of his slaves and that was to finance his move to Washington. He had suffered great remorse of having to sell the slave. No evidence of any kind has been found to substantiate the claim made by the publisher either.

II

JAMES POLK

Children of Sarah and James Polk:

No biological children

The Polks' ward, Marshall Polk, was arrested for embezzling money from the Treasury.

James Polk married Sarah Childress when he was twenty-eight years of age and Sarah was twenty. They had no children of their own and no children lived in the White House during their administration.

The Polks were wards of their nephew Marshall Polk whose father died a month before his birth in 1831. At the time the Polks took their nephew under their care James Polk was a U.S. Representative from Tennessee.

Marshall Polk attended Georgetown University and graduated from West Point in 1852. During the Civil War he joined the Confederate army as a captain of artillery. He was seriously wounded at Shiloh and had to have a leg amputated, but remained in the army being promoted to colonel.

For a time after the war he lived on a farm in Tennessee and published the *'Bolivar*

Bulletin'. He entered the political world in 1876 and served three terms as Tennessee State Treasurer.

Marshall Polk had been found to have embezzled hundreds of thousands of dollars from the treasury from his time as state treasurer. When a customary inspection was about to take place in 1883, Polk quietly disappeared from the state. The study found that hundreds of thousands of dollars were missing. It was discovered that Polk had been embezzling funds in five of the six years he served in office.

The attempted flight of Marshall Tate Polk Jr. from the country sounds like a story from a Wild West movie.

It wasn't too hard to figure out in which direction Polk was headed as he owned a silver mine in Mexico and there was no extradition to the United States. Warrants of arrest were sent to cities along his probable escape route. It shouldn't be too difficult to spot a man with a wooden leg.

Along the way he was recognized on a train by a conductor who recognized him from the notices posted along his likely route. Polk and his servant got off at the next stop trying to escape by horseback. The conductor had the authorities called and gave chase.

Somewhere along the way the conductor and friend confronted him in the Texas scrub just eighteen miles from the Rio Grande where he would have crossed into Mexico. They were able to hold him captive until the authorities arrived.

Polk was charged with embezzlement and sentenced to twenty years in jail. He died while serving time in jail.

12

ZACHARY TAYLOR

Children of Margaret "Peggy" and Zachary Taylor:

Ann Margaret Mackall Taylor – Born: April 9, 1811   Died: Dec. 2, 1875

Sarah Knox Taylor "Knoxie" - Born: March 6, 1814   Died: Sept. 15, 1835

Octavia Pannill Taylor – Born: August 16, 1816   Died: July 8, 1820

Margaret Smith Taylor – Born: July 27, 1819   Died: Oct. 22, 1820

Mary Elizabeth Taylor "Betty"- Born: April 20, 1824   Died: July 26, 1909

Richard Taylor "Dick" - Born: Jan. 27, 1826   Died: April 12, 1879

"Knoxie" married Jefferson Davis who would one day be president of the Confederate states.

Anne Margaret Mackall Taylor was the first child of Zachary and Peggy Taylor and was born near Louisville. Anne grew up on different military posts moving around in her young life. The family settled down in Louisiana for a time where their father commanded the fort at Baton Rouge. Her father fought in the War of 1812. Zachary Taylor successfully defended Fort Harrison in Indiana Territory from an Indian attack commanded by the Shawnee chief Tecumseh.

Being that Anne's life had been lived out on different posts while her father served in the military, it wasn't a surprise when she married a military man herself. She met and married Robert Crooke Wood an army surgeon at Fort Crawford in Wisconsin.

Anne had four children. Her two sons fought in the Civil War for the Confederacy while her husband fought for the Union serving as surgeon general. At the end of the war she was a widow and moved to Germany to live with her daughter, Blandina Dudley von Grabow, who had married a baron and member of the German embassy. She lived the remainder of her life in Germany and died there in 1875.

The second child and daughter of Zachary Taylor was Sarah Knox Taylor a sweet girl named after the fort where her father was stationed and the family was living. She was known to others as Knox or Knoxie, a nickname she assumed from her birthplace.

When the family was living in the Mississippi Delta region Knoxie suffered a severe bout of malaria. She survived, two of her sisters did not.

During her teenage years Knoxie's father was transferred to Fort Crawford, Wisconsin following the Black Hawk War. While stationed at Fort Crawford the seventeen year old Knoxie met Jefferson Davis. Davis would one day be president of the Confederate. When Davis was transferred to another post her father was pleased. He respected Davis but he knew how hard it was on his own wife and family with him being in the military and being moved from post to post. He didn't want that for his daughter. Some of the military posts were quite rugged with the lives of those living there in danger of attack, disease, or hardships. It was a difficult life. He wanted a better life for his daughter.

Knoxie was a determined young girl who had her heart set on Jefferson Davis and unknown to her parents they were communicating with each other through letters over the next few years. Through those letters they planned to marry. Twenty-one year old Knoxie and Jefferson Davis married in 1835 at the home of a family member of the Taylors. Her parents did not approve and did not attend the wedding. They did stay in contact with their daughter after her wedding through mail.

Jefferson Davis and his bride traveled on their honeymoon to visit his brother and sister. While visiting Davis' sister in Louisiana they both came down with malaria. Davis recovered, his young bride did not. Only three months after their wedding the twenty-one year old bride died of malaria.

Margaret Smith Taylor, her mother's namesake, died at the age of one from malaria dying just three months after her sister Octavia.

Mary "Betty" Elizabeth Taylor was the youngest of the Taylor girls.

Betty's mother had insisted on her children receiving good educations and as the children were old enough for school she sent them to live with relatives away from the frontier. She wanted her children to be raised where it was more civilized and away from disease and the hard life they would have had to endure on the frontier. Betty was sent to Philadelphia where she received a good education.

Betty married her father's aide Colonel William Wallace Bliss in 1846.

Zachary's wife was against her husband accepting the nomination for the presidency. She had followed her husband uncomplainingly from one frontier military post to another for nearly forty years of their married life living in tents, log cabins, and army forts; but when it came time to move to the White House she was not happy about the move.

Betty along with other members of her family, with the exception of her mother and brother, accepted an invitation from the outgoing president and his wife the Polks to attend a White House dinner the night before her father's inauguration.

Peggy Taylor delegated her duties of first lady to her daughter Betty. Betty was popular and considered intelligent, sophisticated, and quite a beauty. She lived with her husband in the White House and assumed all the social duties of the hostess of the White House while her husband remained working as her father's aide. Betty was so popular she even had a song written in her honor.

After serving as president for sixteen months the president attended a ceremony celebrating the Fourth of July at the uncompleted Washington Monument in the summer heat. He ate raw vegetables, cherries, and milk. The next day he had wretched stomach pains. He died five days later of cholera morbus with his wife and family by his side.

It was a little over a year after they moved out of the White House following her father's death when Betty suffered another loss with the death of her husband. Six years later she married her second husband Philip Pendleton Dandridge. Her mother died ten days later.

Betty never had children of her own, but during the Civil War her sister Ann and her sons moved to Germany leaving her daughter in Betty's care.

Betty died at the age of eighty-five.

Richard Taylor named after his paternal grandfather Richard Lee Taylor who served in the Revolutionary War was the last of the Taylor children and the only son.

Richard spent his early years on the frontier on different military posts living in rugged conditions; sometimes in tents, log cabins, or army barracks. It was an exciting life for a young boy with Indians and the wild, open frontier. His parents wanted him to have a good education and when he turned ten they sent him to private schools in Kentucky and Massachusetts. When they sent him off to school he didn't know he would only see his father once and then only briefly for the next eleven years.

After attending a Boston prep school he was sent to Europe going to Scotland for two years and to France for another year to further his education. It was a long time for a young boy to go without the guidance of his parents and not to have his father in his life. It would forever create a strained relationship between father and son.

When he returned to the United States he was tutored to prepare him for Harvard. After attending Harvard he found it wasn't to his liking and he completed his studies at Yale. While at Yale he developed an interest and read everything he could get his hands on in classical and military history. This would serve him well in the future. During his time at Yale he became a member of Skull and Bones a secret social club still in operation today that other president's sons and even presidents have been members of. He graduated from Yale in 1845.

The uneasy relationship between Dick and his father was further provoked when his father would write on how he should use his time in order to not to be idle. His father thought his son weak and was impatient with him when Dick became sick when under stress. His father's reaction to him must have exasperated his illness as it appears he never could quite measure up to his father's expectations. Dick suffered from a debilitating disease of rheumatoid arthritis which is triggered by a faulty immune system. His father saw it as a weakness and said, "Better to make no very great calculations as regards to the prominent positions our children are to occupy...they are but rarely realized."

Soon after Dick's graduation from Yale the ongoing controversy over the boundary between Texas and Mexico was escalating and about to turn into a war. Dick met with his father to become his aide-de-camp but came down with a fever and left to recuperate at the family plantation where it was decided he would stay and work. Still in his teens Dick was managing the cotton plantation his family owned in Mississippi.

His father became president in 1849 and Zachary Taylor's only son was not invited to his father's inauguration, the strain between them had become so great. Dick one day without notice showed up at the White House. He was immediately sent home.

His father was determined his son would not become a 'celebrated presidential son' and insisted he run the family's Mississippi plantation. He never saw his father again, not even attending his father's funeral. The strain between father and son had not lessened. An estimated one hundred thousand mourners lined the streets to see the president's funeral march – his son was not one of them.

He had been able to convince his presidential father to purchase a sugar cane plantation in Louisiana. At his father's death the plantation called 'Fashion' was inherited by Dick.

The year after his father's death Dick married Louise Marie Myrthe Bringier. She came from a wealthy family, the daughter of a wealthy French Creole matriarch. The couple had five children.

Dick entered local politics in 1855 and was elected to the Louisiana Senate.

Dick was successful at the sugar cane plantation increasing it's land and labor force to two hundred slaves. He became one of the richest men in Louisiana. Then the freeze of 1856 ruined his crops turning his success story into one of large debt.

He saw that war between the states was imminent and served as a delegate to the Louisiana Secession Convention in 1861. With a heavy heart he voted to withdraw from the Union. When the Civil War began he was asked to serve and while he was opposed to secession he accepted the appointment. Where he may have been lacking in experience in the field; what he was lacking in that aspect he more than made up for with his knowledge of military history and strategy which aided him greatly in combat. He quickly gained respect proving himself to be a competent leader.

His sister had been a bride of Jefferson Davis who died from malaria. Davis however did not forget about his brother-in-law. Dick fought with Stonewall Jackson who kept an eye on Taylor recognizing the brilliant strategist that he was. At thirty-six years of age he was the youngest Confederate officer to attain the rank of major general. President Jefferson Davis would later promote him to lieutenant general making him only one of only three men who did not attend West Point to achieve such a high rank from the south. He was the last of southern generals to surrender east of the Mississippi.

The Civil War took much from Dick Taylor: his sons died of scarlet fever, his wife after suffering so much died young, his plantation had been confiscated and sold, and he fought malaria until his death. He had proven himself; never accepting favors or promotions due to his name but on his own merits for which he was held in high esteem from both northerners and southerners.

He wrote his memoirs about the Civil War, *'Destruction and Reconstruction: Personal Experiences of the Late War,'* one of the most credited reports of the Civil War. The memoir was published just a week before his death. He died at the age of fifty-three.

13

Millard Fillmore

Children of Abigail and Millard Fillmore:

Millard Powers Fillmore – Born: April 25, 1828   Died: November 15, 1889

Mary Abigail Fillmore – Born: March 27, 1832   Died: July 26, 1854

Millard Fillmore's son Powers destroyed his father's presidential papers after the president's death.

Millard Powers Fillmore named after his father was known simply as Powers.

Powers was a Harvard student studying law. He went on to practice law in Buffalo, New York.

His father assumed the presidency after the death of President Taylor, and Powers served as his father's private secretary at the White House.

His mother who was not well during her time in the White House passed away a short time after his father's administration.

His days after serving as the president's secretary Powers practiced law and was appointed a federal court clerk.

After his mother's death his father remarried a woman named Caroline Carmichael McIntosh. Powers was upset about his father remarrying and never accepted his father's second wife. When his father died he pleaded to his son in his will to get along with his stepmother. That plea fell on deaf ears. After his father's death he was involved in a bitter court battle with his stepmother over the property and personal papers in his father's will. Powers won his case.

When he won the court case Powers was awarded his father's presidential papers and many of his personal belongings. He destroyed his father's presidential papers and sold the belongings. By destroying the presidential papers he deprived the public of knowledge of his father's administration and a part of our nation's history. That era would be lost to history due to his spiteful act. From the sale of his father's belongings he donated the money to different charities.

Before his own death he left instructions for his own personal papers which included letters to and from the former first lady and president to be destroyed. His request was that all his papers were burned.

He never married or had children and died without friends.

Mary Abigail, or Abby as she was known, was the Fillmore's only daughter.

Abby was a sweet girl who always put others happiness first. While she wasn't a beauty she had such an appealing personality and generous spirit that people were attracted to her.

Unusual for the times she was educated far beyond what most girls from her times were. She attended a private school and then graduated from New York State Normal School. She spoke fluent French, and could speak Spanish, German, and Italian. She was an excellent student.

She was a school teacher until her father became president and then she moved into the White House to assist her semi-invalid mother who wasn't up to the task of assuming the role of first lady. Even though she was only a teenager at the time, she assisted her mother as hostess of the White House and was very successful at the role.

Abby was only nineteen when she became a hostess for the president's mansion. It was an unexpected move as her father was vice president until the unfortunate death of President

Taylor. It was a young age to assume such a large role but she excelled at it.

Abby like her mother loved music and played the harp, piano, and guitar. She and her mother would often entertain White House guests by performing duets.

Abby like her brother never married. She spent most of her adult life caring for her sick mother and assuming the role of hostess to aid her father. She was a selfless young girl who was admired by all who met her.

Abby was devastated at the loss of her mother when she passed away. Her father had run for reelection which he lost, but her mother even though a semi-invalid insisted on doing what was right and attended the inauguration of Franklin Pierce who was succeeding her husband. The weather was wet and cold, and while waiting after the inauguration for a carriage the already sickly former first lady caught a chill which turned into pneumonia and she died less than a month later.

Abby died a month after her mother's death from cholera at the age of twenty-two.

Franklin Pierce

Children of Jane and Franklin Pierce:

Franklin Pierce, Jr. - Born: Feb. 2, 1836   Died: Feb. 5, 1836

Franklin Robert Pierce – Born: Aug. 27, 1839   Died: Nov. 14, 1843

Benjamin Pierce – Born: April 13, 1841   Died: Jan. 16, 1853

Two months before the inauguration their son Benny was killed,

the only fatality of a train accident.

Jane and Franklin Pierce had three sons. All three sons lived for only a short time. Franklin Pierce, Jr lived only three days, Frank lived for four years, and Benjamin died at twelve years of age. Not one of their sons survived to live in the White House. By the time of the Pierce administration all three of their children were dead.

If opposites do indeed attract Franklin and Jane Pierce are a perfect example. While Jane was religious and couldn't relate to Washington politics and their corrupt, backstabbing ways; Franklin was a former alcoholic who thrived on politics. He had politics in his blood while his wife couldn't fathom how anyone who was a part of Washington society could profess to be a believer in the Bible and it's teachings.

Franklin Pierce, Jr. their first child was born in 1836. The baby lived for only three days. His mother wore black from the day of her child's death until her own death.

Franklin Pierce was elected to the United States Senate in 1837. He was the youngest member of the Senate. His wife associated her husband's political aspirations in Washington as the reason God was punishing the couple and why their first child died. With this mindset when she discovered she was pregnant again she did everything she could to persuade her husband to get out of politics.

Pierce was only twenty-four years of age when he was elected to the Legislature and two years later became Speaker. When he entered Washington, it was as a Representative and then as a Senator.

Their second son Frank Robert was born August of 1839. The proud mother and father breathed a sigh of relief as their son arrived a healthy child. He died at the age of four of typhus fever. After the death of two young children Jane's mental health began to unravel. She again blamed their son's deaths on her husband's involvement in politics.

The Pierces had one remaining child, Benjamin Pierce who was born in April of 1841. He was two years old when his brother died. His parents catered to their one remaining son.

Concerned about his wife's mental health and to appease her, Franklin retired from the Senate and returned to practicing law.

In 1852 Pierce's name was put forth as a presidential candidate. The Democratic Convention was in a dilemma. None of the presidential candidates secured the necessary two-thirds majority of delegates needed for the nomination and a new candidate was needed. Franklin Pierce's name was put forth as a dark horse candidate unbeknownst to the candidate.

Franklin and his wife were out for a carriage ride when a courier approached them informing them of the news. Jane Pierce was so shocked by the news she fainted. Franklin's retirement from politics had come to an end.

His wife prayed for his defeat. Pierce to his credit did no campaigning, but he wouldn't turn it down if he felt the party needed him. He won the election.

Two months before his inauguration President-elect Pierce, his wife, and eleven-year old son Benny took a train trip. The coupling on the train car broke and the train jumped the track and plummeted down an embankment. When the train came to a halt Franklin and Jane were only bruised but their son Benny was dead. He had been killed instantly, the only fatality of the train accident.

Due to their son Benjamin's death, the first lady did not attend her husband's inauguration. It was March before the first lady moved into the White House and even then didn't receive publicly until January of 1855. During the time that she did not see anyone publicly it was her uncle's widow who would stand in as hostess and when she wasn't available Mrs. Jefferson Davis, future First Lady of the Confederacy and wife of the Secretary of War, would stand in for her.

The death of their last child cast a pall over the White House. The first lady was often found writing heart breaking notes to her dead son Benjamin. Franklin returned to drinking while his wife lost her mind and retreated into her own world of delusion where she believed she was still with her sons.

James Buchanan

Children of James Buchanan:

No biological children – never married

The Prince of Wales the first British royal to visit the U.S. was so impressed by Harriet Lane, the president's ward, that he personally invited her to his coronation.

Our only president in history who was a bachelor throughout his entire administration was James Buchanan. He had been engaged when he was twenty-eight. His fiancee after hearing he had been seen in the company of another woman wrote him a letter breaking off the engagement. A few days later she died of an overdose committing suicide. He vowed never to marry after her death and he remained a bachelor.

Buchanan while not married had a large family. There were twenty-two nieces and nephews, seven orphans in his care, and several others he helped support.

A niece he had raised since a young girl was Harriet Lane who would become the acting first lady during his administration. Orphaned at a young age Buchanan had become her full time guardian. While he was her legal guardian he referred to her as his adopted daughter.

Wards of her uncle who was senator at the time, Harriet and her sister Mary Elizabeth were enrolled in the Merritt Boarding School in West Virginia. By the time she had become a ward of her uncle, Harriet was already widely read in classic literature and stayed up to date with current international events through newspapers and magazines.

When Buchanan became secretary of state under President Polk he transferred Harriet to the Academy of the Visitation Convent School in Washington. The school was not only closer to her uncle but had the reputation of high morals and a good academic reputation as well. Her favorite subjects were history, astronomy and mythology. She also studied French, writing, arithmetic and chemistry.

Even at the young age of eleven years of age she was exposed to her uncle's political life maturing her beyond her years. She became her uncle's personal and political confidante which prepared her well for her future role as White House hostess.

When Buchanan's term of secretary of state came to an end he purchased an estate in Lancaster, Pennsylvania called Wheatland where he and Harriet lived while he prepared to run for the presidency. He would become Pennsylvania's only president.

Harriet was often invited to join her uncle and others in political and business meetings. They often sat and discussed their opinions and observations on current events and what they read in newspapers giving her an insight into the political world few other young women were ever allowed to be a part of.

When Buchanan was appointed as minister to Great Britain Harriet joined him abroad. She considered herself during this time as a representative of the United States and eagerly looked forward to being presented to Queen Victoria and Prince Albert. When she was presented to the queen, Queen Victoria and her court were quite impressed with the young American lady who presented herself very well.

Harriet was an expert horsewoman and well read in British literature which endeared her to members of Victoria's family. She formed a permanent and personal friendship with the royal family. Before returning to the U.S. she also traveled to France where she was presented to Emperor Napoleon III and Empress Eugenie.

It isn't known if she attended her uncle's inauguration but it is assumed so. She was there with him to enter the White House for the first time as president and she attended the inaugural ball with him.

Harriet was twenty-seven when she moved into the White House. With the nation uneasy with the threat of Civil War hanging over them she was determined to make the Presidential Mansion a showplace where people would enjoy coming for an evening of entertainment and forget the troubles of the nation.

After the gloom and doom of the previous administration, Harriet was a brilliant change that was welcomed in the White House. The previous administration having practically a nonexistant social life, Harriet Lane threw open the doors and invited the people of Washington in while reinvigorating the social scene.

Harriet was a popular hostess of the White House and well-liked by men and women alike. The women copied her style and the men were equally enthralled by her. The presidential yacht was named after her as well as a U.S. Coast Guard cutter.

For such a young girl Harriet did an astounding job; not only in decorating the mansion but the dinners, balls, and receptions were given praise the White House hadn't received for several administrations.

During her time in the White House she used her position and influence to promote social causes she strongly believed in. She brought in artists and musicians to White House functions promoting culture. She was very popular in her time.

One of the most memorable events during Buchanan's presidency was when the son of Queen Victoria, the Prince of Wales who later became King Edward VII, came to visit the White House. He was the first British royal to visit the U.S. The prince who was nineteen years of age at the time of his visit was greeted in New York with parades and a ball; but he never forgot the White House hostess Harriet Lane who years later he would personally invite to his coronation.

When news had arrived of the prince's imminent visit Harriet wanted to throw an elaborate ball in his honor. Nunc, her nickname for her uncle, put his foot down saying, "No dancing in the White House." The president disapproved of dancing. He refused to lift the ban on dancing in the White House that had been in effect ever since the Polk administration – not even for a prince.

James Buchanan's orphaned nephew James Buchanan "Buck" Henry who was named after his uncle, also lived at the White House during his uncle's administration serving as his private secretary.

His uncle worked him hard insisting that he was to be in his office which adjoined the president's office whenever the president was working. It wasn't uncommon for him to have to put up with verbal abuse from his uncle; but what for him was just too much to bear was when his uncle reprimanded him for growing a mustache. He packed his bags and quit. He was replaced with another nephew who most likely had to tolerate the same treatment.

Harriet didn't marry until the age of thirty-six, not that she didn't have her choice of beaus. She married Henry Elliott Johnston who was a banker from Baltimore.

Harriet had two sons. Both of her sons would die of rheumatic fever and her husbnad of pneumonia.

Harriet and her uncle remained close throughout their lives. At his death she inherited the majority of his estate which was substantial.

She sold Wheatland, the home she and her uncle had lived in, and sold her home in Baltimore, and moved back to Washington living just a few blocks from the White House becoming the grand dame of Washington. She was a wealthy widow between what she was left by her husband and her uncle.

She would return to England for the coronation of King Edward VII, who had visited her in the White House many years ago but never forgot her.

16

Abraham Lincoln

Children of Mary and Abraham Lincoln:

Robert Todd Lincoln – Born: August 1, 1843 Died: July 25, 1926

Edward Baker Lincoln "Eddie" - Born: March 10, 1846 Died: Feb. 1, 1850

William Wallace Lincoln "Willie" - Born: Dec. 21, 1850 Died: Feb. 20, 1862

Thomas Lincoln "Tad" - Born: April 4, 1853 Died: July 15, 1871

Robert Lincoln's life was saved by the brother of the man who would later assassinate his own father.

As newlyweds Abraham and Mary Lincoln lived at the Globe Tavern, a two-story inn in Springfield, Illinois. Their first child Robert was born at the inn and lived there until complaints from other occupants about the baby's constant crying forced them to move to a small cottage with five rooms.

Lincoln loved children and was thrilled when just before Robert turned three another son Edward Baker was born. At the time of Eddie's birth Lincoln was working hard to earn a living to support his family as a lawyer. He rode circuit for several months out of the year and would be away from his young sons as they were growing up for many months out of the year.

Lincoln was elected to Congress and the family moved to Washington, D.C. taking up residence in a boardinghouse. They still didn't see much of their father as he left for work before dawn and it was past their bedtime before he returned in the evening. Later in life Robert would complain that his father hadn't been around much when he was growing up.

Robert was more like his mother's side of the family, upper crust, and was influenced from his time at Exeter and Harvard. He was much more serious than his younger brothers and more reserved. There has been much written about the relationship between Robert and his father; some saying there was a major rift between them. He loved his father and his father loved and respected his older son. Many times when Robert visited the White House his father used him as a sounding board and discussed important matters with him respecting his opinion. It was a different relationship from that of his brothers, but a loving one all the same.

While living in Washington the family would watch concerts at the Capitol and visit parts of Washington including the grounds of the White House. Robert was old enough to remember his father taking him to visit the U.S. Patent Office where they would spend hours in the Model Room amazed at the hundreds of models of American inventions. Abe Lincoln would have a patented invention of his own one day; the only United States patent that was ever registered to a president.

The next year when it was time for Lincoln to return to Washington for the next session of Congress Robert traveled with his father as far as Springfield where the five year old Robert was going to stay with his maternal grandfather. Robert was taken to the state legislature to see where his grandfather was involved in politics.

By the time Robert celebrated his fifth birthday he had traveled over a thousand miles back and forth from Illinois to Washington by stage, rail, canal boat, and steamer.

The Lincolns returned to Springfield at the end of Lincoln's term as congressman and he again took up practicing law.

Eddie who had always been a frail child became extremely ill. After struggling for his life just short of two months the boy died weeks before his fourth birthday. It was later determined that it was tuberculosis that took his life.

Losing his young son would forever affect how Lincoln treated his children showering them with love and finding amusement in their antics, not having the heart to discipline them.

Less than a year after Eddie's death William Wallace, or Willie, was born. A little over two years after Willie's birth their fourth son arrived who was named Thomas but always called Tad which was short for tadpole.

The two younger boys were inseparable; but with seven years between Robert and Willie and nine years between him and Tad the young boys were never close to their older brother.

When Lincoln was away Robert would take over as 'man of the house' and chop the firewood, milk the cow and take it to and from the pasture, and run errands for his mother.

Robert wasn't all work though; as he and a friend were caught taking some lead pipe where a house was being built and then taking the pipe and selling it to the hardware store. When his father discovered what his son had done he and a penitent Robert paid a visit to the store where Robert was made to tell the store owner what he had done, bought the pipe back from him, and returned it to the owner. 'Honest Abe' never raised a hand to his son or raised his voice; but the lesson was learned and remembered.

Abe would pull his youngest sons Willie and Tad for walks in a little wagon. At times during these walks Lincoln would read a book while pulling his sons behind him. On one of these jaunts Tad fell out of the wagon, but his father with his head in his book didn't even notice and kept walking down the road minus one son until a neighbor poked her head out of a window and pointed out to Lincoln that he had lost something along the way.

The Lincoln boys had made quite a reputation for themselves with those who knew them including Abe's law partner. When they visited their father at his office they would pull the law books off the shelves, spill the ink, and scatter the books and papers while their father sat by doing his work and ignoring the pandemonium his sons were causing. Abe's law partner was astounded that there was such a lack of discipline when it came to Abe's children. They were left to run wild and seldom if ever corrected in their behavior.

Tad when only seven years old came down with scarlet fever. He did recover but not before Willie also came down with the fever; not quite as severe a case as his brothers. Tad suffered throughout his life with a speech impediment and some believe that it was brought on by scarlet fever while others believe he was born with a cleft palate.

Willie as young as nine years of age was unusually intelligent. He had a memory that astounded those around him. Springfield photographer J. G. Stewart recalled that Willie "was the brainiest boy I ever saw. His memory was so great that after he had heard a sermon he could repeat it almost word for word."

Willie wanted to be a preacher when he grew up. Willie was a child that showed great promise. He was the most like his father and was very kind, but he enjoyed pulling pranks as much as his brother Tad.

Tad and Willie went to Miss Corcoran's school while living in Springfield. One of the teachers commented that Lincoln would not allow Tad to be pushed in his schooling. The boy had a speech impediment and one wonders whether the other students teased him. Not only did he have to deal with a speech impediment, but his adult teeth came in crooked which didn't help. Tad once said to one of his cousins, "I love you, Johnny, because you are nice to me and don't tease me." His brother Willie was also a champion of Tad's as he would serve as interpreter to those who couldn't understand him when he spoke and was always a friend to his brother.

Thomas Hicks an artist who had come to the State House to paint Abe' portrait was pleasantly amused when he recalls Lincoln bent over working at his desk. Hicks was painting while at the same time watching Tad and his friend who had discovered his tubes of paints. Tad and his friend mixed some blue paint with red and a few other colors into the palms of their hands and spread it on the wall. Liking their art work they added some other colors to their handiwork. Of course, the boys had as much of the paint on themselves as they did on the walls. The artist, perhaps remembering himself as a boy, wore a smile on his face as he watched the boys at their work. Perhaps Abe seeing the look on the artist's face turned to see what the boys were up to. Seeing the boys with paint on their faces and hands Abe calmly sent them home to get washed up.

Robert at sixteen years old left Springfield in 1859 with a friend in hopes of becoming a Harvard student. Robert arrived at Harvard full of confidence, walked into the exam hall, and failed fifteen out of the sixteen tests. That was a humbling experience for him. A year later he took the exams again only to fail yet again. Robert then applied to Phillips Exeter Academy where he hoped to prepare to pass the Harvard exams. He wasn't a great student, but a determined one.

Exeter Academy instilled the values of a gentleman as much as they did academics. He was trained to dress as a gentleman and instill the strict social codes of the Victorian era in which traits he carried with him throughout his life. It is due to this influence and how it changed his life that it was often said of Robert that he was more of a Todd than a Lincoln.

His father was a candidate for the presidency and was traveling making speeches. He came to visit his son at Exeter in hopes of instilling in him the need to study hard. His son had the opportunity for a good education, something Abe had been deprived of.

Robert did study hard and was also involved in athletics. He excelled in sports and enjoyed baseball, football, and track. In his later years he would discover golf, which he said he wasn't very good at but enjoyed it just the same.

It wasn't just sports he 'played' at. Robert was a bit of a prankster, and he along with some friends went through town removing fence posts and signs and taking off with them - all in fun. The fun was over once they were caught. The authorities were going to let Robert off due to his father who had recently been nominated as a candidate for the presidency. Robert stood firm and insisted on being punished equally to his friends. He gained respect from his peers and adults from his actions.

At the end of the year at Exeter he again took the exams for Harvard and this time he passed. His becoming a Harvard student was quite an accomplishment as Harvard was considered, and still is, one of the most prestigious colleges in the states. The education, friendships, and experiences he would encounter during his days at Harvard would be an asset throughout his life.

Only months after becoming a Harvard student seventeen year old Robert's father was elected President of the United States. Instead of living at the White House Robert would be away at college. Students at Harvard were impressed when they found Robert to not feel entitled to special treatment because of who his father was. He acquired a reputation of one of good character who made friends easily.

At the end of the first term the students had six weeks off and Robert used his time off to return home so he could travel with his father to Washington to attend the inauguration.

The train was filled with family and friends close to the Lincoln family who would be there to witness his inauguration. At every stop along the way they were greeted with well-wishers, bands playing, and journalists hoping to get a word or an interview from the incoming president.

Robert was entrusted with his father's inaugural address for safe keeping on the train. His father knowing his words would become part of a historical record, and due to the state of the nation had escaped to a storeroom of his brother-in-laws' store where he could have privacy along with peace and quiet without interruption to write the speech. He took a lot of time working hard on every word and phrase.

On the train Lincoln placed his inaugural address in a black oilcloth bag and gave it to Robert telling him to take care of it. Robert was unaware of what his father gave him for safekeeping or of the importance of what was in the bag. Somewhere along the journey he lost sight of the bag and it was nowhere to be found. It was the one and only time Lincoln's law partner had ever witnessed Lincoln angry and raising his voice at any of his sons.

When the bag was found Lincoln told his son what was in it and handed it back to him telling him to take care of it. Robert most certainly never let it out of his sight again the entire trip.

On the day of the inauguration the Lincoln family was staying at the Willard's Hotel where they were met by President Buchanan. The president and President-elect Lincoln rode together in an open carriage to the Capitol for the inauguration.

Robert stood with pride watching his father sworn in to become the next President of the United States. As he listened to his father give his inaugural address he must have been greatly relieved that the bag had been found, as his father's words were deeply moving to the crowd of about twenty-five thousand people who listened intently to every word.

Robert returned to Harvard just two days after the inauguration. On school breaks he would visit the White House, but the nation was in the midst of the Civil War which began just a month after his father took the oath of office. Robert had little private time to spend with his father on his visits. His father had the weight of the nation on his shoulders.

The Lincolns were the first to have young children living in the White House since the Tyler administration almost twenty years previously. At the time Abraham Lincoln became the 16th president Robert was seventeen, Willie was ten, and Tad was eight.

In the White House Willie would talk to visitors and was known to give impromptu tours. He was the most like his father of all Abe's sons.

Robert while a Harvard student only visited the White House periodically, but the two youngest boys Willie and Tad would leave a lasting impression on those they came in contact with.

The White House gardener became furious when he discovered Tad had eaten all the strawberries he had been carefully growing for a state dinner. In a rage he threatened to tell the first lady what Tad had done. Julia Taft who often looked after the boys reminded the gardener that reporting her son's actions to the first lady would accomplish nothing, that he was after all the Madam's son. The gardener knowing she was right exploded calling Tad "the Madam's wildcat."

The two youngest boys had tutors at the White House. Willie was smart but Tad had a difficult time learning. The boys, mostly Tad, were a handful and tutors didn't last long. The tutors would complain about the boy's behavior and of Tad's lack of interest in learning. When their father heard this he dismissed it saying, "There's time enough for him to learn his letters and get poky." Tad was no longer required to attend classes.

The president had promised the boys he would get them ponies once they got to the White House. The boys enjoyed riding through the streets of Washington with the president following behind on his own horse.

The boys gave the president a lift in spirits at a time when the nation was at war. He could often be found with the boys on his back traipsing through the halls of the presidential mansion. At least for the time he was with them he could forget the great burden he carried.

When Robert came to visit from college he would complain about his brothers lack of discipline and rowdy behavior. Some of the staff and other visitors to the White House silently agreed with Robert, but would never dare voice their opinions on the president's upbringing of his sons.

The president and first lady weren't ones to discipline their children and they were given pretty much free rein to do as they pleased. Abraham said, "It is my pleasure that my children are free, happy, and unrestricted by parental tyranny." However, there was the time Tad sprayed state officials with a hose when his father did spank him.

Tad seemed to have no limits to his mischief. He was known to smear ink on the telegraph desks and hammered nails into one of the secretaries desks.

Tad and Willie had a great time exploring the White House, as have all the presidential children before and after him; but when they discovered the bell system which was used to call staff when needed by the president or first lady Tad decided to have fun and pull the cords on all the bells at the same time. This sent the staff running thinking they were being called due to an emergency. It was the president who figured out who was behind the mischief.

Willie had a better sense of understanding as was seen when Tad threw a ball into a mirror and broke it. When Willie rebuked him for what he had done Tad responded that Pa wouldn't care. Willie reminded his brother that the mirror didn't belong to Pa but that it belonged to the United States government.

Willie liked to have fun just like other boys and was his brother's companion during many of his antics, but he had a serious side to him too and enjoyed having his father read to him and enjoyed drawing and writing poetry. He understood that as the son of a president he was different and of interest to others, but he said, "I wish they wouldn't stare at us so. Wasn't there ever a president who had children?"

When arriving at the White House one day, Seward who was Lincoln's secretary of state arrived with Prince Napoleon who was the nephew of Napoleon I and cousin of Napoleon III. The secretary of state spotted young Willie outside playing and Seward who had befriended the boy gave him a salute. Prince Napoleon honoring the president's son doffed his hat and gave the lad a ceremonious salute. Willie stood and took off his cap and bowed to the ground like a little ambassador.

It had been a cold, rainy day when Willie and Tad took their ponies for a ride one day.

That same night Willie came down with a cold and fever; hours later his brother Tad was also feverish.

Mary Lincoln didn't know what to do as a party had been planned at the White House. She and Abe discussed canceling the party but the doctor reassured them that they should have the party and enjoy it and the boys would soon recover. By the time of the party Willie's fever was worse and he was having a difficult time breathing.

Willie suffered for two weeks before he died, not from riding his pony in the wintry weather but of typhoid fever most likely caused by the polluted water at the White House. The running water was piped into the White House from the Potomac.

The president and first lady were devastated at the loss of their son. Mary closed herself off from everyone including young Tad who was still sick with the fever his brother had died from. It would be others who had to care for Tad who was also grieving for the loss of his brother and constant companion. Tad would recover from his fever, but would forever be a changed boy.

Lincoln looking at the body of his young son Willie buried his face in his hands and cried without shame. Lincoln said, "He was too good for this earth. I know he is better off in heaven, but then we loved him so."

Elizabeth Keckley, born a slave but now a businesswoman and Mary Lincoln's seamstress and friend was called in to console Mary and to care for the dead boy's body. Elizabeth tenderly washed Willie and dressed his body preparing him for his burial.

The Taft boys, sons of Horatio Nelson Taft the U.S. Patent Office Examiner, were the Lincoln brother's best friends. They had been playmates and had come to visit the boys during their illness. They too were mourning the loss of their friend. Mary Lincoln had sent a note to Mrs. Taft to keep the boys home, but Abe had sent for the boys so they could see their friend before he was placed in the casket. He was a compassionate man who knew the boys were also hurting from the loss of their friend. When Bud Taft came to say good-bye to his best friend he was so affected he had to be carried from the room.

The coffin was left open for the family to say their final good-byes and for the staff of the White House and the president's cabinet, but the coffin lid was closed before the funeral. The family had just left the room and the subdued servants came to see Willie for the last time openly sobbing for the little boy whose face had always been lit up with friendliness and affection, and who had just a short time ago been running through the halls. Willie had been loved by those close to him and tears flowed unrestrained. At the funeral, Secretary of Treasury Chase and Secretary of State Seward, senators, ambassadors, and soldiers all struggled with their tears grieving along with the president at the loss of his son.

The White House was covered in black crepe. The casket was removed from the Green Room and in the procession to the cemetery in Georgetown two white horses pulled the hearse carrying the president's son who had never known anything but happiness in his life. The president and his son Robert followed behind the hearse in a carriage drawn by black horses with a terrible storm surrounding the funeral procession. The casket was left in a vault of a friend of the Lincolns until the time it would be moved to it's final resting place in Springfield, Illinois. Little did anyone know at that time that when Willie's casket was taken to Springfield it would not make the journey alone. He would be accompanied by his father - the assassinated president.

Lincoln grieving as he was, still had the demands of the presidency to see to. There was no rest or time off for a grieving father. He received little sympathy from a nation who had lost so many of their own sons to the Civil War.

It wasn't unusual for people to line up in the halls of the White House hoping to be able to have an audience with the president to ask for jobs or favors. Tad noticed a woman who was obviously poor who was crying and listened to her story of how her son was in the army who was ill and she wanted him sent home. Tad immediately went to his father and begged his father to do something to help the woman. His father had a hard time turning any request down from the boy since the loss of Willie. His father in the middle of an important meeting saw the distress the woman's story had brought to Tad and the president excused himself from the meeting, went with Tad to speak to her, and signed the papers so she could bring her son home.

Tad had become tenderhearted and seemed deeply touched by others' hardships. He brought home street urchins and brought them to the White House kitchen to be fed. If the kitchen staff complained, Tad simply went to his father and asked, "Isn't it *our* kitchen?" The president saw to it that the children were fed.

Tenderhearted as he had become; he still enjoyed his pranks and being a young boy.

After Willie died the first lady had shut herself away. The president knowing how difficult this time was for Tad spent as much time as possible with his son. Tad became his father's shadow and was found by his side even when his father had to work late at night. He was sometimes found sleeping on the floor by his father's feet as his father worked. Tad was never turned away and he came up with a special knock on his father's door so his father would know he was there to see him. Even when in an important meeting when Lincoln heard that knock he would stop the meeting and tend to his son.

Tad and his father would walk hand in hand down Pennsylvania Avenue to Fifteenth Street to New York Avenue where there was a quaint little toy shop called Stuntz's. Children would often stand on the sidewalk peering into the toy shop's windows to see the display of the latest toys. The president got enjoyment from watching his son's face light up as he looked around at the treasures inside. In the back of the toyshop sat Joseph Stuntz himself carving wonderful toys such as the wooden toy soldiers Tod was so fond of collecting. It was a joy to father and son to sit and watch the man carve the toys and listen to him tell his tales of the days he was a soldier in Napoleon's war. More often than not, Tad would leave with a new toy soldier or cannon to add to his collection.

After Willie died Tad didn't ride his pony anymore. It reminded him too much of his brother who he sorely missed. On an afternoon when he was out with his parents he spotted some goats and was entertained watching them play. His father happy to see his son smile and laugh again later had one of his staff purchase a pair of goats. He and Tad would play on the White House lawn with them. The goats got to where they recognized Lincoln's voice and would come running when they heard him. Abe was quite amused when he found Tad had tucked the goats in bed with him one evening.

His mother wasn't quite as amused the day Tad tied the goats to a chair and sat on it with the goats pulling him chariot style. He came racing through the East Room of the White House screaming in delight as the goats pulled him in his self-made carriage through the room and out again leaving chaos in his wake as some visiting women from Boston were having tea with the first lady.

The goats weren't the only pets Tad had. Presidential families are often given some unusual pets as gifts. They were given a turkey which was meant to be for their Thanksgiving dinner, not for a pet. Tad was having a great time with the turkey he had named Jack leading it around on the South Lawn of the White House with a noose around it's neck. When Tad discovered his turkey was about to be butchered he ran to his father to save his turkey telling his father, "He's a good turkey, and I don't want him killed." The president gave the turkey a reprieve and he was spared from becoming the Lincoln's dinner.

The White House has had an Easter Egg Roll since the days of President Hayes administration. Children from Washington were all invited to participate. Tad a changed boy since the death of his brother was seen spending the day with a handicapped child watching over him and sharing his own Easter eggs with him that the White House cook had made up special for Tad. Rather than running off and joining in the fun with the other children he spent the day with the boy. He thought to bring his father over to him so the boy could have the thrill and memory of shaking hands with the president.

One day as Lincoln was looking out a window he spotted a fire at the stables and ran to the building calling for help to save the horses. When a guard spotted a tall man racing in the burning stables he realized it was the president. Lincoln was pulled from the fire. Later Lincoln was seen with tears running down his soot covered face. The staff who had tried to save the horses were moved to tears when they learned that Lincoln had been trying to save Willie's pony. Willie's pony and all the horses were lost in the fire.

People are more familiar with the younger sons of the Lincolns due in part that Robert was away at Harvard at the time the Lincolns were living in the White House. Robert did return to the presidential mansion to be with his family whenever he had school vacations.

A strange coincidence happened on one of Robert's visits. On leave from school Robert was traveling to Washington by train. While at the train station waiting for his train he was in a crowd and was pushed forward against a stationary train. Just as Robert had been pushed by the crowd, the train began to move and Robert fell in the space between the train and the platform. He was unable to escape until a bystander reached down and grabbed him by his coat collar pulling him onto the platform. He would surely have been crushed by the approaching train without the aid of the man who helped him. Robert looked to thank the person who had most likely saved his life and recognized his rescuer.

His rescuer was none other than Edwin Boothe, America's most admired actor who was traveling with John Ford, owner of Ford's Theater in Washington. Robert recognized the actor and thanked him by name. Robert Lincoln was saved by the brother of the man who would one day assassinate his own father at Ford's Theater just a few years later.

Robert's visits to the White House were always looked forward to. He was liked and respected by all. While his father enjoyed his young son Tad's company, it was Robert who was a sounding board to his father on events and issues of importance. Robert was there to give his father comfort during the president's despair from the loss of life after the Battle of Gettysburg. Robert's comments would later be some of the only eyewitness recollections of the president that survived the times. They were historic moments and thoughts of a sitting president, due to Robert's conversations with his father they were preserved for history.

Robert's time in Washington on his visits weren't idle. He spent time in hospitals visiting soldiers who had been wounded in battle. While doing so, he had befriended a French soldier who couldn't speak English. Robert who was fluent in French would read the newspaper to him and spend time talking to the young man keeping him company and translating for the medical staff.

November of 1864 was the year Abraham Lincoln was reelected. If you recall the story of the turkey named Jack who had originally been meant for a Thanksgiving meal at the White House but who Tad saved, he was still around at this time. Soldiers from Pennsylvania were quartered on the grounds of the White House at the time of the election. Their tents were set up on the South Lawn where a commission from their state arrived to take their vote for the presidency. Tad burst into his father's office and excitedly pulled his father to the window and pointed at the turkey strutting around the soldiers. The turkey had become a pet of sorts of the men. The president asked his son what his turkey was doing at the polls and asked his son with amusement if he was there to place his vote. Tad answered, "No, he's not of age to vote."

The cheers were deafening when it was announced that President Lincoln had been reelected. A cannon had been placed in the driveway of the White House and was repeatedly fired off. Occasionally a pane of glass in the White House was shattered from the concussion.

Robert had been discussing with his father for years his desire to join the army, but because of his mother's fear of losing yet another son Abe had delayed his son's doing so.

As early as 1861 Lincoln had called for volunteers to fight. Robert could only sit back as fellow students and professors joined the fight. Newspapers and citizens alike made disparaging remarks about Lincoln's own son not volunteering to the point where it was an embarrassment to Robert. After all, he sincerely wanted to join.

Robert pressed his father at every visit to the White House about joining. Privately his father spoke to the first lady who cried that she didn't want to lose another son. Abe knowing it was the right thing to do responded to her, "Many a poor mother has had to make this sacrifice and has given up every son she had – and lost them all." Lincoln didn't want to lose his son anymore than she did, but he knew he could no longer stand in the way of his son's joining. His son now a Harvard graduate he respected Robert's desire to join. The war was close to the end when Lincoln wrote to General Ulysses S. Grant asking if there was a place for Robert with his army. He didn't want him in the midst of battles, but nor did he want his son to be given precedence over others who had fought and served already proving themselves. Robert was brought into Grant's army as one of his own personal staff, a position as a Harvard graduate he was highly qualified for.

Congressman Rice, a friend of Lincoln's recalled in later days the proud look on the president's face when his son entered the room wearing the uniform of a captain. He placed his arm around his son and said to the visitors in the room, "My boy here has just been made a captain on General Grant's staff." Rice recalled vividly the look of fatherly pride on the president's face.

As part of General Ulysses S. Grant's staff Robert Lincoln would be at Appomattox Court House during General Robert E. Lee's surrender. He was outside on the porch at the time of the surrender, but General Grant would later call him inside to be presented to General Lee and be a part of the historical moment. He is one of two sons of a president to have been present at Appomattox Court House during the surrender and signing of the papers ending the Civil War. One from the north and one from the south.

Two days later as Washington celebrated the end of the war, Lincoln spoke from a window overlooking the portico. The crowd cheered as they saw the president and waited silently for his speech. His speech was not one of celebration or of vindictiveness toward the enemy, but one showing kindness toward the Southerners and the wish to bring them back into the Union. His wish was to reunite the states and the people.

General Grant and Robert left for the White House immediately afterward arriving five days later on April 14th, 1865. Robert would be only too happy to inform his father of what he had just witnessed. The United States had been preserved and kept intact. There were still long days ahead with reconstruction to face.

When Robert arrived at the White House the family was having breakfast. Afterward, Robert and his father were enclosed in the presidential office for hours where Robert told his father of the final days of the war and the witnessing of the surrender of General Robert E. Lee.

Mary Lincoln wanted to attend the play *'Our American Cousin,'* being performed at Ford's Theater that evening. The Lincolns invited General Grant and his wife Julia to join them. The Grants were anxious to return home to see their children and thanked them for the offer but declined.

Abe also invited Robert to join his parents at the theater that evening. After having just spent weeks in the field he was exhausted and said he preferred to stay home and go to bed early.

Tad also went to the theater that evening, only he went to Grover's Theater to see *'Aladdin.'* Tad learned of his father's assassination when someone announced loudly throughout the theater, "President Lincoln was assassinated in his private box at Ford's!"

It was a horrifying way to learn of one's own father's death, especially for a twelve year old boy. Obviously quite distraught over the news he was quickly taken from the theater and returned to the White House.

The White House doorkeeper, Thomas Pendel who Tad called 'Tom Pen', was there when the boy returned and ran up the stairs crying, "They have killed papa dead!" With all of his family members away Tad had only the staff to console him. Thomas gathered Tad into his arms to try to comfort him.

The doorkeeper later recalled how he took the boy and tucked him into bed and stayed with him and talked to him until he fell asleep from sheer exhaustion.

It had been approximately 10:15 P.M., Act 3, Scene 2 of the play when Boothe entered the president's box at Ford's Theater and shot the president with a single shot from a derringer. Lincoln had been examined by a physician on site and taken across the street to a boarding house when it was determined the shot would be a fatal one and it was only a matter of time.

Someone was sent to the White House to notify Robert. It was about 10:30 that evening when he heard a disturbance in the hall before someone came and informed him about his father. Robert ran downstairs and finding a carriage waiting for him left immediately for the Petersen House where his father had been taken. He had to fight his way through the crowd to the room where his father was being cared for. Lincoln's physician told Robert that the wound was fatal and there was no hope.

He spent the rest of the evening and early morning watching over his father and comforting his hysterical mother. His father never regained consciousness. Robert remained remarkably calm in such an agonizing situation as he watched over his father suffering only brief moments when his anguish gave way to gut wrenching sobs.

The physicians watched over Lincoln; watching and waiting for the end that was inevitable. The president was pronounced dead at 7:22 A.M. It was only then that Robert turned to Senator Sumner for comfort and broke down completely.

Robert's young life was about to change drastically. At only twenty-one years of age going from a college graduate to the army, never having held down a job, would be solely responsible for his mother and young brother.

Twenty-one year old Robert was the only family member in attendance at his father's funeral. He had traveled by train taking his father's body and that of his brother Willie to be buried in Springfield, Illinois. His mother was too upset to attend and she insisted Tad stay with her in Washington.

After the death of his father Robert apprenticed at a law firm in Springfield until he passed the bar exams and was licensed as an attorney.

Tad now looked to his older brother for companionship and guidance. Robert sought to be not only a caretaker for his brother but an adviser. He prepared Tad for school as his education to date had been practically nonexistent and had doctors tend to Tad's speech impediment hiring an elocutionist to help Tad learn to speak correctly. Tad worked hard at his schoolwork and at pleasing his older brother.

Robert had courted Mary Harlan, the daughter of U.S. Senator James Harlan, for about four years throughout the Civil War. They were married on September 24, 1868 in a private ceremony held in the senator's home in Washington.

When Robert and his wife returned from their honeymoon his mother and Tad had left for Europe where they would live for almost three years. Tad was fifteen at the time they sailed to Europe.

Robert and Mary had three children: a daughter named Mary, a son named Abraham Lincoln II but was called Jack, and another daughter Jessie.

Sometime after President Lincoln's assassination the former first lady approached Congress using the memory of her husband for sympathy asking for money. She did receive some money from Congress, the amount equivalent to one year's salary as president. Not being enough to pay her debts or live on she tried selling the clothing and jewelry she wore as first lady. When her actions were discovered it turned into a scandal that humiliated her son Robert.

Mary and Tad returned from Europe a little less than three years from the time they had departed. Tad was eighteen when they returned. Robert was impressed with the maturity of his brother Tad. He had studied hard and proved to be a good student and had overcome his speech impediment. Robert was happy to be reunited with his brother. The time they had together would be short-lived; two months after their return Tad was dead.

Tad was seriously ill and quickly became bedridden. His condition deteriorated to the point that he would have to sleep in a chair that held him upright so he would not drown in the fluid in his lungs. His sickness was painful for the young teenager. Robert who cared greatly for his brother suffered along with Tad as he cared for him the remaining two months of his life.

Mary Lincoln, the former first lady, was becoming more and more of a concern as her actions were unstable. She had lost three sons and a husband who had been assassinated which had greatly affected her mental health. She traveled for a time and Robert was so concerned about her actions he arranged for her to be attended by a nurse and watched over by others who reported to him. When she returned to Chicago he checked her into a hotel, but he found her actions and conversations so delusional that he checked into the room next to hers where he could keep a close eye on her. He ended up remaining there for the next two weeks. She was found running through the hall of the hotel screaming that someone was trying to murder her. She was so sure someone was trying to rob her that she carried her money, over $50,000 worth of government bonds, on her person through the streets of Chicago. She told anyone who would listen that people were trying to poison her. She had lost all sense of reason.

Robert eventually felt he had no alternative and called on a physician. He also called on Dr. Richard Patterson the proprietor of Bellevue Place Sanitarium. Bellevue Place Sanitarium was a private, upscale sanitarium his mother could spend her time in a stress free environment and get rest and the help she needed.

It was agreed on that Mary Lincoln was in need of care in a sanitarium. Mary would never agree to go, so Robert did what he thought was his only alternative and had her committed through a jury trial. He along with the physicians would have to testify against her. This was a painful thing for Robert to endure, but he felt it was in his mother's best interest.

The procedure was obviously very difficult to Robert as he sat on the witness stand and testified against his mother and had to state in front of others and his mother how he felt his mother's mind had been unsound since the death of his father. His face was pale and his eyes were puffy and red from weeping as he gave an account to those in the courtroom of the actions of his mother that brought him to the point where he thought his mother wasn't safe left in her own care. He broke down weeping, which Robert being a private person must have found humiliating. The scene brought others in the courtroom to tears.

The ordeal was agonizing for Robert her last living son. In the mind of the former first lady she thought her son was conspiring to lock her up to rob her of her money.

She was to be admitted the following day, but in the meantime she tried to commit suicide by poison. She escaped those who were to watch over her until her commitment the following day and approached several druggists requesting camphor and laudanum. One druggist she had approached for the poison recognized her and gave her a placebo and called and notified her son of her actions who came and sat with her until the time of her confinement.

Mary Lincoln was only in the Bellevue Place Sanitarium in Batavia, Illinois for four months. During that time she was in the private part of the house of Dr. Patterson where she could take her meals with the family and go for walks and drives whenever she desired. She was released uncured after undue pressure from friends and the press, but would be under the care of her sister until she fled again to Europe. She went for years where she refused to see her son.

For generations Robert has been vilified and unfairly judged by some for his actions in having his mother committed. His intentions in doing so were to look out for his mother and do what he thought was best for her. He never resented having to care or look out for her; even though he was in his early twenties when the role of care taker for not only his mother but also his brother was thrust on him after the death of his father.

Robert was appointed as the secretary of war under President Garfield at the age of thirty-seven. Upon his arrival in Washington he was pleased to see it was an old friend of the family who would swear him into office. William Crook, Executive Clerk, had been his father's bodyguard during his days in the White House; but unfortunately had not been on duty the night his father was assassinated. Perhaps if he had been maybe history would have turned out differently.

Robert had been invited to a dinner at the home of a business acquaintance where the family had a member of the family who was an invalid who had a nurse to tend to her needs. The family had requested the nurse to serve at the dinner. When the nurse heard their guest was Robert Lincoln who would be at the dinner she said she most certainly would serve at the table, but it would be with a pistol in her hand. When they found out she was the niece of John Wilkes Boothe the nurse was quickly terminated.

Robert again escaped death when he was riding on a train when the railroad car he was in crashed into two different trains traveling a short distance apart. Between the time he was saved by Boothe, brother of his father's assassin; saved from the hand of Wilkes' niece; and the train accident Robert felt very fortunate to be alive.

People and politicians were constantly trying to convince Robert into running for the presidency. His answer to them was, "It seems difficult for the average American to understand that it is possible for anyone not to desire the Presidency, but I most certainly do not."

Robert not only came close to death himself several times, but was close to three different presidential assassinations.

One being when his father was shot. He had been invited to accompany his family to the theater but declined so he wasn't there at the time of the shooting, but he was there when

Lincoln breathed his last.

President Garfield invited Robert to join him on the presidential train and travel with him. Robert was running late and arrived at the train station a few minutes after Garfield. He was only a matter of feet away from the president when Garfield was shot when Robert heard someone yell, "The president has been shot."

The third time would be when President McKinley was shot at the Pan-American Exposition. The Lincolns planned to attend the Exposition and upon arrival at the Buffalo train station was handed a telegram from his secretary informing him that President McKinley had been shot at the Exposition.

Many years later when President Theodore Roosevelt invited him to the White House he turned him down saying, "I am not going and they'd better not invite me, because there is a certain fatality about presidential functions when I am present."

In 1883 Robert Lincoln as secretary of war was a part of President Chester Arthur's presidential party that traveled on horseback for six weeks to see Yellowstone. The presidential party traveled through rough terrain and weather conditions to see some of the country that most Americans had never seen. Up until a short time previously it had been too dangerous to travel due to renegade Indian war parties. They traveled hundreds of miles and saw such breathtaking sites as the Grand Tetons, Jackson Hole, and were fortunate enough to view Old Faithful geyser at Yellowstone.

When President Chester Arthur contemplated running for a second term it was the only time Robert Lincoln said he would agree to have his name on the ballot as vice president. He let it be known it wasn't his desire, but he felt he couldn't turn the president down if he made the request. Fortunately for him the president decided not to run again; which is a good thing as President Arthur was suffering from Bright's Disease and Robert Lincoln would have become president at the death of Arthur who wouldn't have survived a second term of office.

President Benjamin Harrison offered Lincoln the appointment of America's minister to Great Britain, the Court of St. James in London. Robert accepted thinking it would be beneficial to his children to live abroad. During their time in Europe Robert's son Jack was attending school in France. While at school Jack had cut his arm which didn't seem to be a serious wound until the cut became infected. Robert and his wife traveled to

France and when they thought it safe brought Jack to London with them. Doctors were called in who drained the wound several times which developed into blood poisoning. After being bed-ridden for over four months Jack died at the age of sixteen.

Robert became one of the greatest and most respected businessmen of his time. He served as president of Pullman Palace Car Company for twelve years.

Robert Todd Lincoln was considered by historians as one of the most successful of presidential children in our history. During his lifetime he became one of the nation's well-known financiers and business leaders. He was considered a man of money and power. The son of the president who had been born in a log cabin had become a millionaire.

The Lincoln Memorial was completed in 1922 and while in the past Robert Lincoln was pleased when his father was honored at events, but still had turned down making an appearance at most events. The seventy-nine year old presidential son of Abraham Lincoln was honored to join President Warren Harding at the dedication of the Lincoln Memorial in Washington, D.C. This would be Robert's last public appearance.

Robert by now an elderly man was a regal sight nevertheless. He was in need of assistance up the steps to the top of the memorial in his black stovepipe hat similar to what his father used to wear. Robert Lincoln received an ovation from the crowd of fifty-thousand people who had turned up to witness the Lincoln Memorial dedication.

Robert Lincoln owned several hundred acres of property in Vermont where he built a mansion called Hildene. The family would alternate living in Washington and summers at Hildene. Living in Washington for several years he was rarely recognized when he was out in public; which was perfectly satisfactory to him. He never wanted to be treated differently or revered simply because of his name.

In his later years he realized he no longer had the time left to keep putting off contemplating on what to do about his father's presidential papers. He had always thought he would have time to go through them himself, but time was running out. Though the collection had been sought by many, it was ultimately the Library of Congress that Robert Lincoln left them to. There were over twenty thousand documents in the collection including Lincoln's draft of the Emancipation Proclamation and his 1865 draft of his Second Inaugural Address. This would be the largest gift of historical materials to the Library of Congress in American history.

Robert Lincoln was respected not only nationally, but internationally. The *London Times* was quoted, "Seldom do sons of the great achieve the distinction and the glory of their fathers; yet in his way Lincoln served his country well in more than one high position, and in old age he had won the respect and esteem of all who knew him."

Robert Lincoln died in his sleep days before his eighty-third birthday.

For many years people and historians alike were troubled as to why Robert Lincoln chose to be buried in Arlington National Cemetery and not in the Lincoln Tomb alongside the rest of the Lincoln family. Some felt there had been some animosity on Robert's part as to why he chose not to be buried with his presidential father, but the truth was discovered when a letter from Mary Lincoln, Robert's wife, was discovered from a private collection.

The letter revealed Robert had indeed planned to be buried in Springfield at the Lincoln Tomb even up to the time of his death; but that it was his wife who felt Robert "should have his own place in the sun," and she wanted "to give her husband the honor she felt he deserved."

Robert had been a secretary of war and a captain in General Ulysses S. Grant's army during the Civil War and by all rights was entitled to be buried at Arlington National Cemetery. The letter had been written to Robert's cousin, Katherine Helm, explaining Mary's decision to have him buried at Arlington. Mary felt her husband "made his own history independently of his great father," and indeed he had. He loved and respected his father dearly, and his final resting place has nothing more to it than a loving wife wanting her husband to be recognized for his own merits and accomplishments.

The end of the Lincoln descendants died out at the death of Robert's grandson, Robert Lincoln Beckwith, the son of his third daughter Jessie. That would be the end of direct descendants of President Abraham Lincoln.

17

ANDREW JOHNSON

Children of Eliza and Andrew Johnson:

Martha Johnson – Born: Oct. 25, 1828   Died: July 10, 1901

Charles Johnson – Born: Feb. 19, 1830   Died: April 4, 1863

Mary Johnson – Born: May 8, 1832   Died: April 19, 1883

Robert Johnson – Born: Feb. 22, 1834   Died: April 22, 1869

Andrew Johnson, Jr. - Born: August 6, 1852   Died: March 12, 1879

Martha who served as White House hostess during her father's administration milked the cows from the White House dairy every morning.

Andrew Johnson only six weeks after becoming vice president became President of the United States after the assassination of Abraham Lincoln. The new president was fortunate to have escaped death himself, as he had been one of the targets along with Lincoln in Booth's plot.

It was an uncomfortable beginning to Johnson's presidency with Mary Lincoln remaining in the White House for several weeks after her husband's death. After Lincoln's assassination the White House was overcome with soldiers and people coming through and helping themselves to souvenirs from the president's mansion.

When Andrew Johnson moved into the White House he was accompanied by his invalid wife, his daughter Martha who was White House hostess, Martha's husband who became a senator from Tennessee, Martha's two children, Mary a widow who was Andrew's other daughter who would also help with White House hostess duties, Mary's three children, and Andrew Johnson's sons Robert and Andrew, Jr. There would be three generations of the Johnson family living in the White House.

While First Lady Eliza Johnson was inaccessible to the general public due to her illness, she did occasionally attend state dinners and entertained close friends in the family quarters. But the duties as White House hostess were more than her physical condition was up to. The role of hostess was turned over to her daughters Martha and Mary.

Martha, Johnson's oldest daughter, had previously accompanied her father to Washington when he was elected to Congress. She spent time at the White House with President Polk and his wife who had no children of their own. Her father who had a mind of his own and stood on his own principles opposed some of President Polk's policies and Martha's relationship with them was severed by the Polks in order to penalize her father. In the interim Martha had been introduced to the White House scene of social receptions and dinners, experiences which would aid her in her role as White House hostess.

The White House had been open to the public during Lincoln's administration for those who wanted to meet with the president or tour the mansion. It had also been used for barracks for Union soldiers. Due to all the traffic the White House was left in quite a state and had a run down appearance not fit for a presidential home.

Martha rolled up her sleeves and set to work overseeing a cleanup and refurbishing like the White House had never experienced before. What makes Martha's accomplishments even more respectable was she did all this with a Congress who was in the midst of an impeachment trial of her father. Martha had remarkably convinced an unsympathetic Congress to allow funds to restore the White House. She made extensive renovations bringing out a style and grace the White House had sorely been lacking, and in doing so making a name for herself in the history of first ladies.

Martha is a part of the reason the White House has the image it does today. She set a precedent for those that followed her to the White House in treating the home of the president as a place of pride and elegance to be proud of.

Martha is one of the presidential children that left her mark in history as a success story; the exception rather than the rule unfortunately.

A dairy was built in the West Wing where Martha herself milked the cows every morning. There were two Jersey cows which Martha milked and then led out to the White House lawn to keep the lawn manicured. The president's family always had fresh milk and butter available.

During his presidential administration Andrew Johnson received great comfort having his family by his side. It must have seemed to him the nation was against him fighting a stubborn congress and against his impeachment.

Martha's husband, David Patterson, was a senator at the time of his father-in-law's impeachment trial. He voted 'not guilty' during the unprecedented trial of the President of the United States; but to no avail. Andrew Johnson was impeached, yet the two-thirds majority vote was not reached and Johnson would remain in office.

Charles Johnson, the first son of the president, served as an intern to study medicine becoming a physician and a co-owner of a drug store previous to the Civil War. He was opposed to Tennessee seceding from the Union. He joined the First Middle Tennessee infantry which fought for the Union. He served as a surgeon. Even before the Civil War Charles had an addiction to alcohol and drugs. His addiction was fed by his easy access to both drugs and alcohol as a co-owner of a drug store.

Charles was just one of many in the history of president sons whose story is tragic not only in his alcoholism but in an early death. He died while serving in the Civil War at the age of thirty-three after being thrown from his horse. He died instantly when his skull fractured.

Mary, the third child of Eliza and Andrew Johnson, was a widow with three children when she moved into the White House. She assisted her sister Martha as hostess at the presidential mansion during her father's administration.

Mary was different from her sister Martha not only in temperament but also in looks. Mary was a blonde while Martha had dark hair. Mary had a short temper while Martha was a loving, compassionate woman. Regardless of their differences, their father found solace in having his two daughters nearby during his troubled administration.

Mary's first husband, Daniel Stover, was a farmer previous to joining and fighting for the Union in the Civil War. He served as a scout and burned bridges behind enemy lines that were used to transfer Confederate supplies. He came down with tuberculosis while hiding out in caves from the enemy and would not live to see the end of the war.

When Mary moved into the White House she brought her three children along with her. In addition to Martha's two children there were lots of little ones to distract their grandfather during the dark days of his impeachment trial. He watched as the grandchildren played on the South Lawn and would go out to join them and scoop them all up for hugs. The grandchildren had the run of the mansion and when they would interrupt their grandfather he never turned them away, instead he reached out and greeted them with love and affection.

The grandchildren profited by their grandfather's attention as he would take them on picnics, take walks through the woods with them teaching them about nature, and listening to stories their grandfather told.

The grandchildren had two grandparents who truly enjoyed their company. Their grandmother was an invalid suffering from tuberculosis and was ordered to stay inside and be quiet and rest. The grandchildren would sit with her while she taught them to do needlework. Later their grandfather would look over their work with pride as he himself had been a tailor in previous years.

The grandchildren were tutored at the White House. There were many times when their grandfather would visit them in their schoolroom and stay and listen to their music lessons. The grandchildren were a loving and enjoyable diversion.

At the end of her father's presidency Mary moved back to Tennessee with her children and remarried. Her second husband was a man by the name of William Brown. She soon realized she had made an error in judgment and found herself married to a man she did not love. Mary wanted to get a divorce but her father forbid her from doing so. She honored her father's wishes but only until his death. Once the former president passed away she got her divorce.

Robert Johnson, second son and fourth child, of Eliza and Andrew Johnson also fought for the Union. He may have been born in the south but he was against secession. He formed an infantry of Tennessee volunteers who were also willing to fight in order to keep the states united. He was respected by his men, because not only did he lead them but he fought right alongside them. He became a colonel in the Union army, though his drinking problem threatened his position in the army. The problem of what to do about him was put off due in large part of the fact that his father was a senator. His alcoholism became such a problem he was eventually forced to resign. His mother took him to a sanitarium for treatment.

When Robert's father became president he made his son his private White House secretary. After the war his drinking had escalated and it proved to be a bad decision for his father regardless of how good his intentions were to help his son.

In the midst of his father's impeachment trial when the president already had enough to worry about, Robert's behavior was out of control and impossible to ignore any longer. An absolutely vicious battle over impeachment his father was facing, his son as his secretary could no longer handle seeing his father's name lambasted in public, and he faced the problem by drinking even more heavily and bringing prostitutes in the White House. Robert's actions only caused more contempt towards his father by his political enemies.

Robert had at one time been looked upon as a young man with a promising future. Now his future was bleak and fleeting. He returned to make his home in Tennessee and eight weeks after his father's administration came to an end Robert was dead at the age of thirty-five. Some argue he died from alcoholism while others state the case that he committed suicide which was brought on by his drinking.

Andrew, Jr. who went by Frank was the youngest of the Johnson family. He was twelve when his father became president. His father who had been in politics was away from home much of his younger years. Frank loved living in the White House where he finally had a chance to spend time with his father and be close to him.

There was over an eighteen year age difference between him and his brother Robert. He was closer in age to his nieces and nephews than he was to his brothers and sisters. He attended school with his nieces and nephews at the White House being taught by tutors and then went on to Georgetown to further his studies.

After seeing firsthand the pain his two brothers drinking caused his parents he made a vow to them that he would never touch liquor and he lived up to his word.

After the days of the presidency at only twenty-one years of age he tried his hand at journalism and started his own newspaper. The newspaper was called *'The Greenville Intelligencer.'* Initially there was a lot of interest in the paper and he had quite a few subscribers. Over time his readers found the paper to be mainly about his father and his accomplishments. The paper gained a reputation as a propaganda tool and the people lost interest causing the newspaper to fail.

Frank married Bessie May Kumbaugh but they had no children. He was the only son of the former president who married.

The youngest son of Andrew Johnson, his father's namesake, died at the age of twenty-six.

18

Ulysses S. Grant

Children of Julia and Ulysses S. Grant:

Frederick Dent Grant – Born: May 30, 1850   Died: April 11, 1912

Ulysses S. Grant, Jr. "Buck" - Born: July 22, 1852   Died: Sept. 25, 1929

Ellen "Nellie" Wrenshall Grant – Born: July 4, 1855   Died Aug. 30, 1922

Jesse Root Grant – Born: Feb. 6, 1858   Died: June 8, 1934

Finishing an embarrassing 37th out of 41 in his class at West Point, Fred years later left the military holding the second highest military position in the U.S.

Frederick was the first son and oldest child of Ulysses S. Grant and his wife Julia.

His early days weren't extraordinary but memorable all the same to him. The family lived in St. Louis from 1854 - 1859 on the farm where Julia, wife of Ulysses, grew up which was property owned by her father. Fred's first memories of his father are from the days on the farm. Previously his father had been away while serving in the army.

Grant managed the farm for his father-in-law while the family lived there. Grant built his family a log cabin to stay in during their time on the farm and raised crops. Fred trailed after his father as he split logs for the cabin and tended to his crops.

Grant taught his older children to swim and to ride horses. Fred recalls hanging on to the back of the horse hanging on tight trying to appear unafraid in front of his father while his father walked alongside of him telling his son to be brave. Grant would get in the water and teach his children to swim and spent evenings reading to them. He instructed his children in subjects such as arithmetic, reading, and spelling. He loved his children and enjoyed their company. He had missed too much time with them while in the army so when he could he spent as much time as possible with his children.

Fred was ten when the family moved to Galena, Illinois where his father was a clerk in the family store owned by Grant's father which he had established for his sons. Fred attended school while living in Illinois.

Grant spoiled his children with toys and made paper boats for them which they sailed in the rain. Grant was strict when necessary. He rarely had to punish them and when he did all he had to do was show his disapproval which impacted the children more than a harsh spanking ever would. The children thrived on their father's love and attention and it hurt them deeply when he was disappointed in them.

The year after they moved to Illinois was the start of the Civil War. Grant wasn't disappointed to leave the family store as he himself said he was no clerk nor had the capacity to become one, but he was familiar with the army.

Fred was only eleven years old when his father left to become colonel of the Illinois Seventh District Regiment. Fred ran away from school three times to be with his father. He ran away to join his father on the battlefield. His father immediately returned him to school. The second time he ran away and joined the soldiers of his father's army who brought him to the general's camp. He was again returned to his studies. The third time his father relented and kept his son with him.

Fred while just a youngster grew up near the battlefields of the Civil War witnessing military life for himself. While he may have missed out on years of formal schooling, he was certainly schooled in military life.

Colonel Grant was on horseback most of the day traveling amongst the troops while Fred had free rein in the camp. Fred accompanied his father through the Vicksburg campaign and siege causing his father no problems, rather looking out for himself. He would be there to witness every major battle of the campaign. At this point at not quite thirteen, he took in everything he saw and would be able to recall what he witnessed in his later years.

During the Vicksburg campaign Fred contracted a disease and became dangerously ill. He was left in St. Louis to recover. His father unable to turn over his command to anyone else worried by the time he was able to go to see to him that he would have passed on, but he did recover.

Fred heard from first hand experience of the capture of Fort Henry. He advanced with his father and troops to Fort Donelson where they received a major victory which awarded Grant a promotion to major general.

It was exciting times and events for a young boy to experience, yet there were terrifying times too. In his later life he would recall witnessing hardships and the same suffering the troops had to endure. In his older years he would recall how he treasured the time and experiences he shared with his father, "I had the happiness as a child and as a man of being his constant companion in peace and in war."

In 1864 his father was called to Washington to meet with President Lincoln who gave his father command of the entire Union armies. Fred then thirteen years old standing by his father's side experienced a burst of pride when it appeared as if all the citizens of Washington had turned out to welcome Grant with cheers and applause. It would be his father who would a little over a year later return to Washington victorious after General Robert E. Lee himself surrendered to him.

Fred at an early age decided that he too like his father and great-grandfather wanted to have a military career. His great-grandfather had joined the Continental army and was present at the Battle of Bunker Hill. Fred had certainly experienced military life firsthand and had a pretty good idea of what he was getting into by making the decision to follow in their footsteps.

Fred was fourteen when he enrolled at West Point in the year 1866. It would be 1871, five years later before he would actually graduate from what normally took four years. While he may have spent time at military camps and witnessing battles, at the same time his studies had been sorely neglected.

During his time at West Point he racked up an assortment of demerits. When he did graduate he ranked 37th out of 41 students.

By the time he graduated from West Point his father was president. Fred was seventeen at the time his father took the oath of office of the presidency. He remained in the military throughout his father's administration.

Fred was given what was considered a choice job as a personal aide-de-camp to General Philip Sheridan. Sheridan, Atlanta's hero, wasn't particularly pleased at the appointment having said, "Fred is good enough, but there are other officers on my own staff of more merit and claim on my personal kindness." But one can hardly turn down a request by the president.

As General Sherman's aide-de-camp he took a trip to Europe for his first view of foreign lands. Fred was in France just after the Franco-Prussian War and traveled through the Caucasus where he stayed with the son of Emperor Nicholas I and Alexander II. He traveled across the vast steppes toward Moscow enchanted with the troika horses pulling their sleighs and the music of their bells.

Returning home Fred fought Indians out west and became a part of the government's surveying parties in Montana and the Arizona deserts.

Stationed in Chicago he met Ida Honore. In 1874 Fred was married to Ida, daughter of Henry Hamilton Honore. They left to move into the White House. They would have two children, a girl and a boy named after their famous grandparents the president and first lady.

Their daughter would be born in the White House in 1876 weighing in at thirteen pounds. Baby Julia, while a granddaughter of the president and first lady, would one day be a princess in Russia who found herself having to escape Russia during the Bolshevik uprising.

Years later the Grant family would return to Galena after the former president and first lady's trip abroad. Once the former president and sons lost their life savings Fred and his family moved in with the former president and first lady.

Fred's father, war hero and former president, was dying of throat cancer. After the former president had lost his life savings, knowing he was dying he was desperate to leave his family financially stable. He spent his final months writing his memoirs with his close friend Mark Twain as his publisher. Fred for a time would write while his father dictated, but when his throat constricted to the point where it was no longer possible for him to dictate to his son or stenographer he would write the remaining chapters by his own hand pushing through intense pain and suffering to complete the works before his death. The memoirs were finished only five days before his death.

Fred and his brothers assisted their father with his book by verifying through records his statements. Fred himself had witnessed many of the events his father wrote of in his memoirs. The time he had spent with his father when he was but a boy during the Civil War were recalled and put on paper to give the public insight on behind the scenes life during the Civil War. It is the most remarkable writings of any president in history.

In 1887 President Grover Cleveland nominated Fred for secretary of state but the Senate refused the nomination stating that it was only because of who his father was that he was nominated for the position.

With the Spanish-American War Fred served in the army where he saw and experienced battle instead of being a witness to it as he had been during the Civil War. He would eventually be promoted to major general.

After his military days he would be appointed as minister to Austria by President Benjamin Harrison where he served from 1890 – 1893. He also served as a New York City police commissioner.

Fred, like his own father, lost his daughter to a foreign marriage where they would make their homes abroad. Both of them did eventually return to make America their home again.

Fred's daughter Julia who was born in the White House and named after the first lady became a princess in 1899 when she married Prince Michael Cantacuzene of Russia. His estate was one of the largest and richest in the Russian Empire. His property included tens of thousands of acres. He came from one of the oldest families in Russia.

The prince and princess left Russia during the aftermath of the Russian Revolution with her jewels sewn into her clothing. They escaped through Finland to the United States and moved to Sarasota, Florida where the couple later divorced. She became an author about the events leading up to the Russian Revolution. The book was titled, *'Revolutionary*

Days.'

By the time Fred left the military he held the second highest military position in the U.S. He stated he was taking a leave of absence to have some time with his family. In actuality he was to have surgery for cancer, something he had long been afraid of since his father's death. Not wanting publicity of his illness to become publicly known he and his wife checked into a hotel under an assumed name. A few hours after arriving at the hotel he began choking and died. He passed away at the age of sixty-one.

Fred's funeral was attended by President Taft, Vice President Sherman, New York's mayor, and officers of the army along with thousands of citizens who admired and respected the son of President Grant. The army's second General Grant was buried at West Point.

Ulysses S. Grant, Jr., Grant's second son was his namesake, but would be known to all as 'Buck' after his birthplace the Buckeye state of Ohio.

Grant recognizing his young son Buck to be sensitive was careful not to hurt his feelings. There was one instance when he did rebuke his son after he popped the carriage whip and frightened the horses. Buck himself remembered that it nearly broke his heart to know his father was disappointed in him. His father didn't raise his voice to his son, only admonished him that his actions were careless. Buck would remember it for the rest of his life.

During the Civil War there were times when his mother and siblings went to visit their father and his older brother at the military camp. Most of those times Buck chose to stay behind and remain with his grandparents.

Buck was sixteen when his father became president. He would attend Emerson Institute in Washington for two years and then attended Phillips Exeter Academy around 1870. Exeter has quite an impressive list of alumni. Another presidential son Robert Lincoln, son of Abe Lincoln, had also attended Exter ten years previous to Buck. Daniel Webster and Franklin Pierce were other graduates that had gone into politics that had attended this nationally known academy with a record of excellence. Exeter was one of the finest schools in America and would prepare Buck for Harvard.

Buck was educated at some of the best schools even previous to attending Harvard from where he graduated in 1874. After graduating from Harvard he then continued on to study law at Columbia University and graduated from there in 1876. He was admitted to the bar in New York.

He served for eighteen months as White House secretary having the opportunity to work under his father during his administration.

After leaving the White House he accepted the post of Assistant United States Attorney in southern New York.

At the age of twenty-eight Buck married Fannie Josephine Chaffee on November 1, 1880. Fannie was the daughter of Colorado Senator Jerome Chaffee. They would have five children.

The year after his marriage Buck started a Wall Street investment firm with the financial aid of his father-in-law. The funds he was loaned gave him the opportunity to open the New York banking brokerage partnership that would later put him, his brother Fred, and his father in the midst of a scandal and lose their entire life's savings.

He joined the partnership with Ferdinand Ward and initially Buck and his family were making a small fortune. They then convinced their friends to also invest in the company. Little did Buck know that his partner was securing several loans and using the securities for collateral which was illegal. The market fell and the scheme was exposed. Initially Buck and his brother and father who had invested in the company with their entire life's savings were thrust in the limelight as a part of the scandal and threatened with a possible jail sentence. They were able to prove themselves innocent of any wrongdoing. However, their money was gone. The partner did go to jail. The Grants found themselves bankrupt.

Buck was guilt-ridden that he had put his family in this position. A year later his father was dead of lung cancer. In order to not leave the former first lady Julia bankrupt and with nothing to live on the former president wrote his memoirs completing it just days before his death.

Grant's personal memoirs is the greatest book ever written by a United States president. The book is a two-volume set narrative of the Civil War days. The entire book was written while he was dying of throat cancer. The manuscript was handwritten sometimes completing as many as twenty-five to fifty pages a day knowing his time was limited. He was in constant pain as he wrote but persevered in order for his wife and family to be financially secure after he was gone. The original manuscript handwritten by Grant himself is in the Library of Congress.

After Buck's investment firm failure he eventually moved to San Diego, California. His wife was in poor health and it was thought the climate would be beneficial to her. His younger brother Jessie was already living in San Diego with his family. Perhaps that may have swayed him towards choosing this area for his new home.

The family traveled cross-country from New York to California in the former first lady's private railroad car. The former first lady accompanied them on the journey. Their mother spent a few days in San Diego visiting with her youngest son Jessie and then left for Santa Barbara to spend the winter with her daughter Nellie.

While the crash of the market was what exposed the scandal of the brokerage business Buck was involved in, he now benefited from the market crash. He and his wife purchased a three-story mansion which they paid for in gold in the sum of $25,000. The previous owner paid over $100,000 when he had originally purchased the place and he even included the furniture in the sale of the house.

The home was in the Queen Anne style and had twenty-five rooms with a picturesque view of the harbor and was located in one of the most valuable areas in San Diego.

Buck's intentions had been to set up a law practice, which he did only to give it up after a time to invest in real estate. One of the properties he bought was the Horton House Hotel in 1895. He planned to run the hotel and name it after his father and include mementos of his father's time from the Civil War and his presidency.

In 1904 Buck ran for the U.S. Senate in California. He did not win and left politics never looking back.

In 1905 he demolished the old hotel and began building the new hotel to honor his father. They had only gotten as far as putting up the concrete framework of the building when the 1906 San Francisco earthquake put a halt to the construction. No lumber was available for quite some time and building came to a stand still for several years. It was

October of 1910 before the U.S. Grant Hotel celebrated it's grand opening. The hotel is still open today and in 1979 was listed on the National Register of Historic Sites. The former president's portrait remains hanging in the lobby to this day.

Buck's wife Fannie who had been in poor health for some time died in 1909. Four years later, he remarried America Workman Wills who was a widow.

Buck spent his last years running the U.S. Grant Hotel and traveling. He died at the age of seventy-seven.

Nellie, President Grant's only daughter, was Grant's favorite child. Everyone who was around Grant could clearly see how he loved and catered to his daughter. His wife would write about it in her memoirs and it was mentioned by her brothers in interviews they gave. There was no resentment, it was just a fact. Perhaps being the only daughter it was to be expected.

When Nellie was born her father had insisted that she be named Julia after her mother, but when she turned a year and a half she was christened Ellen Wrenshall Grant named after her dying grandmother. But she would be known to all as Nellie.

Nellie was thirteen when she took up residence at 1600 Pennsylvania Avenue. With three brothers they adored their sister and looked after her; as did the press. She became the darling of Washington and even years later when she married and moved abroad the press never forgot her or changed their feelings about her.

Nellie was the first teenage girl in the White House since Millard Fillmore's daughter Abby. The nation was enthralled when young presidential children moved into the White House. She had the personality to draw them in and in their eyes she could do no wrong.

Her parents wanting her to have a good education chose Miss Porter's School in Connecticut. The school was a boarding and day school that excelled in academics and is still operating today with the same valued reputation it held in the 1800's.

Her father accompanied her to the school knowing her mother wouldn't be able to resist Nellie's pleas to come back home. The president left a tearful daughter with a heavy heart and found that by the time he had returned to Washington she had already sent him several telegrams stating that she was homesick and wanted to come home. The president no stronger than her mother when it came to his daughter couldn't resist his daughter's pleas and sent an escort to bring his unhappy daughter back to the family.

Nellie did attend a private school in Washington for a time but she didn't like school and wasn't known to put herself out studying. At the end of a school day the White House carriage had come to pick up the presidential daughter only to be told by the teacher that she hadn't learned her lesson and to come back to pick her up later. After being turned away yet again when the carriage returned Nellie understood she wouldn't be going home until she learned her lesson. The next time the carriage came for her she knew her lesson and was permitted to leave.

The following day the first lady arrived at the school with her daughter. The teacher feared she was about to be rebuked by the first lady, but she was there to thank her for teaching her daughter the lesson that she was plain Nellie and no different from the other students that were sent to school to learn.

When Nellie was in her teens she was invited to parties given by Washington society. She loved to attend parties and dances. She was a typical teenager in that respect with the attitude that life was fun and should be enjoyed.

In the nineteenth century it was common for young men and women of upper class to go on a European tour. The Grants sent Nellie on a European tour with the family of a friend as her chaperone to visit Europe's historic cities and to experience culture to broaden her education.

The seventeen year old Nellie had a grand time. She was treated as American royalty and was invited to balls and parties where she was the guest of honor. She was received by Queen Victoria and was catered to as though she were an American princess. She loved every minute of it.

At the end of the tour she boarded the luxurious steamship *Russia* where her life was about to change. With most of the passengers aboard confined to their cabins due to seasickness including her chaperones, Nellie met and fell in love with a young Englishman by the name of Algernon Sartoris. Algy, as Nellie called him, was handsome and wealthy and twenty-two years to her seventeen years. He was the son of opera singer Fanny Kemble. He was a British officer assigned to the British delegation in Washington.

When Algernon met with the president to ask for his daughter's hand in marriage he was not looked upon with favor. Grant tried to dissuade his daughter from the marriage but the most he was able to do was convince them to put the wedding off for a year. He thought his daughter too young to marry and probably hoped by the end of a year she would have lost interest.

Nellie's family did not approve of the young man she chose to marry, but Nellie was stubborn and as usual her stubbornness prevailed. The White House would have a wedding.

The White House was spruced up with the excitement of *'the social event of the nineteenth century'*. It was certainly the highlight of Grant's administration and something the public anticipated with an excitement not seen in quite some time.

The day of the wedding people lined up around the White House fence hoping to spot the bride in her wedding finery.

The eighteen year old bride entered the East Room on the arm of the president while the Marine Band played Mendelssohn's *'Wedding March.'* The room was decorated with lilies, Florida orange blossoms, and potted plants.

On May 21, 1874 a White House wedding took place that the nation celebrated. The bride looked radiant in her satin gown trimmed in Brussels lace. With two hundred guests looking on the bride and groom stood on a raised dais under a large floral bell and exchanged their vows as the president gazed unseeing at the floor and wept. His daughter would be leaving to live in England.

The couple left Washington in a private Pullman palace luxury car. The train was draped in American and British flags to honor the bride and groom. The following day they would sail for England.

The president was later found in his daughter's room with his face buried in her pillow sobbing. He had lost his little girl.

The nation had fallen in love with Nellie and followed her every move even after she moved abroad.

Unfortunately, it wouldn't be a happy marriage. They would have four children but her husband began drinking heavily; evidently something he had been prone to do even before the marriage. He had a reputation before their marriage of drinking and of a roving eye with the women and perhaps this is why the Grants never approved of the marriage.

Whether Algernon had thought that by marrying a presidential daughter it would open doors for him that would have otherwise remained closed or what his thoughts were on the matter, nothing of the sort transpired. He appeared to become bored with his wife. He began being seen with other women. Rumors flew both in England and in the States.

Nellie remained in touch with her parents writing letters and visiting when possible. When she received a letter from her father in February of 1885 telling her he had been diagnosed with throat cancer she rushed to his side arriving in New York just sixteen days after he had written the letter.

It took a week to cross the Atlantic and mail took some time, but she wasted no time when she read her father's letter. He hadn't asked her to come but that was his hope. He wanted her with him. Regardless of the intense pain he was in he was there to meet his daughter at the dock when she arrived. As she stepped off the steamship he wrapped her in his arms and sobbed.

Her father died July 23, 1885, a war hero and president but it would be as a loving father to his children how he would be remembered.

Nellie returned to England after his death where she obtained a divorce from her alcoholic, womanizing husband. His family felt she had suffered enough at the hands of their son. They didn't blame Nellie for the failed marriage. She was awarded a large income from the Sartoris estate and returned to the United States a wealthy woman.

Nellie would remarry on her fifty-seventh birthday to her childhood sweetheart Franklin Hatch Jones in a quiet ceremony. Franklin was a first assistant postmaster general under President Cleveland. Three months after the marriage she became ill. The last seven years of her life she was paralyzed and an invalid her remaining years.

She was described as one of the most attractive young women who lived in the White House and would be remembered as a darling of the nation.

Jesse the youngest son of the president and first lady was full of personality. Grant enjoyed his son's comical ways which were completely contrary to his own. While his father may have been stoic, it didn't mean he didn't find his son to be quite entertaining and quite frankly a relief to tense days. He enjoyed his company immensely and could often be found on the floor wrestling around with his son or with Jesse on his back using his father for a horseback ride.

Grant enjoyed spoiling his two youngest children. During the Civil War there were times when the family had come to stay at camp with him. Staff officers often found him with his two youngest playing with them as if he was one of their playmates. It was clear to see that he adored his children.

Jesse was eleven when his father became the 18th President of the United States. The grounds in the back of the White House were open to the public at the time they lived there and when the children went out to play they were followed by curious people who watched every move they made. There wasn't the threat of safety in those days as there would be today with presidential families, but the first lady found the situation to be "anything but pleasant." Julia complained to the president and he had the south grounds closed so the children could play without becoming entertainment for the masses.

Jesse loved living at the White House recalling in later years how all the kids from the neighborhood would come over to play. The White House grounds were like one big playground and large enough for him and his friends to play baseball.

Jesse loved exploring the White House finding hidden staircases and areas that he used for play rooms.

Jesse had grown up surrounded by important people who others would simply read about in history books. He grew up in the time of the Civil War where his own father was a war hero and President Abraham Lincoln was a man he had met many times as a young boy. He never desired a military life himself; perhaps seeing too much of it in his younger days. He would attempt to make a career out of being a president's son as an adult and even made a halfhearted attempt at one point to run for the presidency.

While a youngster living in the White House his sister Nellie had been sent to a boarding school and sent her father a telegram saying she wanted to come home. Jesse being sent to school figured if it worked for his sister he would try the same tactic. The president told him to come on home. Once in Washington he had little time for school. Years later even with very little formal schooling he was still able to enter Cornell College. Of course, being a presidential son could have had something to do with smoothing the way for his entrance into college.

The family was able to spend time together and ate most of their meals as a family. Even dinner time seemed to be a time for entertaining his youngest children. The president would roll the bread into little balls and throw them at the kids until the kids were in hysterics. Then there was the time he was at a formal dinner and forgetting himself threw a bread ball at the wife of the British minister. He did not receive the same reaction from her that he did when throwing the bread balls at his children.

The American people knew all about the president's children as they followed them closely. When they learned Jesse loved animals he began receiving pets from sources who were most likely trying to score points with the president in the hopes that it would help their political career. Some of the 'living' gifts came from other countries as well.

Two of his favorite gifts were two ponies he received named Reb and Billy Button. He received a parrot from a Mexican ambassador and a Labrador Retriever from another politician. When the dog arrived the president sought out the White House steward. The president let him know that in the past former pets seemed to live very short lives. The president warned the steward that if anything happened to *this* dog every employee in the White House would be fired. Needless to say, the dog was well cared for and lived a long and happy life.

Jesse enjoyed the pets he received as gifts, but his favorite gift was a telescope. He would set the telescope up on the roof of the White House and he and his father would spend hours watching the stars and studying astronomical charts by lantern light. It was a time they both looked forward to and enjoyed.

Jesse had lots of interests and hobbies that came and went. For a time he enjoyed collecting stamps. Jesse would check letters his father had received from all over the world and confiscate some of these stamps for his collection.

When he found an ad in a newspaper selling a collection of foreign stamps for a mere $5.00 Jesse excitedly sent in his $5.00 for the stamp collection. He waited and checked the mail anticipating the arrival of his stamps. When after a time he still had not received his stamps Jesse told Officer Kelly, a member of the police force assigned to the White House, about his dilemma. Kelly suggested he go to his father and see what he would suggest. Jesse went to his father and complained about the matter asking if maybe the secretary of state or secretary of war would help by writing a letter for him. The president gave it some thought and suggested that his son attend the next cabinet meeting. Perhaps they could come up with a solution to his problem. The cabinet members thought it would be a good idea for Officer Kelly to write a letter.

Using a White House letterhead Officer Kelly wrote to the person who had offered the stamp collection: "I am a Capitol policeman. I can arrest anybody, anywhere, at any time, for anything. I want you to send those stamps to Jesse Grant at once." He sent his letter in the mail and in a matter of days Jesse had his stamps. Jesse learned it sometimes paid off to be the son of a president.

After his father's administration was over his parents planned to travel on a world tour. Jesse was a student at Cornell University at the time but dropped out to travel on the tour with the former president and first lady. Jesse was nineteen. The Grants were treated like royalty throughout the tour.

While in London Jesse wrote to a friend back home about his travels complaining about having to go out every evening to dinner at some Dukes or Earls or Lords. He described it as boring, saying that when traveling to a foreign country you want to actually see the country. He went on to say, "They consider me a prince, and at all the dinner parties I sit ahead of all the noblemen." He was amused at how when he said anything the waiters would interrupt others who were speaking telling them, "His Excellency was speaking."

While some during his foreign travels may have referred to him as 'His Excellency,' Queen Victoria described him as "a very ill-mannered young Yankee."

When his parents headed to Asia on the tour Jesse came home to finish his education. He returned to study at Columbia Law School.

Jesse Grant married Elizabeth Chapman who he had two children with. He and Elizabeth were married for over thirty years. Jesse traveled extensively for much of his life and spent little time at home with his wife and children, so it was ironic that when he filed for divorce he filed on grounds of desertion stating she deserted him. It would be several years before the divorce went through and when it did he married for a second time the week after his divorce was finalized. His second wife Lillian Burns Wilkins was nineteen years younger than Jesse.

Jesse had enjoyed traveling and the royal treatment he received while on the royal tour with his parents and afterward enjoyed traveling throughout his life. When overseas he was treated with more respect as a presidential son than he received in the states. Some of those he met overseas who were enamored to be in the company of a former presidential son convinced him that he should run for the presidency. He had been the son of a Republican president but he himself was a member of the Democratic party. He would run but was not taken seriously and that was the end of his political life.

Jesse had made his home in San Diego and for some years worked for his brother Buck as manager of his hotel the U.S. Grant Hotel. He had also built a casino in Mexico.

Jesse wrote a memoir about life with his father titled, *'In The Days Of My Father General Grant.'* He had a ghostwriter who was largely responsible for the writing of the book.

Jesse died in 1934 at the age of seventy-six.

19

Rutherford B. Hayes

Children of Lucy and Rutherford B. Hayes:

Sardis "Birchard Austin" Hayes – Born: Nov. 4, 1853   Died: Jan. 24, 1926

James Webb Cook Hayes – Born: March 20, 1856   Died: July 26, 1934

Rutherford Platt Hayes – Born: June 24, 1858   Died: July 31, 1927

Joseph Thompson Hayes "Jody" - Born: Dec. 21, 1861   Died: June 24, 1863

George Crook Hayes – Born: Sept. 29, 1864   Died: May 24, 1866

Frances Hayes "Fanny" - Born: Sept 2, 1867   Died: March 18, 1950

Scott Russell Hayes – Born: Feb. 8, 1871   Died : May 6, 1923

Manning Force Hayes – Born: Aug. 1, 1873   Died: Aug. 28, 1874

Webb Hayes was the first presidential son in history to win the Medal of Honor

and is one of only two two presidential sons to ever have received this honor.

The firstborn son of Rutherford B. Hayes was Birchard Austin Hayes who was a young adult by the time his father became president.

Some writers and historians in the past have listed his birth name as Sardis Birchard Hayes, but according to his father's diary dated December 26, 1870 the story is a bit different. Birchard had come home from Cornell University for the Christmas holidays when the topic of his name came up. Here is the story of his name in his own father's words taken from his diary: *"We originally called him Birchard, with no other Christian name. "Simple Birchard" was our phrase about it. When he grew large enough to know that Uncle Birchard's Christian name was Sardis, he took that name also. Finding it was no more agreeable to Uncle than it is to me, we asked him to drop it which he did a few weeks ago. I now offered him for his choice as a middle name either of his ancestral names, Scott, Cook, Austin, Russell, etc., etc. He chose Austin, the maiden name of my grandmother Birchard. So Birchard Austin Hayes it shall be. "*

Birchard and his brother Webb spent a good part of their childhood going from one Civil War military camp after another. The boys would go with their mother to spend winters in the Union Civil War camp with their father in West Virginia. Their father was with the 23rd Ohio Volunteer Infantry.

The 23rd Ohio Volunteer Infantry consisted of not one, but two future presidents. Rutherford B. Hayes and eighteen year old William McKinley. While the majority of the Civil War for their regiment was spent in sheer boredom they did participate in the Antietam Campaign and accompanied Sheridan in the Shenandoah Valley, but the majority of their time was spent in the mountains of West Virginia.

Rutherford and wife Lucy were strong Christians who not only read their Bible daily but lived accordingly, instilling good virtues and character traits in their children by example. Hayes taught his son Birch, "Always do what you know is right."

Before the war's end Birchard moved to Fremont, Ohio to live with his great uncle and namesake Sardis Birchard. He spent seven years under his household while completing his high school education and preparing for college.

Birchard graduated with an A.B. degree from Cornell University and then continued his education at Harvard Law School graduating with a Bachelor of Laws degree. It was when Birchard was at Harvard that his father was elected as the nineteenth president.

After graduating Birchard specialized as a tax and real estate attorney in Ohio.

At the age of thirty-four he married Mary Sherman. They had five boys. Their first son would live only a month past his first birthday and in some records his name is omitted.

Birchard in post-presidential days would work with his brother Webb as adviser in the creation of the Hayes Presidential Center.

James Webb Cook Hayes, Rutherford and Lucy Hayes' second son, was known all his life as Webb. At a later date, like his older brother Birchard he officially changed his name by omitting James.

As a youngster Webb with his brother Birchard spent six months every winter at their father's Union camp during the Civil War. They spent winters in different camps but usually at Camp White in West Virginia.

While at winter camp he became close to General George Cook commander of the unit who later became Webb's godfather. Cook taught the boy his love for the outdoors that he carried with him throughout his life. General Cook taught him how to live off the land and to hunt and fish. In his later years Webb and Cook would make yearly trips into the Rocky Mountains spending their vacations hunting for big game.

When Webb turned ten years old he went to live with his uncle in Ohio joining his older brother. He attended school in Ohio until the time he left for Cornell University in 1873.

Webb attended Cornell University for two years and then left to serve as his father's secretary during his third term as governor of Ohio.

At the time his father was running for the presidency Webb was graduating from Cornell. Webb joined his father at the Republican National Convention working the convention floor to secure the nomination for his father.

Rutherford B. Hayes would win the election in a disputed election. The other candidate, Samuel Tilden, had won the popular vote and Hayes won the majority in the Electoral College securing the election. The election would hold the title of most disputed election in history until the year 2000 with the election between George W. Bush and Al Gore.

Webb had served as his father's private secretary while his father was in Congress and now twenty-one year old Webb became his father's secretary in the White House.

Webb was very successful in business. All the Hayes children would prove to be successful and of good character, traits that had been instilled in them since their youth. Webb became well off financially from his business endeavors. One success story for which he received much credit and financial gain was what would become the multinational Union Carbide Corporation. He would serve as vice president of the corporation for several years. This endeavor made him a rich man.

Having made his fortune in business he had no qualms of leaving it behind to volunteer in the Spanish-American War. He was commissioned a major in the First Cleveland Troop which later became known as the First Ohio Cavalry. Webb would serve with distinction leading troops against the Spanish in Cuba and Puerto Rico.

While fighting in the Santiago de Cuba Campaign he was wounded while crossing the San Juan River. Wounded or not, he wasn't to be left behind and would take part in the assault on San Juan Hill at the age of forty-one. His age certainly didn't slow him down. At an age when most military men would be living their battles only in their memories, Webb was daring and brave in battle going on to serve at the invasion of Puerto Rico.

Webb promoted to lieutenant colonel served in the Philippines with the 31st United States Volunteer Infantry. After a thirty-three day voyage Webb landed in the Philippines. Within hours of landing he learned of a unit of American soldiers who had been captured with no means of escape. Webb heroically broke through enemy lines to reach the Americans and returned the next morning to report on how to rescue the men. His intelligence gave the Americans the information they needed to ensure the safe capture of their men. The American soldiers were saved due in large part to the brave act of this presidential son.

Webb Hayes became the first presidential son in history to win the Medal of Honor for his act of heroism. Even to date, there have only been two presidential sons to ever receive the Medal of Honor.

In 1900 Webb was in China during the Boxer Rebellion. He was a part of the relief force that rescued Westerners both American and British citizens. Future President Herbert Hoover and his wife Lou were in China at the time with Herbert working as a mining engineer. They were numbered among the American citizens who were rescued. Webb was also an observer in the Russo-Japanese War.

In his late fifties Webb would join British and French brigades in Italy fighting in the days before the United States joined in World War I. When America did join in the war, Webb transferred to the U.S. army. He was decorated in both France and Africa for his service for bravery.

Webb married widow Mary Otis Miller when he was fifty-six. They had no children.

As a presidential son his accomplishments are many and his bravery unprecedented; but yet he is most remembered for his creation of the Rutherford B. Hayes Presidential Center. It was the first presidential library created for an American president.

Rutherford Platt Hayes known as Rud, third son of Rutherford Hayes, was in college during most of his father's presidential years. He did come to visit the White House during school holidays. When he arrived he would find his two older brothers also in residence along with his younger brothers and sister. The White House always seemed to be full when he visited between family and friends. He rarely was fortunate enough to have a bedroom to himself and had at times been found sleeping on a cot or couch; and if those were filled up it wouldn't be unusual for Rud to end up sleeping on a billiard table or in a bathtub.

Rud attended Michigan State University and then graduated from Cornell University with a Bachelor of Science degree.

After Rud graduated from college he would travel to an area of the United States few Americans from the east had seen; other than those hardy souls that had moved out west or those searching for riches during the gold rush.

Rutherford B. Hayes would be the first sitting president to visit the West Coast. The president was accompanied by his wife Lucy, two of his sons Webb and Rud, secretary of war and General William Tecumseh Sherman, and a son of the president's cousin who was a lieutenant stationed at one of their stops also joined them for part of their journey.

The group traveled across the plains by special train on the Transcontinental Railroad traveling at top speed of thirty-five miles per hour. At a stop in Wyoming Mr. Charles Smith joined them who was introduced to the others as the youngest member of the president's old regiment in the war.

At Evanston a couple of Shoshone Indians were gazed at in wonder by those traveling in the presidential tour. One of the Indians was in American style clothing while the other Indian was in traditional Indian clothing of buckskin. They saw prairie dogs and antelope and perhaps some buffalo as they watched out the train window.

At one point six people from their party, including presidential sons Birchard and Rud, got out and rode on the cow-catcher of the train while the president and first lady rode with the engineer. They rode like this for quite a distance downhill witnessing magnificent views of mountain scenery and viewing natural wonders.

While in Salt Lake City the boys took a side trip to swim in the lake. They were surprised to find that a person could float without any effort at all even if they didn't know how to swim. They had been warned before entering the water not to let any of the water get into their mouth or eyes due to the salt content. Rud got his mouth and eyes full of the salt water nearly blinding him.

While in the New Mexico Territory they rode in horse-drawn army ambulances with military guards watching over their V.I.P. guests, as they were now traveling in a dangerous area known for Apache raiders and outlaws. At this time there was no railroad in this part of the country.

The group traveled through Nevada and on to Sacramento and San Francisco, California. While in California General Sherman rode up front armed with the driver while aboard the stage coach watching for bandits throughout the territory. This was the wild west.

They covered about ten thousand miles in all on their journey; traveling by train, steamship, army ambulance, ferryboat, and stagecoach. They left in late August and returned in October. The Hayes sons Birchard and Rud had an experience few others of their time would ever be fortunate enough to experience.

Rud would go on to do postgraduate work at the Boston Institute of Technology. He would return to his home base of Fremont, Ohio and eventually become a cashier at the Fremont Savings Bank which was an honorable job at the time and given only to those noted to be trustworthy, upstanding men.

October 24, 1894 Rud married Lucy Platt who was a cousin. They had three children, all boys.

President Hayes' uncle, Sardis Birchard, founded the Birchard Library. Rud was appointed a trustee. When he wasn't working at the bank, Rud spent many hours devoted to the library and brought forth many new ideas which were revolutionary at the time. He had found his calling.

Rud thought of ways to make the library appealing to children by designing an area with child sized furniture and books of interest to children. He came up with the creative idea of sending books to surrounding areas which would become the first traveling libraries. This gave many who previously had no opportunity to read an assortment of books to choose from.

Rud became a founder of the Ohio Library Association and served as commissioner for several years. He became one of the most important figures in developing the national library system.

He eventually moved to Asheville, North Carolina becoming involved in scientific farming and purchasing large areas of land. During the last years of his life he spent his winters in Florida. He remained involved in the communities he lived in serving on different boards and continuing with his work in education of children.

Joseph Thompson, or little Joseph as his brothers lovingly called him, was born on December 21, 1861 while his father was away during the Civil War. General Rutherford B. Hayes longed to see the newest addition to his family and was finally able to arrange for the family to come to Camp White in West Virginia where the 23rd Ohio Volunteer Infantry was being quartered so he could see him. Little Joseph was a year and a half and his father up till this time had only been able to read in letters from the family that he was the very image of his father.

The baby had not been a healthy child since birth. Within a few days of arrival the baby was sick and died of dysentery. He died on June 24, 1863. It would be a heartbreaking time for the family to lose one so young.

The arrival of their next son George Crook Hayes was born on September 29, 1864. He was named after General George Crook who was Hayes' favorite commander. His proud father described him as "stout, and very pretty." Unfortunately, he would be the second son the Hayes lost during the Civil War, as he too lived a short life dying before his second birthday on May 24, 1866 of scarlet fever. His father mourned the loss of his son deeply.

At the time Rutherford B. Hayes became president his three oldest sons who were born before the Civil War were in their late teens or early adults with two of them in college and the other son serving as his private secretary. When the Hayes moved into the White House they had two younger children, nine year old Fanny and six year old Scott.

Fanny, the only girl in the family was born September 2, 1867, when her father was a congressman in the state of Ohio. She grew up in Ohio attending school in Fremont. She grew up in the Hayes home Spiegel Grove.

Fanny being the only girl was catered to by her parents and her older brothers. Being the center of attention didn't stop when she moved into the White House. She and her younger brother Scott enjoyed playing hide and seek with endless places to hide in the presidential mansion, sometimes even convincing Supreme Court justices or senators to join in their games with them.

The first lady had been dubbed "Lemonade Lucy" as no alcohol was served at the White House during the Hayes administration. Alcohol or not, there were many social events that took place at the White House during their time in Washington; one of them being the celebration of their 25th wedding anniversary. The first lady at forty-six years of age and having given birth to eight children wore the same wedding gown she wore to their wedding twenty-five years previously. The president and first lady renewed their vows in front of their friends, family, cabinet members, and Washington society.

First Lady Lucy Hayes held many social events at the Executive Mansion which their two youngest children Fanny and Scott took part in. One of those events was the annual Easter Egg Roll.

The two youngest Hayes children weren't tucked away out of sight as many presidential children have been but were often seen throughout the White House inside and out playing. In the winter they could be seen sledding on the White House lawn and at other times were seen with their mother taking carriage rides through Washington. They were young children that enjoyed having a good time.

Fanny would spend time around the White House secretaries watching in awe as they used the telephones. If she behaved herself sometimes she was allowed to speak into the telephone herself.

Fanny and Scott were tutored in a room that was made up into a schoolroom for them.

As in all First Families before and since, gifts were sent for the children from places all over the world. One gift they enjoyed was a Siamese kitten sent from the American consul in Bangkok. It was the first Siamese cat in the United States and they appropriately named it Siam.

Two of Fanny's favorite gifts that she had hours of fun with were two large dollhouses. One of the dollhouses was a Christmas gift from her parents that they had a White House carpenter make for her. Fanny would spend hours rearranging the furniture and sitting quietly playing in the upstairs hallway where the dollhouses were kept.

Life wasn't all fun and games, as the children at an early age were taught about public service which Fanny would continue throughout her life. On Memorial Day she would join her mother at Arlington National Cemetery to decorate graves of Civil War soldiers.

At the end of Hayes administration the family moved back to Ohio where Fanny would complete her education. Fanny attended school with Molly Garfield whose father became president after her own father. Fanny also attended a boarding school in Connecticut, Miss Sarah Porter's School, where she attended classes with Molly Garfield daughter of the 20th president and Nellie Arthur whose father would become president after Molly's father making him the 21st president.

Fanny still lived at Spiegel Grove with her parents when her mother passed away. It is unfortunate that when the public is asked what they know about former First Lady Lucy Hayes that the answer usually received is that she was known as "Lemonade Lucy" due to not allowing alcohol in the White House.

Lucy Hayes was a woman who worked for what she believed in. A busy mother she still took the time to place an abandoned African-American child in an orphan's asylum where it would be cared for. She taught her own free black servant how to read and write. She worked during the Civil War tending to wounded soldiers, working in tent hospitals in military camps, sewing and cooking for the soldiers, and given the name "Mother of the Regiment," but it seems to be the "Lemonade Lucy" name that stuck in people's minds.

Lucy was a strong advocate working for, not just agreeing with, freed slaves obtaining civil rights. She worked to create an Ohio orphanage for the children of Civil War soldiers, she taught the blind, mute, and deaf patients. Her daughter witnessing these acts of kindness continued on in working for others who needed help.

Fanny became her father's hostess at their home in Ohio and his traveling companion sharing his interest in education and prison reform. After her father's death she continued working with women inmates at a woman's prison in Massachusetts.

Fanny didn't marry until after her father passed away. She married a friend she had known since her childhood days, a navy ensign Harry Eaton Smith. They married at the Hayes home Spiegel Grove and among the guests was President and First Lady McKinley.

She had one child, a boy named Dalton who would precede her in death. The family lived at Annapolis near Washington, D.C. until after WWI. The couple later divorced.

Fanny died on March 19, 1950.

Scott Russell Hayes was six years old when his father became the president. He was born in Ohio at the time his father was serving as Ohio's governor.

At the time the Hayes moved into the White House they had five children still living, having lost three sons to an early death. The White House was usually full of the Hayes children. Some of those 'children' were close to being adults with two away in college who came often to visit; one as their father's personal secretary and then there were the two younger ones who lived at the White House Scott and Fanny.

Scott at just six years old was a very visible presence at the presidential mansion. The Hayes loved animals and Scott was often seen playing with his two dogs and even had a goat that pulled him around the lawn of the White House in a little cart with the dogs running alongside joining in the fun.

Scott and Fanny were tutored in a classroom that was set up on the second floor along with other children from family friends and White House employees. Along with their studies they also had fun dancing, riding horses, and swimming.

Scott had a little difficulty in his studies and received extra tutoring. At six years old it was still hard to sit still when he would rather be out riding his bicycle or playing with his pets.

For a boy his age there was just so much to do and things to see at the White House. There were always people of interest coming and going. Scott was mesmerized by the delegation of Native American Indians who came to visit his father. The Sioux chief Red Cloud called him "a young brave."

Scott and Fanny were often found watching the secretaries at work. They were in residence when the White House had the first telephone installed. They were allowed to sit and watch the secretaries speak into it if they were very quiet. They sometimes got to have a turn speaking into the telephone, probably the first children to ever do so. Their phone number at the White House was number 1.

When Scott celebrated his seventh birthday there were dozens of children there to celebrate with him in the East Room.

At the end of his father's administration the family returned to Fremont, Ohio where they lived at Spiegel Grove the family estate.

Scott attended Cornell University as his older brothers had before him.

After graduating from Cornell he worked for a time at the First National Bank of Fremont and then moved on to the Thompson-Houston Electric Company in Cincinnati, Ohio. The company later became the General Electric Company and Scott was advanced to be in charge of the Cleveland, Ohio office.

Scott worked with a few other firms for a time settling in New York with the Railway Steel Springs Company starting as an assistant sales agent and working up to become vice president of the company. He would eventually become vice president of the New York Air Brake Company. He became quite successful and wealthy.

In 1912 Scott married Maude Wright Anderson. They never had children.

Scott purchased an estate that overlooked Croton Dam which was part of the New York City water supply system. The estate was located a distance of twenty plus miles north of New York City. He named his estate Spiegel Farm after the home he grew up in. It was one of the most spectacular estates in the area.

Scott and his wife Maude often visited his childhood home Spiegel Grove. One of their trips to Spiegel Grove they were accompanied by the soon-to-be President Warren

Harding and First Lady only a few months before he took office.

While on a business trip through Central and South America accompanied by his wife, presidential son Scott Hayes and Maude were involved in a shipwreck off the coast of Peru. The crew got the women off the sinking ship and placed them in a metal tanker and just before the ship sank they put the male passengers in a different tanker.

A storm was brewing in the Pacific when the passengers were rescued by yet another vessel. This vessel was carrying wild animals. The animals stirred up from the storm broke loose aboard the ship. Tigers and boa constrictors were just some of the animals now loose terrifying the passengers. They were rescued yet again and taken to Peru and returned home with an exciting story to tell.

Scott was admitted to the hospital for an operation on a brain tumor but died May 6, 1923, before the operation took place.

Manning Force Hayes, the seventh son, was the only one of the Hayes children that was born at Spiegel Grove.

Manning lived to celebrate his first birthday but died just weeks later. He passed away on his mother's 43rd birthday from what was probably related to dysentery. While as an infant his mother had described him as "the brightest wee baby we have had," his father said of the child that he had not seemed "altogether healthy at any time."

20

JAMES GARFIELD

Children of Lucretia and James Garfield:

Eliza Arabella Garfield "Trot" - Born: July 3, 1860   Died: Dec. 3, 1863

Harry Augustus Garfield "Hal" - Born: Oct. 11, 1863   Died: Dec. 12, 1942

James Rudolph Garfield – Born: Oct. 17, 1865   Died: March 24, 1950

Mary Garfield "Mollie" - Born: Jan. 16, 1867   Died: Dec. 30, 1947

Irvin McDowell Garfield – Born: Aug. 3, 1870   Died: on July 18, 1951

Abram Garfield – Born: Nov. 21, 1872   Died: Oct. 16, 1958

Edward Garfield – Born: Dec. 25, 1874   Died Oct. 25, 1876

Two of the Garfield sons were with their father when he was assassinated.

Eliza Arabella called Trot was the Garfield's first born. Her father had little opportunity to enjoy his young daughter as he was serving in the military during her short life. He had been against the southern states seceding from the nation and served as a major general in the Union Army. He fought in the battles of Middle Creek, the Battle of Shiloh, and Chickamauga.

It was August of 1861 when James Garfield volunteered to join the Union Army. Garfield could see that they faced defeat at the Battle of Chickamauga and rode with his commanding officer as they made their retreat from the battlefield. He rode six miles under enemy fire to rejoin the Union forces. Six miles is a long ride by horseback with little cover while under fire. He was rewarded with a promotion to major general becoming the youngest officer at thirty-one years of age to hold this rank. This occurred three weeks before the birth of his son Harry.

Garfield suffered from jaundice the summer of 1862 and returned home for his wife to nurse him back to health. Lucretia and James had spent a total of six weeks together during their first six years of marriage.

He had little time that he was able to spend with their daughter Trot before she died from diphtheria at three years old.

Harry "Hal" Augustus Garfield was born October 11, 1863 in the midst of the Civil War. He was born a short time after the Garfields moved into their first home. They had previously lived in rooms they rented.

Hal's father was there for the first few days of his life but left days later for Washington. It was a matter of weeks after their son's birth that their firstborn Trot passed away.

Hal would attend St. Paul's boarding school in New Hampshire as would his younger brothers.

Hal was seventeen in 1881 when his father became president. While attending his father's inauguration in the cold, snowy weather his father was the first president to have a march dedicated to him by John Phillips Sousa with the *'Inauguration March'* performed by the U.S. Marines band with Sousa himself conducting. His first act as president after the inauguration was when Garfield bent down and kissed the cheek of his mother who was the first mother of a president to witness her son's inauguration.

Hal was one of five Garfield children living at the White House at the time. Hal was seventeen; his brother Jim fifteen; fourteen year old Mollie, the only daughter of the Garfields; ten year old Irvin; and eight year old Abram.

Hal and his brother Jim had a tutor at the White House to prepare them for college. They were about to attend their father's alma mater Williams College.

As a presidential son Hal experienced the same frustration other presidential sons before and after him experienced – the unavailability of their father's undivided time. When he fell in love and wished to turn to his father for advice he discovered his father was much too busy to have any time to discuss the matter with him. He would have to wait for a month to actually speak to his father on a matter that was of great importance to him. Robert Lincoln before him had made the same complaint saying he could barely get more than ten minutes of his father's time. They wouldn't be the last presidential sons with the same complaint.

Hal would attend his father's alma mater Williams College in Massachusetts and then continued his education studying law at Columbia in New York and Oxford in England.

Hal along with his younger brother Jim were there at the historic time of witnessing their father's inauguration and were also with their father at the Baltimore and Potomac Railway Station in Washington to witness his assassination. The boys only seventeen and fifteen years of age saw their father gunned down right beside them.

Just that morning their father came into their bedroom at the White House while they were trying to catch a few extra minutes of sleep. Their father entered the room singing the song 'I Mixed Those Babies Up' from the opera *H.M.S. Pinafore* and grabbed both his teenage sons tucking them under his arms as though they were sacks of potatoes. His sons wiggled free from their father's grasp as he amazed them by doing a flip, then hopping around the room and balancing on his fingers and toes. The boys were awake now and while their father bounded off for breakfast the boys dressed to join their father.

It was July 2, 1881, when they entered the railway station, not even having time to board the train before Charles Guiteau stepped from the shadows and shot the president. While Guiteau would be convicted of murder and hanged, it wouldn't bring their father back.

Garfield had only been president for four months. Robert Lincoln, oldest son of Abraham Lincoln and Garfield's secretary of war, had just arrived at the train station to see the president off when he heard the shots of the president being shot. It was sixteen years after his own father had been assassinated; and yet there still was no Secret Service or bodyguards protecting the president.

Two months previous to the shooting the first lady became very ill with malaria and was recovering at a resort by the sea in New Jersey. Frail and as sick as she was she returned to Washington as soon as she received word. Her only thoughts now were on tending to her husband.

For two months the president was bedridden being poked and prodded by no less than a dozen doctors trying to find the bullet that was still lodged inside his body. By doing so without taking the precautions used today against infection the doctors did the opposite and set an infection from the germs on their hands while digging for the bullet.

Alexander Graham Bell used his induction balance machine, a type of metal detector, to try to locate the bullet inside the president's body. His attempts were unsuccessful. It wasn't that his machine didn't work but the fact that the president was laying on a bed with metal springs, and due to one of the doctors insisting the bullet was on one side and letting him search on that side of his body only. After his death it was determined the bullet had moved to the other side; most likely due to all the poking and prodding from the doctors.

The Garfield children visited their father by his bedside but it was hard to see their father who had been so full of life lying helpless and suffering. The children would spend most of their time quiet in their rooms, the joy of living in the White House gone.

James Garfield was president for only four months at the time he was shot and would die two months later making his the second shortest presidential administration in history – second only to William Henry Harrison whose administration lasted only one month before his death.

After the days of the White House Hal would graduate from Williams College in 1885 and continue his education studying law at Columbia Law School. He spent his second year of law in Oxford.

He opened a law office with his brother Jim. He would also become vice president of the Cleveland Trust Company.

Hal married Belle Hartford Mason on June 14, 1888. They had six children: two were either stillborn or died within a year of their birth. His children were: James born in 1890; Mason born and died in 1893; Luceilia born and died in 1894; Lucretia, who must have been a twin of Luceilia also born in 1894, but where Luceilia died at birth or within the year, Lucretia lived to be seventy-four years of age; Stanton born in 1896; and Caroline born and died in 1898.

Hal would prove to be one of the success stories of presidential children as would the other Garfield offspring. Hal spent much of his life devoted to education teaching at both Princeton University as professor of politics and professor of contract law at Williams College. He would become the 9th president of William's College.

During his time at Princeton Hal became friends with Woodrow Wilson, who unbeknownst to both of them at the time was a future president of the United States.

Hal remained at Williams College as its president until America became involved in WWI. With the U.S. entering the war President Woodrow Wilson asked Hal to lead the newly created Fuel Administration. It would be Hal's position to control supply and distribution of energy resources. He would have to negotiate for fair prices and allot energy resources as he deemed necessary which made him few friends and earned him the undeserved nickname of 'dictator of the nation's fuel resources.'

By the end of the war he was recognized for his efforts by being awarded the Distinguished Service Medal.

At the end of the war he returned to his role as president of Williams College.

He lived to the age of seventy-nine.

James or "Jim" Rudolph, Garfield's second son was born Oct. 17, 1865 in Hiram, Ohio. Jim studied at St. Paul's School in New Hampshire before moving to Washington.

Jim was fifteen when he moved into the White House where he and his older brother Hal were tutored in preparation for college. Jim and his brother would be attending Williams College as their father had before them.

Jim was interested in sports and was athletic. His favorite sport was baseball which was a new sport in America that had gained a lot of interest ever since Abner Doubleday invented the sport the summer of 1839.

The Garfields were a close family and even with their father as president and a busy man, time was always made for family. The boys were accompanying their father the day he was assassinated. They had ridden in a separate carriage as his father had ridden in the

State Department carriage which didn't allow room for the boys. Hal and Jim were trailing behind their father and Secretary of State Blaine. Jim fifteen at the time watched in horror as his father was shot right before his eyes.

In a matter of minutes Dr. Smith Townsend arrived at the railway station. Townsend, the first to arrive, was the District of Columbia's health officer. While he was the first to arrive there would be nine other doctors who would join him, all who insisted on examining the president.

The president while lying on the floor of the railroad station was examined without the doctor using any precautions against germs right on the floor of the train station. They couldn't have picked a more filthy place to ensure infection in an open wound, but during these times doctors didn't concern themselves about germs. If they would have the president most likely would have lived, as it was infection that ultimately killed the president.

The second doctor to arrive Charles Purvis was one of the first black men in the country to study at a university. He became the first black doctor to treat a president of the United States.

Other doctors arrived and each one poked the president's wound trying to locate the bullet lodged in his back.

It was a terrifying scene for the sons to witness. The night his father was shot Jim wrote in his diary, *"I was frightened and could do nothing but cry."*

Their father was bedridden and suffered for the next two months. His children would visit his bedside only to see their father wither away before their eyes and suffer silently never complaining. Unable to keep down food he lost eighty pounds during the two months he survived.

The children had before enjoyed their father being a president and living in the White House with many wonderful memories of their first few months in the Executive Mansion. They now stayed in their rooms most of the time venturing out only for meals or for an update on their father's condition.

Years later Jim's own grandson would say, "My mother told me he never got over it. My grandfather idolized his father." A fifteen year old having to witness his own father being shot while walking next to him was traumatic.

After his father's death the two oldest boys Hal and Jim studied at Williams College. Jim graduated in 1885 and continued his education at Columbia Law School.

He worked part-time in a law office in addition to his studies at Columbia until he felt he was prepared to pass the bar exams. At that point he returned to Ohio, passed the bar, and then opened the law office Garfield & Garfield with his brother Hal. The two of them practiced corporate law.

Helen Newell had caught Jim's eye and the two of them were married in 1890. Helen was the daughter of the president of the Lake Shore Railroad. They would have four children and remain married until she passed away in 1930. One of their grandsons would one day marry a granddaughter of President Benjamin Harrison.

During the mid-1890's Jim had become friends with Theodore Roosevelt. While they didn't see much of each other they remained in touch throughout the years. Theodore Roosevelt would remember his friend when he became president.

Jim in the meantime won a position on the town council in Mentor, Ohio where he and Helen made their home. The following year he would become a delegate to the Nineteenth Congressional District Convention representing his county for the next two years at the Republican State Convention. Before reaching the age of thirty he would be elected to the Ohio State Senate where he served for two terms.

Growing up in a home where politics was a part of life, he too was now a part of that political world. His belief was that if decent men were in government positions that a corrupt government would become nonexistent. *If only that were so.*

While serving in the Senate he became an adviser to his friend Theodore Roosevelt who was now president. Jim would go on to serve as U.S. Official Civil Service Commission following his years in the Senate, Commissioner of Corporations, Commerce and Labor Department, and then as Secretary of Interior.

When Taft became president he would replace Garfield, and at that time he returned to his law practice in Ohio. Not quite having had his fill of politics in 1910 he tried for the nomination for governor but his efforts on that behalf failed.

Jim Garfield would remain active for much of his life becoming a founder of the Roosevelt Memorial Association serving as its president from 1924 to 1950. He was also involved in charitable institutions.

For a time after his wife's death he would live with his younger brother Abram until he became too ill.

His father would have been proud, not only of Jim but of all the Garfield children. Their father may have passed away while his children were still young, but he along with the first lady had instilled great values and character traits in each and every one of their children.

Mollie is the only Garfield daughter that survived past childhood. She was born in Washington, D.C. while her father was a member of the U.S. House of Representatives.

Garfield would read to his daughter and sons for hours when he had time off. He read some of his favorite authors to them introducing them to good literature. *"It is a pity,"* he wrote, *"that I have so little time to devote to my children."*

In 1881 Mollie attended her father's inauguration and attended the inaugural parade with her friend Fanny Hayes. The outgoing president's daughter and the incoming president's daughter, schoolmates and friends, shared a moment in history.

Mollie attended Miss Mittleberger's School in Cleveland, Ohio. She also attended Miss Porter's Finishing School for a short time. While living in the White House she would attend Madam Burr's private school in Washington. At Madame Burr's she studied French, English, reading, geography, arithmetic, and spelling. Girls of elite families attended Madame Burr's school and received an education above what was the norm at the time for young girls.

The president sent Mollie off to school every morning with a hug before she ran out the door for school. Mollie, fourteen when she moved into the White House would walk several blocks on her own to school everyday. This was several years previous to the time the Secret Service protected presidents and their families.

The first lady protected her children from the press refusing to allow newspaper and magazines from publishing photographs of her children. The president agreed with the first lady. He was determined not to spoil his children or to allow others to do so due to his presidency. *"Whatever fate may await me, I am resolved, if possible, to save my children from being injured by my presidency,"* he wrote. *"Every attempt, therefore, to flatter them, or to make more of them than they deserve, I shall do all I can to prevent, and to arm them against."* They were the first president and first lady to guard their children from the public and the media.

Mollie loved to entertain and whether having learned the social graces and the art of entertaining at the girl's finishing schools she attended or instilled in her from watching the entertainment at the White House she loved to invite her friends over for luncheons and tea parties. A former president's daughter Fanny Hays was often one of her guests.

Before Garfield was shot there had been a newspaper article about presidents being in more danger than the average citizen but the mindset was the president couldn't be protected if someone really wished to do them harm. Garfield agreed. *"Assassination can no more be guarded against than death by lightning,"* he wrote, *"and it is best not to worry about either."* Worry about it or not, he was being watched by someone who had exactly that in mind in regards to the president.

Lucretia, or Crete as the president referred to his wife the first lady, had entertained guests at an open reception at the White House. One of the guests was Charles Guiteau who had been seeking to be appointed an ambassadorship in Paris. He was only one of many who waited daily to see the president in hopes of attaining a position. He became disgruntled when the president denied his request.

Suffering from malaria Crete in a weakened state was sent to the Jersey shore to recuperate thinking the salt air would refresh her and help her in her recovery. She was escorted to the train station by the president for her departure. Crete was visibly very ill. Guiteau who had been waiting to shoot the president saw the condition of the first lady and changed his mind, deciding at the last minute he would not want to have the first lady witness her husband's assassination. It could wait for another day. That day came on July 2, 1881 when he arrived at the train station with his two oldest sons. Guiteau had no concern about shooting the president in the presence of his children evidently.

The days of joy for Mollie ended the day her father was shot by an assassin. She was with her mother sitting by her father's bedside when he passed away.

After the death of her father Mollie would write in her diary, *"Sometimes I feel that God couldn't have known how we all loved and needed him, here with us. I don't think I shall ever learn to say 'Thy will be done' about that."* To lose a father so young who was such a commanding presence in her life left the young girl grieving.

A year after her father's death Mollie was in love with the man who had served as her father's private secretary, Joseph Stanley-Brown, a man she had not cared for when they first met, but one that her father had loved like a son. Mollie confided to her diary, *"I don't believe I will ever in my life love a man as I do Mr. Brown."* She was correct in her thoughts as they would marry and live to celebrate fifty plus years of marriage.

After her father's assassination Mollie had moved with her mother to the Garfield family home Lawnfield in Mentor, Ohio. Her mother had requested that her husband's secretary, the man Mollie had fallen in love with, organize Garfield's papers. He did so and then attended Yale's Sheffield Scientific School. The couple kept in contact through letters until the time they could be reunited. It was a little over six years after the death of her father before the marriage took place.

The former first lady announced wedding plans of two of her children for a double wedding planned for June 14, 1888. Mollie would be marrying her father's former secretary in a double wedding with her oldest brother Harry and Belle Mason.

The wedding would take place in the Memorial Library, the room the former first lady had built to house the president's papers and memorabilia.

Palms, plants, and flowers filled the home with intertwined daisies, roses, white carnations, and ferns while the wedding party would stand under a canopy of the flowers.

Harry and Belle were married first with James, brother of the groom, as best man and the bride's sister May being the maid of honor. May would also be maid of honor for her best friend Mollie. After the first ceremony Mollie in her gown of silk crepe with no veil, as her groom thought it would make her look unnatural, exchanged her vows. A dinner followed the ceremonies for all the wedding guests.

The wedding guests which included former President Rutherford B. Hayes and wife Lucy returned to Cleveland by a special train for wedding guests only.

Mollie with her new husband Joseph left for Kansas to visit Joseph's mother and then left for Europe where Joseph would study at the University of Heidelberg in Germany.

Mollie and Joseph had three children: Rudolph, Ruth, and Margaret. Their son Rudolph worked with his uncle, Mollie's brother Abram in his architectural firm. Their daughter Margaret became a surgeon, and their daughter Ruth worked in publishing and published a book based on her mother's diaries titled, '*Mollie Garfield In The White House.*'

Mollie and Joseph, along with her brother Harry and Belle, celebrated their 50th wedding anniversaries. The couples held a luncheon which included family and friends. Invited but unable to attend, President Franklin Roosevelt sent a note of congratulations to the two couples.

Mollie lived to the age of eighty.

Ten year old Irvin and eight year old Abram were similar to Tad and Willie Lincoln's years in the White House as far as stirring up trouble. The White House staff called the two youngest Garfield boys, especially Irvin, terrors of the White House.

The boys loved riding their bikes and as far as Abram was concerned inside was as much fun as outside. Irvin rode his bike down the formal staircase and raced his brother around the halls and in the East Room making the antiques and mementos of past presidents mere obstacle courses. Abram not causing enough damage of his own invited his friends to come join in on the fun. Of course, the boys would wait until their parents were away from the presidential mansion before pulling these stunts.

The two youngest boys were tutored at the White House but they had a hard time sitting through lessons when they were more interested in having fun.

Garfield had said of his children, "No child of mine shall ever be compelled to study one hour, or to learn even the English alphabet, before he has deposited under his skin at least seven years of muscle and bone." The boys had by now reached that 'seven years of muscle and bone' and were of an age when it was time to take their education seriously. Their father was strict about their education, which paid off as all his children went on to become successful.

On the day of their father's assassination before leaving for the train station he looked in on his youngest sons finding them performing somersaults on their beds. He joined in on their fun showing them how he could do a handspring and singing at the top of his voice along with his sons. That would be the last time they would have the opportunity to play and enjoy their father's company.

As their father lay bedridden and dying in his bed the children would visit him, but it was hard to view their father weak and unable to get out of bed when they were used to a father who had played and wrestled with them.

Both boys full of life did settle down and would attend Williams College like their father and older brothers did before them.

Irvin graduated from Williams College in which he was head of the football team during his senior year. After graduating from Williams College he then went to Harvard Law School. He practiced law in Boston becoming a corporate lawyer. He was head of the Boston law firm of Warren, Garfield, Whiteside and Lamson. He was successful in his law practice and argued cases before the Massachusetts Supreme Court.

Irvin married Susan Emmons in 1906 and they had three children: Irvin, Eleanor, and Jane. He died unexpectedly just before his eighty-first birthday.

Abram, the youngest surviving son of James and Lucretia Garfield also attended Williams College where he received a Bachelor of Art degree. He then attended the Massachusetts Institute of Technology where he earned a Bachelor of Science in architecture. He was a founder and first president of the Cleveland School of Architecture which became part of Western Reserve University.

Abram established his own architectural firm in Ohio. Many of the buildings he designed still stand today as designated historic landmarks.

He served under two presidents, President Theodore Roosevelt and President Coolidge, who appointed him to the National Council of Fine Arts.

Abram married Sarah Granger and after her death he married a bride much younger than himself, Helen Grannis Mathews. He had two children with his first wife: Edward and Mary. He lived to the age of eighty-five.

Edward had been the last of James and Lucretia's children born on December 25, 1874. Garfield had received news that his youngest son, not yet two years old, was seriously ill from whopping cough. He rushed home only to find the boy was unconscious. He would live for a few more days with both his parents praying continuously but he would not survive. His father would live only five years after the death of his son Edward.

21

Chester Arthur

Children of Nell and Chester Arthur:

William Lewis Arthur – Born: Dec. 10, 1860   Died: July 7, 1863

Chester Alan Arthur II – Born: July 25, 1864   Died: July 17, 1937

Ellen Hansbrough Herndon Arthur "Nell" - Born: Nov. 21, 1871   Died: Sept. 6, 1915

Alan and the Prince of Siam were caught swimming nude in the South Lawn fountain at the White House and were nearly arrested.

The Arthurs first child, William Lewis Arthur, named after his maternal grandfather who had been an explorer was born while his father was in the military during the Civil War. His birth came fourteen months after the marriage of Ellen and Chester Arthur. William died at the age of two and a half.

The Arthur's second son, Chester Alan Arthur II, was born at the end of the Civil War just a year after the death of the Arthurs first child.

The Arthurs had three children, two of which survived infancy. Their third child was a girl named Ellen after her mother but called Nell.

Ellen Arthur, Chester's wife, died of pneumonia less than a year before he became vice president. After only six months as vice president President Garfield was assassinated making Arthur the next president.

When Chester saw the condition of the White House he absolutely refused to move in. He initially wanted to build a new presidential mansion but was turned down. Congress did agree to remodel the White House allowing $30,000 for renovations.

The servants quarters were in terrible condition; the septic system was failing and even the paint on the ceiling was peeling off in the kitchen. Chester hired Louis Comfort Tiffany to decorate the state rooms. During the remodeling much of the historic White House furnishings were carted off, twenty full wagon loads and sold to the public at auction. Rooms full of historic furnishings and memorabilia were lost due to the careless handling of these priceless antiques of great historical value having been a part of past presidential administrations.

Presidential son Chester Alan, who preferred to go by Alan, was away at Princeton attending college when his father became president. Alan and Nell came to visit after spending the holiday season in New York. Alan would return to college while Nell for the time being stayed with relatives.

The president wanted his daughter to live with him in the White House but he needed someone to care for her and someone to assume the role of White House hostess. He called on his sister Molly McElroy who had cared for Nellie after her mother's death and seen to her education. Molly came and took over the role as hostess. Her two young daughters May and Jessie accompanied her who were company for Nellie.

Alan was seventeen when his father became president and spent most of his father's administration away from the White House but visited often. Nellie at nine years old enjoyed living at the presidential mansion. Her favorite thing to do was to play in the elevator which was a new invention since her father had the White House remodeled.

The president was adamant about protecting his children from the press. He was quoted, *"I may be the president of the United States, but my private life is nobody's damn business."* And that was enforced where his children were concerned. He would not allow press interviews or photos taken of his children. The press respected him on this point. Future presidents have followed his lead requesting the press to leave their children alone and not exploit them; even though it is sometimes the father as a political candidate that brings the children out using them as a political tool.

After completing his studies at Princeton Alan studied law at Columbia University with the intention that he would one day work in and eventually take over his father's law office in New York. And as the saying goes, *'the best-laid plans of mice and men,'* don't always go according to plan. Alan never did finish his education at Columbia and he never worked a day in his life.

Alan had been catered to most of his life and especially now as a presidential son he had come to expect preferential treatment. Alan brought friends and girlfriends to the White House to stay for holidays and weekends. He would use the presidential carriage riding around Washington and partied on the presidential yacht.

Alan was gaining a reputation as a playboy and he was pointed out by other parents to their children as an example of what not to become. He had earned the title 'Prince of Washington,' and it was not meant as a favorable title.

The Prince of Siam while a guest of the White House nearly got involved in an international incident when Alan and the prince were caught swimming nude in the South Lawn fountain and were nearly arrested.

While Alan appeared to be all fun and games and used his father's name and power instead of standing on his own two feet and becoming a man to look up to; Nellie just a child was the one to be admired. She was a sweet, selfless girl. She often worked towards helping others as a volunteer to charitable needs, collecting toys and clothes and items to donate, and serving hot meals to poor kids because she felt sorry for them and didn't want them to go without. One Christmas holiday she served over two-thousand needy children dinner to be assured they had a nice meal for the holidays.

As different as night and day brother and sister were strangely enough very close and remained so until her death.

Alan cared for his father in his last days. His reasoning and actions are still difficult to understand today, but his father had asked his son to destroy all his personal and presidential papers after his death. After his death Alan began doing just that until others stepped in and stopped him. Due to this act, there is little known or of historical value to give historians insight into the administration of Chester Arthur.

His father had advised his son to stay out of politics. Alan did stay out of politics and business. With the aid of the inheritance he received from his father he traveled to Europe socializing with royalty and celebrities. Some of the friends he made while on his European stay was the Prince of Wales and artists James Whistler and John Singer Sargent. His hobby seemed to be women and partying. His initial plan had been to travel throughout Europe for six months and then return home. He ended up staying in Europe until his health declined.

When the former president died Molly McElroy took in her orphaned niece and cared for her. Nell would eventually marry Charles Pinkerton in 1903 and made her home in Albany, New York.

While in Switzerland at age thirty-six Alan married a wealthy divorcee Myra Townsend Fithian Andrews from California in the year 1900. He returned to America the same year for health reasons. He had suffered respiratory problems related to asthma and bronchitis.

Returning to America Arthur brought the European game of polo with him which was fairly new to America. Vice President Theodore Roosevelt who came to dinner with the Arthurs enjoyed a game of polo while in Colorado.

Alan reunited with his sister upon his return and they remained in touch. Alan and Myra had a son the year after their move to America, Chester Alan Arthur III born in 1901. The couple also had a daughter they named Ellen after his mother but she did not survive.

Nell passed away September 6, 1915. Nell at the age of forty-three had surgery and needed blood transfusions to save her life. Blood transfusions were a fairly new procedure at this time and she died from complications.

During his sixteen year marriage Alan had continued drinking heavily and involved with women other than his wife. They divorced in 1927. He married Rowena Graves in 1934, a woman who was thirty-nine while he was seventy years of age. He lived three years after his marriage dying July 17, 1937 of a heart attack.

22

Grover Cleveland

Alleged Illegitimate Child of Maria Halpin and Grover Cleveland:

Oscar Folsom Cleveland – Born: September 14, 1874   Died: March 9, 1947

Adopted and name changed to: James E. King in 1879 – 5 yrs. after his birth

During the presidential election a scandal of an illegitimate child was revealed.

Grover Cleveland, a bachelor, had been nominated for the office of the presidency. The press uncovered a story during the election revealing a scandal that occurred ten years previous. The press and the public wanted to know - *did he father an illegitimate child?*

Cleveland's campaign at first told him to lie, but Cleveland knew there was no point denying the allegations. His opponent's party came up with the slogan, "Ma, Ma, Where's my Pa? Gone to the White House...ha ha ha." Despite the scandal coming to light Cleveland won the election.

It had been back in the year 1874 when a woman by the name of Maria Halpin gave birth to an illegitimate son. She named Cleveland as the father of the child. At the time he didn't deny it.

Maria Halpin was a beautiful woman who had been widowed during the Civil War who had two children and needed a job to support herself and her children. Experienced as a dressmaker she moved to Buffalo and found work in a department store as a saleswoman.

The story goes that Grover Cleveland saw her and asked a friend to introduce them. They began spending time in each others company. Grover was in his late thirties and as a successful attorney he was probably looked upon as a good catch, and she was certainly a woman he would have been proud to be seen with.

The beginning of the story is when one evening they went out and he walked her home to the boarding house where she was living. She claimed that he forced himself on her. She would now be considered a 'ruined woman.' She threatened to report the rape to the police, but claims he threatened her once she announced her intentions of reporting him to the authorities. As a lawyer and former assistant district attorney he had connections and she knew he could cause problems for her. Of course, every story has two sides to it as does this one. As sordid of a story as this sounds there are official court documents that give her story credence.

At the time he had been a party boy even though a grown man at the time. He was known to frequent places of prostitution and drink an excessive amount of liquor.

When she discovered that she was pregnant she went to confront him with the news. Initially, she said he promised to do the honorable thing and marry her.

After he had time to consider what to do about the matter he made arrangements that she was unaware of. He arranged for a certain doctor to be at the hospital when she was to give birth and to 'take care of her'. The doctor's name was Dr. King.

Maria gave birth to a son and named the infant Oscar Folsom Cleveland, a name she said Cleveland himself had insisted on. Oscar Folsom was his good friend and law partner. Cleveland years later married Folsom's daughter and she would become the first lady.

When the baby was only days old the doctor who delivered him took the baby without the mother's knowledge or consent. The doctor gave the baby to his sister-in-law who was pregnant herself and due in a short time. The doctor insisted she care for the baby even though the sister-in-law Minnie Kendall initially refused. The doctor was insistent and said she would be paid for caring for the infant, but she was to tell absolutely no one. Being in a difficult financial situation she reluctantly agreed.

The doctor again arrived unannounced at his sister-in-law's door one day and told her they were to take the baby to the baby's father. They arrived at a law office. They entered a room where a woman ran to Minnie and snatched the baby from her arms crying and tenderly cradling the child. The man named Cleveland who Minnie had never seen or heard of before told the woman to give the baby back. Minnie could tell by the woman's actions that she was the natural mother of the child. The woman broke down in hysterics.

Minnie returned home that day with the baby and cared for him for a year before the doctor arrived yet again with no prior notice saying the baby was to be returned to it's mother. Minnie was told to get in a waiting carriage and to turn him over to his mother. She did so and upon returning home the doctor insisted she and her husband were to leave town - *immediately.* They were never to tell anyone anything at all about the baby.

With political aspirations Cleveland knew this situation could be the end of his political dreams if one day Maria appeared with the child claiming he was the boy's father. He approached a judge he knew well who drew up papers for Maria to sign giving up all rights to the child.

Papers in hand Cleveland approached Maria offering her money if she would place the child at the Buffalo Orphan Asylum ensuring her he would pay for the child's care. She was promised she could visit him anytime.

Maria did visit the boy quite often. Realizing she had made a terrible mistake she planned to take him when no one was looking. When the opportunity arose, she snatched the boy and ran disappearing with him.

Cleveland again reached out to someone in power convincing them that Maria was unstable and the child was in danger. Again papers were signed without even speaking to Maria or verifying the facts. Maria was found and the child was taken from her with Maria fighting with everything she had in her. The boy was returned to the orphanage.

Maria was bundled into a carriage and taken to a lunatic asylum and admitted as a patient. Once she was under the charge of a caring, honorable doctor who listened to her story he could see for himself she was not insane. He ordered her to be released.

The boy named Oscar was taken to a new home. He was adopted by none other than Dr. King, the doctor who had delivered the boy and taken him from his mother. He and his wife had a daughter that had died and couldn't have any other children. The boy was adopted and given the name of James E. King, Jr. He would be too young to remember the name he had been born with and probably would have no recollection of his mother.

It was ten years later when Cleveland was running for president when the story came out. Maria was approached and offered a great deal of money to tell the newspaper the story wasn't true. She refused. It was Minnie, the doctor's sister-in-law who had cared for him for a time when approached by a reporter who finally told the true story.

Cleveland later came up with the story that he was just one of many men who had 'known' Maria, but since he was the only one of the men who was unmarried at the time he claimed the boy was his.

Oscar, or James as he was called after his adoption, followed in his father's footsteps and became a doctor himself. He was most likely raised in a loving home regardless of how the couple came about having the child. It is uncertain if his adoptive mother even knew of his origins. As a newborn infant he had been kidnapped, his mother's reputation ruined, she was admitted to a lunatic asylum, all in order to cover the tracks of a man's wrong-doings. If James ever knew any of his history either as a child or when grown, he never tried to locate his birth mother or father and never told anyone his birth father was the President of the United States. He may have never been told, and likely wasn't considering the illegality of his abduction and adoption. Considering he was only two years old at the time of his adoption he wouldn't have remembered.

The illegitimate son of Grover Cleveland passed away at the age of seventy-three. He had been married once and divorced with no children.

Two years into his first administration at forty-seven years of age the bachelor president finally settled down and married. He married a twenty-one year old woman, Frances Folsom, the daughter of his law partner Oscar Folsom who his illegitimate son had been named after. When her father died in an accident she had become Cleveland's ward. They were married in the White House - the only president in history to do so.

Grover and Frances would have five children. He was a loving father to his children with his wife Frances. Cleveland served as the 22nd and the 24th president, the only president to serve two nonconsecutive terms as president. You'll meet his other children during his next administration as they were born after his first administration ended.

23

BENJAMIN HARRISON

Children of Caroline and Benjamin Harrison:

Russell Benjamin Harrison (born: Russell Farnum Lord Harrison) - Born: Aug. 12, 1854 Died: Dec. 13, 1936

Mary Scott Harrison "Mamie" - Born: April 3, 1858   Died: Oct. 28, 1930

Unnamed daughter – Born: June, 1861   Died: Stillborn, June, 1861

Children of Mary and Benjamin Harrison:

Elizabeth Harrison Walker – Born: Feb. 21, 1897   Died: Dec. 26, 1955

A goat pulling the president's grandson behind him in a cart

took off running down Pennsylvania Ave. with the president chasing after them.

Benjamin Harrison was the last Civil War general who became president of the United States. His oldest child, Russell Benjamin Harrison, was six years old at the beginning of the Civil War.

Harrison had a law practice in Indiana and that is where his children Russell and Mamie grew up. Mary who was called Mamie was born in Indianapolis.

A second daughter was born to Benjamin and Caroline in June of 1861 but was stillborn. She remained unnamed.

In 1862 a year after the attack at Fort Sumter President Lincoln was in desperate need of more men to join the Union army. Governor Oliver Morton of Indiana was called on to aid in finding additional reinforcements. Benjamin Harrison had gone to the governor's office on a business matter and the governor explained his dilemma to Harrison of the trouble he was having in finding men to volunteer. Harrison volunteered to raise a regiment of volunteers and to join them. He not only raised the required amount of volunteers, but would train them during the day and study military tactics by night. Throughout the war he fought alongside his men with honor and by war's end was a general.

Mamie received her education through public schools while Russell graduated from the Pennsylvania Military Academy and continued his education at Lafayette College in Pennsylvania where he studied mining and engineering.

Russell graduated from Lafayette in 1877 and by years end of 1878, with intervention on his father's part who was a senator at the time, secured the position of assayer at the Original Gold Mines of Montana. It was a desirable position many coveted where he would be in charge of the gold in the state of Montana.

In 1848 when gold was discovered in California at Sutter's Mill the following year people worldwide moved to California in hopes of striking it rich, known as the California Gold Rush. Gold was discovered in Montana in 1852 just a few years after the discovery in California, but it would be 1862 before mining of the precious metal began. The office of the assayer in Montana was established in 1874, but it would be 1877 before operations went into effect. This was one of only five U.S. assay offices where gold discovered and recovered was melted into gold bars.

Russell was very fortunate indeed to secure this position. He moved to Montana where he lived and held this position for eight years.

In 1884 Russell married Mary Saunders, daughter of Senator Saunders. His bride's father had been Territorial Governor of Nebraska under President Lincoln and had been senator of Nebraska for six years up until the year before his daughter's marriage.

Russell and Mary had two children William Henry and Marthena. William Henry would serve in WWI and become a Wyoming congressman. Marthena married and had three children.

There was another wedding in the family the same year, that of Mamie to James Robert McKee of Indianapolis. They also had two children, one which during his grandfather's administration became the "most famous baby in the world." Her children were Benjamin Harrison McKee who would later become known as Baby McKee and her daughter Mary Lodge McKee.

Russell and Mamie along with their mother Caroline who was about to become the first lady attended the inauguration held on March 4, 1889. Benjamin Harrison was dubbed the "centennial president," as his inauguration celebrated one hundred years since the first presidential inauguration of George Washington held in 1789.

Benjamin Harrison's two adult children along with their spouses and children would make their home in the White House. Mamie would live there throughout her father's entire administration helping her mother with the role of White House hostess. After the death of her mother she would assume the role for the last five months of her father's presidency.

The first lady, Caroline Harrison, was influential in convincing Congress to allow funds for repairs in the White House. She had new floors installed and added additional bathrooms, but most important of all, electricity was installed. Electricity in homes was a pretty new idea and both the first lady and the president were afraid of being electrocuted so they left the lights burning all night until the building engineer arrived in the morning who then turned the lights off. They enjoyed the invention and the use of lights but weren't willing to risk the danger themselves.

Another endeavor the first lady became involved in became one of the highlights visitors from all over the world enjoy even today when visiting the White House. While going through the presidential mansion during the renovation period she had discovered bits and pieces of dinnerware from past presidential administrations collecting dust in the attic. Some pieces were chipped or broken and the china had all been discarded and kept tucked away for years.

In the past new residents to the White House were allowed to sell off old china from past administrations and use the funds from the sales to purchase new china. The first lady saw the interest and historical value of the dinnerware. The first lady cataloged past administrations' china and they were later displayed in the China Room where tourists enjoy viewing the display when visiting the White House.

This had been a great find for the first lady who painted china herself. She had been taught by a German artist named Paul Putzki while she lived in Indianapolis. She later had Putzki come to Washington to teach anyone who was interested in the art of china painting.

The first lady was honored with being asked to become the president of the Daughters of the American Revolution, a new organization at the time. She was thrilled to accept the position.

When the Harrison family moved into the White House it wasn't just their children and grandchildren who moved in with them. The first lady's father also came to live with them who was almost ninety years of age. Her father had been living with a widowed sister who cared for him so she moved in too, as did the first lady's widowed niece Mary Lord Dimmick. Mary became the first lady's social secretary. Four years after the first lady's death the president would marry the widowed niece causing an irreparable rift between the president and his children.

When Benjamin Harrison was president there was another Benjamin in the house – Mamie's young son who the president nicknamed Baby McKee. The public and the press were captivated with him and his sister Mary Lodge. The press couldn't get enough of him often ignoring news of public policy over stories about the children.

Baby McKee when taken from the White House for a vacation had reporters grumbling that there would be nothing to write about while he was away. A senator griped about all the newspaper coverage Baby McKee received and offered a new hat to any reporter who could make the claim that they had never written about the boy. Not one reporter stepped forward to claim the new hat.

The press wrote about what the public was interested in and they were infatuated with

Baby McKee. When his mother would take him outside on the White House grounds to play she would walk over to the fence for him to greet his adoring fans.

It wasn't just the press and the public who were infatuated with the president's grandson. The president himself loved being around his grandchildren and often left the Oval Office at noon just so he could join them in their play. He would head out to the South Lawn and play with the grandchildren and their pets.

One of the children's favorite pets was a goat by the name of Old Whiskers. They had a cart the children could ride in that the goat would pull around the South Lawn. One day as the president stood outside waiting for his ride he saw Old Whiskers take off running across the lawn pulling Baby McKee in the cart. The goat took off across the lawn and down Pennsylvania Avenue at top speed with the president, who could easily be described as a bit hefty, running after them waving his cane at the goat and yelling at the goat to stop. Dash, one of their dogs, ran alongside the president barking thinking it was a great game.

The president gasping for breath finally caught up with the goat and cart with a delighted Baby McKee who had enjoyed the ride immensely. They headed back to the White House with tourists and residents of Washington who had witnessed the scene amazed they had seen the President of the United States running down the street after a goat. It made for a great tale to tell.

Everything Baby McKee did was of interest to the public, so when he was taken to Barnum's Circus of course the press had to write about it, knowing the country would be just as delighted in the story as little Benjamin had been in seeing the circus.

When Baby McKee celebrated his fourth birthday, it was the president who passed out cake and ice cream to the children. He enjoyed the party as much as the children.

Benjamin Harrison was a doting grandfather and when a foreign visitor came to lunch with the president one day he was a bit miffed to discover that the president's young grandson would be joining them for their luncheon. As the three of them sat around the table with Baby McKee in his high chair by the president's side he decided he wasn't getting enough attention and as youngsters will do began banging quite loudly on the table of his highchair. The president's guest frowned and showed his displeasure in the entire scene but it didn't bother the president at all; but he told the boy to be quiet to appease his guest. He responded to his grandfather's reprimand by not only banging his hands but now kicking his feet making quite a racket.

"See how he obeys me," the president laughed. In his eyes the boy could do no wrong.

While working in the presidential office the president searched around the room for some papers he had laid on his desk, finally giving up and calling in his secretary to aid him in his search. There sat Baby McKee half hidden behind the draperies with missing papers in hand using the papers to stir the contents of the spittoon.

While Baby McKee may have been a favorite of the press and the president, he cared for each and every one of his grandchildren. The president was worried sick when his granddaughter Marthena, his son Russell's daughter, came down with scarlet fever over the Christmas holidays. The entire White House was shut down and under quarantine. Everyone was worried about coming down with the fever and the White House was literally shut down for days.

The president's daughter Mamie began the tradition of the White House Christmas tree. She wanted the children to enjoy the holidays as if they were in their own home and it is a tradition that has remained in the White House. The president dressed up as Santa Claus for the grandchildren and passed out their gifts.

Russell had become his father's White House secretary while he and his family lived at the presidential mansion, but after a time he and his family moved back to Montana and he purchased the *Helena Daily Journal*. Three years later the paper was shut down by the sheriff pending a settlement of debt.

Russell had become a major stockholder owning more than $500,000 worth of stock in the year 1891. People were suspicious as to how he had come to own such a large amount of stock when he wasn't known to be very successful in business. The *New York Times* claimed fraud suggesting perhaps the president's son had exchanged presidential favors for the stocks; but the accusations were dismissed when there was no evidence proven of any wrong doing.

The same year as the stocks scandal Russell became one of the early members of the newly formed Sons of the American Revolution. The members are males whose ancestors served in the American Revolutionary War. The group had only been formed two years previous to his becoming a member. It is quite an honor to be a member and he was certainly eligible as his father's great-grandfather, yet another Benjamin Harrison, was a signer of the Declaration of Independence and a Governor of Virginia and one of George Washington's chief adjutants.

The president along with his son and his wife and the first lady's niece who had served as the first lady's social secretary set out campaigning for a second term. He would not be reelected.

One month before the 1892 presidential election the first lady passed away suffering from tuberculosis.

In 1893 Benjamin Harrison and his brood would pack up and leave the White House while Grover Cleveland was about to return as the only president to have served two nonconsecutive administrations. Harrison moved to Indianapolis and Mamie and her children accompanied him to get him settled in his new home before moving themselves to New York.

After having a large extended family in the White House which included grandchildren to make every day worth getting up for, he now found himself quite alone – *and very lonely.* His wife of forty years had passed away, both his children had moved on with their own lives, and his grandchildren were no longer a part of his daily life.

Mamie's husband, James McKee, had found work with the General Electric Company in New York which is where they made their new home.

Russell moved to Terre Haute, Indiana in 1894 where he was president of the Terre Haute Street Railway Company a street car company. While living in Indiana their son William was born. Russell would remain with the Terre Haute Electric Railway Company up until the time the Spanish-American War began.

The president had picked back up with practicing law, but his house was empty and he didn't like being alone. He had grown close to his wife's widowed niece while she lived at the White House and while she traveled with them to campaign for his reelection. It would have been unsuitable for a single woman to move into a man's home as a housekeeper or ward. She had lost all her family members by the time they left the White House and c'est la vie, the two married. The former president was sixty-two while she was in her late thirties.

Russell and Mamie were shocked, not that their father wanted to remarry but it was who he planned to marry. She was twenty-five years younger than their father and the same age as his daughter Mamie. The former president's children who had been so close to their father refused to attend the wedding. His son and daughter became estranged from their father. Russell and Mamie his children from his first marriage never spoke to their father or saw him again after he remarried.

In 1897 the former president and his second wife Mary had a daughter they named Elizabeth. By now the relationship with his other two children had become irreparable and permanent. He had desperately pleaded with them to accept their stepmother and their new stepsister but they wouldn't budge. His children wanted nothing to do with either one of them.

His new daughter Elizabeth was born four years after he left the office of the presidency. He was sixty-six years old at the time of his daughter's birth. He lived for only four more years. In those short years he would enjoy his young daughter playing with her and taking her on walks. He died from the flu and pneumonia March 13, 1901.

In bed fighting for every breath his four year old daughter came into his room bringing him a gift of a small apple pie she made him. Too weak to speak, he could only smile to let her know he was pleased with her gift. He died just a few hours later.

When it became evident that the former president's illness would be terminal his daughter Mamie was notified and asked to come. Both of Mamie's children were sick with the measles and she chose to remain with them instead of rushing to her dying father's side to make amends. Eventually when she and her husband did arrive at her father's home he had already passed away. Neither Mamie or Russell attended their father's funeral.

The president's youngest daughter Elizabeth received an exceptional education for a young woman of her time. She earned a bachelor's degree in science and law following with a law degree. She then continued her education receiving a degree in liberal arts. She was admitted to the bar in New York and in Indiana. All of these accomplishments were met by the age of twenty-two, a remarkable feat.

In 1921 Elizabeth married James Blaine Walker an investment banker who was the great-nephew of her father's secretary of state. She was active in her community and published an investment paper for women called *Cues On News*. She appeared on radio and television giving women tips for investing. She was named secretary to the Committee for Economic Development which up until she held the position had been held only by men.

Elizabeth and James had two children: yet another Benjamin Harrison and Mary Jane Walker. Their son graduated from Princeton and Harvard and became a pilot during WWII. Their daughter became a doctor in New York and married Newell Garfield who was President Garfield's great-grandson. Elizabeth, the youngest daughter of President Benjamin Harrison passed away at the age of fifty-eight.

When the Spanish American War broke out Russell volunteered and became a major and inspector general of Puerto Rico. Before war's end he was promoted to lieutenant colonel.

After the war Russell would practice law. He and his wife divorced after two children and many years of marriage. He would enter politics in 1921 and served in the Indiana House of Representatives for two two-year terms of office. He would then serve in the Senate for an additional two terms of four years each.

Russell worked with organizing help for war veterans who fought in the Spanish American War.

October 28, 1930 Mamie died of cancer. She died six years previous to her older brother Russell. She was seventy-two years of age at the time of her death. Her husband died in October of 1942, suffering with failing health he committed suicide at the age of eighty-four.

Russell passed away December 13, 1936 of a heart attack.

Baby McKee grew up but little was known of him after leaving the White House between the estrangement of the family and former president; and the fickle public had moved on to the "new star" of the White House, young Ruth Cleveland dubbed Baby Ruth. But that seemed to suit Baby McKee, now Benjamin, just fine.

As his mom told the press, "He thinks he got enough notoriety when a baby to last him for some time."

Baby McKee, no longer a baby and known now as Benjamin, grandson of former President Harrison worked in overseas banks and in the days before the U.S. became involved in WWI he volunteered as an ambulance driver in France and was a member of the French army.

24

GROVER CLEVELAND

Children of Frances and Grover Cleveland:

Ruth Cleveland "Baby Ruth" - Born: Oct. 3, 1891   Died: Jan. 7, 1904

Esther Cleveland - Born: Sept. 9, 1893   Died: June 26, 1980

Marion Cleveland – Born: July 7, 1895   Died: June 18, 1977

Richard Folsom Cleveland – Born: Oct. 28, 1897   Died: Jan. 10, 1974

Francis Grover Cleveland – Born: July 18, 1903;   Died: Nov. 8, 1995

Esther Cleveland was the first and only child of a president to be born in the White House.

When Grover Cleveland was elected president during his first administration he was a forty-seven year old bachelor with a scandalous reputation. His lesbian sister, Rose Cleveland, served as the first lady up until the time he gave up his bachelor days and married.

Jumping back to Cleveland's first administration, he entered the White House as a bachelor and left it as a married man. It was two years into his first administration he married the twenty-one year old beauty Frances Folsom. When his law partner from New York died in an accident Cleveland became her ward and knew her since she was an infant.

Twenty-seven years younger than the groom the bride stole America's hearts. He is not only the first, but the only president to have been married in the White House. While other presidents have married while in office, Cleveland is the only one to have his wedding take place in the White House.

The wedding took place in the Blue Room. Cleveland actually put in a full day's work before taking his wedding vows. The guests arrived: relatives, close friends, and members of the cabinet and their wives. It was an intimate affair with only twenty-eight guests. The president all decked out in a tux gazed adoringly as his young bride in an ivory colored gown as she entered the room with John Philip Sousa leading the U.S. Marine Band.

The press were anxious to write about the historic event of a sitting president marrying. The press however would be disappointed to learn that they were not invited other than to take a quick peek at the floral arrangements previous to the ceremony. A member of the press had gone so far as to try to bribe John Philip Sousa into letting him crash the wedding as a member of the band.

The couple had requested Reverend Sutherland to omit the word 'obey' in the traditional vows of 'love, honor, and obey' and replace 'obey' with 'keep.'

The couple spent their honeymoon at Deer Park, Maryland where they had been followed by the relentless press. As annoying back then as they are today, they attempted to peer into the couple's windows using binoculars and even went into the kitchens to see what the Clevelands were eating. Cleveland fed up with their lack of privacy on their honeymoon commented on the journalists lack of good breeding.

The public remained enthralled with the first lady. The new first lady had become one of the most popular women ever to serve as hostess for the nation. She retained that title after serving as first lady for two administrations.

At the conclusion of Cleveland's first administration the couple moved to New York City. During their time in New York their first child Ruth was born. She arrived on October 3, 1891 between Cleveland's two administrations. Cleveland would be reelected the year after Ruth's birth after a four year reprieve from Washington.

The Clevelands now were returning to the White House just as the first lady had promised the White House staff they would do when they left four years previously. President Cleveland would be the only president in history to serve two non-consecutive terms.

With the Clevelands triumphant return to Washington for his second administration Ruth was a one year old infant with the first lady already expecting their second child.

The public was excited about not only having a young first lady but with having infants in the White House. Maybe a little too excited. At this time the White House grounds were open to the public and while Ruth's nurse had the infant out for fresh air the little girl was grabbed from the nurse's arms and passed around from one woman to another while they all marveled and gazed adoringly at the child; all while the nurse tried to regain possession of the president's daughter. It was fortunate they were an adoring public and not out to do her harm. In another incident someone tried to cut a curl off Ruth's head for a souvenir.

When evidence was given that revealed there was a conspiracy to kidnap the little girl that was when the president and first lady knew something had to be done, adoring public or not. It was their child's safety that was their main concern. Cleveland had the White House grounds closed to the public. The press who once "adored" the little girl were now claiming perhaps the child was deformed and was being hidden away.

A second child Esther was born to the president and first lady. Esther was the first and only child of a president born in the White House. She arrived six months into Cleveland's second administration. Even though she made history by being the first president's child born in the White House, she was overshadowed during her father's presidency by her sister Ruth who would continue to receive the majority of the attention.

With the threat of having their children kidnapped and trying to give them as much of a normal life as possible the Clevelands moved to a home called 'Woodley' two miles outside Washington. Woodley was a home built by the uncle of Francis Scott Key. The home was also used by Presidents Martin Van Buren, John Tyler, and James Buchanan.

The Clevelands main concern was for the safety of their children. They now had three young girls. Their third daughter Marion was born in 1895 at their summer home at Buzzard's Bay in the town of Bourne, Massachusetts.

The Clevelands wanted a summer home where the family could go to relax. Knowing Cleveland loved to spend his time off trout fishing a friend had recommended the area. After viewing the trout-filled ponds in the area, that was incentive enough for Cleveland. This was an area where Cleveland could forget about stress and be himself.

Cleveland was often seen around town in an old beat-up hat and fishing boots. But even here at their summer retreat that privacy was taken from them when several suspicious looking men arrived at the property and refused to leave.

It was one summer while at the vacation home that the president had a secret surgery the public wouldn't learn about until ten years after the fact.

In the summer of 1893, President Grover Cleveland had discovered a lump on the inside of his mouth which was diagnosed to be a cancerous tumor. Unbeknownst to the public, he disappeared for four days to have surgery on a friend's yacht. All involved were sworn to secrecy.

It was the beginning of his second term as president and the country was experiencing a depression. Cleveland feared if the public were aware of his health issues it would only add additional fears to the stability of the nation with a president suffering major medical problems. Cleveland decided to keep the surgery a secret from the public.

He suffered through a ninety minute operation while seated in a chair that was tied to the mast with a team of surgeons performing the surgery aboard a rocking boat out to sea. The tumor and five teeth were removed along with a substantial part of the president's jawbone while he was sedated only with ether. The president would have to wear an artificial jaw for the remainder of his life.

During the Christmas holidays of 1894 the Clevelands decorated the second floor Oval Room with a Christmas tree. President Benjamin Harrison had been the first to decorate the White House with a Christmas tree, but it was the Cleveland's three little girls who were the first White House children to have a tree with electric lights. The tree was lit up with red, white, and blue electric light bulbs. It had only been three years since the White House had electricity installed.

Many children of the presidents were taught at the White House with tutors or as the Cleveland children with a school set up in the family quarters.

Ike Hoover, White House usher who served forty-two years in the White House and had the opportunity to see many presidential families come and go, remembered well the little Cleveland girls. When asked about the girls he said, "None have been so loved and admired by the White House household as these three little Clevelands."

Cleveland in his days before becoming president was the first sheriff of Buffalo, New York who once had the job to hang a man. He continued to make history in his presidential days when he went down in history several times as the first Democrat elected after the Civil War, he was the only president to have served two nonconsecutive terms, he was the only president to have married in the White House, and his daughter Esther is the first child of a president to have been born in the White House.

He had two children born during his administration: Esther who was born in the White House and daughter Marion who was born during his presidency but at their summer home. The only other sitting president to have a child born during his administration was President Kennedy. Kennedy's third child Patrick born during his administration survived only for a few days.

At the end of his second administration the Cleveland family retired to Princeton, New Jersey. The former president and first lady would have two more children, two boys Richard and Francis. The same year they left the White House their first son Richard, known as Dick, was born October 28, 1897.

In 1903 the couples second son and last child Francis was born. His father was sixty-six years old at the time of his birth. A year after his birth his sister Ruth would be dead and he was only five years old when his father died.

Ruth had never been a strong, healthy child and had health problems throughout her young life. In 1904 she contracted diphtheria. The disease weakened her heart and in only a matter of days she passed away.

An excerpt from Cleveland's diary tells how the family was banned from her room and the household was under quarantine.

Excerpts from Cleveland's 1904 diary read as follows:

January 6th: Dr. Carnochan came at 2:30 and Dr. Wykoff at 3:30. We had been excluded from Ruth's room, but learned that dear Ruth died before Dr. Wykoff came, probably about 3:00 A.M., Jan. 7th.

January 8th: (In a trembling, almost illegible hand) We buried our daughter, Ruth, this morning.

Her death was a shock not only to the family, but to the nation who even after she left the White House still adored the little girl.

It was only four years later that Grover Cleveland himself passed away from a heart attack leaving his young widow behind with four young children. The former first lady was only one of two former first ladies who remarried after their presidential husband's deaths: Frances Cleveland and Jackie Kennedy.

In 1918 Esther married Sir William Bosanquet in a Westminster Abbey ceremony. William Bosanquet was a captain of the British Army and the son of Sir Albert Bosanquet. Captain Bosanquet, fifteen years older than Esther died in March of 1966. After her husband's death Esther moved back to the U.S. with her two children.

In 1962, when Esther at sixty-nine years of age was interviewed about her days in the White House she said she remembered a few things. She had left Washington at the age of four but still had a few vivid memories. Her most vivid memory was when her father let her dip her fingers in his inkwell and make blobs on his papers. She also remembered holidays with the Easter eggs on the South Lawn and Christmas.

Esther lived to the age of eighty-six.

There is a story that has been told to which people still believe to be true today; and that is that the Baby Ruth candy bar was named after Ruth Cleveland. That may or may not be the case; it is what the Curtiss Candy Company insisted on when taken to court by Babe Ruth the baseball player for infringing on his name.

It was in the early 1920's when the candy bar the Baby Ruth first came out. That was seventeen years after the death of little Ruth Cleveland and over two decades after President Cleveland left office. What seems more believable is Babe Ruth, a famous baseball player, was having a tremendous year having hit fifty-four home runs.

Which sounds more logical to you: a candy bar was named after a twelve year old child of a former president that had been dead for longer than she lived or that it was named after one of the most famous baseball players ever to live that was having an outstanding season that had a huge fan base?

If the candy bar company admitted that the candy bar was named after the baseball star they would have had to pay him for the use of his name which would have taken a huge bite out of their profits. So, the question remains as to who it was named after; but whoever it was, you can still find the candy bar on the store shelves today.

Marion, the youngest daughter of the former president and first lady graduated from Westover School and also attended Columbia University Teacher's College. She was married twice; first to William Stanley Dell for eight years and after he died she later married John Harlan Amen. John Amen was a special assistant to the U.S. attorney. After WWII he served on the U.S. legal staff in Germany at the Nuremberg war crimes trials.

Marion very young when she left the White House at the end of her father's administration was excited when First Lady Hoover invited her to the White House for a visit. Being as young as she was when she had lived at the presidential mansion she wasn't surprised when she had no memories as she was shown around. Before leaving she was taken to the second floor where the family quarters are and she noticed a strong musty smell of roses. She didn't think too much about it at the time but later asked her mother if there was anything unusual about the smell where the first families lived. Her mother replied that it smelled of an old house by the ocean with a musty smell of roses.

The two boys born after the family left Washington, Richard or Dick as he was called, the oldest son attended Exeter an excellent preparatory school that was established in the late 1700's where a president and presidential children were listed among the alumni; such as: Franklin Pierce, Robert Lincoln, Ulysses S. "Buck" Grant, Jr., and Richard and Francis Cleveland both attended, along with other very well-known names.

After graduating at Exeter Dick would study at Princeton University where he was a well-liked student who was involved in sports. He left Princeton when the U.S. entered WWI. He joined the Marines and became a first lieutenant. At the end of the war he finished his education earning a bachelor's and a master's degree. He would continue his education at Harvard earning a law degree.

He married Ellen Gailor who he met while on a holiday in Europe.

Francis, the youngest child of the Clevelands, was only five years old when his father passed away. He also attended Exeter Preparatory School and Harvard earning a degree in drama.

He taught school for a short time but his calling was the stage. He had a few roles on Broadway and he, his wife Alice Erdman, and Edward Goodnow a director, founded the Barnstormers which was an acting company. Francis became not only an actor but a producer and director as well.

His father had been a Democrat president, but Francis was a Republican.

Francis and his wife were married for sixty-seven years until her death. He lived to be ninety-two.

25

William McKinley

Children of Ida and William McKinley:

Katherine McKinley "Katie" - Born: Jan. 25, 1871   Died: July 25, 1875

Ida McKinley – Born: March 31, 1873   Died: August 22, 1873

The likeness of their dead daughter was used on campaign buttons and banners leaving people to think their daughter was among the living.

The sounds of children's voices were not to be heard in the halls of the White House during the McKinley administration. No children lived in the White House during this time; however if you were to peek inside the family quarters at one of the bedrooms you would be quite confused with good reason when you saw a little girl's clothes laid out and to hear the first lady speak of her child named Katie as though she were expecting her any minute.

Katherine called Katie was born on Christmas day of 1871, the first year of William and Ida McKinley's marriage. Ida who was very close to her mother named her firstborn after her mother.

Katie was a beautiful little girl who was very much loved.

When Katie was two years old they were expecting their second child. Just a few weeks before the birth of her second child her mother passed away. Believed to be when she was attending her mother's funeral, Ida fell and suffered a concussion and spinal injury which brought on neurological problems.

Ida had previously been quite healthy hiking up to ten miles a day. The fall brought on epilepsy which she would suffer the rest of her life as there was no cure or treatment for it during this time. At twenty-six years of age, a woman who had been in very good physical condition was now an invalid.

Two weeks later her second daughter was born after suffering a difficult birth. The baby was never in good health and died only four months later of cholera. The little girl had been named Ida after her mother.

Ida in poor health suffering from seizures remained most of her time in bed. While his invalid wife was laid up McKinley took over the care of his daughter Katie.

Katie was an adorable child who made friends easily and was a pleasant child who got on well with others. She had blue eyes and blonde hair that hung in long curls.

Ida was suffering not only physically but had become mentally disturbed after suffering the loss of her mother and then the death of her child months later. She became jealous and unreasonable whenever her husband or child showed affection to each other; she wanted them only to show affection to her.

Katie, only a year and ten months after her baby sister died, contracted typhoid fever and died. Katie was only three and a half years old at the time of her death. Some sources say Katie died of scarlet fever while others say typhoid.

After losing her mother who she had been very close to and both her daughters in less than three years time her health declined. She would spend the remainder of her life as an invalid.

Two years later William McKinley became the nation's 25th president. Likenesses of his daughter Katie had been used on campaign buttons and banners and some people were under the impression their daughter was among the living. The president and first lady spoke of their daughter as if she was alive.

The first lady would lay out Katie's clothes across her little chair and displayed a portrait of her. When speaking of her she would speak of her as the age she would have been if she remained alive.

The same obsession didn't apply to baby Ida who had still been a young infant at the time of her death. She was described by those close to the McKinleys as one who "came to earth for only a little while." Frail from the beginning, her death didn't seem to come as a surprise to others.

The president would attend the Pan-American Exposition and become the third president to be assassinated. While standing in a receiving line at the exposition a man later identified as Leon Czolgosz approached with a pistol wrapped in a handkerchief and fired twice at point blank range. The president survived for eight days and then died of infection and gangrene. His last words were, "It is God's way, His will, not ours, be done."

His assassin was executed in the electric chair.

Vice President Theodore Roosevelt after the death of President McKinley was sworn in as the 26th president.

26

Theodore Roosevelt

Children of first wife Alice and Theodore Roosevelt:

Alice Lee Roosevelt "Princess Alice" - Born: Feb. 12, 1884   Died: Feb. 20, 1980

Children of second wife Edith and Theodore Roosevelt:

Theodore Roosevelt, III "Ted" - Born: Sept. 13, 1887   Died: July 12, 1944

Kermit Roosevelt – Born: Oct. 10, 1889   Died: June 4, 1943

Ethel Carow Roosevelt – Born: Aug. 13, 1891   Died: Dec. 10, 1977

Archibald Bulloch Roosevelt "Archie" - Born: April 9, 1894   Died: Oct. 13, 1979

Quentin Roosevelt – Born: Nov. 19, 1897   Died: July 14, 1918

General Omar Bradley called Ted, Jr's fighting and leadership during D-Day "the single bravest act" he witnessed during the entire war.

In 1901 President McKinley had been shot and lingered for eight days before succumbing to the fate dealt him by an assassin's bullet. Once he passed away vice president Theodore

Roosevelt became the 26th president.

After the childless White House of President McKinley the transition in the White House changed dramatically with the arrival of President Theodore Roosevelt, the first lady, and their six active children. Alice his only child by his first wife was seventeen; Theodore, Jr. at fourteen years of age; Kermit twelve; Ethel was ten; Archie seven; and Quentin was three years of age.

The Roosevelt's brood of children attended public and private schools with the exception of Alice who refused to attend school of any kind. She instead would receive tutoring off and on. That fact alone, that she dictated that she would not attend school and got away with it should have been an eye opener to the nation of the type personality of Alice Roosevelt.

Alice was the president's only child from his first marriage with Alice Lee Hathaway who he had married after leaving college. Edith Kermit Carow who would become his second wife had been his girlfriend before going away to college and had been a guest at his first wedding. A few years after the death of his first wife he returned to his first girlfriend and made her his wife.

Roosevelt's first wife passed away two days after the birth of Alice from Bright's disease or kidney failure. Roosevelt's mother died of typhoid fever on the same day as his wife in the same house. Roosevelt found someone to care for his newborn daughter and left for the next two years living in the Dakota Territory spending his time on his ranch driving cattle and hunting.

Theodore never spoke of his wife again; not even to his daughter – *ever*. Theodore had left his newborn daughter with his sister to be raised. Alice spent summers with her maternal relatives the Lees; but it was Auntie Bye who raised Alice the first three years of her life.

After his second marriage, his wife Edith had Alice brought to their home to become a part of their family. Alice would say later in life that she never really felt like she belonged.

As a youngster Alice suffered from a mild form of polio. The muscles in one leg were growing shorter than the other leg and Edith, her stepmother, administered nightly massages and physical therapy by stretching her legs to spare her from disfigurement or other after effects of the disease.

The Roosevelts all had an assortment of pets. Alice had a macaw she named Eli Yale but her most well-known pet was a green garter snake named Emily Spinach that would attend receptions and events with Alice. She would bring the snake in her purse to events and then remove the snake to surprise and scare visitors and guests. Other times she would wear the snake draped around her neck.

Alice is one of the most popular and well-known of all presidential children. Willful and flagrant she was nicknamed 'Princess Alice' by the press; and the nation absolutely adored her, keeping track of her every move wondering what she would do next. She never left them wondering for long.

Alice was always the center of attention and that's the way she liked it. She was the belle of every ball dancing until all hours flirting with all the men. She had a song written about her and a color named after her.

From her maternal relatives the Lees she received an inheritance of $2,000 a year; an amount average Americans couldn't match with their annual salaries at the time.

She indulged and bought herself an expensive red touring car that cost more than what she received from her annual inheritance.

Alice was the first American young lady to smoke out in public; something proper young ladies would never do. When lighting up in front of her father he bellowed, "You shall not smoke under my roof." No problem; she went to the White House roof and smoked.

Instead of being outraged the women and young girls of America loved and enjoyed reading about every escapade of the president's daughter. They wanted to know everything; what she wore, how she styled her hair, who her friends and dates were, what outrageous thing she would do next to make it in the newspapers. In an era when women were expected to know 'their place' and be prim and proper she was anything but; and the country was enthralled with her.

When someone asked President Roosevelt if he couldn't do something about his daughter, he replied, "I can either run the country or attend to Alice, but I cannot possibly do both." Some would say that her behavior was a cry for attention from her father.

When the family was vacationing at their home Sagamore Hill, the Secret Service reported to the president that a man had approached the gate demanding entrance stating he had arrived to marry the president's daughter Alice. The Secret Service unarmed the man as he had been carrying a pistol. They assured the president he was not a threat, but deranged. The president replied, "Of course he's insane, he wants to marry Alice."

In 1905, President Roosevelt was deep in the midst of mediating peace between Russia and Japan for which he would win the Nobel Peace Prize. The president was sending an eighty-three member diplomatic delegation which included seven senators, over twenty congressmen, the secretary of war who would also become a future president Taft; but his real brainstorm came when he decided to include his twenty-one year old daughter Alice as a goodwill ambassador. She would be the *first* First Daughter to serve in this role.

The group sailed out of San Francisco headed to their first stop in Hawaii. Alice being who she is felt it her obligation to keep those on the ship entertained. Shocking everyone on board she jumped into a pool on the ship fully clothed.

Arriving in Hawaii she learned the hula but complained she about suffocated wearing layer upon layer of leis her guests had put around her neck.

The group was welcomed upon arrival in Japan to fireworks and parades. The Japanese treated Alice as a royal as they looked upon her as the Princess Royal of America. The other representatives along on the trip observed how Alice was greeted by all those she met at every stop with awe. The president had been very wise in including her on the trip.

Alice was being entertained with geisha dancing and sumo wrestlers, which didn't impress Alice. She described them as "huge, fat...men as big as Secretary Taft himself." The 'huge, fat Taft' was having secret meetings with the Prime Minister Katsura while the rest of the delegation were being entertained and taken to see shrines and the Cherry Blossom Festival.

Alice was given lavish gifts at every stop and taken to meet the mikado. The emperor never before having shared his private garden with a foreigner honored the president's daughter with a tour.

In Manila she was entertained when Taft himself got up and joined in a traditional dance called the rigadon which he had learned when he was governor general of the Philippines.

The journey lasted four months and it was on the voyage that she began spending time with Nicholas Longworth III a congressman from Ohio. But there was plenty to keep her occupied and entertained during the voyage.

At one of the islands she met the Sultan of Sulu who gave her a ring with a huge pearl and asked her to join his harem. In China she met the Empress Dowager Tz'u Hsi (Cixi), at the summer palace. In Korea she met the emperor and crown prince. She was worn out by all the pomp and circumstance and was ready to return home after such a long journey that was filled with entertainment day and night. The trip had been a huge success giving both Alice and world leaders of the Far East some memories they would not soon forget. The world leaders had been honored that the president's daughter had come to visit their country.

Returning home to Washington Alice began seeing Congressman Nicholas Longworth on a serious basis. While her father may have been relieved to think he could soon turn his unpredictable daughter over to some other man to deal with, her stepmother warned Alice that the congressman had flaws that would surely cause her some misery if she were to marry him. He was much older than Alice (he was thirty-six to her twenty-two), he drank too much, gambled, and had a reputation as a lady's man. But when Alice set her mind to something there was no dissuading her.

The wedding date was set for February 17, 1906. She was about to become the fourth president's daughter to be married at the White House.

Before the wedding gifts arrived from all over the world for the bride. The President of France sent a priceless Gobelin tapestry. The Vatican sent a mosaic. She received exquisite and priceless gifts from the mikado of Japan, the King of Spain, the German kaiser, and the empress dowager of China. Her favorite gift was from Cuba. They had great respect for her father who had a hand in their liberation from Spain and in appreciation sent her an exquisite string of pearls with a diamond clasp. She wore the necklace not only on her wedding day but would wear them for the rest of her life. The pearl necklace is worth half a million dollars today.

The American public also remembered the president's daughter and sent her more practical gifts. She received a wide assortment of gifts including: turnips, apples, a feather duster, and the United Mine Workers sent a train car load of coal for the bridal couple. Most of the gifts Alice never even saw and there were gifts found after her death that were still unopened.

The groom himself overlooked up to now received an unusual gift that arrived with a group of ten Ponca Indians painted and dressed in beaded buckskin clothing. They arrived at the Capital to deliver to the groom a buffalo skin vest. Disappointed not to find the groom in the Capitol they continued down Pennsylvania Avenue arriving at the White House where Eagle Horse the chief delivered the gift to the president for his future son-in-law explaining to the president, "Can a man be boss of his own wigwam if it is so that all the ponies, the beads, the buffalo hides, belong to his wife?"

The Roosevelt-Longworth wedding was the social event of the season. The day of the wedding thousands of people crowded outside the gates of the White House hoping to catch a glimpse of the bride. Amongst the crowd were people selling souvenirs depicting the bride and groom. Alice peeking out the window of her bedroom at the souvenir hawkers and the crowd was delighted all this attention was about her.

Alice wore a gown of white satin with an eighteen foot long train of silver brocade. She carried a bouquet of white orchids and wore the pearl necklace that had been a gift from the Cuban government. She also wore a diamond brooch which was a gift from her parents, a diamond and pearl necklace that was a wedding gift from the groom, and diamond bracelets that were gifts from the German kaiser. Alice was never one to be subtle, and certainly not on her wedding day.

After vows were exchanged the most memorable moment for most of the guests was when Alice brandished a sword belonging to White House aide Major McCauley and cut her wedding cake with the sword to the gasps and astonishment of her guests.

As Alice prepared to leave for her honeymoon while saying good-bye to her family her stepmother hugged her and whispered in her ear, "I want you to know I am glad to see you leave. You have never been anything but trouble." Trouble or not, it seemed a very cruel send off to someone she had raised for the last nineteen years – and on her wedding day, no less.

Congressman Longworth's career certainly didn't suffer by being married to the president's daughter. He went on to become Speaker of the House becoming one of Washington's most powerful men. While he profited from being married to Alice, the marriage itself was a sham. He was an alcoholic and a womanizer. The marriage wasn't a happy one, but Alice never considered divorce.

October 14, 1912 Theodore Roosevelt was shot as he exited his hotel to deliver a campaign speech while campaigning for an unprecedented third term in the White House. In the breast pocket of his coat he had folded in half a fifty page speech so it would fit in his pocket along with a metal spectacles case. He was shot at close range and his notes for his speech and metal glasses case is most likely what saved his life. He insisted on going on and delivering his speech before going to the hospital.

He stood before the crowd to deliver his speech. The crowd was speechless when Roosevelt announced that he had just been shot and unbuttoned his vest to reveal his bloody shirt. He held up his notes for his speech so they could see the bullet holes that had gone completely through each of the pages. "The bullet is in me now, so that I cannot make a very long speech, but I will try my best," he said. You had to admire him for pressing on, foolhardy that it was.

Nick throughout their married life had made no effort in concealing his mistresses or the fact that he was an unfaithful husband, but when Alice took up with Senator Bill Borah she did keep their affair quiet. They had an affair that lasted for years and at the age of forty-one she discovered she was pregnant. It is believed that her husband was sterile as in all his years of running around with numerous women he had no children; legitimate or illegitimate. One has to wonder how she explained her condition to her husband or if she even bothered. If there was ever any doubt as to the paternity of the child's father Alice's diaries did reveal that Senator Borah was indeed the father of her daughter Paulina.

It would have been unusual if Alice wasn't a bit fearful about giving birth. Not only the fact that she was an older first time mother but her own mother had died after giving birth to her. The baby arrived on the very day that her mother and grandmother had passed away, February 14th. In this case both mother and daughter were healthy.

During the Great Depression in 1933, Alice found herself in a bit of a financial bind as many Americans did. To help her financial situation she published an autobiography, *'Crowded Hours: Reminiscences of Alice Roosevelt Longworth.'* With such a popular subject as Alice was the book sold well.

When Nick lost his position as Speaker of the House he was depressed and at loose ends. Suffering from a cold that he couldn't seem to rid himself of he decided to get away and visit the home of his mistress. His body was weak from abuse over the years with his heavy drinking and his cold developed into pneumonia. It soon became obvious to those caring for him that Nick would not survive and in a short time he passed away.

Alice's daughter was only six years old when the man she thought was her father passed away. Nick had adored the little girl and they had been very close regardless of not being father and daughter. The following year when she was seven there was a kidnapping scare. This followed on the heels of the kidnapping of the Lindbergh baby so was taken very seriously; many children of high profile parents were being threatened. Alice had received letters demanding a ransom with instructions of where she was to deliver money if she wanted to keep her daughter safe. Guards were hired to protect their home and her daughter. Over time the threat just seemed to die out with no answers ever received or uncovered as to who was behind the threats.

Alice was not a very good mother, perhaps due to being so self-absorbed she had no time or emotional support to offer her daughter. At nineteen years of age Paulina announced to her mother that she was going to marry Alexander Strum. Alice didn't approve of him seeing in him what she had suffered with her own husband; an abuse of alcohol.

Paulina like her mother was headstrong and married him anyway. At her wedding she wore her mother's pearl necklace she had received from Cuba as a wedding gift. She also wore another item that belonged to her mother; a lace veil that had been a gift from the royal family the Romanovs.

Alice having suffered her step-mother's cruel words at her own wedding Alice repeated history; and on the night before her daughter's wedding she told Paulina that her father that she loved so much wasn't her real father - *and left it at that*. It was a cruel thing to say and do, especially with the timing being the night before her wedding.

History repeated itself yet again when Paulina gave birth to a daughter, but would leave the baby to partake in drinking sprees and parties and being a negligent mother. The baby Joanna had an unhappy childhood.

Alice and her daughter had become estranged, but when Paulina's husband died at the age of twenty-eight from cirrhosis of the liver she and five year old Joanna returned to Washington to live. Paulina turned to alcohol and prescription pain killers and died of an overdose at the age of thirty-one; just five years after her husband's death. Whether the death was a purposeful suicide or not remains unknown.

Alice by then was in her seventies and had just endured a mastectomy but didn't hesitate to take in her granddaughter to raise. She would later undergo a second mastectomy. Never having lost her sense of humor she reported that she was the "only topless octogenarian in Georgetown Hospital."

She had a close relationship with her granddaughter that she never had with her own daughter or anyone else for that matter, except maybe with Auntie Bye who had raised her as a youngster. Their relationship would remain close for the rest of her life; perhaps passing on some of that biting sarcasm she was so well-known for.

Politics was in her blood and was a huge part of her life. She remained a well-known figure throughout Washington society. Some described her as witty, while others thought she was sometimes cruel in what she said about and to people. There definitely was a bite to her tongue; political correctness is not something she ever concerned herself with and that in itself is refreshing – and honest; which you don't find a lot of in Washington.

In her lifetime presidents came and went; she was around from the days of Benjamin Harrison to Jimmy Carter. She let anyone who asked know exactly how she felt about each and every one of them. Some of them invited her to the White House while others banned her from her former home. She was banned by the Tafts, Woodrow Wilson after telling a joke at his expense, and later even by her cousins a few times removed the other Roosevelts.

She got along well with some of the first ladies. Harding who also put up with an unfaithful husband she got along with though she didn't like her husband and Grace Coolidge was a favorite resident of the White House of hers. They both enjoyed attending Senate meetings but again she thought Calvin was bad mannered; but what would she know about that? She didn't vote for the 'other Roosevelt' and was well received by Lyndon and Lady Bird Johnson. He said about Alice that she was "the closest thing we have to royalty." That may have influenced her thinking about Johnson.

She had been around the world and met many people in her lifetime: kings and queens, presidents and first ladies, dowager empresses, prince and princesses, senators and their wives; but in her old age she most enjoyed the company of her granddaughter.

Alice Roosevelt lived to the age of ninety-six; the oldest presidential child to date. She died in 1980 of pneumonia at her home. Many First Families have come and gone, but none so well remembered as 'Princess Alice.'

Theodore Jr., or Teddy, was the second child of Theodore Roosevelt and first son and first child with his second wife Edith. Being a firstborn and bearing his father's name much was expected of him and he didn't disappoint.

When their father had to be away from his family he would write to his children. Young Ted received letters before he could even read so his father would draw pictures in the letter for him. Theodore Roosevelt's most admirable trait was his devotion to his family. Even when separated they were never far from his thoughts.

As a youngster Ted was a daredevil to the point where his father, no stranger to rowdy behavior, wondered if his son would survive his childhood. After listening to some of Ted memories of his childhood his father seemed to encourage his vigorous behavior. When he was about nine years old his father gave him a rifle. Ted looked it over and asked his father if it was real. His father then loaded the gun and shot a bullet into the ceiling. The bullet hole in the ceiling was supposed to be kept a secret from Ted's mom, though it's doubtful she would have missed seeing a hole in the ceiling.

In Roosevelt's pre-presidential days when he worked as a civil service commissioner in Washington his son Ted fondly remembered that he often escorted his father to the office. On the walk his father would talk to him about history. He made it vivid in his son's mind by having his son imagine himself in the role of the historical character he was telling him about. This ensured his son would recall these historical events. When they talked about different battles his father would stop and using the tip of his umbrella would draw the battle plans in the dirt. He instilled in all his sons the necessity for every man to do his part when it came to fighting for their country.

When a guest at dinner asked the typical question of what Ted wanted to be when he grew up, his father swelled with pride when Ted answered that he wanted to be a soldier like his father.

Ted was fourteen when his father became president. Even when he was the president Roosevelt would take time to lead his children on long hikes. If something was in the way they had to climb over it and keep on going as though they were on an obstacle course. He was physically active and so were his children. Perhaps part of the reason President Roosevelt pushed himself so vigorously was he was a very sickly child that his parents doubted would live to see his fourth birthday. He had asthma so bad that many times he didn't have the strength to blow out a candle. As a very young child his father paced the halls holding him in his arms, his father felt he was holding a dying child. You would never know it by seeing Roosevelt as a vigorous adult with no obstacle too strenuous.

Theodore Jr. wise beyond his years said, "Don't you think it handicaps a boy to be the son of a man like my father, and especially to have the same name? I will always be known as the son of Theodore Roosevelt and never as only myself."

The two oldest Roosevelt boys, Ted and Kermit, went to Groton a boarding school in Massachusetts. After graduating from Groton Ted wrote and told his father he was considering going to West Point. He was interested in a military career. His father's dream had been that his son would follow in his footsteps and attend Harvard as he himself had done. He wrote saying as much to his son. Ted went to Harvard.

In 1908, the popular Theodore Roosevelt decided not to run for reelection. After Taft's inauguration in 1909, Roosevelt and his son Kermit left for Africa to hunt big game and to collect specimens to exhibit at the Smithsonian Institution. The hunt lasted a year, but before heading home he left for Norway to accept the Nobel Peace Prize he had been awarded for his invaluable aid in the ending of the Russo-Japanese War.

While his father was on the safari Ted had met the woman of his dreams. They waited to get married until after his father returned. Two days after his father arrived back in the U.S. on June 20, 1910, Ted and Eleanor Butler Alexander married. In their thirty-four years of marriage they would have four children.

Ted was successful in his business adventures previous to WWI making himself a substantial fortune. When war broke out in 1914 is when he found his true calling. As WWI broke out the Roosevelt boys all sought to position themselves to the front lines. Ted ended up on the front lines as a major.

Ted suffered much during the war. Chemical weapons were first used in WWI and Ted a victim of the poisonous gas was blinded by it for days. The gas attacks also damaged his lungs. Ted's leg was damaged by machine gun fire and he found himself in the same

Parisian hospital as his brother Archie. Archie's wife Eleanor was working with the YMCA so she could be close to her husband. She was there to care for him while he was recovering.

He didn't remain laid up any longer than he had to and was soon back at the front. He was now lieutenant colonel and awarded the Silver Star and the Croix de Guerre by the French. His name had been put forward for a promotion and for the French Legion of Honor. It was refused due to the fear that people would think he was merely being promoted due to who his father was; regardless of how well deserved.

Returning to the U.S. after WWI Ted worked relentlessly to assure there would be help for orphans and widows of soldiers. He was largely responsible for the founding of the American Legion.

Ted along with his brother Kermit went on an expedition to hunt for big game on a hunting trip to Asia on behalf of the Chicago Field Museum. The two brothers became the first men from the West to confirm the existence of the giant panda. Up until their discovery most in the zoological world were skeptical that it actually existed. It was a major discovery on their part.

President Warren Harding appointed Ted as Assistant Secretary of the Navy in 1921, and his brother Archie was vice president of the Union Petroleum Company. During his tenure the scandal of the Teapot Dome Scandal occurred. Both brothers were eventually cleared of all charges of any wrongdoing on their part but in the meantime their reputations were damaged.

Ted threw his hat in the political ring and ran for the Republican nominee for governor of New York with aspirations to one day run for president. His cousin Franklin Roosevelt spoke against Ted because of the scandal. Eleanor Roosevelt went even further in her attempts to thwart his political aspirations by following him on his campaign trail in a car fitted with a giant teapot on the roof of the car reminding voters that he had been involved in the Teapot Dome Scandal. He never forgave her for this stunt and it destroyed any possibility he had towards a political career. The fact that he was innocent of any wrongdoing made it all the harder to bear.

He was appointed governor of Puerto Rico by President Coolidge but when his cousin Franklin Roosevelt was elected president he knew his days of presidential appointments had come to an end.

He co-authored a few books, one with his brother Kermit *'East of the Sun and West of the Moon.'*

Ted served during WWII serving as a brigadier general. Initially he was stationed in England but when he learned of the attack that was to take place on Utah Beach he put in a request to lead the assault. His request was denied more than once by Major General Barton who told him there would be no generals taking part in the assault. Ted continued his fight to be a part of the invasion stating that to have a general land in the first wave of attacks at Normandy would boost morale for the men who would most certainly be on a suicide mission. Eventually Major General Barton relented and agreed but only after making it very clear that his chances of survival were practically nonexistent.

It wasn't just the fact that Ted was a general or the son of a president as he had proved himself already on that point. He was not one to use his father's name to assure himself an easy out, but he led his men rather than followed. He was fifty-six years of age and suffering from battle wounds from the last world war and couldn't walk without the aid of a walking stick.

Ted was the only general that stepped foot on that beach with the first wave of troops on D-Day armed with a walking stick and a pistol. In hand to hand combat on that beach he shot and killed a German with that pistol but if he had run out of bullets he probably would have beat him with his walking stick. He stood on the beach with bullets flying over his head and all around him directing the troops to their positions. He was a courageous and inspirational leader for the troops that followed him onto that beach.

Another Roosevelt was on that same beach that day, his own son Quentin Roosevelt II, named after his late brother who had been a fighter pilot and lost his life in WWI. They were the only father and son to fight on D-Day.

The Utah Beach assault was the greatest invasion in history. Once Utah Beach was secured from the enemy General Barton came ashore and was not only amazed but delighted to see that General Theodore Roosevelt, Jr. was alive. He never believed that he would have survived.

General Omar Bradley described the actions of Roosevelt as the "single greatest act of courage" he witnessed in the entire war. General Patton too wrote in his diary that Ted was "one of the bravest men I've ever known."

I don't believe at this point that anyone would agree with what Ted had said as a young adult about "always being known as the son of Theodore Roosevelt and never as myself." He more than proved himself that he certainly stood on his own two feet and made his own place in history.

Ted had proven himself in both world wars. He was awarded every award available to ground forces; including the Medal of Honor which was awarded posthumously.

A few weeks after Normandy Ted confessed to his son that he had been experiencing heart attacks.

His son convinced his father to seek medical treatment. His father agreed but a few hours later on July 12th, 1944, Ted died of a heart attack just five weeks after D-Day. He was buried in Normandy next to his brother Quentin Roosevelt who was killed in the first World War.

Six generals were honored to serve as pallbearers at the funeral of Ted Roosevelt, Jr. Included in the group of generals who served as pallbearers were George Patton and Omar Bradley.

President Franklin Roosevelt presented the Medal of Honor posthumously to Ted's widow. As FDR gave the medal to Eleanor, Ted's widow, the president said, "His father would have been proudest."

Theodore Roosevelt, Jr. is one of the most honorable of presidential sons.

Kermit, second son and second child of Theodore with second wife Edith, was twelve years old when his father became president and they moved into the Executive Mansion. It was his father who officially had the name changed to the White House in 1901. Previous to having the name changed it was called, "President's Palace," the "President's House," and the "Executive Mansion."

Kermit and his brothers and sisters had a great time discovering every inch of the White House. They were a rambunctious lot and could be found swimming in the fountains on the White House lawn, climbing flagpoles, and having a great time discovering all the rooms in the mansion.

The White House not only had the unruly bunch of kids to deal with, but they had pets...*lots of pets.* Kermit had a pet kangaroo rat that was brought to the table to dine with the family. Kermit would set it on the table and it would hop across the table to the president who rewarded it with a lump of sugar.

It was refreshing with all the new life the Roosevelt children brought to the house but they certainly kept the staff on their toes. Kermit and the other Roosevelt children would borrow large trays from the kitchen and use them to slide down the stairs using them as sleds. By the time they returned the trays they were dented and a little worse for wear.

Kermit attended Groton Preparatory School and from there would go on to Harvard.

During the early 1900's Theodore Roosevelt was busy with one of the greatest engineering feats in history, the Panama Canal. President Roosevelt was quoted as saying, "I took Panama and let Congress debate that, while I went ahead and built the canal." It was a marvelous endeavor; over two hundred cubic yards of earth had to be moved.

Typical of Roosevelt he had to get right in the middle of things. He was not one to watch from the sidelines or learn what was going on by reports read while sitting behind a desk. He consulted with everyone involved and went to see it for himself, becoming the first president to travel outside the U.S. while a sitting president. He considered the Panama Canal to be the most historic accomplishment of his presidency, and he had to be involved of every aspect. It was just his way.

1906 was an election year, but at this time in history presidents didn't campaign. It was difficult for him to sit back and not have a hand in things. He wrote to Kermit who was away at school of his fears of not being reelected. His fears were all for not, as he won by the largest vote any candidate had won up to that time in history.

When his father's administration came to an end Kermit was attending Harvard. His father not used to being idle and wanting to remove himself from the limelight had planned a year long hunting trip to Africa that was to be part of a scientific exploration for the Smithsonian Institute. In his freshman year he left college to accompany his father on the safari. His plan was to go on the safari for a year and then return to Harvard.

It would be a memorable trip for father and son. They would have to have a whole crew come along just to carry the supplies. Roosevelt brought along approximately two-hundred crates of food, bedding and tents, arms and ammunition, four tons of salt to preserve skins, books to read, and an enormous American flag he would fly at their camps.

Some of the animals they hunted and shot were elephants, water buffalo, lions, zebras, and rhinoceroses.

After their return Kermit returned to Harvard and finished his education. He finished his four years of study in two and a half years graduating from Harvard in 1912.

The year after his college graduation he would be exploring another continent with his father. They were going to explore the Amazon. His father had learned of an unmapped river and father and son joined an expedition with the purpose of charting the river's course. Kermit and his father collected animal and plant specimens along the journey.

The fifty-five year old former president and his college age son Kermit would go on the adventure of their life. Sometimes adventures don't exactly turn out the way originally planned and that's what happened in this case. They had no idea what they were about to endure. Their supplies were insufficient for the journey, there were two deaths that would occur during the expedition, and the former president and son both came pretty close to losing their own lives along the way.

Their purpose was to chart a river that nobody up to this time knew where it went. This was a challenge to the former president. The river was treacherous with rapids that took a brave soul to face and not turn back. They traversed the river in dugout canoes sometimes taking as long as six days just to travel carrying their canoes and supplies by land around a rapid. They had to do this numerous times. Not only physically challenging, but they also had to endure insects that bit, malaria, torrential rains, and overgrown jungles.

It was a challenge even for the fittest of man. One man drowned along the way and another lost his mind and murdered one of the men in the expedition escaping into the jungle to who knows what end. The former president realizing there was a chance they may not get out alive from the excursion said, "I have already lived and enjoyed as much of life as any other nine men I know, and if I must leave my bones in South America I am quite ready to do so."

Things went from bad to worst when two of their canoes capsized and when Roosevelt rushed into the water to try to save one of the canoes and their already inadequate amount of supplies they had. He hit his leg on a rock which became infected.

Kermit feared for his father's life as his father came down with dysentery and malaria with his temperature rising dangerously high. Kermit watched over him nights fearing his father wouldn't wake up the next morning. Roosevelt so desperately ill considered taking a fatal dose of morphine. Not so much for his pain but for the fact that he didn't want to be a burden to the others on the expedition. Kermit let his father know he was returning to the states with him dead or alive; and if dead he would be a much bigger burden.

Kermit had come down with malaria too, but in order to save the medication for his father he made light of his own illness.

They finished their journey after almost four months time having explored the entire length of the river and charting it's course. They had traveled nearly one-thousand miles. The former president still weak and ill had lost fifty pounds in a matter of weeks.

The year the Amazon expedition ended Kermit married Belle Willard who was the daughter of the U.S. ambassador to Spain on June 11, 1914 in Madrid, Spain. They would have four children: Kermit, Joseph, Belle, and Dirck.

Kermit worked as an assistant manager of a bank in Argentina up until the time he joined the British Army serving in the Middle East. While serving as a soldier of fortune he came upon a house full of Turkish soldiers. On his own, Kermit showed a confidence and bravery that impelled the Turks to turn over their weapons and surrender. For his brave act he was awarded the British Army Cross.

Kermit was the only Roosevelt to come out of WWI unscathed. In WWII he was awarded the Military Cross.

After the war Kermit published the book 'Quentin Roosevelt: A Sketch With Letters' in memory of his brother who died during WWI. He founded the Roosevelt Steamship Company and the United States Line.

Kermit much like his father was an adventurer so he jumped at the chance to accompany his older brother Ted on a hunting expedition across the Himalayas over uncharted mountain passes in search for big game. Nineteen new species were discovered and confirmed including the giant panda on their expedition. When he returned home he co-wrote a book about the expedition with his brother titled, *'East of the Sun and West of the Moon'*.

In 1939 Kermit joined the British forces before the U.S. joined in WWII.

Kermit fought a losing battle with alcohol and put his marriage in jeopardy by taking on a mistress. He also fought an ongoing battle with depression. His wife Belle turned to her uncle President Franklin D. Roosevelt for help. It was an ongoing battle between her and Kermit with his alcoholism and his being an unfaithful husband. The president had Kermit sent to a post in Alaska. It was at this post that Kermit would be involved in establishing a militia of Eskimos and Aleuts. The president thought that having him stationed far from the battlefront would remove any stress.

Kermit looked at himself as a failure and an embarrassment to his family. Unable to face life any longer he one day picked up his gun and shot himself putting a bullet through his head. His mother was never told that he had committed suicide, instead she was told he died of heart failure. He was fifty-three at the time of his death.

Ethel, the only daughter of Theodore and second wife Edith, was born at the family home Sagamore Hill in Oyster Bay, New York. Of all the children she was the one who most favored their mother.

Ethel was a rambunctious tomboy and was ten years old when her father became president. She was seven years younger than her half-sister Alice and had two brothers that were older than her and two that were younger.

Her brothers remembered Ethel as being bossy. Her father being a little more diplomatic about it said, "She had a way of doing everything and managing everybody." She even went so far as to give orders to the staff of the White House.

She was as different as night and day from her sister Alice who 'demanded' to be in the spotlight. Alice was pretty; while Ethel was a bit overweight and not really what you would describe as a cute little girl. She was often in the background but that was fine with her; in fact she preferred it. Her parents would refer to Ethel as 'the perfect daughter.' Later in life when the subject was brought up about Ethel being reticent she replied, "I have an instinct for privacy."

While living at the White House Ethel went to a local boarding school, the National Cathedral School which is located at the Washington National Cathedral in Washington where she stayed all week and came home on weekends. She wasn't very happy about having to stay at school during the week. Her preference was to be home. It was a rough adjustment for her and she had a hard time making friends as they didn't know what to expect of a president's daughter. Ethel graduated from the school in 1906.

In 1908, just two years after graduation and just a few months before the Roosevelt's left the White House Ethel had a Debut and Coming Out Party. She was seventeen at the time and while most girls had their coming out parties at the age of eighteen this would be the only opportunity for her to have her party at the White House.

She met her future husband Richard Derby through her brother Kermit who of all her siblings she was closest to. She would marry Derby who was a surgeon when she was twenty-two. The doctor was ten years older than Ethel. They were married on April 4, 1913 and lived in Oyster Bay. They had four children: Richard, Edith, Sara, and Judith.

It is always the four sons of Theodore Roosevelt who are given accolades for fighting in WWI, but it was Ethel their sister who became the first of the Roosevelt children to see action during WWI. Her physician husband had volunteered in France and Ethel joined him as a volunteer nurse tending to the soldiers in the American Ambulance Hospital. Ethel when joining her husband left her infant son behind with her parents and his nurse. He was her parents first grandson.

This same son, the only son of Ethel and her husband, died at the age of eight of blood poisoning. Their son's death sent her husband into a deep depression which lasted for approximately six years. During that time she had the responsibility of caring not only for her other children and her husband but in maintaining the household and finances.

Ethel worked for several charities and causes; one of those causes being the Red Cross where she volunteered for sixty years. Another cause she was deeply entrenched in was securing low income housing for African-Americans in the Oyster Bay area.

After the death of her mother, Ethel with respect to her family's place in history worked on turning the family home Sagamore Hill into a national historic site remaining on its board of directors until her own death. Not only was she on the board but she sometimes conducted the tours at Sagamore Hill; the place of her birth and childhood home.

On one of those tours she conducted in 1974 she became very defensive when giving an interview along with a tour of her childhood home when the interviewer George Vecsey made a reference to her father as a hunter. Not an unusual assumption on his part since her father shot and brought back hundreds of animals and skins; not only for his personal homes but for museums. Roosevelt's polite but formidable daughter responded to his faux pas by saying, "Don't think of him as a hunter. He was a conservationist. He also helped classify many animals. But he was not a hunter." I think Roosevelt himself would have laughed at that description; as he did indeed go on many 'hunting expeditions' but this was an early example of political correctness.

Ethel like her father not one to be idle was a member of the board of directors of the Museum of Natural History in New York. Her grandfather had been one of the founders of the museum in 1869. She worked with the National Audubon Society assisting with the creation of the Theodore Roosevelt Nature Center on Long Island. Her father had been an advocate of the natural world and had assisted museums in their acquiring animals, botany, and specimens to further educate the public and she did this to honor him.

While her father had been president during the initial building of the Panama Canal and was responsible for acquiring control over the Canal Zone for the U.S., Ethel supported the proposed revision of the Panama Canal Treaty.

Ethel was one to work more behind the scenes than to become one who took the spotlight. She worked for the causes she believed in. Most of the time she remained out of the public eye by her own choosing. She did come out in 1960 making an official seconding speech for the nomination of Richard Nixon at the Republican National Convention. Even then her speech was brief and to the point.

Her husband passed away in 1963 and ten years later she lost her daughter Judith who had suffered from an illness intensified due to to her alcoholism. Even as a baby Judith had not been healthy suffering from acute asthmatic bronchitis.

In her mid-seventies Ethel would travel to exotic places such as Kashmir where on her own she climbed to the top of a steep mountain and to Machu Picchu with the indomitable spirit so much a part of the Roosevelts.

In 1977 Ethel passed away at her home in Oyster Bay, Long Island at the age of eighty-six.

With seven year old Archie and his three year old brother Quentin, it didn't take them long to make themselves at home at the White House. The presidential mansion was a treasure trove for children who were as active as they were.

Archie named for his great-great-great grandfather Archibald Bulloch, an American Revolutionary patriot, screamed with delight as he flew down the main stairway on a tin tray he had borrowed from the White House kitchen. His three year old brother Quentin came crashing down right behind him riding on his own tray. They had even convinced their older sister Alice to join in the fun. If their father hadn't been busy in a meeting and if he could have found a tray big enough, he may have joined in the fun too; as he often joined in on his children's rowdy play. He was just like one of the kids with the first lady stating he was like having another child.

It was 1905 and the Roosevelt children stood and watched as their father was sworn in at his inauguration. He had already completed the remainder of President McKinley's administration, but this time he himself had been elected as the President of the United States. The younger boys squirmed throughout the ceremony; hard to be still at their age.

Archie had pretty much the freedom to do as he pleased as a youngster in the White House. He would ride his bicycle, even walk through the halls on his stilts, and race his siblings through the halls. It wasn't just the younger boys either; Alice was just as likely to join them when they would hide in the seats in the East Room and jump out and scare the staff and visitors alike.

The younger Roosevelt boys had friends that came over to play that was part of a group they called the White House Gang. The boys would meet in the attic to plan out their mischievous deeds for the day. One thing they did that brought lots of fun and memories was when they dropped water balloons from the roof on the guards below or whoever else got within their aim.

President Roosevelt, similar to President Lincoln as far as raising their children was concerned, was more inclined to let their boys have their days of fun rather than to dish out discipline. Their father was a strong advocate in living life to the extreme and he encouraged the same behavior and attitudes in his children. Rather than discipline he many times joined in their fun. If they got too out of hand he would take them outside on long hikes or riding their horses, but if he walked in their rooms and there was a pillow fight going on; well, there was just too much boy left in the president for him to leave without having a little fun himself. It would be just like the president, all decked out in a tux dressed for a formal ball or reception to have to run change his shirt at the last minute after playing a little too vigorously with the kids.

Holidays were unique at the White House and one Thanksgiving when being gifted a large turkey for their dinner the boys were discovered chasing the frightened bird around with hatchets. There's no telling where they discovered the hatchets or what they would have done if they had actually caught the turkey.

Christmas of 1903 the Roosevelts had a party in which they invited hundreds of children where they enjoyed ice cream shaped like Santa Claus and other Christmas decorations. There was music and entertainment.

It was great fun for the younger children and the boys from the White House Gang to see all the interesting people that came through the doors of the White House: celebrities, politicians, and people from different parts of the world. Some of the foreign diplomats used a monocle so the boys took up collecting watch crystals to imitate them. When the first lady was entertaining a diplomat in the family quarters, hearing some giggling he looked up and there through a skylight peering at him he saw four boys all with monocles, which were actually the old watch crystals, imitating him. He was so shocked at his discovery he lost his own monocle in his cup of tea which set the boys off in gales of laughter.

Archie attended the public school in Washington where he would walk to school. He and his brother Quentin would either walk on their own or sometimes ride their ponies. It's hard to imagine a son of a president doing so on their own and as young as they were, but it was safer then and it was the days before they were protected by the Secret Service.

When he was a little older he would follow in his older brothers' footsteps and attend Groton. Archie, unlike his brothers wouldn't remain at Groton for long. He was a little too vocal in criticizing the headmaster, so he finished his studies at Phillips Academy. From Phillips Academy he would continue on to Harvard where his father and brothers had also gone to complete their studies.

After graduating from Harvard in 1916 Archie was prepared to join in the fight of WWI.

Before he left he married his sweetheart Grace Stackpole Lockwood on April 14, 1917. While he was overseas he would first learn he had become a father when he read the news in a Paris newspaper. Months after receiving the good news he was hit with shrapnel which crushed his knee along with other injuries. He came very close to losing his leg to amputation. He was discharged with 100% disability, but not before the French awarded him the Croix de Guerre.

The former president died in his sleep January 6, 1919. It would be Archie who notified his siblings by the telegraphed message, *'The old lion is dead.'*

After Archie was discharged from the war due to his disability he worked in the field of oil and petroleum. Along with his brother Ted he had been caught up in the Teapot Dome Scandal, but both brothers were found to be innocent of any wrongdoing in the scandal. Archie wanting to remove himself from those involved he left the Sinclair Oil Company not wanting to be tainted by their reputation and their part in the scandal. He went on to work in finance very successfully and was the founder of Roosevelt and Cross an investment firm.

Disability or not, during WWII Archie returned to fight again receiving two Silver Stars with Bronze Oak Leaf Cluster, the Bronze Star, and Purple Heart. He was the only soldier in U.S. history to be declared 100% disabled for the same wound in both WWI and WWII.

Archie and wife Grace lived out their lives in Cold Spring Harbor, New York which was close to his childhood home Sagamore Hill. They had four children: Archibald, Jr., Theodora, Nancy, and Edith.

After the death of the former first lady the Roosevelt home Sagamore Hill was sold to the U.S. Park Service and made into a National Historic Site. Sagamore Hill had remained in the family from the time it was built in 1886 until the 1950s, and then was opened to the public with the same furnishings and photos and family mementos displayed that the family enjoyed during their days when they called Sagamore Hill home.

Archie, the sole surviving son of the Roosevelts often came to visit his family home where he had such fond memories of growing up. It must have seemed bittersweet as he gazed at the original furnishings and personal mementos of the family bringing back memories of fond days spent with his parents and siblings. He would gaze at the stuffed animal heads with a memory of his father's love for nature and with every room filled with books. There are 8,000 books in the collection. His father was a voracious reader and even took books with him during his expeditions where at times he was found under a shady tree reading. He had passed his love of books onto his children. It had been a house filled with noise and laughter with active children. As he gazed at the animal skins laid out across the floor of the library and the family photos displayed he must have had a few moments of nostalgia; isn't that what kept drawing him back to his old home?

Archie was proud to be the son of one of the most well-loved presidents in U.S. history. His father is immortalized for all to remember him at Mt. Rushmore.

In 1971 while Archie was driving he and his wife were involved in a car accident that took the life of his wife Grace. Archie lived eight years after her death. He lived his last years in Florida. He died of a stroke at the age of eighty-seven on October 13, 1979.

The White House had initially been called The President's House and was officially called the Executive Mansion, but President Roosevelt passed an executive order naming it The White House; which is what the people of the nation had already been calling it for years. In 1901 the name became official.

Other than the fact that the mansion was painted white, which isn't that uncommon; just what was behind the name The White House? It was back during the War of 1812 when the British who were still ticked off about the American Revolutionary War came back for a second shot at our nation. They planned to burn the city of Washington, D.C., and they did indeed set fire to it.

You remember the story where Dolley Madison saved the painting and other artifacts from the White House before fleeing for safety. When the British arrived at the president's mansion they sat down and enjoyed a sumptuous meal that had been planned for a dinner party that evening and then set fire to the mansion. On the very day that the British determined to burn the city down, Washington, D.C. suffered what was most likely one of the worst storms in the history of D.C. So while the building was burning the British fled; and while it was burned and blackened from the smoke and fire the building was saved. The blackened walls after being repaired were painted white and afterward began being referred to as The White House.

President Roosevelt put his work aside everyday around 4:00 P.M. For what he called 'the children's hour.' This was his time with his children. Children's hour one day would be spent reading to his children, other times they would all play hide and seek, or teach the boys to box and the girls to run or ride.

When they had guests the president thoroughly enjoyed telling them all of his days out west with stories of cowboys, tales of his hunting, or travels.

Three year old Quentin was a charmer. All he had to do was smile and he won you over. This came in handy with his many antics as he was clearly the most rambunctious of the lot and also the president's favorite.

Quentin had walked through the gardens and flower beds on his stilts uprooting the flowers which upset the gardener. When the president admonished him Quentin said, "I don't see what good it does for you to be President. You can't do anything here."

Quentin and his friends that were members of the White House Gang were at the edge of their seats as the president told them the story of the Battle of San Juan Hill with the Rough Riders. While most young children at their age were playing cowboys and Indians, their favorite game of imagination was them being members of the Rough Riders and reenacting the battle. Quentin, of course, played the part of his father. The problem was this time Quentin was using his father's actual sword from the battle which remained as sharp as the day he had used it himself in battle. The fact that the boys had been told never to touch it was obviously ignored in this case. Charlie Taft, the son of the Secretary of War and the future president's son, tripped and fell at the same time that Quentin was swinging the sword and accidentally nicked Charlie's cheek. His cheek began bleeding and the boys were like deers in headlights when they heard someone coming their way. Charlie thinking quick said, "I tripped on the chair." The boys hid the sword and rubbed some of Charlie's blood on the chair. And that is how the reenactment of the Rough Riders came to an end on that day.

The boys in the White House Gang got away with quite a lot as the president found enjoyment and amusement in their play and explorations; but one day they pushed the limits too far when during a sleepover the boys had peppered Andrew Jackson's portrait with spitballs. His father woke Quentin up as angry as he had ever seen him and made him get up and take off the spitballs. His friends were prohibited from the White House for one week.

The Roosevelt children had lots of pets but the most famous pet was Algonquin, an Icelandic Shetland Pony. Archie had been sick with measles laid up in bed for some time, and Quentin knew just the thing to cheer him up. He got his brother Kermit to help him and they brought Archie's pony Algonquin up in the elevator. The pony had seen his reflection in the elevator mirror and the boys had a rough time getting him to leave the elevator. Archie was definitely cheered up at the sight of the pony in his bedroom.

Another incident that occurred with pets of the White House is when Quentin came roller skating into the president's office during a conference his father was having with senators and a few other men of distinction. Quentin had bought four snakes at a pet store and he dropped them on the table in front of the men. The men jumped up and clambered to get away from the snakes. The snakes were rounded up and disposed of, but I would imagine the president got a good laugh out of the scene and probably teased the men relentlessly.

When Quentin became of school age he went to Force Public School in Washington. He never expected to be treated any different from any of the other boys just because his father was president, and he wasn't. His fellow students treated him like all the other boys. Being full of energy, he often danced and sang his way into the classroom. He had a pleasant personality and a sunny disposition. He was distracted easily and at times would be found drawing pictures instead of doing his schoolwork.

Quentin would attend Harvard, his father and older brothers' alma mater. While a university student he attended a ball in Newport, Rhode Island where he met what would become his future fiancee, Flora Payne Whitney. Flora was a great-granddaughter of the shipping and railroad millionaire, Cornelius Vanderbilt. Vanderbilt was one of the country's richest men Initially, neither family was thrilled with their relationship; the Roosevelt family being modestly wealthy and of old money while the Vanderbilt family was flashy with new money. Both families eventually came around and accepted the relationship which all came to naught, as the young couple never had the opportunity to go through with the marriage.

While away at Harvard Quintin would write letters to Flora, a correspondence through letters which would become insightful into the history of America pre-WWII and during the war. The letters wrote of the sinking of the Lusitania in 1916 when 128 Americans lost their lives, his bitter criticisms of the sitting president Woodrow Wilson who was neutral concerning the war, with Quentin writing in a letter, *"We are a pretty sordid lot to want to sit looking on while England and France fight our battles..."* Flora continued to receive letters while he was away in France where he wrote of his training for the U.S. Air Service, his flight training, and shooting down his first German, right up until the time she received notice of his death.

But to go back in time just a bit, Quentin had initially been too young to enlist and when he left Harvard he volunteered for the U.S. Air Service. He proposed to Flora and had to leave immediately for flight school in France.

While attending the flight training school he caught pneumonia in the bitterly cold weather they had to endure while in France and was sent to Paris on leave to recover. While on leave he begged Flora to come to Paris so they could be married. She tried to make her way to Paris, but was unsuccessful. Overseas travel was difficult due to the war.

When Quentin learned all three of his brothers were on their way to the front he was determined to get there too. The older brothers teased Quentin about not yet being in the fight. He would be the last of the brothers to see action in the war, but when their father learned of the brothers teasing his youngest son his father quickly put a stop to it.

When the students of the flight school were finally tested to see who could make it as a pilot and who could not, Quentin proved himself to be worthy. Initially his captain, Eddie Rickenbacker was concerned when he learned a president's son would be in his squadron; but it didn't take long for not only Rickenbacker but the whole squadron to see that not only was he one of the most popular men in the group, but one the men all trusted.

It was May of 1918 when the pilots were sent to the front, a moment he had anticipated for quite some time. When he flew his first patrol he was fearless and his commanding officers warned him to be more cautious. Only days later his squadron would return to their base minus one pilot – Quentin Roosevelt.

The other pilots continuously watched the skies in hopes of his return; they grinned and patted each other on the back when they finally spotted Quentin's plane coming in for a landing.

Quentin once on the tarmac grinning from ear to ear informed the other pilots he had just shot down his first German plane. The pilots cheered and gathered around him as he told his story of how he had pulled away from the squadron to check on some planes off in the distance. When he saw they were enemy planes and there were twenty of them to him being on his own he decided it was best to return to base with the rest of the squadron. He had lost his way for a time and when he spotted what he assumed was his squadron ahead he moved into his spot in formation in the back. It was only later when one of the planes veered off that he spotted the black Maltese cross on the side of the plane identifying it as a German. He was flying in formation with a whole squadron of Germans. He quickly fired a long burst and the plane ahead of him burst into flames and fell to earth. Quentin without wasting any time raced for the military base. The other pilots were amazed at his story and astonished that he made it out of there alive.

Quentin was proud to write home to his father and inform him he had shot down an enemy plane. Three days later the Germans had their revenge.

Quentin was on a routine patrol when he came across German Fokkers led by none other than Hermann Goering himself. He had time to signal the other pilots in his squadron saving their lives, but this time his luck had abandoned him when a German pilot shot Quentin's plane down. Initially, it was thought that Quentin had landed and had become a prisoner of war. Even the pilots who had seen him shot down believed this to be so. He had been shot twice in the head by the barrage of bullets that brought his plane down and he was dead before his plane hit the ground.

The Roosevelts were notified that their youngest son had been shot down, but that his fate was undetermined. The Roosevelts received little peace or rest for days waiting for word on Quentin. Official word was received from General Pershing with his letter giving the official notice. The International Red Cross stated that his death was confirmed.

Quentin at age twenty, the youngest in the family, died in the line of duty. His parents grieved and the former president requested from his children that the next son born in any of their families be named Quentin.

His father never recovered from the pain of his son's death. He died just six months after Quentin's death.

The first lady said after Quentin's death, "You cannot bring up boys as eagles and expect them to turn out sparrows."

27

WILLIAM HOWARD TAFT

Children of Helen and William Howard Taft:

Robert Alphonso Taft – Born: Sept. 8, 1889   Died: July 31, 1953

Helen Herron Taft Manning – Born: Aug. 1, 1891   Died: Feb. 21, 1987

Charles Phelps Taft II – Born: Sept 20, 1897   Died: June 24, 1983

The Senate committee listed Robert Taft, the oldest son of President Taft, as one of America's five greatest senators.

In early January of the year 1900 Taft had received a telegram from President McKinley summoning him to Washington. President McKinley appointed Taft as civil governor for the Philippine islands. After the Spanish-American War the Philippines had come under the United States protection. Taft would go to the islands to set up a civilian government. Taft was initially reluctant to accept the position in what was in a distant part of the world and the job itself would be quite an undertaking, but it would distinguish him in the future for a higher office, one his wife adamantly insisted he pursue – the presidency.

The Taft family boarded the army transport *Hancock* and sailed towards the Philippines where they would make their home for the next few years.

Robert kept himself occupied on the voyage by teaching himself how to play chess from reading a book. He then proceeded to play chess with the officers on board who were dismayed to see that an eleven year old rookie player beat each and every one of them.

Taft's other two children nine year old Helen and two year old Charlie enjoyed their voyage across the seas to what seemed like the other end of the world. When they arrived in Manila they adapted quickly and easily to their life on the Philippine islands.

The two older children Bob and Helen had ponies they could ride about the island while Charlie played with the neighborhood Philipino children learning to speak their language which was a mixture of Spanish, English, and Tagalog. Helen was taught by their governess to speak German and Tagalog.

The Tafts were well received by the Philipinos and while living in the islands they lived like royalty.

When the Taft's oldest son Bob turned fourteen his parents decided that it was time for him to return to the United States to continue his education. After four years in the Philippines Bob sailed home on his own. He would enroll and study at the Taft School which was run by his Uncle Horace. His uncle persuaded him to study subjects he had little interest in. One of those subjects being debate. His uncle looking ahead realized the importance it would be in his future if he followed in his father's footsteps in either law or politics. Bob followed his uncle's advice and entered every debate available. He would not look back and regret it.

President Theodore Roosevelt named Taft his secretary of war and the family returned to the states to live.

Robert or Bob as he was called by friends and family would go on to study at Yale in 1910 where he graduated first in his class. He was a member of Yale's secret society Skull and Bones known as Bones and was a member of his father's fraternity Psi Upsilon. He continued his education in 1913 at Harvard Law School graduating with the class's highest honors. He continued making his family proud when he earned the highest score in the Ohio bar exams.

William Taft's wife Nellie had visited the White House when she was a teenager during the Hayes administration. After her visit she vowed she would one day marry a man that would be the president. When she met and even after they married Taft held no interest in becoming president. Taft's lifelong dream was to be appointed chief justice of the U.S. Supreme Court. He was able to fulfill both their dreams and eventually became the president and chief justice of the Supreme Court becoming the first and only person to have held both positions.

It was Nellie, Taft's wife, who had two secret meetings with President Roosevelt to secure the president's backing towards her husbands' presidential candidacy at the end of his own term.

March 4, 1909 was the day of the inauguration and a severe snow storm made it impossible for the inauguration to take place outside. The inauguration was moved inside the Capitol building. Thousands of men had worked half the night just to clear the snow from the parade route filling hundreds of wagon loads with the snow that blanketed the streets of Washington.

Eleven year old Charlie had already spent quite a bit of time in the White House as a part of the White House Gang with his friends Quentin and Archie Roosevelt, and all this presidential pomp and circumstance must have seemed like old stuff to him. Bored through the procedure of the inauguration he occupied himself by reading the book *'Treasure Island'*.

Once the Taft family moved into the White House the new First Lady Nellie Taft determined she would make some changes. She replaced the all-white staff and replaced many of them with African-Americans who assumed the role of ushers which was considered a highly prestigious position.

She was anything but an idle first lady, though few today know more about her other than she was responsible for the planting of the Cherry Blossoms in what is known as West Potomac Park. The cherry blossom trees are still admired in Washington today.

Some of her accomplishments as first lady are: she changed the president's mode of transportation from horse-drawn carriages to the automobile; her efforts towards providing healthy living conditions resulted in the first official federal act that had been initiated by a first lady; she invited not only Washington society to events held at the White House but others as well giving many the opportunity of visiting the president's home that never had the opportunity to do so before; and the most notable social event during her time as first lady was when she and the president celebrated their 25th wedding anniversary with over five thousand guests.

At the age of forty-eight and just three months into her husband's administration the first lady suffered from a stroke. After the stroke her daughter Helen who was in her second year studying at Bryn Mawr took a leave of absence to help assume the role of White House hostess. After her tenure as first lady, Nellie Taft became the *first* first lady to have her memoirs of her days in the White House published. 'Recollection of Full Years' was published in 1914.

Bob and Helen were both teenagers when their father became president and were both continuing their education at universities. Charlie attended public school during his days in Washington. He would also go on to study at the Taft School, the school his uncle founded where his older brother had previously studied. He finished first at Taft which may have surprised some in his family as he wasn't scholastically minded. While he had the better personality and made friends easier than his older brother it seemed to come as a surprise when he excelled at his studies.

There were some of the White House staff who remained from the previous administration who were familiar with Charlie and his pranks recalling the time at a dinner he hid under the table and tied the guests shoelaces together.

The Roosevelt boys had moved out of the White House, but with Charlie now a resident he kept the White House staff busy. Charlie carved his initials in the presidential yacht which brought the wrath of the president down on him, but his initials would be immortalized forever after with other administrations.

He once worked the White House switchboard while staff was on a break and had a good time talking to people who called the White House; he was one of the first children to listen to a talking machine or a phonograph; he climbed on the roof of the presidential mansion and slid down to the balcony to the floor below; he drove the president's electric car into a tree; but Charlie's most memorable experience was when he witnessed a Wright Brothers flying machine land on the South Lawn.

Not quite as spontaneous or rambunctious as their younger brother Charlie, both Helen and Bob had some favorite memories of their own. One of Helen's being a time when she was vacationing and she put on warpaint and enacted an Indian raid on the other campers.

In 1910 she had a coming-out tea at the White House with over a thousand guests.

Taft was a large man weighing somewhere between three-hundred and three-hundred and fifty pounds during his presidency. Rumor that has lasted through the years, similar to Washington's chopping down a cherry tree but with about as much substance, was that because President Taft was so large he got stuck in the bathtub. As funny a story as it may be, there is no validity to the story. He did order a very large bathtub, but it was for comfort not to being stuck in the bathtub.

In 1913 Taft's administration came to an end and Woodrow Wilson became the next president. During President Wilson's administration war was declared on Germany in 1917 in what became the First World War.

In 1914 Robert married Martha Wheaton Bowers. Martha's father was the former solicitor general in his father's cabinet. His wife would be a political asset for him as his own mother had been for his father.

Robert or Bob Taft, son of the former president, was determined to fight in the war and tried to enlist in the army twice but was turned down both times due to his eyesight. If he couldn't fight he was determined to be an aid in helping the war effort in one way or another and went to work for Herbert Hoover who was running the Food Administration.

At the conclusion of the war in 1918 Bob's work was hardly over. He was faced with two overwhelming tasks. He would be bringing the soldiers home and he would have to find a way to feed the people who were living in Europe where the land was decimated from the effects of the war.

This task would take him to Europe where he would work with Herbert Hoover with the U.S. Food Administration in order to distribute food to those in need. The task seemed insurmountable as the numbers were huge, having three hundred million mouths to feed in Europe and the Middle East. The mission was accomplished and they were even able to build up a surplus to ward off famine. He traveled the areas in need seeing the devastation for himself and was in charge of overseeing the distribution of the food so it would fall in the right hands.

He became the first American to ever receive the White Rose which was Finland's highest award for his efforts. No longer did he see his war work as just sitting at a desk while others fought. His role in the distribution of food was vital to Europe's post-war survival saving more lives than you could begin to count.

In 1920 Bob was elected to the Ohio State House of Representatives serving until 1928. His final two years he served as Speaker of the House.

The former president's lifelong dream of becoming Chief Justice of the Supreme Court became a reality in 1921. He became the only person to have served as both president and a U.S. chief justice, the highest posts in both the executive and the judicial branches of the government.

New Years Eve of 1922, Bob had to leave his home to be sworn into the Ohio House of Representatives. It was a difficult time for him to be away from home as his wife was pregnant and expecting in the very near future. Bob assured her that he would be back in plenty of time and called on his brother Charlie asking if he couldn't be there for her if she went into labor while he was away. He reassured both his wife and his brother that it would be highly unlikely to occur during his absence. Charlie reassured him that he would be available if needed. His own wife was also expecting, so he knew how nervous his brother must have been about leaving.

That very evening Charlie received the call that Martha had indeed gone into labor. He picked her up and took her to the hospital, and when he arrived home his own wife was waiting who was also in labor. On the final night of 1922, two Taft babies were about to be born. Just before midnight Charlie's son arrived first and just a few minutes later born the following year as it was just past midnight into the new year, Bob's son made his arrival.

In 1924 Bob and his younger brother Charlie formed a law partnership.

The former president Howard Taft died March 8, 1930.

In 1938 Bob ran for the U.S. Senate and won. Bob was an opponent of FDR's New Deal as he felt strongly that the New Deal was in opposition to the Constitution. He was also the only senator to oppose the Japanese-American internment camps during WWII. At the time he received a lot of criticism for his stance, but today in hindsight he is praised for his belief and opposition to what was clearly a violation of the Japanese-Americans' civil rights.

Bob Taft's name was put forward three times at Republican National Conventions. He had hoped to be the second son in American history to follow his father into the White House, but it was not meant to be. He sought the presidential nomination in 1940, 1948, and in 1952. His third attempt looked hopeful until Dwight D. Eisenhower's name was put forward. He was not able to defeat the most popular general from WWII for the nomination; and that would be his third and final try for the presidency.

In 1949 Bob's wife Martha, his help-mate and staunch supporter, had a stroke which left her confined to a wheelchair. While Bob had a bit of an abrasive personality, with Martha he was only loving and kind caring for her every need and showing her a tenderness few knew he had in him. His wife now came first, and was first and foremost his priority.

Bob and Martha had four sons: William Howard III who became ambassador to Ireland; his namesake Robert Alfonso, Jr. who would be elected to the U.S. Senate; Lloyd Bowers an investment banker; and Horace Dwight a professor of physics and a dean at Yale.

While Bob was playing a round of golf with President Eisenhower he was feeling some pain and stiffness in his hip. He confided in the president that he hadn't been feeling very well and the president convinced him to go to the hospital for tests without delay. Initially the doctors thought it was minor, perhaps arthritis; but the pain increased and he eventually checked into Holmes Memorial Hospital where they told him his body was full of cancer. Suffering through the pain he continued to work in the Senate.

In 1953 when the Senate was in recess he was admitted to the hospital for surgery, however; it was too late and he passed away from the cancer at the age of sixty-three.

In 1957 a Senate committee listed Bob's name as one of America's five greatest senators.

In 1915 Helen, the only daughter of the Tafts, earned a scholarship and graduated from Bryn Mawr. She received degrees in history, economics, and politics. She later earned a masters degree and a doctorate in history from Yale. Two years later she was appointed dean of Bryn Mawr. She was only twenty-five.

Three years after becoming dean she married a history professor also of Pennsylvania from the Swarthmore College. Helen and her husband Dr. Frederick Manning had two daughters who would marry professors themselves.

A few years after becoming dean she became acting president of Bryn Mawr. She had entered Bryn Mawr as a student in 1909 and had a career at the college which lasted for four decades; from professor of history, chairman of the history department, dean, and acting president.

Helen published the historical books, *'The Revolt of French Canada'* and *'British Colonial Government After the American Revolution.'*

Helen like her mother was a suffragist. She traveled giving speeches on a topic that was near and dear to both her heart and had been to her mothers also; that of the right for women to vote. Her mother had fought the same fight though her mother proposed the idea of women voting, but only for the ones having considerable knowledge about politics.

Helen died at the age of ninety-five from pneumonia in 1987 making her one of the presidential children that lived the longest. There was only one presidential child, Alice Roosevelt Longworth, who lived a longer life. The two as different as night and day; Alice a gregarious, biting woman who was admired but never accomplished a single thing in her life while Helen was a very successful, influential woman.

Charlie was forever looked upon as the fun-loving of the children of Taft didn't seem to be taken seriously when it came to his studies as his older siblings were, so his parents were taken by surprise when he took the Latin prize during his Yale entrance exams finishing first. He would graduate magna cum laude. While a junior at Yale he won the Gordon Brown prize one of Yale's highest undergraduate accolades which is awarded to a junior who excels in the standards of intellectual ability, high manhood, capacity for leadership, and service to the University.

Charlie outgoing and popular at Yale was captain of the Yale basketball team, played tackle on the varsity football team, and president of the debating club. He like his brother, father, and grandfather who was a co-founder was also a member of Skull and Bones. As much as he was enjoying his college years he dropped out when the U.S. entered WWI and enlisted.

Before heading off to war however; there was one thing he had to do first. He married Eleanor Chase. They married on October 6, 1917. Three months after saying their vows he would sail for Europe into a war zone.

Charlie found himself east of Verdun arriving at the tail end of the Battle of Verdun, one of the largest and longest battles in WWI. He was quickly promoted to sergeant-major and sent to study in France at the artillery school.

While in Europe he learned not only of the birth of his first child but of the death of his close friend Quentin Roosevelt whose plane had been shot down by a German fighter pilot.

At the end of the war Charlie returned to finish his education at Yale and graduated in 1918 with a bachelor of arts degree. While at Yale he became a member of the Skull and Bones Society, a secret club that future presidents, sons of presidents, and others of high standing in society were named as members. He remained at Yale for a year coaching football. He graduated from law school in 1921 about the same time that his father's dream came true of being appointed as chief justice of the Supreme Court.

Charlie and Eleanor had a good marriage and would have seven children: five daughters and two sons.

Charlie joined his brother in opening their own law firm in Cincinnati, Ohio. In 1925 he became the youngest president of the YMCA.

The two Taft brothers who shared such a rich history and background found themselves at odds during WWII when Charlie served as Director of U.S. Community War Service and Director of Economic Affairs under President Franklin Roosevelt. His brother Bob who was a senator at the time opposed just about everything FDR stood for.

Charlie was an adviser to the U.S. delegation in 1945 to the San Francisco Conference that led to the creation of the United Nations. He was co-founder of the World Council of Churches and became their president in 1947. In 1955 Charlie was elected mayor of Cincinnati and became known as "Mr. Cincinnati" during his time as mayor. He purchased the Taft family home and in his later years had it restored and turned into a National Historic Site.

Charlie was a loyal Cincinnati Reds fan who like his father loved baseball. He had a large part in the construction of the Riverfront Stadium which was home to the Reds and Cincinnati's Bengals football team. He loved sports which had played a large part in his life during his college years; and not only did he have a love for baseball but was an avid fly fisherman. His car could be spotted driving down the road with a canoe on the roof of his car so he would always be prepared for his next opportunity to fish.

Charlie died at the age of eighty-five in the year 1983.

28

WOODROW WILSON

Children of Ellen and Woodrow Wilson:

Margaret Woodrow Wilson "Nistha" - Born: April 30, 1886   Died: Feb. 12, 1944

Jessie Woodrow Wilson – Born: August 28, 1887   Died: Jan. 15, 1933

Eleanor "Nellie" Randolph Wilson – Born: Oct. 16, 1889   Died: April 5, 1967

Not only did two of his daughters marry during Wilson's administration, but a niece of the president married in the White House, and President Wilson himself married his second wife during his presidency.

Woodrow Wilson left his law practice in order to continue his education at Johns Hopkins University. His desire was to become a college professor. While visiting his uncle he attended the Sunday service at the church where Ellen's father was the pastor. He was immediately drawn to Ellen who he determined very quickly to make his wife. Initially she didn't show much interest in him, but he was able to wear her down and after his relentless pursuit she agreed to become his wife. Being away at school with no opportunity of getting down on one knee and proposing he sent her engagement ring through the mail.

Ellen's mother had passed away and after suffering a nervous breakdown her father was committed to the Milledgeville State Mental Hospital where he committed suicide.

Woodrow was very supportive to Ellen who had offered to break the engagement due to the stigma of her father's mental health issues and suicide. Woodrow not only refused, but offered to take in her two brothers telling her they would always be welcome to live with them as part of their family.

June 24, 1885 Ellen and Woodrow Wilson were married and soon after began their family having three daughters all born within three years of each other. Their daughters were Margaret, Jessie, and Eleanor who was nicknamed Nellie.

Woodrow and Ellen both were highly educated. Woodrow having graduated with a Ph.D. in political science. Woodrow Wilson was the first and only to date president to have earned a Ph.D. Ellen's academic studies were above and beyond that of most women and also of many men of her time.

The girls followed their parents example. Their mother homeschooled her young daughters giving them an extensive education, exceptional to what they most likely would have received had they attended a public school. By the time they did go off to school they were well-prepared.

Woodrow who was now a professor held teaching positions at Bryn Mawr College, Wesleyan University, and Princeton University.

The three Wilson girls were taught by their mother every day. In addition to their basic subjects their mother read to them from the works of Homer, Shakespeare, and other great poets. Their education was well beyond average not only for their age but for their gender.

Professor Wilson had become quite a scholar and during his time at Princeton University had intellectual peers from all over the U.S. and the world visit the Wilson home. The conversations were varied, stimulating, and highly educational. Professor Wilson allowed his young daughters to sit in and listen as long as they were quiet and not disruptive.

By the time the girls were sent off to private schools they were educated far above that of their peers. They attended Mrs. Scott's Private School and later Miss Fine's Private School founded by a Wellesley College graduate. Ultimately they attended Goucher

College. Margaret would also go on to study piano and voice at the Peabody Institute of Music.

The other two Wilson daughters were also students of Goucher College and Princeton University. Jessie graduated Phi Beta Kappa from Goucher.

Early in the year of 1905 Ellen Wilson received notice that her daughter Margaret was suffering from a nervous condition. Her mother said of Margaret, "She has been a nervous child all her life." To give her a break from the pressures of academics her parents sent her on a European trip where she visited England, Scotland, France, Italy, and Germany.

Their father's career in academia was excelling as he had gone from professor to the university president, but he was also showing a great interest in politics. He was elected governor of New Jersey in 1910.

Jessie and Nellie spent a weekend at the country home of a friend of the family who had also invited her nephew Francis Sayre who had recently graduated from Harvard Law School. Jessie and Francis had a lot in common and hit in off. It was love at first sight.

It wasn't long before Francis proposed to Jessie. The fact that her father was involved in campaigning they decided to keep the engagement a secret until after the election.

Their father won the election and was about to become the nation's 28th president. The nation was surprised when they learned that the new President-elect Woodrow Wilson had turned down the idea of having an inaugural ball. In place of celebrating at a presidential ball he chose to spend a quiet evening at home with his family which may have been a disappointment to three young girls in their twenties.

After their father's inauguration the girls moved into the White House with their parents. It was customary at the time for young, single women to live with their parents until they were married. They were all in their twenties when they took up residence in the White House. Margaret was twenty-six, Jessie twenty-five, and Nellie was twenty-three.

The Wilson family checked out all the nooks and crannies of the White House. Margaret chose what is known as the Lincoln Bedroom today for her own space. The criteria for her was there was room for her baby grand piano and space where she could practice her music and singing without disturbing the others.

While looking around the room Margaret had chosen, one of her sisters discovered a plaque under the mantel which read, *"In this room Abraham Lincoln signed the Emancipation Proclamation of January 1st, 1863, whereby four million slaves were given their freedom and slavery forever prohibited in these United States."* It made one stop and realize all the historical events that had happened in the home they now resided in and of the people that had roamed these same halls; people you read and studied about in history. They, too as president's daughters would become part of their nation's history.

Nellie was most like her father, though few would see this side of him. Both father and daughter enjoyed vaudeville and dancing. He loved to sing and would sing along with his oldest daughter Margaret or sometimes sang on his own. All three daughters enjoyed acting with him and listening to him read aloud to them on a quiet evening.

It was an adjustment to the Wilson daughters who were used to having their parents available at all times. Being president was quite different from a college professor, college president, or governor. Nellie when asked in later years about her life in the White House said, "We became goldfish in a bowl. Utter strangers passed judgment on us." It was the same argument most presidential children had, but one of the hardest adjustments for Nellie was not having her father available when she needed him or wanted to discuss something with him. The family was used to spending a lot of time together and now the nation was making demands on his time.

The press and the public were interested in learning about the Wilson girls wanting to know all about them. The two youngest girls were secretly engaged, but the press didn't discover their secret regardless of how much they pried trying to find out everything they could about the president's daughters.

After the Roosevelt boys and Charlie Taft, the White House staff might have thought they would get a breather from the pranks since the girls were older and more mature, but they soon found out that the Wilson girls liked to pop out and scare them. They also fooled the tourists who visited the White House by pretending to be just another tourist themselves.

The family enjoyed spending time with each other. Many times Margaret would entertain the family and guests in her room playing her piano and singing. The president had a nice voice and often sang along to the delight of their guests.

Jessie and Francis had been very good at keeping their engagement a secret so when the

White House announced their engagement it came as a complete surprise to the press and they rapidly sought to find any information they could on the groom and the wedding plans.

The press weren't the only ones to find the engagement a shock. Francis was working in the New York District Attorney's Office. His colleagues and the district attorney learned of his engagement when they read about it in the newspaper. They weren't even aware he knew the Wilson family or had ever been to the White House, so it was quite a shock to those closest to him.

The first lady was not well when making wedding plans for her daughter and before long there would be an additional wedding to plan for.

Jessie's wedding would be the sixth president's child to marry in the White House. The nation had fallen in love with Jessie and were excited to learn of her wedding plans. They admired the fact that both the bride and the groom were down-to-earth and did their best to avoid the limelight.

While initially the bride and groom had planned to have a quiet, simple wedding in the small Blue Room which was more suitable for their personalities; plans changed as wedding plans tend to do. As the president's guest list grew it made it impossible to fit all the guests in the smaller room and they had to have the wedding performed in the East Room.

The day of the wedding arrived and people clamored to be guests of the wedding. The guards at the gate of the White House were on high alert for wedding crashers so when the groom arrived without a ticket he was refused entrance. The guards had been informed that no one without a ticket would be allowed admittance. The groom had completely forgot his ticket not even thinking that he as the groom would need one. Frank did his best to explain to the guard that he was the groom, but received the response from the guard that anyone could make that claim trying to gain admittance and his captain gave strict orders that no one without that ticket or invitation was allowed in. The captain was called in who recognized him and admitted the groom so he didn't miss his own wedding.

Jessie and Frank's wedding would be the first White House wedding to take place since that unforgettable wedding of Alice Roosevelt Longworth seven years previously, so the nation was excited and anxious to celebrate the wedding of another presidential daughter.

A reward had been offered to any reporter who could discover the whereabouts of where the bride and groom were planning to honeymoon. Margaret, Jessie's older sister and maid-of-honor, helped fool the press when she disguised herself along with one of the guests who slipped into a White House limousine so the press would follow them thinking they were the bridal couple. This way the bride and groom could safely leave with their honeymoon plans kept secret. They were successful and the location of their honeymoon was left undiscovered.

Just six months after Jessie's wedding the president would again be walking another daughter down the aisle.

Early days of his presidency when their father had been choosing his cabinet and going over his list with his family, Eleanor or Nellie his youngest daughter said, "I don't really care who you choose, as long as you make that nice Mr. McAdoo secretary of treasury." That should have been the family's first clue.

Nellie had been secretly engaged to a young man she had met while on vacation. Whoever this secret engagement was to there doesn't seem to be any mention of his name anywhere, and he seems to have been forgotten by the wayside once she met William McAdoo.

Nellie had first met McAdoo when he visited the governor's mansion as a guest of the Wilsons. Evidently there was something about him that caught the Wilson's youngest daughter's eye even back then. As she was serving breakfast she spilled the cream and just about spilled the coffee she was serving him that morning before taking him to catch his train.

Once Woodrow became president Nellie and McAdoo were often seen dancing together at social functions at the White House. No one seemed to notice that a romance was budding; perhaps due to the fact that it never crossed their minds that their daughter of twenty-three years of age would be interested in a man who was fifty years old, a widower, father of six children, and a grandfather.

The family became enlightened to the relationship when one evening one of the White House staff entered the Oval Room where the family was and announced that the secretary of the treasury had arrived. As the president went to stand he was informed, "For Miss Eleanor."

It had been at her sister's wedding that Nellie led Secretary of Treasury McAdoo into the Blue Room to teach him the fox trot, a new dance that was all the rage.

McAdoo first proposed to Nellie in January and she at first turned him down. She gave it some thought and after he proposed for a second time she agreed to become his wife. Everyone was quite surprised when their engagement was announced. His children weren't happy with the idea of their father marrying a woman that was younger than some of his own children. The couple was married on May 7, 1914. Nellie was twenty four at the time of her wedding and the groom was fifty-two.

The first lady had not been feeling well for some time but attributed it to her demanding schedule as first lady and that she was getting up in years, though she was only fifty-four at the time. She had taken a fall earlier in the year and her health progressively got worse. The doctors discovered she had Bright's Disease, acute or chronic nephritis or a kidney disease which at that time was fatal. The doctors kept their diagnosis from the president and the family, but it didn't take long for them to realize she was doing poorly.

Due to the health of the first lady the wedding would be a small, intimate affair held in the Blue Room.

The first lady recovered enough to enjoy her daughter's wedding.

After the wedding the young bride immediately went from a pampered adored daughter of a president to a cabinet officer's wife and a member of Washington society. McAdoo's name had even been mentioned as a possible presidential candidate in the near future.

The Wilsons were the only presidential family to have two daughters marry in the White House. People were now asking: 'Will there be a third daughter to marry?' Margaret had served as maid of honor for her sisters but she had no desire to become a bride herself.

Three months after Nellie's wedding, Europe became involved in WWI. The first lady died just three days later in August of 1914. First Lady Ellen Wilson was the third presidential wife to die in the White House during her husband's administration.

After the death of the first lady Margaret stepped in to take over the role as White House hostess; not by choice but she seemed to be the only one available since her two sisters were married and running their own households. She would come to resent the role and the time it took away from her singing career. She wrote a letter to her sister Jessie complaining that guests and callers took up every minute of her time.

She wouldn't have to worry for long, as soon there would be someone else to step in and take over the role. Before the first lady died she told her physician to tell her husband that she hoped he would remarry one day. He didn't wait long.

Sixteen months after the death of the first lady the president remarried. He married a wealthy widow Edith Bolling Galt. The wedding was held at the home of the bride. While Washington society was appalled that he married again so soon, his daughters knew he was desperately lonely. He was the third in the immediate family to marry during his administration.

During his administration not only did his two daughters marry in the White House, but also the president's niece Alice Wilson also had her wedding in the Blue Room during the war. The niece's wedding would be the last White House wedding until 1966 when Luci Johnson, daughter of President Lyndon Johnson, married Pat Nugent.

Margaret saw her father's marriage as a way out for her as the role of White House hostess and she could now pursue her singing career. She made her singing debut with the Chicago Symphony Orchestra at a concert in New York. Margaret sang at a Christmas pageant in 1916 at the Treasury Building as the headline soloist.

When the U.S. entered WWI Margaret worked as a Red Cross volunteer at Washington's Union Station. She worked along with two future first ladies and a former president's daughter: Eleanor Roosevelt, Florence Harding, and Alice Roosevelt Longworth, the daughter of former President Theodore Roosevelt and the wife of a congressman.

Jessie and her husband had a successful and happy marriage. They had three children, one who was born in the White House who was his father's namesake, Francis Sayre, Jr., who would become dean of the National Cathedral. Their other two children Eleanor who was born a year after her brother and three years later another son Woodrow Wilson Sayre.

During WWI Margaret gave concerts for the Red Cross. She spent almost a year in

France entertaining the troops and giving concerts at all the Army training camps. It was a welcome respite for the soldiers to hear songs familiar to them from back home and they were touched that a daughter of a president would come to entertain them and lift their spirits in a war zone.

Margaret gave performances sometimes for just a few wounded soldiers and also to larger crowds. She traveled down roads bombed with craters that they would have to travel to reach some of the soldiers, but it brought the boys from back home comfort and a short time to put aside their fears and concerns of war and enjoy themselves. By the end of the war the concerts had strained her voice to a point where she could no longer sing and she suffered a nervous breakdown from the horrors she had seen.

In 1917 Woodrow Wilson had his second inauguration again declining an inauguration ball thinking they were too costly.

The president's daughters all believed strongly in women's rights. Jessie even led marches and organized protests and relentlessly pushed her father into supporting the 19th Amendment which would allow women the right to vote. His daughters evidently had some influence on their father as September of 1918 he stood before Congress in support of granting women the right to vote.

President Wilson and the first lady traveled to France to attend the Paris Peace Conference at the end of WWI making him the first president to travel overseas during his administration. His daughter Margaret who was already overseas giving concerts was there waiting to greet him when he arrived.

First Lady Edith Wilson was the *first* first lady to attend foreign diplomatic talks. Margaret and the first lady would be two of the five American women permitted to witness the historic signing of the Versailles Treaty which ended the war between Germany and the Allied Powers.

On October 2, 1919 President Wilson suffered a massive stroke. The doctor and first lady withheld information from the public concealing the severity of his condition. While the President lay in his bed on the brink of death unable to function as a president, the first lady a woman who could not even vote, was running the country. It was the first lady who was making all the decisions at this time leaving the country completely in the dark as to who was really running the country and of the president's condition.

When the Hardings moved into the White House and President Wilson could retire in peace the Wilson daughters still actively fought for women's rights. As their mother had before them it was something they each strongly believed in.

In the early 1920's Francis Sayre and his wife Jessie moved to Siam with their three children. Francis Sayre, son-in-law to former President Wilson served as an advisor to the Minister of Foreign Affairs in Bangkok. In recognition to the great work he did while he served in Siam he was honored with a title of high nobility, Phraya Kalyan Maitri, the only American to receive the Thai title.

In 1926 he along with his family returned to Bangkok at the request of King Prajadhipok as an advisor. The children old enough now to remember their time in Siam recalled with great delight the time the king had asked their father if they had ever ridden an elephant. When replying no, the king sent his white elephant decked out in the royal trappings of a 'regal elephant of a king' to their house for the children to ride. They also recalled there were lots of snakes in Siam which has since been renamed Thailand.

While the Sayre family were still in Siam the former president died. Margaret and the former first lady were with him. Eleanor and her husband also came to be with him.

Being the only unmarried daughter her father left Margaret $2,500 a year for as long as she remained unmarried, which in her case was for her lifetime. That was insufficient funds for her to live off of so she started working. For a time it is believed she worked for an advertising firm and later was involved in oil stocks; though it is unclear in what capacity exactly.

Margaret wasn't making enough to live on and had her father's former press secretary look into her father's will. When the first lady got wind of this, thinking her stepdaughter was about to challenge the President's will and hearing the reason behind it, she limited her contact with his daughters and made no offer of financial aid of any kind to Margaret. The former first lady had already been a wealthy widow when she married their father. She had been granted a federal presidential widow's pension and inherited almost the entire bulk of his estate in addition to the mansion they had lived in. She intended to keep every bit of it for herself and was indifferent to Margaret's circumstances.

Margaret had come across a book by Sri Aurobindo, a contemporary of Gandhi. He was a spiritual leader of India who had received his education in England at Cambridge. After studying in England he returned to India. Margaret was interested in his philosophy which was grounded in yoga and meditation and packed up and left the U.S. for India and never looked back.

It was in 1938 she moved to Pondicherry, India where she lived in an ashram under the new name of Nishtha. She lived in India until the time of her death. She died of uremia, kidney problems similar to her mother. She died April 24, 1944 and was buried in India.

In 1928, Jessie gave the introductory speech for the presidential nominee at the Democratic National Convention. Her name had been brought forward as candidate for senator but she declined. Instead, she accepted the role of the Secretary of the Massachusetts Democratic State Committee.

Jessie died at the young age of forty-five from complications following an appendectomy.

Under the administration of President Franklin Roosevelt, Francis Sayre son-in-law and widow of presidential daughter Jessie, became assistant secretary of state and personal representative of the President of the Philippines holding the title of the U.S. High Commissioner for the Philippines. Francis was in the Philippines after the invasion of Pearl Harbor. The submarine USS Swordfish was used for evacuating high-end personnel which included Sayre and Navy code breakers. They escaped by USS Swordfish submarine just days before the Japanese occupied the Philippine islands. Sayre was known throughout history as one of the most successful presidential sons-in-law.

Eleanor, the youngest daughter, sad to say had an unhappy marriage. In her early twenties at the time of her marriage she was immediately thrust in to role of a mother to some children who were older than she was and were clearly unhappy about their father's marriage. She was also in the spotlight with her husband being secretary of treasury and with ambitions to become president himself. It was quite an adjustment for a young girl regardless of how mature she was.

Eleanor, or Nellie, and her husband had two daughters: Ellen Wilson born the year after her parent's wedding in 1915 and another daughter Mary Faith born in 1920.

The couple lived in California where twice he ran for the presidency unsuccessfully. In 1932 he became a senator and two years later Eleanor claiming mental cruelty the couple divorced.

Nellie wrote short stories and a few books about her family. She also worked on establishing the Woodrow Wilson Foundation.

Nellie suffered a cerebral hemorrhage causing her incapacitation and she died two years later at the age of seventy-seven years.

29

WARREN HARDING

Child from Florence Harding's first marriage and stepson of Warren Harding:

Marshall Eugene DeWolfe "Pete" - Born: Sept. 22, 1880   Died: Jan. 1, 1915

Illegitimate child of Nan Britton and Warren Harding:

Elizabeth Ann Britton "Emma" or "Ann" - Born: Oct. 22, 1919   Died: Nov. 17, 2005

Illegitimate daughter; proven by DNA testing in 2015

The president and first lady had secret lives with one illegitimate child

and another abandoned child

With Harding's numerous affairs and scandals during his administration that came to light after his death he has been recorded as one of our worst presidents in American history. The first lady didn't score any higher as far as popularity goes either; and was even accused by some as poisoning and killing the president.

There were no children in the White House during the Harding administration. No children were produced from their marriage; however, they both had secret children.

A young teenage girl by the name of Florence Kling who would one day be First Lady Harding became pregnant by the boy from next door Henry "Petey" DeWolfe. Unmarried and pregnant at age nineteen Florence would later claim that she and the baby's father eloped.

Florence and Petey lived together in the town of Galion while she was pregnant and for a short time after their baby boy was born. While living there they passed themselves off to neighbors and those in the community as a married couple.

The first legal record of any kind was of the birth of the baby boy Eugene Marshall DeWolfe. There is no record of any marriage in any marriage license ledgers. Historians and others doing research on the future first lady have never been able to find concrete proof of a marriage between Kling and DeWolfe, leading them to believe that the future first lady and DeWolfe likely established a common law marriage. They did meet the terms of Ohio common law marriage requirements. Divorce papers were discovered on file in Marion County, Ohio to grant a divorce for Florence from Henry "Pete" DeWolfe.

Florence lived with the baby's father while pregnant and for a short time after the birth of Marshall, but the father was a drunk and often disappeared from their home. Then one day he left and never came back.

Florence broke and unable to support herself and the baby returned to her parent's home. Her father agreed to care for the boy but only if she agreed to give him up forever. Part of the agreement was that she would not have a role in bringing up her son. She agreed to her father's terms and left her infant son with him and never looked back. She wasn't exactly material for 'Mother of the Year Award.'

Marshall was raised by his grandparents while Florence lived on her own giving piano lessons in order to earn an income.

In 1891 when Florence married Warren Harding a newspaper publisher, her eleven year old son Marshall remained under the legal care of his grandfather. It appears that after his mother's marriage he did spend some time with her and her husband. Closer to his stepfather than he was to his mother he wanted to follow in Harding's footsteps and become a "newspaperman" like his stepfather. Harding did spend some time training him as editor and publisher and after he graduated from high school he gave Marshall a job at the *Marion Daily Star* his newspaper.

Marshall contracted tuberculosis and moved to Colorado for a better climate for his health. When he moved to Colorado he purchased a struggling newspaper but was unsuccessful at the venture mostly due to his alcohol problem. Marshall had unfortunately followed in his birth father's footsteps and became an alcoholic. He also had problems with gambling.

While in Colorado he married Esther Neely and they had two children before she divorced him. He would die in Colorado on January 1, 1915 at the age of thirty-four from advanced tuberculosis aggravated by alcoholism.

His body was returned to Marion, Ohio but there would be no announcement in the newspapers, not even the paper owned by his stepfather. The stepson of a future president and first lady was laid to rest in an unmarked grave.

During the presidential campaign the Hardings hid the fact that the future first lady had been "married" and divorced and had a son. When Harding was elected president in 1920, the fact that the first lady was a mother and grandmother was not disclosed.

President Harding a womanizer once told a group of reporters, "It's a good thing I'm not a woman. I would always be pregnant. I can't say no." Harding had a reputation for being quite the womanizer, both before his presidential days and during his time in the White House.

He began an affair with Carrie Fulton Phillips who was not only a close friend of his wife but was the wife of his best friend and neighbor. He met Phillips during his days in Ohio when he was editor of a newspaper. His wife was recovering from kidney problems and Harding's best friend, husband to Phillips, was in a sanitarium being treated for depression after the death of his two year old son.

When the relationship was discovered by Harding's wife he agreed to end the affair, but not being an man of his word the affair continued.

Another friend of his wife who he had an affair with was Susan Peal McWilliams Hodder who gave birth in 1894 to Marion Louise Hodder who is believed to be a child of Hardings. The fact that he supported her until she was an adult pretty much put the question of the child's paternity to rest.

A maid named Rosa Cecelia Hoyle allegedly gave birth to his illegitimate son and committed suicide when he wouldn't leave Florence. Harding is also said to have had an affair with Augusta Cole and that she had an abortion that he set up.

Rumor abounds with Harding and his 'many women' that he slept with which included chorus girls and just about anyone who didn't turn him down. Even Grace Cross his Senate staff secretary is said to have been one of his many paramours.

The relationship between him and Nan Britton lasted for years and with her he had a daughter. A daughter he refused to ever lay eyes on even though he continued his affair with her mother up until the time of his death.

It appears about the only woman he didn't have sex with was his wife. Harding had this to say about her, "There isn't one iota of affection in my home relationship. It is merely existence, necessary for appearance's sake."

Carrie Phillips, his wife's friend he had an affair with, threatened to expose their relationship if she wasn't paid off. Obviously, she was paid off as was revealed when the Library of Congress released letters Harding had written to his mistress. The letters revealed that Harding and the Republican National Committee paid her off to the tune of $5,000 monthly to keep her quiet while he was president. She received funds in the amount of $20,000 - $25,000, which adds up to just under $300,000 today, and that was in addition to her monthly payment of $5,000. It appears blackmail was a pretty lucrative business.

The letters weren't your average love letters between two lovers in an illicit affair; they were more what you would read in a porn magazine. It would have been quite embarrassing to the president to have those letters revealed during his administration. While he did avert that embarrassment; they are now a part of the Library of Congress and public record for the entire world to see for generations to come.

Nan Britton grew up in Marion, Ohio where Warren Harding had been a newspaper publisher.

Harding was married but regardless of that fact women found him attractive. When the young, naive Nan Britton approached the senator about helping her find a job he was flattered that nearing his golden years the young twenty year old was clearly smitten with him. He agreed to help her and made plans to meet her in New York.

Senator Harding did meet Nan Britton in New York. What happened in that New York hotel room was later exposed in a book Nan wrote after the president's death. She wrote of beginning a relationship with the fifty year old senator when she was an innocent twenty year old girl.

The couple had just finished having sex when the New York Police Vice Squad broke down the hotel door having learned of the illicit affair, most likely from the hotel proprietor. The police proceeded to arrest the couple but when they realized that he was Senator Harding the police apologized and left.

Nan and the senator maintained their relationship for the next six and a half years up until the death of Harding. In October of 1919 she gave birth to a little girl Elizabeth Ann who was the illegitimate daughter of Senator Harding. She was born just over a year before he became President of the United States.

Elizabeth Ann had been conceived on a couch in the office of the senator. Nan was thirty years younger than the senator.

When Harding became president he made arrangements with the Secret Service to make monthly payments to Nan for the care of her daughter; while he paid for her care he refused to ever see his daughter.

Even once Harding became president he had secret rendezvous with Nan Britton. The day after he was elected president he met her in a house used by the Republican campaign staff. She also met him many times in the Oval Office. The president took her into a closet and had sex with her. After the first lady almost walked in on them he made arrangements with a Secret Service agent to stand guard and warn him by knocking on the door whenever the first lady was approaching.

The president was undiscerning in carrying on with a young lady who was clearly in love with him and according to close family members of hers she remained in love with him until the day she died.

Nan once arrived at the White House and while visiting the president told him that his daughter was sitting on a park bench in Lafayette Square, and if he would just look out the window he could see his daughter. He refused.

When the president died Nan discovered there was nothing in his will or any provisions made to care for his daughter. Now needing a way to support herself and her daughter she wrote the tell-all book, *'The President's Daughter.'* In the book she told everything: from their first time in a New York hotel room when she was just a young woman, to the places where they met and carried on their affair from the Senate couch in his office to the closet in the Oval Office.

It wasn't the first time a president was accused of an affair, but never before had a woman come forth with an exposé on the private life of a president.

Unable to produce physical evidence since she had followed his orders and destroyed all his personal letters to her she was vilified and accused of lying for money or to destroy the Republican party.

The Harding family denied her claims insisting that the president was sterile. Unfortunately, the press and public believed the family regardless of his tarnished reputation towards women. Nan Britton was abused and accused of being a liar. She would not live to see her claims validated that her illegitimate daughter's father was the president nor would the president's illegitimate daughter live to see the day, but her son would.

Elizabeth Ann turned down all interview requests but she did admit in 1934 that her mother had told her that Warren Harding was her biological father.

Elizabeth Ann graduated from Sullivan High School in 1938. She was enrolled under the name Elizabeth Ann Harding. She had intended to continue her education at Lake Forest College but married Henry Blaesing and moved to California and later to Mt. Hood, Oregon. She raised three sons and lived a private life.

She was a private person and preferred to keep it that way, refusing when her grandchildren tried to convince her to speak out about who she was and of her parentage. Elizabeth Ann passed away in 2005. Her mother Nan Britton had passed away in 1991.

The truth would eventually be revealed through DNA testing, but not in time for Nan or her daughter to have the truth they always knew acknowledged publicly.

Dr. Peter Harding, a grandnephew of the president and retired psychiatrist from California, said as a boy growing up he had heard his family's side of things where they denied Nan Britton's claims stating that President Harding had mumps as a child that had left him sterile. After his own father's death when he found a copy of Nan Britton's book among his things be became curious.

Dr. Harding and his cousin Abigail Harding decided to look into the subject further. Other family members were adamantly opposed to them digging up old skeletons, but Dr. Peter Harding insisted that "people have a right to know who their parents and grandparents are. I think that's just a human right. There was a whole family that didn't know for sure who their father and grandfather was. They deserved to know."

Dr. Harding and his cousin Abigail reached out to James Blaesing, a grandson of Nan Britton and son of the illegitimate daughter Elizabeth Ann. They connected with each other and agreed to have a DNA test performed.

Testing by AncestryDNA found that Elizabeth Ann was indeed the daughter of President Harding. Stephen Baloglu an executive at Ancestry said, "The technology that we're using is at a level of specificity that there's no need to do more DNA testing. This is the definitive answer." The results are 99.9% certain. That leaves little room for doubt or denial.

The results that the DNA testing confirmed that President Harding was the father of Elizabeth Ann Blaesing was first announced by the *New York Times* in 2015.

The results of the DNA testing have put to rest the ninety year old argument and brought new light into presidential history. And yet again, with the aid of DNA testing history has been rewritten.

30

CALVIN COOLIDGE

Children of Grace and Calvin Coolidge:

John Coolidge – Born: Sept 7, 1906   Died: May 31, 2000

Calvin Coolidge, Jr. - Born: April 13, 1908   Died: July 7, 1924

Cal, Jr. was the first presidential son to die in the White House

since the death of Abraham Lincoln's son Willie during the Civil War.

It became common place for Calvin Coolidge to be apart from his family during his days in the legislature. Grace remained at their home raising the boys where she could often be found spending time in the backyard playing ball with the boys. When government was not in session and school was out the family would spend their summer vacations together living with Cal's father at the family homestead in the hamlet of Plymouth Notch in rural Vermont.

During the 1920 presidential election Coolidge initially agreed to having his name put forward as a candidate, but then informed his wife that Warren Harding selected him as his vice presidential candidate. Grace Coolidge didn't necessarily see this as a good thing, as she thought he was worthy presidential material himself. Running on the ticket with

Harding as vice president would remove his chances of becoming president. That, however; wouldn't prove to be true.

Harding did win the election and Calvin Coolidge became his vice president. During his two and a half years as vice president Calvin Coolidge who wasn't known for being friendly and sociable came to realize what an asset his wife was whose personality was far different from his own. Grace was adept at working with people; which was a benefit to the vice president and later to his presidency.

Vice President Calvin and Grace Coolidge were staying at his boyhood home where his father was living in Vermont when they were awoken early one morning to the news of President Harding's death.

In Coolidge's own words of that momentous day, this is how he was notified that his days of the vice presidency had come to an end and he would now become the 30th president.

"On the night of August 2, 1923, I was awakened by my father coming up the stairs, calling my name. I noticed that his voice trembled...I knew that something of the gravest nature had occurred. He placed in my hands an official report and told me that President Harding had just passed away.

Before leaving the room I knelt down and, with the same prayer with which I have since approached the altar of the church, asked God to bless the American people and give me power to serve them...

My first thought was to express my sympathy for those who had been bereaved and after that was done to attempt to reassure the country...

Meantime I had been examining the Constitution to determine what might be necessary for qualifying by taking the oath of office. It is not clear that any additional oath is required beyond what is taken by the vice president when he is sworn into office. It is the same form as that taken by the president.

Having found this form in the Constitution, I had it set up on the typewriter, and the oath was administered by my father in his capacity as a notary public.

The oath was taken in what we always called the sitting room, by the light of the kerosene lamp, which was the most modern form of lighting that had then reached the neighborhood. The Bible which had belonged to my mother lay on the table at my hand. It was not officially used, as it is not the practice in Vermont or Massachusetts to use a Bible in connection with the administration of an oath.

Besides my father and myself, there were present my wife, Senator Dale, who happened to be stopping a few miles away, my stenographer, and my chauffeur."

The Coolidge's oldest son John was at a military camp and standing in line waiting for his breakfast when his captain approached and said, "Your father is President of the United States."

The youngest son Cal, Jr. was working on a tobacco farm when his boss arrived with the news that President Harding had died and his father was now president.

The youngest Coolidge replied, "Yes, I suppose he is." He then calmly proceeded to ask his boss at which location was he supposed to work that day. When one of the other workers who worked along side of the president's son that day, both of them making $3.50 a day said, "If my father was president, I wouldn't work in a tobacco field." Calvin just looked at him and said, "If *my* father were your father, you would." Even as youngsters on summer vacations their father had farmed them out to local farmers to work. His father believed in hard work.

The Coolidge boys both nearly six feet tall were fifteen and sixteen years old when their father became president.

Calvin, Jr. was described as a bit of a prankster but also as a student who took his studies seriously and one who loved to read. The topic most remarked and admired by the public about the youngest son was that he was humble.

When the public learned the Coolidge boys had chores such as mowing lawns and helping neighbors clean out furnaces; that made them seem like every other American boy. While Cal, Jr. played a mandolin and banjo his older brother John played the violin and the piano and loved to sing.

The first summer that the Coolidge's occupied the White House the boys spent the summer in Washington. At the end of the summer the boys attended boarding school at Mercersburg Academy and spent weekends at the White House.

President Coolidge could be hard and quite demanding on his sons. When his son John was away at college at his old alma mater Amherst, he wrote his son a letter. The letter let him know in no uncertain terms that he was sent to college to work and that he expected him to keep his mind on his studies and not to dally at Smith College; the college for women that was located near Amherst.

John was involved not only in his studies but in extra-curricular activities. He enjoyed boxing, acting in the plays the college produced, and singing in the chorus.

President Coolidge, not enough to worry about in running the country, decided he needed to limit his son John's distractions at school and sent a Secret Service agent to act as his bodyguard. The story was that threatening letters had been received and the president wanted his son protected. But John had to wonder if it was really his protection his father was worried about or the fact that he wanted someone to keep an eye on him. The agent had to bunk in the same room as John and be with him at all times except for when he was in class.

When the boys came to the White House on weekends and school holidays their father let it be known they were expected to dress for dinner whether they had guests or not as "this is the President's House" they were informed.

The Coolidge family had all been taught American sign language by their mother who had taught at a school for the deaf before her marriage. When the family wanted to speak to each other without letting others within hearing distance know what they were saying they would communicate with each other by sign language.

The Coolidge family loved animals and had quite a variety of pets during their days at the White House including at one time as many as eleven dogs. Some of the more strange pets they had were a bobcat, lion cubs, a bear, raccoon, and Pygmy hippo.

The president could often be seen walking the halls with Tige the cat draped around his neck. The first lady had a mockingbird she kept for a pet until she discovered that keeping mockingbirds in confinement in Washington was against the law and punishable by a $5 fine and a month in jail. The first lady hated giving the bird up but she also didn't want to embarrass the country by being the *first* first lady to go to jail. Their favorite pets were the white collies Rob Roy and Prudence Prim.

The Coolidge family enjoyed physical exercise. Grace was known for her hiking and swimming while Cal enjoyed golfing and fishing, common activities for a president. Not as common was his fondness in riding a mechanical horse and exercising with Indian clubs; which are pins that resemble bowling pins that you swing around for exercise. The sons enjoyed hiking and swimming with their parents.

Grace was also known for her fondness of baseball, hence given the title 'First Lady of Baseball.' She could often be seen in the stands at the Washington Senators baseball games being played at Griffith Stadium. Cal occasionally joined her to throw out the ceremonial first ball but rarely stayed long enough to see the conclusion of the game. The love of the game was passed down to John who was a Red Sox fan until his dying day.

President Coolidge who wasn't known for letting loose and having a good time refused to let his family dance in public. That didn't stop the first lady and John from learning how to dance the Charleston by the White House butler.

In 1923 President Coolidge became the first president to light the National Christmas tree. They were the *first* First Family to have the National Christmas tree on the grounds of the White House beginning a tradition that is carried out still today.

The sons had sixty friends attend a Christmas party at the White House and left with bragging rights that each one of them had a dance with the first lady.

When the boys arrived at the White House in the summer of 1924, John had just graduated from Mercersburg and in the fall would be attending Amherst College. For the first time in years the boys would be attending different schools. But little did they know this would be their last summer together. After this summer John would rarely come back to the White House. There would be too many painful memories.

Calvin, Jr. was more like his mother than his father. He was very social and full of energy. He spent much of his time at the tennis courts at the White House.

Cal had spent the day playing tennis. Unable to find a clean pair of socks he played without socks and developed a blister on his toe. After completing his games of tennis he treated the blister with iodine and didn't give it another thought. Within hours septicemia or blood poisoning developed. By the time the doctors were called to treat him, it was too late.

His father helpless and worried sick over the condition of his son caught one of the wild rabbits that made the White house lawn their home and brought it in to show his son thinking it would cheer him up.

A son who just days ago was outgoing and full of life was losing the battle as the blood poisoning affected his body. It was more than a decade away before antibiotics were discovered to treat infections such as he had. As the president and first lady watched helplessly as their son was losing the fight for his life he was taken to Walter Reed Hospital. In a matter of days the sixteen year old son of the president was dead.

Cal, Jr. was the first presidential son to die in the White House since the death of Abraham Lincoln's son Willie who had died during the days of the Civil War.

The nation who had admired the young son of the president for his humility and fun-loving personality mourned with the family. Cal, Jr. had once told a friend, "I think you are mistaken in calling me the first boy of the land, since I have done nothing. It is my father who is president. The first boy of the land would be some boy who had distinguished himself through his own actions." He was a humble lad and when news spread of his death thousands of telegrams and phone calls of condolences poured into the White House.

His funeral was held in the East Room. The Coolidge family touched by the nation's outpouring of sympathy and caring ordered the White House gates open to the public.

His brother John years later when being interviewed by Life magazine stated, "Though father was tenderhearted, he rarely showed his feelings. But when they were taking my brother's casket from the White House after the funeral services, my father broke down and wept."

The Coolidge boys were the first Boy Scouts to live in the White House and the Boy Scouts were included in the funeral proceedings. With the gates of the White House open a massive crowd had gathered to be a part of the funeral and show their respects to the sixteen year old first son. The Boy Scouts accompanied the funeral procession to Union Station and kept the lines open for the family to proceed unencumbered. When the funeral train arrived there were Marines in the honor guard who were accompanied by the Boy Scouts when the casket was carried to the graveside. At the end of the service each of the Boy Scouts filed by the grave dropping a rose on the casket as they passed.

Most of Coolidge's 1924 presidential campaign took place while the incumbent president and first lady were in mourning after having buried their son that summer. Coolidge won the election.

The inauguration took place at the East Portico of the Capitol and the oath of office was administered by Chief Justice William Howard Taft the only former president to have also become chief justice. Coolidge's second inauguration was the first time an inauguration was broadcast on the radio.

John Coolidge had missed his father's first inauguration which had taken place in his father's boyhood home but he did attend his father's second inauguration; however, it would only be an overnight visit as his father didn't want him to miss classes. He had arrived that morning and would have to turn around and leave the same evening. There was no inaugural ball.

Perhaps even more important to him than his father's inauguration is the fact that on the train coming in to Washington he met Florence Trumbull the daughter of Governor Robert Trumbull of Connecticut who would become his future wife. Florence was a student at Mount Holyoke College which was a short distance from Amherst the college John attended. After meeting they saw each other every week while attending school and wrote to each other when they were away for summer and school holidays.

John had attended Mercersburg Academy and graduated in 1924. He then attended Amherst College where he graduated in 1928; graduating from both schools while his father was president.

There were two visitors of the president and first lady that received a lot of notice from the public. One of these visitors was Helen Keller the famous deaf author. The other was Charles Lindbergh.

Lindbergh made his historic flight in his plane *The Spirit of St. Louis,* the first solo nonstop flight across the Atlantic Ocean in 1927 at just twenty-five years of age he became an instant national hero. The first lady had tracked his flight by radio. After Lindbergh returned to the United States he visited Washington where President Coolidge and First Lady Grace Coolidge welcomed him at a Washington Monument stand built for the occasion. While visiting with the president and first lady Lindbergh offered to fly the first lady in his plane which she was more than happy to accept; until the president requested that she not do so, saying it would attract unnecessary publicity.

Another historic event the first lady had tracked on her radio was that of Robert Peary's exploration to the North Pole.

March 4, 1929 the Coolidge's attended the inauguration of Herbert Hoover. The president and first lady retired to Calvin's hometown in Massachusetts where he would write his autobiography. January 5, 1933 the president died of heart failure a few months before the inauguration of Franklin D. Roosevelt.

The homestead at Plymouth Notch was left to his son John. He would donate the house with the furnishings to the state of Vermont for the purpose of dedicating the building as a historic site. The public can take a tour and see the home as it was on the night that Coolidge took the oath of office and became president in the sitting room.

John much like his father was a man of few words. He married the young lady he met on the train on the way to his father's second inauguration. Their marriage took place in 1929, just six months after his father left office. John and his wife Florence had two daughters.

John worked for the New York, New Haven, and Hartford Railroad for over a decade and then became president of the Connecticut Manifold Forms Company. He reopened the Plymouth Cheese Corporation in Plymouth at the historic village. He bought buildings in the village of Plymouth which now serve as the President Calvin Coolidge State Historic Site.

John lived to be ninety-three years of age. His last years he lived in Plymouth Notch, where his father grew up and he had spent many summers himself. He would often be found at the Coolidge historic site answering questions about the Coolidge family without ever revealing he was the son of former President Coolidge.

The former first lady wrote her son John a letter in 1932 recalling the day her son Calvin, Jr. died. It is a heartrending letter of her memories of her young son in the last moments of his life. It tells of a loving mother trying to comfort her son and he responded with a flicker of a smile and was gone. The letter can be seen in the collection of the Calvin Coolidge Memorial Foundation.

31

HERBERT HOOVER

Children of Lou and Herbert Hoover:

Herbert Clark Hoover, Jr. - Born: Aug. 4, 1903   Died: July 9, 1969

Allan Henry Hoover – Born: July 17, 1907   Died: Nov. 8, 1993

By the age of two Herbert Jr, oldest son of the Hoovers,

had traveled around the world twice

Prior to becoming president Herbert Hoover worked as a mining engineer and executive in China when Herbert and Lou were newlyweds. It was June of the year 1900 when Lou and Herbert living in the city of Tientsin were in the midst of the area where the Boxer Rebellion broke out. Native Chinese had come to resent foreigners influencing China and the people bringing Western customs into their world. The Chinese were violently attacking and even murdering foreigners during the rebellion. It had become so dangerous that Lou, who would one day become first lady, had tires shot out on her bicycle as she rode through town and began carrying a pistol herself.

In August of 1900 the Hoovers moved to London where their two sons were born. The Hoovers home was in London up until the year 1914, but during this time they traveled to other countries such as India, Egypt, Russia, Australia, New Zealand, and as far away as Japan and Burma.

Three years after their arrival in London Herbert Clark, Jr. was born. By the age of two Herbert Jr. had traveled around the world twice. One of his earliest memories was of a time when they were in Australia where his father worked in the gold mines and he rode in a wagon with his father that was stacked with gold.

Almost four years after the birth of their first son their second son Allan was born, also in London.

The Hoovers remained in London until what would later become known as World War I broke out in the year 1914. Herbert helped organize the return of around 120,000 Americans from Europe; including his wife and two young sons. Lou didn't leave London immediately though, as she helped to create and chair the American Women's War Relief Fund and Hospital. She also helped those that were unable to get home to find housing and aid.

While Herbert stayed behind to organize aid from neutral countries Lou and the two boys returned to the States and lived in California.

For the next two years Herbert worked from London in an effort to distribute and feed war victims distributing over two million tons of food; even convincing German authorities to allow him to send food shipments to war victims inside Germany becoming an international hero. His efforts fed nine million people affected by the war saving them from starvation.

As Lou had done during the Boxer Rebellion in China, she became involved by helping in organizing groups to raise money and send food overseas.

While in California the family lived near Stanford University, the same University where Herbert and Lou had graduated in earlier years with geology degrees. Lou had been the first woman to receive a degree in geology from Stanford, an unusual field for women at the time.

During their time living in California Herbert, Jr. was the water boy for the Stanford Indians football team. He would later return to the university as a student.

It was 1917 before America joined in the war. Herbert Hoover was appointed by President Wilson to take on the role of chief of the U.S. Food Administration which brought their father back home to the States. The Hoovers next move was to Washington.

At the war's end Herbert organized shipments of food for millions of starving people in Europe. The *New York Times* named Herbert Hoover one of the "Ten Most Important Living Americans." His war efforts ended his days in mining as he was now completely immersed in public service; but it was also when others started thinking seriously about him as a political candidate.

The year after America went to war the 1918 – 1919 flu pandemic broke out, the deadliest in modern history. About one in four Americans came down with the flu and approximately 675,000 Americans died from it. One of those who came down with the influenza was Herbert, Jr. He recovered but suffered with hearing loss afterward that affected him for the rest of his life. He would have to wear a hearing aid which in later years would make him ineligible to fight during WWII.

His hearing impairment didn't seem to affect his interest in radio, as at the age of fourteen Herbert, Jr. became interested in radio communications.

Herbert, Jr. attended Stanford University where both his parents had graduated. He graduated with a degree in general engineering and continued his studies at Harvard Business School. Following his graduation at Harvard he won a fellowship from the Daniel Guggenheim Fund where he studied aviation economics. He would combine his love of radio that had captured his interest in his teens and combine it with aviation.

Herbert, Jr. married Margaret Watson in 1925. The next two years they would have two children: Margaret Ann Hoover born in 1926, Herbert "Pete" Hoover III born in 1927, and during his father's presidency they would have their third and final child Joan Leslie Hoover born in 1930.

In 1928 Herbert, Jr. was hired by Western Air Express where he could put his interest in radio communications and aviation to good use. He set up communications systems which would guide radio-equipped aircraft.

Herbert Hoover was elected the 31st President of the United States and on March 4, 1929 his inauguration took place. Hoover became the first president born west of the Mississippi and the only president to have come from Iowa.

Allan, the youngest son, was in college and arrived in Washington for the inauguration but would only stay overnight before he returned to college. This would be the first inauguration to be broadcast not only by radio but to also be recorded in motion pictures with sound.

The two sons, Herbert, Jr. and Allan, were rare visitors to the White House spending little time in the presidential residence. Herbert, Jr. was twenty-five when his father became president and had his own family and career while twenty-one year old Allan was in his college years.

Allan spent most of his father's presidency as a student attending Harvard Business School. He would become a graduate of both Stanford University and Harvard Business School. He didn't like the White House and spent as little time as possible there. He had strong opinions of life at the White House by making the statement, "If I don't get out of here soon, I'll have the willies." He did keep two pet alligators at the Executive Mansion which were often found wandering around loose on the grounds.

 While Allan made it known he didn't care for life in the White House he wasn't beyond using it to his advantage. He once threw a Christmas party inviting over two hundred people. They first had dinner in the State Dining Room and then enjoyed jazz music as the guests danced; the only time President Hoover allowed dancing at the White House during his administration.

It was only a little over six months after the inauguration that the Wall Street stock market crashed in October which was the beginning of the Great Depression.

Regardless of the condition of the nation and with people going hungry, there were dinner guests at the White House daily and they were almost always served a full seven course meal; all while right in the city of Washington families were going without.

Peggy Hoover, daughter of presidential son Herbert, Jr. and granddaughter of the president, had been told by a friend she could no longer play with her because her mother told her the Depression was her fault. Though no fault of the granddaughter of the president the people thought President Hoover was uncaring to their predicament. It was hard to be rational during difficult times when people were going hungry, losing their livelihoods, and their homes.

The president and first lady may have appeared to have been uncaring but the president and the first lady did help others. They never allowed their acts of kindness and giving to be revealed to the press and the public. To them the matter was private.

The president and first lady treated their servants different from past first families. The president or first lady didn't want to see a servant at their work. When the household staff heard bells ringing: two bells for the first lady and three bells for the president, that signaled that they were approaching and the servants were not to be seen.

The household staff would have to duck behind curtains or dash into a closet where they may run into other members of the staff also trying to stay out of sight of the president and first lady. If they weren't quick enough and they were seen there were consequences they would face. This held true even for the gardeners working outside who would have to hide behind a bush or portico if the first lady came out to work in the flower gardens or to walk her dogs.

The Hoover sons were as difficult as their parents. The head butler Alonzo Fields said of Herbert, Jr., "He was like his father in that he did not appear to see others." It was demeaning to the staff and disrespectful.

Allan who spent little time in the White House had a butler replaced just because he didn't like the way he walked. The White House staff were there to make life easier and as comfortable as possible for the president and family. Most of them were members of the White House staff for many years and served several presidential families during their administrations. To some presidential families the staff became like family members, but not to the Hoovers. To be disrespectful in such a manner to people who catered to your every whim was difficult to comprehend.

The first lady had her own opinions about the staff. She insisted all butlers and footmen were exactly the same height. The butlers were required to wear tuxedos during the day and white tails at night. After the food had been served they were then required to stand silently at attention the entire time until they were signaled to remove the dinnerware.

When clearing the tables they better take great care that the silverware didn't clank against the plates unless they wanted to pay the consequences.

What disturbed some of the staff most of all was the fact that the president and first lady didn't even speak to them. The first lady would use hand signals to them to let them know her orders. The president himself never said a word to the staff or even looked at them. It was as if they weren't even there.

Having learned to speak Mandarin Chinese during their time in China the First Family would speak in Chinese around guests or staff if they didn't want others to know what they were saying.

The same year that his father was elected president, Herbert, Jr. was selected as the first president of Aeronautical Radio, Inc. which put his face on the cover of Time magazine.

In 1929 First Lady Lou Hoover began the tradition of decorating a Christmas tree in the White House.

Christmas Eve, the Hoover's first Christmas in the White House, a fire broke out in the West Wing. At the time the fire broke out the Hoover family including children and grandchildren were enjoying their dinner in the State Dining Room with staff and their families. Ike Hoover, Chief Usher, and the staff rushed out to aid in putting out the fire. While the guests at the dinner were becoming nervous at the thought of the fire and the White House going up in flames, the first lady just drew the curtains and took the children to see the Christmas tree telling them stories and handing out gifts.

The president, his sons, and the members of the Cabinet watched the fire from the west terrace. Seeing the fire spread to the West Wing all but the president rushed out to try to save the files and important papers from the Oval Office and adjoining offices. More than one hundred men were fighting to save the White House from being destroyed as the president stood by without lifting a hand to help and watched. The fire was finally put out in the early hours of Christmas day.

The Hoovers gave a Christmas party during the Depression where the guests were asked to bring gifts of toys, clothing, or something children could use or enjoy to be given out to children who would otherwise not receive anything for Christmas.

When gossip spread that the only reason Western Air Express received certain government contracts was due to Herbert, Jr. being a presidential son he stepped down and sent in a letter of resignation. His letter of resignation was not accepted as the company knew the rumors were not true. He had risen rapidly in the company perhaps which was part of the reason the gossip came about, but it was due to his talents not his name. At the age of twenty-six he had been honored by an aviation trade magazine giving him the title of "the radio genius of the industry."

While many corporations were anxious to employ the president's son there was a shadow that hung over Herbert, Jr., the thought that his desirability for employment was more due to his family name than to his own talents. When one offer came to him that he recognized as beyond his capabilities he responded with "my name is not for sale at any price."

Herbert, Jr. a short time after resigning from Western Air Express was diagnosed with tuberculosis and he spent the remainder of 1931 recuperating and resting at a sanatorium in Asheville, North Carolina. He spent his time reading and learning about any new scientific field that offered him the opportunity to challenge his mind while laid up. During his year of convalescence his wife and children lived in the White House.

After his time of convalescence had come to an end he returned for a time to Western Air Express and then went into teaching business economics at the California Institute of Technology.

When his father lost his reelection to Franklin D. Roosevelt in 1932, Herbert, Jr. and his brother Allan purchased the home of their father's birthplace for $4,500. Allan had a large part in restoring his father's home in Iowa. The brothers turned the home into the Herbert Hoover Presidential Library and Museum.

Herbert, Jr. went into the field of exploration geophysics. He founded the company United Geophysical and later founded Consolidated Engineering Corporation.

Allan married Margaret Coberly in 1937. He and his wife had three children; two sons and a daughter: Allan, Jr. born in 1938, Andrew born in 1940, and Lou Henry, named after the first lady, born in 1943.

Allan worked in mining, agriculture, and financing. He was an owner and operator of farm and ranch properties which made him a wealthy man. He was also a mining executive like his father before him and an investment banker.

In his later years Allan would serve in foundations promoting his father's legacy. He died November 8, 1993 at the age of eighty-six.

In 1943 Herbert, Jr. was invited by the President of Venezuela to advise the Venezuelan government during their negotiation of oil contracts with other governments. He had built such a reputation for himself that the following year the Shah of Iran hired his company to advise his country in their negotiations of oil concessions.

The first lady died in 1944 a short time after she and the president moved to the Waldorf-Astoria. The former president who was used to always having people around him lived alone now in the hotel in New York; but his son Herbert, Jr. would drive up from Connecticut just to have dinner with his father when he knew his father would be alone. The former president died at the age of ninety in 1964.

In 1953 President Eisenhower asked Herbert, Jr. to travel to Iran as his special envoy to try and broker a deal between the U.S., Britain, and Iran. Eisenhower pleased with his accomplishment then asked him to become Under Secretary of State which he accepted, serving from 1954 – 1957. His father at age eighty was there to watch his son sworn into office.

Herbert, Jr. considered one of the most successful presidential children died in 1969 at the age of sixty-five.

32

FRANKLIN D. ROOSEVELT

Children of Eleanor and Franklin D. Roosevelt:

Anna Eleanor Roosevelt – Born: May 3, 1906   Died: Dec 1, 1975

James Roosevelt "Jimmy" - Born: Dec 23, 1907   Died: Aug. 13, 1991

Franklin Delano Roosevelt, Jr. #1 – Born: March 18, 1909   Died: Nov 8, 1909

Elliott Roosevelt – Born: Sept. 23, 1910   Died: Oct 27, 1990

Franklin Delano Roosevelt, Jr. #2 - Born: Aug. 17, 1914   Died: Aug. 17, 1988

John Aspinwall Roosevelt – Born: March 13, 1916   Died: April 27, 1981

One of Roosevelt's sons was accused of being involved in an assassination plot. He was accused of offering $100,000 to an 'alleged mobster front man' to assassinate the Bahamanian Prime Minister.

Eleanor Roosevelt didn't have to change her last name when she married her fifth cousin once removed Franklin D. Roosevelt. She was the niece of sitting President Theodore Roosevelt. When planning their wedding First Lady Edith Roosevelt offered Eleanor the

White House for their wedding site. She declined the offer but the president did walk the bride down the aisle.

Between the years 1906 - 1916 the Roosevelt's would have six children. Their first child Anna arrived fourteen months after her parent's marriage on May 3, 1906, weighing in at 10 pounds 1 ounce.

It became obvious fairly quickly that Eleanor didn't know the first thing about children or how to raise them. As a three month old infant Anna suffered from convulsions. The new mother felt the doctor's contempt and disgust about her ignorance on how to care for a baby - and she really didn't know the first thing about taking care of children, nor did she really care to learn. In later years her children while under the care of nannies and their grandmother were much more comfortable with them than they were with their own mother. Eleanor was quite content to let them take over the raising of her children; a job that left her feeling inadequate.

Eleanor would hang Anna, her young infant daughter, outside in a wire contraption similar to a cage so her daughter could get fresh air. Neighbors shocked at the sight of seeing her daughter cared for in such a manner threatened to call the Society for the Prevention of Cruelty to Children. Anna also had her hands tied to the sides of her crib because her mother suspected she might be 'touching herself in an intimate way.'

Jimmy was born in December of 1907 weighing in at 10 pounds 5 ounces. The Roosevelt children were all big babies. The other children followed every few years.

Franklin, Jr., their third child died before reaching eight months of age. Eleanor was away from their home and in New York with Franklin who was at that time working in his law office. They were notified that baby Franklin was near death. Eleanor and Franklin rushed home. The next morning they took the baby by train to New York to consult with a specialist. The specialist informed them that the baby had heart trouble and wasn't expected to live. He died the following morning.

Elliott arrived less than a year after Franklin, Jr's death, the same year his father became senator of New York. He ran as a Democrat in a city that had voted Republican for the last thirty-two years, yet he won the election.

Between the birth of Elliott and the second son to carry the name Franklin, Jr. FDR was appointed as Assistant Secretary of the Navy at the age of thirty-one, the youngest man to hold the appointment in the navy's history. It was a post he would hold for the next seven years.

During the children's young life their mother was away from the children more often than not leaving them in the care of nurses and nannies.

When Woodrow Wilson appointed FDR as Assistant Secretary of the Navy the family moved to Washington. FDR's mother had intimidated her daughter-in-law Eleanor and pretty much run her life from the time she married FDR until they made the move to Washington. When Eleanor fired all the white household staff replacing them with an all black staff her mother-in-law questioned her decision. Eleanor replied, "Mother, you run your house; and I'll run mine."

Eleanor had had quite enough of her mother-in-law bossing her around and making her feel inferior. From the time she had become engaged to her son she had meddled by making them put off their marriage for a year, choosing their homes and furnishing them herself, and taking over with the children.

FDR's mother had told her grandchildren, "Your mother only bore you. I am more your mother than your mother is." She had ruled the roost in the past, but Eleanor was determined that it would be she who was in charge of the house now. The house yes, but the raising of the children was of less relevance.

When Eleanor became pregnant yet again a secretary was hired to help her. The secretary was none other than Lucy Mercer who would later become involved with Eleanor's husband in a romantic relationship that would continue off and on up to the time of his death.

The Roosevelts spent their summers in Canada at Campobello. To get there they would occasionally take the steamer, but usually took a woodburning locomotive riding in a car that had oil lamps and heated by a Franklin stove. At one of the stops along the way was a nearby reservation. Indians would board the train to sell their wares such as blankets and baskets. Jimmy was always afraid of being scalped.

Their summer vacation home at Campobello was a large cottage with eighteen bedrooms with no electricity or telephone. The children spent their summers at Campobello with their mother. Their father joined them when there was a break in his work schedule. It was arranged that Eleanor's doctor who had been there for the arrival of the other four children would come to Campobello in time for the arrival of their fifth child. It was fortunate that the night she went into labor FDR was there. FDR sailed to the mainland for the doctor in the little town nearby. He arrived in time with the doctor to see to the birth of his son Franklin, Jr. #2.

When Franklin, Jr. was just weeks old his nurse had covered his crib with a blue veil over his crib to block the sun. While lying in his crib he had pulled the veil in his mouth sucking on it. When the nurse returned to check on him, his face had turned blue from the coloring in the veil. The nurse was terrified he had been poisoned by the dye.

Eleanor gave birth to their last child John in 1916.

Eleanor often joined FDR and was away from home leaving the care of the children up to nannies. She knew the nannies were more knowledgeable than she was about caring for them and was quite content to leave the children in their care. What she didn't know is that one of those nannies was abusive.

The nanny pushed Anna to the floor and kneeled on her in an attempt to teach her manners. When Jimmy sat watching the nanny as she ate her lunch watching her put hot mustard on her lunch she forced him into eating the entire pot of hot mustard. Another time while they were staying in New York the nanny made Jimmy put on one of his sister's dresses with a sign on his back which read *'I am a liar'* and march up and down the street because he had told her he had brushed his teeth and she didn't believe him.

Elliot's turn of abuse came next when he upset Franklin, Jr.'s high chair and laughed when his brother fell. The nanny shoved him in a closet and in a rage locked the door breaking the key off in the lock. He had been locked inside for three hours screaming for help when his father arrived home. When he discovered his son locked in the closet by the nanny who was supposed to be caring for him he was furious. Amazingly enough she was kept on for several more years and then pulled the same stunt locking Franklin, Jr. in the closet - again breaking the key in the lock.

Would that be the final straw for Eleanor? No, she didn't fire the nanny until the day she went through her drawers and found empty gin and whiskey bottles. It appears that drinking was a larger transgression to the children's mother than abusing her children.

Perhaps it was the fear she would have had to care for the children herself that had caused Eleanor to turn a blind's eye to the treatment of her children.

As much as Eleanor was uneasy around her children the kids loved when their father had time to play with them. Winters he would pull out the sleds and he would join the kids riding down the hills screaming with delight right along with the kids. He would rough house with them and play sports such as hockey while their mother stayed home.

It was decided the boys needed some culture and they were forced into taking weekly dancing lessons in the ballroom of the British embassy with the boys hating every minute of it dressed in white gloves, Eton jackets, and patent-leather pumps.

Christmas holidays were spent at Hyde Park with the house smelling of pine and decorated with Christmas festive decorations. FDR would pick out the tree himself and they would decorate it with ornaments and wax tapered candles. It was a family tradition to decorate the tree with candles; one FDR claimed his own father had decorated their trees with when he was a child. A bucket of water was kept close by just in case of fire.

The Roosevelt rule was the children were allowed to get up on Christmas morning but they couldn't wake their parents until 7:30. The kids would dance around watching the clock as the minutes ticked by until the clock stuck on the half hour then making a mad dash for their father's bedroom. More often than not he heard them coming and was waiting to greet them. Their mother hearing the rowdy, impatient bunch joined them from her own room and was soon followed by their grandmother. After wishing their parents and grandmother a Merry Christmas they ran to dress and then had breakfast and made their way to open their presents in front of a tree that reached fourteen feet decorated with ornaments and wax tapers as such that it could have been featured on Currier & Ives.

Christmas morning the family attended church and that evening their father read to them curled up in front of a fire with a worn out copy of Dickens *'A Christmas Carol'* to them – a tradition he began from his days at Groton school and would continue during their days in the White House.

The summer of 1921 was life changing for FDR. It was customary for them to spend their summers at their vacation home at Campobello. On August 10th FDR fell overboard from his sailboat into the frigid waters of the Bay of Fundy.

He later complained of lower back pain and went for a swim hoping to ease the pain. As the day wore on his legs became weak and within three days he could no longer stand. He was diagnosed with infantile paralysis another name for polio at the age of thirty-nine.

Anna decided she had met the love of her life and arrived home for Christmas introducing the man she planned to marry to the family. Curtis Dall was a stockbroker and a graduate of Princeton. Ten years older than Anna he seemed a misfit for the Roosevelt daughter. She had spent her vacation in Arizona on a ranch and loved the outdoors and animals thinking it would be the life for her. And here she walks in the door with a city-slicker, just the opposite of Anna who had been a tomboy all her life.

Jimmy and Elliott decided to see exactly what Anna's beau was made of and to knock him down a peg or two. After he bragged about the skills he had mastered playing hockey while at Princeton the boys challenged him to a game of ice hockey. He smugly accepted. The boys waited for their opportunity, finding it as he made a dash for the goal and tripped him. Blood flowed from a cut made from a skate blade that sliced his chin. Anna let her brothers know with no words held back how she felt about their actions as she took him inside to clean him up. The boys couldn't help but notice with amusement the scar the groom displayed on his chin on his wedding day.

Anna was twenty years old when she married. According to Anna in later years, she admitted to marrying Curtis to get away from a stressful and complicated home life. She wanted to get out of the house and he was the first to come along and offer her a way out. The marriage lasted six years in which time they had two children. Funny that in her adult life she returned to live with that "stressful family" in the White House.

Anna met her second husband while campaigning for her father for the presidency. John Boettiger who would become her next husband was a reporter for the *Chicago Tribune*.

Jimmy, the second child and first son of Franklin and Eleanor, was educated at Groton an exclusive boy's preparatory school. He continued his education at Harvard and finished at Boston University Law School. While receiving an excellent education at the best schools Jimmy's academics were nothing to brag about.

Jimmy married Betsy Cushing in 1930 which would be his first of four marriages.

Jimmy first entered the business world by going into the insurance business. He started his own insurance agency in 1932, Roosevelt and Sargent. As president of the company he made himself a comfortable living making a small fortune.

While his father was running for president Jimmy was actively campaigning for him and was campaign manager for the state of Massachusetts.

He was twenty-six years old at the time his father became president. He resigned from the insurance firm and went to work for his father in the White House in 1937.

Elliott also attended Groton. He however did not attend Harvard as his brother Jimmy and his father had. He flunked the Harvard entrance exams.

Franklin, Jr. #2 graduated from Groton the year his father became president. Unlike Elliott he had excelled academically and in sports. He was nineteen when his father entered the White House. He would take some time off between graduating from Groton and attending Harvard by traveling to France, England, and Spain.

John, the baby of the family, grew up on the Roosevelt estate in Hyde Park in New York. He attended The Buckley School and Groton and would later go on to Harvard.

John was only five years old when his father contracted polio. He had missed the years when his father played vigorously with his children. To try to make up for this loss, Eleanor not wanting her youngest to miss out on sports and physical activities learned to swim and skate so she could take her youngest children on outings. The family chauffeur taught the two youngest to swim by dangling them in the water on a rope attached to a sturdy pole.

Franklin Roosevelt, better known as FDR, was inaugurated March 4, 1933; the first handicapped president in American history. Due to his polio FDR could not walk; however few Americans at the time realized the extent of his disabilities. Held up by his son Jimmy, FDR approached the rostrum where he took the oath of office. His inaugural speech is most remembered for his words, *"The only thing we have to fear, is fear itself..."*

At one time or another all of the Roosevelt children, most of them were adults by this time, lived at the White House while their father was president; some for a longer period than others.

John, the youngest of the Roosevelt children, who was seventeen years of age and a student when his father became president drove his old, beat up car to the White House gates late one night and was turned away. He was told, "No son of a President would be driving such a junk heap."

Another night when John was looking for a midnight snack from the refrigerator he was frustrated to find the refrigerator locked. The servants had a habit of helping themselves to the contents of the fridge making food loss an issue. Life at the White House was more complicated than at Hyde Park where he grew up.

The Roosevelt's oldest child and only daughter, twenty-seven year old Anna, was seeking a divorce from her husband when she moved into the White House. Her two children nicknamed Buzzie and Sistie would be remaining in New York initially so Sistie could finish her year of school.

Anna wanted to get a quick divorce so she could get married to a reporter she had met while campaigning for her father. John Boettiger, the reporter for *The Chicago Tribune* who was covering her father's presidential campaign would become her second husband. The couple would have to delay their wedding plans for awhile as Elliott was also getting a divorce so he could remarry. Her parents didn't think it would look good for two of his children to get divorced so soon after his election and Elliott refused to put off his own divorce.

Anna's son Curtis, nicknamed Buzzie, moved into the White House when he was three years old along with his six year old sister Anna Eleanor who was nicknamed Sistie. Buzzie was a happy child who loved living in the White House. The press loved having a young grandchild in the White House and Buzzie was all too happy to pose for them as they took photos of him while he played on the South Lawn of the White House.

Buzzie in his later years would write the book, *'Too Close to the Sun: Growing Up in the Shadow of my Grandparents, Franklin and Eleanor'* about his grandparents who he said were the most influential people in his life.

Eleanor uncomfortable with her own children as youngsters did no better with her grandchildren. When she came upon her three year old grandson crying the exasperated first lady told him "to bottle it." She didn't have a reputation for being patient or compassionate toward her grandchildren. She may have been an active first lady but she failed miserably at being the type grandmother that would cuddle her grandchildren and enjoyed spending time with them.

Growing up with a mother who was indifferent and hands off with her children her daughter Anna knew it was important to show her children love; but never having received that love herself she was also a mother who didn't know how to show her children love and tenderness that comes natural to most mothers.

After the grandchildren had moved into the White House the first lady came across Buzzie lying on the floor crying. She looked down at him with exasperation and told him if he must cry to go find a bathtub and cry there; never once asking him what was wrong or trying to soothe his hurt feelings. Later that same day when giving some guests a tour of the family's living quarters they heard crying coming from the bathroom of the Lincoln Bedroom. When they entered the room they found Buzzie sitting in the bathtub crying his heart out – and still received not a bit of concern or compassion from his grandmother. It seemed to be easier for her to show compassion to complete strangers rather than to her own grandchildren.

Looking back at those memories as an adult Curtis would say "empathy eluded my grandmother when it came to family members, or anyone else for whom she felt responsibility." In reflection he said his grandmother had a difficult time being close to others – including family.

It was a different story with his grandfather who he looked upon as a father figure. He once made the remark that when he grew up he wanted to be like his grandfather. His mother gave him a withering look and said, "You can never be like Papa. Who do you think you are?"

The grandchildren had few opportunities to play with other children during their time in the White House. They grew up quite isolated from others of their own age. When other children were brought around Buzzie had no idea how kids were supposed to play with each other or even how to make friends.

The only 'friends' Buzzie and Sistie had were the White House staff who made an effort to pay attention to the grandchildren. Other than the staff they were on their own and had only each other to play with. Only on special occasions or for special events were other children brought to the White House to play. They were hand-picked and arrived with their own nannies who watched over the children with an eagle eye.

One of the events when other children were brought in was for a birthday party for Buzzie. He didn't know any of the children that were invited and never saw them again after the party.

Buzzie and Sistie's days were organized. Their mother would arrive at a set time and read to them and then have a conversation with their nanny as to what she expected them to do that day. As Buzzie would later say, "She would speak about us, but not to us." She was as indifferent and removed from her children as her mother had been with her.

Anna wrote two children's books called *'Scamper: The Bunny Who Went To The White House'* and *'Scamper's Christmas.'* The books were published in 1934 and in 1935. Eleanor Roosevelt would also write a children's book herself a few years later titled, *'Bobby and Betty Come to Washington.'* Ironic that two women who didn't have a clue of how to relate to children would write children's books.

When Anna left the White House to marry her second husband her own children didn't even know she was getting married and had never met the man who was about to become their stepfather. When asked where their mother was they were told she was on her honeymoon. They didn't even know what that was.

After Anna remarried she and her husband moved to New York City where he would be working but left the children behind for a time to remain in the care of their grandparents.

Buzzie and Sistie attended the school The National Research Council for Children. They were driven to school by a chauffeur to a large house where the school was set up. The first time Buzzie had to use the restroom he was taken and shown where it was located and then the teacher shut the door behind him. This was the first time Buzzie had ever gone to the bathroom on his own. Usually his nanny took him and undressed him and when he finished she washed his hands and redressed him. He had never undone his buttons on his own before and for him it was perplexing as he tried to figure out the task of undoing his clothing himself. When he finished his business he walked outside where the teacher was waiting for him. The teacher seeing he had left the toilet unflushed she mentioned it to him to which he replied, "In the White House we never flush the toilet."

It wasn't unusual for the Roosevelt sons to be an embarrassment to their parents with their drinking and partying ways, their divorces, and business deals exploiting the Roosevelt name.

Jimmy the first son was twenty-six when his father became president. He had worked on the campaign to get his father elected. He now felt he could use his father's position to get friends of his government jobs. Just months after his father was in office he was known as 'the man to see.' The press had a field day. Jimmy was even known to brag about it and when things got so bad with the press he was sent to Europe so things would die down.

In 1935 Jimmy became president of National Grain Yeast Corporation a company involved in making industrial alcohol. He again became center stage of gossip when there were rumors of bootlegging. One of the company's backers was Joseph Kennedy, Sr. Word was out that backers of the company were involved with organized crime. At that point Jimmy had no other choice than to resign. Scandal seemed to follow him.

The following year Jimmy entered the Marines as a lieutenant colonel and was assigned as the president's military aide. Fingers were pointed at the president's son yet again as receiving special favors due to his name.

Jimmy got some relief from being the center of unwanted attention due to his brother Elliott. Elliott became a name well-known connected with scandals during his father's presidency and after. Just twenty-three when his father became president he was an opportunist that used his father's name in any way that would be helpful to himself. His name seemed to constantly be on the bad boy list. He was connected with an import-export scandal involving German airplane builder Fokker. As many of the other Roosevelt children did he also had multiple marriages and again there were grumblings about his advancement in the military.

Elliott had first married at the age of twenty-two. The ink was barely dry on the marriage certificate when he decided he was in love with someone else, divorced his first wife, and turned around and immediately married his second wife who just happened to be a Texas heiress.

Elliott had become interested in aviation and pursued his studies in that direction becoming an expert in the field. The year his father became president he went to work for William Randolph Hearst a bitter enemy of his father. He became director of a Hearst radio network. His sister and her husband would also become employed by Hearst in the near future.

The two youngest sons of the president and first lady, Franklin, Jr. and John, were still in school. They would often visit the White House during school breaks.

Both boys were reckless drivers. Franklin, Jr. had been arrested in four different states and had been sued due to car accidents more than once. Both boys drove too fast and what was the most worrisome was when they did this after a drinking spree. One policeman had pulled them over and when discovering they were Roosevelts they were told they should set a better example as sons of the president. They didn't take too kindly to being rebuked.

It wasn't the first time they had an encounter with the police. During his father's first inauguration Franklin, Jr. 'borrowed' a motorcycle from a policeman to see the sights in Washington.

Franklin, Jr. at nineteen was in his second year at Harvard and John was a seventeen year old senior at Groton. Instead of settling down as young men they were both out of control. While the president seemed to find his sons amusing, the first lady did not.

Franklin, Jr. while at Harvard was pursued relentlessly by the press looking for a story. With his reputation as being a bit risqué and a party boy the reporters knew it was only a matter of time before they would have a story. Tired of being followed and chased by the reporters, Franklin, Jr. grabbed one of the reporter's cameras and threw it down breaking it – *and the reporters had their story.*

Life wasn't all fun and games for Franklin, Jr. however; as he did earn a law degree at University of Virginia Law School once he graduated from Harvard. During the Depression he worked in a Wall Street law office as a clerk.

John and Franklin, Jr. the two youngest boys were closer to their mother than the other boys. Perhaps part of that reason is their father had come down with polio when they were young and she tried to step in and do things with them their father had done with the others when they were younger, or perhaps she had become more comfortable in her role as a mother by then. Whatever the reason, she took both of them on a trip to Europe in 1937, a decision she probably regretted.

Determined to keep the two boys from roughhousing in hotel rooms which their father found entertaining at home, she made a point of wearing them out taking them hiking for miles; but all she accomplished was wearing herself out.

The highlight of the vacation as far as the boys were concerned was when Franklin, Jr. held John by his ankles dangling him out of a fourth-story hotel window at Mont-Saint-Michel. The horrified people who witnessed this scene called the police. In Cannes on the French Riviera, a drunk John attacked the mayor making headlines not only in Cannes but also back home.

After completing his education at Groton John went to Harvard as his father and brothers before him had. While a junior at Harvard his father arranged a summer job for him working in the forests of Tennessee for the TVA or Tennessee Valley Authority.

After his wild, youthful days John would settle down and become the least controversial son and was often praised for not trying to use his famous name to make life easier but standing on his own achievements. He would also be the only son not to seek political office.

While Eleanor seems to have been a complete failure as a parent and initially did not want her husband to become president, she excelled in her life of public service. She was the first lady that dramatically changed the role of first lady being active herself in politics. She spoke out for human rights, children's causes, and women's issues.

First lady Eleanor had a newspaper column, '*My Day,*' similiar to a diary. The column covered interesting people she met, her travels, her thoughts, and how she handled the pressures of public life. The article appeared in 90 different newspapers giving Americans a glimpse into the life of a first lady like they had never seen before.

Eleanor worked hard towards helping the country's poor, stood against racial discrimination and during World War II traveled abroad to visit American troops. Criticized by some and praised by others she was the most active first lady in American history. She still holds that title today and she would be a hard one to compete with. She also had the advantage of the most years in the White House which gave her additional time, even so there has been no other first lady in American history that can even come close to her achievements as first lady.

Eleanor Roosevelt was the *first* first lady to give press conferences – to women reporters only; as her husband's press conferences were for men only. She received more press coverage than any other first lady with the exception of Jacqueline Kennedy.

In 1936 Franklin, Jr. became engaged to Ethel du Pont who comes from the famous du Pont family who are rated #15 of America's Richest Families worth over $15 billion dollars today. The media scrutiny became so unbearable to the president's son tht he was quoted as saying, "This is worse than campaigning with father."

The du Ponts were a Republican family that did not care for President Roosevelt and had used part of their fortune to fight against him in the elections. The du Ponts were well-known adversaries of the Roosevelts. The wedding was a bit like Juliet marrying Romeo.

Franklin, Jr. married Ethel du Pont who was named one of the "most beautiful and eligible wealthy bachelor girls of America." Franklin, Jr. was considered quite a catch himself.

The wedding was kept small - a mere 1,300 guests were invited.

The marriage would not be a happy one. They had two children together but in 1949 Ethel filed for divorce on grounds of incompatibility and mental cruelty. He remarried within two months of his divorce and within seven months of the divorce she too was engaged and would remarry and divorce again.

Ethel years later would spend time in a sanitarium, a psychiatric facility for the rich and famous who wished for their treatment to remain undisclosed. She eventually ended her life by committing suicide by hanging herself in her shower with the belt from her robe.

There would be nineteen marriages amongst the five Roosevelt children. Their parent's marriage was a poor example to follow.

The president and first lady lived separate lives. Chief Usher Ward said, "We (meaning the White House staff) never saw Eleanor and Franklin in the same room alone together. They had the most separate relationship I have ever seen between man and wife."

Yet they had six children together. Despite being pregnant and giving birth six times, Eleanor disliked sex. She once told her daughter Anna that sex was an "ordeal to be borne."

While for years there was much speculation about whether the first lady was a lesbian, all deniability pretty much ended when the book *'Empty Without You: The Intimate Letters of Eleanor Roosevelt and Lorena Hicks'* by Rodger Streitmatter came out.

The book included three hundred letters from just a two year period written in Eleanor's own words. These were letters written to a woman who had an adjoining room to Eleanor's in the White House. FDR himself called Lorena Hicks Eleanor's 'she-man.'

Hick's sister burned the letters she found of her sisters from the first lady telling the first lady's daughter Anna that her mother hadn't always been discreet in her letters.

For years historians tried to deny and cover up the relationship, but Eleanor's own son came forward in later years, against his family's wishes, admitting to his mother's relationship with another woman. This does not diminish in any way what the first lady accomplished in her lifetime; so why try to cover it up or deny it? During her lifetime the lifestyle was not widely accepted and was looked upon with disdain.

Anna had moved with her second husband to New York after her marriage while her children remained at the White House. Buzzie would later say his mother's absence for a year in his life had not made much of a difference to him and his sister. They were now told they would be moving to New York to join their mother and her husband.

Once in New York he attended the Buckley School where his uncles had gone. He had settled in and was content at his new school when he learned they would be moving to Seattle where his mother and stepfather would be working for the *Seattle Post-Intelligencer* working for Willaim Randolph Hearst. Anna had another baby a boy named John during their time in Seattle.

John, the youngest of the Roosevelt's children, married Anne Lindsay Clark in 1938. She was a debutante from Boston. John went to work at Filene's Department Store in Boston until the time that America entered WWII.

A third term for the presidency was unprecedented, but for the first time in American history a president was elected for a third term.

Elliott joined the Army the year before America entered the war. At this time Europe was at war but the U.S. was still dragging it's feet about committing itself to become involved. Elliott was commissioned as a captain regardless of the fact that he had no military training. There was an immediate outrage from the press and the public calling it nepotism.

Jimmy moved to California in 1939 with the desire for a new beginning. He worked for Samuel Goldwyn Productions and eventually went into the movie production business becoming president of the company. He would later establish his own company Globe Productions and become a film producer. One of the films he produced was *'Pot o' Gold,'* a romantic musical comedy starring Jimmy Stewart. Jimmy Roosevelt was accused of taking money from the Mafia to finance his movie ventures.

It was the year 1940 when presidential son Jimmy suffered from a perforated ulcer and was hospitalized having to undergo surgery. It was during this time he spent in the hospital that a romance began with one of the nurses. His marriage of ten years with Betsy ended in 1940 and he married the nurse Romelle Schneider the same year of his divorce from Betsy.

Jimmy who had joined the Marines was sent by his father on a secret diplomatic mission to assure oher government leaders that the U.S. would soon be in the war. This was in April of 1941. Little did the president know at that time what the Japanese had planned for the U.S. that forced our country into the war perhaps sooner than originally thought. Some of the government leaders Jimmy met with were Chiang Kai-shek of China, King Farouk of Egypt, and King George of Greece.

December 7, 1941 was the day hundreds of Japanese fighter planes bombed Pearl Harbor. The attack lasted approximately two hours leaving devastation in it's wake. More than 2,000 American soldiers and sailors died in the attack and another 1,000 were wounded. Destroyed were 20 American naval vessels including battleships and over 300 airplanes.

The day after the assault President Roosevelt went to Congress asking for a formal declaration of war against Japan and Germany. They agreed with only one dissenting vote. December 7, 1941 is a day Americans will not forget.

Public sentiment against Japanese even towards those born in America with Japanese roots had turned hostile. 110,000 – 120,000 people of Japanese ancestry living on the Pacific coast were forced to leave their homes and their belongings behind and live in internment camps. It made not a bit of difference that 62% of those interred were American citizens. A law had been passed. President Roosevelt signed the law into effect but the first lady had grave misgivings saying it would forever remain a black eye on America. She was right.

Elliott had entered into the military the year before the U.S. entered the war, but once America entered into WWII Elliott was rapidly promoted to major, then lieutenant colonel, colonel, and brigadier general receiving criticism because of his quick promotions. Every time he was promoted the press and the public hurled vicious accusations about the advantages the president's sons were receiving due to their father's position. In this case their accusations were simply not true.

Elliott had proved himself to be worthy of his promotions by flying three hundred combat missions and participating in the invasion of North Africa, Sicily, and the D-Day invasion of Normandy. He had been wounded not once, but twice; and decorated for valor.

During the war he was awarded the U.S. Air Medal, Legion of Merit, and the Distinguished Flying Cross with Oak Leaf Cluster; made Commander of the Order of the British Empire, and received the French Legion of Honor, and the Croix de Guerre with Palm.

In 1943 Elliott became involved in a scandal concerning purchasing warplanes that involved Howard Hughes. He had been asked by General Arnold to investigate several reconnaissance aircraft under development and to select a successor to the Lockheed P-38.

After being wined and dined by employees of Hughes Aircraft and then shown around their aircraft factory by Howard Hughes himself, Roosevelt recommended the Hughes D-2 which had already been previously turned down by the military as being inadequate. It was determined that the Lockheed XP-58 was further along in development and superior to the Hughes plane. When looked into, it was turned over to the Senate to investigate whether Elliott's choice had been influenced by the Hughes firm spending a substantial sum on entertaining him.

While in Hollywood Elliott had met actress Faye Emerson. His second wife Ruth divorced him after almost eleven years of marriage and six months later he announced that he and actress Faye Emerson were engaged. In no time at all they married at the Grand Canyon in Arizona.

Elliott and Faye arrived at the White House where she met the president and first lady for the first time. While the president enjoyed her company, the first lady wrote to a friend the evening after meeting her, *"Elliott's new wife (his third) is pretty, quiet, and hard, I guess. She seems capable, but I don't think she is more than a passing house guest!"* The first lady had seen so many spouses of her children by this time that she had become a bit cynical; but within a short period of time Faye would become her favorite daughter-in-law.

Another issue with the press came up when Elliott returned to the military after his wedding and ordered his mastiff dog, an extremely large dog, to be shipped to his wife. In order to ship the dog three American soldiers on leave were bumped from their flight to make room for the dog. It didn't take any time at all for the story to reach the press and become a front page story.

During WWII Franklin, Jr. served on a destroyer which was bombed during the Sicilian invasion. After putting himself in harms way to save a critically wounded sailor carrying him to safety he was awarded the Silver Star Medal. Before war's end he would be awarded not only the Silver Star, but a Purple Heart, Navy Cross, and the Legion of Merit. He became a commanding officer of his own destroyer in 1944. He served in both the Pacific and the Atlantic theaters of war.

In 1943 when President Roosevelt met with Winston Churchill at Casablanca his two sons Elliott and Franklin, Jr. were with him.

When the U.S. entered WWII John told his family he was planning on claiming conscientious objector status. The family was able to influence him otherwise and he joined the navy. He would be awarded the Bronze Star and served as lieutenant on the aircraft carrier *USS Wasp* in the Pacific. He didn't have the brilliant military career his brothers had, but all the same he did serve his country.

Anna's husband had contacted General Eisenhower in 1943 about receiving an officer's commission after his father-in-law, the president, made a passing remark about him not being in uniform. When her husband left for the war her father who was not in good health requested for his daughter and her youngest son John to come back to the White House to live. He wanted his daughter near him. His personal assistant had suffered a stroke and his daughter took her place in the office.

Anna liked feeling needed by her father and soon basked in the glory that went hand in hand with working for the president. As the president's health declined she took on more responsibility filling the role of chief of staff, personal assistant, and his social secretary. She often served as his hostess, as the first lady was out of the White House more often than not; and she also had control of who got in to see the president and who didn't.

While an asset to her father she became a distant figure in her son John's life who was also living in the White House at the time. John would later admit he barely remembered her during this time era, as when she wasn't busy working in the White House office she often traveled with the president including overseas trips.

While his mother was a distant figure barely to be remembered, he had great memories of his grandfather, or PaPa as he called him, who as the only child living in the White House during the war years was given special attention. He would put John in bed with him mornings and read the funny papers to him. He easily recalled the wonderful times at the White House swimming in the pool with PaPa, the Easter egg hunts, and the special visit from the Lone Ranger and his famous horse Silver.

His grandfather kept wind-up toys on his desk for when his grandson John came to visit him in the Oval Office. His grandfather as president was more accessible to him than his own mother.

While working for her father she was a witness to many historic moments; but she also witnessed and set up some meetings with other women that put her in a position that would have caused problems with her own mother. Granted their marriage was dysfunctional at best; but she had to keep these meetings and rendezvous a secret from her mother all the same to keep the peace.

FDR's daughter Anna while working closely with her father had noticed that his health was deteriorating. Even though she had been reassured by his personal physician she insisted he get a second opinion and arranged for him to have a physical at Bethesda Naval Hospital. She was not reassured by this doctor's diagnosis. He gave the diagnosis that the president was suffering from heart disease, high blood pressure, and cardiac failure of the left ventricle. He gave him about a year to live and recommended that he not run for a fourth term.

The president did not heed his doctor's warning and he did run for a fourth term. On the day of his nomination he suffered a seizure with his son Jimmy by his side. Months later he began suffering chest pains.

President Roosevelt was running for an unprecedented fourth term. He had already made history when being elected president for a third term, but now he was running again with Harry Truman for his running mate as vice president.

The president invited his grandson Buzzie to join him and Harry Truman for lunch one day. Truman while his running mate he wasn't someone the president knew well. Little did Truman know the true motives behind this lunch. The president made Truman feel at ease while he questioned him, asked his opinions on certain matters, and watched his reactions to different topics the president brought up; all while being measured on his character and trustworthiness. The president was well aware that the odds were agains him on living out his fourth term and unbeknownst to most, he had contemplated on stepping down at the end of the war. He wanted to reassure himself that Truman would be a president who would continue his policies.

At some point the president asked his grandson to excuse himself so he could speak on confidential matters. Buzzie now a teenager, later learned that once he left the table the president told his running mate in strictest confidence about the top secret development of the atomic bomb; that was at that very point in time in it's final stage of production at Los Alamos. It would indeed be President Truman who would later have to make the difficult decision to use those bombs on Japan.

FDR was elected for a fourth term with Truman as his vice president. Due to the ongoing war there would be no parades or inaugural balls. Normally the inauguration is held at the Capitol but this time it was held at the South Portico of the White House; perhaps due to his failing health, though that excuse would never have been verbalized. His fourth term would last all of three months.

The fourth inauguration had been kept short. Roosevelt's inaugural address was one of the shortest in American history lasting only six minutes. Afterward he went inside the White House and collapsed suffering chest pains. The president knew he was living on borrowed time and a few weeks later went over the terms of his will with his son Jimmy and passed the family ring on to him as the eldest son.

His grandson Buzzie recalled what would unbeknownst to him at the time be his last

Christmas with his grandfather. His grandfather gave him a large model of a submarine. It was a gift that had been given to his grandfather by Charles de Gaulle, who at that time was head of the provisional French government during World War II. His grandmother argued with his grandfather that gifts from heads of state shouldn't be given away, to which his grandfather replied that de Gaulle was "just the head of some French committee or another." His grandson got to keep the submarine and treasured what would be his last gift from his grandfather.

Two days after the inauguration FDR left for a secret meeting with Churchill and Stalin that was held at Yalta. The president's daughter accompanied him on the trip. This was the second time the trio had met during the war. The world leaders all agreed to demand Germany's unconditional surrender and began plans for a post-war world.

In the year 2005 the grandsons of those three famous men, the three leaders of WWII: FDR, Churchill, and Stalin met in the Netherlands to review their grandfathers' legacies from that conference of 1945 in Yalta. The three grandsons were: "Buzzie" or Curtis Roosevelt, Winston S. Churchill III, and Yevgeni Dzhugashvili

The president planned a trip to Warm Springs for a rest and a meeting with his longtime mistress Lucy Mercer. While at Warm Springs he suffered a massive cerebral hemorrhage and died.

FDR had been immensely proud of the fact that all four of his sons had served during WWII. By the end of the war Jimmy who started out on the bad side of the public and press thinking he had been given special favors as a presidential son had gained the nation's respect. He returned a war hero.

Shortly after FDR's death his son Franklin, Jr. was awarded the Legion of Merit.

Anna and her husband John attempted to start their own newspaper in Phoenix, Arizona, but it failed and so did their marriage. She would divorce her second husband in 1949. He committed suicide the following year by jumping out of a hotel window in New York City. Anna married for a third time, James Halsted, a physician. She died of cancer in 1975 at the age of sixty-nine.

The Roosevelt's second child Jimmy would be elected U.S. Representative. He served from 1955 – 1965. While running it came out that he had numerous extramaritial affairs while married that dated back to the time of his father's presidency. He resigned during his sixth term when President Lyndon B. Johnson appointed him a delegate to the United Nations. He wrote *'My Parents: A Differing View,' 'A Family Matter,'* and *'Affectionately, FDR: A son's story of a lonely man.'* Jimmy married four times and had seven children. He was the last of the Roosevelt children to pass away. He died of complications of Parkinsons disease and a stroke at the age of eighty-five.

Elliott and his wife Faye moved to Top Cottage a retreat home FDR had built on his land at Hyde Park. In 1948 Elliott's wife Faye was treated for self-inflicted cuts on her wrists. Two years after her suicide attempt she divorced Elliott. Elliott was married five times, remaining with wife #5 for the last thirty years of his life. He had five children and his last wife's four children by a previous marriage adopted the name Roosevelt as their own.

While Elliott had many careers in his lifetime from military, rancher, mayor of Miami Beach, Florida; it seems that his life as an author was the most productive. He wrote numerous books which included a best-selling murder mystery series based on the first lady as the main character.

How much input he had in these books is in question as he worked with William Harrington who did research and was a ghost writer for celebrity writers. The books from the mystery series with the name of Elliott Roosevelt as author continued being published for ten years after Elliott's death with new books coming out up until the time Harrington himself committed suicide.

Elliott also wrote several books with a co-author about his mother and father which caused irreparable damage between Elliott and other family members. To him it was more important the public had the truth and realized while even though they held the title of president and first lady they were still human with faults and weaknesses of their own.

In 1973 Elliott, the son most connected with scandals throughout his lifetime (brother Franklin, Jr. was a close second), was accused of being involved in an assassination plot on the Bahamanian Prime Minister. He offered $100,000 to an 'alleged mobster front man' to assassinate the prime minister paying him $10,000 up front. Now, if this sounds too wild to be true; the check with his signature was produced along with taped conversations. Elliott maintained up until his death that it wasn't true. Elliott was investigated by the Senate in 1973 of his ties to organized crime. He died of heart failure at the age of eighty.

When Franklin, Jr. returned from the war he served in several New York law offices and became involved in politics. In 1946 he served on the President's Committee on Civil Rights for his father's successor Harry Truman.

Franklin, Jr. was looked on as the one son that most closely resembled his father in many ways and some believed he would follow in his father's footsteps. That thought seemed to be reaffirmed when he made a move for a seat in Congress that had been vacated. He would be reelected and served as congressman from New York from 1949 – 1955. He became the second son of FDR's that served in Congress. Twice he would run for governor, but would be defeated both times.

Franklin, Jr. would be named Under-Secretary of Commerce under President Kennedy after his appointment as Secretary of the Navy had been vetoed. He was good friends with President Kennedy and spent time in the White House socially during his administration. When JFK was assassinated and Lyndon B. Johnson became president he appointed Franklin, Jr. as chairman of the Equal Opportunity Commission.

Franklin, Jr. married five times, the first being to an heir of the du Pont fortune who a year after their divorce committed suicide, the second in-law of the Roosevelts to do so and another who attempted suicide. His second wife Suzanne Perrin he married in 1949 and divorced in 1970. His third marriage to Felicia Schiff Warburg Sarnoff lasted six years. When Franklin, Jr. and Felicia divorced he married the following year to Patricia Luisa Oakes who was the daughter of British actor Richard Greene and the granddaughter of gold mining tycoon Sir Harry Oakes. His fifth wife, Linda McKay Stevenson Weicker he remained with until his death in 1988. Between his five wives he had four children. He died on his seventy-fourth birthday of lung cancer.

At the end of the war, FDR's youngest son John had a career as a retailer in California at the Grayson & Robertson stores in Los Angeles. In 1953 he became an investment banker for a short time before moving to Hyde Park the family home he grew up in.

Unlike his brothers and sister who had a long list of marriages and divorces John married only twice. In 1965 John and Anna were divorced after almost thirty years of marriage. After the divorce she moved to Spain where she lived with her former sister-in-law Elliott's third wife the actress Faye Emerson. The same year they divorced John remarried Irene Boyd McAlpin. He had three daughters and a son with his first wife.

John would later become a member of the Republican party, but waited until after the death of his father to change parties out of respect for his father. He wasn't the only brother with Republican ties. His brother Jimmy joined Democrats for Nixon and publicly supported President Nixon's re-election in 1972. Jimmy also supported Ronald Reagan.

In 1956 John was a consultant for an investment firm which he joined in later years becoming a vice president for the company Bache and Company. He managed the Teamsters Union pension funds and became friends with Jimmy Hoffa.

John was an officer and director of the Standard Uranium Company during the Cold War when the U.S. Atomic Energy Commission was seeking sources of uranium in order to produce atomic weapons.

John died from a heart attack in 1987 at the age of sixty-five.

The Roosevelt children were a great source of stories for the press not only during their father's administration but also for years afterward.

33

HARRY TRUMAN

Children of Bess and Harry Truman:

Mary Margaret Truman – Born: Feb. 17, 1924   Died: Jan. 29, 2008

When presidential daughter Margaret was late coming home from dates her father sent the Secret Service after her to bring her home.

The president is dead! Vice President Truman had just left the Senate and was meeting Speaker of the House Sam Rayburn for a drink. Rayburn arriving before Truman ordered him a bourbon and water and delivering the drink he informed Truman the president's press secretary had called looking for him. Truman returned the call and was told to come "quickly and quietly." Aware of FDR's health issues Truman feared the worst. Arriving at the White House Eleanor Roosevelt informed Truman, "The president is dead."

While attending the 1944 Democratic Convention Truman had been offered to run as President Franklin Roosevelt's vice presidential running mate who was running for his 4th term of office. Truman accepted the offer much to the dismay of his wife Bess. Initially angry that he had agreed, she feared that due to FDR's health there was a very real possibility of her husband ending up being the president in his stead. And of course, that is exactly what happened.

Bess Truman had been able to stay in the shadows and out of the limelight while her husband was a senator, but she feared that as vice president there would be unwanted attention paid to her and her husband. She feared for naught; as during her days as the second lady, or wife of the vice president, she remained an unrecognized face in Washington. When it was discovered she would become the first lady the White House Chief Usher admitted he didn't even know what she looked like.

Bess Truman worried that with her husband's name on the ticket running for vice president that something in her past would be discovered which she preferred be left private. When Bess was still a teenager her father who was an alcoholic and deep in debt committed suicide by shooting himself in the head in the bathtub of his home while his family was sleeping. In those times society looked down on the family of someone who had committed suicide. Bess lived with this secret in shame and always feared the 'family secret' would be revealed.

Bess Truman had two miscarriages before their daughter Margaret was born. Margaret would be their only child. A child who was well-loved and close to her mother and father.

Harry Truman played the piano and often played for his daughter as she was growing up. At a young age he encouraged her to take singing lessons. On her eighth birthday she said she wanted an electric train and was surprised to receive not a train set, but a baby grand piano.

The Truman family were a close-knit family and when Truman had been elected to the Senate his wife Bess and daughter Margaret joined him in Washington. Bess never comfortable as a public figure was happier back home in Missouri; so when Congress was on break they would return to their home in Independence, Missouri. Margaret was ten years old at the time and from 1935 to 1942 went to public school during the fall in Missouri and during the spring in Washington she attended Gunston Hall a private school for girls.

When Margaret was enrolled at the school in Washington she was an only child with no brothers or sisters to turn to and no friends in a strange place. By the time she was enrolled at the school the other children already had friends and were familiar with each other. Margaret felt left out until one day the girls decided to have a contest to see who could scream the loudest and the longest. Margaret who was taking singing lessons finally found a way to make the other girls take notice of 'the new girl.' When it was her turn to scream she gave it her all and let out a loud and long scream. At the conclusion of her scream she looked around to see the other girls staring at her surprised. After that, she was accepted.

Margaret continued her education at George Washington University and was a student at the university when her father became vice president graduating with an Associate of Arts degree the same year.

It was a mere eighty-two days that Truman served as President Roosevelt's vice president before the president died and Truman became the 33rd president. During Truman's administration which lasted from 1945 to 1953 he would have the burden of the decision of dropping the atomic bomb on Japan and at war's end would work towards rebuilding a devastated postwar Europe. The task of containing communism from spreading would have to be dealt with; and yet another war the U.S. became involved in, the Korean War.

Pandemonium had broken out at the Truman home. Margaret was preparing to go on a date and was half dressed when her father called telling his family that President Roosevelt had died. Her mother was crying after receiving the news when the doorbell rang. Margaret, not thinking clearly after receiving the news of not only the president's death but the fact that her father would now be president, opened the door forgetting she was wearing only her slip. She was faced with a woman who identified herself as being from the *Associated Press*. Margaret quickly slammed the door.

Life was about to change drastically for the Truman family. They would no longer be a family of obscurity. Margaret would later recall that moment in time saying, "When I opened the door in my slip to that press girl, it was the last time I ever opened a door without finding out who was there. It was at that moment I ceased to be a free agent."

Margaret rushed to the White House with her mother where they would witness the swearing in of her father as President of the United States. The reality of the situation hadn't even had time to sink in. It was only hours after the death of FDR.

Due to the circumstances Truman would be sworn into office in the Cabinet Room. The date was April 12, 1945. It was 7:00 P.M. when Margaret stood by her mother Bess

Truman, Eleanor Roosevelt, members of the Cabinet, and Speaker of the House Sam Rayburn who just a short time ago thought he was wrapping up the end of the day by having a drink with the vice president, now found himself standing watching him being sworn in as the 33rd President of the United States.

Chief Justice Stone had been called to the White House to administer the oath of office. Stone got Truman's middle name wrong while reciting the oath of office saying, "I, Harry Shippe Truman." Truman responded during the oath with his correct name, "I, Harry S. Truman." Truman didn't have a middle name, just a middle initial. At the completion, Harry S. Truman became the nation's 33rd president.

FDR's death was unexpected and so it would be a few weeks before Eleanor Roosevelt and family moved out of the White House. During the time that Eleanor Roosevelt remained in the White House the Truman family would live in the Blair House which was located directly across from the White House. During Truman's second term of office they would return to the Blair House to live while the White House was being refurbished. But for the time being that is where the president made his home and then walked to the White House every day to work.

Truman took office during the midst of WWII. The Truman family were just moving into the White House when Germany surrendered which became known as V-E Day.

President Truman would become the president remembered for making some of the most crucial decisions in history. A request had been sent to Japan to surrender but was rejected. Truman made a decision that he didn't make lightly and only after several meetings with advisers. The decision was to order the drop of atomic bombs on Hiroshima and Nagasaki. It was only then that Japan surrendered.

Margaret was twenty-one years old when she assumed the title of First Daughter. She was a student at George Washington University studying voice, history, and politics. She was working towards a career as a concert soprano which was her life's dream.

Margaret was anything but enthralled with living in the White House. She found the furniture old and the upstairs living quarters a mess. The Roosevelts had lived there for many years and had quite a number of people living in the family quarters, so it definitely had a lived in worn out look which she found most undesirable. You could see marks on the walls where pictures had hung, the carpets were worn, and when she had a friend over for a luncheon the State Dining Room was freezing.

During other administrations presidential daughters assumed the role of hostess when either there was no first lady or the first lady was too ill to assume the role. Margaret Truman often took over the role for her mother as Margaret enjoyed meeting the public and speaking to the press or on camera; a role her mother was only to happy to turn over to her daughter.

The president and first lady had a close relationship with their daughter and it wasn't unusual for the president to confide in her keeping her in the loop. The White House staff nicknamed them "the Three Muskateers."

The Trumans who were private found the White House with it's staff of almost a hundred people a place that took time getting accustomed to. The place was run with military precision with all the staff knowing their place and what to do and when, so it was very well run; but when you're used to your privacy it can be quite an adjustment.

One member of the staff the Trumans never did adjust to was the Chief Housekeeper Henrietta Nesbitt that had been brought in to the White House by Eleanor Roosevelt. The Trumans found themselves wishing Nesbitt had left with Eleanor. When she served the president brussels sprouts he pushed them to the side refusing to eat them. Margaret let Mrs. Nesbitt know the president didn't like them and asked her not to serve them again. The very next night Truman found brussels sprouts on his plate again. A bit more firmly Margaret reminded her not to serve them again. When the following day she served them yet again Margaret called her mother who was at their home in Missouri and told her if Mrs. Nesbitt didn't leave the White House she would.

President Roosevelt had also complained about Mrs. Nesbitt who ruled over her territory with an iron fist, but to no avail. She served whatever was on sale that week and it didn't matter if you liked it or not, president or not.

The first lady requested the rolls be freshly made and not store bought. Mrs. Nesbitt continued serving store bought rolls and insisted they were freshly made. When the first lady requested a stick of butter to take to a meeting where each woman was to bring one ingredient for a dish they were going to make Mrs. Nesbitt refused to give her the butter saying war rationing was still in effect. The first lady was easy to get along with but she would not tolerate insolence. Mrs. Nesbitt was dismissed with no regrets from the rest of the White House staff. Mrs. Nesbitt had her revenge by retiring and writing a book about her White House experiences.

While some found Truman to be quick tempered, he was not one above having a little fun. One story the White House staff told when talking about the Truman family is how when a waiter entered the dining room to serve a meal he found the president, first lady, and Margaret throwing balls of bread at each other at the table. Another time when they had been served watermelon for dessert they started flipping watermelon seeds at each other. The scene is difficult to picture with Truman who had the appearance and reputation of a 'stuffed shirt'.

During the time when Margaret's father was president she graduated from George Washington University. Her father gave the commencement address and presented her with her diploma.

Becoming a First Daughter meant your date would have to walk you up to the front door of your home, which in her case meant being watched over by a Secret Service agent with brilliant flood lights lighting up your every move as if you were on stage. She knew that must have been intimidating for her dates.

Margaret made the decision not to become engaged while living in the White House. She wanted to be assured it was her and not the power of the presidency that attracted her beau. She had a difficult time dealing with wondering if it was her her that her dates cared about, or if it was the bragging rights of saying he was dating the president's daughter that appealed to him.

Living at the White House your friends are anxious to see where you live and what it's like in the family quarters of the White House. She invited a few of her friends over for a slumber party where they slept in the large Lincoln Bed. Margaret found the bed to be uncomfortable and "overpowering, dark and gloomy."

Another time Margaret invited friends over to the White House it was for dinner and dancing. The party took place in the East Room. At some point in the evening some of the couples ventured out to take a look at different rooms in the White House. One couple found themselves in the State Dining Room where a chandelier hanging over the dining table caught the young girl's eye. Mesmerized by the beauty and size of the chandelier she asked the young man she was with to lift her up so she could touch it. When he lifted her up she started to lose her balance and reached out and grabbed the metal arms. Her date walked off and left her literally hanging from the chandelier.

The young girl screaming for someone to come help her down caught the attention of one of the butlers who, more of a gentleman than her date, helped her down. The next day when Margaret told her father about it, wanting him to hear about it from her first fearing he would be angry, she was surprised when her father hearing the story burst out laughing.

While Margaret stood on the roof of the White House with the first lady the president who was flying in the presidential plane, at that time dubbed the *Sacred Cow,* had the pilot buzz the White House. The Secret Service unaware the president had left and was in the plane called in the Washington police and Air Force security thinking someone had taken off in the president's plane. The White House was in panic mode until they realized it was the president himself buzzing his wife and daughter who were on the roof top oblivious to the chaos caused by the plane coming so close to the presidential mansion.

Margaret dreamed of becoming a concert soprano and when practicing the White House staff had to be very quiet and careful as the prima donna insisted that she wasn't disturbed when practicing. Any of the staff who may have had a cold were ostracized and banned from her presence.

Margaret debuted with the Detroit Symphony Orchestra in 1947 on a national radio program which led to future concert tours and a recording contract with RCA. She looked forward to a concert planned at Constitution Hall in Washington where her parents would be able to hear her for the first time live.

Her parents thought her singing was spectacular and praised their daughter, but the next day the president was furious when he read the *Washington Post* and saw a review by Paul Hume the music critic who didn't have the same opinion of their daughter's singing. The review stated that Margaret had "a pleasant voice of little size and fair quality," "cannot sing very well and is flat a good deal of the time."

The president sent the critic a letter which read, *"Some day I hope to meet you. When that happens you'll need a new nose, a lot of beefsteak for black eyes."* This was probably the best thing that could have happened to the critic as it brought him notoriety he never would have received otherwise. Hume later sold the letter from the president for $3,500;

but in the eyes of the public they loved the fact that the president defended his daughter and he gained points in popularity.

Bess Truman was entertaining women from Daughters of the American Revolution while her husband was upstairs taking a bath. It appeared there was a very real threat of one of the chandeliers in the Blue Room could come crashing down on them. The president later joked he was worried he would fall through the floor, bathtub and all, and that he was a bit nervous about appearing naked before Bess's guests.

The floors in the upstairs room sagged and walking across them you felt as though you were on a ship out to sea. The following year when Margaret's piano fell through the floor Congress agreed it was time to fix the problem. In 1948 the Trumans had to vacate the White House and move back to the Blair House across the street so the mansion could be completely renovated.

Nearing the end of his administration Truman stated there was unfinished business to be taken care of so he would be running for reelection. Margaret was involved in campaigning for her father's reelection in 1948 and traveled with him on his Whistlestop campaign. The campaign began in September and they would be riding a special train called *Magellan* which consisted of seventeen cars with diner cars where people could eat, lounge cars where people could sit to talk and relax, and cars where they could sleep.

President Truman, the first lady, and Margaret lived on the train during the campaign with several stops where he gave speeches and met the people. The train tour consisted of a 30,000 mile tour around the United States. Margaret would also meet with the press on the train to be interviewed and was a great aide to her father's campaign.

Her father's second inauguration took place January 20, 1949. It was the most elaborate inauguration held up to that time and the first to be televised. Margaret was there to witness her father taking the oath of office for the second time and danced the night away at her father's inaugural ball.

After the election Margaret and the first lady made a one day trip aboard the presidential yacht where they sailed from Key West, Florida to the island of Cuba.

With the inauguration behind her Margaret was ready to get back to her singing career and began taking voice lessons from Helen Traubel a Metropolitan Opera star. In October she began a concert tour and in November made an appearance with the National Symphony Orchestra at Constitution Hall. The following year she made her first national television appearance on the Ed Sullivan show '*Toast of the Town.*'

In November of 1950 while still living in the Blair House two Puerto Rican nationalists attempted to assassinate the president. The president was not hurt but a police officer was killed along with one of the would-be assassins. After the assassination attempt the president let the Secret Service talk him into being driven to the White House to work everyday instead of walking. He also became more protective of his loved ones. If Margaret was returning home late from a date the president at times sent Secret Service out to bring her home.

When Truman became president after the death of FDR the United States was in the midst of WWII and now in June of 1950 when the Communist government of North Korea attacked South Korea President Truman didn't see any way that the United States could not become involved in aiding South Korea and keep communism from spreading. The president met with his military advisers and they agreed unanimously that whatever had to be done would be done. The president however, was determined to keep the war a limited one and not risk becoming involved in a major conflict with China or Russia.

This was the era of McCarthyism when McCarthy claimed communists had infiltrated the government. Those who worked for the State Department and were gay were believed to be vulnerable to blackmail by the Soviets. McCarthy wished to bring their lifestyle to light and terminate their employment to eliminate any risk. Today this is looked back on as a blight on U.S. history and determined to be a witch hunt. One of those who were affected by this was John Montgomery a close friend of Margarets who committed suicide hanging himself in his home that he shared with Martin Braverman an attorney who was identified as Margaret's boyfriend.

In 1950 Margaret co-starred with Jimmy Stewart in '*Jackpot*' performed on Screen Directors Playhouse on radio. The following years she took trips to Europe with friends and in 1952 went on another concert tour. Margaret when not on tour loved to sing along with her father at the piano, a pastime they both enjoyed.

In January of 1953 it was time for the Trumans to leave the White House. When her father's administration came to an end Margaret moved to New York City where she would continue with her singing career. Even though the former president and first lady moved back to Missouri and Margaret was in New York they still remained close. The year of his retirement the family took a cruise to the Hawaiian Islands together.

Margaret in between singing concerts also filled in for Edward Murrow on his TV Show *'Person To Person,'* where she interviewed her own parents the former president and first lady. For a time she was hostess of a radio show called *'Weekday.'* She co-hosted other television shows and radio programs throughout her career, but singing was her first love.

She had kept her promise that she wouldn't marry while her father was president and she stuck to that promise, but in 1955 she met Clifton Daniel at a dinner party where a romance began between the two of them. They kept their relationship private and it wasn't until just the month before their wedding that it was discovered that the former president's daughter was about to be married. It was four years since she had left the White House.

Clifton Daniel was working in New York when Margaret met him. Previously he had worked as a foreign correspondent for ten years. As a foreign correspondent he had been in war zones during WWII, covered the founding of the country of Israel, and for a time was posted in Moscow. He was currently working for the *New York Times* as an editor.

The couple had four sons together and had a happy marriage. She quit her concert career after she married and wrote an autobiography, *'Souvenir'* which received great reviews. She would also write her father's biography *'Harry S. Truman.'*

First Lady Bess Truman had been known to be a pack rat and after her death Margaret discovered correspondence that dated back from the time her mother and father were engaged while her father was stationed in Europe during the war, letters from her days as first lady, menus, financial transactions, and paperwork which gave great insight into the life of the former first lady. All of this had been tucked away and stored in the cushions of the sofa, behind chairs, under beds, and in closets and the attic. When gathered together Margaret discovered letters that her father had written to her mother from a period of almost fifty years. These letters became a great discovery, historically and personally, and she used this correspondence to write her mother's story called, *'Bess W. Truman.'*

Margaret also wrote books on White House pets, first ladies, and life in the White House which had great insight coming from a presidential daughter.

Margaret would in all be credited for writing over thirty books both fiction and nonfiction. The fiction books were murder mysteries centered around the White House and Washington. As in many celebrities and well-known figures many of the books are written with a ghostwriter. How much input did she actually have in the mystery series is unknown; but she certainly would have had inside information on the White House and about presidential families that made the stories more intriguing and authentic.

Similar to the last president's son's books that were also written with a ghostwriter the books continued for a decade after his death but still listed his name as the author. Margaret also using a ghostwriter, her books also continued long after her death.

Margaret's first murder mystery book was written with William Harrington as the ghostwriter, but from the second book on she worked with Donald Bain who had already ghostwritten about thirty books at that time. He was quoted as saying, "I remember when we first met, Margaret told me, 'I want the Speaker of the House killed.' "We just went from there." Margaret would meet with Bain several times a year and they would discuss scenarios and go over rough drafts, but Bain did the actual writing of the books. After Margaret's death Bain signed on with the Daniel family to continue the series.

It's always great insight to ask a presidential daughter or son after they have been away from the White House for a time about their memories of life in the White House or as a First Family member what it was like. In some cases the story stays the same, the main theme being how it is difficult to lose your privacy. "The only thing I ever missed about the White House was having a car and driver," she once said. Another advantage she said of her White House days was the White House theater where you could request any film, even ones that had just come out. The people you met, traveling by private plane and train, and receiving fabulous gifts. "Some of it was fun, but most of it was not. It was a great view of history being made," Margaret was quoted as saying in 1980.

The downside of living at the White House was you couldn't go anywhere without a Secret Service agent, you had to really watch what you said around reporters, you became public property, and people felt entitled to know everything about you, and comment on your appearance.

Many times former presidents and their families are invited to return to the White House at social events. The Kennedys gave a dinner in honor of former President Truman. Margaret and her husband Clifton attended the event. They visited with the Kennedys before the dinner and were a part of the entourage that made an entrance coming down the Grand Staircase. This was a customary event for the president and first lady but one that Margaret had seldom participated in herself and one her husband was completely unfamiliar with. The president and first lady pause briefly between *'Ruffles and Flourishes'* being played and *'Hail to the Chief.'* Clifton unaware of this part of the ceremony kept on walking and almost ran into Jackie Kennedy. Afterward he rebuked his wife for not letting him in on this part of the ceremony as it would have been quite embarrassing to all of them if he would have run into Jackie Kennedy and knocked her down the stairs.

Margaret continued her career with a television show she co-hosted and a radio program where she interviewed authors. She served as honorary chair of the Harry S. Truman Library.

To date Bess Truman holds the record for the first lady that lived the longest living to the age of ninety-seven. Margaret died in the year 2008 at the age of eighty-three.

34

DWIGHT D. EISENHOWER

Children of Mamie and Dwight D. Eisenhower:

Doud Dwight Eisenhower "Icky" – Born: Sept 24, 1917   Died: Jan. 2, 1921

John Sheldon Doud Eisenhower - Born: Aug. 3, 1922   Died: Dec. 21, 2013

As the Eisenhower's son stepped forward to receive his diploma at West Point;

his father, the Supreme Allied Commander, was at that moment in time

overseeing the invasion on the beaches of Normandy known as D-Day.

It was June 6, 1944 at the United States Military Academy at West Point and John Eisenhower was patiently waiting for his name to be called to receive his diploma. His mother sat in the audience to witness her son's graduation, but his father was unable to attend.

General Eisenhower was in Europe overseeing the Allied invasion on the beaches of Normandy; though no one in the audience was aware of that at the time. Photographers gathered around John and Mamie Eisenhower to record this memorable day, but it would end up being a mere footnote; as the real news of the day would be the Allied invasion of German-occupied Europe.

John wasn't surprised when he learned his father wouldn't be able to be there to witness his graduation from West Point where his father had also graduated. His father was in Europe as Supreme Allied Commander in the midst of WWII. However, he was stunned later that evening when he learned of the D-Day invasion on Normandy. While he was walking on stage to receive his diploma his father was launching the greatest air and sea invasion in the history of the world. There had been no warning or whispered rumors whatsoever of the plans of the invasion.

That very evening John was rushed aboard a Flying Fortress bomber and was flown over the English Channel on his way to meet up with his father. He would witness for himself the site of the D-Day invasion.

Ike had been away on field assignment when his first son was born. Mamie was taken to the post infirmary lying down in the back of a horse drawn cart. No sooner had she arrived and so did their son who arrived within half an hour of their arrival at the infirmary. Ike and Mamie called him "Icky".

Their first child, Doud Dwight "Icky" Eisenhower died in 1921 of scarlet fever in his father's arms at the age of three. Ike and Mamie rarely spoke of their firstborn. Ike wrote in his memoirs of his son, *"This was the greatest disappointment and disaster in my life, the one I have never been able to forget completely."*

The Army was a hard life for Mamie who had grown up in a home where she was pampered and spoiled, and yet she drew comfort and support in the tightly knit Army family, such as when Ike and Mamie had left for Denver to bury their firstborn. It was just a few days before Christmas. When she returned to Camp Meade, Maryland the men and women at the post had taken down their Christmas tree, put the Christmas presents out of sight, packed up the baby's items for them so when they returned it wouldn't be something they had to face during their time of mourning. It was a thoughtful gesture she never forgot.

John Sheldon Doud Eisenhower was the second son of the Eisenhowers. He was born one year after his brother died. He became "the greatest source of happiness in their lives."

While pregnant with their second son in 1923, Ike and Mamie sailed on a troop transport to where he was stationed in Panama. Ike had been assigned as executive officer of the infantry brigade in the Canal Zone. Ike and Mamie found Panama a bit more "exotic" than most places they had been assigned to live while in the military.

The home they lived in stood at the outskirts of the jungle. Their first night in Panama, a bat swooped down at them as they were preparing for bed. Ike stood on the bed, unsheathed his sword, and swung at the bat. The rest of the night was no more restful as a rat gnawed at their bedroom door all through the night. Not only did they have to battle bedbugs by placing the legs of their bed in pans of kerosene, but the cockroaches were enormous and plentiful.

Thousands of people living in the area had died of yellow fever and malaria. Being that Mamie was pregnant and they had already lost one son it was of great concern to them. Before her time to give birth she left for the states to have the baby in a safe environment. Mother and baby returned to join Ike when their son John was two months of age.

John spent time at military bases during his youth where his father trained but rarely lived on base. The family lived in Panama; Fort Leavenworth, Kansas; Fort Benning, Georgia; and the Philippine Islands.

John would celebrate his sixth birthday on a ship headed to Europe. The U.S. wishing to honor veterans from WWI that helped remove the stigma that the United States was an isolationist nation had assigned Major Eisenhower to write a book on historic WWI sites as a guide book for Americans traveling overseas. The guide book showed locations of battle sites, cemeteries, and memorials with the history on the different locations. While in Europe John was able to tour the battle sites with his father receiving a hands-on education of the battles that had taken place at the different sites they visited.

When John's father was sent to the Philippines as chief military aide to General Douglas MacArthur, Eisenhower left ahead of his wife and son and accompanied MacArthur to the Philippines. At the time his father departed, John was attending grade school at the District's Adams Elementary School in Washington where his father had been working under General MacArthur. Unlike most children whose fathers are in the military he was fortunate in being able to spend his grade school years in one school.

Once he graduated he and his mother sailed to join his father. John attended high school in the mountains of Luzon in the Philippine islands. While in the islands his father learned to pilot a plane and John was able to fly with him. Father and son enjoyed hiking and spending time together. Life in the Philippines was an interesting experience; hearing new languages and learning about different customs of the islands; but when WWII broke out the Eisenhower family returned to Washington.

Ike a career military man never tried to persuade his only son one way or another in joining the military or in choosing a career; but seeing the example his father set it wasn't a surprise to anyone when John attended West Point. The year before he attended West Point he attended "Beanie" Millard's West Point preparatory school in Washington.

While attending West Point John spent his free time playing tennis, singing in the choir, tutoring other students, and working on the yearbook. John graduated from West Point a second lieutenant on D-Day. After graduation he left that same evening for London where he was able to be with his father for three weeks flying with him to the site of the Normandy invasion to visit British commanders. After his time with his father he returned to the U.S. for infantry training and then joined the staff of General Omar Bradley in Europe.

As a new second lieutenant John wrote in his memoirs of when he had joined his father in Europe during WWII. *"I was not only his son; I was a young lieutenant who needed on occasion to be straightened out."*

"I asked him in all earnestness: "If we should meet an officer who ranks above me but below you, how do we handle this? Should I salute first and when they return my salute, do you return theirs?"

"Dad's annoyed reaction was short. 'John, there isn't an officer in this theater who doesn't rank above you and below me." A humbling lesson he remembered well.

After his training when John was about to join a platoon overseas he was taken aside by an officer and advised that he would not be placed in a situation where he would be in harm's way. The army could not jeopardize the son of the supreme commander by taking his father's focus off commanding the troops. If he was concerned for his son's safety his father's concentration would not be focused where it needed to be.

At the end of WWII John returned to West Point to teach English while at the same time continuing his graduate studies. He went on to earn a masters in English and Comparative Literature from Columbia University.

June 10, 1947, John married Barbara Jean Thompson just days before her nineteenth birthday. They would have four children including David Eisenhower who would later marry the daughter of another president.

The war being over and the Eisenhowers back in the states never having owned their own home purchased a home on a 190-acre farm near Gettysburg, Pennsylvania.

A grassroots movement had put forth Eisenhower's name as a presidential candidate. Being a popular general of WWII and a war hero he was a favorite in the polls. The election is considered to be the greatest election upset in American history. Eisenhower went on to win the election.

While President-elect Eisenhower had an explosive temper he also had a sense of humor. The bald future president when meeting his future Secretary of the Treasury George Humphrey for the first time, Ike said to the balding Humphrey, "George, I see you comb your hair the way I do."

When Eisenhower was elected president his son John was fighting in the Korean War. As during WWII when his being in harm's way was a concern due to his father being supreme commander, his father was now about to become the President of the United States. By now John had proven himself as a soldier, but yet again was about to have his military career altered due to his father's position. He had been assigned to fight in a combat unit but now was reassigned to the safety of division headquarters.

In hindsight he looked back on the decisions on keeping him out of harm's way and in 2008 he wrote an article for *The New York Times,* titled, *'Presidential Children Don't Belong In Battle.'*

In a radio interview he had been asked the question, 'Did I believe that the children of presidents or vice presidents should be assigned to combat zones?' "No," I declared automatically. "They have no place there."

He shared the story of when as a part of an infantry unit in Korea it was learned his father had become the Republican candidate for the presidency. Initially he had refused orders for being reassigned which would have removed him from combat duty.

As it came near time for John to be deployed he talked with his father about his decision.

His father who had been an officer himself understood his son's decision and accepted it saying he would accept the risk of his son being killed or wounded, but if the Chinese Communists or North Koreans ever took him prisoner and threatened blackmail it would put him in the position of having to resign the presidency.

John understood that his father would accept his decision; but in doing so, if it came to his being captured he must take his own life rather than be captured.

Looking back years later he felt his decision had been unfair to his father and selfish on his part, and that quite frankly the army should never have given him the option of making that decision.

When his father was elected president John accompanied his father on a tour of the battlefront in Korea. John would leave Korea a decorated hero.

President Eisenhower was infatuated with westerns and during his inaugural parade the crowd was entertained by cowboy Monty Montana who was a trick roper who delighted the crowd when he lassoed the new president. Sixty two bands were included in the inaugural parade and two inaugural balls took place to welcome the new president and war hero into office.

The people of America felt they could relate to the first lady as she purchased clothes off the rack rather than having her clothes made by a designer and watched for sales cutting coupons out of the newspaper even while living in the White House.

The first lady's health was an issue and many times Patricia Nixon, wife of the vice president, or the first lady's daughter-in-law would serve as hostess in her stead. Mamie suffered with asthma, a heart condition, and also suffered from an inner ear disorder called Ménière's disease which affected her balance and gave some the idea she had been drinking.

The first lady was said to run the domestic staff in the White House like a 5-star general. While Ike was an early riser the first lady sometimes stayed in bed all day but rarely got up before noon; sometimes even holding meetings while she was still in bed.

The Eisenhower's son John, his wife Barbara, and their four children also lived in the

White House. The president's favorite grandchild was David who the president later named Camp David after. David was the only grandson of the president and first lady.

John served as a White House aide to his father. Aides would often have John give his father any bad news as the president was known to have an explosive temper. Later during his father's administration when the president's health was declining John served as his advisor and protector.

By the time President Eisenhower was in office Secret Service agents were also assigned to watch over the president's family; though I'm sure when they were assigned to watch over the president's grandchildren they didn't expect to have to attend an all-girl's summer camp. They were good sports though, and when twelve-year old granddaughter of the president Barbara Ann camped out with the girls the two Secret Service agents assigned to her slept in tents and danced around the fire joining in the sing-along much to the delight of the other campers.

The granddaughters were often captured in photos on the White House grounds with their grandmother. The grandchildren enjoyed living at the White House and when grandson David was celebrating his birthday he had a western themed party. He enjoyed westerns as much as his grandfather did. Roy Rogers and Dale Evans big western stars on TV at the time were brought in to entertain the children.

The president loved to golf. He initially practiced golf on the South Lawn but had to give it up when people began lining up along the fence, the press showed up, and even people driving by when seeing the president would stop their cars in the middle of the street to get out and take a look. Frustrated, the president gladly accepted when the American Golf Association offered to build him a putting green located in a more secluded area where he could practice in peace. The president was even known to swing a golf club as he walked the halls of the White House and wore his golf shoes inside destroying the floor in the Oval Office with his golf spikes.

President Eisenhower took his golf very seriously and when the squirrels would dig up the greens the president got so mad he told the gardeners to shoot the squirrels. The Secret Service let the gardeners know that would not be acceptable and instead advised them to set traps and remove the squirrels. They did exactly that, removing them to the nearby Rock Creek Park. When the public learned about the fate of the squirrels they were furious and captured squirrels themselves bringing them to the iron gates of the

White House and releasing the squirrels on the grounds.

If the president was winning while playing golf he was in a great mood and would joke around with the other players, but if he was losing he would lose his temper and swear banging his clubs around. His grandson David would mimic his grandfather playing golf right alongside him on the grounds of the White House.

A memory David recalled years after his grandfather's death was when as a teenager he worked on the Gettysburg farm during the summers. He remembers all too well being fired by his grandfather for taking an overly long lunch hour. Hours after he had been fired his grandfather's car pulled up to David's front door to pick him up for a golf date. Not a word was spoken until the third hole. "Near the green Granddad broke the silence. 'I allow all of my associates one mistake a year. You've had yours.'" David remembered that he was rehired that afternoon.

During President Eisenhower's second administration his son John was hired in an executive advisory position. Being his son the president often took out his frustrations blaming his son more than he did the other staff and rarely gave him praise even when well deserved.

When his father's term of office came to an end and the former president and first lady retired to their new home in Gettysburg, John and his family joined the former president and first lady. He was going to help his father draft his memoirs.

John went on "leave without pay" in order to assist his father, and when his two years of leave ran out and the memoirs were still incomplete John resigned from his army commission. This was a very selfless act on his part as he resigned with just a year to go before he could have retired at half pay. He was a significant aide to his father in writing a two-volume presidential memoir, *'Mandate For Change,'* and *'Waging Peace.'*

In 1965 John was approached by G.P. Putnam's in regards to writing a history of WWII's Battle of the Bulge. John with a graduate degree in English, experience in aiding his father in writing his memoirs, and his experience in the military was eager to accept the challenge.

He spent years going through archives discovering pertinent information about the battle, interviewing military leaders and others with firsthand knowledge, and then going to

Europe where he surveyed the battlegrounds and spent time interviewing both Axis and Allied generals. The book, *'The Bitter Woods: The Battle of the Bulge,'* was published in 1969 with excellent reviews and he made a name for himself as a military historian.

John also wrote the story of his father's life and in later years he would publish books on World War I, World War II, the Civil War, the Mexican War, and books on different generals.

The president's favorite grandchild David Eisenhower married Julie Nixon on December 22, 1968. Julie's father had been his grandfather's vice president. At the time of their marriage Julie's father had been elected the nation's 37th president but had not yet taken office. The bride and groom did not wish to be married in the White House but to have a private ceremony. Eisenhower's best man was Fred Grandy, who would later star in the series *The Love Boat* and eventually became a congressman. Julie's maid-of-honor was her sister Tricia. David and Julie live in Pennsylvania and have three children and grandchildren.

The former president offered his grandson one hundred dollars if he would cut his "mop of curly hair" into a neat military style for his wedding. David said he did get a trim just before the wedding, but evidently it wasn't enough to satisfy his grandfather as he never saw the hundred dollars.

John Eisenhower chaired Nixon's 1968 presidential campaign and after Nixon was elected he appointed John as ambassador to Belgium. John received the news of the appointment and shared it with his father who was in the hospital after suffering from a heart attack. John would serve as ambassador to Belgium for two years.

John learning of his father's diagnosis remained with his father as much as possible to be with him until the end. They had time to discuss many things during the former president's confinement and spend valuable time together. At the end his father looked up at his son and said, "Be good to Mamie."

John saw his father's last heartbeat on the monitor and then he was gone. It was March 28, 1969 when he said his final good-bye to his father at Walter Reed Hospital in Washington, D.C. There was little opportunity to mourn with preparations to be made for the funeral of a former president and war hero.

After John finished his stint as ambassador to Belgium he returned to the U.S. and began writing his many military histories. With all he had accomplished to date, which was quite impressive; none held a candle to his achievements as a military historian. His writing career lasted over forty years.

As all presidential sons and daughters struggle to be accepted on their own merits and not to live in their father's shadow, John suffered with the same problem. Almost all presidential children are looked on as the child of a president first and foremost before their own accomplishments are ever recognized and John was not only the son of a president but of a supreme allied commander of WWII.

"His unusual success, while exhilarating to us all, made me feel that among strangers I was always some sort of curiosity," John wrote in *'Strictly Personal,'* his 1974 memoir. He was able to achieve his own success and be recognized for a brilliant historian.

Not only John but also his son David became military historians. The president's grandson wrote: *'Eisenhower At War 1943 – 1945'* and *'Going Home To Glory: A Memoir of Life With Dwight D. Eisenhower, 1961 – 1969'* that he co-wrote with his wife Julie.

David and Julie have devoted their time to writing, teaching, and lecturing. Julie has written several books including one about her mother, *'Pat Nixon: The Untold Story.'* David's first book about his grandfather, *'Eisenhower At War, 1943 – 1945,'* was a Pulitzer Prize finalist in 1987.

John and his first wife Barbara divorced in 1986 after thirty-nine years of marriage. In 1988 John married Joanne Thompson. John Eisenhower died on December 21, 2013. He was buried at West Point Cemetery.

35

JOHN F. KENNEDY

Children of Jacqueline and John F. Kennedy:

Unnamed; "Arabella" Kennedy – Born: Aug. 23, 1956   Died: Aug. 23, 1956 - Stillborn

Caroline Bouvier Kennedy – Born: Nov. 27, 1957   Still Living At The Time Of Publication

John Fitzgerald Kennedy, Jr. - Born: Nov 25, 1960   Died: July 16, 1999

Patrick Bouvier Kennedy – Born: Aug. 7, 1963   Died: Aug. 9, 1963

John Jr., the Kennedy's firstborn son, was the first child ever born to a President-elect.

It was November of 1957 and Jackie was in the hospital about to give birth. The expectant father Senator John Kennedy nervously paced in a waiting room with hopes of good news after a difficult beginning with their attempts to start a family.

The first time Jackie had been pregnant in 1955 she had a miscarriage after three months and learned at that time that carrying and delivering a child would always be problematic for her. The following year pregnant and nearing the end of her pregnancy she began hemorrhaging while eight months pregnant. At the time her husband was off sailing on a yacht in the Mediterranean with friends - *male and female friends.*

It wasn't quite three years after John and Jackie Kennedy were married when Jackie gave birth to their daughter that was stillborn. Receiving the news of his wife and stillborn daughter it never even entered the mind of the senator to return home to comfort his wife. It took the counsel of wiser friends who spoke up reminding him that if he ever planned on running for president, which they knew were his plans, he better get home to his wife unless he wanted to lose every woman's vote in the future.

The stillborn baby girl was never officially named. The name Arabella was one that Jacqueline referred to as the firstborn daughter she lost, though it never appeared on any official record. Her gravestone was simply marked Daughter.

The Kennedys longed for a family and after two failed attempts so far this third pregnancy had gone well. John Kennedy paced nervously waiting to hear word from the doctor. This time the news was good and Jackie delivered a healthy 7 lb. - 2 oz. baby girl that the baby's father would smile on with pride. The proud father described her to friends and family as "fit as a fiddle and robust as a sumo wrestler." Caroline Bouvier Kennedy had arrived.

The Kennedy's marriage would suffer many infidelities throughout their marriage, even into the White House. It was one of the more unfavorable traits the Kennedy men shared.

In 1960 Jackie learned she was pregnant yet again while her husband was running for the office of the presidency. He would narrowly beat Richard Nixon and he became the first Catholic president and the youngest president ever elected in the history of the United States. It had been the first time presidential candidates debated on television and since Jackie was in the final trimester of her pregnancy and confined for these last months she could only watch from home while her husband debated Nixon in what had been a very close and hard fought campaign.

The morning after the election Jackie had Caroline wake her father up. His three year old daughter gave her father a hug and a kiss and said, "Good morning, Mr. President."

Caroline not quite three years old would be assigned her own Secret Service agents. She was the 'darling of the nation' and had captivated the press. Jackie didn't appreciate all the attention by the press of her daughter complaining they were trying to turn her into a Shirley Temple clone. Her father's nickname for Caroline was 'Buttons,' and she was as the expression goes, 'cute as a button.'

The president elect had been at the family home in Palm Beach preparing for his presidency by selecting cabinet members and staff. He came home to spend Thanksgiving with his very pregnant wife and daughter. Jackie's due date wasn't until the middle of December not for about another three weeks, so he returned to Palm Beach after sharing Thanksgiving dinner with the family. He planned to be in Palm Beach for another week or so and then return to be with Jackie for the final days of her pregnancy.

JFK left Thanksgiving evening flying back to Palm Beach on his private plane, *'The Caroline.'* Before the plane had landed in Florida the pilot sent him a message that there was an important message waiting for him on the ground. He learned his wife had been rushed to the hospital having gone into premature labor. He immediately turned around and took a quicker commercial flight back. En route the pilot called President-elect Kennedy to the cockpit where he learned his wife had just given birth to a 6 lb. - 3 oz. baby boy. He was told both mother and son were doing well.

They could deliver this news now, but if it hadn't been for a pediatric resident by the name of Seiler the news may have been very different. The resident after witnessing the newborn turning blue and not breathing inserted a tube into the trachea of the newborn and for several minutes had to breathe air into his lungs before he breathed on his own. On the baby's dismissal from the hospital it was noted the baby suffered from "Respiratory Distress Syndrome" which later became known as "Hyaline Membrane Disease," the same disease his brother Patrick would die of.

John, Jr. was born just three weeks after the election becoming the first child born to a president-elect.

The Secret Service kept the reporters and photographers out of the hospital and kept vigil over Jackie and baby John. An alert nurse had seen a man acting strange outside Jackie's window and reported him to the Washington, D.C. police. The police apprehended the man and discovered that he had on him five sticks of dynamite.

Before JFK was even in office the Secret Service received a report that someone had made threats against the president-elect and he was believed to be in the Palm Beach area. Jackie and the children had joined JFK in Palm Beach to spend the Christmas holiday in Florida. The president-elect was preparing to leave the house to attend church, and his wife and children along with some nieces and nephews who had also come for the holidays walked him out to his car. Richard Paul Pavlick, a retired postal worker from

New Hampshire had been watching the president-elect's home waiting for him to leave. He had seven sticks of dynamite that could be exploded by pressing a switch. He had planned on blowing up JFK, but seeing the children he didn't want to harm them or Jackie. He decided to wait for another opportunity. Before he had another chance to take action he had been tracked down and apprehended.

January 20, 1961 the president took the oath of office while Jackie stood by his side. The children remained in Palm Beach with their nanny as they were too young to understand what was going on; which was made clear when Maude Shaw their nanny and Clint Hill a Secret Service agent watched the live coverage of the inauguration. When they called Caroline to the television so she could see her father take the oath of office she was more interested in getting back to her finger painting.

When the Kennedy family arrived at the White House for the first time Caroline spotted something that caught her eye and held her attention. White House Chief Gardener Robert Redmond had made a snowman on the driveway for the young presidential daughter. The snowman was made up hat and all to greet the new little tenant of the White House.

The Kennedy children brought new life into the White House as they were the youngest children to live in the White House since the days of Grover Cleveland's administration. They were the darlings of the press. The first lady wanting her children to live a life as normal as possible limited the access of the press to her children, but the press was always on the alert for news of Caroline and the most desired photos from the White House were those of the Kennedy children.

It was the press who nicknamed John, Jr. as John-John when a reporter heard the president calling his young son twice in quick succession. His family never called him by that name and as he grew a little older he would correct others telling them his name was John, *not* John John. During the years of the White House it was Caroline who was the bigger draw for the press as John adorable as he was, was still a toddler; but in later years John would overshadow his sister with his good looks and charm that captivated the public and the press.

Caroline and John were very close so when a Secret Service agent made a remark to John about keeping the noise down, big sister stepped in coming to his defense and said, "My, we are grumpy today, aren't we, Mr. Jones?"

The president enjoyed starting and ending his days with his children nearby. Caroline and John would sit and watch cartoons as they ate breakfast with their father. The president was often seen walking the halls on the way to the Oval Office holding the hand of one of his children. Caroline remembered that he didn't really like to read them stories but he made up stories for them. Some of the stories would have Caroline and her pony as the main characters where she won the Grand National horse race. Other stories he would tell had John and Caroline with him on a PT boat where they would sink a Japanese destroyer.

Caroline could often be seen riding her pony Macaroni on the White House lawn. The pony had been a gift from Vice President Johnson. Visitors who had come to see the White House were thrilled when they had the opportunity to watch the president's daughter riding her pony.

When the pony wasn't being ridden he was free to wander the White House grounds. One day as the president glanced out his window from the Oval Office he saw the pony staring into the window. The president watched him for a few minutes then got up and opened the door and motioned for the pony to come in. The pony looked at the president, stood there for a moment as though he were considering the invitation, then turned around and wandered off.

There was a day though when Caroline was out riding the pony when she saw her father in the Oval Office window watching her. She rode the pony onto the portico and right into the Oval Office where the pony left an unpleasant gift behind for the president on the Oval Office rug.

During the Kennedy administration it was commonplace to see his young children with their father in the Oval Office. John loved to play hide-and-seek where his favorite hiding place was under his father's desk where he had discovered a secret panel that opened like a door.

The first lady set up a school on the third floor of the White House for Caroline and several children of the staff. A playground was set up on the South Lawn for the children, but when tourists began lining up at the fence along with tour buses bringing in people to watch them Jackie asked the gardeners to plant rhododendrons along the fence to keep her children from being a major attraction.

When the White House hosted a dinner Caroline loved to peek out from the Grand Staircase to see all the people below dressed up in their tuxes and gowns. The conductor of the Marine Band who had seen the little girl peeking through the balusters began playing 'Old MacDonald Had A Farm' which delighted Caroline who began clapping along. The first lady looked up and spotted her daughter and brought her down to meet the guests.

The first lady spent more time away from the White House than in it. She spent time at a home in Virginia in horse country called Gen Ora that the first lady leased as a get-away. She would stay at the 400-acre farm from Thursdays to Tuesdays for which she received scathing criticism.

The first lady's historical restoration and the tour of the White House she gave during a special on TV is what she is most remembered for as her accomplishments as first lady. Believing the White House should reflect the artistic history of the United States she set to work on not redecorating but in restoring the White House. She planned to do this by bringing back historical pieces from past administrations.

The opposite of hard working First Lady Eleanor Roosevelt, Jackie did little otherwise as a first lady other than to be 'window dressing' or as a "lovely inconsequence" as historian Arthur Schlesinger described her. She was young and elegant so her fashions received international attention and were admired and copied worldwide.

The president and first family spent some weekends and holidays at Camp David. Caroline was able to have her pony Macaroni at Camp David to ride the trails while John loved walking through the woods using sticks he found as imaginary guns or swords.

The camp was rustic, but luxurious. The entire family enjoyed their time there as it was a place that felt removed from the pressures of the presidency. The best part of Camp David to John was the journey to get there. They flew to Camp David on the presidential helicopter.

John was totally mesmerized by the White House helicopter. He loved watching it land and take off, but even more he loved riding in it. John was downstairs watching for the helicopter that was to take them to Camp David. This was a rare treat for him as he had few opportunities to be a passenger.

Clint Hill, one of the Secret Service agents squatted down beside the boy and asked him if he was going to be riding in the helicopter. It was then they heard it overhead coming in to land. Just a toddler and with a very small vocabulary John ran to the window where he could see it land yelling, "Copter! Copter!"

For an adult it is the small things that bring great joy to a child that we find so endearing. President Kennedy and Caroline went to the hospital to visit JFK's father who had suffered a stroke. Caroline spotted a gumball machine and asked, "Daddy, can I please have a gumball?" The president never carried cash on him so he regretted to have to tell her he didn't have a penny for the machine. Seeing the forlorn look on his daughter's face and not wanting to disappoint her he asked his Secret Service agent Paul Landis if he had a penny. Agent Landis handed Caroline a penny and her eyes brightened and with a big smile on her face she walked over to the gumball machine and got her gumball. To see such joy on a child's face when she popped that gumball in her mouth was contagious. Both the president and the Secret Service agent walked down the hall of the hospital with big smiles on their faces.

Caroline stole the show when she wandered into the middle of a press conference her father was giving while dressed in her nightie and robe stomping around in a pair of her mother's high heels. After that scene whatever the president had to say at the press conference was of little consequence.

Holidays are a wonderful time at the White House with the beautiful decorations and an actual sleigh ride on the South Lawn. Jackie was the first lady who introduced the tradition of decorating the White House Christmas tree with a theme. She chose the 'Nutcracker Suite' as the theme for 1961 decorating the tree with toy soldiers, lollipops, sugar plum fairies, gingerbread cookies, and musical instruments. When Caroline entered the Blue Room and saw the tree decorated her eyes got as bright as the lights on the tree.

Christmas holidays were times of tradition and memories for the Kennedy family. Caroline and John put on a play every year wearing costumes depicting Mary and Joseph. In school Caroline would glue sequins onto construction paper ornaments and stick cloves into oranges making pomander balls.

Caroline was talking to her father about the Christmas gifts she hoped to get, but said she wished she could talk to Santa to make sure he knew what she wanted. The president arranged with one of the switchboard operators to play along and he called Caroline to the phone. She answered the phone and listened a minute and then began telling the person on the phone her wish list. After she hung up she said, "I've just talked to Mrs. Santa Claus!" Caroline didn't pick up on the fact that Mrs. Claus who lived in the North Pole spoke with a southern accent.

One of the gifts Caroline received from her Christmas list was a Susie Smart talking doll which she left behind in the Oval Office one day. The talking doll had a tape recorder inside the doll which would record what you said and play it back, hence the talking doll. When the doll was returned the nanny was surprised when she pushed play to hear the president saying words inappropriate for innocent little ears to hear. The nanny tried to erase the tape before Caroline heard it. She was unable to figure out how to erase it and finally just threw out the tape. When Caroline went to play with her doll the nanny explained the doll must have laryngitis and just needed to rest her voice. A Secret Service agent went out and bought a new tape and Susie Smart was miraculously cured of her laryngitis.

The president and first lady were absent for the yearly Easter Egg Roll at the White House choosing instead to continue with their own family tradition with attending church and celebrating Easter with the Kennedy clan. In 1961 people noticed when the Kennedy family left church there was an unusually large amount of Secret Service agents protecting the family. The president and first lady had received an anonymous letter written by supporters of Castro and the new Communist regime in Cuba stating the Kennedy children would be kidnapped and held hostage against any future attack the U.S. might launch against Cuba.

The times the president vacationed in Hyannis Port he enjoyed the time he was able to spend with his children. Having grown up by the sea he was a good sailor having won the Nantucket Sound Star Class Championship Cup, the MacMillan Cup, and the East Coast Collegiate Championships. While he was at ease sailing the yacht he preferred the challenge of sailing in the Victura, a sailboat he received as a 15th birthday present from his parents.

The president took Caroline sailing and having taught her mother to sail he planned to also instruct his children and share his love of sailing with them. As he sailed with four-year old Caroline heading out to sea the president explained to her how to trim the sails and manage the tiller. Caroline listened intently to every word.

The first lady wanted her children to live as normal a life as possible and wanted them to have experiences other children their age took for granted. She would color and decorate Easter eggs with them rather than have Easter eggs decorated by professionals. One year she and the president's sister Jean decided to take their children trick or treating for Halloween. They decided the only way they could pull it off was if they also dressed up so they wouldn't be recognized.

The first lady took a large black garment bag and cut out holes for her eyes and finished off her ensemble all in black with boots, stockings, and opera gloves. She was covered from head to toe and would be going incognito. The president's sister Jean copied Jackie's costume only used a red garment bag with red accessories.

Caroline dressed up as a witch and John as a skeleton and the group headed to the neighborhood of Georgetown to go trick or treating. Hiding behind masks they just might have pulled it off if it weren't for all the Secret Service agents trailing them from house to house.

The president and first lady announced to the nation that they were expecting a baby. John, Jr. was born after Kennedy had been elected but before he became acting president. This child would be the second baby born to a sitting president. The first sitting president to have become a father was Grover Cleveland.

The White House was preparing for the new arrival preparing the nursery while the first lady spent time at Hyannis Port. She would spend the last trimester of her pregnancy taking it easy with family.

The first lady had just taken Caroline to a riding lesson when she turned to Secret Service agent Clint Hill and told him she needed to get home – *immediately!* The doctor arrived at the Kennedy home the same time as they arrived with the first lady. After examining her the doctor explained to the Secret Service the first lady had gone into premature labor and needed to get to the hospital without delay.

In what must have seemed a long time to those standing helplessly by but was only a matter of minutes, they waited for a helicopter to land and they quickly had the first lady aboard flying to the hospital at Otis Air Force Base in Hyannis Port.

The baby wasn't due for another five and a half weeks. This was a real concern. Upon arriving at the hospital she was taken into the delivery room for an emergency cesarean birth. The president had been notified and had left Washington and was on his way to the hospital. The baby arrived before the president.

When the doctor came out of surgery he explained to the Secret Service waiting outside the delivery room that the first lady was fine, but there was some concern with the baby's breathing.

The president arrived and visited Jackie. He spoke with the doctor who explained the condition of his son. After seeing his newborn son in an incubator fighting for each breath the president made arrangements to have the baby baptized without delay. The hospital chaplain christened the 4 pounds, 10 ½ ounce newborn son named Patrick Bouvier Kennedy.

Dr. Drorbrough, a pediatrician doctor who had been called in by Dr. Hughes was the hospital's chief resident of pediatrics from Boston. He was flown in by helicopter to examine the infant. The baby was diagnosed with hyaline membrane disease. The doctor advised transferring him to Boston Children's Hospital without delay. He explained that Children's Hospital was better equipped to care for the baby who was barely clinging to life.

Before Patrick was taken by ambulance to Boston the president made a special request of Dr. Drorbrough. Realizing there was a good chance his son wouldn't survive he asked him to go with him to the first lady's room so she could have a few moments with her newborn son. The first lady reached into the incubator and held the tiny little hand of her son for about ten minutes before he was whisked away. That would be the last time the first lady would see her son.

The president accompanied his newborn son to Boston where the baby was closely monitored. He watched his son through his incubator as the baby fought for his life each breath coming with great difficulty. The tiny body was hooked up to tubes that seemed to cover every inch of his tiny body.

The hospital set the president up in temporary quarters where he could go to rest and pray. It was the middle of the night on August 9th just two days after the birth that the doctors called the president telling him there was no hope and the end was near.

When the president arrived at his son's incubator the team of doctors took little Patrick out of his incubator and removed the tubes from his body and gently laid the infant in his father's arms. It would be the first and the last time he would be able to hold his son. Only three minutes passed as the president held his son before the newborn took his last breath while cradled in his father's arms. Baby Patrick had lived for only thirty-nine hours. The president returned to the room the hospital set up for him, closed the door, and wept.

The first lady had been kept medicated and was sleeping most of the time oblivious to how fragile the life of her newborn son was. It would be her doctor, Dr. Walsh, who had to break the news to her that her son had passed away.

Funeral services were held the day after his death. He had survived only two days. The first lady too weak to attend the services remained in the hospital. As the president looked at the tiny white coffin where his newborn son lay his shoulders heaved, mourning the loss of his tiny son. He embraced his infant's coffin and wept unabashedly. No one walked away with dry eyes.

Three months after the death of their son the president and first lady were leaving for a trip to Texas. They would be flying in the helicopter to the airport and John would fly with them as far as the airport and then be returned to the White House. The ride to the airport was a short one, only six minutes in length; but John loved flying so much that the president had his son and one of his Secret Service agents fly along whenever possible.

As the helicopter landed on the tarmac at the airport the president leaned over and gave his son a hug and said good-bye.

"I want to come," John whined. Tears filled his eyes as the first lady leaned over and kissed him reminding him that his birthday was in a few days and they would be back to celebrate. He only cried harder wanting to fly with his mother and father on the plane.

The president gently reassured his son that they would be back in a few days. John sobbed as his father and mother exited the helicopter. That would be the last time John saw his father.

The president and first lady rode in an open convertible in a motorcade through downtown Dallas. The vice president and Lady Bird followed in another car. The procession left the airport and traveled along a ten mile route where there were crowds of people lined up along the route to see the president and first lady as they drove by.

As their car passed the Texas School Book Depository gunshots were heard. Two of those bullets found their destination and hit the president. The car sped to Parkland Memorial Hospital just minutes away, but it would be too late. The president was pronounced dead. President John F. Kennedy was assassinated on November 22, 1963.

It would be the children's nanny, Maud Shaw, who had the unenviable task of telling the children their father was dead.

The White House became a whirlwind of activity and Caroline seeing a helicopter landing on the South Lawn asked if that was the one bringing her mommy and daddy home. The nanny had to swallow her tears and tell her that her father had gone home to heaven to be with God and her baby brother Patrick; but he would be watching over her.

It was difficult enough for Caroline to understand, but John was so young the nanny tucked him into bed without telling him. She soon had to try to explain to him too that his father was gone. Too young to understand he simply said, "I wonder when he's coming back."

Caroline was going to turn six years old in less than a week and John would be three years old in three days. There would be a large void in their life with their father who had loved them dearly gone from their lives.

The president's closed casket was brought to the East Room of the White House with an honor guard standing watch for the next 24 hours. Nearly one hundred years earlier another president who had also been assassinated President Lincoln also was laid out in this same spot.

The honor guard carried the flag-draped casket and placed it on a caisson pulled by six white horses where it would be taken to the Capitol to lie in state. En route, along Pennsylvania Avenue could be heard the sound of the horses hooves clacking on the street as it passed. The silent crowd were lined up along the route paying tribute to their dead president. Day and night hundreds of thousands of people coming to pay their respects lined up to view the guarded casket. The following day the funeral took place - the day John turned three.

It is approximated that a million people lined the streets along the route of the funeral procession. Millions more watched it from home on their televisions. The funeral mass took place at St. Matthew's Cathedral.

After the funeral service the first lady and her children were standing on the steps of the Cathedral as the casket was removed and placed on the caisson. The military saluted their fallen Commander in Chief. The first lady bent over and whispered in John's ear. He took a step forward, thrust his little shoulders back, and John who had turned three years old that day saluted his father. A moment in time that any who witnessed it will have forever etched in their memory.

United Press International photographer Stan Stearns captured the famous image, the most famous photograph of any presidential child, that immediately comes to people's minds when they think of that day when the little son of the president said his final good-bye to his father standing tall saluting his father's coffin.

On the same day of his father's burial the first lady decided not to cancel the plans made previously for John's birthday party. It was his third birthday. It was important to the first lady to ensure that he would leave the White House with a good memory.

Over time after JFK's assassination the family, her mother and aunts and uncles could see a change in Caroline. She had become moody and removed. Her Uncle Bobby Kennedy said, "She no longer let anyone get close to her. Every time I look at her; I want to go somewhere and cry."

Caroline had been close to her father and was old enough at the time of his death that she remembered him well and had many memories of him. She had a much harder time dealing with his death than John did who was still a toddler at the time. Jackie kept in close contact with a child psychologist in an attempt to help her daughter deal with her father's death. Caroline had always been a sweet, loving child but had now become argumentative and withdrawn often seen walking around with clenched fists.

The former first lady had moved her children to New York thinking a change of scenery would be good for all of them. The children were kept busy with the nanny taking them to the Bronx Zoo, Central Park where they rode bicycles and went roller skating, and the circus at Madison Square Garden.

Their mother also saw to it that they took advantage of the cultural and historical events available in New York City. They visited the Metropolitan Museum of Art and the Museum of Natural History. They visited Liberty Island to see the Statue of Liberty and rode to the top of the Empire State Building. They attended a children's operetta at Carnegie Hall and attended Broadway musicals.

During the holidays the children watched the Thanksgiving Parade along Fifth Avenue and the lighting of the Christmas tree at Rockefeller Center. Regardless of how busy the children were, there was a void in their lives that their father had once filled.

The former first lady had received a gift of an oil painting of the former president as a gift from Secretary of Defense Robert McNamara. When she received it she propped it up against the wall until she could find the perfect spot to hang the painting. When Caroline came in the room and saw it she ran over and began repeatedly kissing the portrait of her father with tears running down her cheeks. Seeing what his big sister was doing her little brother John mimicked his sister and also began kissing the portrait and crying. The first lady seeing her children broke down. She had the painting put away.

The only consistent male role model in John's life was his Secret Service agent Jack Walsh. John really took to him and enjoyed being with him. Jack became a father figure to John. He accompanied him wherever he went. Agent Walsh was a good man and gave John the male attention he desperately needed.

When John began attending the prestigious school at Saint David's there was a time when he was being teased by some of the other children. One day he hauled off and punched one of the bullies. Someone asked him where he learned to fight and he proudly said, "The Secret Service."

The children's uncle, Bobby Kennedy, would include Caroline and John on ski trips with his own family. The Kennedys were a tight-knit family and celebrated holidays and special events together. When Bobby spent time teaching his children to ski he included his late brother's children Caroline and John. John fell and began to whine and his uncle responded by saying, "Kennedys never cry." John answered, "This Kennedy cries."

John had been drawn to anything that flew from the time he was just a toddler in the White House. Between Marine One the presidential helicopter and Air Force One the presidential plane he had early on had a passion for helicopters and airplanes.

After leaving the White House Godfrey McHugh, who had been an Air Force aide to President Kennedy remained in contact with the Kennedy family and often sent John airplane models. One day McHugh received a phone call with an odd request from the former first lady. She explained that JFK had promised his son an airplane when he grew up and she wanted to honor that promise. She asked if he could help her with her quest to fulfill this promise. McHugh promised to look into it and get back with her.

McHugh arranged for a plane from WWII that had been deactivated to be repainted and embossed with the Air Force insignia. Jackie arranged to have the plane moved to the backyard of their home at the Kennedy compound. Ten year old John spent hours at the controls of the plane pretending he was a fighter pilot.

Senator Robert Kennedy was campaigning for the presidency when he too was assassinated. This terrified the former first lady. She said, "If they're killing Kennedys, then my children are targets. I want to get out of this country." This was the same year she married Aristotle Onassis and the family would live on his private island Skorpios in Greece.

Many Americans were upset when they learned the news the former first lady was about to remarry. Onassis was extremely wealthy but he also had a disreputable reputation. Jackie did what she wanted, public opinion never swayed her one way or the other. Onassis was extremely good to her children and genuinely cared for them.

It was only during the flight to Greece that Jackie told her children, just five days before the wedding took place, that she was about to remarry.

Caroline who had become remote and hard to get close to made an attempt to accept her new stepfather, but they never shared a close relationship like John had with Onassis. John had no problem accepting his new stepfather as he looked up to Onassis and thrived having a man in his life who cared for him and spent time with him. John and Onassis got along very well.

Onassis took up a lot of time with the children. He spent time telling John stories and took the children on tours of his private island pointing out different species of birds to them and teaching them about the wildlife. He was patient and kind to Jackie's children.

Onassis knew how to calm the hyperactive John down and would capture his attention telling him about Greek myths. Often when Onassis had to travel to Athens he would take John with him entertaining him and take time showing him around. John admired Onassis and looked up to him.

Onassis had a tree house built on his private island for John and Caroline that was larger than most American homes. He indulged them. He had the means and it was important to Onassis that Jackie's children were happy. When John worried about his pet rabbit flying from America to Greece Onassis had the pilot keep the rabbit with him to make sure it arrived safe and sound.

Caroline and John visited Onassis' private island during summers and school holidays, but attended school in the states. Caroline had a difficult time fitting in and making friends.

President Nixon invited the former first lady along with thirteen-year old Caroline and ten-year old John to visit the White House. It would be the first time, and the last, that Jackie returned to the White House. The visit was private with no press or photographers. It would be the Kennedy and Nixon families only.

The purpose of their visit was for a private unveiling of an official portrait of the former president and first lady which would be hung in the White House. Jackie had been a bit fearful that returning to the White House would be difficult for her children, but they seemed to remember very little of their time there. They enjoyed a private dinner with the Nixon family where John spilled a glass of milk in the president's lap.

At one time Caroline was the media darling of the press. She was the most photographed child of America and had a hit song "Sweet Caroline," written for her by singer-songwriter Neil Diamond. Caroline had become withdrawn and was quite a loner. She may not have won a best personality contest but she was very intelligent. She passed the posh Brearley all-girls private school's entrance exams with ease.

Though book smart Caroline clearly was lacking in social skills. She could be quite rude and came across as self-serving when dealing with others. Two examples of this was when she entered a bank and jumping the line left the bank when told she would have to wait her turn. Another time she entered an ice cream parlor where she made her way to the front. She was told she would have to take a number and wait her turn. Her response was, "I'm Caroline Kennedy." When it was repeated that she would have to wait her turn she turned around and walked out.

While Caroline was attending Concord Academy she turned sixteen which was the age when she would lose her Secret Service protection. It may have felt a bit exhilarating not being under their watchful eye, but at the same time they had always been around to give her a feeling of safety. Something that as a Kennedy she may have been reassured by.

Caroline and John went through the same difficulties all teens go through including peer pressure. Both Caroline and John smoked pot and John even went so far as to try cocaine. However, both sister and brother seemed to do much better than their Kennedy cousins who seemed to be in and out of trouble.

Jackie Kennedy remained very close to her children. She was known to have said, "If you bungle raising your children, I don't think whatever else you do matters very much." While at times she was controlling and demanding, she was also there to steer them in the right direction if they veered off course.

There was a time when photos of the Kennedy children showed them looking much like other teens their age: long hair, unkempt, jeans being their favorite choice of dress. Caroline stopped taking the diet pills her mother had the doctor prescribe for her and put on weight. Jackie was known to be very controlling about her daughter's diet and weight, even to the point of humiliating her in public when she ordered dessert.

One evening Caroline and her mother were having dinner out. When Caroline requested the dessert menu her mother who usually spoke in a soft breathy voice spoke out in a voice loud enough for other diners near by to hear when she ridiculed her daughter saying, "You're not going to order dessert. You're much too fat. Nobody will ever want to marry you."

Caroline while away at school was beginning to spread her wings. She would smoke pot with her friends, drink in excess, smoke cigarettes, and curse like a sailor. She grew out of that faze and ended up emulating her mother by the time she was a young adult. By then she was again standoffish and came across as entitled; traits she never outgrew.

Caroline and John were described as complete opposites: she was an introvert while he was an extrovert. John easily made friends, true friends whose friendships would last his lifetime; while Caroline could probably count on one hand those she considered a close friend and have fingers left over. She demanded her privacy to a point that is obsessive and had a tendency to withdraw from others, while John was always eager to try everything and meet everyone he came in contact with.

Jackie wanted her fatherless son to grow up in a 'manly way.' During his adolescence he attended character building outdoors survival schools. One of those he had attended when he was only ten years of age. He accompanied Anthony Radziwill the son of Jackie's sister to Wales where he learned to sail, canoe, rock climb, and camped out on the moors.

Cousins Caroline and Marie Shriver are very close as John was to Timothy Shriver. When John was fourteen he accompanied the Shriver family on a vacation to Russia. During the vacation his uncle, Sargent Shriver husband to Eunice Kennedy, spent hours telling John stories about his father he had never heard before. By the time he returned home he felt he had a new understanding and respect for his father. No one had ever taken the time before to tell John so much about his father.

The following year Sargent Shriver asked Jackie if John, who was fifteen at the time, could accompany his cousin Timothy on a trip to Central America to work with the Peace Corps. Being that it was John's father who had established the Peace Corps, it was a wonderful opportunity for John to see what it was to give to others who were in need. It would be a lesson that stayed with him for a lifetime.

The boys traveled to a Guatemalan village that just months ago had suffered a major earthquake. They slept in tents and lived off a diet of yellow rice and red beans. They traveled by donkey and bathed in a cold mountain stream. Their duties consisted of helping the Peace Corps volunteers with hauling sandbags, digging trenches, and distributing medical supplies, food, and water.

While in the tenth grade John went on an Outward Bound Survival Trip on Hurricane Island which is an isolated area off the coast of Maine. He was left on the island on his own for three days supplied only with a gallon of water, two wooden matches, and a how-to brochure on outdoor living. John had learned self confidence at an early age and felt there was nothing he couldn't cope with. "John had great self-confidence in his ability to come through these things," said John Whitehead, a trustee of the Kennedy family and family friend.

John was part of a group that went on a trip sponsored by the National Outdoor

Leadership Course on Mount Kenya in Africa where he had to evade a charging rhinoceros. He and a group of other boys and girls were led into the snake-infested African bush where the group got lost and a search party of Masai warriors were sent out to locate them.

In 1975 Caroline had been accepted into Radcliffe College but decided before attending college she would first spend a year in London taking an art course at Sotheby's auction house. She enjoyed spending time at the museums in London and attending lectures, but she also discovered London's night life.

While in London Caroline would be staying with a family friend of the Kennedys, Hugh Fraser who had daughters Caroline's age. The girls took Caroline out on the town and introduced her to a life she was unaccustomed to. While in London she was no longer the shy, removed girl she had been back in the states. She spent her evenings dancing, attending London's theater, and rock concerts. While away from her mother's watchful eye she drank, smoked pot, partied, and ate what she wanted.

An event happened that put her on the front page of the newspapers worldwide. It was early morning and Hugh Fraser was preparing to leave for work but had agreed to drop Caroline off at Sothebys on his way to work. Fraser waited outside for Caroline who was upstairs getting ready. Hugh nodded hello to his next door neighbor who was outside walking his French poodles when the phone rang inside the Fraser home. Fraser, still waiting for Caroline ran in and answered the phone. While on the phone an enormous explosion went off. A bomb had been placed underneath his car destroying it and killing the next-door neighbor who was walking his dogs. Glass flew into the Fraser home cutting him while the explosion knocked Caroline off her feet upstairs.

Scotland Yard suspected the bomb had been planted by the IRA. While Fraser had been the target, if she had been ready on time Caroline would have been in the car with him when the explosion went off.

Jackie tried to convince Caroline to return to the states but Caroline could be just as stubborn as her mother when she had reason to be; and she felt she had that reason. Caroline had been dating Mark Shand, a Brit whose father was an English Lord. Shand's sister is Camilla who is now married to Prince Charles.

While Caroline was in love with Shand the feeling wasn't reciprocated. Since the bomb scare Caroline had been plastered in the London tabloids and the press hounded her wherever she went. Frustrated by the press following her every move Caroline threw a glass of water at one of the photographers which of course became headline news. Shand, a British aristocrat who avoided the press at all cost, dropped Caroline without so much as a word to her.

In September of 1976 Caroline entered Radcliffe College. While she may have gotten away with 'dressing down ' while away from her mother's watchful eye in London, there was no such luck now. Earl Blackwell made his fortune keeping track of celebrities and annually made a list of the ten worst dressed women which the media watched with great interest. Jackie was not amused when she found her daughter's name at the top of Earl Blackwell's 'Worst Dressed List.'

John was attending Brown University where at least half the women on campus wished to date or meet the handsome presidential son. He could have had his pick of girls but he wasn't the type to use his name to take advantage of someone.

While a student at Brown, John pledging for Phi Kappa Psi fraternity streaked across campus dressed only in fish entrails and dog food. He may have been a presidential son but he lived as normal a life as possible wanting to experience the same thing other college students did.

During his second year at Brown the university sent a letter stating he was in danger of being expelled due to his grades. Jackie knew he had a difficult time not only due to the fact that he had ADHD, but also because his Uncle Ted had asked him to campaign for him. John was out campaigning every weekend.

Jackie wrote to the school explaining that in the past she had never asked for special considerations for her children as she felt it did them more harm than good. She wanted her children to be able to make it on their own and not just because they were a Kennedy and given special favors. In this case she explained John had the additional burden other students did not in the fact that he was campaigning. He did pass and eventually received a bachelor's degree in history.

Caroline graduated from Radcliffe College now part of Harvard in 1979 and would later graduate from Columbia Law School in 1988. Having graduated from Radcliffe she began working as a research assistant at the Metropolitan Museum of Art. She followed in her mother's footsteps as a patron of the arts. She remained with the Metropolitan Museum of Art for five years.

While interning at the museum she became friendly with another intern Laura Burke. Laura when asked about Caroline said, "She was a loner but not necessarily by her own choosing. People were afraid to approach her. There's an intimidation factor. People just wanted to do business with her because of who she was. It was always in the air, the celebrity factor. I have to say that she was very nice once you got to know her."

While some thought Caroline being aloof meant she was shy, Caroline herself said, "I'm not as shy as everybody makes me out to be." Caroline made it difficult for others around her to get to know her as she came across as hands-off; while not shy she certainly didn't reach out to others. She suffered what other celebrities go through in wondering who was really interested in being your friend because they liked you, or did they want to get close to you because of who you were.

John could often be seen riding his bike in New York City zipping around corners, cutting through traffic, or riding through Central Park. On his way to school he rode his bike right through a red light and was pulled over by a policeman. After looking at John's identification the policeman looked up and said, "Are you *the* John F. Kennedy, Jr.?" John responded that he supposed he was. The police officer then said, "You're free to go." John surprised the officer by responding, "I broke the law. I'll take the summons." And he did. He paid the fine, and most likely earned the officer's respect.

After John graduated he took a trip to India where he registered for a public health course at the University in New Delhi. He worked to help to organize English lessons for children from the slum areas of Delhi in a program sponsored by Mother Teresa and was able to meet her.

John was considering going to law school, something his mother had been pushing him to do; but what he was really interested in was acting. He had been involved in the drama department and had been encouraged in pursuing acting. He debuted in a play at the Irish Theater on Manhattan's West Side where the director described John as "one of the best young actors I've seen in years."

John wanted to pursue acting by attending Yale Drama School but when he spoke to his mother about going in this direction Jackie threatened to disinherit him unless he went to law school.

John caved and instead of following his passion he bowed to his mother's wishes and went on to New York University Law School. Sharing his shame with the world by becoming front page news when he flunked the bar exam three times, the newspapers ran with the headline, "THE HUNK FLUNKS . . . AGAIN."

Eventually John did pass the bar exam. He worked as a New York City Assistant District Attorney for four years during which time he argued and won six trials. By then he felt he had paid his penance and quit.

A friend of Johns, Steven Styles, described John as "the golden child, you really couldn't help but to gravitate to him. He was good-looking as hell. He also had great empathy." It was hard to find anyone who had a bad word to say about him, not even ex-girlfriends. He was a likeable, friendly guy who never treated people as though they were beneath him. Another friend, Rob Littell, admired him for the way he accepted individuals on their own merit.

Almost everybody in America knew John was good-looking, published a political magazine named *'George'*, and thought he may one day follow in his father's footsteps and get in politics; but what few knew was John was deeply involved in charities spending a great deal of time giving not only financially but giving his time to devote to these causes. He didn't want attention or notoriety, he just wanted to give back making a difference in others' lives. If you only saw John through the eyes of the press and the paparazzi you may have thought he was a spoiled rich kid; which is a shame as there was so much more to John F. Kennedy, Jr.

John worked with inner-city children in Harlem and in Brooklyn tutoring students. He helped start Exodus House, a school for the children of Harlem that many others had given up on. Not only did he help start the school, but he spent hours tutoring the children enrolled in the school. The Robin Hood Foundation was another foundation he was involved in which helped the poor children in New York.

John's Aunt Rosemary, sister to his father, was mentally disabled and this was another cause that he felt strongly about. He established Reaching Up, Inc., a nonprofit organization that trained people who cared for the mentally disabled.

Public service was something John had instilled in him while growing up. The time he spent with the Shrivers gave him hands on experience. It was something he strongly believed in. He had a much healthier attitude in this aspect than his sister who lived isolated behind brick walls.

But John liked his fun, too! He celebrated one Halloween as 'Golden Boy' covered in gold glitter and a loin cloth, another Halloween party he came dressed as Michelangelo's 'David' wearing only a large fig leaf with his body coated with talcum powder which thrilled the women at the party and made the men envious. As a true Irishman he arrived at a St. Patrick's Day party head to toe in green with bell topped ballet slippers that rang out announcing his every step dressed as a leprechaun.

John made headlines when he introduced his Uncle Ted Kennedy at the 1988 Democratic National Convention. John delivered a speech that brought the audience to silence and ended with a three minute standing ovation. The world took notice of this presidential son who they all assumed would one day be up there himself running for office.

Pierre Salinger said, "I heard that speech. I thought, this guy is going to run for office one day. He's got the style and the look." The world certainly already knew who he was and he had the name going for him. Everyone believed it was only a matter of time before the former president's son himself entered the world of politics. If that goal was on his Bucket List he never lived to fulfill that destiny.

In 1987 *People* magazine named John "America's Most Eligible Bachelor" and the following year pasted his face on the front cover with the title of "Sexiest Man Alive." You would have been hard pressed to find a female that argued with either title.

Caroline had very few boyfriends in either her teen or adult years, but John while he never had the reputation of a womanizer like his father and Uncle Ted he did have his fair share of romances. Throughout the years his name was linked with several woman; the most serious being Christina Haag who he had a five year relationship with and actress Daryl Hannah another relationship that lasted for years.

John once said his mother would most likely never approve of any girl he dated. She made it abundantly clear she wasn't happy about some of the women she saw linked in the papers with her son.

One woman in particular that she seemed determined her son end his relationship with was Daryl Hannah. John not understanding what his mother could have against her since she hadn't even met her asked his mother what it was about her she disapproved of. She responded it was because she was an actress (could this attitude be influenced due to her own husband's indiscretions with Marilyn Monroe; one has to wonder), and she didn't want him having a relationship with anyone in the media spotlight. It seems to be an odd response when she herself chose two man who were most definitely *'in the spotlight.'* This appeared to be a case of 'do what I say, not what I did.'

John was one who enjoyed living on the edge, an adrenaline junkie. He enjoyed paragliding and paraplanes, kayaking, and deep-sea diving. As an athlete he enjoyed biking through the streets of NYC, roller-blading through Central Park, swimming, rowing, and playing football. He worked out at a gym almost every day of his adult life.

On his travels he crawled through dark claustrophobic tunnels that were sections of the old Viet Cong strongholds from the days of the Vietnam War. He went scuba diving with a dive team from the 'Vast Explorer,' a salvage vessel hunting for a legendary pirate ship. He kayaked in Iceland. He kept on the go and wasn't still for very long at a time. He had things to do and places to see; and in hindsight living the short life he did he seemed to be trying to fit in a lifetime of adventures in a short period of time.

Caroline's life was gentler and quieter, but productive. At the Metropolitan Museum of Art she coordinated special productions as a staff member of the Office of Film and Television. Some of the films she was involved in have aired on Public Television. She would graduate from law school, marry, and have three children: Rose born in 1988, Tatiana in 1990, and John, named after her father and brother, born in 1993.

Caroline while in law school read a poll in a newspaper that showed 59% of Americans couldn't name the Bill of Rights. She was astonished and inspired at the same time to write the book, *'In Our Defense: the Bill of Rights In Action,'* which she co-wrote with a fellow student, Ellen Alderman. After they completed the first book they wrote another, *'The Right To Privacy.'* She compiled several books on poetry, some which were her late mother's favorite poems and a Christmas book of poetry and scripture.

Caroline from an early age had been encouraged by her mother to have a strong sense of personal achievement. I think she accomplished that goal. She earned a fine arts degree at Radcliffe, trained at Sotheby's, worked in documentary film production for the

Metropolitan Museum of Art in New York, became involved in charities, and is currently serving as Ambassador to Japan.

It was while Caroline was working at the museum that she met her future husband. At the time they met he was an exhibit designer and by the year 1985 they were in a serious relationship. His name was Edwin Schlossberg and he had yet to meet the ultimate challenge - *be approved by her mother and brother.*

A friend of Carolines named Lisa remembers the night Caroline introduced Ed to her family. They were having dinner together. "I remember Jackie being a little distant, not eager to let this new person into the circle, or at least that's how it appeared to me. Jackie seemed to really be looking Ed over studying him as if she were scrutinizing him, perhaps wondering what her daughter saw in him."

At some point during the dinner Ed excused himself and Caroline leaned over to her mother and whispered, "So, Mother, what do you think of him?" Jackie responded, "Well, he's not exactly interesting now, is he?" At that point John jumped into the conversation, not being able to hold back his opinion any longer. "Heck, Mom, let's face it. That guys the biggest bore who ever lived!" Caroline must have been a bit devastated that he hadn't exactly passed the approval test with her family whose opinion meant so much to her.

Ed is twelve years older than Caroline which is the same age difference between her own mother and father. But that's where the comparison ends. While Caroline comes from a strong Catholic family, Ed comes from a devout Jewish family. His family were not blue bloods, but 'new rich.'

If asked to describe himself Ed would have said he was an author, poet, philosopher, conceptual artist, visionary, Renaissance man. You could say he is kind of full of himself; in other words, not a humble man.

Ed designed T-shirts and experimented with printing poetry on aluminum and Plexiglass. He wasn't exactly what you would describe as a success story or self-made man. His work only really began to be noticed when the public learned he was engaged to Caroline Kennedy.

People that worked with Ed described him as opportunistic, shallow, and insincere. I seriously doubt their opinions changed over time. Even some in the Kennedy family years after they had the opportunity to really get to know him described him as a dictator. It seems the only one that really approved of him was Caroline.

Caroline and Ed were married July 19, 1986. It is ironic that as private as Caroline is she chose to have a large wedding with thousands of guests, while her brother who is outgoing and a very public person would choose to run off and have a private wedding.

Caroline decided against backing Democratic Hillary Clinton when she ran in her first presidential campaign even though the Clinton and Kennedy family knew each other. Caroline campaigned for Barack Obama.

Caroline wrote, "I have never had a president who inspired me the way people tell me that my father inspired them. But for the first time, I believe I have found the man who could be that president – not just for me, but for a new generation of Americans." Whether she feels he succeeded in doing so or not is unknown.

President Obama rewarded her for campaigning for him by appointing her as ambassador to Japan, a post that is considered one of the most prestigious in the U.S. diplomatic ranks. In accepting this role she appears to be trying to make a name for herself, not that of her father's daughter or the daughter of Jackie Kennedy; but stepping out from under their enormous shadows and standing on her own accomplishments.

As for her role as ambassador to Japan she has traveled to Kumamoto City to encourage residents in their recovery efforts following an earthquake and made speeches and public appearances. She visited Nagasaki and Hiroshima to meet the survivors of the atomic bomb and visited the Fukushima Dai-ichi nuclear power station. She tweeted on a topic she found deeply disturbing which was the drive hunt dolphin killing.

Living a life in a gilded cage behind brick walls she has twice tried to break out of that prison; once in running for the Senate in the year 2008 which she quickly backed out of as she was ill prepared and had no idea on what policies to stand for. When being questioned on the platform she would stand for she stammered and stuttered not having given much thought to the issues. She had thought she could just become senator and 'make a difference.'

As the daughter of the president whose famous quote was, "Ask not what your country can do for you, but what you can do for your country," perhaps as the sole survivor of her immediate family she felt pressured into becoming involved in public service. Caroline may feel that it is up to her to do something; a role she previously assumed her brother would one day undertake.

Currently there are over two dozen presidential children still alive; though none have received the attention and scrutiny from the press and paparazzi as the son and daughter of President Kennedy. Most presidential children are allowed to go on and live their lives in anonymity, perhaps only occasionally making headlines if ever. Jackie all too familiar with the press had warned her children not to lose their soul to the paparazzi.

"Caroline's attitude regarding the press seemed totally unrealistic," said Andy Warhol. "If you're a bona fide celebrity, you can't very well dictate terms. It doesn't work that way." But then Caroline had been chased by paparazzi her entire life to the point at times where she felt her life was endangered. Anyone who has had a camera thrust in your face and chased every time they walked out their door may understand why she responds to the press in the manner she does.

John met Carolyn Bessette, the woman he would one day marry at a time that he and Daryl Hannah had gone their separate ways. The relationship between John and Carolyn was pretty fast and furious. They had a stormy relationship brought on by her jealousy and her aversion to the paparazzi that seemed to follow John's every move. John was used to them and considered the paparazzi a part of his life; he had been photographed and in the press from the time he was born. Carolyn avoided them at all costs and when photographed she always had a frown on her face. The paparazzi disliked her as much as she disliked them. The 'American Prince,' which is how America looked at John had always been friendly and accommodating with them - *until Carolyn came into his life.*

In September of 1996 John and Carolyn pulled off a coup that left the press stunned. They ran off and were married in a private ceremony that not even family and friends were aware was about to take place. It's amazing they were able to pull it off without word being leaked with his every step under constant scrutiny.

They married on Cumberland Island, Georgia with only a few friends and relatives. Their family and friends had been invited to what they thought was a party. They didn't know they were coming to a wedding until they arrived. At the time of their wedding John was thirty-five years of age and Carolyn was thirty.

Neither Kennedy children chose spouses that the public were endeared to. They didn't even like each others' spouses. Caroline snubbed her sister-in-law and had nothing to do with her. John speaking of his brother-in-law to his close friend Billy Way said, "He's a smug asshole. A real creep." Billy said, "His condemnation of Schlossberg was noteworthy insofar as he so rarely bad-mouthed people."

It was a sentiment shared by many. Ed could be outright rude. Stanley Mirsky a physician who had a weekend home in the Hamptons near the Kennedy's home came across Ed while in town, and since they lived near one another Stan went up to introduce himself. Stan said Ed gave him one of the most hostile looks he'd ever seen and without even acknowledging him crossed the street in order not to have to speak to him. Others have recalled similar circumstances when they were treated with a rudeness that left them standing in their tracks with their mouths open unable to believe what had just happened.

The world assumed John would one day go into politics, but John had another idea in mind. It was in 1995, he realized his dream when he launched *George* magazine. John was the founder and publisher.

John had dreamed of publishing a political magazine for some time and encouraged by Carolyn he partnered with an old friend Michael Bernan. Michael had a background in public relations and marketing but had no experience in publishing. They assumed the two of them could combine their skills, experience, and knowledge and make a success of the magazine. John's dream was of a political magazine that was not solely politics, but a combination of politics and pop culture. The magazine's name *George* was named after George Washington.

John had given up much at the request of his mother even the flying lessons he had loved, but after her death he began resuming the lessons. Back in 1988 his mother had threatened to disinherit him if he continued with the lessons.

Two years after his mother's death he decided to take up flying again. His sister like her mother had in the past did everything she could to convince her brother to give up flying which is ironic since it was she who first took flying lessons herself. Caroline had signed up as a student pilot and had completed half a dozen lessons with an instructor when Jackie used her step-brother Alexander Onassis' fatal crash as an excuse to end the lessons. Without asking Jackie ordered Caroline's flight instructor to take her daughter out of the program.

John and Caroline had many arguments over his flying. Caroline told him, "Nothing's changed except that Mother isn't here. But I still am, and I'm afraid." He kept insisting he would be fine, that he knew what he was doing. For a time he listened to his sister's counsel but he missed flying and one day called her and asked that she support his decision and not give him any more grief about it.

John was a dare devil that pushed the limits. It was less than two months before his death that he flew his ultralight powered parachute into a tree. His wife Carolyn watched in disbelief as he untangled himself from the wreckage and hobbled his way to the house with a grin on his face. He fractured two bones in his ankle which left him in a cast walking on crutches right up to just a few weeks before he made his fatal flight.

The Kennedys were all at Hyannis Port at the Kennedy compound to attend the wedding of Rory Kennedy. Caroline and Ed did not plan to attend as the family had made previous plans to celebrate Ed's 54th birthday on a rafting vacation. John and Carolyn were planning to attend the wedding and were going to fly there in John's Piper Saratoga after first dropping off Carolyn's sister Lauren at Martha's Vineyard.

Friends who were waiting at the airport to meet Lauren became concerned when the plane was late. When time passed and she still had not arrived they began making calls. Ted Kennedy was notified and he began checking around. He discovered their plane hadn't been seen on radar since half an hour before it should have landed. The following morning a fleet of aircraft were sent out on a search and rescue attempt.

By the next afternoon debris from the plane wreck began washing ashore near Martha's Vineyard. Ted learned from the Coast Guard that a person on the shore had spotted something floating in the water and went into the surf to investigate and returned with a suitcase. An identification tag on the luggage identified it as belonging to Lauren Bessette. Throughout the day other debris was washed ashore including a prescription bottle made out to Carolyn Bessette. It was a solemn find for those who discovered contents of the plane which included a bag of kayaking gear John had brought along. Pieces of the plane began to emerge from the surf confirming their worst fears. There was no way the trio could have survived.

Caroline was notified and returned home where she was comforted by Maria Shriver her cousin and closest confidante. Ted Kennedy arrived and soon after he and Caroline walked outside and lowered the flag she displayed in her yard to half-mast. Her brother

John, the last of her immediate family was dead.

The wreckage from the plane crash was discovered at the bottom of the ocean. A Navy ship recovered the bodies and what was left of the wreckage. The cause of the crash was determined to be "pilot's failure to maintain control of the airplane." Being a novice pilot he wasn't trained well enough to fly at night over water which caused spatial disorientation, which is when a person cannot correctly determine their position.

Within days the bodies were cremated and the Kennedy and Bessette families boarded the USS Briscoe as it made its way to the crash site. An officer released the ashes of John, Carolyn, and Lauren into the sea. John was thirty-eight, Carolyn thirty-three, and Lauren thirty-four. Three young lives lost.

John wasn't the first Kennedy to lose his life in a plane crash. There seemed to be a history of fatal plane crashes associated with the family. Joe Kennedy, Jr., the oldest brother of JFK died in 1944 when his WWII bomber blew up over the English Channel. JFK's sister Kathleen known as "Kick" died in an airplane crash four years after her brother's fatal crash while flying from Paris to Cannes. In 1964 Ted Kennedy was being flown from Washington to Massachusetts when his plane crashed killing the pilot and one of Ted's senatorial aides. Ted survived but spent over two months in the hospital recuperating. Ethel Kennedy's parents and one of her brothers were killed in separate plane crashes. In 1973, Alexander Onassis, Aristotle's only son and step-brother to John and Caroline died while piloting a plane in Greece. And now in 1999, John Kennedy, Jr.'s name was added to the list of fatalities.

Caroline has followed her mother's example by living a private life. She refuses interviews and she and her husband have been known to banish friends, employees, and associates from their lives if discovered they have spoken to the press about not only her but her family. Friends of her late brother were shocked when they received a call from her denouncing their speaking to the press even though they didn't have an unkind word to say about him.

Caroline is secure in her future behind her brick walls and her self-imposed prison. The fortunes of Caroline and her immediate family received after the deaths of her father, her mother, and her brother has left her family fortune in an abundance of over $500 million.

36

LYNDON B. JOHNSON

Children of "Lady Bird" and Lyndon B. Johnson:

Lynda Bird Johnson – Born: March 19, 1944   Still Living At The Time Of Publication

Luci Baines Johnson - Born: July 2, 1947   Still Living At The Time Of Publication

Lynda is currently the oldest living presidential child.

Sixteen year old Luci was sitting in Spanish class at Washington's National Cathedral School when a student ran into the classroom crying out the news that President Kennedy had been shot and killed. Luci whose father was the vice president and her mother were traveling with the president and first lady in Dallas. There was no mention if the vice president or second lady had been harmed.

Class was dismissed early as students and teachers alike were stunned into disbelief that the president was dead. Luci was worried about her parents. She walked outside the school in a daze and looked up and saw a Secret Service agent she recognized. He reassured her that her parents were not injured. It was then she realized – *her father was now President of the United States.*

The new First Family included two teenage daughters; Lynda who was nineteen and Luci who was sixteen. They were the first teens to live in the White House in fifty years.

Secret Service agents were immediately assigned to the Johnson girls after the president's death. Their lives were about to change in a way they never imagined. The girls were both still in shock over the assassination and had yet to realize what it would mean to them for their father to be president. They were totally unprepared in becoming part of the First Family. There is no comparison in your father being vice president as there is to your father being the president.

Their father took the oath of office aboard Air Force One while still sitting on the tarmac of the Dallas airport with his wife Lady Bird by his side and First Lady Jackie Kennedy. Jackie was still in her blood stained suit she had been wearing while sitting next to her husband when he was shot. It was the first and last time in American history a president of the United States took the oath of office aboard Air Force One. By the time they landed in Washington there had been a regime change with a different president than the one that had departed just the day before.

When a president goes through the election process he and his family move into the White House immediately after the inauguration. The custom is the morning of the inauguration the outgoing president has the opportunity to say goodbye to the staff at the White House that has served him and his family for the last four or eight years. Around 10:30 A.M. the incoming president and first lady arrive at the White House and are met at the North Portico entrance by the outgoing president and first lady. Both presidents, the outgoing and the incoming, ride in one limousine to the Capitol while the first ladies follow in another.

At that point it is like a well-oiled machine at the White House. Every member of the staff is required to work that day, as for security reasons no helpers from a moving company or outside help can be brought into the White House. The minute the two presidents drive off for the Capitol the move is set in motion. While the oath of office is taking place and the parades are going on everything from the outgoing family is removed and everything is set up for the incoming presidential family. Even clothes are hung in the closets and everything is set up so they immediately feel at home. By the time the newly sworn in president and his family return, usually sometime between 4:00 – 6:00 P.M., they can come in and relax with no signs of the mad scurrying that has taken place for the last five to six hours. They have a chance to rest before it's time to head out for the inaugural balls.

Due to the assassination there were no inaugural balls and it would be sixteen days after

Lyndon B. Johnson was sworn in as the 36th president before the Johnson family moved into the Executive Mansion.

The very night the Johnson family moved in Luci recalls it was a night she will never forget. She had a girlfriend over to spend the night. "Neither one of us knew how to light a fireplace, but we tried anyway," Luci remembers. "It got out of control and I started throwing fruit-juice glasses of water into the fire. To get rid of the smoke I stood on my desk, opened a window, and looked down to see a White House policeman looking up. I was wearing a nightgown." The next few days she spent cleaning smoke off the walls.

A month after the assassination had passed and the period of mourning had come to an end, President Johnson ordered the black bunting draped throughout the White House to be removed. As the symbols of bereavement came down, Christmas decorations went up. It was quite a transformation from a house of despair to the merry signs of the holidays.

Luci had turned sixteen just a few months previous and had been given a new Corvette for her birthday. "I'd just gotten a driver's license," Lucy said. At her age she thought she was just going to start enjoying some freedom with a driver's license and a car; but there would be no way she could drive around in her new Corvette with her friends. That wouldn't be possible now with the Secret Service going everywhere she went.

At sixteen everything is dramatized and it was no different for Luci who proclaimed, "I have been robbed of my youth, my private life." That seems to be a sentiment shared by all teenage First Family members. They feel they have reached an age when they can start having a little independence only to lose it before it really begins; every move they make is being witnessed by the world and under the watchful eye of the Secret Service.

She did discover one of the perks of being a president's daughter when her dog was lost. J. Edgar Hoover Director of the FBI put the dog on the FBI's "Most Wanted" list until he was found.

As far as living in the White House goes the girls found it difficult. It isn't a place where your friends can just drop in to visit when your address is 1600 Pennsylvania Avenue. "You feel so alone," Luci said. While Kennedy was president the first lady had used the third floor solarium for a school for Caroline. The Johnsons turned the area into a recreation room for the girls to use to entertain their friends. The room was supplied with a record player, TV, and soda bar with bar stools. The girls enjoyed their time in their own space with friends and dates and barred the Secret Service.

"I will never be just Luci Johnson," she complained. "I'll always be the President's youngest daughter, always and forever." She was absolutely right. Once you become the son or daughter of a president, that is how the public remembers you first and foremost. If you are highly successful, it is usually thought that it was due to the advantages given you as the child of a president; and if you fail or don't accomplish much with your life, you are judged more harshly than if you were just the son or daughter of a normal citizen. It is hard to live in your parent's shadow. There's nothing to compare to being President of the United States.

Lynda was a few years older than her sister and more mature. When her father became president she was a college student attending the University of Texas. When her family moved into the White House the first lady had her daughter transfer to George Washington University. Initially she lived at the university, but as a First Daughter found the stress too much and moved to the White House along with her roommate from college. It wasn't easy at the White House either as when they tried to study she said the tourists who walked around beneath her bedroom window were noisy and she found it difficult to concentrate.

The press who can be quite harsh in their judgment had Lynda labeled as the brains of the family and Luci as the beauty. It was unfair to both girls and caused friction between them. Lynda was the quieter of the two, while Luci still young and carefree was more outgoing. Lynda unhappy with the way the press had portrayed her became unapproachable, while Luci had a way with the media and became 'their darling.'

When the girls complained about the press following their every move and having cameras in their face everywhere they went the first lady reminded them, "Don't do anything you wouldn't mind seeing on the front page of the newspaper."

Lynda, wise beyond her years said, "Children of men in public life – somewhat like the children of preachers – learn early in life that people expect them to be adults before they are even adolescents."

The girls like most teenage presidential kids resented the Secret Service for invading their private space. They said with them coming on dates with them it was like having your big brother tagging along.

While it's difficult for a teen and their friends at the time to fully understand the need to constantly have Secret Service around, they are very much appreciated for the work they do for the presidential families. They put their lives on the line and give up much in reference to their own personal lives; rarely being able to spend holidays, birthdays, or the time they would like to spend with their own families in order to serve the president and his family. They are indispensable to the First Family for their protection.

Sunday and Monday are the only days the White House isn't open to the public for tours. Every other day the tourists could be heard bright and early through the girl's bedroom window as they tried to sleep. Years later they would find it had been much easier to deal with the tourists coming to visit than to listen to the protestors against the Vietnam War as they chanted and yelled outside the White House.

Several months after President Kennedy's assassination and after LBJ had become president, Lady Bird wrote to her husband to encourage him to consider running for the presidency. His administration would soon come to an end that he had completed in place of President Kennedy and she wanted him to consider running on his own merits; even though she realized the entire family would pay a price. She was very astute.

Years after her husband's death while being interviewed on the television show *'Nightline,'* she read aloud to the viewers part of the letter she had written to him years earlier. *"In the course of the campaign and in the ensuing years,"* she read, *"you – and I – and the children – will certainly get criticized and cut up, for things we have done, or maybe partly-in-a-way have done – and for others that we never did at all. That will be painful."* Lady Bird's prediction came true.

LBJ not only considered his wife's wise counsel, but he followed her advice and ran. The entire Johnson family got out to campaign. Luci said, "My father said, 'Luci, we're in the campaign of a lifetime. It's a sinking ship, and I'm counting on you to bail, baby, bail!'"

Luci campaigned in twenty-six states, over half of the United States. But there were times when enough was enough. As a teen she wanted some time to herself to do what she wanted, so when she overheard her mother and one of the presidential aides talking about her getting out and campaigning that weekend Luci hid in the closet so they wouldn't find her.

President Johnson won the 1964 election. The morning of the inauguration the First

Family had chipped beef on toast for breakfast then dressed while the first lady ran around rushing them all so they wouldn't be late.

They arrived at the U.S. Capitol where the swearing-in ceremony took place. President Johnson made the decision that he wanted his wife to be the one to hold the Bible on which he would place his hand as he repeated the oath of office. This was the first time it had been carried out with the first lady taking part and the tradition is still upheld today.

The president took his oath of office and delivered his inaugural speech behind bullet-proof glass. That was the first time in history it was felt a need to protect the president in such a manner. The assassination of a president forced the changes. It had become a much more dangerous world for the president.

The threat was so serious that the New Mexican Cochiti Indian tribal dancers that would be in the inaugural parade in their native dress were informed they wouldn't be allowed to take part in the event unless they removed the points of their arrows. Secret Service helicopters kept watch over the crowd during the parade watching for any suspicious activity.

There were five inaugural balls that evening. The crowds were so immense it was a nightmare for the Secret Service, especially when the president insisted on getting on the dance floor and dancing the night away.

The night before the girls had attended a 'Young Democrats Dance.' One of the dances was held at The Mayflower Hotel and one was held at The Willard Hotel. Lynda Johnson stood in a receiving line shaking hands for hours at the Mayflower Hotel, while at the same time Luci attending the dance at The Willard Hotel was on the dance floor having a great time dancing The Frug, Jerk, and the Watusi; which is where she earned the nickname 'Watusi Luci.'

After Lynda graduated from college she was given a two month vacation to Europe from her parents. While in Greece she went sightseeing to ancient ruins and was part of a dig with an excavating pick in search of ancient treasures. She unearthed pieces of human bone and old tiles from temple ruins near Corinth. Her next stop was Mycenae which had been a major Greek city during the Bronze Age learning a bit of world history along with her vacation. She attended the wedding of King Constantine and Princess Anne-Marie of Denmark as a representative of the U.S. along with the wife of the U.S. ambassador to

Greece Mrs. Henry Labouisse.

Luci attended the National Cathedral School and once brought her entire class, all sixty-two students for a White House tour.

The fact that the Johnson girls were the first teenage daughters of a president since the days of Alice Roosevelt fifty years previously made them an attractive subject to the press. The media considered the First Daughters fair game. What they did, where they went, how they dressed, even their hairstyles were all subjects that were commented on and criticized. All that attention and criticism can be a bit overwhelming and invasive so when Luci was asked by the press if she had a boyfriend she got a bit irritated and responded, "I'd rather not talk about that, because although I'm the president's daughter. I also have a right to my own private life. Besides, whether, I have a boyfriend or not isn't anything of national significance."

As a teenager Luci had her rebellious moments. She showed this side of her when she had the spelling of her name changed from Lucy to Luci; and in the White House that rebellious streak reared it's ugly head when she knew her mother was entertaining guests and she played her piano *really* loud.

While many presidential family members complain about their lack of time with their busy parents, for the Johnson girls it was just the opposite. Luci said, "I saw more of my parents than I'd ever seen before. I think I was sixteen years old before I ever sat down at a table for lunch or dinner with just the four of us."

Chief Usher West who worked at the White House from the Eisenhower administration through the Nixon administration was delighted to see a lively White House with Lynda and Luci. "They kept the staid old halls jumping. Noise and laughter, dates and dramatics echoed through the historic rooms," West said.

The girls having grown up in a political family had learned early on about public service and in helping others. Luci was proud of her father when he signed the Civil Rights Act into effect on her birthday in 1964. The law outlawed discrimination based on race, color, religion, sex, or national origin.

To some the signing of the Civil Rights Act was seen as the most important legislation in American history. Though not everyone was happy about the end of the days of discrimination, including some of those in Congress. The act had the longest filibuster in the Senate's history. More Republicans voted in favor of the Civil Rights Act than Democrats with 80% of Republicans voting for the bill while only 60% of Democrats voted to pass the bill. Two leaders who worked for equal rights for African-Americans but with extreme differences of how they went about doing so were Malcolm X and Martin Luther King, Jr., who met for the first and only time at the Senate hearings. Even when the act was finally passed many Americans were opposed to it and riots ensued.

First daughter Lynda was curious to know what the public was saying about her father and family and disguised herself and joined a tour through the White House. She thought that would be the best opportunity she had to see what people really thought of them. At the end of the tour she found herself on the outside of the White House fence and being in disguise had to convince the guard at the gate who she was by removing her disguise before she was let back in.

June of 1965 Luci had just graduated from high school and planning on going into nursing. The president had delivered the commencement speech at her graduation. Back home she was dressed in shorts and an oversize shirt sitting with curlers in her hair under the hair dryer as forty friends were quietly sneaking into the solarium for a surprise party. She was completely surprised and even more so when her friends told her since she was going into nursing school they needed a cadaver at the party. They rolled in a body covered in a sheet on a stretcher and an old friend popped up off the stretcher.

Luci met the man she would later marry while on a blind date. Not wanting the press hanging around during the date, she tricked them by hiding her black hair under a blonde wig and using a fake name. She was thrilled she was able to pull this off and still laughs today when telling the story.

An ongoing concern of sons and daughters of the president is in wondering whether a person is attracted to them or is it the glamor of the White House and the bragging rights of 'dating a president's son or daughter.' Lynda Johnson realized it wasn't just the son or daughter of the president that suffered. "The young man gets besieged with, 'What are your intentions?' Did he want to take Lynda out or did he want to take the President's daughter out?" It wasn't easy for the boys either.

Luci became engaged to Pat Nugent. Being a recent convert to Catholicism she chose the largest Catholic church in America for the location of her wedding. The only issue was in the past the church had denied other couples the right to be married there. Here she was a recent convert and she was given permission to have her wedding there causing an outcry. But she got her way and her wedding took place at the National Shrine of the Immaculate Conception in Washington. This would be the first time a sitting president's daughter was married in a church.

Another issue that arose during the wedding plans was the date they chose. They chose August 6th the anniversary date of the day the atom bomb was dropped on Hiroshima. People complained about the date she chose and wanted her to choose another day for the wedding saying it was disrespectful to be having a large celebration on that particular day. She responded to the complaint with a vehement resounding no, she would not change the date. After all she said, she was born after the date the bomb was dropped and the date was her own personal choice and would not be changed.

Seven hundred guests arrived to witness the marriage of Luci Baines Johnson and Patrick Nugent. Approximately another fifty-five million viewers were able to watch the wedding as it was broadcast on television.

Brides have received such a reputation from the day they begin planning their wedding until the moment they are driven off in a limousine heading for a honeymoon of being demanding and unbearable that many have received the label of 'Bridezilla.' In this case however it wasn't the bride but the maid of honor, the sister of the bride. As the bride was being dressed in her gown and the bridesmaids were also dressing and primping for the special day Lynda was constantly complaining about how she looked just the same as the other bridesmaids. She thought she should have something that made her stand out from the others, to mark her as being 'special.'

Priscilla, who was not only the designer of the wedding gown but was tending to the bride and bridesmaids had been listening to Lynda complaining until she had had quite enough. When one last time Lynda began whining to her to "make me stand out," Priscilla reached over and grabbed a pair of scissors and taking Lynda's floor-length veil in hand cut it to elbow length. Priscilla said, "Now you stand out!" That wasn't exactly what Lynda had in mind and she was livid. A replacement veil was quickly made for her by one of the seamstresses who was there to help fit the girls in their dresses.

The drama behind them, the bride made quite an entrance in her gown that had been kept secret from everyone before the wedding. Even the White House staff weren't allowed to lay eyes on the gown before the day of the wedding. The gown was a beautiful princess style A-line skirt with long sleeves and a high collar and a 9' train made of French lace.

The wedding day was taking place in the hot, humid summer months of Washington and the maid of honor Lynda Johnson almost fainted from the heat in the midst of the ceremony. A chair was brought for her to sit through the end of the ceremony.

The reception took place at the White House in the East Room. The wedding cake was seven tiers weighing in at 300 pounds and stood 8'. When it came time to cut the cake the president stepped in to help his daughter. Luci stood on the Truman balcony to toss the bouquet. Perfectly aimed, it landed just a few steps from her sister Lynda.

The newlyweds changed and had made a plan to thwart any plans the press may have had in following them to their honeymoon site. When it came time to leave the bride and groom went through a tunnel that connects the White House to the Treasury Building located next door to the Executive Mansion. There was a car waiting for them in the basement garage with a driver. The couple crouched down on the floor of the car until they had passed the White House and out of sight of any who may have attempted to follow them.

Once Luci was married and off living her new life the press turned to Lynda wondering if she would soon marry. She had been engaged for a time to Bernard Rosenbach but that engagement had been called off. She began dating a White House military aide, and for a time a medical student, but what really captured the media's attention was when she began dating the actor George Hamilton who had the reputation of a playboy and was known as the man with 'the perpetual tan.'

A movie star and a president's daughter: *this was front page news!* Not only were their names linked in newspapers, but gossip columns coast-to-coast kept track of what the two were up to and wondered if a marriage would be announced anytime soon.

George Hamilton and Lynda Johnson met when he was invited to a White House dinner after he had starred in the movie, *'Your Cheatin' Heart'* where he portrayed Hank Williams. A jet-setting romance followed with dates at the Sugar Bowl and the Oscars. He spent holidays at the Johnson Ranch with the family and the two of them went off for a weekend in Acapulco. He flew in from London where he was making a movie to spend New Year's Eve with her, and he was quoted in *'Modern Screen Magazine,'* telling the interviewer when asked about the president's daughter that he could love her "even if she weren't the president's daughter."

When Hamilton threw a birthday party for her at his Beverly Hills mansion people wondered if he would give her an engagement ring. Even though he traveled the world making movies they were seen together enough to keep the rumors going and the press was sure a marriage was soon to be announced.

Unbeknownst to the press and the public who thought they knew everything there was to know about the president's daughter; again she had pulled a fast one. She had met Chuck Robb a Marine officer who was the captain of the White House color guard. She met him while he was working at the White House.

When he had completed his work for the day he met Lynda up in the Solarium. The butlers and some of the White House staff were aware of the romance, but they kept the young couple's secret to themselves.

One morning she went to her parent's bedroom so she could talk to them before her father headed off to the Oval Office for his workday. She made the announcement to her parents of her intentions to marry Robb. Her fiancé was soon going to be leaving for Vietnam so they arranged for the wedding to take place so they would have a few weeks together before he was to leave for Vietnam.

When the engagement was announced the world was stunned. How had she pulled this romance off without a word leaking out? Not only the nation and the press were stunned; but so was George Hamilton. Even so, they have remained friends over the years.

Lynda's wedding would be the 8th White House wedding for a president's son or daughter and the first in fifty-three years. The couple had a traditional military ceremony with an archway of crossed swords.

Lynda in a silk satin, long sleeved gown made her entrance coming down the Grand Staircase on the arm of her father. It was a December wedding and the bridesmaids were dressed in red velvet gowns. After walking his daughter down the aisle when the minister asked, "Who giveth this woman to be married to this man?" President Johnson responded with, "Her mother and I."

Bonnie Angelo, a reporter from *Time* who was covering the wedding was given an area behind a drape that had a little hole cut out so she could witness every moment of the ceremony. Angelo said, "And for that I bought a new velvet dress." She spent the entire ceremony kneeling on the floor behind the partition; but other reporters were envious that she got to attend at all.

Lynda changed out of her wedding gown and the bride and groom were whisked away with the couple being flown off in a helicopter.

By the time Lynda's husband left for Vietnam she was expecting their first child. While he was fighting in Vietnam she returned to the White House to live. Her sister had also returned to live there with her little boy while her husband was also in Vietnam.

Both president's daughters' husbands off in Vietnam they were worried about their husbands while at the same time they had to listen to Vietnam protestors who could clearly be heard from their bedroom windows. Lynda's room faced Pennsylvania Avenue and from her sister Luci's room she could also hear the protestors. Lynda said, "It was distressing to Luci and to me when you could hear the people yelling from across the street all day and all night about the war, particularly since both of our husbands were over there. They were sacrificing and I was pregnant, and they would say things that were very hurtful."

By 1968 the U.S. had already lost 30,000 Americans to the war. President Johnson's approval ratings had dropped to below 40 percent. LBJ's administration would most be remembered for the Vietnam War. Lynda was distraught over her father's presidency being judged due to the war. "How do you think I felt when there were people marching outside the White House shouting, 'Hey, hey, LBJ, how many kids did you kill today?' " she asks.

After his daughter Lynda dropping her husband off for a tour of duty and returning distraught, asking her father, "Daddy, why do they have to go to Vietnam?" Johnson feeling the pain of his daughter made the decision there and then not to seek reelection.

When the president had ordered bomb raids on Hanoi and his daughter Luci found him pacing and clearly stressed over his decision she took him to visit the Benedictine monks at St. Dominic's Roman Catholic Church in Washington where they went to pray.

The young teen girls who had arrived as the newest First Family changed over their five year period of being the president's daughters. Luci said, "It shaped my character; it was a prism through which I would view all other experiences of my life." It wasn't all easy, or all good times; but there were many opportunities available as a presidential daughter. "It was one of life's great privileges to be an eyewitness to history."

Luci was married to Pat Nugent for almost thirteen years. During their marriage they had four children, but the marriage would eventually be annulled by the Catholic Church. She would remarry an investment banker Ian Turpin. Luci and her second husband were married at the Johnson Ranch in 1983. Luci lives in Texas today with her husband Ian.

When Luci married the first time she was attending nursing school but had to drop out as married students were not allowed in the school. In 1995 she registered at St. Edwards University in Austin, Texas and graduated; eliminating the label she carried of being the only woman in her family for the last three generations without a college degree. She graduated at the age of fifty.

"Luci once asked her mother the former first lady how she wanted to be remembered. Lady Bird Johnson responded, "I made a lot of little lists in my life, and I checked a lot of things off." When an interviewer asked Luci the same question, she responded in kind. "I've checked a few things off my own list," she said. And indeed, she has.

Luci is chairman of the board and manages the multimillion dollar media empire LBJ Holding Company. She has served on many boards continuing the public service work that was instilled in her while growing up. Luci is vice president of the BusinessSuites. She has received many awards for her work including the 1997 Top 25 Women Owned Business Awards.

When your father becomes president the whole world has opinions of him and whether they think he did a good job, opinions on everything they do and say. Then they have opinions on the first lady and his children. It can be pretty hurtful to hear your parents slandered and abused in the press or even by people you meet. Luci said, "At some point I learned that I couldn't control what people thought of my parents, my sister, or me."

In the year 2012 while in her early 60's Luci was diagnosed with Guillain-Barré syndrome a rare autoimmune disorder affecting the peripheral nervous system and was admitted to Mayo Clinic. Caught early she experienced a full recovery.

Lynda Bird Johnson Robb when asked about her memories of being a 'president's daughter' replied, "You get to meet an awful lot of interesting people," said Lynda. In looking back she has happy memories of her time in the White House, though some of it was rough; like when her husband was away in Vietnam.

Lynda is currently the oldest living presidential child. Her husband Charles Robb became a Virginia governor as well as senator of Virginia. He was at one time considered a shoo-in as a future presidential candidate. Those predictions came to a screeching halt when rumors of his infidelity and attendance at cocaine parties surfaced. He sent out a letter of confession admitting to partaking in matters "not appropriate to a married man." He said with Lynda's forgiveness and God's, he put that chapter behind him. Lynda stood by him and in a kind but firm way told the *'Washington Post'* it was nobody's business but their own.

Lynda and her husband have three daughters. In her 'post-presidential' life she has used her name and influence with educational programs such as *'Reading Is Fundamental.'* She, too, has served on many boards, one of which was that of her mother's *'Lady Bird Johnson Wildflower Research Center.'* She has been honored with awards for her public service.

37

RICHARD NIXON

Children of Pat and Richard Nixon:

Patricia Nixon "Tricia"- Born: Feb. 21, 1946   Still Living At The Time Of Publication

Julie Nixon – Born: July 5, 1948   Still Living At The Time Of Publication

Trisha Nixon was the most reclusive of any modern day White House daughter. Her sister referred to her as the "Howard Hughes of the White House."

When Nixon graduated from law school he applied to be a special agent in the FBI. He had attended a lecture by a special agent while he was at Duke and the lecture had stirred his interest in a career with the FBI. He went through a physical and testing but never heard anymore from them. If he had, perhaps U.S. history would have had a different story.

Richard Nixon married Pat in the year 1940. During their marriage he ran for nine national political campaigns. He was elected as a U.S. congressman in 1946 and was campaigning for that position while Pat was pregnant with Tricia. Just a matter of weeks after giving birth Pat left baby Tricia with her paternal grandmother, Richard's mother Hannah, and was back on the campaign trail with her husband. Nixon went from congressman, to senator, vice president, to President of the United States.

Tricia and Julie attended public school in Washington during the first phase of their father's political career. Their mother put the girls in the Sidwell Friends private school by the time Tricia was nearing the end of her elementary school years.

A fellow student of Sidwell Friends at the time the girls were twelve and fourteen compared the two sisters saying, "Julie was pretty, cute and bouncy. The kids elected her president of her class and everyone conceded it was because of her and not her father.

Tricia was regarded by almost everybody as very quiet and scared. She never smiled. She was just a plain girl with a funny nose." By the time her father became president the ugly duckling had become a swan and the nation compared her to Princess Grace of Monaco. Perhaps her aloofness was part of the appeal, but by this time she was a pretty, petite young lady with long blonde hair and blue eyes.

The sisters growing up were inseparable but were as opposite as they come. Tricia even as a young girl was introverted and extremely private while Julie was a dark headed pretty girl that was an extrovert and well-liked by all who met her.

In 1960 Nixon ran for the presidency against Kennedy and lost. He ran for governor and lost in 1962. Pat wanted him to get out of politics and he agreed - for awhile anyway. He had decided to run for the presidency again in 1968 and didn't even bother to inform his wife of his decision. She gave in to his wishes and campaigned for him. She became the *first* Republican First Lady to address the National Convention.

She became the *first* first lady to make news when she wore pants in public. She made headlines many times as being the *first* first lady to throw out the ball for a major league team during a World Series game and she was the first to visit a combat zone flying in an open helicopter with the protection of the Secret Service.

President-elect Nixon's youngest daughter Julie announced to her father her plans to marry David Eisenhower. Her father merely nodded but showed no enthusiasm and had no words of congratulations for his daughter. She later complained to her mother about how hurt she had been by her father's reaction. That evening she found a note on her pillow of congratulations from her father.

It isn't clear how the families felt about the marriage. President Eisenhower who had been the 34th president was grandfather of the groom and was widely respected as a World

War II hero. President Nixon, the 37th president and father of the bride will always be remembered as the symbol of the biggest political scandal in American history.

When the Nixon family arrived in Washington for the inauguration they were invited to the White House by outgoing President Johnson, a custom for the outgoing and incoming presidents. Julie and Tricia met the Johnson girls Lynda and Luci who very obviously were not happy about leaving the White House.

The two families traveled together to the Capitol for the swearing in of office to take place. Luci pulled Julie aside and confided in her how much closer she and her sister had become the last year of their father's presidency while their husbands were in Vietnam. They had both returned to the White House to live while their husbands were fighting in the war.

Luci advised Julie, "Don't let all the attention drive a wedge between you and Tricia." She was speaking remembering the strain that had occurred initially between her and her own sister.

It was 1969 during Nixon's first inauguration and it was the height of the Vietnam War. Thousands arrived in Washington for the inauguration, but many came not to cheer the new president but with other plans in mind. They arrived to be a part of the first organized protest at a presidential inauguration since the days of Franklin Pierce in the mid-1800's.

The protestor's plans were to throw rocks, tomatoes, and smoke bombs at the new president as he was driven down Pennsylvania Avenue and to throw horse manure at Vice President Agnew. After the swearing in took place and the president was being driven to where he would watch the inaugural parade the president's limousine had rocks and beer cans thrown at his limousine; all while you could hear in the background demonstrators screaming anti-war slogans.

Due to the anti-war protestors heightened security was a must. On President Nixon's first day of office there was the largest visibility of security ever seen at a president's inauguration; including Washington District police, troops, and National Guardsmen that added up to almost 10,000 members of the security force that were spread out throughout Washington and along the parade route.

When the Nixons arrived at the White House following the inaugural parade the private quarters had been transformed into their own living space. The Nixon girls were delighted to discover Dr. Pepper and Butter Brickle ice cream left in the solarium refrigerator by the Johnson girls. To giggles and sighs of disbelief that they were actually in the White House they had an ice cream party of their own.

Julie was twenty and Tricia twenty-two when their father became president. Many presidential offspring have proved an embarrassment to their parents finding their faces plastered in the newspapers due to something they have done or said; but the Nixon girls would not be listed among that group. "We were well-behaved, but we didn't deserve any Academy Awards," says Julie. "There were no lectures about how we were supposed to act."

The girls did admit that it was quite an adjustment; things you don't take into account when you just look at the glory of living in such a historical home. Julie said, "I guess it's because the phones are always ringing. People are always around. It's not really a home."

Julie had recently been married, so while she did have a bedroom in the White House she didn't stay there often. The first few months after moving in Tricia practically lived in her room. Tricia rarely left the White House saying, "I can't go out in crowds because people always recognize you, but I've found it possible to have a private life." Private, but unusual for a girl her age and in her position.

Julie was married while her father was President-elect. She met the man she would marry while still a young girl back in 1956 at the Republican National Convention in California. He was there as his grandfather President Eisenhower was campaigning for re-election. It was at the convention that Julie's father was nominated as President Eisenhower's vice president. Both Julie and David were eight years old at the time. They would meet again at the White House when David's grandfather was president and Julie's father was vice president.

January 20, 1957 the Nixon family were at the White House for a private inaugural ceremony to swear in President Eisenhower and Vice President Nixon for their second terms. When it was time to leave Julie began to cry. She wanted to play in the White House she told her mother and the first lady. Mamie invited the girls to stay and play with her grandchildren, one of them which would one day be Julie's husband.

The Republican Women's Club of Hadley, Massachusetts deserve credit for bringing the two together again years later. When the club members discovered David was attending Amherst and Julie was only seven miles away attending Smith College, the Club asked the two to be featured speakers at one of their events. Julie and David spoke to each other over the phone about the invitation and decided not to attend the event; but they did make plans to meet each other for ice cream. That was the beginning of their relationship. They were both nineteen when they began dating.

Julie and David had a private wedding. They were married at Dr. Norman Vincent Peale's Marble Collegiate Presbyterian Church in New York with her sister Tricia as her maid-of-honor. They married twenty nine days before her father would be sworn in as president. It was a match that would go down in history due to the fact that the groom was the son of a presidential son and grandson of a president and Julie would be the daughter of a president.

Eisenhower never cared for his vice president and during his time as president he never invited Nixon into the private quarters while the family lived in the White House. David, Julie's husband and grandson of Eisenhower, had spent a lot of time in the White House while his grandfather was president so he showed the family around the family quarters.

He showed them a stairway that was tucked away hidden behind a wall panel in the main hall that led to the third floor. As they entered one of the rooms David headed over to a rug and the family had to wonder what he was doing when he lifted the rug up and pulled out a piece of paper that had been tucked underneath the rug. He proudly showed his wife the note he had left there eight years previously when he was twelve years old that read, *"I will return."*

David Eisenhower later was described by Secret Service agent Ron Kessler in his book, *'The First Family Detail,'* as being a kind person. He was also described as the most clueless person the Secret Service had ever protected. One example was when he bought a new car and planned to drive from California to Pennsylvania to visit his grandmother the former first lady Mamie Eisenhower. The car broke down around Phoenix. David called the local dealership who had the car towed and said they would fix the car.

David called the next day and was told the car was ready to be picked up. When he picked up the car he discovered the only thing wrong with the car was it had run out of gas. That was just one of many similar stories about the former president's grandson.

Tricia, the only daughter of the president who lived at the White House often refused to attend White House functions. Reporters started to write negative comments and complain about her lack of attendance at these events. Her sister who was outgoing and sociable made excuses for her saying, "Tricia is the Howard Hughes of the White House."

Tricia was a blonde beauty who was the most reclusive of any White House daughter since the Victorian era when it was common for a young, unmarried girl 'not to be seen'. Tricia spent most of the time in her private quarters.

One of the staff members of the White House told *'Women's Wear Daily,'* that the First Daughter "slept very late in the morning and then spends a lot of time on her hair and putzes around."

The president responding to some negative press about his daughter said, "Tricia doesn't drink or smoke. On the other hand, she has a great time - she swings." He was referring to a Masked Ball thrown at the White House for the younger crowd. The Temptations and the Turtles were providing the entertainment.

Everyone attending the Ball had to go through the Secret Service first. Before the Ball began the Secret Service destroyed the Turtles' metronome suspecting it might be a bomb. Rumor has it that the band snorted cocaine under a portrait of Lincoln in the White House.

The Turtles were Tricia's favorite band, but evidently the sentiments weren't mutual. "She was wearing organdy and stuff," lead singer Howie Kaylan of the Turtles later described the president's daughter. "She rustled when she walked by.... She had big fat earrings and was perfumed to the gills."

He wasn't the only one who left the event with an 'unadoring' impression of the president's daughter. Barry Goldwater, Jr. had been Tricia's date for the event. By the end of the evening they were on opposite sides of the room.

Another date Tricia went on that flopped was with George W. Bush who would one day become president himself; though no one would have guessed that to be his future at the time - himself included.

It was George W's father, another future president, George H.W. Bush who was working in the Nixon administration at the time who invited his son to meet the president's daughter at a party in honor of the Apollo 8 mission that first orbited the moon.

The two of them went on a dinner date which was a disaster by George W.'s account. George W. was a cocky young guy rather full of himself. At the time of their date he was a young pilot in training in the Texas Air National Guard. During dinner he reached across the table for the butter and knocked over a glass of red wine. Later when he lit a cigarette he was 'politely' asked by Tricia not to smoke. George W. said, "The date came to an end when she asked me to take her back to the White House immediately after dinner."

It seemed matchmakers were doing their best to find a suitable mate for the president's daughter, so when Prince Charles of England who was considered the world's most eligible bachelor at the time came to America, her own father set to work trying to set the two of them up as a match.

Obviously the prefix "prince" in front of one's name is a major draw for unmarried girls, but in this case it drew the girl's father not the girl herself. Tricia was twenty-four at the time and Prince Charles was twenty-one. According to royal biographer Anthony Holden: "Seating plans constantly had Charles and Tricia side by side while the program had them spending all of each day together, even to being left alone with each other in various parts of the White House."

Any aspirations of having his daughter become a princess failed however, as Prince Charles was upset at the obvious attempt to match him up with the president's daughter who he found to be "plastic and artificial."

It was a time when the antiwar demonstrations were taking place outside the White House when the first lady and her two daughters were having lunch with Mamie Eisenhower. During the luncheon a guard outside their open window accidentally dropped a canister of tear gas forcing the women to run from the room.

There were times when the Nixon 'girls,' which consisted of Julie and the first lady in this instance, just wanted to do something normal. The first lady put on a scarf to try to disguise her identity and they walked across Lafayette Park to the Statler Hilton Hotel where they had dinner at Trader Vic's. They enjoyed their dinner and when finished got up and walked out without paying. The manager was in a quandary of how to handle the situation and decided to just send the bill to the White House.

Tricia Nixon gave a televised tour of the White House aired on CBS *'Sixty Minutes,'* where she took reporter Harry Reasoner through private parts of the White House rarely seen by others.

In May of 1970, the First Family was whisked away to Camp David after a National Day of Protest went into effect after the shooting of four students protesting the war at Kent State University.

The President wanted his family to stay at Camp David while the protests went on to keep them safe. The following morning the first lady insisted on returning to be with her husband. The Secret Service tried to convince her otherwise, but she was determined to return to the White House to be there in support of her husband.

The Secret Service wishing to keep the Nixon family's identity secret from Camp David back to the White House for safety reasons brought in an ambulance to enable them to get through intersections that were blocked by the demonstrators. The first lady, the Nixon girls, and Julie's husband were put in a plain sedan. There were hundreds of protestors on the streets. There were police and agents along the route and at the gate of the White House.

Julie described that intense ride as "like a play, removed from reality." She described the feeling she had as a "sick, hollow feeling" in her stomach. At the White House shades were drawn and the lights were off with relentless chants of protestors heard in the background.

It was trying times for the president. Julie said sometimes when the pressure was intense you could hear her father playing the piano softly all alone during the night.

Julie and David Eisenhower were preparing for their graduation at Smith and Amherst Colleges. Anti-war opinions were still strong with protests being the worst at college campuses. It was determined that it would be unsafe even for the graduates to appear at their own ceremonies.

Tricia was planning a class reunion at the White House and when a fellow alumni Grace Slick of the Jefferson Airplane and her date Abbie Hoffman a radical activist arrived at the White House to attend the reunion they were denied entrance. Later Grace Slick admitted that she had planned to put LSD in the punch bowl.

It was in 1964 that Tricia met Ed Cox the man she would marry. Ed became a graduate of Princeton and Harvard. They were as different as night and day in their political inclinations.

In an interview with the press Tricia told them how impressed she was with how intelligent Eddie was. "I think Eddie is more intelligent than I am. " She boasted on his athletic skills. "When he plays squash or tennis, I cheer and get out the pom poms ... I'm very unathletically inclined."

She said she wasn't much good as a cook either. She went on to explain that she could make chocolate chip cookies which were a favorite of Eddie's, and she could make pancakes, eggs, and bacon. "It's really a hard thing to get the bacon right," the President's daughter is quoted as saying. She was obviously smitten.

The Nixons weren't very communicative, even with each other. Tricia kept her engagement a secret for two years before breaking the news to her father. She described her father's reaction as "he was speechless for a moment, but you know how fathers are." It seemed to be a recurring theme with the president pertaining to his daughters.

When the couple announced their engagement to Ed's parents they weren't thrilled at the news. His family was 'old money' with an ancestor that could be dated back to the Revolutionary War times with his own history that connected him to the first president of the United States. That ancestor was Revolutionary War patriot Robert Livingston who had sworn in George Washington as the first President of the United States.

Ed's family looked down their blue-blooded noses at the Nixons believing the Nixons were beneath them. Quite frankly, neither family was happy with their child's choice of a mate. The Nixons weren't happy with their daughter marrying a liberal either.

Tricia who had the reputation of a recluse and very private, unlike her sister who had a private wedding ceremony, instead chose to go with her mother's suggestion of having their wedding in the Rose Garden at the White House. It would be the first wedding to take place in the Rose Garden; which almost didn't happen due to the rainy weather that cleared up just in time for the ceremony.

The wedding was described in *'Life'* magazine as "akin to American royalty." Tricia was featured as the cover story for *'Life'* magazine twice and was described as "the most beautiful of all White House brides." That must have miffed one of the guests at the wedding; eighty-seven year old Alice Roosevelt who *always* had to be the center of attention who had her own wedding at the White House sixty-five years previously.

President Nixon was reelected in 1973, but dark days were ahead for his presidency. An alert security guard just may have changed history when he noticed tape on a door latch outside of the Democratic headquarters at the Watergate office building. And you know what happened from there...or perhaps not; depending on if were you alive at that time in history or if you paid attention in history class.

Watergate was a political scandal such as this nation has never before experienced. There was a break-in at the Democratic National Committee headquarters in Washington in which President Nixon's administration attempted to cover-up their involvement.

The first lady knew nothing about the Watergate scandal until she heard about it from the media. She and Tricia and Julie had been kept completely in the dark about not only the scandal but of the president's involvement. The three of them stood by him giving the president their unconditional support. While Julie truly believed in her father's innocence, the first lady more shrewd in the ways of the world and politics advised her husband to destroy the tapes while they were still part of his personal property. He did not take her advice and it was the tapes, clear evidence in his part in the wrongdoing that did him in.

Nixon was informed by a phone call from his press secretary that the vote was in, voting to impeach the president. Republican leaders met with the president informing him that the Senate would muster the two-thirds vote necessary for his impeachment.

"That was how I learned I was the first president in one hundred and six years to be recommended for impeachment," Nixon remembered. With his future of a disgraced president with his impeachment conclusive with a heavy heart he made the determination to resign; against his family's wishes who wanted him to keep fighting.

While Julie was visiting her father in his office he informed her of his decision. He would resign - *the first president in U.S. history to do so.* Julie went to her mother to tell her of his decision as her father had not been able to do so.

When Julie later recalled that day in her life that she would never forget when she saw her mother crying she said, "For me, those tears that were shed so briefly were perhaps the saddest moment of the last days in the White House."

August 8, 1974, President Nixon went on national television to inform the nation of his decision. The following day the president rose and wrote a one-sentence letter of resignation. This would be the saddest day in the life of Richard Nixon.

He said his thanks of appreciation to the White House staff then went down to the East Room for the final time to say good bye to staff and Cabinet members who were there to see him off.

The White House had a blanket of sadness over it as though there had been a death. The band played *'Hail To The Chief'* one final time as the White House staff and Cabinet applauded and cried. The president as his final act as a president gave a short speech to those who were there to support him.

George H.W. Bush, a future president, was there as Chairman of the Republican Party and would write of the president's departure in his diary which are in the National Archives of the George H.W. Bush Presidential Library and Museum. *'Close to breaking down-understandably... Everyone in the room in tears...I remember Lt. Col. Brennan who has been with him so long-Marine- standing proudly but with tears running down his face....'*

Gerald and Betty Ford stood by in the Diplomatic Reception Room waiting for the president to say good-bye to his staff. Gerald Ford would be sworn in as the next president at noon.

The Fords walked the Nixons out to Marine One the presidential helicopter. The Nixon family boarded Air Force One to head home to California. As the president reached the top of the stairs he turned and gave a final wave with a smile on his face that must have been difficult to muster up. His was a departure in disgrace.

Then President Nixon took his final helicopter flight as president away from the White House. His resignation would be effective at noon. They were flying over Missouri at noon when his resignation became effective. From that time on they were no longer flying on Air Force One, as it was no longer transporting the president. The call sign would now be changed to the number on the tail of the plane. When they landed in

California Richard Nixon, former president, was now a private citizen.

Lives go on, and David Eisenhower would study law and Julie wrote her first book about famous people she met while living in the White House called, *'Special People.'*

Julie and her husband David have become writers with David writing a book on his grandfather titled, *'Eisenhower at War 1943-1945,'* a finalist for the Pulitzer Prize in history in 1987. Together the couple co-wrote the book, *'Going Home To Glory: A Memoir of Life with Dwight D. Eisenhower 1961 – 1969.'*

Julie also wrote a biography of her mother, *'Pat Nixon: The Untold Story.'* They have been speakers at conventions and he lectures in political science at the University of Pennsylvania. They have three children and live in Philadelphia.

A surprise to none, Tricia became very private living in obscurity choosing to be a stay-at-home mother to her one son. They live off Fifth Avenue in Manhattan and she serves on several boards and in addition is involved in the Nixon Presidential Library.

The two sisters who had always been so close went through a major rift on how to spend a bequest for the Nixon Presidential Library. A lawsuit ensued with one sister against the other. The sisters not wanting to dishonor their father's memory have since spoken and settled the dispute that put a strain on their relationship.

Tricia had this to say about being the child of a president, "Once you've been a White House kid, you'll always be a White House kid. It's always part of you." According to Tricia, regardless of what you do with your life after you are long gone from 1600 Pennsylvania Ave., that is how you will always be remembered.

38

Gerald Ford

Children of Betty and Gerald Ford:

Michael Gerald Ford - Born: March 14, 1950   Still Living At The Time Of Publication

John Gardner "Jack" Ford - Born: March 16, 1952   Still Living At The Time Of Publication

Steven Meigs Ford - Born: May 19, 1956   Still Living At The Time Of Publication

Susan Elizabeth Ford - Born: July 6, 1957   Still Living At The Time Of Publication

Susan Ford is the only presidential daughter to have had her senior prom at the White House.

It was a first in American history when under President Nixon's administration Vice President Spiro Agnew resigned, the first vice president ever to do so. He resigned in disgrace after a charge of political corruption. A new vice president would need to be appointed and it would have to be someone of impeccable character. Gerald Ford, a man of integrity and decency, was the man chosen. Ford would be the first vice president in American history nominated under the 25th amendment to the Constitution.

With humble beginnings the new vice president was born Leslie Lynch King, Jr., when at only two weeks old his mother fled with her newborn son to put an abusive relationship behind her. When she remarried her son took on the name Gerald Ford after his stepfather.

As a teen Ford worked at a local hamburger stand and lived an unassuming life. He made a name for himself as a student at the University of Michigan where he played center on the football team earning three varsity letters and was named the Most Valuable Player. He was offered a contract to play with professional teams Green Bay Packers and the Detroit Lions both of which he declined and went on to study law at Yale graduating third in his class. At Yale he was assistant football and boxing coach. He appeared as a male model on the cover of *'Cosmopolitan'* and in a photo layout in *'Look'* magazine.

Ford was a great athlete, not only in football but he was an avid downhill skiier and golfer. He was the most athletic of our presidents even though the press portrayed him as a bumbling fool.

Ford had quite a résumé before he ever entered politics. He volunteered for the Navy during WWII and aboard the carrier USS Monterey he served as the ship's athletic director and as gunnery officer where he saw action in the Pacific Theater. He was awarded the Asiatic-Pacific Campaign medal with one Silver Star and four Bronze Stars, the Philippine Liberation Ribbon with two bronze stars, the American Campaign Medal, and the World War II Victory medal during his service.

It was 1948 when Ford announced his candidacy for the nomination for U.S. House of Representatives where he won thirteen times remaining a congressman until 1972. In 1963 he was appointed by President Johnson to serve on the Warren Commission to investigate President Kennedy's death and served as House Minority Leader in 1965. In 1973 it appeared his destiny was laid out for him when he was chosen to replace Agnew as the vice president.

The Fords had four children. Michael the Ford's firstborn son had always been a good student and never gave his parents a moment of worry. He had been against U.S. involvement in the Vietnam War but still felt it his duty and joined R.O.T.C. at eighteen years of age. While in college Michael was pursuing a law degree but knew the field of law was not a good fit for him. He contemplated on what he really wanted to do with his life and decided on the ministry. He enrolled in Gordon Conwell Theological Seminary. Michael and his girlfriend Gayle announced their engagement while he was a student at the Seminary.

Susan the youngest and the only daughter of the Fords had grown up in Washington and during the summers worked at the White House selling souvenirs and at other times worked for her father in the Capitol; but she never aspired for a political future herself. She found politics boring.

Susan had attended public schools up until she was sixteen at which time her father became vice president. It was the year 1974 when without explanation Susan was ordered by the Secret Service not to leave the family home – *under any circumstance.* Regardless of how much of a fuss the young teen put up about 'being a prisoner in her own home,' there was nothing she could do to change the circumstances.

The family soon learned the reason behind the order. The Symbionese Liberation Army (SLA) a domestic terrorist group had named Susan as a possible kidnapping threat. A note had been found with three names on it. The first name was that of a man who was a school superintendent who had already been shot and killed. The second name was Patty Hearst and the third name was Susan Ford. Patty Hearst daughter of the powerful Hearst publishing family was kidnapped by the group and brainwashed over the months they held her and then was involved in a murder committed during a bank robbery. In hindsight, Susan was very grateful for the Secret Service intervention and protection. "The vice president's family didn't have Secret Service protection back then," Susan said. "I had Secret Service before my mother did."

Up until the time of the threat by the SLA Susan had been boarding at the Holton-Arms School where she attended school. With the threat on her life she moved back home since Holton-Arms an all-girls academy couldn't accommodate her Secret Service agents.

It was August 8, 1974 and Vice President Gerry Ford and wife Betty were at home with their daughter Susan and Steve watching President Nixon's televised resignation speech. Their father who became vice president due to a resignation was about to become the president due to yet another resignation. He would replace two leaders who had resigned in disgrace. Gerald Ford was about to become the only president in U.S. history who ascended to the highest office in the land without getting a single popular or electoral vote.

Michael and Gayle were on their way back to Boston after their wedding. Michael was studying for his masters in preparation for the clergy and his classes were about to resume. Having just arrived at their home in Boston the Secret Service arrived with instructions for them to turn around and return to Washington. They explained that President Nixon had just resigned and Michael's father was about to be sworn in as the next president. The Secret Service handed them plane tickets and rushed them back out the door. Michael was twenty-three years old at the time.

Jack the second son of Gerald and Betty Ford had attended Utah State University where he studied Forestry and was now working at Yellowstone as a park ranger like his dad had before him. He was riding horseback patrol and was oblivious to what was going on in the outside world, completely unaware his father was about to become the nation's next president. He discovered the news when Secret Service agents arrived and he was 'confiscated' and whisked aboard a helicopter and flown to Washington.

The vice president and his wife Betty waited in the Diplomatic Reception Room while President Nixon met with his staff and Cabinet. As the Nixons were prepared to leave the White House for the final time the Fords accompanied them down the red carpet to the presidential helicopter to see them off. As Nixon was about to enter the presidential helicopter he turned around and with a forced smile on his face gave his famous two handed v-sign signaling victory which seemed out of place under the circumstances. He then turned and entered Marine One a broken man. It was approximately 9:00 A.M. and President Nixon's resignation would become effective at noon. At that time Vice President Gerald Ford would be sworn in as the nation's 38th president.

Ford was sworn into office by Chief Justice Warren Burger in the East Room of the White House. After taking the oath of office Ford gave a speech declaring, "The oath that I have taken is the same oath that was taken by George Washington and by every President under the Constitution. But I assume the Presidency under extraordinary circumstances never before experienced by Americans. This is an hour of history that troubles our minds and hurts our hearts." The public had lost faith in the presidency and people holding political office in general. It would be difficult times President Ford would face in restoring that faith.

President Ford had told his children the story of how his high school principal had gathered $100 for a scholarship so Ford would be able to go to college. Unfortunately, his former principal didn't live to see what had become of the man he believed had a great future ahead of him. Ford never forgot the kind act his principal had done for him saying, "Here I stand, because one man invested $100 in my life."

Steve would later reflect on the day his father was sworn in as president. The Nixon administration ended with no forewarning which left the White House staff scrambling to get the Nixon's household items packed and moved out of the White House. The Fords would remain in their home in Washington until the White House staff were prepared for them to move in. The same day Ford had been sworn in as the next President of the United States his wife was fixing the family dinner and Steve told the story of how she looked over at his dad and said, "Gerry, something's wrong here. You just became President of the United States, and I'm still cooking."

The Fords were a humble, unassuming family. His four children were in their teens and early twenties and their lives were about to change in a way none of them could have foreseen. Most First Families have time to prepare for the change they will endure as their father campaigns for the position and usually works towards it for years previous to campaigning, but with the Fords it was literally a matter of hours for it to sink in that their father was about to obtain the highest office in the country – *without ever aspiring to do so.*

Steve had just graduated from high school and was just weeks away from becoming a student at Duke University when his father became president. It was an overnight change in his life as he explained it, "All of a sudden we all got ten Secret Service agents, and life changed."

The first day the Fords moved into the White House Steve called his best friend and told him to come over and check out the place. Of course, no longer could his friends just drop by, but they would first have to be checked out through the Secret Service. When his friend arrived he gave him a tour of his 'new home,' and they went to the third floor Solarium where all presidential children seem to be drawn to as a place to hang out. From the Solarium they discovered a rooftop access and took the stereo on the roof and cranked up the sound on the stereo to the tune of Led Zeppelin playing *'Stairway To Heaven.'* "That was my first night in the White House," Steve recalled with fondness.

"The lease on the house was very temporary, for some of us shorter than others," Steve said years later when recalling his time in the White House. "The White House really belonged to the staff, because they were the ones who were there for four, five, six different administrations. It was truly like living in a museum," Steve said. "Everything dates back to Lincoln or Jefferson. I can remember moving in there – at home usually I put my feet up on the table where we lived in Alexandria, but Mom goes, 'Don't put your feet up there! That's Jefferson's table.'"

The move had little effect on Michael who was married and attending seminary school, but the others all lived there, some for a shorter time than others. Jack, second son of the Fords said, "Living in the White House can be very intimidating. It's an experience of a lifetime, but there's also the feeling that you're living in a museum. There's that feeling that you'll round the corner, wearing just your shorts – and run into a group of tourists." Jack probably wished it was just tourists the day the elevator opened and there he stood in jeans and a T-shirt facing the first lady and Queen Elizabeth II and Prince Philip. He was hardly dressed appropriately for meeting the royal visitors, but the Queen turned to the first lady and said, "Don't worry, Betty, I have one of these at home too." Meaning of course her own son Prince Charles; but it's hard to imagine he would have ever been caught in such attire meeting a head of state.

Steve, eighteen at the time his father became president and having just graduated from T.C. Williams High School planned on moving out shortly to go to Duke University to study oceanography. After giving it some thought he realized he wouldn't feel comfortable with ten Secret Service agents trailing his wake carrying machine guns on a college campus and decided to take some time off. He got up his nerve to tell his parents of his decision. "I walked into Dad's office, which was the Oval Office, and said: 'I don't feel I am ready to go to college. I always had a dream about going out west and being a cowboy.' My dad just about fell over. I am sure he thought that was the dumbest thing that had ever been said in the Oval Office." Both Steve's parents had the insight and the courage to let their son make his own future. "I felt it was a very important time in my life to develop like a normal person."

After his short time in the White House he tied his motorcycle to his Jeep and headed to Montana where for a time he worked on the professional rodeo circuit as a cowboy roper. He did eventually return to complete his education attending Utah State University and California Polytechnical Institute.

Susan, the youngest of the Ford children and only daughter, was seventeen when her father became president and spent the most amount of time in the White House. When the Fords moved into the Executive Mansion once the Nixon family's belongings had been removed, the White House staff showed the family around the private quarters. They were choosing the rooms they would use for their bedrooms when the first lady suggested the room across from their own would be a good choice for her daughter. Susan with a look on her face that the first lady described as priceless, simply said, "I don't like pink." She chose another room on another floor, and while she no longer had pink walls she still begged her parents to let her redecorate and get rid of the blue shag carpet in her room. Susan was one of the few presidential offspring who were content living at the White House. The fact that she now had a bathroom all to herself for the first time in her life helped.

As Susan would write in her book *'Double Exposure'* of her first official tour of the White House, *'We heard about the rooms, their furnishings, and the history behind the building that had just become our home, a feeling of awe swamped me. I kept thinking about all the people who'd stood in these rooms before me, people like Andrew Jackson and Abraham Lincoln. F.D.R. gave many of his fireside chats from here. I could imagine Abigail Adams hanging her laundry to dry in the East Room, and one of Theodore Roosevelt's kids sneaking a pony up the elevator, and all the other wonderful stories about the White House and the people who have lived in it.'*

I imagine it is similar to the many tourists who tour the White House thinking of all those who have walked the halls and made history in the rooms they are walking through; but then again to make your home in the same house as past presidents throughout America's history must make you stop and think every time you sit behind a desk that Thomas Jefferson himself used or where Abraham Lincoln signed the Emancipation Proclamation gives you a renewed appreciation for those men who walked before your own father the current president.

Previously when Ford was being considered for the vice presidency he was asked at the hearing about giving Nixon a pardon if President Nixon should resign. Ford answered, "I do not think the American people would stand for it." But, that is exactly what he did less than a month after being in office. He pardoned Nixon, and it was the one act during his presidency which caused him to lose any chance of being reelected. His reasons for doing so were valid, as he stated, "The tranquility to which this nation has been restored by the events of recent weeks could be irreparably lost by the prospects of bringing to trial a former President of the United States." All the same, the nation was outraged. They thought he had struck a deal with Nixon – which he vehemently denied.

After facing the stress of finding disfavor with the nation after making the decision to pardon Nixon, another situation much more serious to President Ford arose. The first lady had been diagnosed with breast cancer and had to undergo surgery for a mastectomy. The first lady was forthcoming to the nation about her personal health issue and shared the news with the nation in hopes it would help other women who faced the same diagnosis and to encourage others to have mammograms. In 1984 the former first lady and her daughter Susan created National Breast Cancer Awareness Month.

Jack had been working at Yellowstone as a summer job, but as long as his father was president he wouldn't be able to work in the field of forestry for which he had earned his degree. The federal government does all the hiring in national parks in his field of expertise and due to nepotism laws Jack had just become unemployable.

Jack told the story of his and his siblings Secret Service protection. "When my father was first sworn in, there was a debate among us whether or not any of the kids would take protection. Dick Kaiser, head of Secret Service protection detail, sat us down and appealed to us. 'Do you realize that you're putting the president of the United States in a position where he might have to choose between family and country?' It's a heavy thought. So I consented to the protection," Jack said.

Reflecting back Jack said, "In the beginning, you think you have a choice in the matter. In the end, you realize you never really did. Later on, I said to Kaiser, 'Hey, that was a really effective pitch. You had me convinced. I'm sold. You came on pretty heavy.' And I was told, 'Oh, that was just the soft sell. If we hadn't convinced you, we would have shown you some of the more incredible death threats and phone call reports.'" And for each president and their family there are numerous threats, more than most American citizens realize.

There were two assassination attempts on President Ford's life, both perpetrated by women. One of the attempted assassination attempts was by a follower of Charles Manson who ran a hippie cult group who would later be arrested for serial killings. After the assassination attempts the Secret Service made it mandatory for all presidents to wear bulletproof vests when out in public.

The Ford family would come to appreciate the Secret Service not only for the fact that it was due to their protection that their sister remained safe during the threat of the SLA's kidnapping threat, but yet again after the two assassination attempts on their father. So while many presidential children complained about their 'shadows,' and it would be exasperating at times for the young Fords, they also saw the very real advantage of their protection.

Regardless of what was going on in the White House, the Ford children knew they always came first with their parents...*always!* When Susan would barge into the Oval Office or walk in the middle of a press conference to ask her father for her allowance the press found it amusing; and it put the president in a different light, making him a dad first and foremost. Regardless of what was on his plate his children still treated him just like an ordinary dad.

A short time before the Ford family moved into the White House their dog, a Golden Retriever, had passed away. Susan conspired with David Kennerly White House photographer and they plotted to get the president a puppy. Susan walked into the Oval Office with the little golden ball of fur and her father and the dog became immediate best buddies. The president himself walked the dog they named Liberty as often as possible. One morning Liberty awakened the president with the need to be walked, and so the president in his bathrobe and slippers took the dog outside to take care of business. When he returned he found the elevator wouldn't work and the stairs, due to security concerns, was locked at night and had yet to be unlocked. Ford had to bang on the walls with Liberty barking by his side in an attempt to rouse someone to let them in. While Liberty was a White House resident she gave birth to nine puppies.

Jack, twenty-three and newly unemployed due to his father's new job lived in the White House for a time. Steve also lived there for a few months before he headed out west. Susan was the sibling who lived there the longest. She would complain that with all the servants in the White House she still had to make her own bed due to her mother's rule. Their mother also insisted Steve and Jack had to cook their own breakfast. The Fords wanted their children to grow up unspoiled and able to make it on their own. Their time in the White House would be short, and they wanted it not to be a rude awakening once they set out into the 'real world.'

Michael was off at seminary school and well grounded. To avoid the press he even took a job under an assumed name to avoid any publicity. Jack was a different story. He tended to blurt out things to the press without thinking which embarrassed his father and gave him cause for concern. He was written up in the press for dating celebrities such as

Bianca Jagger. He brought George Harrison formerly of the Beatles home to the White House to meet his father.

Another celebrity Jack dated that delighted the press was Chris Evert the tennis star. The two went out to dinner after a Washington tennis tournament. She later described their first date. "We didn't agree on one thing the whole night," she said. "You name it and we disagreed." Some may have thought the relationship would have ended before it started, but they continued to see each other.

The media had become alert to the fact of how much time the two of them were spending together and began following them in hopes of a story. The media followed their every move and even when they went jogging or bike riding that became a story and made it into *'People'* magazine. Chris was getting tired of being chased by the press. "It would have been nice to get to know Jack without reporters following us everywhere we went," Chris complained. She had already come to the conclusion that Jack would make a great friend but that was the only future the two of them had – as friends.

Steve understood about how the press made it awkward when it came to dating. Not only did a girl have to deal with the press wondering who she was and flashing cameras in her face, but there was also the Secret Service everywhere you went. That could be pretty intimidating. "First dates were always bizarre," Steve explained. "I'd call for a reservation and say, 'I'd like a table for two, and I'd also like another table for two – but way across the room, please."

Steve and a friend both fun loving teens decided to pull a prank on his Secret Service. They were able to lose the agents when they were at his ranch in Montana while out horse back riding. When they were a distance away they shot four rifle shots into the air and came galloping back with Steve slumped over his saddle. "The guy comes running out and the first words he uttered, I swear, were, 'My career! My career!'"

Steve had never even ridden a horse before he was eighteen and had decided to become a cowboy. It's no wonder his father looked at him like he had lost his mind when he told him of his decision to move out west and become a cowboy. Once he was settled in after moving out west he took rodeo lessons and became a member of the L.A. Rough Riders a professional rodeo team.

Back at the White House Susan was receiving criticism from her mother's assistant

Nancy Howe about her chosen mode of dress – blue jeans. Nancy wanted her to stop wearing jeans as the public was watching her every move and what she wore. Susan replied, "I will always wear jeans." She did manage to get out of those jeans on occasion, such as when she stepped in for her mother to take on the role of White House hostess. But the moment the event was over, she was back in her jeans.

Susan and her mother had a great relationship. "I'll come home from school in the worst mood, and she'll cheer me up...I don't know what I'd do without her," Susan said. "My mother and I are very close. I guess you could call us best friends."

Susan wrote a monthly column for *'Seventeen'* magazine during her stint in the White House which was very popular among modern teen girls. This experience helped later when she went on to write mystery novels with the main character who was a First Daughter living in the White House.

Susan is the first and only presidential daughter to have her senior prom held at the White House. Each student who planned to attend the prom had to provide the Secret Service with their name, birth date, and Social Security numbers to be checked out. Evidently everyone passed muster as there is no record of any student being excluded; other than Gardner Britt who had been Susan's boyfriend up until a short time before the prom. They got into an argument over the Equal Rights Amendment and Susan broke up with him leaving her without a date. Susan invited Billy Bales, a twenty-one year old pre-med student of Washington and Lee University.

Before the prom began, Susan with her date and three other couples had dinner aboard the presidential yacht, the *Sequoia,* while they sailed down the Potomac for a sunset cruise. The prom was a huge success with two bands playing while the students danced the latest dances the Bump and the Hustle in the East Room until 1:00 A.M.

On the 4th of July Susan and a few of her friends shot off some fireworks from the White House grounds which is illegal to do in Washington, but like Susan said, 'Who's going to come behind the White House gates and arrest you?'

On her 18th birthday she had a party on the South Lawn with friends from Vail, Colorado where the family often went to ski. The kids had a great time dancing, cooking out burgers and hot dogs; and having just come of legal age were even allowed to have some beer while they watched fireworks off the Truman Balcony of the White House.

Susan had taken an interest in photography while watching Kinnerly the White House photographer who had taken the time to give her pointers and get her started. She also had the opportunity to sign up for a workshop with Ansel Adams. She attended Mount Vernon College for Women, which is now part of George Washington University. When her father lost his reelection she changed to the photojournalism school at the University of Kansas where she was able to work for a time as a photographer on the *'Capitol Journal'*, a newspaper in Topeka, Kansas. In the ensuing years she has worked with the *'Associated Press,' 'Newsweek,' 'Ladies' Home Journal,'* and even had the opportunity to work in film.

After the Fords moved out of 1600 Pennsylvania Avenue the Ford's children went their own way as young adults.

Michael after studying at Wake Forest and Gordon Conwell Theological Seminary became an ordained minister and joined the ministerial staff of the Coalition for Christian Outreach at the University of Pittsburgh; and as of 1981 leads the Office of Student Development at Wake Forest. He and wife Gayle have three children.

Years after leaving the White House Jack would say that his time in the presidential home was a time he enjoyed. He was the only one of the Ford children who had ever seriously considered the possibility of a political career. In 1996 with the experience of six Republican conventions behind him, he was asked to serve as executive director of the host committee for the San Diego Republican Convention. He was co-founder of California Infotech, a company that supplied electronic information kiosks to malls. He married Juliann Felando in 1989 and they have two children.

In 1975 while his father was still president Steve worked for the National Geographic Society studying and tracking grizzly bears in Montana. He owns his own ranch in California where for a time he bred Thoroughbred racehorses and was involved in the race horse industry in the capacity of owner, breeder, manager, and race track executive serving as associate vice president of Turfway Park Race Course in Kentucky.

Steve was offered a small part in a Western which opened the door to a career as an actor. He has had a successful twenty-year career as an actor in Hollywood. He has appeared in over 800 hours of film and television. He played on a soap opera *'The Young and the Restless'* for six years and was in several movies with well-known actors. He played in *'Eraser'* with Arnold Schwarzenegger, *'Contact'* with Jodie Foster, *'Armageddon'* with

Bruce Willis, *'Heat'* with Robert DeNiro and Al Pacino, *'When Harry Met Sally'* with Meg Ryan, *'Starship Troopers,'* and *'Black Hawk Down.'* He has been a guest star on dozens of television shows. Steve hosted the prime-time series *'Secret Service'* – a topic he was all too familiar with.

Steve served three years on the board of directors of The National Cowboy Hall of Fame in Oklahoma City and currently serves on the board of directors for the President Gerald Ford Museum. He is still involved in acting and is a motivational speaker. Some of the topics he speaks on are: 'Inside the White House & Hollywood: Getting To The Top With Character,' 'Beyond the Limelight: Overcoming the Struggle,' and 'Leadership With Character.'

Steve has never married, but did father an illegitimate child at the age of twenty-three. His son was born in 1980. Steve acknowledged that he did father the child and assumed parental responsibilities for his son. Steve and the child's mother reached a settlement concerning visitation rights and support for the child but chose to keep the details private.

The former first lady had suffered from alcoholism for years which progressively got worse in the years after they left the White House. The family had an intervention and she sought help. After her recovery she helped to establish the Betty Ford Center where people can go to seek help overcoming their own addictions. By the former first lady coming forward and being open about her addiction and how she was able to overcome the problem aided many others to admit to their own problems and find help.

One of those who also struggled with alcoholism and went into treatment at the Betty Ford Center was her own son Steve. He had struggled for some time himself with battling alcohol during his days of trying to make a living as a part-time actor. "I had been living a secret life on the road," he told the Drug Education Council in a recent interview. But then "one day my life just came crashing down."

Steve has been sober now for several years and as a motivational speaker speaks on the topic of his addiction and his road to recovery. But Steve understands alcoholism is a lifelong struggle. "My addiction is sneaky," he said. "It's always outside the door, doing pushups, waiting for me to fail."

Susan attended the University of Kansas but quit before she graduated. While staying with her parents she met her father's Secret Service agent Charles Vance who was sixteen years her senior and divorced. They married in 1979 when Susan was twenty-one. The couple had two children together but divorced in 1988.

Susan has worked as a photojournalist and currently serves on the board of the Betty Ford Center. She has now added her name to the list of other presidential children who became authors. She has written two White House mystery books with the main character being the First Daughter who is a photojournalist with the setting at the White House. The books she published are *'Double Exposure'* and *'Sharp Focus.'*

In an interview Susan said she remembers her years in the White House as a fairy tale. She remembered the most comfortable room was the Solarium on the third floor which faced the National Mall. "You weren't afraid to break anything," says Susan. "It was like a normal living room. You felt comfortable in there." On the other hand, she remembered one of the rooms on the second floor she described as "a creepy room." Her fondest memories seem to be involved with family.

On her very last night in the White House Susan slept in the Lincoln Bedroom, the room she had heard where others have said they have seen a ghost. While Susan tried to fall asleep the first lady made 'ghost sounds' from the hallway. "That's the kind of thing she did," said Susan.

Today Susan lives in the southwest with her second husband Vaden Bales who she married in 1989. Her life almost ended with no warning, when in the year 2010 at the age of fifty-three she was exercising at a gym when she went into sudden cardiac arrest. Ford says she was *"extremely lucky"* that while she was in the gym, a surgeon had just come in and was able to shock her back with an automated external defibrillator. Before this occurred she wasn't even aware of having any heart problems.

Susan had a close relationship with her mother and today she continues representing the Ford family in public service events. Susan shared one of her mother's life lessons she had instilled in her. "As my mother says, 'You give back, you don't give up. You can always choose to help others. If you do, it will change you.'"

39

Jimmy Carter

Children of Rosalynn and Jimmy Carter:

John William "Jack" Carter - Born: July 3, 1947   Still Living At The Time Of Publication

James Earl "Chip" Carter III - Born: April 12, 1950   Still Living At The Time Of Publication

Donnell Jeffrey "Jeff" Carter - Born: Aug. 18, 1952   Still Living At The Time Of Publication

Amy Lynn Carter - Born: Oct. 19, 1967   Still Living At The Time Of Publication

First Daughter Amy Carter was charged by a run away 6,000 pound elephant at a pet show and saved by a Secret Service agent.

Jimmy Carter's ascent to the presidency was nothing less than phenomenal. Up until two years before he became president he was an unfamiliar face and unknown name. From peanut farmer to the president - *who would have ever dreamed that was a possibility.* Even his own mother when told he was going to run for president asked him - *president of what?*

The Carters had four children. Jack, the firstborn, would spend his summers working at his father's peanut farm, the farm Jimmy Carter took over after his own father's death. Jack's earnings began at ten cents an hour; it didn't always pay to be the boss' son.

Summers were spent cleaning in preparation for the harvest. During peanut season you would work until you just couldn't work anymore and then get up the next day and do it all over again. Jack got a raise when his father was in the Senate and he worked as a page a few times making $5 a day.

In the days when the kids were growing up, the family (pre-Amy days as their sister was a late addition to the family) would spend summers in Central Florida at a fishing camp off Lake Harris. Their parents would go off fishing for the day and the boys were left on the shore where Jack remembered playing with alligators. He remembers his time of vacations as spent in the Panhandle of Florida or Central Florida where his parents mainly fished and the kids hung out and entertained themselves in natural settings.

Jack fondly remembers the times the family took vacations, this one in particular in which the three boys were all from about the age of seven to twelve. They were camping and a black bear broke into their cooler and ate all the bacon. During their camping trip Jack remembered his parents having an argument because his mother told his father she wasn't sleeping one more night in a tent. His father was mad because the hotel cost $24 a night, but his mother won the battle.

Jack was taken along on a hunting trip with his dad and his Uncle Billy. They left him on his own in a deer stand with the instructions of 'just make sure before you shoot, it isn't a human'. After hours of boredom, a twelve year old can only stand so much sitting still and doing nothing, Jack decided to head back to the truck. On the way there he heard some rusting in the bushes and could see a hide so knew it wasn't human. He shot at it and heard in return a loud squeal. He had shot a pig. His shot only hurt it and you could hear it squealing for miles and miles. The pig was wounded, but not mortally. That experience turned Jack off from hunting for the rest of his life.

Jack graduated from high school in Plains, Georgia with a graduating class of twenty-five. High school had been a breeze where he never really had to study so he was ill-prepared when it came to college. Georgia Tech decided Jack needed to take some time off so he transferred to Emory where they came to the same conclusion. He then tried Georgia Southwestern for a semester and then went back to Emory. College had become like a ping pong game at this point going back and forth from one college to another and none of it taken seriously. Jack was involved in a car accident and that was when he decided that "he and college weren't on the same path," and at twenty years of age quit.

At the suggestion of his father he joined the navy in April of 1968.

During his navy days Jack was on a salvage ship off Pearl Harbor and later for a time was in Vietnam. He served on the salvage ship USS Grapple (ARS-7) where they would try to find planes that had gone down and raise them up from the sea. When he returned to the states he attended a nuclear power program where in a drug bust he admitted to smoking marijuana, taking THC, and LSD and spent his last month in the navy in a stockade and received a "less than honorable" discharge at the same time that his father had been elected governor.

After Jack's discharge from the navy he enrolled at Georgia Tech yet again and this time graduated. He continued his education earning a law degree at the University of Georgia. During this time he had married and was living in the carriage house behind the Governor's Mansion with his first wife Judy Langford Carter. After completing his education in 1974 he was a representative for the state of Georgia at a Democratic mid-term election.

During his father's campaign for the presidency Jack and his wife helped to campaign for his father. At the time he had just become an associate in a law firm. Jack himself stated that after being used for his name because of his father's position he threw away his years in law school and became involved in the grain elevator. He found his niche in the commodities market.

While his brothers and sister were living in the White House Jack was moving in his own direction making his own way in life.

Chip, the Carter's second son, ran into trouble early in life when he found himself sent to the principal's office after throwing a chair at his teacher. It would prove to be just the beginning of worries for his parents.

While Chip was in college he ran with a crowd involved with drugs. It was an introduction to a lifestyle that he brought with him to the White House when his father became president.

Chip had campaigned for his father making appearances and giving speeches when his father was running for governor. Chip met his future wife Caron in 1970 during the Georgia gubernatorial campaign when his father was elected governor of Georgia. Chip and Caron married in 1973 living in a mobile home in Plains, Georgia while he worked at his father's peanut warehouse. When his father became president they left the days of living in a mobile home behind and moved into the White House.

Of the three Carter boys Jeff, the youngest son, was the most studious and down-to-earth. He married his wife Annette Jene Davis in 1975.

Amy was only a toddler when her father was running for governor. The two year old was often left with her grandmother while her parents were off campaigning. Her father became governor in 1970 and President of the United States in 1976.

Amy grew up in the Governor's Mansion where tourists wandered throughout their home. Later in the White House the family would have their private quarters, but in the Governor's Mansion you may have to walk through a crowd of visitors just to get to another room. Rosalynn recalled that "everybody made a big fuss over the baby when they saw her and she'd just walk straight through and look straight ahead" as if they weren't even there.

The governor and his wife were busy and needed someone to look after three year old Amy. Rosalynn Carter chose Mary Prince to care for her daughter. Prince was part of a prison trustee program. It had been less than a year since she had received a life sentence for killing a man outside a bar in Georgia. Prince was in her mid-twenties, an African American inmate who would move from the Georgia penitentiary to the Governor's Mansion to care for the governor's daughter. If she thought that was a big step up; she would have been astonished to know that in four years she would be moving to the White House. From prison to the White House; who would have ever imagined?

Jack, Amy's older brother who was almost twenty years her senior, recalls a time in the Governor's Mansion when Hubert Humphrey was visiting. Amy who was four years old at the time was sitting in his lap smearing brownies all over his face while he completely ignored her and kept talking.

Jimmy Carter's next stop was the White House. It was election night and the family was in a hotel while waiting for the results to come in. Jack who had an adjoining room to his parents in their hotel received a visit from Dan Ackroyd and John Belushi. Ackroyd had been portraying his father on "Saturday Night Live" so he was a little embarrassed to how he would be received by the Carter family, but they all thought he was quite entertaining in his role as the prospective president.

The peanut farmer had been elected the next President of the United States. His nine year old daughter Amy showed up at her father's inauguration with a book so she wouldn't be bored.

In a break from custom the new president and first lady departed from their bulletproof limousine and walked hand in hand with nine year old Amy between them down Pennsylvania Avenue. Carter's children and their families also left their limousines and walked behind their father. Jack walked down Pennsylvania Avenue carrying his son Jason on his shoulders.

President Jimmy Carter became the first president from the south in 128 years, the first Democrat in the White House in 8 years, and the first president since President Lyndon Johnson to be of the same party that controlled Congress.

Amy was not happy about moving to the White House. She wouldn't be coming alone though. Mary Prince would be coming along to care for her. When Carter had won the presidency her work release from the prison was terminated and she was sent back to prison. The first lady believed in Prince's innocence and wrote to the parole board securing the prison inmate a reprieve so Amy's nanny could come to live and work for them at the White House. The president had himself assigned as her parole officer.

Amy was the first young child to live in the White House since the days of President Kennedy and his young children. While the Kennedy children were adorable and photogenic; Amy had large glasses, dressed in clothes that looked homemade, you could easily call her homely, and lacking in social skills. But, she was a child of the White House so the press made her a subject of pursuit.

Amy didn't want to just sit upstairs in the family residence. There was this great big, new house she was living in to explore. The first lady said Amy would sometimes go downstairs during the public tours, but "people made such a fuss over her" finding the president's daughter as part of their tour group that she quit going. The White House was a big, lonely place for Amy as her brothers were much older than she was and it was similar to being an only child in a strange, new place where you didn't know anyone.

Jack only visited the White House once or twice a year, but Chip worked with his father and moved into the White House with his wife Caron. Their son was born in 1977 while they were residents of the White House, but Chip had often been seen at social functions without his wife. Rumor has it that when he announced to his father that he was divorcing his wife his father threw him out and for a time his wife and six month old son remained in the White House while Chip returned to Plains, Georgia. Chip and first wife Caron were divorced in 1980 during Carter's presidency and he would return to Washington while his wife Caron and their baby James Earl IV moved back to Plains where she taught disabled children.

The days of the hostage crisis in Iran were a blight on Carter's presidency. Iranian students at a Texas college campus attacked the president's son Chip. He wasn't hurt in the attack due to the protection of the Secret Service.

Chip ranked pretty high as one of the least liked presidential children by both the Secret Service and the White House staff. He was old enough 'to know better' but abused marijuana and alcohol in the White House. He was notorious for trying to pick up women asking if they wanted to have sex in the White House. He was a source of embarrassment and went against all principals the president and first lady stood for - *but yet they allowed it to continue.*

Chip seemed to think that being a presidential son would be all that was needed to draw women to him. That was not the case with rock star Linda Ronstadt. He came across as a starry eyed fool relentlessly pursuing the longtime girlfriend of California Governor Jerry Brown, his father's main rival in the Democratic nomination of 1980. Ronstadt looked at the president's son as a bothersome pest in his relentless pursuit of her. It was definitely a one-sided infatuation.

Jeff had married and he and his wife Annette lived in the White House while he attended George Washington University. He was a good student and spent his time studying.

Inevitably when someone thinks of Amy Carter it is of the photos of the day the little girl was sent to public school looking lonely and forlorn as she made her way through a cordon of photographers by herself with downcast face and a sad look on her face. President Carter wishing to make a statement sent his daughter to public school; a first for the child of a president since the days of Theodore Roosevelt.

Followed by a mob of photographers the little girl looked absolutely miserable. The

Washington Post described Amy as forlorn. In later years when the first lady was asked about that infamous day of sending her daughter off to school said, "I remember when she went to school the first day in Washington. Everybody was so distressed because Amy looked so lonely. That was just her normal life." Amy attended the Washington public school for less than a year before transferring to an elite private school.

Amy was lonely and had a hard time making friends initially. For most children it was odd having Secret Service agents around but over time they didn't even notice them; and the agents themselves gave them their space. But Amy was different; which she proved yet again when she was asked what she wanted for Christmas and she responded with "a chain saw."

Amy's best friend in the White House was her Siamese cat named Misty Malarky Ying Yang. For a time she had a dog named Grits that had been a gift from a teacher. Not having a dog for a pet the teacher felt sorry for her as she was pretty much growing up as an only child at the White House. While two of her brothers also lived at the presidential mansion they were married and having their own children. The dog was a Border Collie mix born on the day her father had won his presidential election. The dog was named Grits due to the family coming from the South and the president's campaign slogan where he referred to himself as Grits. The dog wound up being returned to the teacher. When the first lady was asked by the press where the dog was, she responded that Amy was off to summer camp and didn't have time for a dog.

The White House home to every president since John Adams had always been respected and revered in the past; but not so with the Carters. The president's sons smoked pot unabashedly in the presidential mansion without fear of reprisal. More than one staff of the White House commented about the president's sons and their drug use in the White House. One said, "I would regularly have to move bongs." The president and first lady did nothing to stop their sons illicit drug activity in the White House.

Willie Nelson had been invited to perform at the White House and stayed overnight as a guest. That evening along with Chip they made their way to the roof of the White House and smoked pot. Willie Nelson commented on his visit to the White House roof with the president's son. "A beer in one hand and a fat Austin torpedo in the other. Nobody from the Secret Service was watching us," Nelson said. "The roof of the White House is the safest place I can think of to smoke dope."

Chip at this time was separated from his wife and was living a lifestyle that as an adult most parents would have at the very least kicked them out of their house, but Chip thought he was untouchable being who his father was. And it wasn't just himself; a dozen Marines who had been stationed at Camp David had to be transferred due to smoking pot with the president's son.

He thought he couldn't be taken down, but about six months after his father became president he was advised to leave Panama City, Florida by the Secret Service. They had been notified that the dive where he was hanging out was about to be involved in a drug raid. He refused to leave forcing the Secret Service to call the president and inform him of what was going on. The president then called his son and said, "You get your ass out of there. You'll do what the Secret Service tells you to do."

Third son Jeff graduated with honors from George Washington University. His degree was in geography and he specialized in computer cartography. His favorite place in the White House was on the roof, not to smoke dope but to look through his telescope. He was not the first or the last of presidential family members to enjoy the breathtaking views from the same site. He would call the Smithsonian 'dial-a-phenomenon' to learn what was happening with the planets and stars at the time and try to find the activity through his telescope. When he spotted comets or asteroid showers he called the family up to enjoy the views with him.

For entertainment Amy enjoyed bowling and watching movies. She would roller skate around the pillars on the North Portico and even at times in the East Room. She had a tree house on the South Lawn she and her friends played in and they enjoyed tea parties out in the fresh air protected by the Secret Service. Amy was taking violin lessons and she and the other students from the music class played at the annual Congressional Christmas party in 1977.

The president and first lady invited Amy to join them for a state dinner for the President of Mexico. I'm sure they regretted their decision after the whole nation criticized their daughter for what they deemed her rude behavior. Amy was seated next to the foreign minister who was already upset when he saw it would be a child seated next to him for this special event, but when Amy pulled out a book and read during the entire meal the press criticized her bad manners. Rather than admitting that it had been a mistake not only to bring a child to such an important event in the first place, where she ignored the dinner guests and read a book throughout the meal, President Carter defended his daughter's actions, "We always read at the table when we were growing up."

Amy was criticized by many during her time in the White House. Some of the White House staff called her bratty while a Secret Service agent said, "She was spoiled rotten." A German reporter called her "a lamentably spoiled, perpetually tired, whining brat with miserable manners."

An Air Force One steward described the First Daughter's actions aboard the presidential plane saying she would purposefully leave a mess for him to clean up. "Amy would look at me and pick up a package of open soda crackers and crush them and throw them on the floor. She did it purposely. We had to clean it up." When something was said about it to the president, he of course denied that she made the mess intentionally.

The president and first lady had to sleep in separate rooms while aboard Air Force One due to the way it was set up. Amy would make herself at home in the room where her mother slept and turn on her music. Not to disturb her daughter, the first lady instead of telling her it was time to turn the music off would go sleep on the floor in the president's room.

The Carter "children" were all catered to and it didn't seem to be benefiting them by their actions, between the boys drug use and Amy's bratty ways. Now that the boys were adults, whether they acted like it or not, it appears that the president and first lady had given up on them and there was no consistency with disciplining their daughter, which they rarely did. Her father would never say no to her, and when they did tell her to do something she just did what she wanted.

Amy was a well-known enough figure to have been mocked on a "Wayne's World" skit in the late 70's featured on Saturday Night Live. It was cruel and in poor taste to be picking on a nine year old and it was in large part due to this action that future presidential families put up barriers when it came to their children demanding the press leave them alone.

The president and first lady had been invited to an annual event Ethel Kennedy hosted for one of her charities. It was called the Hickory Hill Pet Show but was more of a circus atmosphere including a petting zoo and large animals. The event took place at the Kennedy compound and was well attended by celebrities, locals, and the public with thousands attending the event. It was a wonderful event everyone looked forward to. The president and first lady had plans but sent Amy with a team of Secret Service agents due to the large crowd. There were approximately three thousand people in attendance that particular day.

The highlight of the event was a six-thousand pound elephant. The day was going well until the enormous elephant broke loose and came charging right at the president's daughter. The elephant was charging towards Amy and within twenty feet of her when one of the Secret Service agents scooped Amy up and took off with her leaping over a fence with her in his arms. It was over almost as quickly as it began, but understandably so, Amy was terrified. She had to be taken to the hospital emergency room to be checked out since she had some abrasions.

Former First Lady Jackie Kennedy who had attended the event said, "I just don't understand. Why, with so many thousands of people here, why in the world that elephant went after Amy Carter!" Ted Kennedy explained, "Well; isn't it obvious? The elephant must have smelled the peanuts on the kid." Obviously in jest, he was referring to the president's history as a peanut farmer.

When President Carter was running for reelection during a debate with Ronald Reagan the president brought up the fact that he had asked his thirteen-year old daughter Amy what the most important issue of the election was. The president explained that she answered, "The control of nuclear arms." The press notorious for finding faults of a candidate was on him like white on rice about the fact that he asked his teenage daughter for advice. He was ridiculed by not only the press but the opposing political party. This was just one more instance where Amy found herself in the press and ridiculed for something she thought was said in a private conversation with her father.

The presidency of Jimmy Carter left it's mark in history as being a president during a time of high inflation with long lines at the gas pumps and rising energy costs. Many consider President Carter to be one of our nation's worst presidents. He is remembered more for what he has done after his days in the White House than what he did as president.

After the days of the presidency, presidential children go on to make lives for themselves; some influenced by their fathers devote their lives to politics while others stay as far from it as possible.

Jack, oldest son of the Carters, moved to Chicago and worked for the Chicago Board of Trade. He started his own investment company. Jack and his first wife Judy had two children and eventually divorced. He tried his hand in politics and ran unsuccessfully for the United States Senate in Nevada. He is living with his second wife Elizabeth in Bermuda. They have four children combined.

Chip became president of Friendship Force an Atlanta based nonprofit international cultural exchange organization. After the days of his father's presidency he married a second time to Ginger Hodges and they had one child. They too divorced and he is married to his third wife Becky Payne. Chip served as city councilman and participated on the Democratic National Committee. The couple live in Atlanta, Georgia. When asked about his days of living in the White House he said, "It really is a fishbowl; anything you say, you're going to hear back somewhere. But you can talk to your family because everybody's going through the same thing."

Jeff was co-founder of the company Computer Mapping Consultants. He is a computer consultant and remains married to his first wife Annette. He like his sister has remained elusive from the press.

In December of 2015 Jeff's twenty-eight year old son Jeremy passed away. He had not been feeling well and laid down to rest. When his mother checked on him she discovered his heart had stopped. She gave him CPR, he was resuscitated and rushed to the hospital where his heart again stopped. The Carter family chose not to have an autopsy done which leaves many wondering why. With no history of heart problems why would a healthy twenty-eight year old suddenly die and why wouldn't his family want to know the cause. On a blog one of his brothers stated that he had a battery of tests done just weeks prior to his death and nothing had been found wrong with his heart.

Amy served as a page in the U.S. Senate during her summer vacation in high school. She attended her senior year at Woodward Academy and went on to Brown University. It was during her sophomore year at Brown University that she became involved in political activism participating in sit-ins and protests with activist Abbie Hoffman. She protested CIA covert actions and South Africa's apartheid. She was arrested in 1986 during a demonstration for protesting CIA recruitment at the University of Massachusetts. She was acquitted. When asked what her parents thought of her arrest, she replied, "My parents told me they were proud of me," she said. "Every time a person sacrifices themselves for a larger injustice, it aids in the cycle of change," said the former president's daughter. "I really don't like it when there's a political action involving many students, and there's a story written about me, and not the action," Amy said. -- *Did she really think that as a former president's daughter the news story wouldn't be focused on her? A president's daughter being arrest – that's news.*

Jimmy Carter when interviewed about his nineteen-year old daughter being arrested replied, "Amy's been arrested four times, three for protesting apartheid and this last time for what she considers, and I consider, illegal activity of the CIA in Nicaragua," said Carter, who declared himself "a very proud father."

Amy was dismissed from Brown University for academic reasons. She would later earn a master's degree in fine arts and art history.

In 1996 Amy married James Wentzel who designed websites. She wore a vintage style wedding dress and was married at the home of her late grandmother. In place of a rose petal aisle she walked down a path strewn with magnolia leaves. She refused to be given away as she stated "no one owned her." She kept her own name. Vows were exchanged under an arbor from an old swing set she decorated with vines and baked her own wedding cake. Her one son Hugo was born in 1999.

Amy is on the board of counselors of the Carter Center established by her father. She illustrated her father's children's book, *'The Little Baby Snoogle-Fleejer'* and his book *'Christmas In Plains.'*

She remains out of the public's eye refusing to speak to the media and refusing all interview requests. Not once since her days as First Daughter has she made a public appearance.

Most presidential children may have found living in the White House difficult at times, but in hindsight looked at their time as a part of the First Family as an experience few are offered and appreciate the people they met, their travels, and experiences as something to look back at fondly - *not so with Amy Carter.*

40

Ronald Reagan

Children with first wife Jane Wyman and Ronald Reagan

Maureen Elizabeth Reagan - Born: Jan. 4, 1941   Died: Aug. 8, 2001

Michael Edward Reagan - Born: March 18, 1946   Still Living At The Time Of Publication

Christine Reagan - Born: June 26, 1947   Died: June 26, 1947

Children with second wife Nancy and Ronald Reagan

Patti Davis - Born: Oct. 23, 1952   Still Living At The Time Of Publication

Ronald Prescott Reagan "Ron" - Born: May 20, 1958   Still Living At The Time Of Publication

Maureen was physically abused by her first husband, Michael was sexually abused as a child,

Patti claims she was mentally and physically abused by her mother.

Of all presidential families theirs was the most dysfunctional of them all.

While it might sound very glamorous to have grown up with two parents who were movie stars, it was anything but for the Reagan children.

Maureen and Michael's mother was Jane Wyman, Reagan's first wife. Maureen, the daughter of two movie stars, was not your typical pampered Hollywood child. She learned at a very early age to become self reliant. It was a lonely existence for a child whose parents worked in a fantasy world and she was often left to amuse herself.

Around three years of age Maureen began asking her parents for a brother, a playmate. Her father would have been only too happy to give his daughter her wish as he wanted a son. Maureen's birth had been difficult and it was assumed there would be no more children for the Reagan family. One day her parents told her she was about to receive the thing she wanted most in her life. When she came downstairs there was her new baby brother. What she had really wanted was an older brother, one who could talk and play with her. They had adopted a three day old baby boy they named Michael.

Maureen and Michael's mother Jane Wyman was a movie star that played some serious roles. She would remain in character even when off set. Maureen remembered it was sometimes hard to recognize her own mother; such as when she played a lead role as Ora Baxter in *The Yearling* for which she won Best Actress.

Maureen was entranced by watching her parents acting. When guests came over they were entertained by a father daughter vaudeville routine they performed for their guests. By the time she was in kindergarten she had already decided she too wanted to be an actress. She told her father there was no need for her to go to school anymore as she knew she wanted to be an actress when she grew up. Her father was able to convince her she would need to go to school to learn to read so she could read her scripts and to write so she could sign autographs. That seemed to make sense to his five year old daughter so she resigned herself to go to school.

In 1947 their mother gave birth to a little girl who was born four months premature. She died the same day she was born living only a matter of hours. The baby was named Christine Reagan.

WWII was ongoing and while Reagan was unable to serve overseas due to being nearsighted, he did serve at the San Francisco port of embarkation. He tried to get a waiver to serve overseas but was denied. He became a filmmaker making government films to promote the war effort making 300 training and propaganda films.

During his time in the service while busy making films for the government his wife's career had flourished and she had become a major star. To his surprise she announced she was getting a divorce. Maureen was seven years old and Michael was only three.

At the age of four Michael learned he was adopted when his sister told him she had a secret. She told him he was adopted. "I didn't know what that meant, only that the way she said it made it sound like something bad," Michael said. "My mother explained that it meant that I was special." But he never felt special again after one of his classmates taunted him with the fact that he was a bastard and was given away because his mother didn't want him.

The same year of her parent's divorce Maureen was sent to boarding school at Chadwick School. It was a tumultuous year; first in losing her father to divorce and now being removed from her mother's life except for an occasional weekend. Michael for the time being was sent by bus every day to a pre-kindergarten class, but by the time he turned six he too was sent to the same boarding school as his sister. Due to the difference in gender and age they didn't see much of each other even though they attended and lived at the same school. This was an especially difficult time for Michael being so young and being shuffled from one home to another and now also sent off to boarding school at such a young age.

Michael still remembers how he cried himself to sleep every night and being teased by the other children. Many of those children only attended the school during the day and then went home, but Maureen and Michael were only allowed to go home every other weekend. On the weekends they had to remain at school their father and Nancy who he was dating at the time would drive up to visit. On the weekends they could leave school it would be their father and Nancy who would pick them up; their mother was too busy.

When their father was dating Nancy, also an actress, she was very kind to his children. Their own mother suffered mood swings and the only time she showed her children any concern was when they were sick. While Nancy was dating their father she joined in on their Saturday outings and would arrive with their father to pick them up from school. She let Michael sit on her lap during the drive home. It was attention and loving care he never received from his own mother, and starving for affection he soon came to love the woman who would be his stepmother. But once they got married and there was a new baby on the way things changed. He was seated in the backseat now where he again felt left out.

When Michael was seven years old he was sent to day camp during the summer. While there one of the counselors saw that he was lonely and desperate for attention. Taking advantage of that fact the counselor molested him. Michael was ashamed and never told anyone about it until he was an adult.

Michael looked forward to the days his father picked him up as he loved visiting him at the ranch. His father spent time teaching Michael and Maureen how to ride horseback. Michael loved riding the horses. One day when he and his sister arrived at the ranch there was a palomino in the corral. He was a golden color with a white stripe down his face. His father picked Michael up and put him on the back of the horse and asked him what he thought of it. His father explained that the horse belonged to a man who had bought it for his son and he was training the horse for him. Michael thought that was a lucky boy and wished he could have a horse just like this one.

The day before Christmas when they were at the ranch his father told him it would be his last chance to ride the horse as it was a Christmas gift for the owner's son. Michael raced out to the stall in tears. It was going to break his heart to have to say good-bye to the horse. When he went out to the barn and opened the top part of the stall the horse stuck his head out of the stall. The horse had a big red bow around his neck with a note that said, 'Merry Christmas, Michael. Love, Nancy and Dad.'

Christmas Eve when he went to his mother's house he was so excited he couldn't contain his excitement as he told his mother about the horse. She responded with a hostility he didn't understand. What he didn't know at the time was his mother and father had struck a deal that his father would give him the horse for Christmas and his mother would give him the saddle and bridle. She must have realized afterward that her gift wouldn't bring the same excitement as his father's gift of the horse and regretted making the deal.

Not being able to sleep wondering what he had done to make his mother so unhappy with him he decided to see if Maureen was awake. As he walked in the hall his mother had just come out of her bedroom carrying the bridle and saddle. When she saw her son she was furious. She said, "Here's my Christmas present to you, Michael. You can go down and put it under the tree yourself!" She then dropped the saddle and bridle at his feet, went into her bedroom and slammed the door.

Maureen and Michael spent the summer at their father's ranch. While at the ranch his father had bought Michael a pet goat named Heidi. When it was time to leave to go to their mother's house he and Maureen decided it would be nice if their mother could meet the goat. They made plans that when it was time to leave they would hide Heidi in the backseat of the car and hide her under their jackets.

Not usually anxious to leave the ranch their father thought something was up when he found them both waiting in the backseat of the car all ready to go. On the drive to their mother's house their father heard a noise in the back of the car and asked, "That isn't Heidi by any chance, is it?" The kids started laughing and Heidi popped her head up over the back of the seat. When their father dropped the kids off at their mothers he didn't hang around to see if she was as enthralled as the kids were over the goat.

Michael and Maureen guided the goat to the backyard but when they opened the door Heidi beat them inside. The kids ran after the goat and as they turned the corner into the living room it was just in time to see the look of horror on their mother's face as Heidi left an unpleasant gift on her brand new white carpet.

It didn't take any time before their mother was on the phone screaming at their father to come get that goat. By the time he arrived to pick up Heidi the goat had made a meal out of all the roses in the rose garden. Their father tried to hide the grin on his face as he wrestled Heidi into his car but was having a hard time doing so.

Michael admitted later in life that he would often act up just to get attention from his mother, but the response from her more often than not was ten hard whacks with a riding crop on each leg. It wasn't unusual for his mother to yell at him or ridicule him in front of others in public. What was unusual was to receive any words of comfort or signs of love from her.

Maureen and Michael received a call at school one day with the news from their father and Nancy that they had gotten married. That was a complete surprise to his children who hadn't been told of any marriage plans or even been invited to the wedding. The same year they were married Patti was born. Up until that time Nancy had treated Maureen and Michael as her own children, but things were different now. They soon noticed they had become irrelevant. They would discover they were now part of two dysfunctional families.

Michael and Maureen were to spend Halloween with their mother one year when she introduced them to a man named Fred Karger. Fred had a daughter a few months younger than Maureen and she went trick-or-treating with Maureen and Michael. When they returned with their bags of goodies their mother told her children she was to be married. She didn't mention when the wedding was to take place. This was the first they had ever met the man who was to be their stepfather. The next morning when they woke up the cook told them their mother had eloped. Needless to say, they weren't invited to their mother's wedding either. When she returned from her honeymoon she was busy at the movie studio and Fred was busy composing music; neither of them had the time or the inclination to be parents. So yet again; Maureen and Michael were shipped off to boarding school.

When Michael was taken to be enrolled at St. John's Military Academy he wasn't even aware it was yet another boarding school until his Mother said, "I'll see you Saturday."

Maureen and Michael spent little time with their father and their father's new family. They didn't spend enough time together to make any shared memories and were more like strangers than family. They rarely even saw each other at this time in their lives.

Once when Mom picked Michael up from school she told him she had a surprise for him. She gave him a standard size poodle whose name she said was Stuffy. She told him it was his dog and he was responsible for his care. Michael took good care of him and became very attached to the dog. Another time when he arrived for a visit at the house he immediately ran off to look for Stuffy and when he couldn't find him he asked his mother where his dog was. She told him she gave him to a new family. He was heartbroken.

When Maureen graduated it would be without her father and stepmother's presence due to Nancy giving birth at the time to her stepbrother Ron. Maureen had become distant from her family and barely noticed their absence from this important event in her life. By this time she called Nancy "Dragon Lady," though never to her face as she could be quite intimidating. Unlike her brother Michael she never did live with her father and stepmother. Though they were at odds at this time in her life, she would resume a relationship with both her father and stepmother later in her life.

While Michael was a student at St. John's Military Academy his sister Maureen was sent to Marymount Girl's School, a Catholic boarding school in New York. She rarely saw either parent while she was living on the other side of the country from her family. After a year of attending Marymount College she dropped out to become an actress. She did get a few parts and was in *Sex and the Married Woman* and had a part in a movie with Elvis

Presley *Kissin' Cousins*. She had bit parts in television shows and sang in nightclubs, but she didn't have much success of either acting or singing as a career.

In the early 60's Maureen was living in Washington, D.C. and working as a secretary having given up on acting. With no family and few friends when she met John Filippone, a policeman who worked near her apartment building, she was vulnerable and desired to get married and feel emotionally connected to someone. He was ten years her senior and knowing him for only a short time she called and announced to her father she was getting married.

The marriage took place in the living room of a friend with the bride wearing a $10 white lace dress with the guests comprised of her father and stepmother Nancy, but not her own mother.

Maureen learned very quickly that the marriage was a mistake. Within days of the marriage she discovered her husband was an abuser. While initially it was verbal abuse it soon turned violent. He would fly into rages over nothing.

Maureen was ashamed and didn't confide in anyone. At this time there weren't shelters battered women could turn to for support and refuge. People during this time didn't want to get involved or not knowing how to handle the situation had a tendency to feign ignorance or look the other way. Neighbors hearing what was going on did call the police, but when they showed up he locked Maureen in the bathroom and told them he was only moving furniture around. Being that he was a policeman himself they didn't pursue it. The beatings continued and he threatened to kill her if she left him. It finally took the intervention of someone higher up in the police force to put a stop to it when he began stalking her after she finally did find the courage to leave him.

Michael had gone to live with his father and stepmother. Frustrated with her son, his mother had taken him to a psychiatrist who told her that her son had a deep desire to be a part of a family. The psychiatrist suggested perhaps she should consider letting her son live with his father for a time. Michael was thrilled when his father asked if he would like to come live with them. He thought he would finally be part of a family. He had a younger sister Patti who was about seven years old at the time and a new baby brother Ron. He would be the big brother that his stepsister and stepbrother would look up to were his thoughts. Most of all, he longed to be accepted and loved.

His father was on the road traveling working for GE at this time. Nancy intimidated everyone in the household from staff to her own children and it didn't take long before her and Michael were at odds with each other. Michael tried to talk to his father about the situation but quickly learned to never make the mistake of speaking against Nancy to Dad, a lesson each of his children would learn over time.

Michael passed back and forth between parents and boarding schools and in addition being adopted and feeling unwanted hadn't received much praise or the love and attention he strongly desired. When it came to school he didn't make much effort when it came to studying so he wasn't surprised when his report card arrived with barely passing grades.

Nancy after seeing his report card said to Michael, "You're not living up to the Reagan name or image, and unless you start shaping up it would be best for you to change your name and leave the house."

As an adopted child he had always wondered where he came from and why he was given up for adoption so he seized this opportunity and said, "Why don't you tell me the name I was born with so at least when I walk out the door I'll know what name to use." His court records had been sealed, but somehow Nancy found a way to get the information from his adoption. A few days later she told him his birth name was John Flaugher and his father had been in the army. While on leave he had an affair and left the woman pregnant as he shipped off overseas, never to return or to acknowledge his son.

The information an adopted child may want to learn about their roots isn't always easy to hear. He asked Nancy if his birth parents were married. She said no. That confirmed that the taunts the children had thrown at him as a young boy that he was a bastard were true then. It was hard to hear, especially from someone who was not taking his feelings into consideration of how this information may affect him.

While thinking it all over, he later said he remembered being surprised that Nancy had been so cruel. How could she not have been more understanding to his being adopted when her own father had abandoned her when she was only a year old. From the time she was a toddler she had been raised by surrogate mothers as her own mother was an actress and was on the road acting on the stage more than she was home with her daughter. It wasn't until she was fourteen that her mother remarried and she was adopted by her stepfather. Even then, he was a perfectionist and she could never meet his expectations and never measured up. Regardless of how hurt and disregarded he felt, he had no one to turn to. He had never felt more alone.

Away at boarding school in 1964 with the Christmas holidays approaching and not even enough money in his wallet for gas to get home for the holidays he called Nancy and explained his situation. She responded to his dilemma by saying, "We've sent you enough money. If you've squandered it, that's your problem. I'm not going to send you more!" *Merry Christmas!*

Not wanting to be the only student left behind at school during the holidays Michael called his mother. In the morning a special delivery letter arrived with a check. The letter told him they would spend the holidays together with friends at Lake Tahoe. He met his mother and they took a train to the snow topped mountains of the Sierra Nevadas. They spent the holidays on the ski slopes and had what Michael described as the most memorable Christmas of his life.

In 1964 Maureen married David Sills who was a lieutenant in the Marine Corps. He, like Maureen was also interested in politics; but they too would divorce. In 1981 she married Dennis Revell who she remained married to up until the time of her death.

In 1952 Ronald Reagan and Nancy Davis had married and seven months later Patti arrived. Her mother would later explain to her that she was born two months premature. A 7 lb – 3 oz "premie" who her mother said was kept in an incubator for the first two months since 'she was early.' Patti wasn't convinced. A 7 lb premie was pretty hard to accept, but in those days "good girls" didn't have sex before marriage. Patti had to bite her tongue when in her college days her father explained to her that he and her mother had waited until they were married to have sex and he expected the same from his daughter. She said she didn't bother responding as she figured by this time he had even convinced himself the story was true.

Patti sometimes appeared in television commercials with her parents when she was young. As an adult she became a part-time actress having roles in *The Love Boat* and was in the film *The Pink Panther.*

In 1958 Ron was born, the last of the Reagan children. While many people referred to him as Ron, Jr. he wasn't really a Junior as his father's middle name was Wilson and his was Prescott. He was an adorable baby and would become the favorite child of his mother.

Nancy had a way of intimidating everyone around her, so even when very young Patti would turn to her nanny for comfort instead of her mother. She never had the opportunity to get too close to any of the staff as her mother went through maids, nannies, cooks, and gardeners on a revolving door basis.

Patti attended school with children of other movie stars; those of Tony Curtis, June Allyson, Jimmy Stewart, Judy Garland, and Angela Lansbury. Her home often had guests that she had seen in movies such as Mary Martin who had played Peter Pan and Roy Bolger who would perform his scarecrow dance for her from Wizard of Oz. Other stars who were often guests at their home were Frank Sinatra and James Arness of Gunsmoke who was a neighbor and had a son who performed feats on his skateboard that impressed Patti so much he became her first crush.

It wasn't until fourteen year old Michael moved in with the family that Patti discovered her family was larger than she had known. She was seven years old and up to this point in her life she was clueless that she had a teenage stepbrother and a stepsister who was eighteen. She had seen Maureen a few times in the past but she had never been told that she was a part of the family. Patti said she probably never would have been told if it weren't for the fact that Michael moved in with them. Michael went to boarding school during the week but came to live with them on weekends. She already had a one year old brother Ron, but she was excited about having a big brother too. When she discovered she also had an older sister though she burst into tears. It was Maureen who told her that she was her sister. Maureen had been shocked to discover Patti didn't even know she existed or that she had a sister. When Maureen asked her father why she hadn't been told, he just said they hadn't gotten around to it yet.

Patti as an adult would write several revealing books about the inner circle of her family and the abuse she received from her mother. She would reveal that the first time she remembered her mother hitting her was when she was eight years old, something that would continue until she finally moved out on her own. "By the age of eight, I was already afraid of my mother," Patti said. As Patti got older and more defiant the abuse escalated, sometimes suffering the abuse on a daily basis. Her father was blissfully unaware or lived in complete denial.

When Patti was nine years of age she was with her mother at the grocery store that had a bakery with a window where people could watch the bakers at work. Children watched in amazement the baker's magic transformation of cakes being decorated and faces being put on gingerbread men. The bakers would come out with a tray of cookies for the children. Patti's mother told her she wasn't to stand there with the other children as she was overweight and couldn't have a cookie.

With her mother preoccupied talking to someone in the produce section Patti joined some other children and waited eagerly as one of the bakers approached her with his tray of cookies. She didn't see her mother coming until she grabbed her arm yelling at her, "I told you that you couldn't have any cookies." People stopped their carts and were staring at my mother making a scene. Her mother dragged Patti down the grocery aisles throwing items into the cart.

On their way home her mother was angry and driving too fast and was pulled over by the police. She was able to talk her way out of the ticket, but after the policeman left she slapped her daughter across the face blaming her for getting pulled over and almost getting a ticket.

One day at the house her mother started hitting her, not just once or twice, but beating her on her head until a family friend of her fathers who was visiting jumped up and pulled Nancy off her daughter. He told her, "Don't ever do that in front of me again." But he never said a word about the incident to his friend Ronald Reagan.

As Patti got older she began noticing that her mother was taking prescription pills – pretty frequently. Patti said that was blamed on her too, saying I got on her nerves and was making her sick. When her father mentioned that Patti's actions were causing her mother to be sick Patti told her father about how her mother treated her when he wasn't around. His answer was, "That never happened." There was no point in trying to tell him any differently – *he never listened to or believed anyone but Nancy.*

Ron was easygoing and escaped the wrath of their mother during his youth. The intercom in Patti's room and Ron's room was left on day and night. Locks had been removed from their doors. There was never such a thing as privacy. With intercoms in both their rooms Patti said she used to time it and see how long it would take for her mother to come in and separate her and her brother. They were never allowed to play together. Five minutes was the record before her mother came in and separated them.

Vacations and holidays were spent at the ranch where the family would go horseback riding. That seemed to be the time their father spent the most time with his children, while involved in an activity he loved more than anything else, riding horses. He would spend hours with them giving them hands on instructions on how to handle the horse. This is where their father was most comfortable. Patti said, "The ranch was an escape for me. It was the only time I really got to spend anytime with my father."

As many teenage girls do, Patti poured her heart out in her diary writing of her insecurities and loneliness. Writing in her diary gave her an outlet and comfort since there was no one who would listen or that she could confide in. "I walked out of the bathroom one day and discovered my mother reading it and then confiscating it," Patti said. "There was no such thing as privacy in our home. When I look back at some of the things that happened as I grew up I realize my mother needed to control everything and everybody around her."

Patti had been sent to boarding school at Orme School in Arizona where she would stay for the next five years coming home only for holidays and summers. Once when I got out of the car my mother said, "Patti, you have a fat butt." Most young girls this age are sensitive to criticism about their physical appearance and Patti was disturbed by her mother's comment about her weight. "That was when I began taking diet pills," Patti said.

Patti became addicted to pills and by the time she came home the next Christmas her bones stuck out and her face was shrunken. Her mother didn't say anything about her being fat anymore, but neither did she seem distressed over the obvious fact that her daughter had become anorexic. Years later when talking about her pill addiction to a friend she asked Patti in a joking manner, "You mean you didn't 'Just Say No'?" That had been Nancy's mantra as first lady in fighting the war on drugs. Not only didn't she say no, she would later experiment with LSD, Quaaludes, and even cocaine. "I'm lucky to be alive," Patti admitted.

Patti was away at Orme School when one day Michael was shocked to receive a phone call from a sister he had little to no contact with. She was fourteen at the time and told Michael, "I have fallen in love with a dishwasher." Her big brother was twenty-one by this time and had a driver's license and a car so she wanted him to come sign her out of school so she could run away with the dishwasher. Michael was in a tough spot. He felt flattered that his stepsister had turned to him asking for help, but considering her age and the circumstances he knew he had to do something but he wasn't sure what. Patti had made him promise not to tell their dad or Nancy. He called the family's business manager to ask for advice who told Michael to leave it in his hands and he would take care of it. He of course called Patti's parents who came and took her out of the school and out of the reach of the dishwasher. Patti never forgave Michael for betraying her trust, though surely she must have known she was putting him in a predicament.

"When my father was running for office he put a lot of emphasis on children. I never could understand this, as it sometimes seemed to slip his mind that he himself was a father and had children," Patti said. "He would sometimes look at us like he didn't know who we were. And Michael and Maureen who were away at boarding school were never mentioned. Out of sight; out of mind. All of us kids were eventually sent off to boarding schools."

By this time Ronald Reagan had been elected as governor of the state of California. During the time when her father was governor Patti a young teen knew she needed to turn to her father and let him know what was happening between her and her mother while he was away. She met his plane and told him she needed to talk to him.

She poured her heart out to him with tears running down her face confiding in him of the abuse she had suffered at her mother's hands. She froze when she heard the tone of her father's voice knowing what was coming. He accused her of lying and said, "Why do you make up these things?" She began crying uncontrollably. "What I'm hearing is just not the truth." He said. Patti walked out feeling broken, knowing her father would never accept the truth.

Michael having grown up with two parents who were actors also wanted to give acting a try and appeared in the television series *Falcon Crest* that his mother starred in. Three out of the four Reagan children tried their hand at acting, but it is doubtful if any of them would have ever secured a role if their last name hadn't been Reagan.

While his father was governor Michael became involved in boat racing. Again his name gave him opportunities that would have otherwise not been available with sponsors wishing to use the Reagan name to sell events. Michael didn't care. He was having a great time racing all over the country and while he never won any inboard races he always finished as one of the top five of ten racers in the nation.

Michael was living the life of an irresponsible bachelor and getting himself deep in debt.

The more in debt he got the angrier his parents became. They thought it was time he grew up and became responsible with a steady job.

Michael was asked if he would be interested in entering a two-day race during the spring of 1967. The competition was fierce. Michael longing for the publicity in hopes of impressing his father surprised everyone by winning the race. They became the Outboard World Champions of 1967. The papers ran with the headlines 'Governor's Son Wins Outboard Championship.'

Michael at twenty-six years of age had plans to marry a friend of the family's daughter who had just graduated from high school and had just turned eighteen. The wedding took place in Hawaii with his sister Maureen and his mother there, but his father and Nancy were not. He was deeply hurt when he later learned his father and stepmother chose instead to attend the wedding of Tricia Nixon instead of their own son's wedding.

When the business Michael was working for went bankrupt he and his wife Julie moved to Mobile, Alabama to be close to his wife's parents. Michael found work with a real estate company selling campsite property but with the job came a lot of traveling. While he was on the road working his wife was having an affair with a married man who also worked for the same company Julie and Michael worked for. Julie wanted to have a baby and Michael in hopes of saving his marriage agreed. About the same time she discovered she was pregnant she asked for a divorce.

Michael has never seen his son from his first marriage. He and his wife made an agreement that she wouldn't have him charged with back pay for child support if he would sign the divorce papers and give up all rights to his son. Michael an adopted child himself gave up his own son who would be adopted by the man his wife was having an affair with that she ended up marrying. Michael said, "He has never known his biological father, as I never knew mine."

Michael remarried in 1975 to a woman who was understanding and strong and supported him through paying off his financial debts. She was there to support him emotionally when he broke down and told her about being molested as a child. He and his wife Colleen have two children together.

When Michael and Colleen first discovered they were expecting their first child Michael was thrilled he would be giving his parents their first grandchild. Their son Cameron was born in 1978. His mother Jane Wyman and his sister Maureen visited at the hospital to meet the new addition of the family and to offer their congratulations; but his father and Nancy again were conspicuously absent. To make matters worse they drove right by the hospital on their way to the ranch the same day but didn't stop to see their first grandchild.

At the age of twelve Ron announced to his parents that he was an atheist and would no longer attend church with his parents. He has remained firm in his non-belief and declares himself an "unabashed atheist who is not afraid of burning in hell."

Ron in his teen years drove around in an old, beat up car and let his his grow long as was the fad of the times for young teens. With his sister moved out of the house he and his mother began having their own heated arguments many times about her listening in on his phone calls, his hair, and the music he listened to.

Patti left home and lived a hippie lifestyle with drugs, dead-end relationships with men, and even had a tubal ligation which insured she would never have children and repeat the cycle of an abusive relationship between parent and child. Years later she regretted the impulsive act and had the tubal ligation reversed but has remained childless. Oddly enough, she would change her name dropping the family name of Reagan and changing it to Patti Davis her mother's maiden name. She became estranged from her family during these years.

One evening Patti was surprised to see her brother Ron walk into the restaurant where she was working. They hadn't seen each other in quite some time and had not been in touch. He told his sister he had run away from home and asked to stay with her.

That evening in her apartment brother and sister sat up and talked. He confided in her that he and his mother were constantly arguing. When he confronted his mother about listening in on his phone calls she raised her hand to hit him. He told his sister he blocked her hand with his arm. He confided that his mother had never tried to hit him before but he remembered all the times she had slapped Patti and he said he had decided she wasn't going to do that to him. He told his mother as much. That's when he left home. He was sixteen at the time.

Ron stayed overnight at Patti's and went back home the next day feeling he had made his point. Patti pondered why her mother had gone to such lengths to keep her and her brother apart as they were growing up.

Patti had a relationship with Bernie Leadon, the guitarist of the group The Eagles. They lived together for a time. She eventually married Paul Grilley a yoga instructor in 1983, but they later divorced remaining friends. She posed nude for Playboy and wrote *'The Way I See It,'* a tell-all autobiography about her family which exposed her dysfunctional family to the world. Her brothers and sister stopped speaking to her when the book came out. They felt she had gone too far in her scream for attention.

In 1976 Ron was attending Yale but dropped out during his first semester having earned a scholarship to New York City's Joffrey School of Dance. This was a total surprise to his parents but Ron was a rare talent who made the cut at the Joffrey Ballet. People began to speculate on whether he was gay. Ron refused to admit or deny the allegations of his sexual preference.

Ron like his sister had a rebellious streak and he held up under the pressure when he chose to become a ballet dancer against his parent's wishes. People thought at the time that any male who was a ballet dancer must be gay. His parents didn't think their son was gay, but they read the allegations and wondered if it could be true.

At the time Ron was studying ballet at the Stanley Holden Dance Center in Los Angeles and was living with his parents. His parents had left on a trip but returned home early unexpectedly. They arrived home and found the cook serving Ron and a young lady in bed and was informed when they questioned the maid that Ron had her preparing candlelight dinners for him and the young lady – in his parent's bed. That must have removed his parent's lingering doubts about his sexuality.

When Ron's father was running for the presidency, Ron said if Ronald Reagan hadn't been his father he would have voted for Walter Mondale in the 1984 presidential election.

When their father was running for the presidency his children from his second marriage were nowhere to be found at fund-raising dinners and political events. Ron let it be known he hated politics and to count him out as far as campaigning went. And Patti, well Patti was off doing her own thing unwilling to be there to support her parents. Ron's children from his first marriage campaigned relentlessly for their father.

Three out of four of Reagan's children tried their hand at acting. Only Ron didn't feel the draw of the stage except as a dancer; unless you count his stint on *Saturday Night Live* where he performed in a skit dancing in his underwear during his father's second term.

Ron was living with Doria Palmieri who he had met when he was twenty while a dancing student at the Stanley Holden Dance Center where she worked. They were having trouble making ends meet with him as a young aspiring ballet dancer. Doria worked as an editor at *Interview* magazine. Doria once confided in Patti that when she met Ron she was surprised that Ron was living in such a small apartment and how sparsely furnished it was. She said he even ate his cereal with water because he didn't have enough money to buy milk. She couldn't understand how his parents who were wealthy and in a position to help didn't offer their son any assistance. Ron only made $11,000 a year as a ballet dancer and lived in poverty much of the time during his dancing career.

Ron and Doria struggled financially. At a time when his father during his presidency was speaking to the nation about the economy, his own son stood in an unemployment line. They were barely making ends meet when Ron offered his parents an original Andy Warhol print as collateral against a loan. He had received the print as a gift from Andy Warhol who he had befriended in New York.

Nancy did not welcome Doria into the family with open arms. She told anyone who would listen that she was too old for Ron. There was a seven year age difference.

When the family had been invited to a Christmas party being given by a friend of the family she told Ron he couldn't bring Doria because they didn't have enough plates. The friends throwing the party were multimillionaires. Did she seriously think her son would buy that story? Ron arrived at the party with Doria on his arm. Patti came up to Doria and whispered, "You're very brave. She's not going to make it easy for you, you know."

Ron and Doria arrived at the Republican Convention where his father was to be announced as the nominee. The old saying, 'If looks could kill' would have been apropos. Nancy didn't want Doria to be there and she made no bones about it. Ron insisted that Doria would go on stage with the rest of the family when his father was introduced as the nominee. Nancy absolutely refused. Ron let his mother know if Doria couldn't be there, then neither would he be there. A truce was finally drawn when Nancy promised her son she would treat Doria better in the future if Ron would go on stage without her. That truce probably lasted about ten minutes after they left the stage.

A month after his father won the presidential election Ron and Doria were married in New York by a justice of the peace. They had slipped into a judge's office in New York planning to pick up a marriage license. The judge suggested he marry them on the spot to avoid a media frenzy. The bride and groom were decked out with the bride in a bulky sweater, blue jeans, and cowboy boots. The groom was in jeans, a sweatshirt, and running shoes. A Secret Service agent was Ron's best man. The press found out about the marriage before Ron's parents did.

Ronald Reagan became the oldest president in American history being just a month shy of his 70th birthday at the time he was sworn into office. He was also the first president to have been divorced.

All of the Reagan children now adults, regardless of how estranged they had become were in attendance to witness their father taking the oath of office, to view the inaugural parade, and for the inaugural balls.

Maureen who had been distant from her father and Nancy who she called "Dragon Lady" at one time became closer than any of the other Reagan children to them during their time in the White House spending as much time as possible in the Executive Mansion.

Michael and Colleen loved the pomp and circumstance of the events leading up to and the inauguration and balls. They felt like a million bucks as they were whisked through traffic in limousines that brought traffic to a stop all around them. They would be the hosts for the inaugural ball at the Washington Hilton Hotel.

Patti most comfortable in jeans and casual attire let her mother convince her into wearing a red Adolfo gown for the inaugural ball while brother Ron and his wife Doria who now could legitimately stand on stage with the rest of the Reagans seemed to enjoy themselves at the inaugural events. Even though Ron's beliefs were far different from his fathers as far as what he stood for he was proud of his father.

For once the family stood reunited at the inauguration, an event that wouldn't happen again until the assassination attempt on their father's life; and even then, though together at the White House and hospital they were distant.

Nancy got a taste of what she would be experiencing during her years as first lady in the White House when the critics and political enemies attacked her for her extravagant inaugural gown which cost $25,000. Her handbag alone cost more than the annual allowance of food stamps for a family of four. During her time as first lady she would often accept 'loans' of designer gowns which instead of being returned to the designer as was intended, the gowns would end up in Nancy's closet - a wardrobe that was valued at over a million dollars.

The first lady received relentless criticism from spending too much money decorating the White House and on her clothes during an economic recession. There were complaints about her not having enough input towards social concerns and for being too involved in the affairs of the presidency and personnel of the White House. It was even hinted at that she had violated the Government Ethics Act of 1977 concerning designers loaning her gowns and her failing to return the gowns instead keeping them as 'gifts.'

At one point the first lady had the lowest approval rating of any first lady since such statistics had been kept. Low approval rating or not, she was most definitely the most powerful first lady in the last forty years. She did her work behind the scenes; but those on staff and in the cabinet knew not to cross her or they would pay. What the first lady needed was a cause – she chose drug abuse and used the slogan 'Just Say No.'

Sixty nine days into his presidency there was an assassination attempt and President Reagan was shot. The Secret Service were the ones that informed his children of what had happened. The first lady hadn't thought to contact her own children let alone the children from her husband's first marriage to let them know what had happened.

The Secret Service arranged for an Army C-140 transport plane to take Patti, Michael and his wife Colleen, Maureen and Dennis to Washington. Ron at the time was traveling with the Joffrey Ballet and was performing in Nebraska but had left and was en route to Washington.

When Patti saw the others she thought to herself how none of them had reached out to each other, even in a time like this. "What kind of family is this?" she wondered. "Even a bullet can't bring us together." The only connection they had was their father who was lying in the hospital after having been shot.

None of them knew any details other than what they had been told by the Secret Service or what they heard on the television as they waited for their flight.

Ron and Doria arrived in Washington the night before the others and had been at the hospital with his mother to see their father. The following morning the first lady, Ron, Doria, and Patti left for the hospital. When Maureen and Michael arrived they were told by Nancy they wouldn't be able to see their father until later as he was too weak to visit with them. They were angry that Ron and Patti had been allowed to see their father but they weren't. Ron and Patti were in their father's room and when they came out they just walked past Maureen and Michael without saying a word.

Their father was still recuperating when his oldest daughter Maureen married Dennis Revell a man twelve years younger than her. This would be her third marriage but the first time she would be a bride as a First Daughter. Since her father was laid up and recuperating at Camp David it would be the president's brother who escorted Maureen down the aisle. Her brother Michael was a guest at the wedding as was her mother Jane Wyman; but Patti and Ron were not. The wedding took place at the Beverly Wilshire Hotel and Maureen being a proponent of the Equal Rights Amendment had the word 'obey' stricken from the vows they exchanged.

Maureen loved visiting the White House saying the place took her breath away. In all the years she visited the Executive Mansion she said she never lost the feeling of wonder and history.

Other than the Oval Office the Lincoln Bedroom was the place most visitors wanted to see. The bedroom has a sitting room with an oversized ornately carved rosewood bed measuring nearly eight-foot by six-foot with a large headboard and footboard that came from the Victorian era. Mary Lincoln had special ordered the bed for Lincoln, though it is doubtful he ever had the opportunity to sleep in it. During Lincoln's era the room was used as an office and for Cabinet meetings. It still today has some historical memorabilia from the Lincoln administration. It was here that President Lincoln signed the Emancipation Proclamation.

Maureen and her husband came and stayed overnight in the Lincoln Bedroom which had a history of ghost tales told about visitations that occurred in the room. Even Winston Churchill said he had seen strange sightings.

Maureen and Dennis swore the room was haunted. They both insisted they had seen Lincoln's ghost. "I'm not kidding," Maureen said. "We've really seen it." The president just laughed when they insisted they had seen something in the room, but his own dog

Rex wouldn't go in the room. He would stand at the doorway and bark peering at the ceiling. The president went in to look around himself but didn't see anything. He wondered if perhaps the dog was hearing an electronic signal sent by the Soviets and had the Secret Service bring in communications experts to have the room checked. Nothing was found or detected.

Maureen ran for the Senate in California but her father refused to endorse her candidacy. When a reporter asked the president about his daughter running for office his response was, "I hope not."

Maureen who had campaigned for her father and other Republican candidates was elected as co-chairperson of the Republican National Committee; something that had never been done in the past for the child of a president.

Patti kept her distance from the White House while her father was president visiting only four times in the eight years he was in office. "I hated the White House," she reported. "It's like this tiny claustrophobic town. There are eyes and ears everywhere."

In 1984 the fight between the first lady with her stepson Michael received a lot of press. For years there had been resentment and tensions brewing, but when Michael had been falsely accused by the Secret Service of stealing, for which it was later revealed he was innocent, the fight between the two escalated to the point where he and his family had been excluded from the family Thanksgiving plans.

Larry Speakes, President Reagan's press secretary wrote in his White House memoir *'Speaking Out,'* "There always seemed to be a controversy about when the Reagans had last seen the kids and who was coming for the holidays – *if anybody.*

Michael the only Reagan child who had children resented the fact that the president and first lady were involved in the grandparent program where he watched the president and first lady on television holding a child in their arms, reading to them, or showing them attention, when his own children the president's only grandchildren had been neglected by their grandparents. Michael knew of many times that Nancy had been near their home while on shopping trips and never stopped to visit him or his children. In fact, it was quite sometime before they even met their only granddaughter.

When Nancy announced to the world that she and the president were estranged from

Michael it caused an even greater rift between them. It would take a meeting with the president's pastor as mediator to sort the problems out. His sister Maureen had inserted herself into the problem forgetting about her own problems with her father and Nancy from the past. It seemed once he became president all was forgotten on her end. Maureen heard about the meeting and showed up in the pastor's office and told her brother she didn't care if they ever worked out their problems or if he ever got back with the family again.

Six year old Cameron and eighteen month old Ashley were at the meeting with their parents. That was the first time the president and first lady had ever laid eyes on their granddaughter. But the meeting was successful and they worked things out with Nancy apologizing for the first time in their relationship. Michael told his father, "You know, you've never told me that you love me." His father looked surprised but told his son, "Michael, I love you."

Problems from the past were repaired but people don't change overnight, if at all. The president and first lady were in their own world needing only each other to be complete which left their children feeling like outsiders. Michael was peeved when he read how Nancy said how wonderful it was to be a grandparent. Michael and his family lived in Los Angeles, a city the president and first lady often visited but never took the time to stop and see their own grandchildren.

Unfortunately that wasn't the end of the family problems. In the summer of 1986 the Reagan offspring were invited to the ranch for a BBQ for a special event. The White House photographer wanted some family photos. The Reagans were a family very removed from each other. Cameron, Michael's son was eight years old at the time and his daughter was three. Nancy leaned over and whispered to Michael asking what his kids called his mother. "Grandma," Michael answered. Nancy frowned and said, "They'll have to call me something else. How about they call me Nanny?" she asked. "I've had nannies," Michael answered, "and you aren't a nanny; and my son has known you as Grandma for eight years, even though he hasn't had the opportunity to call you that to your face." Nancy turned around and smiled for the cameraman and put on a front for the public and press.

All of the Reagan children wrote at least one book about their family. Michael was writing a book about his life and his family titled, *'On The Outside Looking In.'* He knew before the book was published he needed to forewarn his parents about what had happened to him when he was seven years old and had been sexually molested by a counselor at a summer camp. He had told no one until just recently when he broke down and told his wife, but as part of the healing process he wrote of it in his book.

At the age of seven a counselor he had trusted had molested him and took photographs of him. Michael had been ashamed and had carried his 'dirty secret' on his own shoulders for thirty-five years feeling he couldn't confide in anyone. He had been afraid if his father knew what had happened he would reject him. Michael knew he had to tell his parents before they read about it in the book or it was revealed in the press; but how do you tell something like that? He thought his father would be ashamed of him.

When he was invited to the ranch for a visit he knew this was the time to unburden himself and tell his father. Initially he tried to talk but couldn't get it out and instead began crying. When he was able to get the story out his father was shocked. Nancy was very comforting and they both stood by him. They were there for him when he really needed them and the burden he had carried on his own all these years was lifted. His family still loved him. That was all he ever wanted - their love.

The next step he knew would be to tell his mother Jane Wyman. And he needed to tell her soon before the book came out. Michael called his mother telling her he needed to talk to her in person. She responded that she was too busy and to just tell her whatever he had to say over the phone. Michael hung up.

The next time he spoke to his mother on the phone she told him she heard he had a book that was going to be published soon. What she said next hurt. She said, "I can't believe you have anything to say at this time in your life that's worth reading." Again when he told her he needed to see her she told him again she was too busy, so he told her over the phone. There was dead silence over the phone. When she did speak she said they needed to talk and she would call him in a few days. When she did call it was to cancel their plans to get together for Mother's Day.

Michael had never searched for his birth parents as he was afraid it would upset his parents, so when he finally decided to go ahead with the search he did so in part due to the fact he thought his children deserved to know their medical history and to know about their roots. He sent a letter to both his parents explaining what he was doing and why. He didn't hear back from his mother which was typical, but his father responded immediately helping him with his search by putting him in contact with someone who could help him. Michael wrote to the Department of Social Services who sent him a six page letter giving him insight into his parents, the circumstances of his adoption, and his parent's health history – but no names were included with the information.

Michael learned that his mother had actually met his birth mother who had answered many questions his mother had. His mother never told him about having met his birth mother, even now all these years later.

A strange thing happened. Michael received a call from a woman who had been a bridesmaid in his wedding to his first wife. She left a message that if he was interested in finding out about his birth family to give her a call. Out of curiosity to find out what she could possibly know he called her. She told him she had met a man while on a business trip who told her he was his half-brother. Michael was concerned that knowing who his father was perhaps this was a scam, so he gave her a list of questions to ask the man. She called Michael after speaking to him and it became apparent there was no doubt that this indeed was his half-brother. When they got together his half-brother told Michael how his mother had told him about his brother while on her death bed. The brothers had met in a private meeting and there was an instant bond between them. Michael finally found his roots and a brother who became a brother more than in name only.

Having received the information in the letter from Social Services he had discovered it hadn't been easy for his birth mother to give him up. He learned from his brother that she had passed away. He told Michael his mother knew who he was since even though names weren't exchanged at the time she met the woman who would adopt her son, she recognized her due to the fact that she was a famous movie star. She had followed her son through his life through articles written in newspapers and from television during the time of his father's presidency.

Maureen, just one of the Reagan's children to have written a book about her famous father threw herself into the fight against Alzheimers once her father appeared on national television announcing to the world that he had been diagnosed with the dreaded disease that destroys your memory. Before her work was done she was credited with raising $60 million for the Alzheimers Association. Two years later she was diagnosed with malignant melanoma the deadliest form of skin cancer. The disease spread throughout her body and she lost her fight and passed away in August of 2001.

At Maureen's funeral President of Uganda Yoweri Museveni spoke praising the former president's daughter for her interest in human rights in his country.

During Maureen's work in Uganda she and her husband Dennis met a young girl Rita Mirembe who they later adopted and brought back to the U.S. with them.

During her father's presidency Patti had publicly fought against everything her father stood for and wrote books exposing the dysfunctional Reagan family bringing their family problems to the attention of the nation. Eventually she would resolve those issues with her parents after learning her father was suffering from Alzheimers. Patti had written both novels and non-fiction books; some of which were not very well received from family members. At the end she was there for her parents; for her father as his mind slipped away and he forgot who his children were and for her mother to give her support during these trying times.

Michael has become a successful radio talk show host and publisher of the *Monthly Monitor* newsletter. He also maintains the Reagan Information Interchange and has written a few books himself.

Ron who was always the closest of the siblings to his parents once said, "Ronald and Nancy were in a circle that no one else could enter...not even their own children."

Ron was married to Doria for over thirty years who passed away in 2014 from complications from a progressive neuromuscular disease. He and his wife never had any children.

Ron has become a former talk radio host who hosted a syndicated late-night talk show for a time and a political analyst most noted for his liberal views, a contrast from his own father's views. He waited until his father left the White House to make his own political views known in order for it to not appear he was doing so because he and his father were on bad terms; which was not the case, he just had a different viewpoint from that of his father.

When friends of his he knew from his days in the ballet began dying of AIDS he helped produce a documentary on AIDS and became a spokesman to help fund the cause of AIDS research.

Ron lives in Seattle far removed from his other siblings. The siblings all reunited with their parents when they learned of the former president's battle against Alzheimers. The years of hurt feelings became inconsequential now. They stood by their mother and father when they needed them the most. Their father was losing his memories with his dementia and their mother was losing the love of her life.

When the former president passed away in 2004 there was a huge show of love and support from the American public who had not forgotten their president who had been one of the most popular presidents in American history. As the funeral motorcade made its way to the National Cathedral people stood by the roadside as they passed waving, some saluting, others visibly crying.

The month after his father's death Ron spoke at the Democratic National Convention about his support for embryonic stem cell research in hopes of a cure or treatment for those suffering with Alzheimers.

In 2011 Ron joined his siblings becoming the last of them to publish a book about his father titled, *'My Father At 100: A Memoir.'*

Ron seemed to accept his parents distance with equanimity. In a documentary about his father Ron observed, "In our house, there were Nancy and Ronnie – and then there were the rest of us." There was no resentment in his words, it's just the way it was.

41

GEORGE H. W. BUSH

Children of Barbara and George H.W. Bush:

George Walker Bush – Born: July 6, 1946   Still Living At The Time Of Publication

Pauline Robinson Bush "Robin" - Born: Dec 20, 1949   Died: Oct. 11, 1953

John Ellis Bush "Jeb" - Born: Feb 11, 1953   Still Living At The Time Of Publication

Neil Mallon Bush "Whit" - Born: Jan. 22, 1955   Still Living At The Time Of Publication

Marvin Pierce Bush – Born: Oct. 22, 1956   Still Living At The Time Of Publication

Dorothy Walker Bush "Doro" - Born: Aug. 18, 1959   Still Living At The Time Of Publication

George W. is the 2nd presidential son in American history to also become president.

George Herbert Walker Bush would become the last of the World War II presidents. He was the first vice president to become president himself since the nations 7th president Andrew Jackson in the year 1837.

George H.W. Bush graduated on his eighteenth birthday in 1942 and on the same day enlisted in the navy and served during WWII. During his stint in the war he became the youngest pilot in the navy.

George H.W. Bush's service in the military was complete and now at the age of twenty he returned to complete his education at Yale and married nineteen year old Barbara Pierce. George and Barbara Bush have now passed the record for the longest married presidential couple celebrating seventy plus years. Previously the record had been held by John and Abigail Adams who had set the record at fifty-four years.

The Bushes and Adams had something else in common. They were the only two presidents whose sons also became presidents.

While still a student at Yale their first child George W was born. After graduation the family moved to Odessa, Texas where George, Sr. learned the oil business. After a short time in Texas they picked up and moved out to California. Barbara was expecting their second child. She gave birth to a little girl they named Pauline Robinson in memory of Barbara's mother who had died in a car crash when Barbara was seven months pregnant. The little girl was always called Robin and her three year old brother George was very protective of his little sister. A few months after Robin was born the Bush family returned to live in Midland, Texas.

George W at age four already had quite a vocabulary, but not the typical vocabulary a parent would be proud of. He swore, was loud, and had quite a temper. One of his mother's ways to respond to his swearing as he was growing up was to wash his and his brothers' mouths out with soap when they used foul language - an act that would horrify mothers today.

Barbara had given birth in 1953 to their third child and second son John Ellis. He would always be called Jeb a name made up from his initials. Jeb was just a newborn when his parents learned of their young daughter Robin's illness. Barbara noticed three year old Robin was listless. She was usually so full of life that when she told her mother she thought she might just stay in bed all day her mother was concerned.

They paid a visit to their pediatrician to have Robin checked. The doctor gave her young patient an examination and had her blood drawn. The next day Barbara was told to return to the doctor's office with her husband but to leave Robin at home. Hearing this they feared what they were about to hear. The doctor told them their daughter had leukemia and had the highest white blood cell count she had ever seen. With compassion she told them the cancer was too advanced to treat. The doctor explained that Robin probably only had a few weeks to live and recommended they let nature take its course and let her die at home surrounded by her loving family.

Her father was unwilling just to give up without trying everything they could to save their little girl's life. They couldn't live with themselves if they didn't feel they had tried everything possible. At three years old her life had just begun. George's father had an uncle in New York who was president of Memorial Sloan-Kettering Cancer Center. They arranged to take her there to see if there was anything that could be done to save their daughter.

George and Barbara decided to keep the news of his sister dying from her brother George W. When it came to his little sister he was gentle and loving. They knew he would take it hard. He knew she was sick but wasn't aware of just how sick when his parents flew her to Memorial Sloan-Kettering Hospital.

Jeb was left as a newborn and spent the better part of the first year of his life being raised by a housekeeper, neighbors, and family friends while his mother was in New York caring for her dying daughter. With very limited contact with either parent and being passed around like a football in a game of scrimmage Jeb as an infant had no one to bond with.

Robin was admitted at the Memorial Sloan-Kettering Cancer Center where she would remain for the next seven months going through tests and treatments. Barbara remained with her daughter while her father flew back and forth fitting in work and checking on his two sons left behind.

Barbara felt she had to remain strong in Robin's company and wouldn't allow anyone to cry in front of the little girl. Her mother held Robin's hand as she received blood transfusions and was by her side through all the tests she had to endure. Barbara who was only twenty-eight at the time was going prematurely gray.

The day came when George received a call from the hospital to come immediately. He flew all night but by the time he arrived Robin had slipped into a coma. Both her mother and her father were with her when she passed away. Her mother said, "One minute she was there, and the next she was gone."

George and Barbara held their little girl one last time. Barbara combed Robin's hair and they said their good-byes.

The day following their daughter's death Barbara and George went golfing. Today people just shake their heads in amazement when they hear that and ask themselves, *'Who does that sort of thing?'*

There was no funeral or any type of memorial service for Robin. Her parents signed papers donating her body for research in hopes it would help other families not to have to endure the same pain they were going through. They were in hopes by this act a cure could be found for this disease that struck young children.

Eventually little Robin's body would be laid to rest in a cemetery in New York. In the year 2000 they had her moved to the future final resting place where her parents, former President George H.W. Bush and former First Lady Barbara Bush, will also be buried upon their deaths at the George H.W. Bush Presidential Library.

George W was at school when he saw his parent's car drive up having returned from New York and rushed out to see his parents and his sister Robin. But Robin wasn't with them. "That's when we told him," Barbara said. "In the car."

It had been just a month and a half before her fourth birthday when Robin died of leukemia. When told by his parents that she was gone he asked them, "Why didn't you tell me?" He never had a chance to say good-bye.

George W was only seven at the time and his little brother Jeb was only a few months old. His parents were in their late twenties having to face the deepest loss of their life.

After Robin's death her father said, "We learned the true meaning of grief when Robin died."

His father was often away with work and his mother was suffering from depression. George W did what he could to make his mother smile or laugh. Many close to the family see this as a pivotal point in forming George W's personality and how he would respond with stress and pain throughout his life.

Two years later Neil was born giving George W and Jeb another brother. Marvin was born the following year. It would be another three years before Doro arrived completing their family.

George W never had the relationship with his brothers and younger sister that he had previously with Robin. He would bully his younger brothers around.

George W's favorite past time was baseball. He would one day become the first president to have been in the Little Leagues. He had been a catcher on the local Little League team. He was a bad sport though and when his team wasn't winning he would swear and want to quit.

George W ran with an unruly bunch of boys who appeared to have little parental supervision. There was a gully that when it rained was full of frogs. George W and his friends would shoot the frogs with their BB guns and once put a firecracker in a frog's mouth, threw it, and watched it blow up.

George W attended public school from grade school through junior high. He would never be noted for being a good student. Not only didn't he take his studies seriously, but he was a cut-up and had the reputation as the class clown. He became a frequent visitor at the principal's office. His parents thought perhaps he would do better at The Kinkaid School which was a prep school.

Left as a newborn when his sister was dying wouldn't be the only time in his life Jeb was left with others to raise. George Sr. as president of the oil company the Zapata Offshore Company moved to Houston in 1959 leaving six-year old Jeb, four year old Neil, and three year old Marvin along with the family dog with a babysitter in Midland, Texas. George W was away at prep school. Their parents lived in an apartment in Houston for four months with their kids left behind back in Midland.

Dorothy Walker or Doro was born after her parents moved to Houston. Her father ever since they had lost Robin had longed for another little girl.

At the age of thirteen George W attended the Kinkaid School while his parents were in Houston. He attended the school for two years until one day his mother informed him he would be attending Andover an exclusive school halfway across the country in Massachusetts. Andover is a prestigious boarding school that ranks at the top of schools in America. The yearly cost are equivalent to attending an Ivy League college.

Andover excelled in academics but George W struggled to keep up. He had a difficult time even passing the basic requirements and would end up graduating near the bottom of his class.

When George W was in his early teens he had attended events with his father and learned people skills by watching his father when he was working on a political race. He noticed how his father gave the person he was speaking to his undivided attention and would remember people's names. This left an indelible impression on George W. He also would learn people's names and use the same listening skills. These skills made him popular amongst the other students at school.

George W could be quite entertaining. He convinced his fellow students during lunch one day to have a contest to see who could use a knife to fling a pat of butter at the wall and make it stick. He had a knack for making people laugh. He was the quintessential party boy.

George W tried out for sports but spent the majority of the time sitting the bench. When he was called up to play one day he had a different viewpoint from one of the referee's calls that angered him so much he threw the ball at a player on the other team. George W was ejected from the game as he continued with his poor sportsmanship that had remained with him since he was younger. Never very good in athletics but enjoying the camaraderie of the jocks he became head cheerleader during his senior year of high school.

A slacker in his studies George W became interested in American history after being inspired by one of his professors. George W gave Professor Lyons credit for his interest and chose history as his major in college. While he may have picked history as his major he showed a complete lack of interest in what was going on in the world around him. History was being made right in front of his eyes, but he appeared to have no interest. This was during the time of the Cuban Missile Crisis, racial unrest, and the Vietnam War; but George W was impervious to the national events that was consuming the minds of the other students.

When it came time to apply for colleges George W had his mind set on attending Yale even though his grades were barely passing and would not have attracted the interest of a school such as Yale. The dean at Andover tried to convince George W to apply elsewhere as a backup plan. Amazingly enough he was accepted at Yale; not due to his grades as they didn't reach the expectation of an Ivy League school, especially one as notable as

Yale; but due to the fact that his father and grandfather were alumni. Name and privilege paved the way for him opening doors for him that otherwise would have been slammed shut.

Before entering Yale George W would spend his summer working on his father's campaign for the Senate. This experience more than anything served him in the future for when his father ran for the presidency and when he himself ran for governor and the presidency. George W took time off at Yale to return home in November to be with the family for the election results. When his father lost the election George W broke down sobbing. Losing was not something the Bush family was accustomed to.

George W was one of Yale's most popular students. He was a poor student but majored in partying. His grades averaged in the low 70's and he was in the bottom fifth of his class. But it was his swagger and personality that appealed to his fellow students. He never would have been voted 'Most Likely To Succeed', but he was good for entertainment.

Like his father before him he became a member of the exclusive Skull and Bones Club which is considered the most secret society in America. In addition to his father, William Taft another past president had also been a member.

George W while in college was arrested while he and some frat brothers, all drunk at the time, decided to steal a Christmas wreath to decorate their dorm The Deke House. George W and his friends were taken to the police station and charged with disorderly conduct until a friend of the Bush family stepped in and charges were dropped. That however would not be his last intimate acquaintance with the law. During his senior year while attending the Yale/Princeton game he became one of the spectators who following the game attempted to destroy the vintage wooden goalposts. George W was sitting on the crossbar still attempting to tear off a piece when the police arrived and caught him in the act.

Fourteen year old Jeb remained behind in Houston in the care of family friends when his parents moved to Washington. From there he was sent to attend Phillips Academy at Andover boarding school.

When once questioned as to why his parents were constantly leaving their children with neighbors, friends, and babysitters, Jeb a bit touchy on the subject replied, "At least we weren't put in a kennel." His father was a distant figure in his life growing up. He was either off on business traveling or campaigning. This family closeness that Barbara Bush always tried to portray just wasn't a reality – but sounded good politically.

With his father gone so much of the time it was up to their mother to be the disciplinarian and with four boys she had plenty of practice. Jeb called her "The Enforcer."

Neil, the third son of the Bushes was described as one of the nicest kids in school. In fact, his brothers called him "Mr. Perfect" as he was growing up. He was the one in the family who was least likely to suffer the disciplinary wrath of their mother. Neil described his mother as an advocate of corporal punishment and said she would "slap around" the Bush children. She was the one in the family who instilled fear in her children; not their father.

Doro was described by her brothers as thoughtful and always thinking of others. She was eight-years old when her parents moved to Washington after her father had been elected to Congress. While living in Washington Barbara was heavily involved in the social and political life. Her children had mostly been sent off to boarding schools, but Doro who was in the fourth grade at the time was living at home.

Barbara was hardly ever around for her children. Doro was pretty much on her own at eight-years old. When she had problems with her schoolwork it would be the mothers of her friends who were there to help her, not her own mother. For a woman who later in life as first lady would claim literacy as her platform it seemed an unusual pick considering the fact that as her children were growing up when their house should have been filled with books there were none to be found.

The mother of one of Doro's friends, who found Doro in her care quite often, described Barbara as being detached from her children. As a mother herself she couldn't understand that Barbara concerned herself more with Washington's social life than caring for her children or seeing that their needs were met. In other words, she found Barbara to be "less than a devoted mother."

While attending St. Albans School in Washington Neil was diagnosed with suffering with dyslexia which made it difficult for him in his studies. Even so, he was able to enroll in Tulane with yet again the influence of the Bush name.

Three years after moving to Washington George H.W. Bush was appointed by President Nixon as U.S. Ambassador to the United Nations. When her parents made the move to

New York Doro moved with them. They lived at the U.N. ambassador's residence at the Waldorf Astoria Hotel.

Jeb, like his older brother George W and his father had before him, attended Phillips Academy. It was here he had to repeat ninth grade and was nearly expelled due to poor grades. The school had a zero tolerance ban on drugs and alcohol. Jeb was using marijuana and hashish at this time. He would have been expelled if it weren't for the intervention of his father. By his senior year he had improved his grades enough to find his name on the honor roll.

Marvin the youngest son attended Andover and he like his brother Jeb also had to repeat the ninth grade. The following year Marvin along with some friends were caught doing drugs. While his friends were expelled, his father stepped in and Marvin was allowed to stay at the school to complete his sophomore year. At the end of the school year he was sent to Woodberry Forest School an all-male boarding school. He attended Woodberry Forest School until he graduated in 1975 and from there went on to the University of Virginia where he graduated with a B.A. degree in English.

After graduating Marvin worked for Shearson, Lehman Brothers and then John Steward Darrel & Company along with a few other jobs until he eventually founded his own investment firm Winston Partners, L.P. Marvin stayed out of politics.

George W for most of his life seemed lost with no direction and no idea of what to do with himself. Up to this point in his life he had excelled only in partying. With only a week before graduation and a looming threat of being shipped off to Vietnam George W flew to Houston to meet with Lieutenant Colonel "Buck" Staudt who was Commander of the 147th Fighter Group of the Texas Air National Guard. With graduation directly ahead of him the odds were great that he would be sent to fight in the Vietnam War.

With graduation looming George W determined that being a part of the National Guard was his best option to keep him from being sent overseas. He wasn't the only one to think so, as the waiting list to get into the National Guard was over a year and a half long wait; but it is assumed the Bush family pulled strings to put George W at the top of the list. At the time he was the son of a congressman and the grandson of a former senator.

George W graduated in 1968 with a B.A. degree. He graduated with a C average. Years later when he was president Yale announced they would be giving him an honorary degree. Over two hundred furious members of the Yale faculty signed a petition protesting the honor declaring it was undeserved from such a "mediocre man."

George W himself admitted, "I was never a great intellectual." That's probably one of the smartest and most humble statements he ever made.

George W was admitted into the National Guard after graduation just twelve days away from losing his student draft deferment. He was admitted the same day he applied avoiding the normal year and a half long waiting list.

Being admitted into the National Guard ahead of everyone else on the waiting list isn't where his preferential treatment ended either. He skipped Officer Candidate School but still received a special commission as a 2nd Lieutenant, regardless of the fact that he didn't have the qualifications. That commission enabled him to get into flight school regardless of his low scores. He scored 25% on a pilot aptitude test; the absolute lowest acceptable grade and 50% for navigator aptitude.

George W skipped all his medical exams once they began testing for drugs which included a nasal cavities exam for cocaine use. A month after the random drug testing was announced Bush stopped attending Guard duty and was removed from flight status.

George W failed to show up for a year – there are no records to be found that he attended drills or service for nearly a year, but yet received an honorable discharge and then ended his service almost a year early in order to attend Harvard Business School.

George W at twenty-seven years of age didn't take his studies at Harvard any more serious than he had anything else in his life to this point. He sat in class flying paper airplanes around the room spitting tobacco juice in a cup with his cowboy boots propped up on his desk. His grades reflected how serious he took his studies – they were mediocre at best.

After miraculously graduating from Harvard with a business degree George W returned to Texas and with the aid of his father found work in the oil business. It would be with his father's help that got him every job he ever had; and even with his family name and connections which helped him in his election of governor of Texas and the presidency.

Now away in high school Jeb at the age of seventeen was involved in Andover's student exchange summer program. He was sent to Guanajuato, Mexico where he taught English as a second language and assisted in the building of a school in Ibarrilla. This is where and when he met his future wife Columba. He was seventeen and she was sixteen when they met. She was the first and only girl he ever dated.

This was a time when the country was sending troops over to Vietnam and Jeb at eighteen pulled a low lottery number in the draft. Panicking when he saw his number was #26 he confided in his parents that he was considering becoming a conscientious objector. Perhaps having second thoughts he went ahead and had his physical and with a loud sigh of relief the draft ended one day before Jeb could have been called.

Jeb instead of following in his father and brother's footsteps and attending Yale chose to attend the University of Texas. Jeb would graduate Phi Beta Kappa and magna cum laude with a B.A. in Latin American studies. The days of having to repeat a grade well behind him he completed college in two and a half years.

Jeb would be the first of the Bush children to marry and the first to have children. Jeb married Columba in 1974 four years after they met. He was fluent in Spanish but his wife spoke no English.

Jeb's parents were concerned when their son announced he was marrying a young Mexican woman who didn't speak English. He had never even dated anyone else. Jeb converted to Catholicism when he married his wife. His parents didn't meet her until the day of the wedding.

In 1974 President Nixon resigned after the Watergate scandal came to light and President Gerald Ford offered George H.W. Bush his pick of several diplomatic posts. George chose the position of Chief of the U.S. Liaison Office in the People's Republic of China.

When George and Barbara Bush left for China their daughter was left behind. She along with brothers George W, Neil, and Marvin paid their parents a visit in China in June of 1975. It was unusual for the family to all be together as they basically grew up in other parts of the country separate from their parents as they were each shipped off to different boarding schools. For a change they were all together; with the exception of Jeb who was already married at the time. It was Doro's 16th birthday and she had never been baptized and even though the Chinese government banned freedom of worship to their own countrymen Doro became the first person to ever be publicly baptized in the People's Republic of China since the days the Communist party took over the country back in

1949.

Doro was a sweet but shy girl. Many years of her life she may have felt like an only child with her brothers away at boarding schools and basically only spending time with them holidays and summers at the family home in Kennebunkport, Maine. Doro too would be sent away to school. She attended Miss Porter's School which was a private all-girl's school in Connecticut. This is an excellent school that had such famous alumna as: Jackie Kennedy Onassis, Gloria Vanderbilt, Princess Anastasia of Greece and Denmark, the Rockefeller daughters, and another presidential daughter Nellie Grant daughter of President Ulysses S. Grant.

After his marriage Jeb went to work in an entry-level position in the international division of Texas Commerce Bank. The job was given to him by a friend of his fathers. Three years later in 1977 he was sent to Caracas, Venezuela to serve as a branch manager and vice president. From entry level to vice president in three years was quite a coup.

Neil graduated from Tulane University. He had earned undergraduate and graduate degrees in international relations and business administration. He then followed in his father's example by going into the oil business; not in Texas however, but in Denver, Colorado.

In 1976 George W's drinking and partying caught up with him when he was visiting the family's home in Kennebunkport, Maine and was arrested for DUI.

George W had reached the age of thirty when his father confided in a friend, Washington attorney Gene Theorous, that he feared his son would never amount to much. At this point, George W seemed all too eager to prove his father right.

George W met Laura and three months after they met they were married. They were both thirty-one years of age and neither had been married before. She was a school teacher and a librarian and they were as different as two people could be. Not only were they complete opposites in personality; but she was a registered Democrat.

A short time after the marriage George W ran unsuccessfully for the House of Representatives. Even though he lost the campaign it was a way of introducing his name and intentions into the political arena.

Laura and George W at age thirty-four found themselves to be expectant parents after years of trying unsuccessfully to have a child. She smoked two packs of cigarettes a day. She had been told it was doubtful she would ever conceive. With the aid of a fertility doctor their wait was over just as they had completed papers so they could adopt a child. They discovered they were expecting twins when they went in for a sonogram test. The pregnancy was difficult and Laura developed toxemia and was hospitalized during her last trimester. The twin girls were born five weeks early but were in good health. The twins were named after their maternal and paternal grandmothers: Jenna and Barbara.

A married man in his mid-thirties and father of two little girls George W was still drinking heavily. His drinking was out of control and causing problems not only in his marriage but with his family. For a time his own mother stopped speaking to him. His family didn't want to be around him when he was drinking and his wife gave him an ultimatum – *several times, with no success.*

In the days before he gave up drinking at the age of forty George W became a born-again Christian during the time his father was vice president. Even so, it didn't appear to be enough to change his ways. He continued his drinking and obnoxious ways and one member of the church he attended described George W's lifestyle as un-Christian.

It would be almost a decade after George W and Laura's marriage before he finally gave up drinking. When later asked what finally made him give it up he said, "I'm afraid I might do something to embarrass my father."

Marvin married his wife Margaret in the year 1981. When Margaret was only five years old she had been diagnosed with a rare form of ovarian cancer. While she survived the cancer she had to have her ovaries removed and was unable to have children.

In 1984 just a few years after their marriage, Marvin who was twenty-eight years of age, athletic, and in good shape began having serious abdominal pains and began losing a lot of weight. He was diagnosed with ulcerative colitis. Initially, he attempted to just live with the disease being treated with medication and watching his diet, but he kept getting worse.

He returned to the hospital in 1986 with internal bleeding and having lost thirty pounds. He had emergency surgery where part of his colon was removed and created a colostomy. He would have to undergo a second surgery the following year removing his entire colon. This was a life saving surgery. Afterward he became a spokesperson for the Crohn's and

Colitis Foundation.

Marvin and Margaret adopted two children. The family lives in Alexandria, Virginia.

Doro would go on to attend and graduate in 1982 from Boston College with a degree in sociology. The same year she graduated she married William "Billy" LeBlond and worked as a bookkeeper in her husband's construction business. They had two children before they divorced in 1990.

When George H.W. Bush ran for the presidency George W moved his family to Washington to work on his father's campaign. He served in the capacity of campaign adviser and even though he was the son of the presidential candidate he received $5,000 a month plus expenses.

In 1980 Jeb moved to Florida and began a career in real estate development. In 1986 he became Florida's Secretary of Commerce where he served until the year 1988 when he joined his father's campaign for the presidency; where unlike his brother George W who was paid well for his work on the campaign, Jeb worked as an unpaid volunteer. Neil also worked on his father's campaign. It was while he was working on the campaign that Neil met and married Sharon Smith.

By now George H.W. Bush had made a name for himself in Washington after serving as congressman from Texas, Ambassador to the United Nations, Chief U.S. Liaison in China, Director of the C.I.A., Chairman of the Republican Party, and vice president under President Reagan. He won the election and would become the nation's 41st president.

At the time of George H.W. Bush's inauguration all of his children were adults. None of the children would live in the White House during their father's presidency, but a few years later presidential son George W would also become president and take up residence in the White House.

On the day of his father's inauguration George W rose before dawn and walked down the uninhabited route of what would be the inaugural parade down Pennsylvania Avenue. The streets that were deserted now would be filled with thousands of spectators in just a matter of hours.

George W and family, along with his brothers, his sister, and their families all attended their father's inauguration along with several inaugural balls that evening.

George W had worked on his father's campaign, but now that his father had been elected president that left George W at loose ends unsure of what to do with himself. George W and his family moved back home to Texas.

Marvin, the least political son of the bunch, was the only son not involved in his father's first presidential election due to his medical problems. When his father ran for re-election he spent some time campaigning with the other family members.

At the end of his father's presidential election Jeb and his family moved to Miami where he resumed his work in real estate. In the past he spread out his interests in his desire to become a millionaire spreading himself thin by not only working in real estate but also selling shoes and working for a mobile phone company. He had now became a minority owner of the Jacksonville Jaguars a professional football team and was involved in a project selling water pumps in Nigeria. Some of the people he became involved with in his business ventures were unscrupulous with questionable character.

Neil was looked on for a time as the one in the family most likely to succeed. He had the brains of the family and he had the looks. He was the best public speaker in the family. If his father had secretly hoped Neil would follow in his footsteps one day those dreams came to a screeching halt in 1988 about the time his father was about to become president. Neil's name was all over the news and making headlines connecting him with the Silverado Savings and Loan that went bankrupt with Neil as director. He would eventually be cleared of any wrongdoing, but his name had been tainted with being involved in the investigation and being one of the higher-ups.

Neil now also lives in Texas where he moved in the early 1990's. He initially worked as an investment consultant arranging international contracts. He has developed a reading program for youngsters called Ignite! which is an alternative educational program. The program is set up to aid children with dyslexia and attention deficit disorder.

Able to raise over $20 million in the educational software start-up Neil himself admitted, "I probably have access to people who probably wouldn't meet with a development-stage company." Again, having the name Bush and his father's influence behind him certainly didn't hurt any.

Rice University Professor Bob Stein said, "There is a family pattern here where the Bush sons - Jeb, Neil, and George W – have benefited tremendously by their connections through their father."

When Doro divorced her first husband she moved back to Washington with her two children to be close to her parents. The first lady however would not allow her daughter and grandchildren to move into the White House so Doro rented a small house in Bethesda, Maryland. She found work at the National Rehabilitation Hospital.

Doro met Robert Koch a former aide to House Democratic Leader Richard Gephardt. They married in 1992 at Camp David. She is the only presidential offspring to have had her wedding take place at Camp David.

The wedding was held in the chapel which is simple and rustic. When the bride and groom knelt at the altar during the wedding ceremony the guests began laughing. The bride and groom were puzzled as to what their guests found funny during such a solemn event. Someone, most likely one of her prankster brothers, had put Bush/Quayle '92 stickers on the soles of the groom's shoes.

Doro already a mother of two had two more children with her second husband. Doro and her family live in Bethesda, Maryland. She serves along with her brother Jeb as co-chair of the Barbara Bush Foundation for Family Literacy.

Doro is personable with a sense of humor and has been involved in the campaigns of her father and brother's presidential campaigns. To date that is six presidential campaigns between her father and George W's election and re-election campaigns and two unsuccessful presidential campaigns for her brother Jeb.

Doro has written a book about her father titled, *'My Father, My President: A Personal Account of the Life of George H.W. Bush.'*

Doro is a founding partner in BB&R Wellness Consulting and she studies with a Western teacher of Buddhist meditation.

George W a baseball fan all his life learned that the Texas Rangers were up for sale and he along with some friends invested in the team becoming part owner. He became managing general partner. It was his face that was seen by the public as the owner of the baseball team. He attended nearly three hundred home games sitting by the dugout amongst the fans. On Opening Day his father the president would always be there to throw out the first pitch.

George W served as managing general partner for five years, but what he really desired was to be baseball commissioner. That offer was never put on the table and eventually he sold his share of the team.

George W again worked on his father's campaign for re-election for the presidency. His father lost the election after losing a lot of support due to breaking a campaign promise of not raising taxes. People have long memories and did not forget him saying, "Read my lips: no new taxes."

Jeb having the same desire to become involved in politics as his father ran for governor of Florida in 1994. It was the same year his brother George W became governor of Texas; but while his brother George W won his election, Jeb did not. Four years later he would try again and this time won the election. Then again in the year 2002 he ran again for reelection becoming Florida's first two-term Republican governor.

During George W's campaign for governor of Texas in an attempt to reach out to Texas hunters he went on a dove hunt. Instead of shooting doves he ended up shooting a protected species of songbird and was fined and publicly embarrassed. But George W had a way of owning his mistake and making a joke of himself saying, "Thank goodness it wasn't deer season. I might have shot a cow." This was the side of George W that endeared him to the people.

George W won the election for governor. George W and Jeb would become the first brothers to be simultaneous governors since the Rockefellers. Both brothers had their sites set on a higher office; they both wished to follow in their father's footsteps and become president. Again, George W would win his election and his re-election; twice Jeb lost his bid for the presidency.

Newly elected Governor George W Bush and family would now make their home in Austin in the Governor's Mansion. His twin daughters were thirteen years old. Four years later he would be reelected. Behind closed doors, people many of which were his father's political allies, were already pushing him to run for the presidency. While Laura never showed her reluctance in his running for the presidency in public, in private she did question her husband if that was what he really wanted to do. She would have been just as happy digging in the dirt and working in her garden at home, but she supported her husband's decision.

When it was announced that George W Bush was running for the presidency classmates from Yale said George W was the last guy you'd ever expect to see in the White House. The memory they had of him was not as a good student or someone you would take seriously, or someone you would expect to have a bright future, but as a guy that drank a lot and was just out for a good time. Stories came out from other students who had attended Yale with him admitting to having sold him cocaine or doing coke with him.

Even so he was a Bush and that was enough for some people thinking 'the acorn didn't fall far from the tree' in hopes that he was an extension of his father. While George W certainly wasn't a mirror image of his father there were many similarities: They both attended Andover and then Yale, they were both members of Skull and Bones Club, his father flew an Avenger over the Pacific in WWII while George W flew an F-102 Interceptor Jet in the Air National Guard during the Vietnam War, they were both in the oil business, his father had been an All-American playing on Yale's baseball team while George W was part owner of the Texas Rangers baseball team, his father ran a mile a day as president while George W ran three miles when he was president. The only time son surpassed his father is when he was elected to a second term of office; whereas his father lost his bid for reelection. It appeared George W with no clear path of his own had spent his life attempting to follow in his father's footsteps.

November 7th on election night the Bush family gathered together to wait for the results. It appeared for a time that Al Gore was about to become the nation's next president. The hold up was Florida, a state with his own brother Jeb as governor that should have easily gone to George W; but it was back and forth first being announced that the state had gone to Gore then to Bush. But then Florida was declared to Bush and at 2:00 A.M. the networks declared Bush the nation's next president.

Al Gore made the call and conceded. But then again, it was announced Florida was back and forth – a race too close too call. Less than two hours after Al Gore had made the call to concede he called back and retracted his concession.

The wait to discover who would be the next president continued for the next thirty-six days as Florida had a recount. It finally took a ruling from the Supreme Court before George W Bush was announced as the winner of the presidential race. He would become only the second son of a former president to also become a president; an event in history that had not occurred since our 6th president John Quincy Adams became president. Still to this day some argue that George W. Bush stole the presidency. But like it or not it wasn't the popular vote that won him the presidency. This was the fourth time in history a president won the election after not receiving the most popular votes but by electoral votes. The last time this occurred was in 1888 when Benjamin Harrison won the presidency. It would happen again in 2016 when Donald Trump won the presidency.

George hadn't even been in politics for seven years when he was elected president. If that surprised some, they would be even more amazed with the 44th president Obama who would follow George W Bush into office with even less experience or time served in politics. And the election after Obama was elected president, Donald Trump would assume office after having *never* served a single day in politics.

Jeb's wife has always hated being involved in a political family and wanted no part of it. She was nowhere to be found when he was campaigning either for governor or president. Unhappy as she was to be involved in a political family she certainly hasn't minded the benefits of being a part of the Bush family. She has very expensive taste in clothing and jewelry. In the year 2000 she took out a loan spending over $42,000 in a single day on jewelry. The *Washington Post* discovered that wasn't the only day she was such a spendthrift. At the same store where she purchased the jewelry she had spent over $90,000 over a fourteen year period of time.

It was in 1999 when Columba embarrassed her husband Jeb then governor of Florida when she flew back into the country after a shopping spree in Paris. It made all the newspapers how she *"misled"* Customs agents about the amount of money she spent on the items she purchased on her shopping trip claiming the items value to be $500 when she had actually spent $19,000.

George W, a presidential son, was about to become the 43rd president and on inauguration day Laura Bush held the same Bible used by George Washington, and the same Bible his father and several other presidents used when they took the oath of office. The president and first lady attended nine inaugural balls that evening but still made it back to the White House before midnight.

George W had only been president for eight months when the September 11 terrorists attacks occurred on American soil, a name came to be known as 9/11. In response George W launched what he called a War on Terror which included the war in Afghanistan and in 2001 the war in Iraq.

George W won his reelection for the presidency and unlike his father he would serve for two terms. After leaving the White House he and Laura returned to live in Texas where he wrote his memoirs *'Decision Points.'*

Since leaving the White House George W has taken up oil painting. He has painted portraits of world leaders, family members, and two self portraits of himself in the shower and bathtub that wound up displayed on the internet.

Marvin until the year 2000 served on the board of directors for Securacom, a company which maintained security for the World Trade Center Towers. After the September 11, 2001 terrorist attacks Securacom and Marvin Bush were severely criticized in the media.

Neil has three children with his wife Sharon. Neil one day sent his wife of twenty-three years an email informing her he wanted a divorce. What he failed to mention is he had been having an affair with a woman who worked for his mother. After the divorce, Sharon who had been a member of the Bush family for over two decades was shunned by her former in-laws.

The divorce turned rather ugly and disclosed some facts about Neil the Bush family would have rather had never been revealed.

He was having an affair with Maria Andrews the married wife of Houston oil baron Robert Andrews. At the same time Neil was divorcing his wife Maria was also notifying her husband she wanted a divorce. The two of them later married. Sharon accused Neil and his brother Marvin of using cocaine at Camp David during their father's presidency. It was also disclosed that Neil had enjoyed the company of a couple of prostitutes when he was traveling in Asia.

Jeb is the father of three children: George P, Jeb Jr, and Noelle. All three of his children have been arrested.

Jeb was a man with a goal. He set a goal and worked hard and reached his goal. He was a millionaire by the time he was thirty-five. Having met his goal to become rich - what he now desired was power.

Jeb is an introvert and says about himself, "I am kind of antisocial." But when running for office he pushed himself to step out of his comfort zone and became a polished candidate; yet he came across as stiff and disingenuous. He had the family name and felt it was his for the asking. But the destiny he had felt all he had to do was ask for was out of his grasp. Twice he ran for the presidency and twice failed, not even becoming the Republican nominee – not even coming close. Where he failed, it is assumed his son George P. is now being groomed for the next generation of the Bush dynasty.

For a man who used the platform of the importance of family life, Jeb was not one to have a handle on family. Regardless of how the Bushes have always tried to portray themselves as "a close family" they really are clueless as to what that really means.

As Jeb was growing up his parents never put their children first. They were often farmed out to family and friends or sent off to boarding schools as they had places to go and things to do. Houston, Washington, New York, China.

Jeb at fourteen had been left behind with family friends and then sent off to boarding school. Jeb's two oldest children would also be sent off to prep schools and the youngest sent to boarding school. Their father was busy campaigning; all the while espousing to other parents the importance of time with their children and having dinner together as a family. With his own son in a boarding school four hundred miles away there weren't too many family dinners being shared. When Jeb spoke at "Family Day" at the Capitol and was questioned by a journalist if he wished he had spent more time with his own children as they were growing up, Jeb chose to walk away rather than answer the question.

Jeb's political dreams put undue stress on his marriage and family. His marriage was struggling. His teenage daughter Noelle was on drugs and his sons Jebby and George P were out of control. His wife blamed Jeb and his political dreams.

All three of Jeb's children were arrested at one time or another: shoplifting, drugs, sexual misconduct, breaking and entering, public intoxication, resisting arrest. When you can't control your own family are you really in a position to try to run a country? But Jeb had always thought he would be the one to follow in his father's footsteps and become president.

Jeb had the mentality that "Some are born to rule, while others are born to follow." He has an elitist attitude and feels his privilege is owed him.

In his unsuccessful attempt at the presidency for the second time in 2016 he pledged on national television that he would endorse the Republican candidate left standing at the end. Initially there were seventeen candidates, and then there was one – Donald Trump. In the end Jeb refused to be a man of his word and refused to endorse Trump or to vote for him.

Bill Paterson, chairman of the St. Lucie County/Republican Party called Jeb's public opposition to Trump "a shame" that will be difficult for many to forgive. Not learning from his own father's error when he wasn't a man of his word, ("Read my lips...no new taxes), Jeb has now done the same. "He welshed on a promise that he made and that's never a good sign," said Paterson. A man is as good as his word, and he has proven to not be a man of his word - *and that is how he will be remembered.*

Little has been seen or heard of from the former President George W Bush since his retirement from office, but he was seen in July of 2016 along with President Obama and First Lady Michelle Obama at a Dallas policeman's memorial service honoring five slain police officers. His actions at the somber affair left many in disbelief and shaking their heads at his totally inappropriate behavior. This was a 'memorial service,' a very serious matter where George W was seen turning around from his front pew and making faces at the press in the back of the church. Then later while on stage he was holding hands with his wife the former First Lady Laura Bush and First Lady Michelle Obama during a rendition of *'The Battle Hymn of the Republic'* all while former President George W was on stage smirking and dancing. Even Laura couldn't control his antics this time.

If George W's actions at the Dallas memorial wasn't bad enough, the *entire* Bush family angered a vast majority of the Republican people who had put both George W and his father George H.W. into office when both former presidents along with brother Jeb, who had officially agreed on national television that he would back the Republican nominee, then refused to do so.

It became public knowledge that the Bush family were voting for Democratic nominee Hillary Clinton instead of the nominee from their own party Republican candidate Donald Trump. The Bushes lost the respect and admiration of many Americans by this act and may very well have lost any chance of any future Bush running for office to not be held accountable. As voters proved in the past when George H.W. Bush wasn't re-elected after breaking his campaign promise of "no new taxes," voters may prove yet again just how long their memories are and how long they can hold a grudge that any future Bush with political aspirations may very well inherit.

42

Bill Clinton

Child of Bill and Hillary Clinton

Chelsea Victoria Clinton: Born: Feb. 27, 1980   Still Living At Time Of Publication

Alleged Illegitimate Child of Bill Clinton and Black Prostitute Bobbie Ann Williams

Danney Williams: Born: Dec 7, 1985   Still Living At Time Of Publication

Chelsea was taught to drive by the president at Camp David in an armored Secret Service car.

Bill Clinton was forty-six when he was sworn in as the 42nd president in 1993; which made him the second youngest elected president. The youngest was his hero John F. Kennedy.

Chelsea was the only child of Bill and Hillary Clinton. She was born and raised in Little Rock, Arkansas; the only home she would know until she moved to Washington when her father was elected president.

Chelsea while growing up in Little Rock attended public schools. She was an exceptionally smart little girl who skipped the third grade.

The Clintons indoctrinated their daughter when she was only six years of age to the dark side of politics. Facing Bill's reelection campaign for governor they were only too aware of some of the stories that may come out. Being of school age they knew it was only a matter of time before word would spread to their daughter and they were concerned of what she may hear about her father. Her mother and father sat her down and explained they were going to play a game.

It was explained that during the campaign her father's enemies and political opponents may say terrible things. Her mother and father would get in Chelsea's face and say harsh things about her father and shake their fingers in her face. Chelsea ran from the room in tears, but regardless her parents were relentless in their "game playing." They would continue with this for weeks on end while their six-year old daughter dissolved into tears.

Hillary explained their actions as role-playing so Chelsea would be aware of what it felt like to have someone you love attacked - *anyone else would have described it as mental or child abuse.* Her parents kept at her until they felt she had become hardened to the attacks and she had learned to hide her feelings and show no emotion.

Chelsea while still in elementary school would confide in friends about her parents. "They yell at each other a lot," Chelsea said at eight years of age. She could hear her parents screaming and fighting with each other while she hid in her room as they screamed and threw things close by. Her parents were either oblivious or unconcerned as to how their fighting was affecting their daughter.

Chelsea's parents were busy people with her father as governor of Arkansas and her mother as the first lady of Arkansas and the first woman partner in The Rose Law Firm. The Clintons pushed their daughter from an early age to become independent.

While thirteen years of age and in the seventh grade after reading an article in a Science class about the cruelty towards cattle in slaughterhouses and of the harmful effects red meat has on the body, Chelsea made the decision to become a vegetarian. She remained a vegetarian up until the time she was married.

When her father was elected president Chelsea who had been born and raised in Little Rock, Arkansas moved to Washington. At the age of twelve it's difficult to leave all your friends behind. To make the adjustment easier on her, her parents had several of her friends stay over for a sleepover her first night in the White House.

There were estimated to be a million people present to celebrate the inaugural festivities. Approximately $33 million dollars were spent for the inaugural celebrations. Bill Clinton's wife and daughter stood by him as he took the oath of office which made him the first Democratic president in twelve years; since the days of Jimmy Carter.

At twelve years old Chelsea became the first child to live in the White House since the days of the Carter administration.

The Congressional Luncheon was held after the oath of office and from there the Clintons were taken by limousine down Pennsylvania Avenue. The president and first lady exited the limousine the last few blocks before they arrived at the White House walking down Pennsylvania Avenue waving to the crowds. Chelsea, exhausted by the stress of the move and from the excitement of all the ongoing activities joined her parents for a few steps but was tired and cold and got back in the limousine and rode in comfort the rest of the way.

The president and first lady attended eleven inaugural balls that evening. Chelsea joined them for a short time and then returned to the White House.

The White House staff helps the First Family children adjust to life in the White House by planning a scavenger hunt for them while their parents are at the inaugural balls. The scavenger hunt includes historical items from past administrations to search for. Chelsea along with several of her friends from Little Rock that had been invited to join her for a slumber party roamed through the White House looking for such items as the Gettysburg Address and the hidden staircase between the second and third floors.

The first four years that Chelsea called the White House home she had seventy-two sleepover guests. Her parents often invited her old friends from Little Rock to stay with their daughter flying them into Washington to keep her company. Chelsea was also allowed to sleep over with friends at their house with her Secret Service agents nearby.

Chelsea was only the second First Daughter to have been an only child of the president. Margaret Truman was the first.

Socks, Chelsea's cat, was brought along with the family to stay with them while living at the White House. His first night at his new home he threw up on the West Hall carpet;

something the White House staff reluctantly admitted he did quite often during his years at the White House.

As a twelve year old First Daughter Chelsea was at an awkward stage in her life. She had braces, pimples, and frizzy untamed hair. While her mother had a make-over before arriving in Washington Chelsea did not; and she became a target for late night TV show hosts, comedians, and even a senator to ridicule.

Rush Limbaugh a radio and television talk show host and political commentator said on his television show, "You may know that the Clintons have a cat Socks in the White House. They also have a dog." He then held up a photo of Chelsea.

Senator John McCain made a remark at a 1998 fund-raiser asking the crowd, "Why is Chelsea Clinton so ugly? Because her father is Janet Reno." He was referring to the long-lasting rumors of Hillary being a lesbian. It was cruel and incredibly insensitive to attack the first lady through her young daughter - especially for a man in his position.

Saturday Night Live also mocked Chelsea's appearance. It was at this point that the Clintons demanded the press leave their daughter alone, making it very clear that she was off limits.

Former White House daughter Margaret Truman also wrote to the editor of *The New York Times* expressing concern for the young president's daughter and requested they leave her alone and not invade her private life.

After being ridiculed on television it was from that time on Chelsea was off-limits and was rarely photographed and never interviewed. The president himself made the statement, "We really work hard on making sure that Chelsea doesn't let other people define her sense of her own self-worth. It's tough when you are an adolescent."

While living in Little Rock Chelsea had always attended public schools, but once she became a First Daughter she attended the upscale, private Quaker Sidwell Friends School which is described as "the Harvard of Washington's private schools" and is a favorite of presidential families. The school is run by Quakers and at the time Chelsea attended the school the tuition ran $14,000 annually.

Eighth grade Chelsea was made to clean her own room, make her bed, and clean up behind herself and her friends when they enjoyed the White House theater. Her parents wanted her to have experiences that normal teens experienced and to keep her grounded; and like most teens her bed went unmade most days. But her life was anything but normal. After all she lived in the White House, had her own assigned Secret Service agents who trailed her every move outside the Family Quarters, traveled worldwide, and met famous people.

The president and first lady did their best to make their lives normal as far as a family life including their daughter. They tried to have dinner together on a regular basis and would watch the latest movies together in the White House theater. Chelsea and her father enjoyed the latest action movies. They would spend time together taking walks, riding bikes, playing cards, or just sit around talking.

When asked about life in the White House Chelsea years later said of the experience, "I was very aware of why we were there and that I was living among history," she says. "One of the things that my parents did was talk with me about their work. So at the end of the day, over dinner, I would tell them what I learned in biology class and my mother would tell me about advocating for women's health around the world, and my dad would talk about the budget fight or what was happening in advance of a trip he was planning to Russia. I knew that we were having a different type of conversation than most of my friends."

While vacationing on Martha's Vineyard their first summer as a presidential family they joined Jackie Kennedy, her daughter Caroline and husband, and Ted Kennedy for a cruise. "Caroline is one of the few people in the world who can understand Chelsea's unique experiences," Hillary later wrote in her autobiography. After that summer Chelsea looked upon Caroline as a friend and role model.

Chelsea and some of the other students from her school spent a day with members of the White House staff who took them to different departments where staff members then taught the students how to cook, clean, and flower arranging. They spent time with the chefs, florist, and housekeeping staff who took the time with the students giving them lessons they would never forget. How many students can say, "I learned to make this recipe from the White House chef or I learned to make this flower arrangement from the White House florist? It was a unique experience. Chelsea proudly made her parents meals she had learned to prepare and beamed with pride when the flower arrangement she made was displayed in the Red Room.

Chelsea, like every other teen in America looked forward to the day when she could drive; even though she wouldn't be allowed to drive on the streets of Washington or anywhere else for that matter without Secret Service protection. The president himself taught his daughter to drive at Camp David using one of the Secret Service armored cars. When the first lady asked her how her driving lessons went Chelsea replied, "I think he learned a few things."

For Chelsea's 16th birthday her parents arranged a party for her and thirty friends at Camp David. The kids were taken to Camp David on a bus and once they arrived they were entertained by having a paintball battle with U.S. Marines in the woods followed with bowling and movies afterward.

The fact that it was her 16th birthday the chef wanted to fix something special for her and contemplated what he could do to make it a special event for Chelsea. When he discovered she wanted to get a car and a driver's license he had his answer. He made her a cake and decorated it with a handmade license and a car that was made out of spun sugar.

Chelsea had breakfast with her father each morning before heading off to school. After school she often did her homework in the president's study located off the Oval Office. Her father helped her with her homework and sometimes asked his aides to do some research to help her.

As a First Family member one of the perks is the travel to exotic places. Chelsea was able to travel to many different countries. She traveled to Russia with her parents and traveled with the first lady on a two week tour of Africa and a ten day tour in South Asia where they visited Mother Teresa's orphanage in Calcutta, India and visited mosques in Pakistan. But one of the places she had especially looked forward to visiting was the Taj Mahal.

It was at the Taj Mahal that Chelsea gave her first public comment. She said, "When I was little, this was sort of the embodiment of the fairy-tale palace for me. I would see pictures of it and would dream I was a princess or whatever. Now that I'm here, it's spectacular."

Chelsea was liked by most of the White House household staff. Betty Finney, one of the maids when asked about Chelsea said, "Teenagers, you're thinking rudeness. That was never, ever Chelsea." The staff has seen their share of unruly First Family members, but

Chelsea was not one of them.

That is not the same opinion others had of her. She, along with her parents, called the Secret Service agents who were there to protect them 'pigs.' White House florist Ronn Payne recalls the day he was in the second floor kitchen when a Secret Service agent walked into the room to let her know it was time for school. She was on the phone with a friend and said, "Oh, I've got to go. The pigs are here." The angered Secret Service agent reminded her it was his job to protect her. Her response was, "Well, that's what my mother and father call you."

Chelsea would often tell the chef not to worry about cooking for her as she would be making her own dinner. The dinner she made herself more often than not was Kraft macaroni and cheese.

When the idea of their daughter going off to college was in the foreseeable future the first lady not particularly wanting her daughter eating out or making a habit of eating fast food during her college days decided it would be a good idea for Chelsea to be a little more self-reliant and learn to cook healthy meals for herself.

Executive Chef Walter Scheib recalled, "I got a call from Mrs. Clinton asking if I would teach Chelsea how to cook." The summer before Chelsea headed off to college she spent some time in the kitchen with the chef and staff learning to make some healthy vegetarian meals. "She was an extremely quick study and as everyone knows now she is very, very bright," Chef Scheib said. "She's a very intense person who didn't take this opportunity lightly. She respected us tremendously in terms of us offering her our time."

When Chelsea was about to graduate, the president had been asked to give the commencement address at the Sidwell Friends School graduation being the first president to do so since President Theodore Roosevelt. Beforehand Chelsea told her father, "Dad, I want you to be wise – *briefly.*"

Chelsea had achieved academic distinction when named a National Merit Scholar at the age of seventeen.

When Chelsea arrived at Stanford University she came with an entourage which included the president, the first lady, dozens of Secret Service agents, and over two-hundred reporters. The dorm room she would be staying in had bullet-proof glass and surveillance cameras were placed in the hallways. While she was on campus she would be discreetly followed by her Secret Service agents who were dressed in casual clothing such as students would wear so as to not be too obvious.

Chelsea was an eighteen year old freshman when the Monica Lewinsky scandal was smeared on the front of every newspaper and tabloid and it was all you would hear about when you turned on the television.

The Lewinsky scandal would not be the first scandal the Clintons were involved with, nor would it be the last; but it was certainly one of the most visible and talked about between the press and the American people with the outcome being the president being impeached.

A student who knew Chelsea recalls that Chelsea's demeanor drastically changed during this time. She changed from being that friendly girl to shutting down.

When the newspapers began plastering "The Sex Scandal in the Oval Office" on the front pages the first lady called Chelsea at Stanford and strongly suggested to her daughter that for the time being it would be best if she stopped reading the papers. The following week Chelsea was brought back to Washington to show the nation that the First Family was a strong united family.

While her parents were doing their best to shield Chelsea from the scandal of her father's infidelities she was suffering from the stress. She was rushed to the campus hospital with severe stomach pains where the doctors concluded the pains were brought on by stress. Chelsea over the next several months would be rushed to the hospital several more times suffering with severe stomach pains.

Matt Pierce, another student at Stanford, was dating Chelsea at the time the scandal came to light. He would become her support who helped her through these rough times. She was receiving little to no support or comfort from her parents who at the time were too self-absorbed in their own problems to take their daughter's feelings into consideration.

The first lady continued to tell her daughter that none of the stories of her father's infidelities were true, but when Chelsea next visited the White House she discovered that not only the American people were being lied to but she also was being lied to. At this point in time the only time her parents were speaking to each other is when they were screaming at each other. While they showed the public a picture of unity, they were anything but. By the time Chelsea headed back to Stanford she wasn't speaking to her father.

When Chelsea arrived home for the summer she spent hours locked in her room, even her parents were locked out. Chelsea often heard her father from the floor above yelling and screaming how Kenneth Starr and the "vast right-wing conspiracy" was out to get him – *not once taking responsibility for his own actions.*

When her father was backed into a corner with no way out he finally admitted on television that he had lied. At this point the only news Chelsea was receiving on the whole sordid affair was like everyone else – from the news. When she heard her father admit to his guilt on television his daughter was devastated.

Her father never asked for his daughter's forgiveness as he had stated he had done on national television. He never even talked to her about it; and neither did the first lady.

At this point Chelsea realized her parents had been less than honest with her and she decided to find out for herself what the true story was. She read *The Starr Report,* an investigative account of the president by Independent Counsel Kenneth Starr. It was quite an eye opener, but something no daughter should ever have to discover about her own father. After discovering the truth Chelsea was hurt and for a time had nothing to do with her father.

How do you ever regain that trust when the father you looked up to all your life lied to you month after month and after discovering the hidden life he has been living. He lied to his wife, to his daughter, the American people, and he lied under oath to a federal grand jury committing perjury.

The president would be impeached for lying under oath to a federal grand jury and for obstructing justice. He was only the second president in American history to have been impeached. The only other president to have been impeached was Andrew Johnson in 1868.

In the year 2000 Chelsea had completed three years of college when her mother was preparing to run for the Senate. Chelsea delayed her last year of school so she could help with her mother's campaign. She was still off-limits to the press but was seen more often by the public through photographs and on television with her family.

It was during her mother's campaign that Chelsea would step in and take over some of the White House hostess responsibilities. Once her mother won her campaign Chelsea returned to Stanford to complete her senior year. In 2001 Chelsea graduated with honors with a B.A. in history.

After graduating from Stanford Chelsea went on to study at Oxford in England and in 2002 began a summer internship with the World Health Organization in Geneva. She would continue her studies at Columbia University in New York.

Chelsea was named as one of the 25 Most Intriguing People of 1996 and again in 2002 by *People* Magazine.

After graduating from Oxford Chelsea moved to New York City and accepted a job as management consultant at McKinney & Company. She worked there for three years and then worked for another three years on Wall Street as an analyst at Avenue Capital Group, a hedge fund owned by Marc Lasry a major financial backer of both her father and mother. She then went back to school to get a masters from Columbia.

Initially when her father tried to persuade Chelsea to become involved in The Clinton Foundation she declined. However much she wanted to step out of the Clinton shadow and become her own person she kept getting pulled back into fulfilling her parent's dreams.

She did not want to be seen as someone valuable only due to her last name, but as most former presidential children will admit, once their father became president their name opened many doors and offered opportunities that would otherwise not have been available to them.

Being called back to campaign for her mother when she ran for president in 2008 is the same time she came to the realization the power of having the Clinton name. At this point, she embraced that power and never looked back.

During her mother's first campaign for the presidency Chelsea stepped out of the shadows and no longer was just a former president's daughter tucked away out of sight. She had her first experience speaking before thousands of people and while public speaking isn't something she excels at, as an associate of Chelsea's said, "She realized she has a voice that people wanted to hear from."

But that voice would not be heard from with the press. During her mother's 2008 campaign Chelsea did not give interviews or answer any questions from the press. She made no exceptions. She was approached by a nine-year old who was reporting for *Scholastic News* asking Chelsea if she thought her father would make a good "first man." Chelsea replied, "I'm sorry. I don't talk to the press, and that applies to you."

Those in the close circle of the Clintons were still protecting her as if she were still a young girl in the White House. When you are out there campaigning for your mother and putting yourself in the public eye it is expected that you will respond to questions from the press; but in Chelsea's case her mother's campaign sent out a message to the press that they were not to talk to her daughter. Those who defied that rule would learn there was a high price to pay.

Her mother lost the campaign for the presidency, but the Clintons weren't going away any time soon.

In 2011 Chelsea was hired by NBC as a special correspondent. Chelsea was just one name whose parent was a political figure that would be hired by NBC over time. They would also hire Jenna Bush daughter of George W and Meghan McCain daughter of John McCain for the draw of their names more than for their talent.

Chelsea's time at NBC was not a success story. The feeling of those working at NBC was that she had been hired to curry favor and to gain access to the Clintons. When discovered she was being paid $600,000 for a part-time job no less (which averaged out to be $27,000 a minute), the rest of the staff at NBC were understandably upset. There were very few full time hires that received such a salary and they were ones who had experience in the field. Her salary was explained that it was due to her being a star, and according to an insider she started acting like one.

Staff at NBC were confused as to why someone who would never even speak to the press would be hired. An NBC veteran said, "She'd walk by with the imperial stare, looking forward, and interacted not at all." She still wasn't speaking to the press, even though she was now their co-worker and supposed to be one of them.

Some at NBC said they may have been able to overlook the hiring of the former president's daughter and her extravagant salary if she had been any good, but her segments were stiff and unimpressive. As the insider put it, "NBC has made a lot of bad decisions in the last few years, but hiring Chelsea Clinton has to be near the top."

Rumors that had been hinted at in the past resurfaced stating Hillary had affairs with both Vince Foster and Webb Hubbell during her time at The Rose Law Firm, but that isn't where the rumors end. It is said that Webb Hubbell is actually Chelsea's biological father. There is certainly a strong resemblance, which was much more pronounced in her younger years – *and in the days before her plastic surgery.*

For those who think the Hubbell – Chelsea rumor is coming from the "vast right-wing conspiracy," author Robert Morrow has admitted that Bill Clinton himself told him that Chelsea was Webb's offspring.

The former president also confided the information of Chelsea's paternity to former Clinton aide Larry Nichols who claims Bill confirmed the rumors that Chelsea's real father is Webb Hubbell, stating that Bill dropped the paternity bombshell during a conversation the two were having at the Arkansas Governor's Mansion during a conversation they had in 1984.

It is said that Chelsea has had four plastic surgeries to date, the first at the age of eighteen. The surgeries weren't to enhance her looks but to shut down rumors of her paternity so she didn't resemble Hubbell according to unsubstantiated rumors. It is said she had an extensive chin implant, her lower lip was cut down to about half it's original size, a nose job, and cheek implants. In addition she has since had her hair straightened, streaked and lightened since her days in the White House which all together has drastically changed her looks since her days when she lived at the White House.

But back to the rumor of her paternity which is a pretty strong accusation. An *Enquirer* reporter decided to put rumors to the test and went to work to receive items from both Hubbell and Chelsea that could be sent off for DNA testing.

The *Enquirer* reporter posed as a fan at a book signing of Webb Hubbells and collected some items consisting of a brand new Sharpie pen along with a Starbucks drink he had been drinking from.

Chelsea's items to be used for DNA testing were going to be a little more difficult to obtain due to the fact that she certainly wasn't going to volunteer them and she was constantly surrounded by Secret Service agents and an entourage from The Clinton Foundation.

The perfect opportunity came when Chelsea spoke at Harvard on a college tour. The *Enquirer* reporter posed as a college student and approached Chelsea asking her to sign the first lady's biography, *'Living History.'* She came prepared with a new Sharpie pen and a clean copy of Hillary's book. Chelsea signed the book and with the Sharpie pen tucked inside returned them to the undercover reporter who then sent the samples to a genetics lab, a nationally recognized laboratory that specialized in paternity testing.

The forensic examination of the samples did not prove or disprove that Webb was Chelsea's father. The official report stated the tests were "inconclusive," "does not discount the possibility." *So the rumors will continue.*

Chelsea met Marc Mezvinsky, the man who would become her husband in 1992 at a retreat the Clintons attended during their White House years. At the time they met Chelsea was twelve and Marc was fifteen.

In later years Chelsea and Marc were both students at Stanford. During his college days he was described by a friend as "a total playboy." Marc and Chelsea had a friendly relationship once they met again at college, but a platonic one until Chelsea's boyfriend broke up with her and she turned to Marc for comfort – and the rest is history.

Marc an investment banker is the son of two former members of Congress so he was certainly familiar with the political life when he proposed to Chelsea over the Thanksgiving holiday in 2009.

Chelsea and Marc were married on July 31, 2010 in an interfaith ceremony; she is Methodist while he is Jewish. They married in Rhinebeck, New York at the exclusive Astor Courts facility with four hundred guests.

The couple had the airspace above Rhinebeck shut down for the twelve hours surrounding the ceremony to avoid the paparazzi. Who other than the Clintons would have the clout to shut down airspace.

The couple set up housekeeping in New York City. In 2013 the former president and first lady helped the couple buy a 5,000 square foot apartment for approximately $10 million in Manhattan in the Flatiron District. It is valued at $15 million today. Their apartment is the length of an entire city block.

Chelsea would join The Clinton Foundation and the name would be changed to The Bill, Hillary, and Chelsea Foundation. But the incoming daughter who immediately received a big title and position was viewed by many already entrenched in the foundation, who had worked hard to receive their promotions by proving themselves through their work, viewed it as yet another unearned opportunity handed to Chelsea due to her last name.

Many in the foundation felt she was coming in and throwing her weight around and has been described as "a spoiled brat and diva." While others who work with her at the foundation admit to her intelligence, diligence, and dedication to the job. Those tasked with managing Chelsea's public persona faced an uphill battle. As even a close friend of Chelsea's described her by saying, "Some people find her a little distant."

It was during her mother's second attempt at the presidency that The Clinton Foundation came under intense scrutiny. Between receiving donations from foreign governments that aren't "friendly or of like-mind" of the U.S. that were received while Hillary was secretary of state. It is debated and looked into whether or not "favors" were being sold.

At the same time both the former president and then current secretary of state were receiving speaking fees up to a million dollars for Bill and up to $500,000 for Hillary from foreign governments, corporations, and other sources. It is fiercely debated on whether or not our global policies have been shaped by large donations received from The Clinton Foundation. Now that Chelsea's name and position is deeply connected with the foundation, she too will be held accountable.

Chelsea Clinton, who it is hinted at as a possible future congressional candidate, has been tainted by The Clinton Foundation. The former editor-in-chief of *The New York Times Magazine* and author Ed Klein states that from his knowledge of Chelsea Clinton "she is even more unlikable than her mother." He said, "She throws her weight around at both the Clinton campaign and at The Clinton Foundation and is arrogant, smug, and always thinks she's the smartest person in the room. Many people left the organization because of her."

As many other former presidential offspring, Chelsea wrote two books. '*It's Your World: Get Informed, Get Inspired, and Get Going!*' is a book geared towards middle school age.

The book received mixed reviews from critics. Chelsea also co-wrote the book *'Governing Global Health: Who Runs the World and Why'* in 2017 also with poor reviews. Not only is the book dull, but it doesn't even address the question that is the subtitle of the book 'who runs the world and why.' It appears that writing and public speaking are not her strong points.

Chelsea Clinton has become a mother herself. She had a daughter, Charlotte Clinton Mezvinsky born in September of 2014 and during her mother's second run for the presidency gave birth to a son, Aidan Clinton Mezvinsky born in June of 2016.

Chelsea again worked on the Clinton 2016 presidential campaign for her mother. The former first lady and presidential wanna-be Hillary Clinton made history twice during her 2016 campaign. She was the first presumptive nominee of a major political party who was under criminal investigation by the FBI while running for president and she became the first woman in the U.S. to win a major political party's presidential nomination.

The former presidential daughter even now as an adult while working on her mother's presidential campaign received the same "hands-off" rule with the press.

Journalist Jack Shafer had a valid question when he asked: 'Why is the press treating a wealthy, 35 year old political operative like she's still a White House kid? Chelsea Clinton has been treated hands off like no other presidential daughter before or since. Why exactly does she warrant this special privilege? The now 36 year old occupies the status of an American princess.'

He has a point. George W Bush's daughters certainly didn't receive the same hands off treatment Chelsea has been given; nor have any other presidential offspring. She's a big girl now; she's not a young teenage daughter which would be understandable if left alone. Chelsea is a grown woman, a wife and mother, a board member of Barry Diller's IAC who is paid $300,000 a year with additional stock awards. She receives $65,000 for speeches, she is a college graduate from Stanford, Columbia, Oxford and a successful business woman; does that sound like someone who is incompetent to speak with the press?

So exactly how long is this "hands-off" approach from the press going to be tolerated? Considering the free pass her mother received from the mainstream media during her 2016 presidential campaign they fear the Clintons and will continue to kowtow to their every whim.

Chelsea has agreed to be interviewed but only by those who are "friendly" and adhere to the Clinton's terms; such as Ellen DeGeneres, Extra, Jimmy Kimmel, and Katie Couric who fawns all over Chelsea like a big, slobbering Saint Bernard puppy. Anytime anyone dared asked any questions that were too probing for her liking she has a tendency to shut down.

During the 2016 presidential campaign when the FBI was investigating presidential hopeful Hillary Clinton it was revealed that Hillary had sent her daughter emails containing classified information for which she was not cleared to receive, all during the time her mother was secretary of state. Chelsea's email was sent to her under the pseudonym Diane Reynolds. The question many asked is why use a pseudonym other than the reason being that they were very much aware that her receiving classified information was against the law.

Chelsea was also mixed up in political controversy when on the night of the attack on the Benghzai diplomatic compound her mother emailed her admitting the attack came from a terrorist group affiliated with al-Qaeda, while at the same time insisting to the American public that it was due to a video.

While it is said that Chelsea and her parents are very close, one of Hillary's close friends who wished to remain unnamed said in an interview, "Unlike Hillary's relationship with Huma, her relationship with Chelsea is remote and somewhat cold. Chelsea is not a warm person. I've never seen them embrace or kiss on the cheek or show any sign of affection, except when they're in public and putting on a show."

It's a well-known fact to the inner-circle of the Clintons that Chelsea was jealous of Huma and would treat Huma respectfully only while her mother was around, but with undisguised contempt when her mother was out of the picture. Chelsea considered herself to be her mother's right hand person, but with Huma in the picture she often had to take a back seat.

"Chelsea desperately wanted her mother to win the presidency. She desired to be co-president," said a Clinton family confidant. "Chelsea thought she would become her mother's chief political advisor."

Having her mother as president would have set Chelsea up for life. She could have received large speaking fees and book contracts. She would have a platform on which to run for public office herself, and she would become more than a former presidential daughter. She had big plans.

During the campaign the former president often tried to give Hillary advice on how to run the campaign and how to reach out to the public; something he had been good at during his own campaigns and something that his wife was desperately failing at.

"Chelsea would take her mother's side against her father, becoming angry with him and loudly telling him to back off," a friend of the Clintons said. "I've seen her point a finger right in his face. He literally bites his tongue. He's afraid of Chelsea's temper, and he's worried she'll yell at him in public the way she does when they're behind closed doors. She can be verbally abusive." Like her parents who are known for their volcanic tempers, Chelsea seems to have inherited this trait.

The Clintons' dreams came to a crashing halt when Hillary Clinton lost her bid for the presidency for the second time in one of the most contentious presidential races in American history when she was defeated by Donald Trump.

It will be interesting to see where Chelsea goes from here. She is young, still in her thirties. She will now have to redefine herself with her plans to return to the White House in a position of power unfulfilled, and with the light shone on the inner dealings of the Clinton Foundation with donations having just about dried up now that the "Pay-to-Play" deal is off the table. But perhaps Chelsea plans to throw her hat in the political arena herself. It's certainly looking that way.

The New York Post has reported that the Clintons have their eye on Rep. Nita Lowey's place when she retires and are grooming Chelsea to take the position herself. Rep. Lowry represents an area in Westchester County which included Chappaqua where the former president and first lady live. *The New York Post* reported the Clintons purchased the house next to theirs for Chelsea and her family so she will be living in the district if Lowey's position becomes available; and at Lowey's advanced age it is only a matter of time before it will be.

When asked not too long ago, Chelsea admitted that running for office one day is absolutely a possibility.

One can only hope not. It appears the nation is rather tired of political dynasties such as the Kennedys, Clintons, and Bushes. The only thing she has to offer is her name and running on the coattails of her parent's accomplishments. She has a real problem connecting with people and comes off as entitled, and as she herself has admitted, "She hasn't found her way and lacks focus in her life." But seriously; I think this nation has had quite enough of the Clintons.

Chelsea's current estimated net worth as of 2017 is $15 million.

Does Chelsea have a mixed race half-brother? Well that depends on two things: if she is indeed Bill Clinton's biological daughter and if Danney Williams is Bill Clinton's son. Chances are that a definitive answer for either of those questions will remain elusive.

During Clinton's administration the story broke that he had fathered an illegitimate, black son with an Arkansas prostitute in 1985. The story, like Chelsea's paternity, remains unproven to this day.

While Bill Clinton denied it from the time he was notified the prostitute was pregnant with his child and he continues to deny or ignore it today, he could put the whole matter to rest with a simple DNA test but refuses to do so.

The people of Little Rock, Arkansas certainly believe it to be true.

During the '90's Danney Williams came forward requesting Bill Clinton to volunteer to give a DNA sample to answer the question once and for all: Was Bill Clinton his father?

Bill Clinton never knew his own biological father, or for that matter was never certain who his natural father was. In his case, he was born three months after his mother Virginia buried her husband. But the facts are that her husband had been away in the service in Europe just eight months before and the baby was full term. This started the local gossips talking. His mother was known as a "loose woman" who had spent most of her nights in dance halls and partying while her husband was overseas.

She tried to lie her way out of the accusations pointed her way by first saying her husband returned a month earlier than he did and then changed her story to the baby being born early; but the doctors and nurses who attended the birth debunked her story saying the baby was most definitely full term. At eight pounds and six ounces that was a fact hard to deny.

Questions would hang over his head throughout his life as to who his father really was. He even confessed to friends in Arkansas that he had grown up wondering who his father really was. So, Bill could certainly understand Danney's desire to have his own paternity question answered.

It was during the time Bill Clinton was governor in 1983 when he was out jogging and he came across Bobbie Ann Williams and several other African-American hookers who were out 'plying their trade' not too far from the Governor's Mansion. That day Bill stopped and talked to the hookers and then continued with his run. Three days later he was back and paid Williams for her services which he partook of behind some bushes.

Two weeks later Clinton made arrangements to have Williams and two other hookers picked up and taken to a small house in a secluded spot. Williams would later describe the house in minute detail. It was a house owned by Clinton's mother that Bill used so frequently that the neighbors had become friendly with his driver and security.

While Bill Clinton has always denied this from ever happening, Buddy Young a former Arkansas state trooper admits that he and another trooper were paid quite handsomely for escorting the governor and prostitute Bobbie Ann Williams to Bill's mother's house.

The following year Bobbie Ann Williams was still working the area known as "Hooker's Row" where she had originally met Bill Clinton when she saw him again and told him she was pregnant. He laughed and told her it couldn't be his baby.

Initially even her own family had doubts as to the legitimacy of her story until she gave birth to a white baby. She claimed that Bill Clinton had been the only white man she had been with. Friends and family said as the boy got older his looks favored the former governor Bill Clinton.

Friends of the Clintons in Little Rock were aware he had fathered a black child, but Bill wasn't worried. Who would people believe: the word of a hooker or the governor? Knowing his sexual background and his penchant for not telling the truth, more people than not very well would have believed the hooker.

Bobbie Ann Williams and her sister Lucille Bolton took lie detector tests by two separate investigators and both times the results were that the women were telling the truth.

Lucille, the aunt who had custody of the boy went so far as to go to the Governor's

Mansion to try to get financial aid for the boy; but she was never allowed to see the governor. She then left word for him but never heard from him.

Bobbie Ann's husband Dan Williams drove up beside the governor one day while he was out jogging and confronted him about the boy. According to Mr. Williams the governor reached into the pocket of his running shorts and pulled out a wad of money and threw it in the car window without saying a word and just kept on jogging.

Robert "Say" McIntosh, a black activist, tried to assist Bobbi Ann and her son by going to the tabloids with the story. It was only then that Bill Clinton responded to the claims and in a meeting behind closed doors with Democrats insisted he didn't have a black baby. But the Clintons like to play with words; such as the time he said, "He didn't have sexual relations with that woman." Well; in this case he could very well say he didn't have a black baby. Danney was no longer a baby, but a young man. So, the way the Clintons look at it, they aren't *actually* lying. Bill Clinton continued to refuse to give his blood sample for DNA testing.

In 1999 *The Star* claimed they had run DNA tests and there was no match. *World Net Daily* reported that no DNA tests had been conducted despite what the media was reporting.

Clinton defenders have made the claim that *The Star* magazine conducted a DNA test proving Bill Clinton was not William's father saying Bill Clinton's friend, Phil Bunton, who was editor at the time claimed there was no match, but in an interview with *WND, World Net Daily,* Bunton admitted no blood sample was obtained and *The Star* magazine never published a story documenting a laboratory test.

If the story of Bill Clinton fathering the son of a prostitute is untrue as Bill Clinton has claimed in the past, then all he has to do to put the story to rest is to have a DNA test and be done with it. *But, it's doubtful that's ever going to happen!*

43

GEORGE W. BUSH

Children of Laura and George W. Bush:

Barbara Pierce Bush – Born: Nov. 25, 1981   Still Living At The Time Of Publication

Jenna Welch Bush - Born: Nov. 25, 1981   Still Living At The Time Of Publication

Barbara and Jenna are the only twins of a president in American history.

George W Bush won the presidency in the most highly controversial presidential race in modern history. That would change come the presidetial election in 2016. It would finally take the United States Supreme Court to finally declare who would become president over a month after the election took place, and then the outcome was determined by a vote of 5 – 4. This disputed election may have just been warming up the nation for what was to come in the near future in the 2016 election of our 45th president in the presidential race of Hillary Clinton against Donald Trump.

There were many momentous events that occurred on George W's watch; but by far the event to leave the largest impact on our nation was September 11, 2001.

George W had only been president for a mere eight months when notified that a plane had hit the World Trade Center. It was assumed it was a terrible accident until a second plane hit and then the world knew – *America was under attack.*

When it was next reported that American Airlines flight #77 had been hijacked it was assumed it was headed towards the White House, but wound up crashing into the Pentagon killing all on board as well as 125 people who had been inside the Pentagon. Later after it was looked into it was thought that due to the angle of the sun the pilot was unable to locate the White House. The Pentagon however; was a target that was impossible to miss.

The president who had been speaking at an elementary school in Florida had been rushed aboard Air Force One once it was realized the crashes were intentional. Secretary of State Condoleeza Rice spoke to the president while he was aboard Air Force One and informed him of a call that had just been received at the Emergency Operations Center beneath the White House. The ominous caller simply said, "Air Force One is next." It was determined it was no idle threat by the mere fact that the caller had known how to call into the nerve center.

The president was informed that he and Air Force One were in grave danger. To lessen the threat while in the skies Air Force One climbed to an altitude of 40,000 feet and two fighter jets joined them flying off each wing to ensure the president's safe arrival to the secure location he was being flown to.

The Federal Aviation Administration ordered all commercial airliners to land at the nearest airport which had never been done before. All commercial fights were grounded.

Unfortunately, the call to 'ground all flights' came in too late to save those on United Airlines flight #93. Five minutes after the call was made they crashed. United flight #93 had also been hijacked and was headed towards Washington. Several passengers on board had been able to make phone calls and had been made aware of the other planes being hijacked and of their fatal outcome. Some heroic passengers rose up and overcame the hijackers causing the plane to crash into a field instead of it's original target. While their target had been thwarted from being reached, all on the flight were killed.

The first lady was safe but the nineteen-year old twins of the president were away at college. At Yale Barbara heard the news on her clock radio and heard another student sobbing uncontrollably a few doors down. Jenna at the University of Texas was woken up by the Secret Service pounding on her dormitory door. Both girls were quickly whisked off to secure locations.

By the time the first lady was able to reach her daughters by phone both girls were practically hysterical. Once commercial flights resumed both girls flew to Washington to spend the weekend at Camp David in the company of their parents. It was a time when the whole nation was reaching out to loved ones.

It would be some time before America felt safe again. This was a day that would go down in history that would be memorable to all; who would always remember where they were when they heard the news and remember the shock as they watched the events unfold over the television.

Going back to the year 1981 when Ronald Reagan was president and George W's father was the vice president was the same year the twins were born. Laura and George W had suffered with fertility issues and had begun the adoption process when it was discovered Laura was pregnant.

With almost two months to go before reaching her due date Laura Bush was suffering from toxemia and had been on bed rest. After two weeks it was determined they couldn't wait any longer to deliver the babies in fear of the mother's health.

The fraternal twins arrived five weeks early by cesarean section; first Barbara arrived weighing in at five pounds and four ounces with Jenna arriving just one minute later at four pounds twelve ounces. The girls were named after their grandmothers.

Neither parent had any previous experience with babies and now here they were with two babies. Their mother said, "They just seemed to cry all the time." Dad would try to comfort his crying babies by holding them and marching around the room singing the Yale fight song to them. Their dad who would one day be governor of Texas and then president of the United States changed their diapers and took over nighttime feedings to give mom a break.

Barbara and Jenna Bush are the first recorded twins of an American president. Andrew Jackson had adopted one of his sister-in-law's twin boys; but the Bush girls hold the title of the only biological twins of a president.

Even by three years of age the girls had developed their own personalities. The sweet little girls riding around their yard on their tricycles are the same girls who went to preschool where Jenna kicked the class bully in the shins.

Their mother would read to them every night teaching them at an early age to love books. They continued with their love of reading and so did their mother who as first lady promoted reading and literacy.

When the twins were six years old their family moved to Washington so their father could work on their grandfather's presidential campaign. While living in Washington and while their parents were campaigning they were able to spend time with their grandparents, known to the nation as George H.W. and Barbara Bush.

The last week of the campaign coincided with Halloween. The twins were thrilled that they were able to wear their Halloween costumes aboard the vice president's plane. Barbara dressed as a vampire and Jenna as a pack of Juicy Fruit gum.

Flying on board Air Force Two with their grandparents the girls entertained themselves by stuffing wads of paper into the plane's toilets which Grandma Bush herself had to remove. Two heads are better than one and what one twin didn't come up with the other did keeping each other entertained.

Barbara and Jenna were seven years old when their grandfather became president. The entire Bush family and all their children had arrived for the event. Little did anyone know at the time that twelve years later they would be back to see another Bush sworn in as president – the twins' father and son of the incoming president.

For two seven year old girls all the pomp and circumstance of the inaugural events became a bit tedious and no longer held their attention. Chief Usher Gary Walters asked the Chief Florist Nancy Clarke if she could entertain the twins for awhile. They had been watching the parade but had become restless after sitting still for so long.

Nancy knew she would need to come up with some type of activity to keep the girls busy. She took the girls up to the guest bedrooms where they would be staying so they could see the colors of their room and then took them down to the flower shop and let them roam through the rows of colorful and fragrant flowers and pick out their own flowers to make an arrangement for their room.

The girls were captivated looking through the wide assortment of beautiful flowers of all shapes and sizes picking out flowers here and there, changing their minds, and looking some more until they decided they had exactly what they wanted. Nancy showed the girls how to arrange the flowers. They were mesmerized and were awfully proud of the end result of the arrangements they made. They never forgot the time they had spent with Nancy and on their future visits to the White House made a point of visiting Nancy and watching her at work arranging flowers to be used throughout the White House.

The girls were very close growing up and would remain so. Barbara would later write an article for *Vanity Fair*, 'We Have Our Own, Unspoken Language' on her memories of the time she and her sister spent together growing up. "We were each others constant slumber-party guest, sous-chef, backup singer, or lead vocalist. We were never bored under the dome of Jenna's expansive imagination, digging for buried treasure in our neighbor's backyard, or playing pioneer, two barefoot girls lost in the unexplored woods … of suburban Dallas. We went on nature walks in the alleys and howled at the summer moon."

Their family had moved back to Texas after their grandfather won the election for the presidency. Their father became part owner of the Texas Rangers baseball team. The girls grew up as comfortable at the baseball stadium as they were in their own home. Texas days are hot and humid and the girls could sometimes be found seeking shelter in the air conditioned suite where they would sing and dance and spent many nights huddled under a blanket with their parents on brisk Texas nights while watching America's favorite pastime.

They made wonderful memories together including the times each night after their showers when 'the three Bush ladies,' would line up in the hallway singing songs from the Pointer Sisters while dancing – "three tone-deaf Texans" as they described themselves who just loved to dance and spend time together.

Their father won the election for governor – not once, but twice. He became the first Texas governor in history ever to be reelected to a consecutive four year term. There have only been two presidential sons ever elected governors – George W and Jeb Bush. Both brothers would later run for the presidency, with only George W succeeding in following in their father's footsteps and moving into the Oval Office. George W had made history by being only the second presidential son to become president; the other being the 6th president John Quincy Adams, son of the 2nd president John Adams.

Being that the girls were fraternal twins they not only looked different but they had very distinct, different personalities. Jenna was blonde, out-going, and very sociable always known as the rowdy twin while Barbara was a quiet, studious brunette. But they both liked to have fun and when their father won his election for governor the girls teased him that they were going to dye their hair flaming red for when he was sworn into office. The family moved into the Governor's Mansion in Austin.

Once the girls reached high school Barbara played softball and soccer, made the National Honor Society, and was someone who came up with her own unique fashion style. She preferred vintage clothing and she was voted "Most Likely To Appear On The Cover Of Vogue" by her classmates. Barbara is the avowed clotheshorse of the two sisters.

Barbara was about to become Homecoming Queen her senior year at half time, but unaware of the honor that was about to be bestowed on her she arrived at the football game wearing flip flops and casual clothing. Barbara was a very pretty girl and though she has always been described as the quieter of the two she has her father's competitive spirit.

Jenna was active in student government and wrote for her school newspaper. Her classmates predicted the accident prone Jenna would be "most likely to trip on prom night." She was class president during high school and was a popular student. As described by one of her classmates, "She was this great character, really funny, like a stage comedian, and a bit of a klutz who'd fall out of her chair."

While different the girls share many of the same preferences. The girls being typical Texans love Tex-Mex but are diversified enough to also share a love for sushi. They finish each others sentences and then break out in laughter. Barbara enjoyed her sister's antics such as the time she stuck two jalapeños up her nose to amuse her sister and ended up burning the insides of her nostrils.

At sixteen the girls went their separate ways for two unique experiences. Barbara spent a year at the boarding school Saint Stephens in Rome, Italy while Jenna headed off to Spain to study and live with a local family.

While living in Spain Jenna met a friend named Mia who she would meet up with again on a graduation trip to Spain where the girls walked the Camino de Santiago de Compostela (the Way of Saint James), a five-day, 75-mile segment of the spiritual trek through the Pyrenees Mountains on a medieval footpath.

Barbara and three friends went on a graduation trip to Moscow, St. Petersburg, and Prague.

When it was time to choose colleges Jenna chose to stay in her home state and attend the University of Texas in Austin while Barbara chose Yale becoming the 4th generation of the Bush family and the first female from her family to attend the Ivy League university.

When their parents told their daughters that their father planned to run for the presidency they were adamantly opposed to the idea. The thought of being hounded by the press and everything they did reported on all while being followed everywhere by the Secret Service was something they were adamantly opposed to. Being typical teens they thought the world revolved around them and many times confronted their father asking him why he "was doing this to us" arguing, crying, with many scenes of drama taking place in the Bush household on the topic. Every time the subject was brought up the girls cried and begged their father not to run.

The girls had made it very clear their feelings on the topic and refused to have any part in their father's campaign. It was selfish and hurtful to their father, but their parents didn't push them to do anything they didn't want to do.

By this time the girls were away at college. Barbara had left for New Haven, Connecticut where she spent a week camping in the wilderness as part of Yale's outdoor orientation program. She enjoyed the experience as their mother had instilled a love of the outdoors in both her daughters.

Barbara and a roommate moved into a centuries old dorm at Yale. Barbara was involved in softball and cross-country. She became a member of Kappa Alpha Theta. Jenna back in Texas moved in to Hardin House a private dorm at the University of Texas with two roommates.

It was during their father's campaign for the presidency when they first got a taste of being presidential daughters when they became newsworthy. Barbara had been caught using a fake ID at a bar and Jenna was attending frat parties where at one party she had become drunk and was dancing with another student when the two of them fell to the floor.

In the age of the internet it didn't take long for the embarrassing photo to be spread on the internet and in the newspapers. While their actions weren't any different from many teens at college and away from home for the first time, other students didn't have to suffer the humiliation of seeing their actions displayed on the front page of the newspapers and reported on by the media every time they turned on TV; and then there was the problem of being viewed on YouTube which would still be available to be seen long after the media had moved on to another story and long after they had outgrown their party days.

On election night the twins joined their family to await the news on whether or not their father had won the election. At 2:00 AM the networks declared George W Bush as the nation's next president. Al Gore called to concede. But then less than two hours later Al Gore called back to retract his concession when it was announced that it was too close to call in Florida. For the following thirty-six days no one knew who their next president was going to be as there was a recount taking place in Florida. On December 12th it was finally announced that George W Bush would be the nation's 45th president.

On Christmas night back home for the holidays Jenna complained of pains and was rushed to the emergency room at St. David's Hospital where she underwent an emergency appendectomy. Less than two weeks after it was announced that Laura Bush would become first lady she spent her Christmas evening sleeping beside her daughter in her hospital room. Her priorities were always family first.

The twins who had been nowhere to be found during the hard work of the campaign were more than happy to come to celebrate the inaugural balls and parties. Nineteen years of age for their father's first inauguration it would be one of four they would attend. The first inauguration they attended at seven years of age was when their grandfather became president, they attended both of their father's inauguration, and were there to witness their father's successor the first black president in American history when he took the oath of office.

"It's living history, and it's not something that many people get to do," Jenna said about attending presidential inaugurations.

There have only been two times in history when both parents of a president have been in attendance at the inauguration to witness their son being sworn into office. The first time was in 1961 with John F Kennedy and the second time was in 2001 when George W Bush was sworn into office.

Not everyone in attendance at the inauguration was in Washington to celebrate. Thousands of demonstrators arrived in Washington for the sole purpose of protesting the controversial outcome of the presidential race. The president's limousine was pelted by a tennis ball and an egg thrown at them in anger.

But the party went on. The president danced with his wife and his daughters. While twirling his daughter Jenna on the dance floor she had a moment of embarrassment with a wardrobe malfunction. They attended several inaugural balls before returning to the White House where the immediate family was staying, their grandparents the former president and first lady, along with about twenty other relatives.

Though the girls rarely stayed at the White House during their father's administration, they were given rooms for the occasions for when they did visit. Jenna's room had once been the bedroom of Caroline Kennedy, Lynda Bird Johnson, and Chelsea Clinton. Barbara's room next door had previously been claimed by John F. Kennedy Jr., Luci Johnson, and Tricia Nixon.

It's hard not to be in awe as you walk the halls and see the rooms, some still furnished from past presidential administrations and think of the historical events that had occurred in these very rooms and thinking of who had also walked these same halls. The room that Jackie Kennedy had once used as their family dining room had long ago been used to remove Alice Roosevelt's appendix, the daughter of Teddy Roosevelt. Then you visit the most famous of rooms in the family quarters, the Lincoln Bedroom; which Lincoln never used for a bedroom but actually used the room as an office. It is said it was in that very room that he signed the Gettysburg Address, considered one of the most important speeches in American history. If walls could talk, the stories you would hear...

The girls spent very little time at the White House during their father's administration but they did celebrate their twentieth birthday having a party at Camp David inviting twenty of their friends. They had dinner and set up a karaoke machine and had a great time.

As First Daughters the girls had Secret Service agents assigned to protect them. The girls were teenage college students and just wanted to be like the other students. They didn't want the Secret Service following them and they didn't make it easy on their agents who considered watching over the Bush daughters a nightmare.

"Jenna and Barbara treated the agents as if they were the enemy," one of the agents said.

"Instead of letting us know where and when she was going, Jenna would just run out and jump in her car and go. Similarly, when Barbara was attending Yale she would sneak out of her dorm eluding her agents."

Jenna often called her father complaining about the agents. The president would call the special agent in charge and tell them to back off. One agent who was assigned to protect First Daughter Jenna responded, 'What if something happens to her?" Considering the times and the threat of Al-Qaeda along with the kidnapping risk of being a presidential daughter the girls didn't take the risk factor into consideration.

When the girls were underage and going to the bars their agents would try to warn them, but their job was to protect them from bodily harm - not to protect them from themselves.

Initially the press honored the fact that the presidential daughters were young college students who just wanted to live a life out of the spotlight; but the girls and their behavior with their underage drinking, using fake ID's, and being arrested changed all that. They became the brunt of jokes on late night talk shows. Jay Leno joked that Jenna was learning to play a new musical instrument: the Breathalyzer.

Their mother had a tendency to indulge her daughters more than she does discipline them, giving them leeway understanding how difficult it was for her daughters who just wanted to live a normal life like the other students and not be under the spotlight. Grandma Bush was another story. She told it like it was, and when on *The Tonight Show* with Jay Leno when he asked the girl's grandmother, former First Lady Barbara Bush about the girl's partying and using fake ID's she replied, "That is not what they should have done. It was stupid. They are smart girls – they know they shouldn't have done that."

The first lady gave her daughters 'the talk' on the risks of alcohol. Their father who had his own drinking problems in the past had quit drinking and the first lady's father had also overcome his drinking problems. Their mother told the girls, "Nothing good happens when you are drunk."

It would be very difficult when the girls finally did mature to lose their reputation of party girls. Especially with YouTube, blogs, cell phone cameras, and the paparazzi. Their actions would be out there for all to see long past their days of partying. Jenna learned that years later when she was a teacher and one of her students asked her what he would find out about her if he googled her. "Oh, please don't do that," she responded.

When Jenna's actions were the top news stories of the media another previous presidential daughter Luci Johnson reached out to Jenna sharing advice her own mother had given her as a First Daughter. Her mother had told her, "Don't do anything that you wouldn't want to read about on the front page of *The New York Times*, because if you do, it will be."

George W certainly understood about bad choices. While he was attending Andover alcohol was strictly forbidden to the students. George W had never been one to follow by the rules and had designed an official stickball membership card that 'appeared' to carry the imprimatur of Andover. He passed out the cards to other students and told them they would serve as fake ID's. All the same information found on a driver's license was printed on the cards and at the bottom was the signature of the High Commissioner who assigned himself the nickname Tweeds Bush after political legend Boss Tweed. Students went off campus and attempted to pass off the cards as official ID's so they could drink; so when it was reported to him about his daughters using fake ID's he couldn't very well act too righteous.

The girls had wanted no part in their father's campaign and still hadn't made any appearances on his behalf as First Daughters; though they didn't mind indulging in the perks of foreign travel on the taxpayers' dime.

Barbara traveled with her mother one summer to England and Italy but chose not to go with her sister Jenna and the first lady when they flew to Europe to visit Hungary and the Czech Republic. White House spokeswoman Noelia Rodriguez let it be known to the press ahead of time that Jenna was traveling as a private citizen – although it was the government, or actually the taxpayers, who would be paying her way – and she was not to be photographed or approached by the press. She let the photographers know in no uncertain terms that when Jenna joined her mother on her public appearances they were to avert their lenses from the First Daughter.

"She doesn't want her picture in the paper, so she avoids the times that there are a lot of press," Laura Bush told White House reporters." The first lady chose to coddle her daughters who were now young adults, instead of telling them to grow up and be positive role models as the president's daughters.

Washington Post writer and author of *'The Perfect Wife'* Ann Gerhart said, "all of the noblesse, but none of the oblige"—pampered blue bloods who had shown "little interest in any of the pressing issues their generation will inherit nor shown empathy for the struggles facing their mother and father."

Slate columnist Michael Crowley commented on the president and first lady's parenting skills, "permissive, laissez-faire parents more interested in shielding their daughters from prying eyes than in drumming solid values into them." While it may have sounded a bit harsh and judgmental, the girls weren't doing anything to improve public opinion.

February 1, 2003 the country suffered another tragedy when the space shuttle Columbia exploded upon it's reentry toward Earth. All seven astronauts lost their lives as debris and remains rained from the skies over Texas. It wouldn't be the only historic event for the year. The country was about to declare war against Iraq. George W's administration suffered many horrific national events.

As the president's daughters the girls were getting an earful on people's strong feelings on the topic of war. Barbara back at Yale had been approached by a teaching assistant in one of her classes who told her she would give her an A in the class if she would tell her father not to go to war. Students themselves worried about their own possibilities of having to go off and fight in a war on foreign land had passionate opinions.

The girls had matured throughout their years in college and the world began to see their maturity as Barbara in the summer before her senior year traveled with her parents to Africa to launch the President's Emergency Plan for AIDS relief. She described her trip as "life-changing." The twenty-one year old presidential daughter who had before seen life as something to be enjoyed and indulged herself in the past was a different young woman that returned from that experience in Africa.

Previous to the trip she had thought she would work in the field of architecture, in design; but after that fateful trip to Africa where she was so moved by what she saw she would eventually become founder and CEO of Global Health Corps, a nonprofit organization that pairs young volunteers with health and development organizations.

In Africa she met a little girl who from judging by her size Barbara had assumed was about three years old. When she asked the girl's mother she learned the girl was actually seven but malnourished and she was born HIV positive. The little girl who had been so excited about meeting an American president died soon after their visit. Along with that memory Barbara met some people who left quite an impression on her. They were committed health care workers who were there to help the young girl and other people with the health epidemic they were suffering. While Barbara was there she saw hundreds of people lined up waiting in the street for medicine.

When she returned to Yale she enrolled in Yale's comprehensive survey course on AIDS. She would for a time live and work in Cape Town, South Africa, working at the Red Cross War Memorial Childrens Hospital which treated AIDS patients.

A few months before school was to end Jenna let her father know she wanted to work for him in his reelection campaign. Both of his daughters would for the first time work campaigning for their father in his final political race. They brought along many of their friends from school to also work on the campaign. Initially they answered phones at headquarters and traveled with their parents on some of the campaign stops. Nearing the end of the campaign the girls were also going out giving speeches which included a speech at the Republican Convention and introducing their father at the National Republican Convention.

After graduating from college Jenna moved to Washington and for a time called the White House home. When asked what it was like to live in the White House she replied, "I feel like it's filled with millions of ghosts. I'm not kidding. I have heard ghosts, I really have." Many other First Family members have made the same claim.

Jenna worked as an assistant teacher at The Elsie Whitlow Stokes Community Freedom Public Charter School. It is a school where 90% of the students come from low-income homes. Jenna takes her job very seriously and the kids love her. On Dr. Seuss's birthday she arrived at her classroom dressed as the Cat in the Hat, she spent time teaching students to read, and she took her class to the White House to watch *The Chronicles of Narnia* in the White House theater.

She is not the same girl who the public is more inclined to remember as a party girl. After all, that made much more titillating news than the fact that she is now following in her mother's footsteps teaching under-privileged children. She admits that these days she is likely to be in bed by 9:00 PM reading and asleep by 10:00. As Jenna will tell you,

"People change, you know."

After a year and a half. She took a leave of absence from her teaching position to work at an internship for UNICEF in Latin America. When her internship was compete she returned to the charter school.

In 2005, a year after the twenty-three year old twins graduated from college Jenna joined the first lady on a goodwill tour of Africa. They would travel from Cape Town to Dar Es Salaam, Tanzania where Barbara was a volunteer at a hospital for young AIDS patients; and Barbara then joined her mother and sister for a journey in Africa. While Jenna had stayed out of the public eye in the past she stepped out of her comfort zone committing herself to not just being a tag-along but an asset to her mother on the tour.

On a stop in Tanzania Jenna bought necklaces and bracelets made by the local women who were selling the jewelry to support their families. Children that had come out to entertain the first lady found themselves joined by Jenna who got up and danced and sang with them and hula-hooped with the children of Africa. They made a stop at the Fann Hospital for HIV/AIDS patients in Senegal where the first lady and Jenna had a tour of the vegetable garden that provided the patients with healthy food.

When Jenna is around children she is transformed. Her face lights up and she loses all intimidation. In Mozambique at a pediatric hospital for children she met a little boy who she introduced herself to and the First Daughter and the young boy did a three-part handshake which is an African greeting. She was quite at ease with the children as they were with her. At a Rwanda church she held an AIDS infected baby on her lap as she listened intently to stories of the people's lives and of the hardships they endured.

They did have an opportunity to enjoy the wildlife and spectacular scenery with both girls along on a journey through the Madikwe Game Reserve where they viewed lions and elephants and other wild animals in a natural habitat, but it was the people they met that left the biggest impact.

After she returned from her stint in Africa Barbara would later join her mother on a diplomatic trip to Liberia in January of 2006 and in February accompanied her to the Vatican City where she met Pope Benedict XVI.

Jenna had worked for almost a year with UNICEF in Central America where she had met an AIDS orphan by the name of Ana. Ana had HIV/AIDS from birth and lost both her parents to the disease. As a teen the youngster had been sexually abused and when she met the presidential daughter she was at that time trying to make a new life for herself. Jenna had been so touched by her story that she would later write a book called *Ana's Story.*

In 2007 Jenna returned with her mother to Africa and encouraged others there that told of being sexually abused and due to the abuse became HIV-positive. Jenna was deeply moved and told the girls they weren't alone and told them of Ana's story. This is the Jenna the press never bothered to show you.

Jenna wrote a second book, this one with her mother which is meant to encourage children to read. It is titled *'Read All About It!'* Jenna and her mother also co-wrote a picture book titled, *'My Great Big Backyard,'* paying tribute to our national parks.

Jenna and her mother had gone rafting down the Grand Canyon and camped out under the stars when she was a teenager and it was there she shared her mother's love of the outdoors.

Barbara traveled with her parents to the Beijing Olympics in 2008. On the trip she also visited South Korea and Thailand. While in Thailand they visited the Mae La Refugee Camp and the Mae Tao Clinic.

A Burmese doctor by the name of Dr. Cynthia Maung who calls the clinic home told of how she had fled Thailand back in 1988 when she was in her late 20's. Her country had been in chaos when she left. Troops fired at demonstrators who protested the junta and the troops would also round up demonstrators and drown them. She had escaped by walking through the treacherous jungles at night and sleeping during the day. When she finally crossed the border her life in a refugee camp began where she set up a clinic to treat refugees. She is considered the Mother Teresa of the Burmese.

The other stop they made before attending the Olympics was at the Mae La Refugee Camp. Nobody who was born in the camp has ever set foot outside due to Thai law requiring them to remain confined to the camps. The president and family were greeted by young refugees performing a traditional Burmese dance, a dance that came from the land over the mountains – a land they had never actually set foot in but would continue their customs and traditions.

Jenna while working in her father's presidential campaign had met Henry Hager. He had previously worked as a White House aide and is the son of former Virginia Republican Party Chairman John Hager. He had passed what Jenna described as "the boyfriend test" since he was able to keep up with the president during a mountain bike ride; but the president kept his pride when Henry was unable to get in front of him – smart guy, way to get on the good side of your future father-in-law.

Henry asked the president for his daughter's hand before proposing to Jenna in the summer of 2007. Jenna and Henry had camped out at Maine's Acadia National Park. After hiking to the top of Cadillac Mountain, the highest peak on the east coast and as the sun was rising Henry proposed. They were married May 10, 2008.

Jenna didn't want to become a White House bride but chose instead to have a private wedding at her parent's ranch. The location of the ceremony overlooked a small lake which was the old cattle watering hole – perfect for a Texas style wedding.

The night before the wedding there was a fierce storm and a rain so hard you couldn't hear the person who was standing right next to you. Hail and wind followed. The tops of the tent where the wedding reception was to be held were filling with water and sagging. The trials and tribulations of having an outside wedding. The next day the oppressive Texas heat dried everything out in time for the ceremony.

The president drove the bride to the ceremony site in a pickup truck and then her emotional father with a tear or two sliding down his cheek walked his daughter down the aisle as as a mariachi band played 'Here Comes the Bride.'

The Bush girls were at the inauguration of 2009 to see their father leave office as the incoming president Barack Obama made history when he took the oath of office as the first African-American president.

No longer a presidential daughter and living in New York in relative peace Barbara released a video in connection with the Human Rights Campaign, the nation's largest LGBT civil rights organization in regards to New York legalizing same-sex marriage.

Barbara had worked with AIDS patients in Africa and after graduating she along with a few friends put their minds to work in how to promote and recruit people to work towards global health. Her connections as a Bush opened many doors; she's upfront and admits to that, but it was for a good cause. She and her friends started Global Health Corps for which at the age of twenty-six she became chief executive.

Dr. Peter Piot who helped discover Ebola said, "I'm a big fan of the Global Health Corps. They engage non-medical people in global health." *The New York Times*, Nicholas Kristof reported about Global Health Corps. "I was initially suspicious of Global Health Corps, wondering how young people, often with no medical training, could be useful."

Global Health Corps provides opportunities for young professionals from diverse backgrounds to work on the front lines. A logistics expert who worked on a drug supply chain in Tanzania, improving drug access. And architects worked on designing clinics in Rwanda with less air flow, so tuberculosis patients would be less likely to infect others. The program gets plenty of praise from health professionals and has been very effective.

The twins come from two Republican presidents in the family, yet neither one is a registered Republican. While Barbara is not formally affiliated with any political party and explained in an interview with *People*, "I don't really label myself as Republican or Democrat." Speaking for herself and her sister, she said, "We're both very independent thinkers." In the 2016 presidential race she was seen in the Democratic Hillary Clinton camp – not as an adversary, but as a supporter.

Her father, a president who ran on the platform of pro-life, Barbara in 2017 is planning a Planned Parenthood fundraiser and will be the keynote speaker.

Jenna in the days since Washington has become an author, an editor-at-large for *Southern Living* magazine, and also adds her name to the list of political daughters who have become a correspondent for NBC news.

Henry and Jenna's first daughter Mila was born in April of 2013 and their second daughter Poppy, followed in August of 2015.

Jenna was there in 2014 as a correspondent for the *Today* show to interview her grandfather former President George H.W. Bush, on his 90th birthday when he was about to make his parachute jump. He had made similar jumps on his 80th and 85th birthday. This would be his last.

During the interview Jenna asked him, "What's your birthday wish on your 90th birthday?" The former president responded, "For happiness for my grandkids," and after only a moment's hesitation added, "Make sure the parachute opens."

Now that the Bush twins are grown they still have slumber parties and will teach the next generation of Bush girls, Jenna's daughters Mila and Poppy, to howl at the moon and sing and dance to the Pointer Sisters like they did with their mother – perhaps all three generations together.

44

BARACK OBAMA

Children of Michelle and Barack Obama:

Malia Ann Obama – Born: July 4, 1998   Still Living At The Time Of Publication

Natasha Obama "Sasha" - Born: June 10, 2001   Still Living At The Time Of Publication

The Obama daughters were the first African-American presidential children in American history.

History was made when our 44th president took the oath of office becoming the first black American president. Not only did he make history as our nation's first black president, but he won the presidency with the largest margin of victory of any Democratic candidate in history. An outsider, an unknown junior senator becoming President of the United States was unprecedented.

Barack was only forty-seven when elected president making him the third youngest elected president in history. Seeming to have come out of nowhere, he had only been a part of the political scene as a United States Senator as of 2004; and in just a matter of a few years in 2008 he was elected as President of the United States.

Barack Obama's past was unlike that of any any other president before him. His father, a black man from Kenya, was a polygamist. He already had a wife and children in Kenya when he married and had a son with a white woman by the name of Stanley Ann who was living in Hawaii. The son's name was Barack Hussein Obama II, who became our 44th president.

After divorcing her first husband Barack's mother would marry another foreigner, a man from Indonesia known as Lolo Soetoro. She and her son moved to Indonesia where they lived in Jakarta in a home with no running water or electricity. Barack at this time went by the name Barry. This is the name he went by from his younger days up until the time he ran for office.

He would return with his mother and step-sister to Hawaii at the age of ten. At the age of fourteen he was left in Hawaii by his mother who returned to Indonesia. He was raised by his white grandparents.

In the days before Obama became president he made three trips to Africa to explore his ancestry; the first trip being in 1987. He returned in 2006 as a U.S. Senator telling the people of the village of Kogelo located in Kenya that he was proud to come back home. When he became president rumors were rampant that he was actually born in Kenya; which would have made him constitutionally disqualified to be president. Obama would return to Africa in the years 2009 and 2013, but did not return to the land of his ancestors – perhaps fearing the old rumors of his place of birth would be resurrected.

In 1992 Barack and Michelle married. Malia Ann was born July 4, 1998 and Natasha, who goes by Sasha, arrived June 10, 2001.

Obama ran for the Senate in 1997. Off continuously campaigning it was often left up to Michelle to raise the girls as Barack was seldom home. Michelle had help as her mother stepped in and cared for the girls when needed.

When she could Michelle would join Barack on the campaign trail. As a "partner in crime" she urged Posedel, Barack's campaign staffer, to go with her to McDonalds for a Big Mac. This is hard to picture today as when Michelle was first lady her platform was all about exercise and nutritious foods. It was Barack at this time who watched what he ate. He would never have considered eating at a fast food restaurant but as Michelle said to Posedel, "He's not around. We can eat what we want."

Obama did win the Senate race. In 1997 he was sworn in to his first term in the Illinois Senate. In 2004 he won the election to the United States Senate. At that time who would have ever dreamed that in four years he would be elected president. Perhaps his daughter did. After her father was sworn in for the Senate Malia asked her father, "Daddy, are you going to be president?" He just smiled.

He had become only the second black man elected to the United States Senate since the days of Reconstruction, and in four years would become the first black man elected as President of the United States.

During his days as U.S. Senator Barack lived part time in Washington and part time in Chicago. Michelle and the girls were living in Chicago where the girls attended school at the Lab School, a private school associated with the University of Chicago. They lived in a 6,400 sq foot home. In a short period of time they had gone from being in debt to the tune of hundreds of thousands of dollars from school loans to living in a mansion valued at close to two million dollars.

The girls grew up close to their grandmother, Michelle's mother Marian Robinson. She was involved in their lives and there to help out when needed caring for them while their parents were off campaigning. The girls had busy schedules with soccer practice, tennis lessons, or ballet. Saturdays were spent with their mother and friends having a pizza lunch and an occasional movie.

They were brought up by their mother to be self-reliant as she had been when she was growing up. When the girls were just starting school they were given their own alarm clocks and told it was up to them to get themselves up and off to school on time. They had to get themselves up, dressed, make their beds, and come in for breakfast. They had a full-time family caregiver and a full-time housekeeper to do the things Michelle said she "didn't fully enjoy; such as cleaning, laundry, and cooking."

Holidays with young children are always festive occasions and were no different for the Obamas. They spent Christmas holidays in Hawaii visiting Barack's grandmother who had raised him. His grandfather had passed away in 1992 before either of the girls were born. In Hawaii the girls would spend time at the beach swimming, snorkeling, and bodysurfing at Kailua Beach; a nice contrast from Chicago winters back home. While Barack's grandmother passed away before she saw the boy she raised become president, the family continues to this day spending their Christmas holidays in Hawaii.

When Barack announced to Michelle that he intended to run for the office of the presidency she was concerned how that would affect their daughters' lives. She wanted their lives not to be disrupted any more than necessary. She was determined to keep them well-grounded.

When they told the girls that their father was running for the presidency Malia said, "Shouldn't you try to be vice president first?"

Michelle told Barack he could run for the presidency on two conditions: one was that he had to give up smoking – *that didn't happen*; though he did try to hide it from the public. The other condition was that if he lost the presidential race that was it. She said she wouldn't go through another election.

The girls followed their mother's lead and gave a condition of their own. They had wanted a dog for a long time but due to Malia's asthma had never been able to have one. The girls had been online doing research looking into breeds of dogs that were hypoallergenic. They were not to be deterred. Their mother said, "Win or lose, when the election is over we're getting a dog."

Barack was busy and away from his family often campaigning. The girls had webcams so they could keep in touch with their father and keep him up-to-date on their own lives. Little Sasha would ask her dad, "What city are you in, Daddy?" as he was on the road campaigning.

Regardless of how busy their father was on the campaign trail he always made time for his daughters. They were after all "Daddy's girls." When home or when the girls were available to travel with him he would often take his girls out roller skating, to play putt putt golf, or just to spend some quality time with Malia and Sasha.

When Malia was asked what it felt like to get up in front of large crowds with their parents while her father was campaigning she answered, "I realize the people aren't here to see me. I'm just a kid." But the crowds loved it when the girls appeared. It's hard to miss the face of boredom on their faces as they sat through speech after speech. After all, they are just kids and they had heard it all before.

The Obamas made appearances in many places to campaign, one of those places was the Iowa State Fair. "We're here for the State Fair," Michelle would tell the crowds; which wasn't exactly true. They were definitely there to campaign. They were trying to reach out and secure votes and having a good time with their daughters.

Malia and Sasha convinced their father to ride with them on bumper cars. They enjoyed carnival games in between their father's campaigning and being stopped as they wandered through the fair shaking hands and talking to the people.

Michelle would tell the people, "I just want some stuff on a stick – a corn dog, a Snickers bar...doesn't matter what it is. Just has to be on a stick." As first lady who later pushed healthy eating, she wouldn't be caught today eating any of the foods she had enjoyed at the fair that day.

There were times when the girls traveled with them on the campaign trail and other times they stayed home with their mother or grandmother. Their parents would sometimes split up and campaign separately to reach out to more people. Michelle angered many Americans while campaigning in Wisconsin when she made the comment, "For the first time in my adult life, I am proud of my country because it feels like hope is making a comeback."

Michelle repeated the statement later the same day and this time in front of television cameras. Realizing Michelle was at times coming across as "an angry, black woman" the campaign staff realized she could be a liability in the campaign as well as an asset. The comment angered *many* Americans.

Malia had tagged along to one of the events where both her father and Hillary Clinton were speaking. Malia, ten years old at the time, made a pretty remarkable comment for a girl her age. She said, "You know this is a pretty big deal. If Daddy wins, he'd be the first African American to be a nominee. Because there was slavery, and there were people who couldn't do things because of their race." Her mother smiled at this enlightening thought for such a young girl, but then Malia continued, "But it would also be a big deal if a woman won. Because there was also the time when women couldn't vote. So it would be a big deal either way." - Probably not what Michelle wanted to hear.

It became evident during the campaign that Barack was to become the nominee, but yet Hillary Clinton refused to concede. Michelle was livid, "Why doesn't she just do the right thing and bow out gracefully?" This was an act that Hillary would repeat when she ran again in 2016 against Donald Trump; not as the nominee but as the presidential candidate.

A month later Hillary Clinton still refused to concede. Her supporters told her without mincing words that she had lost and for the good of the Democratic party she needed to concede with no further delay. It still took her another two days and then she did so through email, not even having the courtesy to make the call of congratulations.

On election day the Obamas brought along Malia and Sasha to witness their parents voting. They arrived at the Beulah Shoesmith Elementary School on the South Side of Chicago to vote. Obama later joked about his wife Michelle taking so long to vote, "I had to check out to see who she was voting for." For Michelle it was a moment to savor.

Malia and Sasha were sent off to school just like any other day. When school was out they had a treat of getting their hair done and got dressed up and enjoyed a family dinner out at a steak house before heading over to the Hyatt Regency Hotel where they would watch the returns on TV.

For a time the family mingled with the larger crowd watching the results filtering in downstairs. The family quietly went off to watch the results in their hotel room with family and Secret Service only in the room. All eyes were glued to the TV watching as the election results came in. The family was subdued, unlike those downstairs who were jumping up and down and cheering as each state's winner was announced.

Just four years into his first Senate term a young black man had just made history. At 11:00 PM CNN's Wolf Blitzer announced that Barack Obama had just been elected the 44th president of the United States.

The Obamas made their way to Grant Park where the victory rally was being held for campaign workers and supporters where they watched the results come in over jumbotrons. Barack, Michelle, Malia and Sasha Obama went on stage with the crowds erupting in cheers and waving American flags in celebration, holding up cell phones taking photos to capture the moment. Sasha holding the hand of her dad while Malia held her mother's hand they waved to their supporters.

"A new dawn of American leadership is at hand," Obama said to his supporters. It was a night none of them would ever forget.

The girl's grandmother who had been caring for the girls while their parents were off campaigning told Malia that night, "Well, surely your mother's not going to make you go to school after being up this late at night; that would be cruel." The girls had been up way past their normal bedtime waiting for the election results and then the celebration afterward, but their mother was one for sticking to a strict schedule and sure enough the next morning the girls were sent to school.

The Obamas moved to Washington a few weeks ahead of the inauguration in order to get their daughters enrolled in school and be there when the new semester began. They would be attending the Sidwell Friends School, a school that had seen other presidential children as students. Though both girls would be attending the school their campuses were in different locations. The middle and upper grades campus was located in Washington but the campus Sashsa would attend for lower school was located in Bethesda, Maryland. The final year Sasha spent there as a First Daughter the tuition during the school year of 2015 – 2016 was $37,750 with an enrollment of less than 1,200 students.

In November after the election the Obamas arrived at the White House where they were met by the outgoing president and first lady to give them a tour of the home they would be living in for at least the next four years. As we all know now, they remained there for eight years after being reelected.

The Bush girls, Barbara and Jenna, were also there to welcome Malia and Sasha and show them around. It has become a tradition not only for the outgoing president to leave a letter to their successor but also for the outgoing presidential children to leave a letter for the incoming First Family. While the Bush girls spent little time themselves at the White House it was a very nice letter they left for Malia and Sasha reminding them that they father was "dad" and basically to disregard the harsh criticism they were sure to hear.

The Bush daughters would write yet another letter eight years later as the Obamas prepared to leave the White House about the memories they would take with them, as elite members of former First Children. It is unknown at this date whether Obama's daughters did the same for incoming presidential son Barron Trump.

On their initial visit to the White House the Bush girls took ten-year old Malia and seven-year old Sasha to meet the White House staff who would become important people in their lives over the next few years. They showed them around the family quarters and showed them how to slide down the banisters as so many presidential children had also done in the past.

The girls' grandmother who had been so much a part of their lives would be moving with them to the White House to continue helping with the girls. She was a bit more lenient with the girls than their mother. The first lady, the "Nazi of clean eating," made the rule that the girls were to only be allowed dessert on weekends, but when grandma was in charge they were allowed ice cream regardless of what day of the week it was.

The Obamas stayed at the Hay-Adams Hotel until the Blair House was available as they had arrived in Washington earlier than expected to get the girls set up in school. Ten days before the inauguration they took Sasha and Malia to visit the Lincoln Memorial. It was no longer "just the family"; they were now accompanied by Secret Service everywhere they went. It was a chilly night in Washington, something they were accustomed to from their days in Chicago as they walked up the steps of the Lincoln Memorial. On the way out their parents pointed out the Capitol where in a few days their father would be taking the oath of office and pointed out the Washington Monument and other historic sites of Washington, D.C.

When the Obamas became the new residents of the White House Sasha was the youngest child to live in the White House since John Kennedy, Jr during the Kennedy administration. Sasha was seven when she moved into the White House.

The night before the inauguration there was a 'Kids' Inaugural' titled "We Are The Future" with entertainment for the younger crowd. Malia and Sasha enjoyed watching the Jonas Brothers who were favorites of Malia and Sasha.

Michelle arrived at the inauguration dressed in an Isabel Toledo designer dress covered in a coat and sheath, J. Crew jade leather gloves to offset her lemongrass color dress, a pair of Jimmy Choo pumps, and sporting 2-carat diamond stud earrings valued at $20,000. Malia wore a a deep blue coat and Sasha wore pastel shades of orange and pink.

As her father prepared to take the oath of office Malia took photos with her own camera. Michelle held the Bible of Abraham Lincoln, the first time it had been used since Lincoln himself used it for his own inauguration in 1861. Malia and Sasha watched their father wearing matching grins from ear to ear and after being announced as the next president Sasha gave her father a thumbs up.

The oath of office had not gone smoothly though with both the president and the chief justice stumbling over the words. Following the oath of office was the customary Congressional Luncheon. Chief Justice Roberts whispered in the president's ear that it was his fault that the oath of office had not gone smoothly and apologized. It was about that time that Senator Ted Kennedy collapsed to the floor suffering a seizure. Already ill and battling brain cancer the senator was rushed by ambulance to the hospital.

The Obama girls had returned to the White House during the Congressional Luncheon until the time of the inaugural parade. That evening the girls had their own party as their parents attended ten inaugural balls.

The girls enjoying their first evening in the White House watched 'Bolt' and 'High School Musical 3' in the White House Theater – a place they planned to make good use out of during their time in the White House.

The White House staff sets up a scavenger hunt for the new First Family members to not only entertain them while their parents are at the inaugural balls but so they will become familiar with the different rooms in the White House. The last clue on the scavenger hunt they discovered was the Jonas Brothers who paid the girls a surprise visit. They played a few songs to entertain the girls and posed for pictures with them leaving them with some lasting memories of their own from inauguration night. That was their first experience of one of many perks they would receive as First Daughters.

As First Daughters they would have advantages and perks, but they also had the same chores they had back home in Chicago. This wasn't due to the White House staff, but at the insistence of their mother.

After a day's worth of worrisome discussion over whether the president had been properly sworn into office due to him transposing a few words in the oath after being incorrectly prompted by the chief justice, advisers determined it would be best to re-administer the oath.

The following evening Chief Justice John Roberts administered the oath of office again at the White House Map Room. Only after the act was completed were reporters informed. They were told that rather than have someone challenge the legitimacy of his presidency it was best to have a do over.

The legitimacy of his presidency would be challenged, not due to the errors when he took the oath of office but due to his questionable place of birth. Some said he was born in Africa and disputed the fact that he was born in Hawaii. That debate, the "birther controversy," continued for quite some time and some still question his place of birth.

The girls reminded their father of the promise he had made before he ran for the presidency – a dog. When Senator Ted Kennedy learned about their father's promise and of the president's daughters desire for a dog he gave them the gift of a six month old black and white Portuguese water dog. The puppy was named Bo. They would later get a companion for Bo, a completely black Portuguese water dog they named Sunny.

The dogs had become so popular there was even a plot to kidnap one of the Obamas' dogs which was thwarted when the Secret Service found the man who planned to kidnap one of the dogs holed up in a hotel room in Washington with a cache of weapons and ammunition in his vehicle.

As the Clintons had done with Chelsea, the Obamas kept their daughters out of the limelight and about all the public saw of them were photos that came sanctioned from the White House or captured "staged moments." The media and the public were rarely given a glimpse into their day to day life and so much of the Obama girls life during their White House days remains a mystery. We have learned basically what they want us to know and see only what we are allowed to see.

It was tumultuous times when the Obamas moved to the White House; it was post-9/11 and also many Americans weren't ready to see a black man as their president. While Julian Bond, Civil Rights legend, stated on *'The Colbert Report'* that there were more threats than with any other previous presidents, it is unknown as to where he received this unconfirmed information. The Secret Service doesn't discuss the number of threats against any president, but Secret Service Director Mark Sullivan at that time stated that the number of threats was at the same level as other presidents in the past.

There are always threats, which the staff of the White House learned first hand when on the night of November 11, 2011 Oscar Ortega-Hernandez parked his car on Constitution Avenue, rolled down his window and shot his semiautomatic rifle into the White House several times. Snipers on the roof standing just 20 feet from where one bullet struck and another agent stationed directly under the second-floor terrace where the bullets struck were surprised when they got the call over the radio from their supervisor, "No shots have been fired. . . . Stand down." They were informed the noise was backfire.

At the time of the shooting the president and first lady were out of town and Malia was out with friends but expected home at any moment. Sasha and her grandmother were inside the White House at the time of the shooting. It was only four days later when the truth was revealed when an observant housekeeper discovered a broken window and a chunk of concrete on the floor outside the Yellow Oval Room which is inside the First Family living quarters. At least seven bullets had hit the family's private residence.

The Secret Service failed when it came to this attack on the White House. The president and first lady were livid when they learned the truth and the fact that they felt their daughters had been in serious danger. They hadn't even been told anything about the incident until Reginald Dickson assistant White House Usher told her about what the housekeeper had found not realizing the first lady had not been informed about the shots fired during their absence.

One of the greatest perks of First Families is the travel. Malia and Sasha have had the opportunity to travel the world accompanying their parents many times on visits abroad. On one such trip they made with their mother was a trip to South Africa where they met former President Nelson Mandela.

The girls have made new friends since their move to Washington and have enjoyed sleep overs and spending time at Camp David where they were often able to invite friends to accompany them. Sasha played on a basketball team. Malia played varsity tennis and attended school dances.

The girls take selfies and roll their eyes at their father's lame jokes like most typical teens. They have grown up to where they now prefer to be entertained by Chance the Rapper over watching Disney movies which they enjoyed when they first moved to the White House. Perhaps the only difference between them and their friends; besides living at 1600 Pennsylvania Avenue, was the rule their mother laid down, "No cell phones before the age of twelve."

Obama was elected for a second term in 2012 and the girls had grown with Malia then fourteen and ready to begin her first year in high school and Sasha the baby of the family at eleven who had easily grown a foot since her first day in the White House. The girls were spotted taking selfies between events at the 2013 inaugural parade. It appears the first lady gave in to her rule of no cell phones before the age of twelve.

Malia and Sasha traveled with their mother and grandmother to China in 2014 on a Goodwill Tour where they sometimes appeared to be bored and churlish, not very interested in the historic sites they visited. They were able to see such historic sites such as the Great Wall of China, visited the Chengdu Panda Base in Sichuan province, toured the Xi'an city wall which is a 600-year-old city wall which is the oldest and most well-preserved defensive city wall in the country, the Museum of Terracotta Warriors in Xi'an, watched a Peking opera performance at the Summer Palace in Beijing, and visited the Forbidden City.

Malia celebrated her sixteenth birthday while living at the White House, an event all teens look forward to as it is whey they can finally learn how to drive. Their first opportunity for a bit of freedom.

The first lady, a guest on the Rachel Ray show said, "Driving for Malia, I think, gives her a sense of normalcy, like the rest of her friends are doing." It was the Secret Service who taught her how to drive; after all, it had been about eight years since her parents had driven a car themselves and it was feared their driving skills might be a bit rusty.

At sometime during a First Family's time in the White House they know without a doubt they are going to be a target for criticism and even though it is almost an unspoken rule by this point to leave young presidential children alone that doesn't always happen. Republican congressional aide Elizabeth Lauten was forced to resign after posting on her Facebook page a criticism on Obams's daughters saying they were "dressing like bar floozies."

They certainly weren't dressed like "bar floozies" the night they attended their first White House State Dinner. Malia looked like Cinderella as she held out her floor length strapless gown out in front of her admiring it as she walked the red carpet. Both girls looked very grown up in their Naeem Khan dresses – each dress cost about what an average American makes in six months time.

The first lady spilled the beans while on the David Letterman show letting the world know that even though you are first lady when there is a teenager in the house you still have to put up with attitude. She spoke of dealing with a sulky teenager and their moods.

The first lady said, "We have one who generally stays here," the first lady said, gesturing with her hand to show an even keel. "And then we have one we call our grumpy cat, our salty biscuit. You just never know what you're going to get from that one."

Of course everyone wanted to know to which First Daughter she was referring to, but when asked she would only say, "I'm not saying – they could be watching," she said. "But they know who they are."

While First Daughters the Obama family visited Carlsbad Caverns, Yosemite National Park, Yellowstone, and the Grand Canyon. The girls seemed unimpressed and seemed to barely tolerate their father and his enthusiasm for the sites. They seemed much more interested when taken to New York on a shopping trip.

The Obama girls probably traveled more than any other presidential children. Some of the travel spots they visited were: China, Liberia, Morocco, Spain, Cuba, Germany, Brazil, South Africa, Great Britain, Amsterdam, and Italy. And those are just the travel spots abroad...

During the Obamas eight years in office travel expenses cost taxpayers more than $96 million - an outrage to many Americans.

The Obama daughters are not the first presidential children to grow up in the age of social media; just look at how the Bush daughters were exposed to their escapades. Malia was also exposed during a visit to Brown University while searching for the university she wanted to attend. While at Brown a photo was taken of her at a college frat house standing in front of a beer pong table with a bong on the table in front of her. The photo went viral on social media.

Malia has been caught on camera smoking pot at a concert and while on their summer vacation at Martha's Vineyard had to be hauled out of a house party by the Secret Service when they discovered the cops were about to raid the party.

Malia was seen in Amsterdam drunk and dancing the night away till 3:30 A.M. and then left when it was discovered that the daughter of the president was at the nightclub. Not exactly headline news unless you're a member of the First Family and then it appears as though the world is just waiting for you to make one wrong move and catch you in the act.

After Malia's "fall from grace," she disappeared for about three months. When you saw the family or her sister she wasn't with them and the media not being able to help themselves 'assumed' she was off to rehab.

Malia took an educational trip to the Cordillera Real mountain range in Bolivia and Peru with a group of teens. Three brothers led guided hikes across the mountain range. The teens had chores to do on the hike such as cooking and cleaning up. The guides had been informed that they would be hosting an important American dignitary but were unaware of who it was. The teens arrived with some bodyguards, but it wasn't until Bolivian journalists broke the story after the hike was completed that the guards became aware of the fact that they had escorted the president's daughter on the hike.

One of the guides when later asked said, "She spoke Spanish very well and was mesmerized by the Bolivian landscape." The travelers lived with a family in a tiny town in central Bolivia during the eighty-three day journey where the teens traipsed the mountains and jungles of Bolivia and Peru.

All in all, the eight years have passed with little controversy as far as Malia and Sasha go. Tucked away in their castle, or prison as some presidential children call the White House; mainly out of sight of the public and prying press they have stood up well to the demands and spotlight of a presidential family.

The president has said his daughter Malia wants to become a filmmaker and over past summers interned in Hollywood as a production assistant on the CBS sci-fi thriller 'Extant' where she did little more than coffee runs but had the opportunity to be on set and see things in action. The next summer she interned in New York on the set of HBO's 'Girls.' She also had an internship for a time at Smithsonian's National Zoo.

Malia graduated from high school the last summer they were in the White House and decided to take a gap year before entering Harvard in the fall of 2017. In her White House years she has gone from a fifth grader to now standing about six feet tall. She learned to drive and began dating while a First Daughter. When her father discussed his daughter dating to comedian and television host Steve Harvey he joked that he's "got men with guns following them around."

Sasha herself was able to experience what it was like to be a part of the working world when she worked at 'Nancy's', a fast food seafood restaurant on Martha's Vineyard. She worked the cash register and bussed tables for a few hours each day for a week while under the protective eye of the Secret Service.

The Obamas final Christmas as the First Family at the lighting of the White House Christmas tree Sasha lip-synced "Sunday Candy" along with Chance the Rapper entertaining the crowd.

There's a new president in the White House now, but the Obamas plan to remain in Washington for at least the next two years while Sasha finishes high school and Malia will become a Harvard student. The Obamas are leasing the home of former Bill Clinton press spokesman Joe Lockhart, a 8,200 sq foot home with nine bedrooms and 8 ½ baths, but will no longer have the White House staff to care for their every need.

Leaving the White House the first lady had told Ellen on her show that she thought it was going to be "a tough time" for her daughters to leave the White House and return to civilian life.

The little girls who had first come to be First Daughters are little no longer; they leave now with Malia at eighteen years of age and Sasha at fifteen. While news of the girls as First Daughters was closely monitored by the White House on what was allowed to become public knowledge, they appeared to have handled growing up in the spotlight pretty well, but still have at times shown a streak of independence along with some attitude.

45

Donald Trump

Children with first wife Ivana and Donald Trump

Donald John "Don" Trump Jr.- Birth: Dec 31, 1977   Still Alive At Time of Publication

Ivanka Marie Trump - Birth: Oct. 30, 1981   Still Alive At Time of Publication

Eric Frederick Trump - Birth: Jan 6, 1984   Still Alive At Time of Publication

Children with second wife Marla Maples and Donald Trump

Tiffany Ariana Trump - Birth: Oct. 13, 1993   Still Alive At Time of Publication

Children with third wife Melania and Donald Trump

Barron William Trump - Birth: March 20, 2006   Still Alive At Time of Publication

Ivanka will hold the title of the most glamorous and influential

First Daughter throughout history.

Donald Trump our 45th president is the first president to have never served a day in politics before taking the oath of office. Americans fed up with empty promises in the past from politicians, the rising debt, and not liking the direction they were seeing their country headed voted him in as the nation's next president. Vice President Pence, the polar opposite of President Trump being a quiet, respectful, humble man told Congress that President Trump had marshaled a movement unlike any other before him in American history.

The election for the 45th president was the most contentious election in history, and the problems between the two parties didn't come to an end once Donald Trump became our president.

What happened to our nation who came together as 'Americans' who cared for one another regardless of race, religion, or political party after 9/11? Since when have Americans become so devisive and put their own interests ahead of what's best for the country? Today there is such contention between one political party over another that instead of working together as President Trump says to "Make America Great Again," some are chanting the mantras of propaganda put out by the mainstream media and those with an agenda such as George Soros. It appears they have drunk the Kool-Aid.

Never before has a newly elected president rolled up his sleeves and gotten to work so quickly and accomplished so much so soon after being elected – *even before taking the oath of office*; to work on our nation's existing problems which he inherited from the last administration: a debt of almost $20 trillion, racial division the worst it's been in decades, the issue of immigrants coming into our country illegally, and the very real threat of Isis.

President Trump will most assuredly hold the record of "M*ost Accomplished*" the first 100 days of taking office. The only thing getting in his way and slowing him down are those on the left who are doing everything they can to impede his progress and RINO's in Congress, rather than choosing to do what is best for America.

President Trump is the first president to have been married three times. He's also the first president who had a doll made in his likeness, bad hair and all, that spoke well-known phrases from the TV show *The Apprentice*.

President Trump's third and current wife, the new First Lady, will be the nation's 2nd foreign born first lady. The first foreign born first lady was the wife of our 6th president John Quincy Adams in 1825.

First Lady Melania Trump was born in Yugoslavia and is the *first* first lady to be a naturalized, rather than birthright, citizen of the United States. She became a resident of the U.S. in 2001 and an American citizen in 2006. She speaks an impressive five languages. In addition to her native language Slovenian, she also speaks English, French, Italian, and German.

First Lady Melania was a former model and is a first lady with grace and style that will rival the former first lady of the Camelot era, First Lady Jackie Kennedy, who was known for her elegance.

Melania married Donald Trump in 2005 in what can only be described as a fairy tale wedding that took place in the groom's palace in Florida, the estate having a net worth of between $200 - $300 million. The bride wore a $100,000 Dior dress that drew audible gasps from the guests with the 1,500 sparkling crystals embedded in the gown that took laborers 550 hours to hand sew. The bridal couple was serenaded by Billy Joel. The guests were all names and faces both famous and familiar to the world. The guests feasted on caviar and Cristal as they celebrated the marriage of Donald and Melania Trump.

Melania has traditional values and her priority is family – always family first. There is no nanny raising their son Barron. She feels that raising a child is a mother's duty, a duty she takes very seriously. Because that is her focus, her platform as first lady will be towards helping women and children, both issues she feels strongly about. She will be adamant in combating cyberbullying. I'm sure her stance on this issue was only reinforced when her own ten year old son was attacked on social media shortly after the election.

Melania said, "Our culture has gotten too mean and too rough, especially to children and teenagers. It is never OK when a 12-year-old girl or boy is mocked, bullied, or attacked. It is terrible when that happens on the playground. And it is absolutely unacceptable when it is done by someone with no name hiding on the internet."

There was very little seen of Melania during the campaign and during an interview between Ivanka and *People* magazine the subject was brought up. Ivanka a mother herself defended Melania's decision. "She made a decision I totally respect which is that she has a young son, he needs stability, he needs routine. My father's traveling so frequently and she is an unbelievably consistent, loving, and reliable figure in Barron's life."

The first lady will remain living in Trump Tower in New York with the youngest member of the first family the Trump's son Barron, at least until the end of the school year. Rumor has it she may remain living there instead of at the White House. So while the first lady may not be immediately taking on the task of hostess or first lady it remains to be seen what her plans will be as far as her role in the White House. Perhaps she will be as elusive as First Lady Jackie Kennedy who spent more time at Glen Ora, the family's horse farm, than at the White House and was seldom there other than to hostess state dinners and for special events.

Donald Trump is the first presidential candidate to have ever financed his own campaign. He is in nobody's pocket and will not be influenced due to campaign donations. Ivanka and her two brothers Don, Jr and Eric, children of first wife Ivana, were often on the campaign trail endorsing their father during the campaign making several public appearances, speeches, and speaking to the media.

Ivanka introduced her father after she gave a speech where she spoke up on the subject of her own political views, "Like many of my fellow millennials, I do not consider myself categorically Republican or Democrat."

Ivanka will easily hold the title of the most glamorous and influential First Daughter throughout history.

She's pretty, articulate, smart, and powerful; and like her dad she knows how to get things done. Ivanka has no plans to take an official White House job. Due to the nepotism laws she is unable to take an official position which is a shame, because it is believed she would do a remarkable job. It is assumed she will have an active role in her father's administration; just what her role will be remains to be seen, but she will be a highly visible force in the Trump administration and around Washington.

Ivanka and her husband Jared Kushner, who will serve as senior advisor to the president, are Washington's new power couple and a couple that is well-liked and admired.

President Trump's two oldest sons Don, Jr and Eric will be remaining in New York to take over the reins of their father's business. Donald Trump made his fortune as a visionary in real estate and building.

Donald Trump chose to go into real-estate as his father had before him but he made his own name and chose his own style. Even though his father was successful and he was a millionaire, Donald Trump's decision to follow his gut instinct and go his own way turned out to be a huge success story. What made him so successful was his ability to execute – he did what he said he was going to do; and if his first days in the Oval Office are any indication, he is continuing to do just that – living up to his word.

If baseball had been more lucrative in his younger days his memoirs may have had a different ending. He was a great baseball player, good enough to get into the major leagues. Major League scouts had sought him out looking him over and they liked what they saw. He decided to stick with what he knew and what he knew he could be good at, and that was real estate.

Donald Trump is the father of five children between three wives. He has three children with his first wife Ivana, Czech model Ivana Trump. Their children are Don, Jr., Ivanka, and Eric.

With both parents so busy with business, what was the secret of success to raising such well-grounded "rich kids" who weren't your typical spoiled children? First wife Ivana's answer was to instill great values in her children and to keep them busy. "I see so many kids which are my friends' children and they're so messed up. They drink, they're on the drugs, they don't want to work, they have no ambition. They get all the money in the world. Why they should get up before eleven o'clock? They're real losers."

Their mother was determined to keep them busy and out of trouble. "Every mother knows that idle children get into trouble. If both parents are working, they have nothing to do, they come home, and they go out on the street. My kids don't have time for nonsense," Ivana said. The Trump children never got something just because they wanted it. "If they want something they work for it. Even for their weekly allowance, they can't just spend it on nonsense."

So exactly how much did they get for allowance one might wonder. Don, Jr got $5 a week, Ivanka got $3, and Eric got $1. "They have to know the value of money or else they will be spoiled," their mother explained.

It had been the same for Donald Trump when he was growing up. His father was wealthy enough that his children wouldn't have to work, but he insisted that they do so. He was determined that his children would appreciate the value of a dollar and unless they worked for it they would never understand that lesson. Donald Trump recalled in his youth when he came home and told his father that his friend's father had bought his son a $45 baseball glove and he would like one too. His father said no, that if he were simply given things he wouldn't appreciate the value of the item. The lesson was learned and it was passed on to his own children.

Don, Jr and Eric are six years apart and have always been very close and still are to this day. They will tell you their first memories are not of Fifth Avenue in a glitzy penthouse but of the outdoors in Czechoslovakia. Their grandparents lived with them a few months during the year and they spent their summers with their grandparents in what later became known as the Czech Republic.

Their grandparents lived in what can only be described as a blue-collar environment, a far cry from their home environment in New York City. Their grandfather who was an outdoorsman took the time to teach the boys to hike, hunt, and fish; to appreciate the outdoors – there were no video games to play or time spent wasted in front of a television. Ivanka stayed at home with her grandmother and watched her cook. The children were taught never to waste food from their grandparents who came from a place that worked hard for everything they had.

Don, Jr. knows those lessons were instilled in him as he explains, "I look at a plate of food that's three-quarters eaten and think, 'Well, she'd be screaming at me.' " Don, Jr. the oldest who spent the most time with his grandparents was very close to his grandfather. He learned to speak Czech when young before his grandparents became fluent in English. He would also learn French while in school making him multi-lingual.

Ivanka admits that their grandparents were a big influence in their lives, but she readily admits that about the only Czech she can speak are the curse words.

Both their maternal and their paternal grandparents were very involved with their grandchildren. Ivanka's grandfather Trump would hold up a shiny silver dollar in front of Ivanka and ask her if she would like that silver dollar. "Before I can give it to you, you need to ask your grandmother if she has chores for you to do." Not one to turn down a shiny trinket the young Ivanka was only too eager to earn that silver dollar. She would skip off to help her grandmother with her chores until she earned that silver dollar. It was never just given to her. Her grandfather made it very clear: If you want something, you have to work for it. There weren't going to be any handouts in the Trump family.

Ivanka a beautiful young woman who always looks like a fashion model outfitted in the latest fashions, many of them her own, admits that as a child she may have been dressed up in dresses with lace and frills but as a young girl she had the heart and soul of a tom boy. Being the only girl in the family and with a mother who often tromped around construction sites in a hard hat it's not unusual to imagine that Ivanka's favorite play toys were Tonka trucks, erector sets, and LEGO's. When she was six years old one of the guys on the construction crews that worked for her father showed her how to work the manual levels on a bulldozer, a life size Tonka truck. A girl's dream come true.

Ivanka as a little girl all dressed up at her father's Trump Taj Mahal in Atlantic City said she held her own turning more than a few heads when she screamed her head off for her favorite boxer getting to see such greats as Mike Tyson, Evander Holyfield, and Sugar Ray Leonard.

Trump Towers was completed shortly after Ivanka was born and the Trump family lived on the 68th floor. Like most girls she had posters of her teen idols on her walls, but unlike most other little girls the Trumps' neighbors were people like Michael Jackson, Steven Spielberg, and Johnny Carson. And unlike most of her peers her family had a spectacular view of New York's skyline and Central Park with a waterfall in their living room.

Ivanka as a young girl would follow her mother around while she worked on the Trump Plaza. That was their special time together and a time that Ivanka relished. In the mornings her mother brought Ivanka with her and Ivanka described that experience as "like being taken to the world's most magical playground."

Once her mother made her rounds Ivanka was allowed to go off on her own to play. She enjoyed spending hours exploring the hotel, snooping around all the different areas, and riding the elevators up and down endlessly.

Ivanka admits that there were times when she would have traded it all for a little more time with her parents. Working more hours of the day than not, neither her mother or her father were around much when she was growing up. Her and her brothers grew up with two nannies and a bodyguard. While all children would like more time with their parents, Ivanka said her parents made sure they had the love and attention they needed. "I was blessed with two of the best parents in the world. My brothers and I had some world-class role models."

"Donnie's always been my best friend, a mentor," Eric said, "In a way, he raised me. My father, I love and I appreciate, but he always worked 24 hours a day."

Yet whenever the Trump kids called their father in his office he always took time to talk to them regardless of what he was in the middle of or who was sitting in his office.

Eric remembers his childhood as being normal, but then what did he have it to compare to? Did he even know what a normal childhood was like? Most people would describe the upbringing of the Trump children as anything but normal.

The family took vacations together often in Aspen, Colorado where they skied. Their mother who had once been a star athlete on the Czech ski team taught her own children to ski at an early age. They were quick learners and natural athletes themselves.

Ivanka told the story of how competitive her father is when at the age of eight when on the slopes at Aspen she was racing her father. "At one point I remember thinking it was rather bizarre that I had started moving backwards up the hill," Ivanka said. Then she realized her father had hooked his ski pole around her and was pulling her back up. He was that determined to win.

Eric laughs at his own memory. "He would try to push me over, just so he could beat his ten-year-old son down the mountain."

Even as adults they still enjoy their time on the slopes. "We're the first people on the mountain and the last ones off," says Eric. "We're always taking runs together. We're die-hard skiers."

Eric, the youngest of the children with Donald's first wife, doesn't speak any Czech but did learn French in school. He is a businessman following in the family business and a former reality TV personality. All three of the Trump children had a role in the reality TV show their father starred in called *The Apprentice* and later their stepbrother Barron would make his debut on the show.

Eric recalls his days when he was around five or six spending time in his father's office quietly building Lego cities while his father was working. He would travel with his father joining his father on jaunts to visit different job sites and negotiating deals. He was getting a feel for his future whether he was aware of it at the time or not.

Ivanka at the age of eight was admitted to the School of American Ballet in the Lincoln Center. It is considered quite an honor and a feat of accomplishment to be admitted into the program. What other little girl do you know of that can brag that Michael Jackson came to see her perform in her ballet recital? Their neighbor Michael Jackson who lived one floor below them in the Trump Tower when he heard about the recital came to see her perform.

Their father never one to go too far away from business was more likely to stay home when Ivanka and her mother traveled around the world. At times her brothers came along, but not always. By the time she was twenty-eight she could count over one hundred countries she had visited. Some of the places she visited in her travels were to France, China, Argentina, and Egypt. Working in a senior position in her father's company she continues to add to the list of places she has visited.

When Donald Trump divorced his first wife Don, Jr was twelve, Ivanka was nine, and Eric was seven. Divorce is hard enough on children but when stories of your father's sex life are front page news on the tabloids and the media confronts the children asking them if the stories are true made it even more difficult.

Don, Jr blamed his father for the divorce and didn't speak to his father for a year. Their mother received custody and the children lived with her following the divorce. Eric believes that his divorce brought on a deeper bond between him and his brother and sister.

Their father would remain in their lives, but with his long hours at work they were raised by their mother Ivana and their grandparents. Don, Jr. and Ivanka looked out for Eric and essentially helped to raise him even though they themselves were young.

Donald Trump had been involved with Marla Maples even before he was divorced from his first wife. Marla gave birth to their daughter Tiffany in 1993. Donald and Marla were married two months after the birth.

Marla was at Trump's estate Mar-A-Lago in Florida awaiting the birth of their daughter while Donald was in New York working. When she went into labor he flew to Florida and was there to witness the birth. Donald chose the name Tiffany after the prestigious jewelry retailer.

Donald Trump's second marriage to Marla Maples lasted only six years, three of those years while a divorce negotiation was taking place. Marla became a single mother to Tiffany and raised her in Calabasas, California. Tiffany was living clear across the United States from where her father was living in New York. Marla brought her daughter to New York a few times a year so she could visit her father and have some time with him.

Tiffany spent about two weeks a year at Trump's estate in Florida Mar-A-Lago, and other than the time she visited him in New York there wasn't much contact other than that as far as a relationship with his daughter during her youth. Donald did help with financial obligations such as the expenses at the Viewpoint School she attended which ran at over $31,000 a year.

The Trump children were accosted by the media during their parent's divorce asking them about their father's affair with Marla Maples. The Trump children were aged seven to twelve and yet the press were actively pursuing them asking them questions that were totally inappropriate to be addressed to a child. To protect her children from the rumors and the press Ivana sent her children to boarding school.

The boys attended The Hill School a university-preparatory boarding school in Pennsylvania. Ivanka attended the Chapin School. Chapin is an exclusive all-girls prep school on Manhattan's Upper East Side. She transferred to Chaote Rosemary Hall a prominent boarding school in Connecticut once she reached high school at the age of fifteen.

"My parents were fine with spending lavishly on their childrens' education. It wasn't about pampering or spoiling us but investing in our future," Ivanka said. "I realized early on I wasn't a responsibility to my parents, but a responsibility to myself above all. To do the right thing and carry myself with pride and confidence and dignity. To preserve and protect the family name and reputation."

The Trump children were home for summers. They were all three expected to work during the summers, not to sit around wasting time or getting in trouble. Their father put them to work on his construction sites. They would learn the business from the bottom up and learn every aspect of the business so if they later came to work for their father they would know the construction business well. If they chose to go elsewhere to work they would still have instilled in them a good work ethic.

Many of those summers Don, Jr worked at the Trump Marina in Atlantic City. His job was in mooring boats to the dock all day. He worked hard for little pay making only minimum wage plus tips. He was treated the same as the other employees doing the same job.

Don, Jr said, "Even in college we were very fiscally responsible. I had 300 bucks a month; anything I wanted beyond that, I had to work for."

At the age of fifteen, Ivanka was put to work shadowing the foreman who was working construction on Trump World Tower. Other than at the age of five when she got to work a bulldozer it was her first experience with working in construction and she was hooked. That just may have been the experience that would later bring her to work for the family business. She loved every minute of it.

Ivanka says that neither she nor her brothers ever looked at their father for a handout or as an ATM machine. If they wanted something they had always been taught they would have to work for it. It made them appreciate what they had.

Eric was put to work one summer doing landscaping with a crew at the Trump's country estate Seven Springs. Whatever project their father was currently working on he found work for them to do. He wanted each of them to learn the terms, the materials they were working with, how to recognize good quality and good workmanship, and the process of each project from the ground up. It would prepare them well for their future. He never gave them a free pass, nor did they expect it. Their father believed it was important for them to learn to do hands-on work to prepare them for the future regardless of what career they would choose for themselves – family business or not.

"He made us work," Eric said, "and I think that's what a great father does. Every summer I was working. I was either mowing lawns at some of our properties, laying tile with some of our stonemasons, or some other job."

"They are acutely aware of what being a Trump does for them, as well as what it costs them, and they do not hold it against anyone who may think it's all a gravy train," former teacher of the Trump sons Matt Ralston says. "There's a graciousness about both of them that is endearing."

While Ivanka's mother had been a model Ivanka herself never thought about doing the same even when at the age of ten she was approached by a modeling agent. She never thought about it again until she ran into the same agent about three or four years later and was again approached. That's when she began to consider the benefits.

After giving the offer some serious thought she began doing some modeling while a student at Chaote. She would model between classes and exams, but her studies came first. Her very first shoot was for *Elle* magazine. For Ivanka this was just a way to make some money, which ended up being quite a lot, but it wasn't something she planned to do for a lifetime career.

Don, Jr graduated from The Hill School in Pennsylvania. Initially after graduation from The Hill School Don, Jr considered joining the Marines, but instead went on to the University of Pennsylvania's Wharton Business School following in his father's footsteps. Don graduated with a B.S. degree in Economics.

For awhile in his youthful college days Don, Jr went through a time when he flaunted the Trump name and became a party boy drinking too much. In his own words, there for a time he "was a bit of a brat." He says his father repeatedly told him not to drink, not to smoke. He didn't always listen and admits he had a drinking problem while in college, but those days are far behind him.

His own father Donald too, had been in his own words "a little wise-guy, a brat who never respected authority." Donald Trump once gave one of his teachers a black eye. Donald's father, Fred Trump, decided what his son needed was discipline and training and thought the perfect place for him to learn that was at military school. So when he was entering the seventh grade Donald Trump had been sent to New York Military Academy.

Eric graduated from The Hill School as his older brother Don, Jr had, but he chose a different route and went to Georgetown University.

People assume life is easy because you come from a family that is well-known and well-off, but that isn't always so. "People are more critical of you. There are stereotypes," says Eric who says he was under the microscope. "People often call you spoiled because you grow up in a prominent family."

Discipline and manners were instilled into the Trump kids at an early age. You weren't likely to see or hear about the Trump children bouncing on the bed in a hotel room or causing chaos. That disciplined behavior instilled in them at an early age remained with them through their teenage years and into young adulthood. Whereas you often read or heard about other "rich kids" getting into trouble with drugs or in the nightclub scenes, that wasn't the case with the Trump kids.

Eric said, "We knew our family had a reputation to uphold. We're one of the last families you'd ever see going to a club and dancing on tables," said Eric. "The family name is very important to us, and we'd never let it get disgraced."

"Although we were privileged and traveled around the world extensively and had the best education, we were expected to work hard," recalls Eric.

While both boys are Trump's sons through and through and proud of it, they don't have the braggadacio gene. Influenced by their mother's upbringing of them and that of their grandparents they are humble and appreciative.

As a fellow alumni who remains in touch with Eric, Clare Fieseler put it, "Eric has Trump genes, but he doesn't have the Trump brand. I've always admired that he is uniquely his own in that way. Less bombastic, more thoughtful. Less self-aggrandizing, more humble. Less Trump. More Eric."

Once Don, Jr graduated and with a degree in hand he wasn't sure if he was ready to spend his life working in real estate and working the long hours his father put in. He felt he had worked for his father from the time he was born, going to work with him as early as age five or six and tagging along. Then every summer the boys were put to work in one capacity or another. Still having a bit of the youthful rebellion in him he had displayed during his college days he packed up his truck and moved out west.

For about a year and a half he lived out of the back of his truck, hiked and explored the spectacular Rockies, enjoyed hunting and camping out with the stars overhead, and made gas and food money by becoming a bartender in Aspen. To say his parents weren't thrilled with this choice he had made was an understatement. But in time the prodigal son packed up and returned to New York and joined the Trump organization in the year 2001. When he joined the family business he quit drinking. "Drinking in moderation wasn't something I was good at," Don, Jr admitted.

By the age of twenty-six Don, Jr had become a senior executive in his father's company. He 'earned' the title. If he hadn't been a hard worker and deserving of the title it never would have just been given to him because he was a Trump.

Working for his father had some disadvantages Don, Jr learned in 2004 when he planned to take a two week vacation. His father let him know he wasn't happy with him taking so much time off. He suggested to his son that he take up golf for leisure since you can go play for three hours and then come back to work. His father is a tough boss to work for.

Eric once he graduated also joined the Trump family business in 2006.

Ivanka graduated from Choate and then attended Georgetown University for two years and from there transferred to the Wharton Business School as an undergraduate. Ivanka graduated in 2004 cum laude with a bachelor's degree in economics. Before joining the family business she worked for Forest City Enterprises to get some experience.

She had been out of college for a year and was twenty-four years old when she joined the Trump family business. At the age of twenty-five Ivanka was about to become the youngest director on the board of a publicly traded company in the U.S. This was not a family business, but a public company. Her appointment was subject to board approval.

She became vice president of her father's real estate company. The Trump siblings have all had to deal with the attitude that just because their last name is Trump and because of who their father is that their positions were handed to them on a silver platter.

Ivanka and her brothers didn't rise to their positions in the company by birthright or foregone conclusion. Ivanka said, "My father is definitely not the kind of guy who'd place his children in key roles within his organization if he didn't think we could surpass the expectations he had for us."

All the siblings have been faced with this accusation or questioned at least once in interviews or in conversations, and many have incorrectly assumed it is due to their name alone that they hold the positions they do in the Trump organization, but this is quite simply not the case. Donald Trump is a savvy businessman and if he felt his children weren't up to the task they would not be put in that position.

Ivanka says she understands why an outsider might dismiss her success as just a form of nepotism. A strong woman who knows she has earned her place in the business has this to say about the matter. "I've learned to ignore it. Rise above it. I refuse to let the opinions of others define how I see myself, how I carry myself, how I get through my days."

Ivanka modeled as a means for some income and even as young as she was at the time knew it wasn't something she wanted to do as a career move. She could see the drawbacks by observing the other models and how catty they were, the constant unhealthy concern over their weight, securing a job that other models were also vying for, and their lack of education. It was for her a short term deal.

Her first magazine cover was on *Seventeen* in 1997 when she was sixteen. In addition to magazine covers for *Forbes and Harper's Bazaar* to just name a few she has also done ads for Tommy Hilfiger and Sasoon. She has done fashion shows for big names such as Versace. She was good and made very good money modeling so her father was surprised when she gave it up to continue her education. "She was a very successful model, and she just gave it up and went to Wharton," he said.

Don, Jr met his future wife through his father – *twice, actually!* They were at a fashion show when Donald Trump walked up to model Vanessa Haydon with his son introducing the two of them. Later that same day forgetting he had introduced them previously he did so again. Vanessa recalls she responded by saying, "Yeah, we just met, five minutes ago."

Don, Jr and Vanessa were both at a New York restaurant attending a birthday party about two months later when they were introduced yet again by a mutual friend. Initially neither one of them remembered the other. Then as Vanessa recalls, something clicked and she remembered how they had previously met. It's a story they enjoy telling to this day.

Don, Jr would one day find his face on the tabloids being called "tacky" and a "cheapskate" after proposing to his girlfriend Vanessa in the manner he did. The reason behind the smear on his name was how he proposed.

In a moment which some deemed should be intimate and private, he had been offered a deal he couldn't pass up on a four-carat engagement ring that was valued at $100,000. If he agreed to propose in what the tabloids called "a publicity stunt" in the presence of paparazzi and photographers at Bailey Banks & Biddle, then the ring was his. So on bended knee at the Bailey, Banks & Biddle jewelry store he proposed.

The prospective bride wasn't complaining, she seemed to enjoy being in the spotlight. And you have to ask yourself; who wouldn't have done the same thing in his place. Tacky or not, he got the ring...*and the girl.*

Don, Jr and Vanessa were married in November of 2005 at the Mar-a-Lago estate in Palm Beach, Florida. The bride and groom were both twenty-seven at the time of their marriage. The groom's aunt, his father's sister, Judge Maryanne Trump Barry of the United States Court of Appeals for the Third Circuit officiated. The bride designed her own gown. They spent their honeymoon in Fuji and Mexico. As of the year 2017 Don, Jr and Vanessa have five children: Kai, Chloe, Donald III, Tristan, and Spencer.

Don, Jr and his sister Ivanka became instant celebrities when they became part of the cast of their father's TV show *The Apprentice*. It wasn't the first time Donald Trump was featured on a television show. He was often a guest on *SNL*. Ivanka remembers her father in those roles. "I grew up watching my father on '*Saturday Night Live*,' " she said. "You may remember, in some of those skits, they had him dressed up like a chicken."

One of the most popular shows on the first season of *The Apprentice* was when Donald Trump sent the contestants out to see who could make the most money from setting up a lemonade stand on the streets of New York City. Perhaps his idea came from his own children when they were growing up and an experience they had.

The Trump kids themselves had a lemonade stand when they were young. For kids a lemonade stand is a fun way to make some money. Your mother supplies the items you need, she makes the lemonade for you, and she supplies the cups. You sit back and smile and look cute and reap the benefits. So this sounded like a great idea to the young Trumps.

Of course, there was no way their mother would allow them to set up a lemonade stand on the streets of Fifth Avenue or in the lobby of Trump Tower. That would have been fodder for the tabloids and a security risk. But the Trump kids were determined. So, that summer when they were at their summer home in Greenwich, Connecticut their mother finally relented but with certain conditions.

First of all, the kids would have to pay for their own supplies: lemonade, sugar, and cups. The cost of the supplies would come out of their profits. If they lost money on their endeavors it would be up to them to pay off the debt. They would be held accountable.

The Trump kids quickly agreed and were excited about their enterprising venture. The first problem they discovered was their location. With real estate in your background the one thing you learn early on is *'location, location, location.'*

The Trumps summer home was at the end of a cul-de-sac in an affluent community where the homes were on large properties and isolated from each other. They could only see one other house, so how would people know about their lemonade stand. There was no traffic, no cars, no one out walking who would see them. It was quite the dilemma. But the Trump kids are quite enterprising – they learned from the best.

In the end they used their marketing skills by selling their lemonade to their bodyguard, their parents' chauffeur, and the household staff. So while they didn't make a profit, they didn't lose money either.

Ivanka's first independent venture was her jewelry line. It was in the year 2007 that she launched her fine jewlery collection where she formed a partnership with a diamond vendor, Dynamic Diamond Corp. to design and create the *Ivanka Trump Fine Jewelry*. Regardless of the shape the economy was in it was a success story beyond her wildest expectations.

There is the saying, 'Find a need and fill it.' That's exactly what Ivanka did when in addition to her jewelry line she expanded into fashion. She realized that no one was designing fashions with the young professional woman in mind. In addition to the jewelry she now has added clothing, shoes, handbags, and accessories.

Not one to just blankly use her name for a selling tool she let those in the field she would be working with know, 'I'm serious about this; I'm not just a name, licensing a product without any involvement.' She is a mother, wife, and business woman and she knows what it means to be a modern millennial and this is the market she was designing for.

Oprah Winfrey called Ivanka a role model for the twenty-first century woman. That's quite an endorsement.

Ivanka and her achievements were noted by the Wharton Club of New York, an alumni club of the Wharton School of the University of Pennsylvania, her alma mater, who awarded her the Joseph Wharton Young Leadership Award in 2012 "for being a Wharton alumnus who, early in her career, has demonstrated great potential for leadership and lasting impact."

Ivanka has her own fashion line and holds the title, along with her brothers, as executive vice presidentof the Trump organization. She has also written two books in the category of business.

It was publishers who approached her about writing the books. Initially she was surprised by the request for her to write a book. Her comment at the time was, 'I don't want to look like I'm telling people I have all the answers. I'm twenty-seven.' But after thinking it over she realized that most business success and how-to books are written by successful business men who are sixty to seventy years old. Few people heard the voice of a young, successful business woman and clearly the publishers felt she had something worthy to say. Her book ' *The Trump Card: Playing to Win in Work and Life'* was a best seller. She also wrote ' *'Women Who Work: Rewriting the Rules for Success.'*

Ivanka realizes that with the last name of Trump she and her siblings will always be living in their father's shadow regardless of any accomplishments they achieve on their own. Now that their father has become president, that shadow has become even larger. "We've all made peace with the fact that we will never be able to achieve any level of autonomy," says Ivanka. "No matter how different a career path we choose from our parents, people will always say we wouldn't have gotten there if it hadn't been for our name."

Eric, the youngest of Donald Trump's children with his first wife, stands 6'5," even taller than his father. His father proudly says of his son, "He's never had problems. He's never gotten into trouble. A good boy, a good kid."

Eric graduated from Georgetown University located in Washington, D.C. with a degree in finance and management graduating with honors. He admits that there was a time when he considered choosing another career, and as most young boys do he had dreamed of becoming a fireman or fighter pilot in his youthful days; but as early as his high school days his dreams turned more towards working in the family business. He readily admits his father's influence had a profound impact on his decision making in ultimately choosing his career path.

In 2006 at the age of twenty-three he started his own charitable foundation, the Eric Trump Foundation, with the purpose of raising money for terminally-ill children and cancer patients at St. Jude Children's Research Hospital.

Eric in addition to holding the title of executive vice president of development and acquisitions for the Trump organization has executed the acquisition of the Kluge Winery and Vineyard in Virginia creating Trump Winery.

"We entered the wine industry with one goal in mind: to create the best wines anywhere in the world," says Eric, president of the Charlottesville, Virginia winery and executive vice president of development and acquisitions at The Trump Organization. "I am thrilled by our tremendous success and the fact that we are not only competing, but winning against the finest wines produced anywhere in the world."

It appears the Midas Touch has been passed on to the Trump children. They are all hard-working, successful, productive citizens who are positive role models. The Trump sons are about to reign over their father's multi-billion dollar empire as their father takes over his new position as President of the United States.

As much as Don, Jr admires his father and emulates him in many ways business wise, he will be the first to tell you, "I'd like to be more like him when it comes to business, but I think I'm such a different person...His work persona is kind of what he is." But for Don, Jr he has a work life and a private life. He can leave it behind him as he enjoys taking time off with his wife and five children to get away and enjoy being a family man.

The youngest of the Trump children is Barron, son of Donald and third wife Melania. He was born in March of 2006, a year after his parents were married. His father named him Barron after a pseudonym he had used himself for many years.

With a twenty-eight year age difference between the oldest and the youngest of the Trump children, Barron is closer in age to his nieces and nephews than he is to his brothers and sisters. By the time Barron was born his brothers and sister were living away from home and were married with two of them having their own children.

Barron like his brother Don, Jr. is multilingual. He speaks English, Slovenian, and French. He learned Slovenian as he speaks it with his mother and with his maternal grandparents who immigrated and live in New York.

Barron looks up to his father and even at a very young age watched his father closely mimicking him. Anthony Senecal the family butler said when Barron was almost three years old one day he was sitting in his high chair when he saw Senecal and said, "Tony, sit down. We need to talk." He was and is very mature for his age.

At five years of age he was learning how to be "the boss." His mother said, "He fired nannies, fired housekeepers. And it's very cute, you know? And then he hires them back." Perhaps one day he will be the next boss on *The Apprentice.*

While he may be seen infrequently as a First Son he has already made several appearances on TV. He was on *The Apprentice* several times and has been on *The Oprah Show* twice.

He enjoys dressing up in suits like his father. He takes golf lessons, tennis lessons, and plays basketball. He plays golf with his father quite regularly, an activity and time together the two of them enjoy. Like his siblings before him he enjoys playing with LEGOS and building large scale models. He likes to draw and is knowledgeable on the computer. He isn't one to ever complain that he is bored. He is used to entertaining himself and can always find something to do to keep busy.

Ivanka and Jared Kushner met in 2007 when they were introduced by someone who thought they would work together well in their business ventures, never even thinking that they would also make a great couple. They were both twenty-five at the time they met. Today when Ivanka and Jared remember that first business meeting where they met they say, "The best deal we ever made!"

They dated for two years before they made it official. For a short time there was a break up due to Jared's parents having an issue with Ivanka not being Jewish. They insisted that she convert before she would be accepted.

When the couple got back together Ivanka went through a conversion process and did convert to Judaism. Ivanka and Jared observe Shabbat and keep kosher and their daughter goes to a religious school similar to Jared's own upbringing.

At their wedding Jared's father spoke in an emotional speech where he talked about his initial reservation that Ivanka wasn't Jewish before admitting that he soon changed his mind when he realized just how much the couple loved each other. It could be his mind was changed because she converted, but nevertheless the couple makes a great pair and are well matched.

Jared's parents are Democrats who are longtime donors to the Democratic party and donated to Hillary Clinton's Senate race in the year 2000. It's not known who they voted for in the 2016 presidential election, but it became public that Jared's younger brother Josh refused to vote for Jared's father-in-law for the presidency. Regardless of their political differences the two brothers remain close and haven't let it come between them.

Ivanka and Jared seemed destined to become a couple. They both came from families heavily involved in real estate, they both attended Ivy League Schools, they both held high positions in their fathers' companies, and they were both *very* ambitious; so there were certainly a lot of similarities. Ivanka admits that those similarities are important. "If I was married to somebody who, even if beneath the surface, didn't like the fact that I work so hard or didn't support my ambitions.....I think it would be very hard to build a solid foundation on that."

Somehow regardless of how full their lives are their marriage appears to be in perfect harmony. Ivanka wisely said, "You realize in life not that many things matter that much, but your choice of spouse is really everything."

Ivanka and Jared were married in a Jewish ceremony that took place at the Trump National Golf Club in New Jersey in 2009. The day of the wedding the bride went for a hike in which she posted to Twitter, "Everything is simply perfect! I'm getting married today!" Days before her 28th birthday she was about to become a bride. She wore a stunning Vera Wang gown inspired by Grace Kelly with her sister Tiffany as one of her bridesmaids and Barron was ring bearer. They honeymooned in Africa.

Today Ivanka and Jared have three children: Arabella, Joseph, and Theodore who was born during her father's presidential campaign. Ivanka's children have a nanny who is Chinese and is teaching the children to speak Mandarin.

Ivanka has an estimated net worth of $150 million. That doesn't all come from family, but from hard work. Her husband Jared's net worth is even higher, which has been estimated as high as $200 million.

Big sister Ivanka stepped up to the plate when Tiffany spoke to her about needing some financial assistance when she was still a teen. She wasn't expecting anything and didn't take it for granted, but admitted she could use some financial help.

Without Tiffany's knowledge Ivanka helped her little sister out. "I went to our father and suggested he think about surprising Tiffany with a credit card for Christmas, with a small monthly allowance on it."

Donald Trump gave her a budget of $500 a month. It was enough to fill her basic needs and to still allow her to have some spending money. It was enough to still keep her on a budget and according to a friend she was very frugal going so far as to calculate down to the last penny how much her part of the bill was when she and her friends ate out.

Ivanka helped her seventeen year old sister Tiffany get an internship at *Vogue* during the summer of 2011.

Tiffany had thought perhaps she would like a career as a singer, but it doesn't appear that is her destiny. She did release a single in 2014 called 'Like A Bird,' but it gave her self satisfaction but not much else.

Tiffany grew up away from her stepbrothers and stepsister in her younger days but when it was time to go to college she moved from the west coast to the east coast to be closer to her father and to attend his alma mater the University of Pennsylvania.

Tiffany has always looked up to her older sister and Ivanka is there to help Tiffany with sisterly advice when needed. Not only has Ivanka given her younger sister advice about boys, but these days the advice is more towards political and what styles and color suit her best while on camera. Ivanka with years of experience in modeling and being in the fashion business is a good one to turn to for such guidance.

Tiffany graduated during her father's presidential campaign. During her time in college she was of age to drink but unlike many who are at college and away from home for the first time she didn't go wild though some have tried to portray her as a party girl. Perhaps how she came about being labeled as such was in part due to her upbringing in California with friends such as the Kardashians (before the days they became famous) and other spoiled rich kids. While she is in the sorority Kappa Alpha Theta and likes to have fun she took her studies very seriously and it paid off as she got all A's in her major studies in Sociology and Urban Studies.

She graduated from U of Penn in 2016 and is interested into going into law and is looking into Harvard. As a Trump it is assumed she will become another high achiever in whichever path she chooses.

For now though Tiffany is best known for being what some call "the forgotten daughter" of President Trump, a First Daughter and is well-known for being one of the "Rich Kids of Instagram," where she shows photos and notes the lives of the glitzy side of her life. Her posts often include photos of friends who also come from rich backgrounds including Kyra Kennedy, daughter of Robert F. Kennedy, Jr; Gaïa Matisse, great-great-granddaughter of famous artist Henri Matisse; and E.J. Johnson, the son of basketball star Magic Johnson. It was the *New York Post* and *The New York Times* who labeled them as the "rich kids of Instagram" and the "Snap Pack."

Eric and girlfriend Lara Yunaska had been together for six years before he popped the question. Lara, an associate producer at the TV program *Inside Edition*, and youngest son of Donald Trump were married November 8, 2014 at Mar-A-Lago in Palm Beach, Florida with Ivanka's husband Jared Kushner officiating the wedding. Eric's brother Don, Jr was his best man and sister Ivanka was a bridesmaid. Ivanka's daughter Arabella was the flower girl and the ring bearer was the bride's dog Charlie making it a real family affair.

Just a few weeks before the wedding the bride had been in an accident while riding her horse and had broken both her wrists. Still healing at the time of the wedding she was still bandaged up which she hid one hand behind her bouquet and the other by tucking her arm into her husband's arm.

The thirty year old groom and thirty-one year old bride honeymooned in Africa and France. As of 2017 Eric and his wife do not have any children.

The older Trump kids were all campaigning for their father's 2016 presidential election, including Tiffany who after graduating became more visible. She joined the others at campaign appearances and while her sister Ivanka has had years to become comfortable in the spotlight as a businesswoman, it was all pretty new to Tiffany. She spoke at the 2016 Republican National Convention on the second night and was endearing when in her speech she said, "Please excuse me if I'm a little nervous. When I graduated college a couple of months ago, I never expected to be here tonight addressing the nation. I've given a few speeches in front of classrooms and students, but never in an arena with more than 10 million people watching." You have to give her credit – that's not an easy thing for anybody to do.

While many wondered about Tiffany and how exactly she fit into the family coming from her father's second marriage, her mother being *"the other woman"* who many say was responsible for the break-up of the marriage of their father and their mother; Ivanka has always looked out for her younger sister and said in an interview with *People* magazine, "She's my little sister. I've been close to Tiffany her whole life, and I really love her."

After graduation Tiffany moved into an apartment not too far from Trump Tower. She is studying for the L.S.A.T. and hopes to be accepted at Harvard to study law. Not feeling the same compulsion to follow in her father's and siblings footsteps and going into real-estate she wants to become a lawyer. Tiffany is still a work in progress and it remains to be seen what her future holds. Whatever she chooses, she will now always be thought of first and foremost as a First Family member.

It is rare to hear a word against the Trump offspring. While there are many people out there who loudly criticize their father, all in all it appears the Trump children have made a good and lasting impression on others.

While Don, Jr was campaigning for his father in Arizona he came across a woman whose car had broken down. Many motorists sped past without giving a second thought to stopping and helping the stranded motorist – until Don, Jr came upon her. He pulled over and regardless of the fact that he was dressed in a suit and ready to speak in front of thousands of people he stopped and helped her push her car to the side of the road and offered her a bottle of water. He made sure she had someone coming to help her before leaving and never mentioned who he was or who his father was. He didn't do it for press coverage; only because it was the right thing to do. Besides; where were all the other good Samaritans? She was grateful for the help and as they were getting ready to leave someone asked her if she knew who he was. Shocked to hear who had stopped to help she was thrilled when he agreed to take selfies with her before he was on his way.

The youngest of the Trumps, ten year old Barron, was rarely seen during the presidential election. His mother preferred to keep him focused on his studies, keep his life as normal as possible or as possible as that is with his father running for the presidency, and she preferred to keep him out of the spotlight. In hindsight, she was very wise to do so.

Barron was only seen three times on the campaign trail. He was in attendance during a rally in South Carolina, he was there for his father's Republican National Committee acceptance speech, and again was there for his father's presidential victory speech.

When Barron was on stage with his family for his father's acceptance speech he had been up for a solid twenty-four hours without sleep. This was a ten year old boy who was still keeping his schedule going to school, had traveled from New York to Cleveland, had been up all night to hear the results amidst all the commotion and excitement, and it was 3:00 in the morning. By the time the family went on stage he was struggling to stay awake.

It didn't take long for the opposition to attack. Rosie O'Donnell, a comedian and television personality with her best years behind her and a mother herself who should have been more compassionate, tweeted despicable remarks about the young son of the presidential hopeful. It was totally out of line and she received a lot of backlash for her remarks. Presidential children, especially those so young, have been out-of-bounds and for the most part left alone since Chelsea Clinton suffered the humiliation of being made fun of on *SNL*. The children aren't the ones running for office – *and a ten year old boy; how low can you go?*

Perhaps this is the reason presidents keep the First Family members so well-guarded and rarely seen. Is it any wonder when you have people who are willing to stoop so low as O'Donnell and a writer from *SNL* who also attacked the president's young son in a tweet less than twenty-four hours after the inauguration.

People in both political parties stood up for him, even Chelsea Clinton, the daughter of President Trump's rival in the presidential race, defended him and pretty much told people to leave him alone. Of course she then had to add in barbs about his father which took away from her act of kindness, instead coming across as a political ploy. I'm sure when she heard the hurtful remarks it brought back some painful memories of her own from her days as a young presidential daughter.

Another person who tweeted standing up for the president's son was Monica Lewinsky. If the name is unfamiliar to you it is only due to your young age, as she was "the White House intern" involved in the sexual activities in the Oval Office with President Clinton during his administration.

Although the younger Trumps learned their business savvy from their father, Donald Trump also learned a thing or two from them about the internet and social media. It was his kids who introduced him to Twitter and Facebook teaching him the advantages of using social media; and they must have been great teachers, because all through Trump's campaign he was "tweeting" away. His "tweets" made national television. The president discovered this was a great means to reach people and a great way of getting around the mainstream media.

While most rich kids are pretty much raised by nannies, that isn't the case with Barron Trump. In his case, his mother who is now First Lady has always been a hands-on mother. She is there to greet him every morning cooking him breakfast and taking him to and from school, which will now be under the watchful eye of the Secret Service, and helps him with his homework. He is smart with his favorite subjects being math and science, and according to his father he is very good with computers.

Love him or hate him: *President Trump was elected our 45th president.* For some he offers hope for some big changes while others are still in mourning over the election results.

Today Don, Jr is thirty-nine and Eric is thirty-three, both executive vice presidents who are taking over, for the time being anyway, a business empire worth billions as their father works from the Oval Office. While each family member is competitive, they work well together. The brothers were each others' best man, they have breakfast together nearly every business day and "catch up," and remain each others' best friend. They have learned from the best and now have the opportunity to step out from under their father's shadow and test their mettle.

Ivanka along with husband Jared Kuchner are now living in Washington in the neighborhood of Kalorama. They will actually be neighbors with the Obamas who will be living a mere two blocks from them, but it is doubtful either of them will be dropping in for a social visit.

Jared has become White House senior advisor. Ivanka's role is undetermined, but she will definitely have a role as Washington hostess, presumably stepping in for the First Lady when needed, and in addition will advise her father on matters of relevance to her such as maternity leave, women's issues, and climate control.

The public having seen little of the young presidential son enjoyed watching him in a candid moment playing peek-a-boo and high five's with his nephew entertaining him while the newly sworn in president was signing papers for cabinet posts immediately after taking the oath of office.

While youngest son Barron will remain living at Trump Tower in New York at least until the end of the school year, he was in Washington for his father's inauguration. He got out and walked in the inaugural parade alongside his parents waving to the crowd. It will be the first time in over half a century that the president has a young son. There hasn't been a young First Son since the days of John Kennedy, Jr who was just a toddler when he lived in the White House.

Will Barron become America's poster child for the 'American Royal Prince,' the title the media once laid on the shoulders of young John Kennedy, Jr? Barron certainly has the looks and the demeanor. He is just aloof enough to have a special appeal. It will be interesting to have a young presidential son in the White House again and watch him in the years that he will hold the title of the president's son.

Barron currently attends school in Manhattan at the Columbia Grammar & Preparatory School and plans to finish the 2016 - 2017 school year there. It is a prestigious private school that runs approximately $45,000 per year. The plans are for the First Lady and Barron to remain at Trump Tower until the end of the school year so as to not disrupt his life anymore than necessary. Understandably Barron is a bit nervous about leaving behind a school and friends he is familiar with and go to a new location. If a new school in or near Washington for the fall of 2017 has been chosen, it has not yet been disclosed.

For the rest of the school year Barron will be escorted to school by the Secret Service and NYPD. The streets will be blocked off in a "rolling pattern" for the few minutes as they travel to and from the school for safety purposes. Routes will be changed on a daily basis for safety concerns.

Barron while not spoiled like you would expect with all that he is accustomed to, it will definitely be a "step down" in the world when he moves into the White House. After all he currently has his own entire floor in the Trump Tower penthouse and that's just one of the places he calls home. But don't think of him as a spoiled rich kid. He is as well-grounded as his other siblings. It won't be the Trump children you'll have to worry about during the Trump administration that you may see making headlines due to what they say or do – perhaps more of a concern will be their father the president.

Anita McBride, a former chief of staff to former First Lady Laura Bush said people are fascinated with first families. The Trump family especially promises to captivate the public's interest.

As the president, will Donald Trump bring *The Apprentice* role with him to the White House – he promised to drain the swamp; will he be using his famous line, "You're Fired!" Yes, he certainly will and has already done so. He has already proved himself that he meant what he said; it didn't take him long to do so either. The first few days in office and he is cleaning house...What's next remains to be seen; but don't blink or you'll be sure to miss something.

Bibliography

Books:

Adler, Bill *The Kennedy Children: Triumphs And Tragedies* (1980) F. Watts

Aldrich, Gary *Unlimited Access: An FBI Agent Inside The Clinton White House* (1998) Regnery Publishing

Algeo, Matthew *The President Is A Sick Man: Wherein The Supposedly Virtuous Grover Cleveland Survives A Secret Surgery At Sea And Vilifies The Courageous Newspaperman Who Dared Expose The Truth* (2011) Chicago Review Press

Andersen, Christopher *The Day John Died* (2000) William Morrow

Andersen, Christopher *George And Laura: Portrait Of An American Marriage* (2002) William Morrow

Andersen, Christopher *Bill And Hillary: The Marriage* (1999) William Morrow

Andersen, Christopher *Barack And Michelle: Portrait Of An America Marriage* (2009) Harper Collins Publishers

Anthony, Carl Sferrazza *America's First Families: An Inside View Of 200 Years Of Private Life In The White House* (2000) Touchstone

Anthony, Carl Sferrazza *Florence Harding: The First Lady, The Jazz Age, And The Death Of America's Most Scandalous President* (1998) William Morrow

Barzman, Sol *The First Ladies: Intimate Biographical Portraits Of The Presidents' Wives From Martha Washington To Pat Nixon* (1970) Cowles Book Company

Bayne, Julia Taft *Tad Lincoln's Father* (2002) University of Nebraska Press

Bongino, Dan *Life Inside the Bubble* (2013) WND Books

Bowen, Catherine Drinker *John Adams And The American Revolution* (2001) William S. Konecky Associates

Bradley, Kimberly Brubaker *The President's Daughter* (2006) Yearling

Brandus, Paul *Under This Roof:The White House And The Presidency--21 Presidents, 21 Rooms, 21 Inside Stories (*2015) The Lyons Press

Brower, Kate Andersen *First Women: The Grace And Power Of America's Modern First Ladies* (2016) Harper

Brower, Kate Andersen *The Residence:Inside The Private World Of The White House* (2016) Harper

Bush, Barbara *Barbara Bush:A Memoir* (2015) Scribner

Bush, George W. *41: A Portrait Of My Father* (2014) Crown Publishers

Bush, Laura *Spoken From The Heart* (2010) Scribner

Byrne, Gary *Crisis Of Character: A White House Secret Service Officer Discloses His First Hand Experience With Hillary, Bill, And How They Operate* (2016) Center Street

Cantacuzene, Princess Julia *Revolutionary Days* (1999) R.R. Donnelley & Sons Company

Chernow, Ron *Washington: A Life* (2011) Penguin Books

Clarke, Nancy with Matheson, Christie *My First Ladies:Behind The Scenes With First Ladies Michelle Obama, Laura Bush, Hillary Clinton, Barbara Bush, Nancy Reagan, And Rosalynn Carter* (2011) Sellers Publishing

Cordery, Stacy A. *Princess Alice: A Biography Of Alice Roosevelt Longworth* (2008) Penguin Books

Cross, Wilbur and Novotny, Ann *White House Weddings* (1967) McKay

Date, S.V. *Jeb: America's Next Bush*

Davis, Patti *The Way I See It: An Autobiography* (1992) Putnam

Davis, Patti *The Long Goodbye* (2004) Alfred A. Knopf

Eisenhower, Julie *Special People* (1977) Simon & Schuster

Emerson, Jason *Giant In The Shadows:The Life Of Robert T. Lincoln* (2012) Southern Illinois University Press

Felsenthal, Carol *Princess Alice: The Life And Times Of Alice Roosevelt Longworth* (2003) St. Martin's Griffin

Flexner, James *Washington:The Indispensable Man* (1994) Back Bay Books

Ford, Susan and Hayden, Laura *Double Exposure* (2003) St. Martin's Press

Ford, Susan and Hayden, Laura *Sharp Focus* (2003) St. Martin's Press

Gherman, Beverly *First Son And President: Story About John Quincy Adams* (2006) First Avenue Editions

Gould, Lewis L. *The Presidency Of William McKinley* (1980) Regents Press of Kansas

Grant, Ulysses S. *Personal Memoirs Of U.S. Grant* (1989) Easton Press

Hagendorn, Hermann *The Roosevelt Family Of Sagamore Hill* (1965) The Macmillan Company

Hill, Clint and McCubbin, Lisa *Five Presidents: My Extraordinary Journey With Eisenhower, Kennedy, Johnson, Nixon, And Ford* (2016) Gallery Books

Hill, Clint and McCubbin, Lisa *Mrs. Kennedy And Me* (2012) Gallery Books

Keckley, Elizabeth *Thirty Years A Slave and Four Years In The White House* (1968) Arno Press

Kelley, Kitty *The Family: The Real Story Of The Bush Dynasty* (2004) Doubleday

Kennedy, Caroline and Alderman, Ellen *In Our Defense: The Bill of Rights In Action* (1992) Avon Books

Kennedy, Caroline *A Family Christmas* (2007) Hyperion

Kessler, Ronald *The First Family Detail:Secret Service Agents Reveal The Hidden Lives Of The Presidents* (2015) Crown Forum

Kessler, Ronald *In The Presidents Secret Service:Behind the Scenes With Agents In The Line Of Fire And The Presidents They Protect* (2010) Crown Forum

Kierner, Cynthia A. *Martha Jefferson Randolph, Daughter of Monticello: Her Life And Times* (2014) The University of North Carolina Press

King, Norma *Ivana Trump: A Very Unauthorized Biography* (1990) Carroll & Graf Publishers, Inc.

Klein, Edward *Guilty As Sin: Uncovering New Evidence Of Corruption And How Hillary Clinton And The Democrats Derailed The FBI Investigation* (2016) Regency Publishing

Lachman, Charles *A Secret Life: The Lies And Scandals Of President Grover Cleveland* (2013) Skyhorse Publishing

Lanier, Shannon and Feldman, Jane *Jefferson's Children: The Story Of One American Family* (2002) Random

Lawson, Don *Famous Presidential Scandals* (1990) Enslow Pub Inc

McAdoo, William G. *Crowded Years: The Reminiscences Of William G. McAdoo* (1931) Houghton Mifflin

McCullough, David *John Adams* (2002) Simon & Schuster

McCullough, Noah *First Kids: The True Stories Of All The President's Children* (2009) Scholastic Inc.

McElroy, Robert *Grover Cleveland: The Man And The Statesman (1923)* Harper & Brothers

Millard, Candice *Destiny of the Republic: A Tale Of Madness, Medicine, And The Murder Of A President* (2012) Anchor Books

Nagel, Paul *Descent from Glory: Four Generations Of The John Adams Family* (1983) Oxford University Press

O'Brien, Cormac *Secret Lives Of The Presidents* (2009) Quirk Books

O'Brien, Cormac *Secret Lives Of The First Ladies* (2009) Quirk Books

O'Reilly, Bill and Zimmerman, Dwight Jon *Lincoln's Last Days, The Shocking Assassination That Changed America Forever (*2012) Henry Holt

O'Reilly, Bill *Kennedy's Last Days* (2013) Henry Holt and Co.

O'Reilly, Bill and Fisher, David *Legends And Lies: The Patriots* (2016) Henry Holt and Co.

Park, Lillian Rogers *My Thirty Years Backstairs At The White House* (2008) Ishi Press

Pryor, Cheryl *The Big Book Of Presidential Trivia* (2016) Arlington & Amelia

Pryor, Cheryl *The Big Book Of First Ladies* (2016) Arlington & Amelia

Quinn-Musgrove, Sandra L. and Kanter, Sanford *America's Royalty: All The President's Children* (1995) Greenwood

Randall, Ruth Painter *Lincoln's Sons* (1955) Little, Brown & Company

Randolph, Sarah N. *The Domestic Life Of Thomas Jefferson* (1947) Thomas Jefferson Memorial Foundation

Reagan, Maureen *First Father, First Daughter: A Memoir* (1989) Little, Brown & Company

Reagan, Michael *Making Waves* (1996) Thomas Nelson Publishers

Reagan, Michael *Michael Reagan:On The Outside Looking In* (1988) Zebra

Reagan, Nancy *My Turn: The Memoirs Of Nancy Reagan* (1989) Random House

Rhatigan, Joe *White House Kids* (2015) Imagine

Roosevelt, Curtis *Too Close To The Sun: Growing Up In The Shadow Of My Grandparents, Franklin And Eleanor* (2009) Public Affairs

Roosevelt, Elliott and Brough, James *Mother: Eleanor Roosevelt's Untold Story* (1973) Dell Publishing

Roosevelt, Elliott and Brough, James *Rendezvous With Destiny: The Roosevelts Of The Oval Office* (1975) Putnam

Roosevelt, Elliott and Brough, James *An Untold Story: The Roosevelts Of Hyde Park* (1973) Dell

Sadler, Christine *Children In The White House* (1967) Putnam

Seager, Robert *And Tyler, Too: A Biography Of John & Julia Gardiner Tyler* (1963) Easton Press

Seigel, Beatrice *George And Martha Washington At Home In New York* (1989) Simon & Schuster

Shaw, Maud *White House Nannie* (1966) The New American Library, Inc

Shepherd, Jack *Cannibals Of The Heart: A Personal Biography Of Louisa Catherine And John Quincy Adams* (1980) McGraw-Hill

Slater, Robert *No Such Thing As Over-Exposure: Inside the Life and Celebrity of Donald Trump* (2005) Prentice Hall

Slevin, Peter *Michelle Obama: A Life*   (2015) Knopf Publishing Group

Streitmatter, Rodger *Empty Without You: The Intimate Letters Of Eleanor Roosevelt And Lorena Hickok* (2000) Da Capo Press

Truman, Margaret *The President's House: A First Daughter Shares The History And Secrets Of The World's Most Famous House* (2004) Ballantine

Truman, Margaret *First Ladies: An Intimate Group Portrait Of White House Wives* (1996) Ballantine

Truman, Margaret *Harry Truman* (1993) Avon Books

Whitcomb, Claire and Whitcomb, John *Real Life At The White House: 200 Years Of Daily Life At America's Most Famous Residence (2003)* Taylor & Francis, Inc.

I have consulted several websites to gather, compare, and confirm information. The following sites proved to be especially valuable, but are by no means intended to be all-inclusive. There have been thousands of news reports and articles concerning the presidents and some of these were used to verify facts or to garner information for further research for the book.

News reports, articles – magazines and newspapers, internet coverage, independent sources:

The New York Times, Washington Post, The Wall Street Journal, Vanity-Fair, The Chicago Tribune, Baltimore Sun, Oregon News, USA Today, Scouting Magazine, Library of Congress, Bloomberg, Newsweek, People, CNN, World News, Rolling Stone, The San Bernardino County Sun, Los Angeles Times, New York Daily News, The Guardian, Associated Press, CBS News, Smithsonian, PBS, Vogue, Mental Floss, History.com, White House History, Eyewitness To History, Carl Anthony Online, Carl Sferrazza Anthony, Wordpress, Presidential Libraries, White House History, Potus-geeks/livejournal, Politico, A Short History Blog, West Point, Hannahirossblog, Texas Monthly, American-Presidents, Express.co.uk, The Fix, From the Wilderness, tvovermind.com, GQ, Kansas City Star, franbeque.com, upi – United Press International, psu.edu – Pennsylvania State University, RealChange.org, The Living New Deal

www.ingramcontent.com/pod-product-compliance
Lightning Source LLC
Chambersburg PA
CBHW081828170426
43199CB00017B/2675